ALTERNATIVE TRAVEL DIRECTORY

1997

*The Complete Guide To
Work, Study, & Travel Overseas*

GENERAL EDITOR
Clayton A. Hubbs

CONTRIBUTING EDITORS
Rick Crowder, Susan Griffith, Cynthia Harriman,
Deborah McLaren, William Nolting,
Susan Sygall, Kathy Widing, Arline K. Wills

Transitions Abroad Publishing, Inc.
Amherst, MA

Contributing editors:
Kathy Widing (Chapter 1), Arline K. Wills (Chapter 3),
Cynthia Harriman (Chapter 5), Susan Sygall (Chapter 6),
Rick Crowder (Chapter 7), Deborah McLaren (Chapter 8),
Susan Griffith (Chapter 17), William Nolting (Chapters 10, 16)

Published by Transitions Abroad Publishing, Inc.
P.O. Box 1300, Amherst, MA 01004-1300

Manufactured in the United States of America

ISBN 1-886732-03-5
Third Edition

Cover and book design by Jason Whitmarsh

CONTENTS

STUDY

Present Constraints and Future Challenges, 90: *Education abroad programming has never been so diverse in its forms, locations, and approaches, but numerous contraints limit its pace.*

WORK

Working Abroad: Experiencing a Foreign Culture from the Inside, 288: *Any individual with guts and gusto has the potential for funding themselves as they travel to the corners of the globe.*

INTRODUCTION

In 1977 I launched *Transitions Abroad,* a magazine of practical information for independent travelers who go abroad to live, work, study, or travel for reasons other than those connected with mass tourism. The title "Transitions" was meant to suggest the changes that occur when travelers leave home behind and truly immerse themselves in a new environment.

Many of the first writers for *Transitions Abroad* were students, just back from a semester or year of travel and study abroad. Writing in the first issue, Gary Langer, then a student at the Univ. of New Hampshire, described staying at a Jerusalem guesthouse of an old Armenian called Mr. A. Those who sought out Mr. A were travelers, not tourists:

"Travelers and tourists, the distinction is simple: Tourists are those who bring their homes with them wherever they go, and apply them to whatever they see. They are closed to experience outside of the superficial. Travelers left home at home, bringing only themselves and a desire to see and hear and feel and take in and grow and learn. Tourists do not go to Mr. A's. They would not appreciate him, nor he them. And the main reason travelers go to Mr. A's is for Mr. A."

Taken out of context, Langer's contrast between travelers and tourists may sound a bit exaggerated and smug (after all, we are all in one sense tourists when we travel to another country). But the distinction has long been made between those who seem to travel more to confirm what they already know than to gain new understanding of themselves and of others. One thinks of Mark Twain's 1860s satirical novel on American travelers who brought so much cultural baggage with them that they were only "In-a-Sense" Abroad.

The stereotypical tourist—whether of Twain's time or ours—doesn't so much abandon his own familiar environment for the sake of engaging with a new one as have himself transported to a foreign place, taking with him as much of his familiar environment as possible. He views the unfamiliar people, places, and culture through the windows or walls of the familiar and pretends that he is still at home. If he must speak to the natives he does so loudly, thereby giving them every opportunity to understand him.

The modern traveler, on the other hand, is increasingly interested in experiencing new people, places, and cultures on their own terms and precisely because they are unfamiliar. The transition is not simply a passage from one place to another; it is a change in perspective and perception.

Interest in alternative travel, or travel for enrichment, grew rapidly in the 1970s and 1980s, in part a result of international air travel becoming affordable to a much larger group of people. In 1989 *Travel & Leisure* magazine commissioned Louis Harris Associates, Inc. to survey thousands of traveling Americans to find out why they traveled. To their surprise, the interviewers found that three travelers out of four took their last trip to improve their minds, to gain new perspectives, and to meet new people. Asked to name their dream vacation, only 10 percent named a place in the U.S. The conclusion of the pollsters was that international travel for personal growth was increasing more rapidly than any other form of nonbusiness travel.

In 1991 Arthur Frommer wrote: "After 30 years of writing standard guidebooks, I began to see that most of the vacation journeys undertaken by Americans were trivial and bland. . . . Travel in all price ranges is scarcely worth the effort unless it is associated with people, with learning and ideas. To have meaning at all, travel must involve an encounter with new and different outlooks and beliefs. . . . At its best, travel should challenge our preconceptions and most cherished views, cause us to rethink our assumptions, shake us a bit, make us broader-minded and more understanding."

"Not to have met the people of other cultures in a nontouristic setting," Frommer concludes in *The New World of Travel*, "is not to have lived in this century."

Detailing the ways and the means to meet people of other cultures in a nontouristic setting has been the major purpose of *Transitions Abroad* since its beginning 20 years ago. In each issue of the magazine we select and publish the most important sources of information on alternative travel along with a selection of programs and other opportunities for the curious and independent-minded.

We revise and update this information continuously. At the end of each year we bring it all together in one volume: the *Alternative Travel Directory*. The three sections—Independent Travel, Study Abroad, and Working Abroad—contain our selection of the major alternatives to mass tourism.

Independent Travel. The experience of travel involves a continuum or a progression from the familiar to the new. On the one extreme are the unadventurous packaged tourists or mass tourists described above who spend a good portion of their trip in a literal bubble being whisked along on a guided tour, usually in an air-conditioned bus. They make virtually no decisions on their own and are taken, on a fixed schedule, from one attraction (often man-made for their benefit) to another. They observe and photograph but rarely actively experience their surroundings.

On the other extreme are those relatively few travelers who avoid the tourist scene altogether and strike out on their own. They are on no fixed schedule or itinerary and settle where they like for as long as they like, finding casual work when necessary to cover their modest expenses or to pay for moving on.

Between these two extremes are those of us in that growing group of travelers who like to go on our own, often to pursue a particular interest, but only after enough planning and preparation to insure that our limited time and money will be well spent. We don't want to be bound to a group or have our experience spoiled by hordes of tourists; on the other hand, we want to be comfortable and feel sufficiently secure to accomplish our goals.

Travel Abroad. The travel resources and programs in the first nine chapters are grouped under the heading of independent or "life-seeing travel." The latter term comes from the concept of the Scandinavian School for Life (adult continuing education schools to enrich the mind, sometimes but not always to teach a vocational skill) which we described in the first issue of *Transitions Abroad* in 1977. Axel Dessau, director of the Danish Tourist Office, is credited with applying the concept to tourism. Visitors to Denmark are able to engage in activities that match their particular interests—for example, educators may visit schools and stay in the homes of teachers.

The fact that similar home and hospitality exchanges are proliferating throughout the world--as more of us travel from one foreign host's home to another rather than to tourist hotels--is just one indication of the increasing desire on the part of international travelers for an authentic engagement with the local people. For more and more travelers, including the readers of *Transitions Abroad*, life-seeing has replaced sightseeing.

Chapter 1 is a country-by-country guide to the best guidebooks and background reading to consult as you begin to make your overseas travel plans.

Chapters 2 through 7 cover the best travel information resources and selected programs for seniors, for families traveling with children, and for persons with disabilities.

Chapters 8 and 9 cover the major resources and programs exemplifying culturally and environmentally responsible travel, the fastest growing of all forms of alternative travel. How precisely one defines responsible travel and how one travels responsibly is a central topic of each issue of *Transitions Abroad* and of Dianne Brause's Introduction to this first section of the *Alternative Travel Directory*.

Study Abroad. In Chapter 10 we list the most useful resources for learning opportunities abroad.

Whereas all travel is at least potentially educational, the programs for people of all ages described in chapters 12 through 15 are structured learning experiences. Those organized for undergraduates carry academic credit. Older adults are welcome to take part in most academic programs for no credit, usually at a reduced price.

Working Abroad. There is perhaps no greater learning opportunity and no more rewarding form of travel than getting to know your hosts by working alongside them—whether as an unpaid volunteer or a well-paid professional. The resources, organizations, and programs described in this section make you aware of all that's available.

Chapter 16 is the most detailed and comprehensive existing review of information on jobs abroad.

Chapter 17 covers employers and organizations offering short-term jobs abroad.

The final three chapters, 18 through 20, outline the opportunities for volunteering, interning, and teaching abroad.

Whatever your age, whatever your reason for travel, we think you'll find the overseas travel alternative you're looking for here. If not, let us know and we'll try to include it in the next issue of *Transitions Abroad* and next year's edition of the *Alternative Travel Directory*. Our address is Transitions Abroad, P.O. Box 1300, Amherst, MA 01004-1300; trabroad@aol.com; www.transabroad.com.

Clay Hubbs
Amherst, MA
December 1996

INDEPENDENT
TRAVEL

Long-distance travel has become a way of life
and the world has become a smaller place.
It can also become a better place as a result
of our first-hand mixing and access to seeing, tasting,
experiencing, and understanding one another's cultures.

—DIANNE BRAUSE, PAGE 14

Traveling Responsibly
Travel As a Positive Force for Change

By Dianne Brause

What is responsible travel and how does one do it? These questions come somewhat naturally to me since I have a strong desire to travel and also a strong commitment to being responsible in my actions. For more than 10 years, I have been writing for the readers of *Transitions Abroad* about the various nuances of the possible answers to these questions.

Responsible travel has to do with the awareness of how our actions affect the people and the places we visit.

If you are a "socially responsible" traveler your choices will support—or at least not harm—the people hosting your stay and their relationship to their own culture.

If you are an "environmentally responsible traveler" (ecotourist) your actions will support or improve the ecosystem of the place you were visiting.

If you are a "sustainable traveler," you and others like you could continue to act in the same way for a very long time without significantly lowering the quality of life of the people or the health of the environment hosting you.

Travel as a Positive Force. Travel is transformative—for the traveler first of all. It changes us, and it changes the places we visit. Since we have been raised in a throw-away culture we are apt to be as casual about throwing away someone else's heritage and connection to place as we are in throwing away our own.

But a new breed of travelers, including the readers of *Transitions Abroad*, is consciously trying not to repeat this part of the past. For all of us, long-distance travel has become a way of life and the world has become a smaller place. It can also become a better place as a result of our first-hand mixing and access to seeing, tasting, experiencing, and understanding one another's cultures. But much of this potential lies buried in a rush to "develop" tourism destinations throughout the world for the entertainment of the relatively well off at the expense of the poor.

It will take a major leap in consciousness for all of us to understand that just because we can pay the prices to go on vacation to a Club Med, cruise the Caribbean, join an African safari, scuba dive off the coral reefs of Belize, or visit a "primitive tribe" in Borneo, we and our money may not really be welcome or of help to the people or place visited. In fact, our presence may actually lower the quality of life of the average person from that country and damage the environment as well. These costs are frequently not factored into the price for our leisure-time adventures.

The False Promises of Tourism. Some years ago many Third World countries were led to believe that tourism would help bring them out of their "less-developed" state and into a flourishing economy. Their leaders—mostly representing a wealthy minority—set in motion a series of actions to attract investors, create a tourism infrastructure, and put themselves at the forefront of progress. Unfortunately, this required enormous loans and an increasing debt burden, especially for the poorer people of the countries who receive little or no benefit from the money invested.

The original thinking was flawed, and many thousands of Third World poor have had to leave their families and communities as a result of tourists' desire to have a cheap vacation in the sun. Those who remain are fast losing what has been the glue of their lives and cultures in exchange for fairly fleeting jobs as bellboys, guides, dishwashers, chamber maids, and sexual playthings. As the traditional stewards of the lands are lost, so are the lands, their resources, and the knowledge of how to preserve them in a sustainable manner. In addition, an understanding of the secrets of nature, including the uses of plants and animals for healing, is disappearing with the blink of an eye and the buzz of a chainsaw.

But thanks to a growing awareness of the destructiveness of mass tourism and the benefits of community directed tourism, the picture may be changing. Socially and environmentally responsible travel will eventually have the same prominence as socially responsible investment has begun to have.

Ten years ago it was unusual to hear travelers ask the hard questions of tour operators, cruise lines, hotel chains, and airlines which have begun to move the travel industry towards more awareness and sensitivity to how their policies affect the peoples and the environments that they depend upon to sell their products. Now codes of ethics are proliferating that ask tour operator and traveler alike to act in ways that are fair, respectful, and non-harmful to both the people and the place visited.

Returning the Gifts. Ecotourism, the fastest growing segment of the tourism industry, has many definitions. But in its true form green travel derives from the fact that many modern travelers are longing to return to the wilds and find the innocence and idealism they once lived by; to let go of the immense stress to get ahead; to do something worthwhile for themselves and for others. They want to raft the wild rivers of the world (and chip in some money to save them from being dammed up); or live in the home of an indigenous person; or help to build a simple dwelling alongside a poor villager in Africa; or stand up against our government by going to Cuba; or help a scientist dig up the lost remains of a culture and people we do not yet know.

In exchange for the resources expended in the act of travel we each need to make a commitment to give back in a way that is connected to the gifting that we receive while on our journey. There are thousands of ways of doing this—from "adopting" a child from the country you visit so that they have enough food and clothing to attend school, to buying or selling articles of clothing made by the people you visit (at fair prices), to starting a campaign to protect a particular species or piece of land, to writing letters to your congressperson about how foreign aid should be given out in the form of micro-loans to village people. As one who is moved by the richness of another part of the world, a responsible traveler will have some "response" to make in appreciation for the privilege of being accepted and hosted as a guest at the table of the stranger.

Traveling responsibly is one way to further a world of peace, understanding, and respect for all beings.

Travel for Mutual Benefit. So next time you hop in the car for a weekend jaunt or spread out the maps to decide where to go on your summer vacation with the family, please take a moment to imagine how you could plan a vacation that would relax or invigorate you while also making real contact with people you don't already know. Or do something which will support the health and future of the environment.

One of the encouraging aspects of this game is that no one can claim to have a perfect score. Start with small steps. Before you know it, it could become a contest with yourself or your friends and family to see who can come up with the most creative and rewarding way to travel, a way that adds to the well-being of the planet and her inhabitants.

The pages that follow provide an extensive selection of ways to combine responsible travel and personal reward.

CHAPTER 1

TRAVEL
RESOURCES

As international travel continues to rise, travelers are becoming more and more savvy and demanding about the quality of information on their destinations. The trend is toward longer stays in one place and greater involvement with locals. While they still require practical information on lodging, transport, and other basics, travelers are eager for information of a cultural, historical, and political nature.

Publishers are responding to this demand for greater detail and greater depth of coverage with an expansion of specialized titles.

The other strong trend in travel titles is towards "series" guides. It all begins with a single title. If the format or formula of that title works, another title is published and a series is born. The original series dates back to the early 1900s with the well-loved travel guides of Karl Baedeker. Today there are over 50 titles in the series. Arthur Frommer's *Europe on $5 a Day* produced a small industry in this country. Frommer Guides now number over 100 titles; the selection includes series within series of walking guides, guides for children, shopping guides, etc. Travelers come to trust their favorite guidebook series, its style and its familiar layout, and reach for them to begin planning a trip.

We begin our annual selections of key travel resources with a description of series guides, then list the series associated with each region or country at the start of each section.

Individual classics still stand alone. These distinctive books--*Europe Through the Back Door, People's Guide to Mexico, Journey of One's Own, Pocket Doctor,* to name a few--are listed within the appropriate planning, regional, or country sections.

For specialized guidebooks and resources for seniors, families with children, students, and persons with disabilities see the appropriate sections of this book. Additional directories of useful information on independent and specialty travel can be found in *The Traveler's Reading Guide* by Maggy Simony (Facts on File) and *Good Books for the Curious Traveler* by Theodora Nelson and Andrea Gross (two volumes, Europe and Asia and the South Pacific, Johnson Books). New this year is

Anderson's Travel Companion: A Guide to the Best Fiction & Non-fiction for Travelling by Sarah Anderson (Scolar Press).

Unless ordering information is included, all the books listed below are available in bookstores.

Guidebook Series

Access Guides (Harper Collins). Well-organized guides with informative walking routes. Titles on London, Paris, Rome, Barcelona, Venice/Milan/Florence, Mexico, Caribbean, Budget Europe, Montréal, and Québec City. New this year: French Wine Country.

Alive Guides (Alive Publications/Hunter Publishing). Excellent all-purpose guides include Venezuela Alive and similar titles for Virgin Islands and Guatemala.

Around the World Program (McDonald and Woodward). A new series sponsored by the American Geographical Society provides substantive introductions by authorities to single countries. Titles include: Japan, Switzerland, Fiji, Australia, Malta, and Brazil.

Baedeker's Guides (Macmillan). The oldest sightseeing series covering major cities, regions, and countries. Many European titles plus Japan, Mexico, Caribbean, Israel, Turkey, Bangkok, Hong Kong, Singapore, Tokyo, Jerusalem, Australia, Brazil, and Nepal. New this year: Scotland, Tuscany.

Berkeley Guides (Fodor's Travel Publications/Random House). Budget guides, with offbeat and adventurous travel ideas. Written by Berkeley students. Titles include: Eastern Europe, Mexico, France, Central America, Europe, Italy, Paris.

Berlitz Travel Guides (Berlitz Publishing). These insightful and literate guides provide the independent traveler with good background as well as practical information to the destination. Titles cover: Australia, Mexico, Caribbean, Ireland, France, Canada, Turkey, Spain, Portugal, Israel, Singapore, Costa Rica. New this year: Cuba, Travel Photography. Also from Berlitz is the Discover series. Lots of good background and pre-trip information. Titles include: France, Italy, Prague, Israel, Singapore, Loire Valley, Normandy, Pyrenees. New this year: Portugal, Tuscany, Egypt.

Best Places to Stay Guide (Houghton Mifflin). Excellent selection of quality lodging. Available for Asia, Mexico, and the Caribbean.

Birnbaum's Guides (Harper Collins). Consistently excellent guides for moderate budgets and up. Titles available for many countries of Europe, Europe as a whole, Mexico, South America, Caribbean, Eastern Europe, London, Paris, Rome, Florence, Venice, Ixtapa/Zihuatanejo, Cancun/Cozumel, Vancouver, Puerto Vallarta.

Blue Guides (W. W. Norton & Co.). Incredibly detailed British series covering history, culture, walks, driving tours, etc. Many titles on European destinations, plus Egypt, Istanbul, Jerusalem, Morocco, Denmark, Barcelona, Tuscany, Amsterdam, Albania, Southwest France, Sweden. New this year: Tunisia, Jordan, Budapest.

Bradt Guides (Globe Peqout Press). Reliable guides originating in the U.K. covering unusual and less traveled destinations for the adventurous traveler. Titles include: Albania, Antarctica, Burma, Estonia, Lebanon, Senegal, Zanzibar. New this year: Africa by Road, Eritrea, Malawi, Madagascar Wildlife, Mozambique, Venezuela, Hiking in Romania.

Cadogan Guides (Globe Pequot Press). Usually excellent, all-purpose guidebooks at moderate prices. Titles on many parts of Europe, plus Australia, Caribbean, India, Thailand/Burma, Turkey, Morocco, Amsterdam, Southern Spain, Mexico, Ecuador and the Galapagos, Paris, Sicily, Cyprus, Malta, Germany,

Southwest France, Brussels, London, Southwest Ireland. New this year: Andalucia, Henry Kelly's West of Ireland, London Markets, The Algarve, Crete, Northern Spain, Central Asia, Tuscany, Dordogne and Lot, Provence.

Citywalk Series (Henry Holt & Co.). Good historically-oriented walking tours. Titles include: Pariswalks, Praguewalks, Romewalks, Florencewalks, Beijingwalks, Berlinwalks, Jerusalemwalks, Londonwalks, Madridwalks, Venicewalks, Viennawalks.

Culture Shock! Series (Graphic Arts). Guides to customs and etiquette of various cultures. Titles include: Thailand, China, Pakistan, France, Great Britain, Israel, India, South Africa, Burma, Canada, Philippines, Australia, Korea, Nepal, A Globe-Trotter's Guide, Ireland, Morocco, Switzerland, Syria, Vietnam, Successful Living Abroad: Wife's Guide. New this year: Turkey, Germany, Denmark.

Customs and Etiquette in . . . (Talman Company). Pocket guides to the customs, manners, and culture of each country. Available for: Arabia and the Gulf States, China, Germany, Russia , Greece, Hungary, Japan, England, India, Israel, Thailand, Singapore.

Day Trips Series by Earl Steinbecker (Hastings House). Oriented to public transportation. Titles: Day Trips in Britain, France, Germany, Holland, Belgium, London, Italy, Europe, Archaeological Mexico.

Driving Tours (Macmillan). Interesting regional driving routes with lots of tips and sightseeing information. Titles include: Britain, France, Ireland, Mexico, Scotland, Austria, Australia, Scandinavia, Switzerland.

Exploring Rural Europe Series (Passport Books). Driving tours of 1 day to 1 week acquaint the traveler with the history, character, and cuisine of the region. Titles for France, Germany, Ireland, Greece, Portugal.

Eyewitness Guides (Dorling Kindersley Publishing). Well designed with lots of color and illustrations, many in 3-D. Good for art and architecture. Titles include: London, Paris, Rome, Prague, Vienna, France, Provence, Venice. New this year: Italy, Loire Valley, Seville and Andalucia.

Fielding's Guides (Fielding Worldwide). Good general guidebooks for all budget levels. Titles: Europe, Italy, France, Caribbean, Holland, Switzerland, Portugal, Brazil, Amazon, Southeast Asia, Vietnam. New this year: Borneo, Sydney, Thailand, Vietnam. Also new this year is a series of Fielding's pocket-size guides called Fielding's Agenda. Titles include: London Agenda, Paris Agenda, Rome Agenda.

Fodor's Guides (Fodor's Travel Publications/ Random House). The largest all-purpose series. Titles include: France, Germany, Great Britain, Europe, Italy, Paris, Caribbean. New this year: Cuba, South Africa. Fodor's Exploring Guides: Well-organized guides with good maps, color photos, detailed information on sights, and lots of trivia and interesting facts. Titles include: Paris, Germany, Spain, Rome, Thailand, Australia, Caribbean, Florence, Mexico, Prague, Turkey. New this year: China, Egypt, Israel. Also Fodor's Affordable Guides for the cost-conscious traveler.

Frommer's Guides (Macmillan). Solid, all-purpose favorite of many travelers. Frommer's comprehensive series covers all price ranges from deluxe to inexpensive. The Dollar-a-Day series is more budget oriented. City guides available for many major cities. Frommer's Walking Tour Series include: Paris, London, Berlin, England's Favorite Cities, Venice, Tokyo, Spain's Favorite Cities. New this year: Nova Scotia/New Brunswick/Prince Edward Island, Prague. Frommer's Food Lover's Companion Series. Titles include: France, Italy. Frommer's Irreverent Guides. Titles include: Amsterdam, London, Paris, Virgin Islands.

Indonesia Guides (Passport Books). Excellent

coverage of the islands of the Indonesian Archipelago. Titles include Bali, Java, Spice Islands, Sumatra, Underwater Indonesia, and more.

Insight Guides (APA Publications). In-depth background, historical, cultural discussion with good destination information. Guides to most international destinations. Titles include: Japan, The Nile, Great Barrier Reef, Mexico City, Madiera, Iceland, Costa Rica, South Africa, Switzerland, Jordan, Belize. Insight Compact Guides, introduced last year for European cities, have now expanded to include Bahamas, Costa Brava, Bali, Burgundy, and Beijing.

Karen Brown's Country Inns and Itineraries Series (Globe Pequot). Offers some great choices throughout Western Europe. Primary selections, organized as part of an itinerary, can be quite expensive but there are usually moderate and sometimes low-cost alternatives as well. Each of the 8 books is revised biannually. Titles include: Austria, France, England, Germany, Italy, Spain.

Knopf Guides (Knopf). Heavy focus on art and architecture with lots of photos, drawings, and plans. Titles include: Amsterdam, Istanbul, London, Vienna, Egypt, Provence, Ireland. New this year: Louvre, Bali.

Let's Go Guides (St. Martin's Press). Still the best all-purpose budget guides around. Thoroughly updated annually. Titles available for Europe, Britain/Ireland, France, Greece, Israel/Egypt, Italy, Mexico, Spain/Portugal/Morocco, Germany/Austria/Switzerland, London, Paris, Eastern Europe. New this year: Southeast Asia, Central America.

Lonely Planet Guides (Lonely Planet Publications). On a Shoestring Guides: Ultra-low-budget guides of considerable reputation. Titles: Africa on a Shoestring and similar titles on Eastern Europe, Northeast Asia, South America, Southeast Asia, West Asia, Central America, Western Europe, Mediterranean Europe, Scandinavian and Baltic Europe, and Middle East. Travel Survival Kits: Excellent guides for the adventurous traveler. All-purpose, all price ranges with plenty of low-cost choices. Wide range of titles throughout Africa, Asia, Oceania, South America. New this year: Austria, Central Asia, Denmark, Jamaica, Romania and Moldova. City Guides: Beijing, Prague. Walking/Trekking Guides. Titles include: Australia, New Zealand, Nepal, Patagonia, Switzerland, Turkey. Also this year a new line of travel literature: "Journeys," with titles on Australia, Japan, New Guinea, and Syria.

Maverick Guides (Pelican Publishing). General guidebooks covering accommodations, sights, background, etc. Titles include: Thailand, Bali and Java, Prague, Berlin.

Michelin Green Guides (Michelin Guides & Maps). The very best sightseeing guides. Good maps and historical notes. English language titles cover much of Western Europe, Mexico, Canada, Belgium, Atlantic Coast (France). New this year: Brussels, Tuscany.

Moon Travel Handbooks (Moon Publications). These guides provide a thorough background in cultural, historical, and political coverage, as well as exhaustive practical information aimed at getting travelers the best value for their money. Titles include: Nepal, Central Mexico, Northern Mexico, Indonesia, Southeast Asia, Bali, South Pacific, Tahiti, New Zealand, Fiji, Egypt, Cancun, South Korea, Micronesia, Yucatan, Pakistan, Belize, Jamaica, Outback Australia, Bangkok, Thailand, Moscow/St. Petersburg, Tibet, Costa Rica, Japan, Alberta and Northwest Territories, Atlantic Canada. New this year: Mexico, Vietnam, Cambodia and Laos.

Nelles Guides (Seven Hills Books). Cover culture and history plus basics on lodgings, sights, and getting around. Good maps. Titles available: Cyprus, Morocco, Paris, Spain (North and South), Turkey, India (North and South), Provence, China, Cambodia/Laos, Bali, Philippines, Moscow/St. Petersburg. New this year: Corsica, Israel, Portugal, South Africa.

New Key Series. Good all around general guidebooks with strong emphasis on ecotourism and the environment. Titles include: Costa Rica, Cancun and Yucatan, Belize. New this year: Ecuador, Guatemala.

Off the Beaten Track (Globe Pequot). Good for driving itineraries. Titles include: Spain, Austria, Switzerland, France, Scandinavia, Czech and Slovak republics, Poland. New this year: Western Canada.

Passport's World Handbooks (Passport Books). The original book in the series is the old reliable South American Handbook. Other titles following the same format include: Caribbean Islands, Mexico/Central America, India, North Africa, East African. New this year: Egypt Handbook, Sri Lanka Handbook, Nepal and Tibet Handbook, Pakistan Handbook.

Rick Steve's Series (John Muir). Offers budget travel insights on the sights, cities, and regions of Europe. Also tips on transport, lodging, and dining. Titles include: Europe, Italy, Scandinavia, France, Great Britain, Baltics and Russia.

Rough Guides (Penguin). For independent budget travelers. Americanized versions of the Rough Guides are written with a political awareness and a social and cultural sensitivity that makes them unique. Close to 40 titles, including many European destinations, plus Mexico, Kenya, Morocco, Peru, Yugoslavia, Czech Republic, Poland, Nepal, Holland/Belgium/Luxembourg, Prague, Barcelona, Egypt, Thailand, Tunisia, England, Corsica, Pyrenees, Tuscany/Umbria, Sicily, London, India, Moscow, Romania, Germany, Canada. New this year: Costa Rica, First-Time Europe, Goa, West Africa.

Sierra Club Adventure Guides (Sierra Club Books). Fine guides to every adventure under the sun. Titles available: the Caribbean, East

Africa, the Pacific, Trekking in Pakistan and India, Adventuring in North Africa, Adventuring in Belize. New this year: Central America.

Travelers' Tales (O'Reilly and Assoc.). Not regular guidebooks with sights and lodgings, but a collection of travelers' tales from experienced travelers. Titles include: Mexico, France, Thailand, India, Women's World. New this year: Brazil, Hong Kong, Spain.

Travellers' History Series (Interlink). Concise background of a city or country with historical information on sights, monuments, and important historical characters. Very easy to reference for the traveler. Titles include: England, Scotland, France, Paris, Spain, China, India.

Travellers' Wine Guides (Sterling Publishing). Beautifully illustrated series from England for those who want to taste or buy wine or simply explore the wine country. France, Germany, Italy, Spain.

Treasures and Pleasures of. . . (Impact Publications). New series designed for people who want to appreciate local cultures by shopping from artists and craftspeople: Caribbean, Hong Kong, Thailand, Indonesia, Singapore and Malaysia.

Virago Women's Travel Guides (Ulysses). Practical advice for women travelers plus background with the slant on women. Titles include: Paris, Rome, London.

Walking Easy (Gateway). New series for recreational walkers of all ages. Titles include: Italian Alps, Swiss Alps, French Alps.

Planning Guides

1996 International Travel Health Guide by Stuart R. Rose ($17.95 plus $3 shipping from Travel Medicine, Inc., 351 Pleasant St., Suite 312, Northampton, MA 01060; 800-872-

8633). Updated annually; recommended by U.S. State Department.

A Journey of One's Own: Uncommon Advice for the Independent Woman Traveler by Thalia Zepatos (The Eighth Mountain Press). Detailed advice on practical matters for women traveling abroad alone.

Adventure Holidays 1996: Your Complete Guide to Thousands of Active Vacations Worldwide (Vacation Work). Bicycling, windsurfing, canoeing, and more.

Adventure Vacations by Richard Bangs (John Muir Publications). Two hundred adventures organized by expedition outfitters.

Adventures Abroad: Exploring the Travel/ Retirement Option by Allene Symons and Jane Parker (Gateway Books). Introduction to vacation and retirement living in 17 countries by the authors with first-hand experiences of people living abroad. Information on housing, medical, cost of living, laws, finances, etc.

Adventures in Good Company: The Complete Guide to Women's Tours and Outdoor Trips (The Eighth Mountain Press). Profiles more than 100 companies worldwide that offer trips for women.

AIDS and International Travel (Council Travel with Stanford Univ. and San Francisco AIDS Foundation). Free from Council. Sound advice to international travelers.

Alternative Accommodations by John E. Sullivan (Travel Insider Press). Short-term stays and rentals worldwide.

Backpacking and Camping in the Developing World by Scott Graham (Wilderness Press). How-to adventure guide.

Budget Lodging Guide, B&J Publications, P.O. Box 5486, Fullerton, CA 92635; (800) 525-6633. Lists more than 600 institutions

worldwide with bed and breakfast, including 41 in London.

Bugs, Bites and Bowels by Dr J. Howarth (Globe Pequot). A Cadogan series guide on healthy travel covering prevention, diagnosis, and cure.

Cooking Schools. Directory of culinary vacations and short cooking classes for the non-professional cook. $13 postpaid from Athabasca Univ., Educational Travel, Box 10,000, Athabasca, AB TO6 2RO Canada.

Courier Bargains: How to Travel Worldwide for Next to Nothing by Kelly Monaghan. $17.50 postpaid from The Intrepid Traveler, P.O. Box 438, New York, NY 10034. Complete guide to courier travel in U.S. and around the world.

Do's and Taboos Around the World: A Guide to International Behavior by Roger Axtell (John Wiley & Sons). Practical and often humorous advice for the business and pleasure traveler on what to do and how to avoid doing the wrong thing in other cultures. Titles include: Gestures: Do's and Taboos of Body Language Around the World, Do's and Taboos of Using English Around the World.

Earth Mapbook Environmental Atlas (Interarts). Newly updated compact world atlas: clear maps, lots of information.

Ford's Freighter Travel Guide (Ford's Travel Guides). Very informative. Updated semi-annually.

Hostelling International (International Youth Hostel Federation). Listings of Youth Hostels throughout the world for all age travelers. Two annual volumes: Europe/Mediterranean and Africa/Americas/Asia/Pacific.

International Travel and Health 1996 (World Health Organization). Vaccination requirements and health advice.

Language Schools. Directory of hundreds of language learning vacations around the world. $13 postpaid from Athabasca Univ., Educational Travel, Box 10,000, Athabasca, AB TO6 2RO Canada.

Passport to World Band Radio (International Broadcasting Services). Hour-by-hour, country-by-country listings for world band radio programming.

Pocket Doctor by Dr. S. Bezruchka (Mountaineers). A compact health guide for the traveler.

Shaw Guides, edited by Dorlene V. Kaplan (Shaw Associates, 10 W. 66 St., #30H, New York, NY 10023). The Guide to Academic Travel describes courses, tours, and programs worldwide sponsored by 258 colleges, organizations, travel companies, and individuals. The Guide to Arts and Crafts Workshops gives details on 237 sponsors of workshops in 28 countries. The Guide to Cooking Schools contains detailed descriptions of 307 cooking schools worldwide plus information on 144 vocational programs. The Guide to Photography Workshops & Schools contains descriptions of more than 300 workshops and tours and nearly 1,000 career programs worldwide.

Smart Vacations: The Traveler's Guide to Learning Adventures Abroad (St. Martin's Press). Features more than 700 institutions and organizations that sponsor 1- to 6-week learning vacations abroad for adults.

Smartest, Smallest, Savviest Book of Travel Secrets by Natalie Windsor (Corkscrew Press). Pocket-size book full of practical tips.

Staying Healthy in Asia, Africa, and Latin America by Dirk Schroeder (Moon Publications). Deals with illness prevention, health supplies, suggestions on eating and drinking.

The Archaeology Handbook: A Field Manual and Resource Guide by Bill McMillon (John

Wiley & Sons). Comprehensive how-to and where-to guide for volunteers.

The High School Student's Guide to Study Travel, and Adventure Abroad, compiled by Council (St. Martin's Press). All the information teenagers need to plan a trip abroad.

The Safe Tourist—Hundreds of Proven Ways to Outsmart Trouble by Natalie Windsor (Corkscrew Press). Lots of travel tips.

Tips for the Savvy Traveler by Deborah Burns and Sarah May Clarkson (Storey Publishing). Hundreds of valuable tips from planning to coming home.

Transformative Adventures, Vacations and Retreats by John Benson (New Millennium). Worldwide organizations offering programs for personal change—meditation retreats, health spas, etc.

Travel and Learn by Evelyn Kaye (Blue Penguin). Educational travel programs offered by museums, colleges, and universities.

Travel Books Worldwide: The Travel Book Review. $36 per year (10 issues), Canada $48, rest of the world $72 or £42 per year from: Travel Keys Books/Travel Books Worldwide, P.O. Box 162266, Sacramento, CA 95816-2266. A 12-page newsletter devoted to new travel books.

Travel by Cargo Ship (Cadogan).

Vacation Home Exchange and Hospitality Guide by John Kimbrough (Kimco Communications). Guide to opportunities for vacation home exchanges all over the world. Information on associations/agencies that will put you in touch with contacts. Call (209) 275-0893.

Volunteer Vacations by Bill McMillon (Chicago Review Press). More than 500 opportunities worldwide, 5th edition, revised and expanded.

Work Your Way Around the World by Susan Griffith (Peterson's Guides, 7th edition). Provides excellent first-hand information on short-term jobs.

Work, Study, Travel Abroad: The Whole World Handbook (St. Martin's Press). Essential resource for students and learning travelers of all ages from Council.

World's Most Dangerous Places by Robert Young Pelton and Coskun Aral (Fielding Worldwide). A collection of first-hand experiences in places deemed dangerous (war zones, political unrest, unsafe areas) or forbidden (by State Department) all over the globe. Advice on avoiding scams, regions to be aware of, protecting yourself, etc. Some areas covered: The Gulf States, The Golden Triangle, Cuba, Eastern Turkey.

Africa/Middle East

Series: Baedeker, Bradt, Berlitz, Blue Guides, Cadogan, Citywalks, Culture Shock!, Customs and Etiquette, Fodor, Frommer, Knopf, Insight, Let's Go, Lonely Planet, Michelin, Moon Handbooks, Nelles, Passport World Handbooks, Rough Guides, Sierra Club, Simple Etiquette, Traveller's History. **Distributors:** Rafiki Books (45 Rawson Ave., Camden, ME 04843; 207-236-4244, fax 207-236-6253): Over 200 titles on Africa.

Africa's Top Wildlife Countries by Mark W. Nolting (Global Travel Publishers). Excellent reference by an authority on African wildlife.

Africa: Literary Companion by Oona Strathern (Passport Books). Compilation of literature, background, and cultural information.

African Customs and Manners by E. Devine and N. Braganti (St. Martin's Press). Dos and taboos on the African continent.

Ancient Egypt by Delia Pemberton (Chronicle Books). An architectural guide for travelers.

Backpacker's Africa by Hilary Bradt (Bradt Publishing). Best hikes in 17 countries. 3rd edition.

Bicycling in Africa by David Mozer (International Bicycle Fund, 4887 Columbia Dr. S., Seattle, WA 98109-1919). How to do it, with supplements on 17 separate countries.

Cycling in Kenya by Kathleen Bennett (Bicycle Books). Biking and hiking safaris.

Engstrom's Guide to Egypt and a Nile Cruise by Barie Engstrom (Kurios Press). Includes walking tours of archaeological sites.

Guide to East Africa by Nina Casimati (Hippocrene Books). Solid, thorough, all-purpose guide.

Guide to Jordan by Christine Osborne (Hippocrene Books). Lots of history and background notes, good itineraries.

Guide to Lebanon by Lynda Keen (Bradt Publishing).

Guide to South Africa by Briggs (Bradt Publishing). Complete guide to South Africa after the recent radical political changes.

Israel on Your Own by Harriet Greenberg (Passport Books, 2nd edition). Excellent all-purpose guide to independent travel—in all price ranges.

Kenya: A Visitor's Guide by Arnold Curtis (Bradt Publishing). Good orientation by long time resident.

Lebanon: A Travel Guide by Reid, Leigh and Kennedy (Pelican Publishing). Latest general guide to Lebanaon.

Namibia: Independent Traveler's Guide by Scott and Lucinda Bradshaw (Hippocrene). A must for anyone making their way across the country's vast expanse by plane, train, 4-wheel drive, bus or foot.

Off the Beaten Track in Israel by Ori Devir (Adama Books). The places the tourist never sees.

Saudi Arabia Companion Guide by Gene Linsdey (Hippocrene). Good general guide to the area.

Spectrum Guides (Hunter Publishing). Beautifully photographed, good cultural and background information. Available for: Kenya, Seychelles, Zimbabwe, African Wildlife Safaris.

The Heart of Jerusalem by Arlynn Nellhaus (John Muir Publications). Practical guide.

The Safari Companion: A Guide to Watching African Mammals by Richard Estes (Chelsea Green Publishing). Good reference for the person on safari.

Albania

Series: Blue Guides, Bradt.

Asia

Series: Cadogan, Fielding, Insight Guides, Lonely Planet, Moon Handbooks, Passport Handbooks, Rough Guides.

A Traveler's Guide to Asian Culture by John Gottberg (John Muir Publications). Excellent background by an Asian specialist.

All Asia Guide (Charles E. Tuttle Co.). 17th edition. Comprehensive guide to the continent.

Asia Pacific Business Travel Guide (PATA). Up-to-date practical travel information.

Asia Through the Back Door by Rick Steves and Bob Effertz (John Muir Publications). Inexpensive ways to experience the region.

Staying Healthy in Asia, Africa, and Latin America by Dirk Schroeder (Moon). Excellent, compact.

Teaching English in Southeast Asia by Jerry O'Sullivan (Passport Books). Practical information on finding a job, teaching and living in Cambodia, Hong Kong, Indonesia, Malaysia, Singapore, Thailand, Laos, Philippines, and Vietnam.

The Traveler's Guide to Asian Customs and Manners by Elizabeth Devine and Nancy Braganti (St. Martin's Press).

Australia

Series: Baedeker, Berlitz, Culture Shock!, Driving Tours, Fielding, Fodor, Frommer, Insight Guides, Lonely Planet, Maverick, Moon, Nelles, Rough Guides, Sierra Club.

Australia by Rail (Bradt Publishing).

Australia: Where the Fun Is by Thalassa Skinner and Lauren Goodyear (Mustang Publishing). Practical information for young travelers.

Bicycle Touring Australia by Leigh Hemmings (Mountaineers). Cycling tours of the most popular and accessible areas.

Bushwalking in Australia by John and Monica Chapman (Lonely Planet Publications).

Exploring Outback Australia (ISBS). Illustrated guide to accommodations, walks, and Aboriginal culture.

Outdoor Traveler's Guide to Australia by Sharon Cohen (Stewart, Tabori, and Chang). Superbly photographed guide to the Australian park system and the country's unusual wildlife.

Stepping Lightly on Australia by Shirley LaPlanche (Globe Pequot). Traveller's guide to ecotourism in this land of diverse flora and fauna.

The Australian Bed and Breakfast Book by J. and J. Thomas (Pelican). Stay in private homes with friendly hosts.

Austria

Series: Baedeker, Berkeley, Berlitz, Blue Guides, Citywalks, Driving Tours, Exploring Rural Europe, Eyewitness, Fodor, Frommer, Insight Guides, Karen Brown, Knopf, Let's Go, Lonely Planet, Michelin, Off the Beaten Track, Rick Steves.

Walking Easy in the Austrian Alps (Gateway Books). Hiking guide for active adults.

Baltic Countries

Series: Bradt, Lonely Planet, Rick Steves.

Benelux

Series: Baedeker, Berlitz, Blue Guides, Cadogan, Daytrips, Eyewitness, Fodor, Frommer, Insight Guides, Knopf, Michelin, Rick Steves, Rough Guides, Virago Women's Guides.

Backroads of Holland by Helen Colijn (Bicycle Books). Scenic excursions by bicycle, car, train, or boat.

On the Rails Around France, Belgium, Netherlands, and Luxembourg by Roger Thomas (Passport Books). Routes, maps, transport information.

Bulgaria

Series: Rough Guides.

Bulgaria: A Travel Guide by Philip Ward (Pelican). Comprehensive.

Canada

Series: Access, Baedeker, Berlitz, Birnbaum, Culture Shock!, Fodor, Frommer, Insight Guides, Let's Go, Lonely Planet, Michelin, Moon, Off the Beaten Track, Nelles, Rough Guides, Sierra Club.

Adventure Guide to Canada by Pam Hobbs (Hunter Publishing). Best outdoor and adventure attractions in all provinces.

Canada Compass Guide (Random House). History, background, maps, and resource information. Nicely illustrated.

Canadian Bed & Breakfast Guide by Gerda Pantel (Chicago Review Press). 1,500 choices including chalets, farmhouses, and city homes.

Cycling Canada by John M. Smith (Bicycle Books).

Guide to Eastern Canada and Guide to Western Canada by Frederick Pratson (Globe Pequot). Both guides provide thorough information on all aspects of travel in Canada.

Montréal Ultimate Guide, Toronto Ultimate Guide, and Vancouver Ultimate Guide (Chronicle). Comprehensive guides covering all aspects of travel to these three Canadian cities.

New Series of Canadian Guides (Formac Publishing/7 Hills). Titles available for Nova

Scotia, New Brunswick, Prince Edward Island, Manitoba, Halifax.

Nova Scotia and The Maritimes by Bike by Walter Sienko (Mountaineers Books).

Outdoor Traveler's Guide to Canada by D. Dunbar (Stewart, Tabori and Chang). Superbly photographed guide provides the active traveler with information on the national parks and outdoor recreation possibilities.

Vancouver Best Places by K. Wilson (Sasquatch Books).

Caribbean/West Indies

Series: Access, Baedeker, Berlitz, Birnbaum, Cadogan, Fielding, Fodor, Frommer, Impact, Insight Guides, Lonely Planet, Moon, Nelles, Passport World Handbooks, Sierra Club.

Adventure Guide to ... Barbados, Dominican Republic, Jamaica, Puerto Rica, and the Virgin Islands (Hunter Publications). Practical guides for the adventurous traveler.

Caribbean Afoot! by M. Timothy O'Keefe (Menasha Ridge Press). A walking and hiking guide to 29 Caribbean islands.

Diving Bermuda by Jesse Cancelmo and Mike Strohofer (Aqua Quest Publications). Diving sites, information on marine life, shipwrecks, and travel in Bermuda.

Diving Off the Beaten Track by Bob Burgess (Aqua Quest Publications). Diving in various Caribbean destinations.

Dominican Republic by Jack Tucker and Ursula Eberhard (Hippocrene).

Fielding's Caribbean by Margaret Zellers (Fielding Worldwide). Considered by many to be the best guide to the area.

Getting to Know Cuba by Jane McManus (St. Martin's Press). Discusses the U.S. travel ban, required travel documents, travel within Cuba, etc.

Guide to Cuba by Stephen Fallon (Bradt Publishing).

Outdoor Traveller's Guide to the Caribbean by Kay Showker (Stewart, Tabori and Chang). Enticing guide covers the Caribbean's natural history and outdoor activities.

Recommended Island Inns Caribbean by Kathy Strong (Globe Pequot Press). Well done.

Rum and Reggae by J. Runge (Villard). An insider's guide to the Caribbean.

Undiscovered Islands of the Caribbean by Burl Willes (John Muir Publications). Undiscovered is a relative term, but good ideas abound.

Central America

Series: Alive, Berkeley, Bradt, Culture Shock!, Fodor, Frommer, Insight Guides, Let's Go, Lonely Planet, Moon, New Key, Passport World Handbooks, Rough Guides, Sierra Club.

Adventure Guide to Belize by Harry S. Pariser (Hunter Publications). Practical guide for the adventurous traveler.

Belize: A Natural Destination by S. Wotkyns (John Muir). Focus on nature travel.

Choose Costa Rica by John Howells (Gateway Books). Wintering and retirement in Costa Rica (includes Guatemala).

Costa Rica Traveler's Literary Companion by B. Ras (Whereabouts Press). Compilation of literature, background, and cultural information.

Costa Rica's National Parks and Preserves by Joseph Franke (Mountaineers). Guide to these beautiful natural areas.

Costa Rica: A Natural Destination by Ree Strange Sheck (John Muir). Focus on nature travel.

Diving Belize by Ned Middleton (Aqua Quest Publications). Diving sites, information on marine life and travel in Belize.

Guatemala Guide, Belize Guide, Costa Rica Guide by Paul Glasman (Passport Press). Comprehensive guides for these three countries.

Guatemala: A Natural Destination by R. Mahler (John Muir). Focus on nature travel.

Honduras by Eric Hamovitch (Ulysses). Off the beaten track.

Honduras and Bay Islands Guide by J. Panet (Open Road). Good all-around guide.

Latin America by Bike by W. Siekno (Mountaineers). From Mexico through Central America to the tip of Argentina.

Maya Road by J. Conrad (Hunter Publications). Covers Yucatan, Belize, and Guatemala. Thorough guide to travel.

Maya Route: The Ultimate Guidebook by S. Ritz and R. Harris (Ulysses). Covers Yucatan, Belize, and Guatemala. Good coverage of wildlife reserves, bird sanctuaries, outdoor activities, sites, and practical information.

New Key to Belize by Stacy Ritz (Ulysses). Good detailed information on Belize.

On Your Own in El Salvador by Jeff Brauer. New. Comprehensive.

South and Central America: Literary Companion by Jason Wilson (Passport Books). Compilation of literature, background, and cultural information.

The Costa Rica Traveler by Ellen Searby (Windham Bay Press). Good background notes. All price ranges.

The New Key to Costa Rica by Beatrice Blake and Anne Becher (Ulysses Press). Good all-around guide to Costa Rica, now in its 11th edition. Blake is a resident of Costa Rica and gives knowledgeable, up-to-date advice.

Traveller's Survival Kit: Central America by Emily Hatchwell and Simon Calder (Vacation Work). Extensive practical information and town-by-town guide to the seven countries of a poorly represented region.

China/Hong Kong

Series: Baedeker, Berlitz, Blue Guides, Culture Shock!, Fodor, Frommer, Impact, Insight, Lonely Planet, Maverick, Moon Handbooks, Nelles, Rough Guides, Travelers' Tales.

Biking Beijing by Diana B. Kingsbury (China Books). Tours through Beijing to popular tourist destinations.

China Bound by Anne F. Thurston (National Academy Press). Prepares long- and short-term visitors for everyday life in China.

China Regional Guides (Passport Books). Includes Fujian, Xian, Beijing, Yunnan.

China: A Literary Companion by A.C. Grayling (John Murray). Collection of literature by native authors, visitors, and observers.

Imperial China by Chris Chan (Chronicle). An architectural guide for the traveler.

Trekking in Russia and Central Asia: A Traveler's Guide by Frith Maier (Mountaineers).

You Want to Go Where? A Guide to China for Travellers with Disabilities by Evelyn Anderton and Susan Sygall (Mobility International USA, P.O. Box 10767, Eugene, OR 97440; $9.95 postpaid). Excellent resource.

Czech Republic and Slovak Republic

Series: Baedeker, Berlitz, Berkeley, Blue Guides, Citywalks, Eyewitness, Fodor, Frommer, Insight Guides, Knopf, Let's Go, Lonely Planet, Nelles, Off the Beaten Track, Rough Guides.

Prague Traveler's Literary Companion by P. Wilson (Whereabouts Press). Compilation of literature, background, and cultural information.

The Czech Republic by Astrid Holtslag (Hippocrene). For the budget-conscious.

Visitor's Guide to Czechoslovakia by Andrew Beattie (Hunter Publishing). Comprehensive (except dining and accommodations) guide with good regional information and driving itineraries.

Europe

Series: Access, Baedeker, Berkeley, Berlitz, Birnbaum, Blue Guides, Bradt, Cadogan, Fielding, Fodor, Frommer, Insight Guides, Let's Go, Lonely Planet, Michelin, Nelles, Rick Steves, Rough Guides.

Are You Two ... Together? by L. Van Gelder and P. Brandt (Random House). A gay and lesbian travel guide to Europe.

Best European Travel Tips by John Whitman (Meadowbrook). 2,001 tips for saving money, time, and trouble in Europe.

Biking Through Europe by Dennis and Tina

Jaffe (Williamson Publishing). Excellent, well-researched.

Cambridge Guide to the Museums of Europe (Cambridge Univ. Press). Over 2,000 entries, includes art collections and cathedral treasures.

Camp Europe by Train by Lenore Baken (Ariel Publications). Touring and camping information using public transport.

Eastern Europe by Rail by Rob Dodson (Globe Pequot). Practical guide.

Eurail Guide—How to Travel Europe and All the World by Train by Kathryn Turpin and Marvin Saltzman (Eurail Guide Annual). Comprehensively covers train travel throughout the world.

Euroad: Complete Guide to Motoring in Europe by Bert Lief (VLE Ltd.). Maps include driving times and distances in miles; documents required. Seven-language autocar vocabulary.

Europe 101: History and Art for the Traveler by Rick Steves and Gene Openshaw (John Muir Publications). Wonderful.

Europe by Bike: 18 Tours Geared for Discovery, 2nd edition by Karen and Terry Whitehill (Mountaineers). First-rate.

Europe by Train by Katie Wood and George McDonald (Harper). Comprehensive rail guide to Europe including Russia and CIS.

Europe for Free by Brian Butler (Mustang Publishing). Good resource.

Europe on 10 Salads a Day by Greg and Mary Jane Edwards (Mustang Publishing). Vegetarian and health-food restaurants across Europe.

Europe the European Way by James F. Gollattscheck (Gateway Books). Living (or extended stays) in the world's great cities for $2,000 per month for two.

Europe Through the Back Door by Rick Steves (John Muir Publications). The best "how-to" and preparation book for Europe with lots of useful hints and information.

Europe Through the Back Door Travel Newsletter, Rick Steves, ed. Quarterly. Free from Europe Through the Back Door, Inc., 120 4th Ave. N., Edmonds, WA 98020. Our favorite travel newsletter.

Exploring Europe by Boat by B.R. Rogers and S. Rogers (Globe Pequot). Practical guide to water travel in Europe.

Festival Europe! by Margaret Johnson (Mustang Publishing). Fairs and celebrations throughout Europe.

First-Time Europe: Everything You Need to Know Before You Go by Louis CasaBianca (Rough Guides). Step-by-step planning guide for low-budget independent travelers.

Manston's Travel Key Europe by Peter Manston (Travel Keys). The best guide to the practical: how phones work, rules of the road, laundromats, etc. Also Italy and Britain.

Michelin Red Guides (Michelin Guides & Maps). Comprehensive symbol-oriented guides to restaurants and hotels throughout Western Europe.

Mona Winks: A Guide to Enjoying Europe's Top Museums by Rick Steves and Gene Openshaw (John Muir Publications).

Moto Europa by Eric Bredesen (Seren Publishing). P.O. Box 1212, Dubuque, IA 52004; (800) 387-6728. In-depth details on renting, driving, buying, and selling a car.

On the Rails Europe, edited by Melissa Shales (Passport Books). Routes, maps, transport information.

Rick Steve's Europe Through the Back Door Phrase Books (John Muir). French, Italian, German, Spanish/Portuguese, and French/Italian/German (3 in 1).

Ski Europe by Charles Leocha (World Leisure).

Take Your Kids to Europe by Cynthia Harriman (Mason-Grant Publications). Practical, up-to-date, how-to guide. P.O. Box 6547, Portsmouth, NH 03802; (603) 436-1608.

Teaching English in Eastern and Central Europe by Robert Lynes (Passport Books). Practical information on finding a job, teaching and living in Czech Republic, Slovakia, Poland, Hungary, Romania, and Bulgaria.

Thomas Cook European Timetable, $24.95 plus $4 shipping from Forsyth Travel Library, Inc., 9154 W. 57th St., P.O. Box 2975, Shawnee Mission, KS 66201-1375; (913) 384-3440. Rail schedules for over 50,000 trains on every European and British main line.

Touring Europe by Michael Spring (Fodor's Travel Publications/Random House). How to plan day-by-day personal itineraries.

Travel Guide to Jewish Europe by Ben Frank (Pelican). Jewish historical sites, Holocaust memorials, neighborhoods, restaurants, etc.

Traveling Europe's Trains by Jay Brunhouse (Pelican). Detailed itineraries.

Understanding Europeans by Stuart Miller (John Muir Publications). Insights into European behavior, historical and cultural heritage.

Walking Europe from Top to Bottom by Susan Margolis and Ginger Harmon (Sierra Club Books). Follows the Grande Randonnée Cinque on a 107-day journey. (You can do smaller portions.)

Walks (VLE Ltd.). Easy-to-follow maps for the 13 major cities of Europe.

France

Series: Access, Baedeker, Berkeley, Berlitz, Birnbaum, Blue Guides, Cadogan, Citywalks, Culture Shock!, Driving Tours, Daytrips, Exploring Rural Europe, Eyewitness, Fielding, Fodor, Frommer, Insight Guides, Karen Brown, Knopf, Let's Go, Lonely Planet, Michelin, Nelles, Off the Beaten Track, Rick Steves', Rough Guides, Virago Women's Guides.

Bed and Breakfasts of Character and Charm in France (Rivages Guides).

Camping and Caravanning France (Michelin Publications). Campgrounds, town plans, location information, plus facilities.

Cheap Sleeps in Paris and Cheap Eats in Paris by Sandra A. Gustafson (Chronicle). Guides to inexpensive lodgings, restaurants, bistros, and brasseries.

France by Bike: 14 Tours Geared for Discovery by Karen and Terry Whitehall (Mountaineers).

France on the TGV by Mark Beffart (Mustang). Travel throughout France on the world's fastest train.

French Country Welcome 1997 Gites de France, available from Ulysses Books and Maps, 4176 Saint-Denis, Montreal, PQ H2W 2M5 Canada; 514-843-9882.) Information on 3,200 B and B's throughout France.

Hotels and Country Inns of Charm and Character in France (Rivages Guides).

Literary Cafes of Paris by Noel Riley Fitch (Starrhill Press). Sit in famous Parisian cafes and read about the writers who made them famous.

On the Rails Around France, Belgium, Netherlands and Luxembourg by Roger Thomas (Passport Books). Routes, maps, transport information.

Paris for Free (Or Extremely Cheap) by Mark Beffart (Mustang Publishing). Hundreds of free and inexpensive things to do in Paris.

Paris Inside Out by Les Amis de la Fonderie (below). An insider's guide for resident students and discriminating visitors on living in the French capital.

Paris-Anglophone by David Applefield (Les Amis de la Fonderie, 104-106 Rue Eduard Vaillant Montreuil du Bois, 93100 Françe; (011-33-48-59-6-58). Directory of the English-speaking world in Paris.

The Unknown South of France: A History Buff's Guide by Henry and Margaret Reuss (Harvard Common Press). A guide to the history and culture of the south of France.

Through the French Canals by Philip Bristow (Talman). Exploring the waterways of France.

Undiscovered Museums of Paris by Eloise Danto (Surrey Books). Guide to little-known, hard-to-find (and major) museums and galleries.

Walking Easy in the French Alps (Gateway Books). Hiking guide for active adults.

Wild France (Sierra Club). Travel and nature guide to wilderness areas of France.

Germany

Series: Baedeker, Berkeley, Berlitz, Birnbaum, Blue Guides, Cadogan, Citywalks, Customs and Etiquette, Daytrips, Driving Tours, Exploring Rural Europe, Fodor, Frommer, Insight Guides, Karen Brown, Let's Go, Michelin, Off the Beaten Track, Rick Steves, Rough Guides, Traveller's History.

Germany by Bike: 20 Tours Geared for Discovery by Nadine Slavinski (Mountaineers).

Greece

Series: Baedeker, Berlitz, Blue Guides, Cadogan, Customs and Etiquette, Exploring Rural Europe, Fodor, Frommer, Insight Guides, Knopf, Let's Go, Lonely Planet, Michelin, Nelles, Off the Beaten Track, Rough Guides, Traveller's History.

Greece on Foot by Marc Dubin (Mountaineers). Fine hiking guide.

Greece: A Literary Companion by Martin Garrett (John Murray). Collection of literature by native authors, visitors, and observers

Greek Island Hopping by Richard F. Poffley (Passport Books) Valuable advice on ferrries, island itinerary planning.

Hungary

Series: Baedeker, Berlitz, Blue Guides, Customs and Etiquette, Fodor, Frommer, Insight Guides, Lonely Planet, Nelles, Rough Guides.

Budapest: A Critical Guide by András Török (Zephyr Press). Detailed inside information.

Hungary: An Insider's Guide by Nicholas T. Parsons (Hippocrene). A classic.

People to People Czech-Slovakia, Hungary,

Bulgaria by Jim Haynes (Zephyr Press, 13 Robinson St., Somerville, MA 02145). Latest in a series of books on Eastern Europe for travelers who want to experience life as the locals live it. Lists over 1,000 locals to contact.

Indian Subcontinent/ Himalayas

Series: Berlitz, Cadogan, Fodor, Frommer, Insight, Lonely Planet, Moon Handbooks, Nelles, Passport World Handbooks, Rough Guides, Travelers' Tales.

Bhutan: Himalayan Kingdom by Booz (Passport Books). Good overall coverage, focuses on background, history, etc. (not the practical).

India by Stanley Wolpert (Univ. of California Press). A concise and comprehensive guide to Indian history and culture by an authority.

India by Rail (Hunter Publishing).

India Guides (Passport Books). All-purpose guides with planned itineraries and good orientation. Titles include: Museums of India, Bhutan and Bombay/Goa, Delhi, Agrand Pakistan, Jaipur, The Hill Stations of India, The Kathmandu Valley.

India, Nepal & Sri Lanka: The Traveler's Guide by Peter Meyer and Barbara Rausch (Riverdale Co.). Popular German budget-oriented guide for the young adventurer.

India: A Literary Companion by Palling (John Murray). Collection of literature by native authors, visitors, and observers.

Nepal Trekker's Handbook by Amy Kaplan (Mustang). Valuable advice.

Northern India: Rajasthan, Agra, Delhi by Philip Ward (Pelican). First-person account by well-informed writer.

Silk Route by Rail by Dominic Streatfield-James (Trailblazer).

Tibet: Roof of the World (Passport Books, 3rd edition). Good overall coverage, focuses more on background, history, etc., than on practical travel information.

Travelers' Tales: India, edited by James O'Reilly and Larry Habegger (O'Reilly & Assoc.). An anthology of travel writings.

Trekking in Indian Himalayas by G. Weare (Lonely Planet).

Trekking in the Annapurna Region by Bryn Thomas (Trailblazer).

Trekking in Nepal by Stephen Bezruchka (Mountaineers, 6th edition). Detailed guide.

Trekking in the Everest Region by Jamie McGuinness (Trailblazer).

Trekking in Tibet: A Traveler's Guide by Gary McCue (Mountaineers).

Indonesia/ Malaysia/Singapore

Series: Berlitz, Bradt, Culture Shock!, Customs and Etiquette, Fielding, Impact, Indonesia Guides, Insight Guides, Knopf, Lonely Planet, Maverick, Moon Handbooks, Nelles, Passport World Handbooks, Rough Guides.

Indonesia Travel Guide by Richard Mann (Singapore National Printers). A complete guide to Indonesia's archipelago of 13,667 islands. Available from ISBS: (800) 944-6190.

Java and Bali Insider's Guide by Jerry LeBlanc (Hippocrene).

Thailand, Malaysia, Singapore by Rail by Brian McPhee (Bradt).

Ireland

Series: Baedeker, Berkeley, Berlitz, Birnbaum, Blue Guides, Cadogan, Customs and Etiquette, Culture Shock!, Driving Tours, Exploring Rural Europe, Eyewitness, Fodor, Frommer, Insight Guides, Karen Brown, Knopf, Let's Go, Lonely Planet, Michelin, Nelles, Off the Beaten Track, Rick Steves, Rough Guides, Traveller's History.

Bed and Breakfast Ireland by Elsie Dillard and Susan Causin (Chronicle). Guide to over 300 of Ireland's best B and B's.

Ireland by Bike: 21 Tours Geared for Discovery by Robyn Krause (Mountaineers).

Ireland: Complete Guide and Road Atlas (Globe Pequot). Comprehensive guide, organized by regions. Information on cities, villages, highlights, and driving tours. Sixteen pages of color road maps and street maps.

Joyce's Dublin: A Walking Guide to Ulysses by Jack McCarthy (Irish Books & Media). Fascinating.

See Ireland by Train by Fergus Mulligan (Irish Books & Media). Compact, helpful resource.

The Visitor's Guide to Northern Ireland by Rosemary Evans (Hunter Publishing). Comprehensive and nicely illustrated.

Wild Ireland (Sierra Club). Travel and nature guide to wilderness areas of Ireland.

Italy

Series: Acccss, Bacdckcr, Berkeley, Berlitz, Birnbaum, Blue Guides, Cadogan, Citywalks, Daytrips, Driving Tours, Exploring Rural, Eyewitness, Fielding, Fodor, Frommer, Insight Guides, Karen Brown, Knopf, Let's Go, Lonely Planet, Michelin, Nelles, Off the Beaten Track,

Rick Steves, Rough Guides, Traveller's History, Virago Women's Guides.

Bed and Breakfasts of Character and Charm in Italy (Rivages Guides).

Bicycle Tours of Italy by Hendricks (Penguin). Cycling tours covering several regions of Italy.

Cento Citta: A Guide to the "Hundred Cities and Towns" of Italy by Paul Hofmann (Henry Holt). A book for the traveler who wants to go beyond the major tourist cities.

Cheap Sleeps in Italy and Cheap Eats in Italy by Sandra A. Gustafson (Chronicle). Guide to inexpensive, charming lodgings and restaurants.

Literary Cities of Italy by William Whitman (Starrhill Press). Guides the traveler by foot and water taxi through the cities that have inspired some of the most brilliant Italian writers.

Northern Italy: A Taste of Trattoria by Christina Baglivi (Mustang). Eat with the locals.

Teaching English in Italy by Martin Penner (Passport Books). Practical information on finding a job, teaching, and living in Italy.

Undiscovered Museums of Florence by Eloise Danto (Surrey Books). Guide to little-known, hard-to-find (and major) museums and galleries.

Walking Easy in the Italian Alps (Gateway Books). Hiking guide for active adults.

Wild Italy (Sierra Club). Travel and nature guide to wilderness areas of Italy.

Japan

Series: Berlitz, Cadogan, Customs and Etiquette, Fodor, Frommer, Insight Guides, Lonely Planet, Moon Handbooks.

Budget Guide to Japan by Ian McQueen (Kodansha). Japan on the cheap for independent travelers.

Coping with Japan by John Randle with Mariko Watanabe (Blackwell). Helpful sourcebook.

Cycling Japan by B. Harrell (Kodansha).

Gateway to Japan by June Kinoshkita and Nicholas Palevsky (Kodansha). Revised edition. Comprehensive guide: good maps, place names also in Japanese characters. By the same authors: Gateway to Tokyo.

Hiking in Japan by Paul Hunt (Kodansha). Mountain trails, maps, great geological notes.

Japan Unescorted by James K. Weatherly (Kodansha). Independent traveler's guide.

Japan Vacation Planner by Charles Northup (Stone Bridge Press), P.O. Box 8208, Berkeley, CA 94707. Pre-trip planner filled with resources.

Japan: A Literary Companion by Harry Guest (Passport Books). Compilation of literature, background, and culture.

Ski Japan! by T.R. Reid (Kodansha).

Teaching English in Japan by Jerry O'Sullivan (Passport Books). Practical information on finding a job, teaching, and living in Japan.

Korea

Series: Culture Shock!, Fodor, Insight Guides, Lonely Planet, Moon Handbooks.

Malta

Series: Blue Guides, Cadogan, Insight Guides.

Mexico

Series: Access, Baedeker, Berkeley, Berlitz, Birnbaum, Bradt, Cadogan, Daytrips, Driving Tours, Fielding, Fodor, Frommer, Insight Guides, Knopf, Let's Go, Lonely Planet, Michelin, Moon Handbooks, Nelles, Passport World Handbooks, Rough Guides, Travelers' Tales.

Adventure Guide to Baja California by Wilbur Morrison (Hunter Publications). Practical guide.

Backcountry Mexico by Bob Burleson and David Riskind (Univ. of Texas Press). Well-written how-to-do-it guide.

Baja by Kayak: The Ultimate Sea Kayaking Guide to Baja by Lindsay Loperenza (White Cloud).

Bicycling Mexico by E. Weisbroth and E. Ellman (Hunter Publications).

Choose Mexico by J. Howells and D. Merwin (Gateway Books). Guide for those interested in retiring or residing in Mexico.

Diving Cozumel by Steve Rosenberg (Aqua Quest Publications). Diving sites, information on marine life, archaeological sites, and travel.

Hidden Mexico: Adventurer's Guide to Beaches and Coasts by R. Bruns (Ulysses). For the coastal traveler.

Mexico by Rail by G. Poole (Hunter Publications).

Mexico West Book by Tom Miller (Baja Trails). Detailed guide to West Coast of Mexico. Excellent for the driver.

Mexico: A Hiker's Guide to Mexico's Natural History by Jim Conrad (Mountaineers). Steers hikers through Mexico's natural landscape while illuminating its natural history.

New Key to Cancun and Yucatan by Richard Harris (Ulysses). Good detail and information.

The Best Mexican Travel Tips by John Whitman (Harper & Row).

The People's Guide to Mexico by Carl Franz (John Muir Publications). A wonderful read—full of wisdom, too.

The People's Guide to RV Camping in Mexico by Carl Franz (John Muir Publications). Extensive camping information and advice.

The Yucatan: A Guide to the Land of Maya Mysteries by Antoinette May (Wide World Publishing). Includes Tikal, Belize, Copan. A respected guide focusing on cultural considerations.

Travelers' Tales: Mexico, edited by James O'Reilly and Larry Habegger (O'Reilly and Assoc.). An anthology of travel writings and personal accounts.

Myanmar (Burma)

Series: Bradt, Culture Shock!, Fielding, Insight Guides, Lonely Planet, Moon Handbooks, Passport World Handbooks.

New Guinea

Series: Lonely Planet, Indonesia Guides.

Bushwalking in Papua New Guinea by Riall Nolan (Lonely Planet Publications).

New Zealand

Series: Berlitz, Fielding, Fodor, Frommer, Insight Guides, Lonely Planet, Moon, Nelles.

New Zealand by Bike by Bruce Ringer (Mountaineers, 2nd edition). Bike tours through scenic countryside.

The New Zealand Bed and Breakfast Book by J. and J. Thomas (Pelican). Lists over 300 private homes and hotels.

Pacific

Series: Lonely Planet, Moon Handbooks, Sierra Club. Lonely Planet and Moon Handbooks have many titles that focus on this area by island groups and individual islands. Titles include: South Pacific Handbook (Moon Handbooks), Micronesia (Lonely Planet), Fiji (both companies), Vanuatu (Lonely Planet), Samoa (Lonely Planet).

Adventure Guide to South Pacific and Adventure Guide to Micronesia by T. Booth (Hunter Publishing). Practical guides for the active traveler.

Adventuring in the Pacific (Sierra Club). For the adventurous traveler.

Philippines

Series: Culture Shock!, Insight Guides, Lonely Planet, Moon Handbooks, Nelles.

Poland

Series: Bradt, Insight Guides, Lonely Planet, Off the Beaten Track, Rough Guides.

Hiking Guide to Poland and Ukraine by Tim Burford (Bradt).

People to People Poland by Jim Haynes (Zephyr Press). One of a series of books on Central Europe for travelers who want to experience life as the locals live it. Lists over 1,000 locals to contact.

Poland by Marc Heine (Hippocrene Books). A fine history-laced guided tour, especially of southeast Poland.

Polish Cities (Pelican). A guide to Warsaw, Krakow, and Gdansk.

Portugal

Series: Baedeker, Berlitz, Birnbaum, Blue Guides, Cadogan, Citywalks, Exploring Rural Europe, Fielding, Fodor, Frommer, Insight Guides, Let's Go, Michelin, Off the Beaten Track, Rick Steves, Rough Guides.

Traveller's Portugal by Anthony Hogg (Boerum Hill Books). If you have a car, these are great itineraries. Excellent history section.

Romania

Series: Bradt, Lonely Planet, Rough Guides.

People to People Romania by Jim Haynes (Zephyr Press). One of a series of books on Central Europe for travelers who want to experience life as locals live it. Lists over 1,000 locals to contact.

Romania Travel Guide by L. Brinkle (Hippocrene). Good background.

Russia and the NIS

Series: Baedeker, Berlitz, Blue Guides, Cadogan, Customs and Etiquette, Fodor, Frommer, Insight Guides, Knopf, Lonely Planet, Moon, Nelles, Rick Steves, Rough Guides, Traveller's History. **Distributors:** Russian Information Services, 89 Main St., Montpelier, VT 05602; (800) 639-4301. Free catalog.

Complete Guide to the Soviet Union by Victor and Jennifer Louis (St. Martin's).

Explorer's Guide to Moscow by Robert Greenall (Zephyr Press).

Georgian Republic by Roger Rosen (Passport

Books). Comprehensive guide to this diverse area. First guide in English.

Russia Survival Guide by Paul Richardson (Russian Information Services). Comprehensive guide with practical information.

Trans-Siberian Rail Guide by Robert Strauss (Hunter Publishing). Excellent.

Trekking in Russia and Central Asia: A Traveler's Guide by Frith Maier (Mountaineers).

Where in Moscow by Paul Richardson (Russian Information Services). Practical information, maps, and information on the city.

Where in St. Petersburg by Paul Richardson (Russian Information Services). Practical information, maps, and information on the city.

Scandinavia

Series: Baedeker, Berlitz, Blue Guides, Culture Shock!, Driving Tours, Fodor, Frommer, Impact, Insight Guides, Lonely Planet, Nelles, Off the Beaten Track, Rick Steves, Rough Guides.

Visitor's Guides (Hunter Publishing). Touring guides with suggested routes and information on sights, places of interest, town tours, background. Available for: Denmark, Norway, Finland, Sweden, and Iceland.

Slovenia

Series: Lonely Planet.

South America

Series: Alive, Berlitz, Bradt, Cadogan, Fielding, Fodor, Frommer, Insight Guides, Lonely Planet, Passport World Handbooks, Rough Guides, Travelers' Tales.

Adventure Travel in Latin America: Where to Backpack, Camp and Find Adventure in Mexico, the Caribbean, Central America and South America by Scott Graham (Wilderness Press). This guide should be a real help.

Apus & Incas: A Cultural Walking and Trekking Guide to Cuzco, Peru by Charles Brod (Inca Expeditions). Good orientation.

Backpacking and Trekking in Peru and Bolivia by Hilary Bradt (Bradt).

Best Places to Stay in South America by Alex Newton (Hunter).

Hayit's Budget Travel: Venezuela by Beatrix Diel (Hayit). New addition to a German budget travel series.

Latin America by Bike by W. Sienko (Mountaineers). Covers Mexico, through Central America all the way to the tip of Argentina.

South America's National Parks by William Leitch (The Mountaineers). An introduction to South America's great ecological treasures.

South and Central America: Literary Companion by Jason Wilson (Passport Books). Compilation of literature, background, and cultural information.

Traveler's Guide to El Dorado and the Inca Empire by Lynn Meisch (Viking Penguin). A superb practical guide.

Traveler's Guide to Latin America Customs & Manners by N. Braganti and E. Devine (St. Martin's Press). An important aid in understanding Latin American culture.

Spain

Series: Access, Baedeker, Berlitz, Birnbaum, Blue Guides, Cadogan, Citywalks, Culture Shock!, Driving Tours, Exploring Rural Europe, Eyewitness, Fielding, Fodor, Frommer, Insight Guides, Karen Brown, Let's Go, Michelin, Nelles, Off the Beaten Track, Rick Steves, Rough Guides, Traveller's History, Travelers' Tales.

Choose Spain by John Howells and Bettie Magee (Gateway Books). Guide to living or extended stays in Spain and Portugal.

Islamic Spain and Northern Spain: The Road to Santiago de Compostela (Chronicle). Informative introductions to architectural styles for the traveler. Northern Spain focuses on the renowned "pilgrim's route."

Paradores of Spain by Sam and Jane Ballard (The Harvard Common Press). Unusual lodging and restaurants.

Spain: A Literary Companion by Jimmy Burns (John Murray). Collection of literature by native authors, visitors, and observers.

Trekking in Spain by Marc Dubin (Lonely Planet Publications). Gives both day hikes and overnight treks.

Wild Spain (Sierra Club). Travel and nature guide to the wilderness areas of Spain.

Switzerland

Series: Baedeker, Berlitz, Blue Guides, Bradt, Culture Shock!, Driving Tours, Fodor, Frommer, Insight Guides, Karen Brown, Let's Go, Lonely Planet, Michelin, Off the Beaten Track, Rick Steves.

Switzerland by Rail by Anthony Lambert (Bradt Publishing).

Switzerland: The Smart Traveler's Guide to Zurich, Basel and Geneva by Paul Hofmann (Henry Holt).

Walking Easy in the Swiss Alps by C. and C.

Lipton (Gateway Books). Hiking guide for active adults.

Walking Switzerland the Swiss Way by Marcia and Philip Lieberman (Mountaineers). Great ideas.

Taiwan

Series: Culture Shock!, Insight Guides, Lonely Planet.

Guide to Taipei and Taiwan by Joseph Nerbonne (W.S. Heinman). Best guide to the area. All-purpose, good language aids.

Thailand

Series: Berlitz, Cadogan, Culure Shock!, Customs and Etiquette, Fielding, Fodor, Frommer, Impact, Insight Guides, Let's Go, Lonely Planet, Knopf, Maverick, Moon Handbooks, Nelles, Passport World Handbooks, Rough Guides.

Chiang Mai: Thailand's Northern Rose (Passport Books). Good general and planning information on this area of Thailand.

Diving in Thailand by Collin Piprell (Hippocrene). Best diving sites with information on preparation, facilities, etc.

Thailand Travel Guide by Sam Fang (Singapore National Printers). Contains comprehensive and concise facts for visitors on business or pleasure. Available from ISBS; (800) 944-6190.

Thailand, Malaysia, Singapore by Rail by Brian McPhee (Bradt).

Travelers' Tales: Thailand, edited by James O'Reilly and Larry Habegger (O'Reilly & Assoc.). An anthology of travel writings and personal accounts.

Turkey

Series: Baedeker, Berlitz, Blue Guides, Cadogan, Fodor, Frommer, Insight Guides, Knopf, Let's Go, Lonely Planet, Nelles, Rough Guides, Traveller's History.

Strolling Through Istanbul by Hillary Sumner Boyd and John Freely (Methuen/ Routledge, Chapman, Hall). A classic that focuses on the city's antiquities.

Trekking in Turkey by Marc Dubin (Lonely Planet Publications). Trekking information for this country of varied terrain.

Ukraine

Hiking Guide to Poland and Ukraine by Tim Burford (Bradt).

Language and Travel Guide to Ukraine by L. Hodges (Hippocrene). Good resource.

United Kingdom

Series: Access, Baedeker, Berkeley, Berlitz, Birnbaum, Blue Guides, Cadogan, Citywalks, Customs and Etiquette, Daytrips, Driving Tours, Exploring Rural Europe, Eyewitness, Fielding, Fodor, Frommer, Insight Guides, Karen Brown, Knopf, Let's Go, Lonely Planet, Michelin, Nelles, Off the Beaten Track, Rick Steves, Rough Guides, Traveller's History, Virago Women's Guides.

AA/Ordnance Survey Leisure Guides (Hunter Publishing). Handsomely illustrated touring guides with good maps. Titles cover Ireland, Scotland, and many parts of England.

An American's Guide to Britain by Robin Winks (Charles Scribner's Sons). A very knowledgeable insider's guide. Excellent.

Best Bed and Breakfasts: England, Scotland,

Wales 1996-97 by Sigourney Wells (Globe Pequot Press). Alphabetically by county.

Best Hotels of Great Britain and Best Restaurants of Great Britain (Globe Pequot).

Cheap Eats in London and Cheap Sleeps in London (Chronicle Books). 100 inexpensive places to eat and sleep.

CTC Route Guide to Cycling in Britain and Ireland by Christa Gausden and Nicholas Crane (Haynes Publishing). First rate. Not available in U.S.

Cycle Tours in the U.K. (Ordinance Survey). Four different guides, each providing many different one-day trips in the U.K.

Cycling Great Britain by Tim Hughes (Bicycle Books).

England by Bike: 18 Tours Geared for Discovery by Les Woodland (Mountaineers).

Fodor's London Companion: The Guide for the Experienced Traveler by Louise Nicholson (Fodor's Travel Publications/Random House). Unique, nonseries title. Includes 12 walking tours.

Literary Britain by Frank Morley (Harper & Row). Packed with information.

Literary Villages of London by Luree Miller (Starrhill Press). The author has mapped her favorite walks past the London homes and haunts of celebrated writers.

London for Free by Brian Butler (Mustang Publishing). Hundreds of free things to do.

On the Rails Around Britain and Ireland, edited by Neil Wenborn (Passport Books). Routes, maps, transport information.

Passport Guide to Ethnic London by Ian McAuley (Passport Books). A guide to history, food, culture—neighborhood by neighborhood.

Scotland Activity Holidays (Seven Hills). Practical details.

Scotland Bed and Breakfast (British Tourist Authority). Over 2,000 B and B's listed.

The Best of Britain's Countryside—Heart of England and Wales by Bill and Gwen North (Mountaineers). Two-week drive and walk itinerary for northern England and Scotland, southern England, heart of England and Wales.

Undiscovered Museums of London by Eloise Danto (Surrey Books). Guide to little-known, hard-to-find (and major) museums and galleries.

Where to Stay in England: B and B's, Farmhouses and Inns (British Tourist Authority).

Where to Stay in England: Hotels and Guest Houses (British Tourist Authority).

Wild Britain (Sierra Club). Travel and nature guide to wilderness areas of Britain.

Vietnam/Laos/Cambodia

Series: Bradt, Fielding, Insight Guides, Lonely Planet, Maverick, Moon, Nelles, Passport World Handbooks.

Guide to Vietnam by John R. Jones (Bradt). Every province and area of interest is described in detail, along with fascinating ethnic and cultural information.

Vietnam: Traveler's Literary Companion, edited by J. Balaban and N. Qui Duc (Whereabouts Press). Compilation of literature, cultural and background information.

Worldwide Destinations

Home from Home (Seven Hills Book Distributors). Annual U.K. guide contains details on homestays, home exchanges, hospitality exchanges, and school exchanges worldwide.

Inn Places: Worldwide Gay and Lesbian Accommodations (Ferrari).

Jewish Travel Guide by Stephen Massil (Sepher-Herman Press). A comprehensive survey for the Jewish traveler. Provides listings of Jewish organizations throughout the world.

More Women Travel (Penguin). From Rough Guide series.

Places of Interest: Worldwide Gay and Lesbian Guide (Ferrari).

Specialty Travel Index: Directory of Special Interest Travel. Biannual, $10 per year. STI, 305 San Anselmo Ave., San Anselmo, CA 94960; (415) 459-4900. Lists adventure travel tour operators that have programs worldwide.

U.S. State Department Travel Advisories. Available through Inter-L or by calling (202) 647-5225, these periodic advisories alert U.S. travelers to health and safety risks worldwide.

Women Travel, edited by N. Jansz and M. Davies. From the Rough Guide Series (Penguin). Compilation of women's experiences, advice, and practical information.

World Music, from the Rough Guides Series (Penguin). References and information on music spanning the globe.

KATHY WIDING is a freelance travel writer and the Travel Book Editor for Transitions Abroad.

CHAPTER 2

Special
Interest
Vacations

The following listing of specialty travel vacations was supplied by the organizers. Contact the program directors to confirm costs, dates, and other details.

Australia/New Zealand

Trek Australia/New Zealand. Fourteen-31 days exploring Australia and New Zealand with a small (13 max.) international group. Hostelling-International accommodations. Explore the Great Barrier Reef, the bush and outback, and parks. Dossier available on request.

Dates: Monthly departures year round. Cost: From $1,289, includes transportation, accommodations, sightseeing, park fees. Contact: Roadrunner Worldwide, 6762A Centinela Ave., Culver City, CA 90230-6304; (800) 873-5872, fax (310) 390-1446; amadlax@attmail.com.

Austria

Wiener Internationale Hochschulkurse. German courses at the University for beginners and advanced students, perfectionist courses (6 levels). Lectures on German and Austrian literature, music, linguistics, Austria. Special courses: translation into German, commercial correspondence, business German, medical terminology, communication, phonetics, Vienna waltz, choir singing. Language laboratory. Excursions.

Dates: Jul 6-Aug 2, Aug 3-30, Aug 31-Sep 20. Cost: Course fee (4 weeks): Approx. ATS4,300; accommodations: Approx. ATS6,000. Contact: Magister Sigrun Anmann-Trojer, Wiener Internationale Hochschulkurse, Universität, Dr. Karl Lueger-Ring 1, A1010 Wien, Austria; (011) 43-1-405-12-54 or 405-47-37, fax 405-12-5410.

Belize

CHAA Creek School of Caribbean Cookery. Our week-long culinary course combines half days of cooking classes with food-related touring to Mayan sites, local markets, and native kitchens. Special emphasis on tropical ingredients, the foods of Belize, and decadent desserts. Enjoy staying at a jungle lodge on the Macal River while learning how to create gourmet meals.

Dates: Jun 1-Dec 15, alternate weeks. Cost: $1,500 per person, based on double occupancy. Contact: Bill Altman, CHAA Creek, P.O. Box 53, San Ignacio, Cayo, Belize, Central America; (011) 501-92-2037, fax 92-2501; chaa_creek@ btl.net.

Canada

Alaskan Grizzly, Rocky Rambler, Hostelling Treks. Two weeks exploring Canada's Rocky Mountains and Alaska's wilderness travel with a small group from many different countries, staying in Hostelling International-approved accommodations. Hike a glacier, view spectacular wildlife, raft wild rivers. Detailed trek dossier available upon request.

Dates: Weekly departures, May-Oct. Cost: From $859. Contact: Roadrunner Worldwide, 6762A Centinela Ave., Culver City, CA 90230-6304; (800) 873-5872, fax (310) 390-1446; amadlax@attmail.com.

Hollyhock Seminar and Holiday Center. Over 60 workshops and seminars in the practical, creative, healing, and spiritual arts. Example: writing, singing, dancing, T'ai Chi, yoga, meditation, drumming. Gourmet vegetarian cuisine; hot tub; vacations welcome without taking a workshop.

Dates: Apr-Oct. Cost: Includes tuition, accommodations and meals. From CAN$500-CAN$1,300 per week depending on accommodations choice. Contact: Hollyhock, The Registrar, Box 127 Manson's Landing, BC, V0P 1K0, Canada; (800) 933-6339, fax (604) 935-6424; hollyhock1@aol.com.

Northern Lights Alpine Recreation. Mountaineering and hiking trips to earnest participants with a sincere interest in meaningful wilderness experiences. Scheduled and customized guided trips. Introductory to experienced. British Columbia Rockies and Purcell Mountain Ranges.

Dates: Year round. Cost: $80 per day, 8-day trips $535-$610. Guiding only. Participants responsible for transportation, equipment, and food. Contact: Kirk or Katie Mauthaer, Box 399, Invermere, BC, V0A 1K0 Canada; (250) 342-6042.

Purcell Lodge Outdoor Programs. This full service modern lodge is situated on a remote mountain top accessible only by helicopter. Hiking, snowshoeing or cross-country skiing in pristine alpine meadows, scenic ski tours, and powder telemark skiing, native study, and photography. Packages include delicious home cooked meals and snacks, deluxe room with mountain views, guiding and ski instruction services.

Dates: Dec-Apr, Jun-Oct. Cost: From CAN$130 per person per night American plan. Contact: Places Less Travelled Ltd., P.O. Box 1829, Golden, BC V0A 1H0, Canada; (250) 344-2639, fax (250) 344-5520; places@ rockies.net.

Costa Rica

Instituto de Lenguaje "Pura Vida." Only minutes from the capitol in the fresh mountain air of Heredia. Intense total immersion methods of teaching. Morning classes and daily cultural activities all conducted in Spanish, maximum 5 students per class. Teachers hold university degrees. Latin music and dance lessons, tours, trips, parties. Learn Spanish fast.

Dates: Classes for all levels start every Monday year round. Cost: Language only, 20 hours per week $230; total immersion, 35 hours per week with homestay $370; children's classes with homestay $370 per week, daycare available. Contact: Instituto de Lenguaje "Pura Vida," P.O. Box 730, Garden Grove, CA 92642; (714) 534-0125, fax (714) 534-1201; BS7324@ aol.com.

Language School on Wheels. See the country and learn Spanish. Travel to Costa Rica's beaches, volcanoes, and rainforests aboard comfortable converted coaches. Study Spanish enroute or on the beach from local teachers. Call for trip dates or have us custom design a tour to fit your group. Immerse yourself in the country.

Dates: Feb 1 and Mar 15, 1997. Cost: $449 (land), $101 (food). Contact: Green Tortoise Adventure Travel, 494 Broadway, San Francisco, CA 94133; (800) 867-8647, fax (415) 956-4900; www.greentortoise.com.

Europe

European Hostelling Trek. Eleven-24 days from London, includes all accommodations, transportation in your own mini-coach, sightseeing in all major cities, breakfast daily and plenty of time to explore on your own: Amsterdam, Rhone Valley, Prague, Budapest, the Alps, Italy, France, Ireland, and Wales. Detailed trek dossier on request.

Dates: Monthly departures year round. Cost: From $999. Contact: Roadrunner Worldwide, 6762A Centinela Ave., Culver City, CA 90230-6304; (800) 873-5872, fax (310) 390-1446; amadlax@attmail.com.

European Snowboard Tour. Chamonix, France is the crown jewel of alpine sports. Experience European culture, art, architecture, and more while snowboarding with other young people (ages 18 to 38) in the legendary French and Italian Alps. Participate in your favorite outdoor sport for 1 week, in another country, in a friendly international resort atmosphere. Make lifelong friends, take your boarding global.

Dates: Mar 21-29, 1997. Cost: From $1,050. Contact: Julio Buelna, Global Travel Etc., P.O. Box 86226, San Diego, CA 92138; (800) 290-4276, fax (619) 299-5293; goglobal@adnc.com.

Mozart's Europe. Follows Mozart on his sojourns in Austria, Czech Republic, Germany, Italy, and Switzerland. Attendance at 9-10 world-class concerts. Meetings with musicologists and musicians. Unique experiences in music such as listening to Mozart's own piano.

Dates: Spring and fall. Cost: Approx. $3,500 (land only). Contact: Norman Eagle, Now Voyager Tours, Deer Lane, Pawlet, VT 05761; (802) 325-3656.

Wine and Walking Weekends. Tutored by wine expert Jon Hurley, enjoy delicious food, stay in English country houses, and take lovely, gentle walks in the Wye Valley.

Dates: Year round. Cost: £165-£195 includes accommodations, 2 breakfasts, 2 dinners, 2 tastings, guided walks, all wines. Contact: Jon Hurley's Country House Wine and Walking Weekend, Upper Orchard, Hoarwithy, Herefordshire HR2 6QR, U.K.

France

Enjoy French in a Chateau. Château de Mâtel (17th century) offers residential courses for adults in General French, Intensive French, Cooking. On 32 hectares of parkland near Roanne city center. Close to Burgundy, Beaujolais, and city of Lyons. Single, en suite, and shared rooms available. One through 12-week courses. Tennis, pool, horse-riding, kayak.

Dates: Every Sunday Apr-Nov. Cost: From $999 full board and classes in Chateau. Contact: Dr. C. Roberts, 204 via Morella, Encinitas, CA 92024; (619) 632-1923 or (800) 484-1235 #0096 or Joe Davies, 3473 Camino Valencia, Carlsbad, CA 92009; Tel./fax (619) 591-4537 (modem) or Ecole des Trois Ponts, Chateau de Matel, 42300 Roanne, France; (011) 33-77-70-80-01, fax 77-71-53-00.

FPI Piano Festival. The French Piano Institute presents a 2-week piano festival in Paris each July for advanced performers, teachers, and music lovers. Total immersion in French piano repertoire is offered by internationally acclaimed guest artists who appear in concert and conduct daily master classes on style and interpretation.

Dates: Jul 7-20, 1997. Cost: $1,248 up, includes tuition, lodging, most meals. Contact: Gail Delente, French Piano Institute, 9908 Old Spring Rd., Kensington, MD 20895-3235; (301) 929-8433, fax (301) 929-0254.

Egypt with a cruise on the Nile. From 1-7 weeks. University students may earn from 4-6 credits from Hebrew Univ.

Dates: Jun 13-Aug 1, 1997. Cost: $1,095-$4,995 land only plus roundtrip airfare. Contact: Arthur D. Greenberg, Israel Archaeological Society, 467 Levering Ave., Los Angeles, CA 90024; (800) 477-2358, fax (310) 476-6259.

Greece

Greek Folk Dance and Folk Culture. Dance courses for beginners and advanced, combined with apprenticeship in costumes, headdresses, handicraft, music, stage management.

Dates: Jul-Sep. Cost: $120 per week. Contact: Alkis Raftis, Greek Dances Theater, 8 Scholiou St., Plaka, 10558, Athens, Greece.

Ireland

Walking and Trekking Holidays. Countryside Tours, set up in 1990, is the specialist in providing leisurely guided and more challenging self-guided hiking tours. A varied program includes all the major areas of interest such as Kerry, Connemara, Wicklow Mountains, and Ulster. Good food, comfortable accommodations in Irish guesthouses.

Dates: Please ask for brochure. Cost: IR£420 for guided tours, from IR£205 for self-guided tours. Contact: Nick Becker, Countryside Tours Ltd., Glencar House, Glencar, County Kerry, Ireland; (011) 353-66 60211, fax (011) 353 66 60217; country@iol.ie.

Israel

The Israel Archaeological Society. The Israel Archaeological Society's Expedition 1997, invites the participation of students, seniors, and families at archaeological digs in Israel and Jordan; work hard, but sleep in comfortable hotels. We will also visit archaeological and historical sites in Israel, Jordan, Syria, and

Jamaica

Private Sailing Groups—Small Groups. Visit various Jamaican destinations in one trip and experience true Jamaican culture and natural beauty. Enjoy sailing aboard Sapphire Cat, a 39-foot catamaran with personalized itineraries, allowing every voyage to be an exclusive experience. Numerous options are available for activity and special interests. Sapphire Cat offers 4 private bedrooms, 2 bathrooms, and fully equipped kitchen.

Dates: Available by reservation year round. Cost: Starting at $450 includes many amenities. Contact: Heave-Ho Charters Ltd., 11A Pineapple Pl., Ocho Rios, Jamaica, W.I.; (809) 974-5367, fax (809) 974-5461; heaveho @toj.comm.

Mexico

ACS Baja Expeditions. Baja lagoons and the Sea of Cortez (Mar): 11-day trip aboard the Searcher to San Ignacio Lagoon, Magdelena Bay, and the Sea of Cortez. Trip begins in San Diego and ends in La Paz. San Ignacio Lagoon basecamp (Feb): A 5-day whale adventure from San Diego, offers 3 full days in San Ignacio.

Cost: $1,200-$2,500 includes safari-style accommodations, meals, whale watching, etc. Contact: Linda Lewis (310) 438-8960 or ACS, P.O. Box 1391, San Pedro, CA 90733; (310) 548-6279, fax (310) 548-6950; asc@pobox.com.

Spanish Language in Guanajuato. We work with our students one-on-one or in small groups (2 to 5 students), tailoring instruction to each student's needs. We teach people of all ages and from many nationalities. Highlights: homestays with families, sports, movies, field trips, hikes, cultural events—all this taking place in the most beautiful colonial setting of Mexico.

Dates: Year round. New classes begin every Monday. Cost: $925. Includes lifetime registration fee, group classes (5 sessions per day Monday-Friday), and a homestay with 3 meals daily for 4 weeks. Lower price for fewer weeks. Contact: Director Jorge Barroso, Instituto Falcon, A.C., Guanajuato, Gto. 36000 Mexico; Tel./fax (011) 52-473-2-36-94, www.infonet.com.mx/falcon.

Yoga Vacation in Mexico. Enjoy a tropical yoga vacation in Islas Miyeres, a tiny island just off Mexico's Turquoise Coast: an ideal place for a truly relaxing yoga vacation, offering sun-washed days on white coral and sand beaches, meditation and Hatha Yoga classes, and delicious vegetarian meals.

Dates: Nov 1997 and Winter 1998. Cost: $695, includes program, double room accommodations, and 3 vegetarian meals daily. Contact: Ashram Reservation Center, Rt. 1, Box 1720, Buckingham, VA 23921; (804) 969-3121, fax (804) 969-1303.

Papua New Guinea

Trans Niugini Tours. Nature and cultural programs are operated in 3 distinct areas, namely the Highlands, the Sepik Area, and a marine environment on the North Coast. Each area has its own distinct culture and environment, with comfortable wilderness lodges located in each.

Dates: Weekly departures during 1997. Cost: $714-$3,570 per person (land cost). Contact: Bob Bates, Trans Niugini Tours, P.O. Box 371, Mt. Hagen, Papua New Guinea; (800) 521-7242 or (011) 675-542-1438, fax 675-542-2470; 100250.3337@compuserve.com.

Scotland

Highland Walks. Guided walking in Highland and islands: ecology, history, coastal, glens. Jean Stewart's 10th year of showing folks around her favorite Highland haunts—and ensuring their comfort.

Dates: Easter to end Oct. Cost: From £365 full board, guide. Contact: Jean Stewart, Island Horizons, Junipers, Lochcarron, IV54 8YL, Scotland; (011) 44-1520-722232, fax 722238; horizons@m0506.demon.co.uk, www.glen.co.uk/rc/horizons.

South Africa

Cheetah Trail Hostelling Safari. Three-week hostelling trek, roundtrip to Johannesburg, includes entrances to game parks, national parks, museums, caves, ostrich and crocodile ranches. Travel with a small group (12 maximum) of people from all over the world. Detailed trek dossier on request.

Dates: Monthly departures year round. Cost: $1,199. Contact: Roadrunner Worldwide, 6762A Centinela Ave., Culver City, CA 90230-6304; (800) 873-5872, fax (310) 390-1446; amadlax@attmail.com.

South America

Incan/Mayan Trail Hostelling Treks. Three 2-week treks exploring Mexico, Peru, or Argentina/Chile with a small, international group, utilizing youth hostels and camping. Explore native ruins, lush jungles, unspoiled beaches, and amazing mountains. Detailed dossier available upon request.

Dates: Monthly departures year round. Cost: From $839, includes transport, accommodations, entrances to parks and archaeological sites, adventure excursions, and some meals. Contact: Roadrunner Worldwide, 6762A Centinela Ave., Culver City, CA 90230-6304; (800) 873-5872, fax (310) 390-1446; amadlax@attmail.com.

Sweden

Uppsala Univ. International Summer Session (UISS). Sweden's oldest academic summer program focuses on learning the Swedish language. All levels from beginners to advanced. Additional courses in Swedish history, social institutions, arts in Sweden, Swedish film. Excursions every Friday. Extensive evening program includes both lectures and entertainment. Single rooms in dormitories or apartments. Open to both students and adults. Credit possible.

Dates: Jun 22-Aug 15; Jun 22-Jul 18; Jul 20-Aug 15, 1997. Cost: SEK21,000 (approx. $3,000) for the 8-week session, SEK12,000 (approx. $1,715) for the 4-week session. Includes room, some meals, all classes, evening and excursion program. Contact: Dr. Nelleke Dorrestÿn, Uppsala Univ. Int. Summer Session, Box 513, 751 20 Uppsala, Sweden; (011) 31-71-541 4955, fax 71-5417705; nduiss@worldaccess.nl.

United Kingdom

Crafts and Arts Courses. Week and weekend courses in painting and drawing, blacksmithing, calligraphy, gardening and garden design, glass engraving, photography, pottery, sculpture, silversmithing, soft furnishing, textiles, woodcarving and woodworking. Courses for different levels of ability, from complete beginners to master classes, run parallel to 7 full-time Diploma courses.

Dates: Year round. Cost: Short course (residential) 5 days £349; weekends £146; 7 days £469. Contact: Heather Way, Public Relations, West Dean College, West Dean, Chichester, W. Sussex PO18 0QZ, England; (011) 44-1243-811301, fax 811343; westdean@pavilion.co.uk.

Study in London. Fall, spring, or academic year study abroad program offering regular university courses in liberal arts, business or performing arts at Middlesex Univ. University housing, on-site orientation program, 12-15 undergraduate credits per semester. Qualifications: Sophomore or above in good academic standing.

Dates: Fall: mid-Sep-late Dec; spring: early Feb-early Jun. Cost: Approx. $6,400 per semester. Includes tuition, fees, room and board, and insurance. (Non-New York state residents add $750 per semester.) Contact: Office of International Education, SUNY New Paltz, HAB 33, New Paltz, NY 12561; (914) 257-3125, fax (914) 257-3129; international@newpaltz.edu, www.newpaltz.edu/oie.

Worldwide

Adventure Travel for Women. Join the oldest adventure program for women on fun and educational outdoor vacations. Come along as we canoe in Minnesota, backpack the Grand Canyon, sea kayak and hike in Alaska, bicycle through Ireland and New Zealand, and visit other beautiful places around the world. We welcome women of all ages who have adventuring spirits.

Dates: Year round. Cost: Varied. Contact: Peggy at Woodswomen, 25 W. Diamond Lake Rd., Minneapolis, MN 55419; (612) 822-3809 or (800) 279-0555, fax (612) 822-3814.

American-Int'l Homestays. Stay in English-speaking foreign homes in over 30 countries. Explore foreign cultures responsibly. Learn foreign languages. Perfect for families or seniors. Learn how other people live by living with them in their homes.

Dates: Year round. Cost: From $49 per night. Contact: Joe Kinczel, American-Int'l Homestays, P.O. Box 1754, Nederland, CO 80466; (303) 642-3088 or (800) 876-2048, fax (303) 642-3365; ash@igc.apc.org.

Archaeological Fieldwork Opportunities. The AFOB is an international guide to excavations and field schools with openings for volunteers, students, and staff. Designed to introduce both student and amateur archaeologist to the experience of actual excavation, it is available every year on January 1. Over 250 opportunities listed. Price: $15. Call (800) 228-0810.

Dates: Year round (mainly summer). Cost: Varies. Contact: Susanna Burns, Archaeological Institute of America, 656 Beacon St., Boston, MA 02215-2010; Tel./fax (617) 353-9361; aia@bu.edu, http://csaws.brynmawr.edu:443/aia.html.

Customized Special Interest Trips. Information—customized tours—travel planning: eco and special interest outdoor adventures—hiking, canoeing, biking, snorkeling, natural history, birding, etc. Clothing optional recreation. Cultural exchanges. World peace. Health. Permaculture. Rainforests. Also budget travel.

Dates: Year round. Cost: $55-$255 per person per day inclusive. Contact: Peter Bentley, Sense Adventures, P.O. Box 1466, Murwillumbah, NSW 2484, Australia; (011) 61-414-854-255.

Earthwatch. Unique opportunities to work with leading scientists on 1- to 3-week field research projects worldwide. Earthwatch sponsors 160 expeditions in over 30 U.S. states and in 60 countries. Project disciplines include archaeology, wildlife management, ecology, ornithology and marine mammalogy. No special skills needed—all training is done in the field.

Dates: Year round. Cost: Tax deductible contributions ranging from $695-$2,800 support the research and cover food and lodging expenses. Airfare not included. Contact: Earthwatch, 680 Mt. Auburn St., P.O. Box 9104MA, Watertown, MA 02272; (800) 776-0188, (617) 926-8200; info@earthwatch.org, www.earthwatch.org.

Educational Adventures. Educational Travel off the beaten path in Asia and South America. Customized for individuals and small groups. "Classrooms without Walls" offer cultural, craft /art, religion, holy site, traditional healing and folk medicine, and natural history/environmental travel study programs, and "Trekking with a Mission" in the world's special and untouristed places.

Dates: Year round. Cost: Vary. See free catalog. Contact: Myths and Mountains, Inc., 976 Tee Court, Incline Village, NV 89451; (800) 670-MYTH (6984), (702) 834-4454; edutrav@sierra.net, www.mythsandmountains.com.

Offshore Sailing School. Learn to sail, bareboat cruising preparation, live aboard cruising. Courses meet the needs of varying sailing abilities from beginners to advanced. Offshore has awarded diplomas to over 78,000 successful sailors over 30 years.

Dates: Year round. Cost: Start at $895 including course and accommodations. Contact: Steve and Doris Colgate's Offshore Sailing School, 16731 McGregor Blvd., Ft. Myers, FL 33908; (800) 221-4326, fax (941) 454-1191; offshore@packet. net, www.offshor-sailing.com.

Penn Summer Abroad. Academic programs granting Univ. of Pennsylvania credits. Courses focusing on language, culture, economics, theater, anthropology, Jewish studies, cinema, art history, traditional folk medicine, performing arts, and religion. Several programs offer homestays, some offer internships.

Dates: Mid-May-late Aug (2-8 weeks). Cost: Tuition: $1,420 per course. Living costs vary. Contact: Elizabeth Sachs, Penn Summer Abroad, College of General Studies, Univ. of Pennsylvania, 3440 Market St., Suite 100, Philadelphia, PA 19104-3335; (215) 898-5738, fax (215) 573-2053.

World Affairs Council Tours. Council trips offer all the sightseeing and cultural highlights of quality touring plus access to political leaders, journalists, and other local experts who give behind the scenes views and briefings. Enjoy an insider's view of Egypt, China, Albania, Sweden, Provence, Borneo, Baltics, Oman, and other destinations. Includes substantive trip materials.

Contact: Joan Russell, Travel Director, World Affairs Council of Philadelphia, 1314 Chestnut St., Philadelphia, PA 19107; (215) 731-1100 or (800) 942-5004, fax (215) 731-1111; wac@libertynet.org.

CHAPTER 3

SENIOR TRAVEL RESOURCES

Seniors' requirements are often different from others in matters of travel abroad. While college students carry little more than a backpack and an ATM card, mature travelers, even experienced ones, generally follow a more organized approach.

Health and safety are paramount concerns. In making your travel plans first of all be aware of the advisories issued by the Department of State that warn about security and health risks in all parts of the world. Embassies and consulates abroad will assist in finding legal, medical, and financial aid when needed.

Trip insurance is advisable in case an emergency forces you to cancel your plans, since penalties for default are usually extremely high. Be sure you shop around and understand the fine print to be certain your policy covers everything. The same is true for medical assistance programs. In the unlikely event of medical evacuation, such a policy covers the exorbitant cost for a relatively small amount.

Seniors also want to know how to get medication and find a doctor who speaks English and what to do if a passport or suitcase is stolen or a connection missed or a rental car damaged.

The following resources will not only help you get ready to go but will help assure a safe and pleasant journey.

How to Phone Home

Auto Europe Wallet Card. Toll-free telephone access codes to reach AT&T, MCI, and Sprint in 20 countries; (800) 223-555.

International Travel Guide from MCI. Covers 100 countries, 108 pages; (800) 792-4685.

Worldwide Calling Guide from AT & T. 44 pages; (800) 545-3117.

Budgeting

Traveling Money, Bank of America National Trust and Savings Association, Box 37000, San Francisco, CA 94137; (415) 622-6390. Questions and answers about money management while traveling. $1.

Unbelievably Good Deals and Great Adventures That You Absolutely Can't Get Unless You're Over 50 by Joan R. Heilman. Contemporary Books, 1995, $8.95.

Your Travel Dollar, Household Financial Services, 2700 Sanders Rd., Prospect Hts., IL 60070; (312) 564-6291. $1.

General Guides

American Society of Travel Agents. Call their Consumer Affairs department at (703) 706-0387 if you need their help to mediate a travel dispute.

Get Up and Go: A Guide for the Mature Traveler by Gene and Adele Malott, 1989. $10.95 from Gateway Books, 2023 Clemons Rd., Oakland, CA; (800) 669-0773.

Mature Outlook, a travel magazine available by subscription from 6601 North Clark St., Chicago, IL 60660; (800) 336-6330.

The Seasoned Traveler by Marcia Schnedler. Country Roads, 1992, $10.95.

Taken by Surprise: Travel after 50 and **Taken by Surprise: Travel after 60** by Esther Mock. R & E Publishers, 1991, $2.98 each.

Travel and Older Adults by Allison St. Clair. ABC-CLIO Publishers, 1991, $45.

Travel Easy: The Practical Guide for People Over 50. Available from AARP Books, 1865 Miner St., Des Plaines, IL 60016; (800) 238-2300.

Travel and Retirement Edens Abroad by Peter A. Dickins. Available from AARP Books, above.

Health and Safety

A Senior's Guide to Healthy Travel by Donald L. Sullivan, 1994. $14.95 plus $3.50 shipping from Career Press, Inc., 3 Tice Rd., P.O. Box 687, Franklin Lakes, NJ 07417.

American Lung Association. For advice on traveling with oxygen call (800) 586-4872.

Citizens' Emergency Center, U.S. Dept. of State, 2201 C St., NW, Washington, DC 20520; (202) 647-5225. Handles emergency matters involving U.S. citizens abroad.

Dept. of State Publications. Send $1 for each to: Supt. of Documents, U.S. Government Printing Office, Washington, DC 20402; (202) 783-3238: Your Trip Abroad. Publication #9926. General travel information on passports, visas, immunization, etc. A Safe Trip Abroad. Publication #9493. Security tips for travel to high crime or terrorism areas. Travel Tips for Older Americans. Covers health and safety as well as basic travel advice. Tips for Travelers to specific areas overseas.

Health Information for International Travel, Supt. of Documents, U.S. Government Printing Office, Washington, DC 20402; (202) 783-3238. $14 (prepaid). Discusses health precautions and immunizations for travelers to foreign countries.

International Assn. for Medical Assistance to Travelers, 417 Center St., Lewiston, NY 14092; (716) 754-4883. Provides a directory of English-speaking doctors in 450 cities in 116 countries. Also information on health risks and immunizations worldwide.

International SOS. Emergency medical evacuation coverage; (800) 523-8930.

The International Health Guide for Senior Travelers by Robert W. Lange, 1990. $4.95 from Pilot Books, 103 Cooper St., Babylon, NY 11702; (576) 422-2225.

Travel Assistance International, (800) 821-2828. The largest global support system for travelers. Provides emergency medical payments, transportation, referrals, monitoring, and interpretation services. Also insurance for medical, trip cancellation, baggage, accidental dismemberment, and death.

Senior Tour Organizers

AARP Experience (from American Express), P.O. Box 37580, Louisville, KY 50233; (800) 927-0111 or (800) 745-4567.

American International Homestays. Arranges visits any time with different English-speaking families for 1 week each in Russia, Mongolia, Uzbekistan, Beijing, Prague, Budapest, Krakow, Berlin, the Baltics, Shanghai, India, and Australia. Visitors have private rooms and opportunities to learn from hosts about local culture. American International Homestays, Inc., P.O. Box 7178, Boulder, CO 80306; (800) 876-2048, fax (303) 642-3365.

Archaeology Abroad, 31-34 Gordon Sq., London WC1H OPY, England. Lists worldwide archaeological digs with details of staffing needs and costs.

Earthwatch Expeditions, 319 Arlington St., Watertown, MA 02172; (617) 926-8200. Be a paying volunteer on scientific expeditions worldwide.

Elderhostel, 75 Federal St., Boston, MA 02110; (617) 426-8056. Educational adventures for older adults. Sponsors over 1,800 nonprofit, short-term programs in 45 countries. Must be 55 or over; younger spouses are allowed.

Eldertreks, 597 Markham St., Toronto, Ontario, Canada M6G 2L7; (800) 741-7956, fax (416) 588-9839. Exotic adventures for the young at heart over 50 crowd.

Gadabout Tours, 700 E. Tahquitz, Palm Springs, CA 92262; (800) 952-5068.

Grand Circle Travel, 347 Congress St., Boston, MA 02210; (800) 248-3737. More than 200 programs worldwide. Free booklet: "Tips for Mature Travelers."

Grand Travel, 6900 Wisconsin Ave., Suite 706, Chevy Chase, MD 20815; (800) 247-7651.

Insight International Tours, 745 Atlantic Ave., Boston, MA 02116; (617) 482-2000.

Interhostel, 6 Garrison Ave., Durham, NH 03824; (800) 733-9753. Over 50 educational travel programs per year worldwide for mature travelers age 50 and up.

Familyhostel, 6 Garrison Ave., Durham, NH 03824; (800) 733-9753. Ten-day learning and travel programs in foreign countries for families (parents, grandparents, school-age children).

Saga Holidays, "Road Scholar" Programs, 222 Berkeley St., Boston, MA 02116; (617) 451-6808 or (800) 621-2151.

Smart Vacations: The Traveler's Guide to Learning. Council. 1993. 320 pp. $14.95 from Council. Adult traveler's guide to learning abroad includes, in addition to study tours, opportunities for voluntary service, field research and archaeological digs, fine arts, and more.

Senior Ventures Network, 1250 Siskiyou Blvd., Ashland, OR 97520-5050; (800) 257-0577.

September Days Club, 2751 Buford Hwy., NE, Atlanta, GA 30324; (404) 728-4405.

Sun Holidays, 26 6th St., Stanford, CT 06905; (800) 243-2057.

Volunteer Vacations by Bill McMillon. Chicago Review Press, 5th ed., 1995, $13.95. Includes 500 opportunities worldwide plus personal stories.

Single Travelers

The Single Traveler. P.O. Box 2176, Northbrook, IL 60065-2176, Northbrook, IL 60065-2176; (847) 714-1334, fax (847) 272-6788. Annual subscription (6 issues) $29.

Golden Companions, Box 754, Pullman, WA 99163; (208) 858-2183. Helps people over 45 find traveling companions. One-year membership fee $94.

Handbook for Women Travelers by Maggie and Gemma Ross. Piatkus Books, 5 Windmill St., London W1P 1HF, England; (011) 44-631-0710.

Mesa Travel Singles Registry, P.O. Box 2235, Costa Mesa, CA 92628; (714) 546-8181.

Partners in Travel, 11660 Chenault St., #119, Los Angeles, CA 90049. Services for single travelers over 50.

Singleworld Cruises and Tours, 401 Theodore Freund Ave., Rye, NY 10580; (800) 223-6490.

Society of Single Travelers, Travelcare, 3000 Ocean Park Blvd., Suite 1004, Santa Monica, CA 90405; (310) 450-8510.

Travel Companion Exchange, P.O. Box 833, Amityville, NY 11701; (516) 454-0880. $48 yearly, $5 sample newsletter. Widely recommended listings and newsletter for travelers seeking companions.

Travel Match, P.O. Box 6991, Orange, CA 92667; (714) 997-5273.

Travel Share International, P.O. Box 30365, Santa Barbara, CA; (805) 965-4955.

Transportation

An American's Guide to Getting Around Europe. Guidelines on types of transportation, discounts by charters, rental car rates. April 1995 issue of Kiplinger Magazine, 1727 H St., NW, Washington, DC 20006.

Eurail Guide Annual by Kathryn Turpin and Marvin Satzman. Published by Eurail Guide Annual, $14.95. How to travel Europe and all the world by train.

Euroad: Complete Guide to Motoring in Europe by Bert Lief. VLE Ltd., P.O. Box 444, Fort Lee, NJ 07024; (201) 585-5080. Maps, 1995, $7.95. Driving times, distances, and seven-language car vocabulary.

Exploring Europe by Boat by B.R. Rogers and S. Rogers. Globe Pequot, $12.95.

Fly Rights: A Consumers Guide to Air Travel spells out federal regulations on overbooking and gives advice on frequent flyer programs, disabled passenger accommodations, travel scams, airline health and safety issues. Send $1.75 in check or money order made out to Superintendent of Documents, Consumer Information Center, Dept. 133-B, Pueblo, CO 81009.

How to Select a Package Tour. U. S. Tour Operators Assn., 211 E. 51st St., Suite 12B, New York, NY 10022; (212) 944-5727. Free.

Ocean and Cruise News. Ratings, classifications, and features of ships. World Ocean and Cruise Liner Society, P.O. Box 92-T, Stanford, CT 06904. $28 for a year's subscription (12 issues).

Rail Europe. A complete source for train travel in 33 European countries including rail passes, rail and drive packages, and tickets. Free brochure; (800) 4-Eurail.

Tips on Renting a Car, Council of Better Business Bureau, 1515 Wilson Blvd., Arlington, VA 22209; (703) 276-0100. $1 with long SASE. Guide to getting the most service for your money from car rental companies.

TravLtips Association. Unusual cruises: freighters, yachts, expeditions. Membership includes magazine and free reference book. $15 a year. P.O. Box 580218-C9S, Flushing, NY 11358; (800) 872-8584.

Volunteering and Other Options

Golden Opportunities: A Volunteer Guide for Americans over 50 by Andrew Carroll. Peterson's Guides, 1994, $14.95.

National Senior Sports Association, (800) 282-6772. Golf vacations.

Nature Expeditions International, (503) 484-6529 or (800) 869-0639. Accompany scientists on expeditions.

Over the Hill Gang, (303) 790-2724. Ski vacations for those over 50.

Seventy Plus Ski Club, (518) 399-5458.

Smithsonian Study Tours, 1100 Jefferson Dr., SW, Washington, DC 20520; (202) 357-4700. Study tours and seminars providing a combination of study, discovery, adventure, and vacation.

ARLINE K. WILLS is the Seniors Travel Editor for Transitions Abroad. She lives in Lynnfield, MA.

CHAPTER 4

SENIOR TRAVEL PROGRAMS

The following listing of senior travel programs was supplied by the organizers. Contact the program directors to confirm costs, dates, and other details. If you do not see the program you want in the country of your choice, look in the "Worldwide" listings at the end of the section for programs located in several different regions.

Australia

Special Interest and Study Tours. Personalized programs for individuals and groups of all ages. We combine education, recreation, accommodations (homestay available), and transportation. Based in tropical Cairns with coverage throughout Australia. Subject areas include: aboriginal dreamtime and culture, Great Barrier Reef, rainforest and savannah. Diving, environmental interpretation, flora and fauna, bird watching, tropical islands and wilderness, adventure safaris and farmstay.

Dates: Year round. Start any date. Cost: Prices and customized itineraries on application. Contact: Murray Simpson, Study Venture International, P.O. Box 229A, Stratford Qld., 4870 Australia; (011) 61-70-411622, fax 552044; svi@ozemail.com.au; www.ozemail. au/~svi.

Ecuador

Academia Latinoamericana de Español (Quito). Ecuador's number-one private Spanish language institute in former diplomat's mansion with swimming pool, hot tub, sauna, sport facilities. Instruction by university-trained teachers, all one-on-one. Customized study programs tailored to the individual. Select host family accommodations. Excursions to haciendas, Indian markets, etc. College credit available and internships.

Dates: Year round. Cost: One-week tuition, lodging, meals $294. Contact: Suzanne Bell, Admissions Director, U.S., 640 East 3990 South, Suite E, Salt Lake City, UT 84107; (801) 268-4608, fax (801) 265-9156; latinoa1@spanish.com.ec, http://ecnct.cc/academia/learnspa.htm.

Europe

Untours. Fully equipped private apartments in areas off the beaten path. Live among the locals and set your own itinerary with the help of our resource books and on-site staff. Destinations: Paris, Prague, Budapest, Vienna, and smaller towns in Provence, Tuscany, Ticino, Bernese Oberland, Central Switzerland, Austria, Rhineland Germany, and Holland.

Dates: Every 2 weeks. First term starts Mar 26, last term starts Oct 22. Cost: $1,411-$2,323 (2 weeks, includes airfare from east coast gateway). Contact: Idyll Untours, P.O. Box 405, Media, PA 19063; (610) 565-5242, fax (610) 565-5142; untours@netreach.net, www. netreach.net/~untours.

Mexico

Copper Canyon. Outstanding cultural and natural history rail trips. The most dramatic train ride in the western hemisphere. Deeper, wider, greener canyons than Arizona's Grand Canyon. Tarahumara Indian culture, nature walks, birding, waterfalls, spectacular vistas. Historic tours, small groups, personal attention. In-depth interpretation of the Copper Canyon and its people.

Dates: Year round. Cost: $1,695 per person for 8-day trips. Contact: S&S Tours, 865 El Camino Real, Sierra Vista, AZ 85635; (800) 499-5685, fax (520) 458-5258; ss@theriver. com.

El Bosque del Caribe, Cancun. Take a professional Spanish course, 25 hours per week and enjoy the Caribbean beaches. Relaxed family atmosphere. No more than 6 students per class. Special conversation program. Mexican cooking classes and excursions to the Mayan sites. Housing with Mexican families. College credit available.

Dates: Year round. New classes begin every Monday. Group programs arranged at reduced fees. Cost: Enrollment fees $75, $175 per week, 1 week with a Mexican family $150. Contact: Eduardo Sotelo, Director, Calle Piña 1, S.M. 25, 77500 Cancún, Mexico; (011) 52-98-84-10-38, fax 84-58-88; bcaribe@mail. interacces.com.mx.

Intensive Spanish in Cuauhnahuac. Cuauhnahuac, founded in 1972, offers a variety of intensive and flexible programs geared to individual needs. Six hours of classes daily with no more than 4 students to a class. Housing with Mexican families who really care about you. Cultural conferences, excursions, and special classes for professionals. College credit available.

Dates: Year round. New classes begin every Monday. Cost: $70 registration fee; $600 4 weeks tuition, housing $16 per night. Contact: Marcia Snell, 519 Park Dr., Kenilworth, IL 60043; (800) 245-9335, fax (847) 256-9475; lankysam@aol.com..

Language Institute of Colima. The Language Institute of Colima Mexico offers a system of total immersion with classes held throughout the year Monday-Friday. Students live with local host families and attend 6 hours of instruction daily; no more than 5 students per class. Many extras, including beach excursions, are included.

Dates: Year round, Monday-Friday. Cost: Registration $80; tuition $415 1st week, $345 after 1st week (for shared room), $445 1st week, $375 after 1st week (for private room). 10% discount for 6 or more. Contact: Dennis Bourassa, Language Institute of Colima, P.O. Box 827, Miranda, CA 95553; (800) 604-6579, fax (707) 923-4232; colima@northcoast.com, www.northcoast.com/~colima

Retire in Mexico Program. Led by the publisher of Retire in Mexico Updates & Business News, this fully escorted, fun, educational experience explores Ajijic (Lake Chapala), the number one retirement haven outside the U.S. Exclusive seminar (Health Care, Immigration, Real Estate and more), fabulous meals, lakeside hotel, a chance to meet local retirees, and much more.

Dates: Sep and Nov 1996. Contact for 1997 schedule. Cost: $689 (double occupancy) land only. Contact: Retire in Mexico, 40 4th St., Suite 203, Petaluma, CA 94952; (707) 765-4573, fax (707) 778-1080.

Philippines

Little Children of the Philippines, Inc. LCP is a not-for-profit, interdenominational Christian agency to help develop caring communities for poor children on Negros Island in central Philippines. LCP has service programs in 7 communities covering health, housing, education, livelihood (agriculture, handicrafts), and peace formation. Research opportunities also available, especially involving handicapped and street children.

Dates: Volunteers may negotiate their own period of service during 1997. Cost: From East Coast: approx. $1,200 roundtrip airfare, $120 per month for food. Dormitory bed free. Contact: Dr. Douglas Elwood, 361 County Rd. 475, Etowah, TN 37331; Tel./fax (423) 263-2303.

Peru

Rainforests of Peru. If you have always wanted to see the rainforest but thought it could never be more than a dream, explore the possibilities with International Expeditions. The world leader in nature travel, we offer small group, ecologically responsible expeditions to the Peruvian Amazon. Now there are 2 ways to enjoy the adventure: by land, in rustic but comfortable lodges, or by air-conditioned riverboat. Write or call for color brochures.

Cost: Eight-day programs, all-inclusive from Miami start at $1,798; optional Cusco and Machu Picchu Extension $1,098. Contact: International Expeditions Inc., One Environs Park, Helena, AL 35080; (800) 623-4734, fax (205) 428-1714.

Spain

Spanish for Seniors. Frequently called Spain's leading school of Spanish, Malaca Instituto has designed a course for senior citizens. Offered at levels from beginner to advanced, the program combines studying highly practical everyday Spanish (for the market, restaurant, booking hotels, etc.) with a program of cultural and social activities. On-site residential accommodations are recommended.

Dates: Oct 14, 28; Nov 11, 25; Dec 9, 1996/ Feb 3, 17; Mar 3, 17, 31; Apr 14, 28; May 12; Oct 13, 27; Nov 10, 24 1997. Cost: Course: from PTS55,000; accommodations from PTS32,540. Contact: Bob Burger, Malaca Instituto, c/Cortada 6, Cerrado de Calderon, 29018 Malaga, Spain; (011) 34-5-229-32-42, fax 229-63-16.

Worldwide

American-Int'l Homestays. Stay in English-speaking foreign homes in over 30 countries. Explore foreign cultures responsibly. Learn foreign languages. Perfect for families or seniors. Learn how other people live by living with them in their homes.

Dates: Year round. Cost: From $49 per night. Contact: Joe Kinczel, American-Int'l Homestays, P.O. Box 1754, Nederland, CO 80466; (303) 642-3088 or (800) 876-2048, fax (303) 642-3365; ash@igc.apc.org.

Earthwatch. Unique opportunities to work with leading scientists on 1- to 3-week field research projects worldwide. Earthwatch sponsors 160 expeditions in over 30 U.S. states and in 60 countries. Project disciplines include archaeology, wildlife management, ecology, ornithology and marine mammalogy. No special skills needed—all training is done in the field.

Dates: Year round. Cost: Tax deductible contributions ranging from $695-$2,800 support the research and cover food and lodging expenses. Airfare not included. Contact: Earthwatch, 680 Mt. Auburn St., P.O. Box 9104MA, Watertown, MA 02272; (800) 776-0188, (617) 926-8200; info@earthwatch.org, www.earthwatch.org.

Eurocentres Language Schools. Immersion course of 20-25 hours per week for beginners to advanced levels. Learn in small classes with students of all ages from around the world. Full organizational social calendar with extended excursions available to students. Homestay living is available, college credit option.

Dates: Begins monthly all year long. Cost: Depends on school and length of stay. Contact: Eurocentres, 101 N. Union St., Alexandria, VA 22314; (703) 684-1494 or (800) 648-4809, fax (703) 684-1495; 100632.141@compuserve.com, www.clark.net/pub/euro cent/home.htm.

Study/Travel for Teachers and Retirees. Teachers and retirees travel overseas with professors from California, who lecture to them enroute. Tour directors are aboard too. Program is in its 13th year.

Dates: Christmas holidays, spring break, summer. Cost: Range from $1,500-$4,000 (includes airfare). Contact: Joseph Jeppson or Peggy Searle (800) 527-3137, or write: Community College Tours, P.O. Box 620620, Woodside, CA 94062.

Travel-Study Seminars. Learn from people of diverse backgrounds about their economic, political, and social realities. Emphasis on the views of the poor and oppressed. Programming in Mexico, Central America, South Africa, and China/Hong Kong. Call for a free listing of upcoming seminars.

Dates: Ongoing. Cost: $1,000-$4,500 depending on destination and length of trip. Contact: Center for Global Education, Augsburg College, 2211 Riverside Ave., Box TR, Minneapolis, MN 55454; (800) 299-8889, fax (612) 330-1695; globaled@augsburg.edu, www.augsburg.edu/global.

CHAPTER 5

FAMILY TRAVEL RESOURCES

Interested in taking the whole family overseas without taking out a second mortgage? Skip the hotels and high-priced rental villas. Look instead into some of the reasonably-priced rentals available below— some for as low as $200 per week. And don't forget youth hostels!

An increasing number of hostels offer family rooms for four to six people. If you're still daunted at the prospect of traveling with the family in tow, see our selection of family travel books for a wealth of advice.

This year we've also added Internet resources to our list. The World Wide Web is a great place to find an overseas penpal, learn some basic foreign vocabulary, or read about other travelers' experiences. Try our recommended sites—or simply look for your own by typing "kids travel" or "family travel" into your favorite Web search engine.

Once you decide on your destination, we offer several suggestions for meeting other families, plus a range of language and cultural programs. While these programs tend to be more expensive than the do-it-yourself options, they're especially appropriate for older pre-teens and teens. Why send the kids off to Camp Gitcheegoomee this summer when the whole family can learn Spanish in Costa Rica or Chile?

Inexpensive Rentals

While U.S. agencies offer properties starting at about $600 per week, you can rent a house for as little as $150 through many local Tourist Offices in Europe. Or try going directly to some of the following European sources.

British Tourist Office, (212) 986-2200. Ask for a free booklet called "City Apartments" for a selection of reasonably-priced family-sized apartments in cities throughout Britain.

FriFerie Danmark, Liselejevej 60, 3360 Liseleje, Denmark; (011) 45-42-34-63-34, fax 34-64-53. Catalog in German and Danish only. Rentals start at about $200 per week off season and $350 midsummer.

Chez Nous, Bridge Mills, Huddersfield Rd., Holmfirth HD7 2TW, England; (011) 44-484-684-075, fax 685-852. Directory of French rentals owned by Brits. They charge only for ads; prices are reasonable ($150 per week plus) since there's no commission. And there's no language gap in making arrangements.

German Tourist Offices. Many regional tourist offices publish excellent color-photo guides. Three good ones:

Familienferien, Schwarzwald, Fremdenverkehrsverband, Postfach 1660, 79016 Freiburg im Breisgau, Germany; (011) 49-761-31317, fax 36021.

Fröhliche Familienferien, Neckarland-Schwaben Touristikverband Lohtorstraße 21, 74072 Heilbronn Germany; (011) 49-7131-629661, fax 68638.

Urlaub auf Bauern-und Winzerhöfen, Rheinland-Pfalz Tourist Office Schmittpforte 2, 55437 Ober-Hilbersheim, Germany; (011) 49-6728-1225, fax 6728-626.

Irish Cottage Holiday Homes. Cork Kerry Tourism, Tourist House, Grand Parade, Cork, Ireland; (011) 353-21-273-251, fax 273-504. Good variety of listings from £100 to £500 per week. Also ads for agencies.

Maison des Gîtes de France, 35, rue Godot-de-Mauroy, Paris, France, 75009. Source for thousands of inexpensive, simple rural rentals in France. French language may help in arranging terms. Write for order blank for 90 regional guidebooks, which cost about $6 each.

Fjordhytter, Lille Markevei 13, 5005 Bergen, Norway; (011) 47-5-23-20-80, fax 23-24-04. Lovely photo catalog in English with very detailed descriptions. Prices start at $165 off season to $350 high season.

Destination Stockholm, Skårgård AB, Lillström, S-18023 Ljustero, Sweden; (011) 46-8-542-481-00, fax 414-00. Cottages in the Stockholm archipelago, starting at about $200 in the off season and $350 in mid-summer. Book 7 to 8 months ahead for high season.

Italian Farmstays. Three good sources for farm rentals and B&Bs in Italy:

Agriturist, Corso Vittorio Emanuele 101, 00186 Rome, Italy; (011) 39-6-685-2342, fax 685-2424. Send money order for LIT35,000 for their Italian catalog.

Terranostra, Via Magazzini 2, 50122 Florence, Italy. Send a money order for LIT43,000 for catalog.

Turismo Verde, Viale Ettore Franchini 89, 00155 Rome, Italy. Send money order for LIT18,000 for catalog.

Swiss Farmstays. Enjoy Switzerland's bucolic beauty with a farmhouse vacation. Some lodgings include a kitchen; others offer meals with the inhabitants.

Fédération du Tourisme Rural de Suisse Romande, c/o Office du Tourisme, 1530 Payerne, Switzerland; (011) 41-37-61-61-61.

Ferien auf dem Bauernhof, Buchungszentrale Verein, Raiffeisenbank, 5644 Auw AG, Switzerland; (011) 41-57-48-17-09.

Ferien auf dem Bauernhof, Schweizer Reisekasse (REKA), Neuengasse 15, 3001 Bern, Switzerland; (011) 41-31-329-66-33. Color photo directory with over 150 listings direct from REKA or from Swiss NTO. Text is in German, with English key and booking info.

Family Adventure Travel

Hostelling International, AYH, 733 15th St., NW, Suite 840, Washington, DC 20005; (202) 783-6161. Affordable hiking and biking trips in U.S., Europe, and Israel, usually for ages 15 and up. Or plan your own hosteling trip: many hostels have family rooms for all ages.

Society for the Protection of Nature in Israel. Operates 1- to 14-day hikes and nature explorations—even a camel tour—in different parts of Israel. Expert environmental guides and low costs; accommodations are in the group's field study centers or hostels. Children age 10 and up welcome. (800) 323-0035.

Overseas Adventure Travel, 625 Mt. Auburn St., Cambridge, MA, 02138; (800) 221-0814. Intercultural adventure trips for families and individuals. Families can choose a Galapagos Wildlife Adventure, a Serengeti Safari, or a Costa Rica natural history trip.

Journeys, 4011 Jackson Rd., Ann Arbor, MI, 48103; (800) 255-8735. Specially-designed socially-responsible family trips include Himalayan trekking and African safaris plus trips to Australia, the Galapagos, Belize, Panama, Vietnam, the Amazon, and Costa Rica.

Wildland Adventures, 3516 NE 15th St., Seattle, WA 98155; (206) 365-0686; fax (206) 363-6615. Family trips to Costa Rica, Honduras, Belize, Peru, the Galapagos, Turkey, Africa, and Nepal. Some trips include homestays and other intercultural opportunities.

Backroads, 801 Cedar St., Berkeley, CA 94710-1800; (800) 462-2848. Family biking and walking trips in the U.S., Canada, Czech Republic, France and Switzerland. Children of all ages welcome.

Butterfield & Robinson, 70 Bond St., Toronto, Ontario, Canada M5B 1X5; (800) 678-1147. Pricey deluxe family walking and biking trips in Italy, Holland, Morocco, Canada, and Belize for families with teenagers.

Hometours International, P.O. Box 11503, Knoxville, TN 37939; (800) 367-4668. Walking tours in England, much cheaper than

Backroads or B&R. Also Israeli "Kibbutz Home" program, apartment and villa rentals, plus B and B's in Britain, France, Italy. Small fee charged for catalogs.

Family Cultural Travel

LEX America, 68 Leonard St., Belmont, MA 02178; (617) 489-5800. Arranges family homestays in Japan with 25,000 member families. Standard 2-, 4-, or 6-week summer or autumn program. Or they'll design a custom program—for instance a homestay to mesh with a business trip.

AmeriSpan Unlimited, P.O. Box 40513, Philadelphia, PA 19106; (800) 879-6640; info @AmeriSpan.com, www.AmeriSpan.com. Family language programs in 12 countries in Mexico, Central and South America. Families stay with a host family; there are a range of childcare options and older kids can study along with Mom and Dad.

Language Study Abroad, 1301 N. Maryland Ave., Glendale, CA 91207; (818) 242-5263. Another family language program in Cuernavaca, Mexico. Children's program for ages 1-10; teen classes 10-15. Host families.

FamilyHostel, 6 Garrison Ave., Durham NH 03824; (800) 733-9753. FamilyHostel offers 10-day trips to Austria, Wales, France, and the Czech Republic (destinations vary yearly) to adult traveling with school-age kids. Trips mix education and recreation plus a chance to meet local families.

Making Friends, Meeting People

World Pen Pals, 1690 Como Ave., St. Paul MN 55108; (612) 647-0191. Links more than 20,000 kids per year (ages 12-20), in 175 countries. Send $4.50 and 9" x 4" SASE for each pen-pal desired (14-16 year olds especially needed).

International Penfriend. Overseas contacts for adults and kids. Send $4 for current issue of World Contact magazine. World Contact, Box 355T, Neffs, PA 18065-0355.

Zephyr Press, 13 Robinson St., Somerville, MA 02145; (617) 628-9726. Zephyr publishes a series of "People to People" guides for Russia, Poland, Romania, Czech Republic/Slovak Republic, Hungary/Bulgaria, Baltic Republics. $14 each. While not geared specifically for family travelers, the guides are a good source for family contacts.

SERVAS, 11 John St., Suite 407, New York, NY, 10038; (212) 267-0252. An international co-operative system of hosts and travelers established to help build world peace, goodwill, and understanding. Families and individuals are welcomed as members. $55 annual membership.

Other Family Resources

Traveling with Children. Dan and Wendy Hallinan, 2313 Valley St., Berkeley, CA 94702; (510) 848-0929. An experienced traveling family arranges home rentals, airfares, and special itineraries for other traveling families, especially in Europe.

Family Travel Times. Published by Travel with Your Children, 40 5th Ave., New York, NY 10011; (212) 477-5524. $40 per year. Quarterly newsletter of worldwide family travel news. Rarely any budget or alternative travel information.

Traveling-With-Kids Books

Travel with Children by Maureen Wheeler. Lonely Planet. $11.95. The definitive guide to Third World travel with kids, covering both logistics and cultural interchange. Third edition now adds first-person stories from other travelers.

Adventuring with Children: An Inspirational Guide to World Travel and the Outdoors by Nan Jeffrey. Excellent overseas and domestic advice for active families who want to backpack, sail, bicycle, or canoe. $14.95 from Menasha Ridge Press, 3169 Chaba Heights Rd., P.O. Box 43059, Birmingham, AL 35243; (800) 247-9437.

Best Places to Go: A Family Destination Guide by Nan Jeffrey. Recommendations and specifics on budget, culturally-aware family visits to Europe, Central and South America. $14.95 from Menasha Ridge Press (above).

The Traveler's Toolkit: How to Travel Absolutely Anywhere. Not specifically for families, but a great "attitude" book that will help new travelers feel comfortable taking on the world. Menasha Ridge Press (above).

Kidding Around London, Kidding Around Paris, Kidding Around Spain. Guide series written for kids instead of parents, suitable for good readers 8 or older. A solid but unexciting mix of history and sightseeing. $9.95 Paris or London, $12.95 Spain, from John Muir; (800) 285-4078.

Kids Love Israel; Israel Loves Kids by Barbara Sofer. New second edition includes lodging, camps, language, food, plus over 300 sightseeing ideas for the whole country. $17.95 from Kar-Ben Copies, 6800 Tildenwood Lane, Rockville, MD 20852; (301) 984-8733.

Children's Book of London, Children's Book of Britain. Usborne Guides. Available through BritRail, 551 5th Ave., Suite 702, New York City, NY 10176; (800) 677-8585. Usborne guides are all fairly good but are not widely available in the U.S.

Kids' Britain by Betty Jerman. Pan Macmillan Books, Cavaye Place, London SW10 9PG, England. A comprehensive guidebook available in England but probably unobtainable here. Lists every conceivable site in England, with costs. Buy it when you get to London.

Guide de la France des Enfants by Marylène Bellenger. Editions Rouge & Or, 11 rue de Javel, 75015 Paris, France. If you can read French, pick this one up in Paris. Exhaustive guide to sites all over France for kids up to 15.

Take Your Kids to Europe by Cynthia W. Harriman. Not simply a list of where to go, but a good intercultural guide to how and why to travel in Europe with children. Second ed., $13.95 plus $2 S&H to Mason-Grant, Box 6547, Portsmouth, NH 03802; (603) 436-1608.

The Family Travel Guide by Carole Terwilliger Meyers. A collection of first-person accounts from families who have traveled all over the world, with specific tips. $16.95 from Carousel Press (below).

The Family Travel Guides Catalog. Carousel Press, P.O. Box 6061, Albany, CA 94706-0061; (510) 527-5849. Most of the books mentioned in this list—and dozens of others—are available through Carousel Press. Send $1 or 55¢ and a long SASE for catalog.

Vacations with Children. Box 67, Suffern, NY 10901. A new travel-books-for-kids catalog with guides, games, activity books for kids, parents, grandparents. Write for catalog.

Internet Resources

A small sample of online family travel resources. All URLs start with http://.

www.ncrsa.com. Extensive list of language courses with dates and costs. Indexed by language or by country, including family and teen options. National Registration Center for Study Abroad, Box 1393, Milwaukee, WI 53201; (414) 278-0631.

www.travelaus.com.au. Scroll down to "Categories" and pick "Family" for a comprehensive list of family activities and accommodations in Australia—no description, but complete contact info.

www.kidscom.com/. A "communication playground" for kids 4-15 in English, French, Spanish, or German. One option: fill in your specs for a penpal—say, French, age 14, girl, likes skiing—and find your e-mail soulmate.

www.worldwide.edu/. My favorite travel site. "Planning Guide" includes basic vocabulary in 17 languages (with sound files), penpals, travel programs. WorldWide Classroom, Box 1166, Milwaukee, WI 53201-1166; (414) 224-3476.

www.bpe.com/travel/. Wonderful compendium of first-person travel experiences from all over the world.

www.family.starwave.com/. The Family Planet site offers a very thorough collection of family travel resources in the U.S. and abroad.

CYNTHIA HARRIMAN is the author of "Take Your Kids to Europe" and a passionate advocate of family travel. She welcomes readers to call her at (603) 436-1608 with additional resources for family travel outside of Europe.

CHAPTER 6

DISABILITY TRAVEL RESOURCES

Persons with disabilities are participating in increasing numbers in all forms of international educational exchange, voluntary service, and independent and group travel. They are a vital component in the global citizen diplomat movement. All exchanges and travel programs need to recognize the importance of including them.

The following organizations and planning guides will assist the approximately 49 million travelers with disabilities in the U.S. to find the option that best meets their needs.

Organizations

Mobility International USA (MIUSA), P.O. Box 10767, Eugene, OR 97440; (541) 343-1284, voice and TDD, fax (541) 343-6812. MIUSA is a national, nonprofit organization whose purpose is to promote and facilitate opportunities for people with disabilities to participate in international educational exchange and travel.

Society for Advancement of Travel for the Handicapped, 347 5th Ave., Suite 610, New York, NY 10016; (212) 447-7284. Membership $25 for students and seniors, $45 others. Publishes quarterly newsletter, SATH News.

The Travelin' Talk Network, P.O. Box 3534, Clarksville, TN 37043-3534; (615) 552-6670, fax (615) 552-1182. Membership registration fee is on a sliding scale: $1 for SSI recipients to $50 for businesses. Members (located all over the world) provide specific information and services to disabled travelers. The Travelin' Talk directory ($32.50 plus $2.50 shipping) contains member information and the services they offer travelers. Other resource listings include travel and tour agencies specializing in travel for people with disabilities. Travelin' Talk Newsletter, with updates on tours, trips, and other activities, is available in large print and on audio cassette tape.

Planning Guides

A World of Options edited by Christa Bucks (Mobility International USA, 3rd ed., 1997). Contact MIUSA (above) for price. A comprehensive guide to international exchange, study and volunteer opportunities for people with disabilities with more than 1,000 resources on exchanges, rights, travel and financial aid; includes personal experience stories.

Able to Travel from the Rough Guide series (Penguin). True stories by and for the disabled, plus practical travel information.

Access to the World: A Travel Guide for the Handicapped by Louise Weiss (Henry Holt). $16.95. To order call (503) 233-3936.

Adventures in Good Company: The Complete Guide to Women's Tours and Outdoor Trips 624 SE29 Ave., Portland, OR 97214 by Thalia Zepatos (The Eighth Mountain Press, $16.95); (503) 233-3936.

Exotic Destinations for Wheelchair Travellers by Ed Hansen and Bruce Gordon. Lists over 100 hotels in Hong Kong, Macao, Singapore, Taiwan, and Thailand. $14.95 from Full Data Limited, Opera Plaza, 601 Van Ness Ave., San Francisco, CA 94102.; (800) 842-8338.

Guide for the Disabled Traveller by The Automobile Association, Norfolk House, Priestly Road, Basingstoke, Hampshire, RG24 9NY, U.K. Lists places to visit selected from AA publication, Days Out in Britain and Ireland. Includes information on accessibility and accommodations at sites of interests, restaurants, and lodgings. £3.99.

Holidays in the British Isles 1996: A Guide for Disabled Travellers by Royal Association for Disability and Rehabilitation (RADAR), 12 City Forum, 250 City Rd., London ECIU 8AF, U.K.; (011) 44-71-250-3222. Over 1,000 places

to stay in all parts of the U.K. and Republic of Ireland. £13 postpaid.

Including Women with Disabilities by MIUSA. Forthcoming. Contact MIUSA (above) for ordering information. Will include model projects by and for women with disabilities, personal experiences, and resources.

International Telephone Directory for TDD Users by Telecommunications for the Deaf, Inc.; 8719 Colesville Rd., Suite 300, Silver Springs, MD 20910; (301) 589-3786 or (301) 589-3006 TDD.

The Diabetic Traveler Newsletter, P.O. Box 8223 RW, Stamford, CT 06905.

The Very Special Traveler, TVST, P.O. Box 756, New Windsor, MD 21776. Bimonthly newsletter ($25 a year) providing travel information and advice for people with disabilities.

Travel Notes from Howard McCoy, Accessible Journeys, 35 W. Sellers Ave., Ridley Park, PA 19078; (610) 521-0339. Newsletter on special needs travel to exotic destinations.

Travel Tips for Hearing Impaired People by American Academy of Otolaryngology; (703) 836-4444.

Vacances Pour Personnes Handicapees by Centre d'Information et de Documentation Jeunesse, CIDJ, 101, quai Branly, 75740 Paris, Cedex 15, France. Forty-one pages of addresses for holidays in France, including information on cultural activities, tourism, and sports. To order send 6 International Reply Coupons.

Wheelchair Through Europe by Annie Mackin. Chronicles author's travels throughout the continent by power chair; emphasizes budget travel and offers how-to tips. Graphic Language Press. $12.95.

You Want to Go Where? A Guide to China for Travellers with Disabilities by Evelyn Anderton and Susan Sygall. MIUSA The title says it all. $9.95 postpaid from MIUSA (above).

Tour Agencies

Accessible Journeys, Howard J. McCoy III, 35 W. Sellers Ave., Ridley Park, PA 19078; (800) TINGLES.

Alaska Snail Trails, James G. Stone, P.O. Box 210894, Anchorage, AK 99521; (800) 348-4532.

Alaska Welcomes You, Paul Sandhofer, P.O. Box 91333, Anchorage, AK 99509; (907) 349-6301.

Barrier Free Travel, Ian J. Cooper, 36 Wheatley St., North Bellingen, NSW 2454, Australia; (011) 61-066-551-733.

Big Apple Greeters, Alexander Wood, 1 Centre St., 19th Floor, New York, NY 10007; (212) 669-3602.

Breckenridge Outdoor Education Center, Scott Ingram, Breckenridge Outdoor Education Center, P.O. Box 697, Breckenridge, CO 80424; (303) 453-6422.

Destination World, I Can Tours, Lynette Wilson, P.O. Box 1077, Santa Barbara, CA 93102; (800) 426-3644.

Disabled Kiwi Tours, Allan and Shona Armstrong, Disabled Kiwi Tours, East Coast Highway, P.O. Box 550, Opotiki, New Zealand; (011) 64-7315-7867.

Flying Wheels Travel, Inc., Barbara Jacobson, 143 W. Bridge St., P.O. Box 382, Owatonna, MN 55060; (800) 535-6790.

Free Again Tours, Ron Kjellesvik, 1000 Figueroa, Unit 36, Wilmington, CA 90744; (310) 518-1444, fax (310) 547-3169.

Gateway Travel, Linda Abrams, 23A Middle Neck Rd., Great Neck, NY 11021; (516) 466-2242.

Hospital Audiences, Inc., Tricia Hennesey, 220 W. 42nd St., 13th Floor, New York, NY 10036; (212) 575-7663.

Mobility International USA, Susan Sygall, P.O. Box 10767, Eugene, OR 97440; (541) 343-1284. Voice and TDD.

Over The Rainbow Disabled Travel Service, David McKown, 186 Mehani Circle, Kihei, HI 96753; (808) 879-5521.

Paradise Found Chris Parker, 101 Crescent Ave., Suite C, Louisville, KY 40206; (800) 680-5926.

Search Beyond Adventures, Steve Anderson, 400 S. Cedar Lake Rd., Minneapolis, MN 55405; (800) 800-9979.

Tailored Tours, Julia Brown, P.O. Box 797687, Dallas, TX 75379; (800) 628-8542.

Wilderness Inquiry, Tracy Fredin, 1313 5th St. SE, P.O. Box 84, Minneapolis, MN 55414; (800) 728-0719.

Travel Agencies

Able to Travel/Partnership Travel, Inc., Joe Regan, 247 N. Main St., Suite 308, Randolph, MA 02368; (800) 986-0053.

Escape Artists, Bonnie Lewkowicz, 1427 Grant St., Berkeley, CA 94703; (510) 526-4477.

Hinsdale Travel Service, Janice Perkins, 201

E. Ogden Ave., Suite 100, Hinsdale, IL 60521; (708) 469-7349.

Holiday Care Service, Imperial Buildings, 2nd Floor, Victoria Rd., Horley, Surrey, RH6 7PZ, U.K.; (011) 44-1293-771500.

Wheelchair Journeys, Carol Lee Power, 16979 Redmond Way, Redmond, WA 98052; (206) 885-2210.

Wheelchair Travel, Ltd., Trevor Pollitt, 1 Johnston Green, Guildford, Surrey, GU2 6XS, England; (011) 44-483-233640.

SUSAN SYGALL is the Director of Mobility International USA, a nonprofit organization whose purpose is to promote international educational exchange and travel for persons with and without disabilities. She may be contacted at P.O. Box 10767, Eugene, OR 97110.

CHAPTER 7

DISABILITY TRAVEL TOURS AND PROGRAMS

The following listing of international travel tours and programs for persons with disabilities was supplied by the organizers and by Rick Crowder, the director of the Travelin' Talk Network, a membership organization providing information and services to disabled travelers. He may be contacted at P.O. Box 3534, Clarksville, TN 37043.

Access-Able Travel Service. We supply accessibility information for mature and disabled travelers. See us at our internet site http://www.access-able.com

Contact: Access-Able Travel Service, P.O. Box 1796, Wheat Ridge, CO 80033; (303) 232-2979, fax (303) 239-8486; carol@access-able.com.

Accessible New Zealand Wide Tours. Fully assisted tours using accessible vehicles. Individual or groups of up to 12. Personalized or set itineraries. Nursing care available. Relax and enjoy. We go at your pace. Total package or vehicle and driver hire.

Dates: Year round. Cost: Very reasonable but can vary considerably. Contact: Disabled Kiwi Tours, P.O. Box 550, Opotiki, New Zealand; (011) 64-7-3157867, fax 7-315-5056; kiwitour@wave.co.n3 or Allan and Shona Armstrong and John Hall (315) 4040.

Information and Services. International information point (member of Mobility International) in cooperation with tour operator TAMM (member of FfIT) for disabled travelers and holiday makers. European branch of Travelin' Talk.

Dates: Year round. Cost: Dependent on services requested. Contact: Tourism for all Switzerland, Hard 4, 8408 Winterthur, Switzerland; (011) 41-52-222-57-25, fax 52-222-68-38, Telescrit 52-222-71-89 (TDD).

Mobility International USA (MIUSA). MIUSA sponsors international educational exchanges to countries around the world, including the U.S. Exchanges include delegates with and without disabilities ages 15 and up. Delegates participate in leadership training, disability rights workshops and recreational activities.

Dates: Vary. Cost: Vary, scholarships available. Contact: Carole Patterson, MIUSA, P.O. Box 10767, Eugene, OR 97440; (541) 343-6812, fax (541) 343-1284; miusa@igc.apc.org.

Travel for Disabled People. Package trip for disabled person in Quebec or elsewhere. Touristic guide, "access tourism," for accessible places in Quebec.
Dates: Year round. Cost: Different price. Contact: Kéroul, 4545, avenue Pierre de Coubertin, C.P. 1000, Succ. M, Montréal, Canada H1V 3R2; (514) 252-3104, fax (514) 254-0766; keroul@craph.org, www.craph.org/keroul.

Accessible Tours. Accessible Tours plans and books your airfare, hotels, and sightseeing, keeping in mind your needs and budget. If needed all arrangements will be wheelchair accessible, including cars with handcontrols or vans with lifts.
Dates: Anytime. Cost: Varies. Contact: Lois Bonanni, Directions Unlimited, 720 N. Bedford Rd., Bedford Hills, NY 10507; (800) 533-5343 or (914) 241-1700, fax (914) 241-0243.

Dialysis at Sea. Dialysis at Sea Cruises, the only complete medical and travel service of its kind anywhere, arranges cruises for dialysis patients on a large variety of cruise ships and destinations, offering the best group rates available (dialysis treatments additional). Each cruise sets sail with a licensed nephrologist and experienced staff of dialysis clinicians.
Dates: Four to 5 departures per month. Cost: $549 per person to over $10,000 per person. Contact: Loretta McCollum Powell, Dialysis at Sea, 107 13th Ave., P.O. Box 218, Indian Rocks Beach, FL 34635; (800) 544-7604 or (813) 596-7604, fax (813) 596-0203.

Neverland Adventures. Devoted exclusively to providing tours specifically designed by and for challenged travelers. The staff chooses the locations by researching areas for a wheelchair-friendly excursion.
Contact: Neverland Adventures, Rod Gothe, 27 Masters St. Caufield, South, Melbourne, 3162, Australia; Tel./fax (011) 61-39-52335191; in U.S. Andy at (800) 717-U-CAN.

Photographic Safaris. Byseewah is a 15,000-hectare game farm near Etosha National Park in Namibia. Accommodations in thatched rondawals, with solar lighting. Swimming pool, game drives, and photographic opportunities of places and people, birds, and wild game including elephant and rhino.
Dates: 1997. Cost: On request. Each safari tailor-made. Contact: Byseewah Safaris, Box 495, Outjo, Namibia; fax (011) 264-651-4294; satellite tel. (011) 871686490286, satellite fax: (011) 871686490287.

Services for Handicapped Travelers. Janice Perkins, a wheelchair traveler and professional travel agent, provides a liaison between disabled clients and travel suppliers.
Dates: Year round. Cost: Varies according to services provided. Contact: Janice Perkins, Hinsdale Travel Service, 201 E. Ogden Ave., Hinsdale, IL 60521; (708) 469-7349 or (708) 325-1335 or (708) 325-1342, fax (708) 469-7390.

Travel for Mobility-Impaired. Accessible Journeys operates tours exclusively for mobility-impaired travelers to destinations such as Africa, India, Nepal, and China.
Dates: Varies. Cost: Starts at $2,500 per person. Contact: Howard McCoy, Director, Accessible Journeys, 35 W. Sellers Ave., Ridley Park, PA 19078; (800) TINGLES or (610) 521-0339, fax (610) 521-6959; moretravel@aol.com.

Travel Turtle Tours. Offers small escorted tours for people with disabilities. Destinations include Australia, Hungary, Israel, Italy, and Prague. Travel Turtle Tours is owned by a woman with a disability who says, "We do not want accessibility to be a state of mind; it's a reality. And, our pace is slow."
Contact: Carroll Driscoll, 197 Candlewood Isle, New Fairfield, CT 06812; (800) 453-9195; fax (203) 746-5577.

CHAPTER 8

RESPONSIBLE TRAVEL RESOURCES

The scope of environmentally responsible tourism and ecotravel continues to expand. The initial concepts of "walking lightly on the planet" and "taking only photos, leaving only footsteps" has evolved into opportunities for travelers to become more actively involved in the communities and environments they visit.

Responsible travel involves not only environmental and cultural protection, but also local participation in and ownership of tourism projects. Innovative programs insure that travelers' dollars go directly into communities and not into the deep pockets of foreign-owned tourism companies. What follows is a selection of key responsible travel groups and publications, our first go at a comprehensive listing. As always, readers' comments are welcome.

Organizations

Adventure Travel Society, 7500 E. Arapaho Rd., Suite 355, Englewood, CO 80112; (303) 770-3801. Information center on adventure travel and ecotourism. Coordinates an annual Adventure Travel Conference in different countries throughout the world.

American Univ.'s Costa Rica Study Tour offers 12 weeks in Washington, DC and 3 weeks in Costa Rica studying tourism and development. Contact World Capitals Programs, Dublane House-Tenley Campus, American Univ., Washington, DC 20016-8080; (202) 895-4900.

Annapurna Conservation Area Project (ACAP), ACAP Headquarters Ghandruk, Ghandruk Panchayat, Kaski District, Nepal. An international project that uses trekkers' fees to protect the environment and culture of the Gurung people in north central Nepal.

Bicycle Africa. David Moser, (206) 628-9314. How-to tips with good information about travel clubs and good places to go on a bike.

Center for Global Education, Augsburg College, 731 21st Ave. South, Minneapolis, MN 55454; (612)330-1159. Offers enlightening travel programs (some for college credit) to developing countries. See the culture and learn about current issues from local people.

Center for Responsible Tourism, P.O. Box 827, San Anselmo, CA 94979; (415) 258-6594. Publishes a monthly newsletter highlighting innovative tourism projects around the world. They are one of the only responsible travel centers in the U.S. and have helped hundreds of travelers, educators, people in other counties. Subscribe—they need your support!

Center for Third World Organizing, 3861 Martin Luther King, Jr. Way, Oakland, CA 94609; (415) 654-9601. An excellent resource for information about progressive politics, actions, and organizations in the U.S. and abroad.

Conservation International, 1015 18th St., NW, Suite 1000, Washington, DC 20036; (202) 429-5660. Provides technical assistance to innovative programs in developing countries; has information about conservation studies and language programs.

Cousteau Society, Project Ocean Search, 930 W. 21st St., Norfolk, VA 23517; (804) 627-1144. Good marine guidelines and information about threats to the world's precious oceans.

Earth Island Institute, 300 Broadway, #28, San Francisco, CA 94133-3312; (415) 788-3666. Publishes "How Green is Your Tour: Questions to Ask Your Tour Operator." Their sea turtle program offers tours to Mexico where participants learn about and help monitor endangered turtle species.

Earthwatch, 680 Mt. Auburn St., Watertown, MA 02272; (617) 926-8200. Offers paying volunteer work with scientists around the world.

Earthwise Journeys, earthwyz@ teleport.com, is an interlink for "earth-friendly travel to discover our global community."

Ecotourism Association of Australia, P.O. Box 3839, Alice Springs, Northern Territory 0871, Australia; (011) 61-89-528-308.

Ecotourism Society, P.O. Box 755, North Bennington, VT 05257; (802) 447-2121. Designs ecotourism training programs, codes for nature tourism planning, has lots of resources.

Ecotrans E.V., c/o Herbert Hamele, Adelgundesnstr, 18 D-80538 Munchen, Germany.

Ecoventure is helping develop a database, BaseCamp, to provide travelers with information on ecotourism. Contact ziegler@wsu.edu or Ronald Ziegler, Washington State Univ. Libraries, Pullman, WA 99164-5610; fax (509) 335-6721.

Ecumenical Center on Third World Tourism, P.O. Box 925, Bankghen, Bangkok 0900, Thailand.

Ecumenical Coalition on Third World Tourism, P.O. Box 24, Chokrakhebua, Bangkok 10230, Thailand; (011) 66-2-510-7287. The oldest center for responsible tourism—a great information resource, particularly about Asia, for tour operators, agents, educators planning travel programs.

Elderhostel, 80 Boylston St., Suite 400, Boston, MA 02116; (617) 426-7788. For travelers over 50. Friendly, educational travel programs around the world for seniors.

Environmental Traveling Companions, Fort Mason Center, San Francisco, CA 94123; (415)

474-7662. Trips for people with physical and cultural disabilities.

Europe Conservation, Via Fusetti, 14-20143 Milano, Italy; (011) 39-2-5810-3135.

European Center for Eco Agro Tourism, P.O. Box 10899, Amsterdam 1001 EW, The Netherlands. Promotes eco-agro tourism, a sustainable tour option for people with green thumbs.

Global Exchange, 2017 Mission St., Suite 303, San Francisco, CA 94110. Solidarity tours to places like Cuba, South Africa, Chiapas. Publishes Bridging the Global Gap and Beyond Safaris: A Guide to Building People-to-People Ties With Africa, and an information-packed newsletter.

Global Service Corps, 300 Broadway, Suite 28, San Francisco, CA 94133; (415) 788-3666 ext. 128, fax (415) 788-7324; gsc@igc.apc.org, www.earthisland.org/ei/gsc/gschome.html. Cooperates with grassroots groups in Costa Rica to send paid volunteers for 2- and 3-week programs.

Global Volunteers, 375 E. Little Canada Rd., Little Canada, MN 55117. Sends volunteers to short-term community projects in selected countries.

Golondrinas Cloudforest Conservation Project, Calle Isabel La Catolica 1559, Quito, Ecuador; (011) 593-2-226-602 fax 2-222-390. A conservation organization conserving 25,000 hectares of cloudforests on the northwest slopes of the Andes. They have volunteer and educational programs, an agroforestry program, and offer a four-day trek through the Cerro Golondrinas area.

Institute for Central American Development Studies (ICADS) ICADS, Dept. 826, P.O. Box 025216, Miami, FL 33102-5216, or ICADS, Apartado 3-2070, Sabanilla, San Jose, Costa Rica; (011) 506-225-0508; icadscr@expreso.

w.cr. Field course in resource management and sustainable development and interdisciplinary semester internships programs focusing on development issues from ecological and socio-economic perspectives.

Ladakh (India) Project, P.O. Box 9475, Berkeley, CA 94709; (510) 527-3873. An educational program that supports innovative grassroots development efforts of the Ladakhi people who live on the western edge of the Tibetan Plateau in India. Good resource materials on counterdevelopment, books, videos.

Office of Study Abroad, The Univ. of Kansas, Lawrence, KS 66045; (913) 864-3742 offers a semester at the port town of Golfito on the southern Pacific coast of Costa Rica in anthropology, ecology, biology, and Spanish.

One World Family Travel, 81868 Lost Valley Ln., Dexter, OR 96431; (503) 937-3357; dianbr@aol.com. *Transitions Abroad* contributing editor Dianne Brause publishes a directory of alternative travel resources.

OTE Okologischer Tourismus in Europa, Bernd Rath, Am Michaelshof 8-10, 53177 Bonn, Germany. Responsible tourism organization; resources in German.

Our Developing World, 13004 Paseo Presada, Saratoga, CA 95070; (408) 379-4431; fax 408-376-0755. Educational project bringing Third World realities to North Americans. Community programs, teacher training materials, resources library. 1997 study tour to Central America.

Rethinking Tourism Project 1761 Willard St., NW, Washington, DC 20009 202-797-1251; DMcla75001@aol.com. An educational and training program for indigenous people who are developing sustainable, alternative tourism. The project offers professionals with scientific, environmental, academic, and technical assistance expertise and volunteers with opportunities to share their skills, resources, and knowledge with indigenous communities throughout the Americas. 1997 programs in the Amazon (Spanish necessary) and Alaska.

School for Field Studies, 16 Broadway, Beverly, MA 01915-4499; (508) 927-7777. Field studies and hands-on opportunities for high school and college students concerned about the environment in places like rainforests.

Sea Turtle Restoration Project, 300 Broadway, Suite 28, San Francisco, CA 94133; (800) 859-SAVE; earthisland@igc.apc.org. Organizes 1- and 2-week conservation projects in Costa Rica and Mexico.

Sierra Club, 730 Polk St., San Francisco, CA 94109; (415) 923-5630. Publishes good travel guides, offers conservation-focused tours.

Smithsonian Research Expeditions, Smithsonian Institute, Washington, DC 20073-0577; (202) 287-3210. Fairly luxurious tours, some to developing countries, the U.S., national parks, etc.

South American Explorers Club. A network with centers in South America for backpackers, hikers, mountaineers, and other interested travelers. Their magazine is a good resource.

Talamanca Association for Ecotourism and Conservation, Puerto Viejo de Talamanca, Limon, Costa Rica. Local environmental organization that offers ecotourism programs.

TERN: Traveler's Earth Repair Network, Friends of the Trees, P.O. Box 1064, Tonasket, WA 98855; (509) 486-4276. Micheal Pilarski authored book, "Restoration Forestry: An International Guide to Sustainable Forestry Practices" which includes a section that is a resource guide on ecotourism. TERN is a networking service for travelers who want to make a positive contribution to the environment.

Tourism Concern, Froebel College, Roehampton Ln., London, SW15 5PU, U.K. Excellent resource on issues related to tourism: land rights, displacement, general responsible tourism information.

Tropical Science Center, Apartado 8-3870, San Jose 1000, Costa Rica; (011) 506-22-6241. Offers open-air classrooms and labs for tropical science students and professionals.

Univ. of California at Los Angeles, Field Study Program, UCLA Extension, P.O. Box 24901, Los Angeles, CA 90024; (213) 825-7093.

Univ. Research Expeditions Program, Univ. of California, Berkeley, CA 94720; (510) 642-6586. Volunteer programs for travelers of all ages. Director Jean Colvin has developed codes of conduct for researchers working with indigenous peoples and codes for travelers going to the same areas.

Wildlife Conservation International, P.O. Box 68244, Nairobi, Kenya; (011) 222254-221-699. Information about ecotourism projects in Kenya.

World Wildlife Fund, 1250 24th St., NW, Washington, DC 20037; (202) 293-4800. Offers ecotours throughout the world.

Publications

Adventuring In... The Sierra Club Travel Guide Series.

All Asia Guide (Charles E. Tuttle Co.). A practical Asia guide.

Asia Through the Backdoor by Rick Steves and Bob Effertz (John Muir Publications). Asia on the cheap and off the beaten path.

Beyond Safaris: A Guide to Building People-to-People Ties With Africa. Global Exchange,

San Francisco, CA; (415) 255-7296. A bit old but still one of the best resources for socially conscious travelers in Africa. Lists organizations.

Directory of Environmental Travel Resources is available for $10 from Dianne Brause, One World Family Travel Network, 81868 Lost Valley Lane, Dexter, OR 97431.

E Magazine. The Earth Action Network, Westport, CT; (203) 854-5559

Earthtrips by Dwight Holing (Conservation International).

Eco-Vacations: Enjoy Yourself and Save the Earth by Evelyn Kaye. Blue Penguin Publications, 147 Sylvan Ave., Leonia, NJ 07605.

Ecotourist Guide to the Ecuadorian Amazon by Rolfe Wesche. The Pan-American Center for Geographical Studies and Research, 3er piso, Apartado 17-01-4273, Quito, Ecuador; (011) 593-245-1200.

Green Travel Mailing List. For green travel resources on the Internet. To subscribe contact majordomo@igc.apc.org.

Green Travel Sourcebook by Daniel Grotta and Sally Wiener Grotta (John Wiley & Sons Publishers).

Indigenous Peoples and Global Tourism. Project Report by Deborah McLaren, The Rethinking Tourism Project, 1761 Willard St., NW, Washington, DC 20009 USA. $6 postpaid.

Indonesian Travel Guide by Richard Mann (Singapore National Printers).

Lonely Planet Guides. Books on every country in Asia plus some regional.

Natour: Special edition on ecotourism. Contact editor Arturo Crosby, Viriato, 20, Madrid, Spain; (011) 91-593-0831.

Nature Tourism: Managing for the Environment edited by Tensie Whelan (Island Press, 1991, $19.95). Guidelines and essays on nature tourism.

Structural Adjustment, World Trade and Third World Tourism: An Introduction to the Issues by K.T. Ramesh, Ecumenical Center on Third World Tourism, P.O. Box 35, Senanikhom, Bangkok 10902, Thailand. Contours, August 1995.

DEBORAH MCLAREN is the coordinator for the "Rethinking Tourism" project. She works with communities designing alternative tourism projects worldwide. Contact her at 1761 Willard St., NW, Washington, DC 20009; Dmcla 75001@aol.com.

CHAPTER 9

RESPONSIBLE TRAVEL TOURS AND PROGRAMS

The following listing of responsible travel programs was supplied by the organizers. Contact the program directors to confirm costs, dates, and other details. If you do not see the program you want in the country of your choice, look in the "Worldwide" listings at the end of the section for programs located in several different regions.

Africa

Bicycle Africa Tours. Village-based, cross-cultural bicycle tours to all parts of Africa. Cycling difficulty is moderate. Each program is different, but all focus on the diversity of the culture, social institutions, and environment, as well as the complexity of the history, economy, culture, and society. Programs are led by African studies specialists.

Dates: Jan (Uganda), Feb (Kenya/Tanzania), Apr (Tunisia), Jun-Aug (Zimbabwe), Oct-Nov (Senegal/Mali), Nov (Burkina Faso/Togo/ Benin). Cost: $990-$1,290 plus airfare for 2 weeks. Includes food, lodging, guides, and fees. Contact: David Mozer, Director, International Bicycle Fund/Bicycle Africa, 4887 Columbia Dr. S. #T-7, Seattle, WA 98108; Tel./ fax (206) 767-0848; intlbike@scn.org; www. halcyon.com/fkroger/bike/bikeafr.html.

Bushman Trail. The Ju/wasi are participating in a sponsored research project on predators such as leopard in Bushmanland, and travelers will join them as they track the animals across their rugged Namibian habitat.

Dates: Mar 6, Apr 10, Jun 12, Jul 10, Aug 7, Aug 21. Cost: $3,200 per person. Airfare not included. Contact: Baobab Safari Company, 210 Post St., #911, San Francisco, CA 94108; (415) 391-5788, fax (415) 391-3752.

International Travel Seminar. Explore the changes taking place in southern Africa. Look at the historical struggle against apartheid in South Africa, the political and economic dynamics in this region, and the future of southern Africa. Participants meet with the poor and disenfranchised, women's groups, cooperatives, and alternative political parties, as well as decision-makers from government, business, and church. Three or 4 trips are offered per year, including South Africa, Namibia, and Uganda.

Dates: Trips of 15-20 days throughout the year to South Africa, Namibia, and/or Uganda. Cost: $3,500-$4,500 depending on the length of the trip. Contact: Travel Seminar Division, Center for Global Education, Augsburg College, 2211 Riverside Ave., Box 307TR, Minneapolis, MN 55454; (800) 299-8889, (612) 330-1159, fax (612) 330-1695; globaled@augs bu rg.edu, www.augsburg.edu/global.

Private Safaris. Individually designed safaris in Kenya. Private safaris in custom-built 4-wheel drive Toyota Land Cruisers, each with 2 photographic hatches. Professional guides and safaris with own group.

Dates: Year-round except Apr, May and early Jun. Cost: $400 and up land only (based on 3-4 people in one vehicle). Contact: Sherry Corbett, Perry Mason Safaris, P.O. Box 1643, Darien, CT 06820; Tel./fax (203) 838-1345.

Argentina

I.I.C.A.N.A. One, 2-, 4-, and 8-month Spanish language programs, offered year round. Course work includes grammar, video and audio exercises, conversation, Argentine history, geography, and literature. Limited internship opportunities available. Apply 10 weeks before start date.

Dates: Start dates for 1996: Feb 5, Jun 17, and Aug 26. Cost: $1,400 (1 month); $2,200 (2 months); $3,800 (4 months); $5,500 (8 months). Contact: Mottay America, P.O. Box 29361, Atlanta, GA 30359; (770) 908-8352; mottay@aol.com.

Instituto de Lengua Española para Extranjeros (ILEE). Located downtown in the most European-like city in Latin America. Dedicated exclusively to teaching Spanish to foreigners. Small groups and private classes year round. All teachers hold a university degree. Method is intensive, conversation-based.

Student body is international, mostly European. Highly recommended worldwide (all travel guides, British and German universities, etc.). Ask for individual references in U.S.

Dates: Year round. Cost: Four weeks intensive program (20 hours a week) including homestay $1,400; 2 weeks $700. Individual classes $19 per hour. Registration fee (includes books) $100. Contact: ILEE, Daniel Korman, Director, Lavalle 1619 7th C (1048), Buenos Aires, Argentina; (011) 54-1-375-0730, fax 864-4942; www.worldwide.edu/argentina/ilee/index.html. In U.S.: David Babbitz; (415) 431-8219, fax (415) 431-5306.

Asia

China and Hong Kong in Transition. Talking with a wide range of people in Beijing, Shanghai, and a rural area, assess how China's economic changes affect political and cultural realities. In Hong Kong, pursue questions about the colony's future. Meet with pro-China and pro-democracy legislators, and people from labor, women's, and foreign investment sectors. (Occasionally other programs are offered in Southeast Asia.)

Dates: Mar 31-Apr 13, 1997. Cost: $4,295 from San Francisco. Includes airfare, lodging, food, program. Contact: Travel Seminar Division, Center for Global Education, Augsburg College, 2211 Riverside Ave., Box 307TR, Minneapolis, MN 55454; (800) 299-8889; globaled@augsburg.edu, www.augsburg.edu/global.

Cross-Cultural Travel. Meet people from very different cultures and explore natural environments beyond the reach of ordinary travel. Himalayan adventures in Nepal, Tibet, Ladakh, Bhutan. Central Asia trips in Pakistan, China. Combine with Southeast Asia explorations in Burma, Thailand, India, Laos, Cambodia, Vietnam. Also year-round departures for learning experiences in Africa and Latin America.

Dates: Year round. Cost: Varies. Contact:

William Weber, President, Journeys International, 4011 Jackson Rd., Ann Arbor, MI 48103; (800) 255-8735 or (313) 665-4407, fax (313) 665-2945; journeysmi@aol.com, www.journeys-intl.com.

Himalayan High Treks. We offer hiking trips in Nepal, India, Bhutan, and Tibet. Our goal is to make tourism benefit the indigenous people and culture of these areas. We take no more than 8 people in a group and provide them with quality equipment, experienced staff and guides. We are environmentally responsible and a portion of cost goes to nonprofits working in the region. (Internships available.)

Dates: Year round. Cost: $1,600-$4,600. Contact: Effie Fletcher, Himalayan High Treks, 241 Dolores St., San Francisco, CA 94103-2211; (800) 455-8735, fax (415) 861-2391; effie@well.com.

International Travel Seminar. Themes for trips to Southeast Asia include the impact of tourism, post-Vietnam war society, refugees, and the environment. Call for current trips.

Dates: Trips of 10-20 days to Thailand, Laos, Vietnam, Hong Kong, and China. Cost: Varies. Contact: Travel Seminar Division, Center for Global Education, Augsburg College, 2211 Riverside Ave., Box 307TR, Minneapolis, MN 55454; (612) 330-1159, fax (612) 330-1695.

Orangutan Conservation. In cooperation with the Orangutan Foundation International, Bolder Adventures offers a series of orangutan research study tours. Participants support the work of Dr. Birute Galdikas, who has spent 25 years studying these endangered primates. The 10-day programs take place at Camp Leakey on the island of Borneo in Indonesia.

Dates: Jul 7, Jul 21, Aug 4, Aug 18, Sep 15, Oct 6, Nov 6, Nov 3, 1997. Cost: $2,100 land cost only. Contact: Bolder Adventures, Inc., Southeast Asia Travel Specialists, 3055 Center Green Dr., Boulder, CO 80306; (800) 642-2742, fax (303) 443-7078; bolder@southeastasia.com, www.southeastasia.com.

Travel-Study Seminars. Visit with Asians from China, Hong Kong and Indochina as their countries undergo profound economic changes. Pursue critical questions, such as: Do these changes also bring political pluralism? What impact do economic changes have on the education and outlook of youth? On the natural environment? Who benefits from economic restructuring? Call for more information on current trips.

Dates: Varies. Cost: Approx. $3,800-$4,300 depending on length and destinations. Contact: Center for Global Education, Augsburg College, 2211 Riverside Ave., Box 307TR, Minneapolis, MN 55454; (800) 299-8889, fax (612) 330-1695; globaled@augsburg.edu, www.augsburg.edu/global.

Australia

Adventure Plus +. Hands-on learning with Australian natural history professional. Sail, snorkel, dive, and explore the underwater sealife in the Great Barrier Reef; sea kayak to remote islands; hike, bike, and camp in the rainforest and the outback, home of the Aboriginal people. Your environmentally and culturally sensitive Australian adventure will be tailor-made to meet your individual or group needs. All participants are encouraged to follow the Guidelines for Responsible Travel.

Dates: Year round. Cost: Call for information, free newsletter, and brochure. Contact: Ms. M.J. Kietzke, CTC, Co-Op America Travel-Links, 120 Beacon St., Somerville, MA 02143-4369; (800) 648-2667, fax (617) 492-3720.

Educational Nature Trips. Educational nature trips outback: wildlife and rock art, rainforest and coral reefs. Also active adventures in the natural environment: river canoeing, sea kayaking, hiking and biking. Snorkel or scuba dive the Great Barrier Reef and Coral Sea. Weekly departures. Join 1- to 12-day expeditions designed for the individual traveler or small groups.

Dates: Call program for information. Cost: Between $80 and $160 per day (all inclusive). Contact: The Adventure Company, P.O. Box 5740, Cairns, Queensland 4870, Australia; (011) 61-70-514-777 or 70-514-888; advent ures@adventures.com.au. In U.S.: (800) 388-7333.

Belgium

Environmental Information Centre. Technical management of Environmental Information Centre for Young People (library with books, magazines, reports, etc. on nature conservation). Intern also takes part in management and activities of environmental conservation youth organization.

Dates: Spring, summer, fall—min. 4 weeks. Cost: Call for details. Contact: NATUUR 2000, Bervoetstraat 33, 2000 Antwerpen, Belgium; (011) 32-3-2312604, fax 2336499.

Belize

Science and Conservation Expeditions. Six-week expeditions working on projects in support of science and conservation for the long term benefit of the ecosystems of the rainforest and the reef. We have completed a mapping project in the rainforest using global positioning systems. Future projects will involve construction of a scientific basecamp and work on the reef.

Dates: Throughout the year. (Recruiting for 1997 and 1998.) Cost: £2700. Contact: Trekforce Expeditions, 134 Buckingham Palace Rd., London SW1W 9SA; U.K.; (011) 44-171-824-8890, fax 171-824-8892; trekforce@ dial.pipex.com, http://ds.dial.pipex.com/ town/parade/hu15.

Canada

Canada's Canoe Adventures. Canoeing and sea kayaking adventures for all ages and abilities. Canada's Canoe Adventures welcomes those who are seeking an experience of a lifetime that will evoke memories for generations to come. Over 45 trips to all parts of Canada, including: Algonquin Park, Quetico Temagami, Quebec, Seal, Tweedsmuir, Bowron Lakes, Queen Charlottes, Johnstone Strait, Nahanni, Coppermine Mountain, and many more. Winter paddling to Belize, Baha, Costa Rica, and Bahamas. Proceeds donated to water conservation projects operated by the Canadian Recreational Canoeing Association.

Dates: Year-round. Cost: CAN$250-$5,000. Contact: Canada's Canoe Adventures, P.O. Box 398, 446 Main St. West, Merrickville, ON K0G 1N0, Canada; (613) 269-2910, fax (613) 269-2908; staff@crca.ca, www.crca.ca/.

Wilderness Lodging. Purcell Lodge is Canada's finest remote mountain lodge. It sets a new environmental standard in sustainable tourism development. A few miles beyond the crowds of Banff and Lake Louise lies true solitude. A spectacular helicopter flight leaves the familiar far behind. Inside, the comfort of a fine country manor. Outside, your own natural paradise. Peaceful walks in alpine meadows, guided ski tours in stunning surroundings.

Dates: Late Jun-early Sep, Dec-Apr. Cost: All-inclusive American plan $130 per night. Contact: Russ Younger, Manager, Purcell Lodge, Places Less Travelled Ltd., P.O. Box 1829, Golden, BC, Canada V0A 1H0; (250) 344-2639, fax (250) 344-5520; places@ rockies.net.

Wilderness Lodging. Mount Assiniboine Lodge is only accessible by hiking trail or scheduled helicopter services. This historic log lodge and its cabins are located on a scenic bluff overlooking the iridescent blue of Magog Lake. Towering above both the lodge and the lake is Mount Assiniboine and its glacier. One of the tallest peaks in the Canadian Rockies, this mountain is world renowned for its similarity to the famous Matterhorn in the Swiss Alps. This World Heritage Site is a must see.

Dates: Late Jun-early Oct, Feb-Apr. Cost: All-inclusive American plan including guides from $75 per night. Contact: Paul Leeson, Manager, Mount Assiniboine Lodge, Places Less Travelled Ltd., P.O. Box 1829, Golden, BC, Canada V0A 1H0; (250) 344-2639, fax (250) 344-5520; places@rockies.net.

Yoga Study and Retreats. Yasodhara Ashram, a vibrant spiritual community founded 33 years ago by Swami Sivanada Radha, offers yoga courses, workshops, spiritual retreats. Situated on Kootenay Lake in the mountains of southeastern British Columbia, the atmosphere is conducive to reflection, meditation, and renewal. The 10 Days of Yoga, an introduction to ashram courses, is offered every quarter. Programs for young adults are offered at this certified post-secondary institute.

Dates: Year round. Cost: Varies. The 10 Days of Yoga is CAN$825 (CAN$170 deposit). Contact: Yasodhara Ashram, Box 9, Kootenay Bay, BC VOB 1XO, Canada; (604) 227-9224 or (800) 661-8711, fax (604) 227-9494; yashram@netidea.com.

Central America

Central American Eco-Tours. One-week tours in each country emphasize national parks and indigenous cultures. Small groups study diverse ecological systems with English-speaking naturalist guides, visit native cultural centers, archaeology sites, hike, swim, boat, cloud forests and craker lakes. B and B lodgings. Tours benefit local people and ecology projects.

Dates: Jan and Feb, 1997 and 1998. Cost: $800 per week plus discount airfares. Contact: Dr. B. Phillips, Casas Americas, 613 S. Circle Ave., Barrington, Il 60010; (847) 516-4921, fax (847) 516-9079; leftknee@ix.netcom.com.

International Travel Seminar. More than 20 trips are offered each year to Nicaragua, El Salvador, Guatemala, and Mexico to meet with the poor and disenfranchised, women's

groups, cooperatives, and alternative political parties, as well as decision-makers from the government, businesses, and churches. Programs are designed to bring you face-to-face with Latin American people's struggle for freedom, justice, and human dignity.

Dates: Trips of 7-14 days throughout the year. Cost: From $1,300-$2,500 (includes airfare, food, lodging, and program). Contact: Travel Seminar Division, Center for Global Education, Augsburg College, 2211 Riverside Ave., Box 307TR, Minneapolis, MN 55454; (800) 299-8889, (612) 330-1159, fax (612) 330-1695; globaled@augsburg.edu, www.augsburg.edu/global.

Update on Guatemala, El Salvador and Nicaragua. Program focuses on people and socio-economic development at the grassroots level. Visit schools, clinics, argricultural development projects, women's and human rights organizations, purchase crafts from their makers, and meet trade unionists. Limited to 10 participants.

Dates: Guatemala and El Salvador Jun 25-Jul 9, 1997. Nicaragua Jul 9-16, 1997 (including the Atlantic Coast and its new university). Cost: Guatemala and El Salvador $2,199 (plus Nicaragua $2,995). Price includes airfare from San Francisco or Los Angeles, 2 meals daily, simple lodging, land transport, transfers to and from accommodations, guides, translators, and facilitators. Airfare subject to change; later return possible. Contact: Vic or Barby Ulmer, Our Developing World, 13004 Paseo Presada, Saratoga, CA 95070-4125; (408) 379-4431, fax (408) 376-0755; vic_ulmer@vval.com.

Chile

Ecolé—Lost Forest Treks. Ecolé and Lost Forest Treks invite the casual adventurer on a 2-week, 3-part trek through southern Chile's wilds. Pristine wilderness, live volcanoes, trackless fjords, hot springs, ancient forests, native cultures, Spanish instruction. Get to know this spectacular country with U.S. and Chilean conservation activists. We can help you get involved.

Dates: Dec-Mar. Cost: Land cost $1,680. Contact: Ecolé, P.O. Box 2453, Redway, CA 95560; Tel./fax (800) 447-1483; ecole@asis.com, www.asis.com/ecole.

Costa Rica

Casa Rio Blanco Rainforest Reserve. Volunteers maintain trails, map, develop educational materials, teach, garden, etc. Also available: 1 paid position in lodge helping with cooking and cleaning. Room, board, and $30 per week. Minimum of 3 months.

Dates: Four-week sessions throughout the year. Cost: $150 per week, includes room, food, laundry, materials. Contact: Thea Gaudette, Casa Rio Blanco, Apdo 241-7210, Guapiles, Pococi, Costa Rica.

Costa Rica EcoAdventure. From cloudforests and volcanoes to tropical rivers and beaches, this 8-day ecological adventure lets you discover and experience some of the country's most beautiful and diverse ecosystems. This escorted exploration includes visits to Carrillo National Park, Poás and Arenal volcanoes, Caño Negro, Carara Reserve, Jaco Beach, and Manuel Antonio Park and more.

Dates: Year round. Cost: Varies. Contact: Charlie Strader, Explorations Inc., 27655 Kent Rd., Bonita Springs, FL 34135; (800) 446-9660, fax (941) 992-7666; cesxplor@aol.com.

Costa Rican Language Academy. Costa Rican owned and operated language school offers first-rate Spanish instruction in a warm and friendly environment. Teachers with university degrees. Small groups or private classes. Included free in the programs are airport transportation, coffee and natural refreshments, excursions and Latin dance, Costa Rican cooking, music and conversation classes

to provide students with complete cultural immersion.

Dates: Year round (start anytime). Cost: $135 per week or $220 per week for program with homestay. All other activities and services included at no additional cost. Contact: Costa Rican Language Academy, P.O. Box 336-2070, San José, Costa Rica; (011) 506-221-1624 or 233-8914 or 233-8938, fax 233-8670; crlang@sol.racsa.co.cr. In the U.S. (800) 854-6057.

Horizontes Nature Tours. For over 12 years, Horizontes has been operating quality personalized travel programs for people interested in nature observation, conservation, education, soft adventure, and meaningful interaction with local people. We operate custom-designed groups and individual itineraries for renowned international tour companies, universities, and nonprofit organizations worldwide, plus a wide selection of package tours.

Dates: Custom trips, 1-day and multi-day package tours available year round. Cost: Contact us for our current 24-page color brochure and price list. Contact: Terry Pratt, Marketing, Horizontes Nature Tours, P.O. Box 1780-1002 P.E., San José, Costa Rica; (011) 506-222-2022, fax (011) 506-255-4513; horizont@sol.racsa.co.cr.

Spanish Immersion Program. The Institute for Central American Development Studies (ICADS) offers 30-day programs of Intensive Spanish Languages—4 1/2 hours daily, 5 days a week. Small classes (4 students or less) geared to individual needs. Extra lectures and activities emphasize environmental issues, women's studies, economic development, and human rights. ICADS offers optional afternoon internship placements in grassroots organizations. Supportive informal learning environment. Homestays and field trips. A great alternative for the socially conscious.

Dates: Programs begin first Monday of each month. Cost: One month $1,150 (includes airport pick-up, classes, books, homestay, meals, laundry, lectures, activities, field trips, and placement). Ten percent discount after first month. Contact: Sandra Kinghorn, PhD, Director, ICADS, Dept. 826, P.O. Box 025216, Miami, FL 33102-5216; (506) 225-0508, fax (506) 234-1337; icadscr@expreso.co.cr.

Dominican Republic

Spanish, Development, Culture. Individual and group programs focused on (1) learning Spanish as a Second Language, (2) adaptation into Hispanic culture, (3) development themes on poverty, migration, sustainability, health, environment. Individually designed programs can include urban/rural homestays, with different degrees of immersion. Fifteen years experience.

Dates: Designed according to participant's needs. Cost: Varies with program ($1,530 per month immersion). Contact: Rafael Paz or Sobeya Seibel, Entrena, EPS-P-4507, Box 02-5261, Miami, FL 33102-5261; (011) 809-567-8990 or 541-4283, fax 566-3492.

East Africa

East Africa with the Experts. Join America's most distinguished museums, zoological societies and wildlife organizations on safaris to East and Southern Africa. Trips are led by outstanding local naturalists and feature excellent accommodations in the best reserves for animal viewing. Park East Tours has been a leader in travel to East Africa for over 30 years and is the 1996 recipient of the Africa Travel Association Award for Outstanding Achievement in the Promotion of Responsible Tourism to Africa.

Dates: All of 1997. Cost: From $2,995 to $5,995 (depending on program, land and air from New York). Contact: Marcia Gordon, Park East Tours, 1841 Broadway, New York, NY 10023; (800) 223-6078 ext. 316 or (212) 765-4870 ext 316, fax (212) 265-8952.

Ecuador

Galapagos Islands. Sail these magical, volcanic islands in maximum comfort and safety aboard a 48-passenger expedition ship, the M/V Corinthian, or a 20-passenger motor yacht, the M/Y Eric, Flamingo and Letty or a 10-passenger motor sailor, the M/S Sea Cloud.

Dates: Year-round departures. Cost: Three nights $600-$800; 4 nights $800-$1,050; 7 nights $1,500-$1,850. Contact: Galapagos Network, 7200 Corporate Center Dr., #309, Miami, FL 33126; (800) 633-7972 or (305) 592-2294, fax (305) 592-6394; gpsnet@aol.com.

Golondrinas Cloudforest Project. The Cerro Golondrinas Cloudforest Conservation Project offers a unique 4-day journey from the páramo (4,200 m) to the subtropical (1,000 m). Your luggage is carried by horses and local farmers welcome you with home-prepared meals. Through this experience the Project aims to share with you the magnificent tropical highlands and heighten your awareness of the importance of nature conservation. Your visit will also benefit the local farmers, who learn from you while earning an alternative income.

Dates: Year round, starting from Quito every Friday. Cost: $50 per person per day. Contact: Fundación Golondrinas, Attn: Piet T. Sabbe, Calle Isabel la Católica, 1559, Quito, Ecuador.

Natural History Workshops in the Galapagos Islands. Specializing in comprehensive, educationally-oriented, professionally-led 11-day natural history tours of the Galapagos Islands. Special programs include history-oriented trips that follow Darwin's route as well as National Science Teacher Association (NSTA)-sponsored tours offering 3 graduate credit hours.

Dates: Monthly departures on 16-passenger yachts. Cost: Approx. $2,800. Airfare not included. Contact: Galapagos Travel, P.O. Box 1220, San Juan Bautista, CA 95045; (800) 969-9014, fax (408) 623-2923; 74072.1127@compuserve.com.

El Salvador

El Salvador Encounter. A Third World immersion experience with a faith-based perspective. An intensive week of listening to Salvadorans describe their struggles through the war and hopes for the future, celebrating new life with the Church, visiting historic sites, and reflecting on how our faith is informed and challenged by what we see. El Salvador Encounter will design seminars for your church or community focusing on your interests: theology, education, women, ecology, politics, and economics. Or join nationwide groups throughout the year.

Dates: One- to 2-week "tours" throughout the year. Cost: $65 per day includes room and board, guide, translation, etc. Contact: Stan de Voogd, 1135 Mission Rd., San Antonio, TX 78210; (210) 534-6996; crispaz@igc.apc.org.

France

Enjoy French in a Chateau. Château de Mâtel (17th century) offers residential courses for adults in General French, Intensive French, Cooking. On 32 hectares of parkland near Roanne city center. Close to Burgundy, Beaujolais, and city of Lyons. Single, en suite, and shared rooms available. One through 12-week courses. Tennis, pool, horse-riding, kayak.

Dates: Every Sunday Apr-Nov. Cost: From $999 full board and classes in Chateau. Contact: Dr. C. Roberts, 204 via Morella, Encinitas, CA 92024; (619) 632-1923 or (800) 484-1235 #0096 or Joe Davies, 3473 Camino Valencia, Carlsbad, CA 92009; Tel./fax (619) 591-4537 (modem) or Ecole des Trois Ponts, Chateau de Matel, 42300 Roanne, France; (011) 33-77-70-80-01, fax 77-71-53-00.

Painting in Calvisson. Calvisson is an old Mediterranean village 15 kms west of Nîmes. A personal introduction to the South of France. Welcome to a 15-century dwelling by Régis, an artist, and Corrine, a historian of art.

They offer you a comfortable stay in a privileged place, painting courses, and guided tours of the area.

Dates: Open year round. Cost: Full board: FF350 per day. Painting course FF40 per hour. Guided tours FF200 per person for full day. Contact: Corinne Burckel de Tell, Grand Rue, 30420 Calvisson, France; (011) 33-4-66-01-23-91, fax 01-42-19.

Village Stays. Set in the heart of the old village of Calvisson, this 15th century house has been restored with patience and talent by its owners and offers you tastefully furnished guestrooms. Calvisson is located 15 km west of Nimes in front of the beaches of Camargue. Painting courses and guided tours of the area.

Dates: Year round. Cost: Double room FF280, single; FF230, suite (3 persons); FF330 with breakfasts, meals FF75 with wine. Contact: Corinne Burckel de Tell, Grand Rue 48, 30420 Calvisson, France; (011) 33-466-012391, fax (011) 33-466-014219.

Guatemala

Eco-Escuela de Español. The Eco-Escuela de Español offers a unique educational experience by combining intensive Spanish language instruction with volunteer opportunities in conservation and community development projects. Students are immersed in the language, culture, and ecology of the Petén, Guatemala—an area renowned for its tropical forests and ancient Maya ruins. Ecological activities integrate classroom with field-based experiences.

Dates: Every Monday year round. Cost: Classes $60 per week (based on 20 hours of individual instruction per week, Monday-Friday). Room and board with local families $50 per week. Registration fee $10. Contact: Eco-Escuela, Conservation International, 1015 18th St. NW, Suite 1000, Washington, DC 20036; (202) 973-2264, fax (202) 887-5188; m.sister@conservation.org.

India

Certificate Course. This certificate course is for 3 months on "Indian Culture, Gandhian Thought, and Peace Studies." Send for brochure.

Dates: Nov 20, 1996-Feb 17, 1997. Cost: $10 form fee plus $750 course fee after securing admission. Contact: Coordinator, Peace Research Centre, Gujarat Vidyapith, Ahmedabad 380014, India; (011) 91-79-446148, fax 79-429547.

Global Village or Global Pillage? Just Transitions, a nonprofit organization, takes groups of concerned individuals to India to witness the impacts of "economic globalization" on ordinary citizens, and network with activist organizations resisting globalization because of the adverse economic, environmental, and social impacts of these changes. Emphasis is on connecting the root causes of similar problems in India and the U.S., and what we can and need to do in our communities to support the resistance movements in India and the U.S.

Dates: May 23-Jun 22; Jul 11-Aug 10; Dec 18-Jan 17, 1998. Cost: $2,750. Includes roundtrip airfare to India, all accommodations, food, local travel, and program costs within India. Limited scholarships available. Contact: Amit Srivastava, Just Transitions, P.O. Box 420675, San Francisco, CA 94142; Toll Free: (888) 345-JUSTICE; amit@igc.apc.org.

Indonesia

Science and Conservation Expeditions. Six-week expeditions working on projects for the long term benefit of the rainforest and ecosystems. A chance for trekkers to experience challenge and adventure. Age 17 and over. Projects include building a turtle hatching pen and constructing a scientist base camp and research center.

Dates: Throughout the year (recruiting for 1997 and 1998). Cost: £2700 for 4 weeks. Contact: Trekforce Expeditions, 134 Buckingham Palace Rd., London SW1W 9SA, U.K.; (011) 44-171-824-8890, fax 171-824-8892; trek force @dial. pipex.com, http://ds.dial. pipex.com/ town/parade/hu15.

Ireland

Irish Language and Cultural Programs. Irish language programs at all learning levels for adults are offered by Oideas Gael, which also offers cultural activity learning programs in hillwalking, dances of Ireland, painting, tapestry weaving, Raku-Celtic pottery, and archaeology.

Dates: Apr-Sep, 1997 (weekly). Cost: $140 plus accommodations (from $80 per week). Contact: Liam O'Cuinneagain, Director, Oideas Gael, Gleann Chohm Cille, County Donegal, Ireland.

Walking and Trekking Holidays. Countryside Tours, set up in 1990, is the specialist in providing leisurely guided and more challenging self-guided hiking tours. A varied program includes all the major areas of interest such as Kerry, Connemara, Wicklow Mountains, and Ulster. Good food, comfortable accommodations in Irish guesthouses.

Dates: Please ask for brochure. Cost: IR£420 for guided tours, from IR£205 for self-guided tours. Contact: Nick Becker, Countryside Tours Ltd., Glencar House, Glencar, County Kerry, Ireland; (011) 353-66 60211, fax (011) 353 66 60217; country@iol.ie.

Italy

American Univ. of Rome. Programs for students of international business, international relations, Italian civilization and culture, Italian studies. Credits fully transferable through affiliations with U.S. institutions. Housing in studio apartments. All courses (except language classes) in English. All programs are designed to provide students with studies of immediate relevance in a highly competitive job market.

Dates: Fall and Spring semesters plus May/ Jun summer sessions. Cost: $4,475 per semester, tuition/housing $2,350. Contact: Mary B. Handley, Dean of Administration, American Univ. of Rome, Via Pietro Roselli 4, Rome 00153, Italy; (011) 39-6-58330919, fax 583 30992.

Kenya

Conservation Expeditions. Trekforce's most recent projects are based on the improvement of the water supply for local people and animals in the northern savannah of Kenya.

Dates: Twice yearly. Cost: £1800 for 4 weeks. Contact: Trekforce Expeditions, 134 Buckingham Palace Rd., London SW1W 9SA, U.K.; (011) 44-171-824-8890, fax 171-824-8892; trekforce@dial.pipex.com, http:// ds.dial.pipex.com/town/parade/hu15.

Mexico

Copper Canyon. Outstanding cultural and natural history rail trips. The most dramatic train ride in the western hemisphere. Deeper, wider, greener canyons than Arizona's Grand Canyon. Tarahumara Indian culture, nature walks, birding, waterfalls, spectacular vistas. Historic tours, small groups, personal attention. In-depth interpretation of the Copper Canyon and its people.

Dates: Year round. Cost: $1,695 per person for 8-day trips. Contact: S&S Tours, 865 El Camino Real, Sierra Vista, AZ 85635; (800) 499-5685, fax (520) 458-5258; ss@the ri v e r. com.

Educational Community. Cemanahuac offers intensive Spanish language instruction by native speakers: academic credit, graduate and undergraduate; Latin American studies classes, with emphasis on the social reality of Mexico; strong field study programs led by anthropologists; rural studies program in a Mexican village; summer programs for educators; volunteer opportunities near the school; family stay program; special classes for professionals.

Dates: Year round program. New classes begin every Mon. Group programs arranged at reduced fees. Cost: Registration fee $90 (one-time fee); weekly tuition $190; housing with 3 meals per day $17 (double), $23 (single). Contact: Vivian B. Harvey, Educational Programs Coordinator, Apartado 5-21, Cuernavaca, Morelos, Mexico; (011) 52-73-18-6407 or 73-12-6419, fax 73-12-5418; 74052.2570@compuserve.com.

Intensive Spanish in Cuauhnahuac. Cuauhnahuac, founded in 1972, offers a variety of intensive and flexible programs geared to individual needs. Six hours of classes daily with no more than 4 students to a class. Housing with Mexican families who really care about you. Cultural conferences, excursions, and special classes for professionals. College credit available.

Dates: Year round. New classes begin every Monday. Cost: $70 registration fee; $600 4 weeks tuition, housing $16 per night. Contact: Marcia Snell, 519 Park Dr., Kenilworth, IL 60043; (800) 245-9335, fax (847) 256-9475; lankysam@aol.com.

Mar de Jade Mexico. Tropical ocean-front responsible tourism center in beautiful unspoiled fishing village near Puerto Vallarta offers unique study options: enjoy great swimming, snorkeling, hiking, and boating; study Spanish in small groups taught by native speakers. Or join the longer work/study program that includes working in development projects such as health clinic, teaching, or working in the community of Mar de Jade itself.

Dates: Year round. Cost: For 21 days: room (shared occupancy), board and Spanish classes

(12 hours per week of Spanish and 12-15 hours per week of community work) $865. For daily room and board $45. Contact: In Mexico: Mar de Jade, A.P. 81, Las Varas, Nayarit, 63715, Mexico; Tel./fax (011) 52-327-20184; In U.S.: P.O. Box 423353, San Francisco, CA 94142; (415) 281-0164.

Spanish Language in Guanajuato. We work with our students one-on-one or in small groups (2 to 5 students), tailoring instruction to each student's needs. We teach people of all ages and from many nationalities. Highlights: homestays with families, sports, movies, field trips, hikes, cultural events—all this taking place in the most beautiful colonial setting of Mexico.

Dates: Year round. New classes begin every Monday. Cost: $925. Includes lifetime registration fee, group classes (5 sessions per day Monday-Friday), and a homestay with 3 meals daily for 4 weeks. Lower price for fewer weeks. Contact: Director Jorge Barroso, Instituto Falcon, A.C., Guanajuato, Gto. 36000 Mexico; Tel./fax (011) 52-473-2-36-94, www. infonet. com.mx/falcon.

Travel/Study Seminars. Learn from Mexicans of diverse backgrounds about their economic, political, and social realities. Emphasis on the views of the poor and oppressed. Programming in Cuernavaca, Mexico City, and Chiapas. Call for a free list of upcoming programs.

Dates: Ongoing. Cost: $800-$1,900 depending on package, destination, and length of trip. Contact: Center for Global Education, Augsburg College, 2211 Riverside Ave., Box 307TR, Minneapolis, MN 55454; (800) 299-8889, fax (612) 330-1695; globaled@augsburg.edu, www.augsburg.edu/global.

Nepal

Cultural Experience Tours. The kingdom of Nepal is a land of ancient history and culture.

Insight Nepal offers individual or group tour programs for those interested in exploring Nepal's diverse geographical and cultural environment through a variety of opportunities, including a Nepali homestay, language training, and lectures, as well as trekking in the Himalayas and an elephant safari in the jungle.

Dates: Feb-Apr and Sep-Nov 1996. Cost: $900-$1,800 (depending on the length of the program). Contact: Naresh M. Shrestha, Director, Insight Nepal, P.O. Box 6760, Kathmandu, Nepal; (011) 977-1-418-964, fax (011) 977-1-416144.

Himalayan Health Expedition. Twenty-three-day trip. For medical students, professionals of all disciplines, anyone interested in public or international health. Led by Nepalese physicians. Visits to modern facilities and 12-day trek to remote villages. See healing trances and rituals of shamans, pundits, and Tibetan healers in villages. Trek past famous Himalayan peaks. Maximum elevation about 12,000 feet.

Dates: Jan 3-25, Oct 17-Nov 18, 1997; Jan 9-31, Oct. 9-31, 1998. Cost: Land $2,595; air approx. $1,900 roundtrip from Los Angeles. Contact: Lillian Jenkins, Coordinator, Journeys International, 4011 Jackson Rd., Ann Arbor, MI 48103; (800) 255-8735 or (313) 665-4407, fax (313) 665-2945; journeysmi@aol.com, www.journeys-intl.com.

New Zealand

Dolphin Encounter (Kaikoura). An opportunity to swim with or watch the dusky dolphins in their natural habitat off the Kaikoura coast. At Dolphin Encounter, we let you take part in this experience, so you can witness the beauty, grace and intelligence of these wonderful creatures. Wetsuit, snorkel, and flippers provided.

Dates: Oct-May. Cost: NZD$80 to swim; NZD$55 to watch. Contact: Lynette Buurman, Dolphin Encounter, 58 West End, Kaikoura, New Zealand; (011) 64-3-319-6777, fax (011) 61-3-319-6534; info@dolphin.co.nz.

Nature Trek. Combine tramping adventure with exploring New Zealand's natural history. This small group tour (up to 9 passengers) covers North and South Island within 18 days. The tour educates people about nature and conservation. The guides have extensive knowledge of New Zealand's natural history and are keen to pass this information on to clients through commentary and questioning.

Dates: Every second Tuesday of the month, Oct-Mar. Cost: $2,200 (all inclusive). Contact: NZ Nature Tours Ltd., Frank Hildebrandt, P.O. Box 27-508, Wellington, New Zealand; (011) 64-4-3853687, fax 2928839, 100252.1302@compuserve.com, http:///nz.com/nz/commerce/clanztours/.

North America

Trek America. Small group adventure camping tours. USA, Canada, Alaska, Mexico, Guatemala, and Belize. We do the driving and supply all the camping equipment. National and state parks, big cities and small towns, famous places and hidden wonders. Tours from 7 days to 9 weeks from 14 cities.

Dates: Year round. Cost: $40-$120 per day (avg. $60 per day). Contact: Jeff Hall, Trek America, P.O. Box 189, Rockaway, NJ 07866; (800) 221-0596, fax (201) 983-8551; trekamnj@ix.netcom.com.

Pacific Region

Hawaii's Kalani Oceanside Eco-Resort. Kalani Educational Eco-Resort, the only coastal lodging facility within Hawaii's largest conservation area, treats you to Hawaii's aloha comfort, traditional culture, healthful cuisine, wellness programs, and extraordinary adventures: thermal springs, a naturist dolphin beach, snorkel pools, kayaking, waterfalls, crater lake, and spectacular Volcanoes National Park. Ongoing offerings in yoga, dance, hula, mythology, language, and massage. Or participate in an annual week-long event: men's/women's/couples conferences, dance/music/hula festivals, yoga/meditation/transformation retreats. Our native staff and international Volunteer Scholar participants welcome you.

Dates: Year round. Cost: Lodging $45-$85 per day. Camping $15. $550-$1,100 per week for most programs, including meals and lodging choice. Contact: Richard Koob, Director, Kalani Eco-Resort, RR2, Box 4500, Kehena Beach, HI 96778-9724; (800) 800-6886 or (808) 965-7828 (call for fax info); kh@ilhawa ii.net, randm.com/kh.html.

Papua New Guinea

Trans Niugini Tours. Nature and cultural programs are operated in 3 distinct areas, namely the Highlands, the Sepik Area, and a marine environment on the North Coast. Each area has its own distinct culture and environment, with comfortable wilderness lodges located in each.

Dates: Weekly departures during 1997. Cost: $714-$3,570 per person (land cost). Contact: Bob Bates, Trans Niugini Tours, P.O. Box 371, Mt. Hagen, Papua New Guinea; (800) 521-7242 or (011) 675-542-1438, fax 675-542-2470; 100250.3337@compuserve.com.

Peru

Amazon and Andean Expeditions. Unique experiences seasoned by adventure, spirituality. Capture a new perspective on culture that will enrich your life. Trips are tailored by Peruvian culturalist Milly Sanojama.

Dates: Year round. Cost: $2,175 2 weeks including Miami. Contact: South American Expeditions; (800) 884-7474; milly@loop.com.

California Institute for Peruvian Studies (CIPS). CIPS, working under a special permit from the Peruvian government, is conducting archaeological expeditions in the Acari River Valley of south coastal Peru. Sites span from 1200 B.C. through the arrival of the Spaniards.

Archaeological field schools, Feb-Aug 1997 will be taught by specially selected professionals and include excavation, textile and pottery analysis, field methods, cultural history, physical anthropology, museology, and more. To date over 100 sites have been located. Few sites have been collected, mapped, photographed, and documented. College credit is available. Flexible independent adventure travelers are encouraged to apply. Space is limited.

Dates: Mar-Sep 97. Cost: $800-$2,300 depending on time spent at sites. Machu Picchu, Colca Canyon, and the Amazon included in some field schools. Ask for details. Contact: CIPS, 45 Quakie Way, Bailey, CO 80421; (303) 838-1215 or (800) 444-1285 for application.

Peru Expedition. A 13-day expedition around southern Perú, including colonial and modern Lima, Paracas National Reserve, Mazca mysterious lines, Arequipa white city of volcanoes, Cusco Inka's capital with wonderful Machu Picchu and Tambopata jungle reservation in Madre di Dios. Group minimum: 2 people.

Dates: Year round. Cost: Land costs: $1,195. Contact: Hector Isola, Andean Tours, Schell 319 OF305, Lima 18, Peru; (011) 51-1-4467992, fax 4456097; postmaster@andean tours.com.pe.

Russia and the NIS

Off the Beaten Path. Unique, flexible, and affordable travel opportunities for individuals and small groups. MIR is a 10-year veteran specialty tour operator with representation in Moscow, St. Petersburg, Kiev, Irkutsk, Ulan Ude and Tashkent. Homestays, Trans-Siberian Rail Journeys, Central Asian Explorations, Mongolian Adventures, European Brewery Adventures. Customized independent and group travel.

Dates: Year round; scheduled departures for tours. Cost: Homestays from $35 a night; full packaged tours from $1,295. Contact: MIR Corporation, 85 S. Washington St., Suite 210, Seattle, WA 98104; (800) 424-7289 or (206) 624-7289, fax (206) 624-7360; mir@igc.apc.org, www.kiss.com/fr/mir.

Scotland

Action Breaks: Activity Holidays. Scottish Conservation Projects Trust is Scotland's leading charity involving people improving the quality of the environment through practical conservation work. The courses range from dry stane dyking, footpath creation, and management to wildlife habitat creation and management and tree planting. Ages 16-70 years welcome.

Dates: Annually Mar-Oct (40 courses in program). Cost: £5 (£4 unwaged) plus membership fee £20 overseas applicants. Contact: Scottish Conservation Projects Trust, Balallan House, 24 Allan Park, Stirling FK8 2QG, Scotland, U.K.

Siberia

Lake Baikal Discovery Tours. Small group ecotours with English-speaking naturalist guide. Study eco-systems unique to Lake Baikal, live with Russian, Buryat, and Innuuyet families; visit sacred sites of Buddhist, Shamanist, and Russian Orthodox cultures; swim, boat, trek around lake. Trips benefit local eco-projects through non-profit REAP.

Dates: Jul and Aug. Cost: $3,300. 17 days including international airfares. Contact: Dr. B. Phillips, Reap Travel Service, 613 S. Circle Ave., Barrington, Il 60010; (847) 516-4921, fax (847) 516-9079; leftknee@ix.netcom.com.

Switzerland

Bookbinding and Book Restoration. Centro del bel libro is a professional school for artisanal bookbinding and book restoration. Courses are offered on the quarter system.

Dates: Call or write for information. Cost: Call or write for information. Contact: Christina Bordoli, Director, Centro del bel libro, Ascona, 6612 Ascona, via Collegio, Centro culturale B. Berno, Switzerland; (011) 41-91-791-72-36, fax 791-72-56.

United Kingdom

English Adventures Cultural Tours. One- and 2-week world-class walking/literary/cultural fun tours in the English Lake District, home of William Wordsworth and Beatrix Potter. Also, excursions to James Herriot's Yorkshire Dales, Hadrian's (Roman) Wall, and William Wallace's (Braveheart's) Scotland. Small 12-person groups. Private suites in a grand Victorian mansion.

Dates: May-Sep, 1997. Cost: One-week tour $1,495; 2-week tour $2,395. Some discounts offered. Contact: English Adventures, 803 Front Range Rd., Littleton, CO 80120; Tel./fax (800) 253-3485.

United States

River Rafting Expeditions. Adventure is for everyone. All ages are welcome and no experience is necessary. River journeys are 2-6 days through National Parks, wild and scenic rivers Green and Colorado Rivers. Incredible whitewater or moderate and scenic stretches. Choose paddleboats, oarboats, motorized rafts, or inflatable kayaks. Color brochure and video to view. Specialty: Family Goes to Camp, women only.

Dates: May 3-Sep 25, 1997. Cost: $322-$887. Contact: Lee Griffith, Sheri Griffith Expeditions, Inc., P.O. Box 1324, Moab, UT 84532; (800) 332-2439 or (801) 259-8229, fax (801) 259-2226; classriver@aol.com, www.griff ith exp.com.

Vietnam

Vietnam Reconciliation Untour. Stay in family-run guesthouses and plan your own itinerary with the help of on-site staff people who will happily share their culture and perspective. Learn from experience and interaction with local people. All proceeds are invested with the Vietnamese, through micro enterprise and loans to community improvement projects.

Dates: Every other Wednesday, starting Jan 8; departure is 2 days prior. Cost: $2,013-$2,312 (2 weeks, includes airfare from NYC or LA). Contact: Vietnam Untours, Idyll, Ltd., P.O. Box 405, Media, PA 19063; (610) 565-5242, fax (610) 565-5142; untours@netreach. net, www.netreach.net/~untours.

Wild Card Adventures. Visit remote hill tribe villages and unspoiled native markets, mystical islands and caves, ancient ruins and pagodas. And the world's most friendly people. Go first class or "go native" with professional English-speaking Viet guides. Trek, cycle, float, or buffalo. Customized budget tours. Special small group services.

Dates: Monthly 10-21 day tours (start first Sunday of month). Cost: $1,630-$2,185. Contact: Wild Card Adventures, 751 Maple Grove Rd., Camano Island, WA 98292; Tel./fax (360) 387-9816.

Worldwide

Adventure Travel for the Discerning Traveler. Culturally and eco-conscious hiking and walking treks within remote countries and areas.

Dates: Year round. Cost: $1,000-$5,000 per person land costs. Contact: Steve Conlon, Director, P.O. Box 398, Worcester, MA 01602; (800) 233-4499, (508) 799-4499; sconlon@ world.std.com, www.gorp.com/abvclds.htm.

American-Int'l Homestays. Stay in English-speaking foreign homes in over 30 countries. Explore foreign cultures responsibly. Learn foreign languages. Perfect for families or seniors. Learn how other people live by living with them in their homes.

Dates: Year round. Cost: From $49 per night.

Contact: Joe Kinczel, American-Int'l Homestays, P.O. Box 1754, Nederland, CO 80466; (303) 642-3088 or (800) 876-2048, fax (303) 642-3365; ash@igc.apc.org.

Backroads Wallking/Hiking Vacations. Distinctive walking and hiking vacations worldwide, including South Africa, Belize, Costa Rica, Bali, Alaska, and Utah. Backroads also offers bicycling and multisport adventures worldwide. All offer a sense of renewal and discovery, as well as unsurpassed support and accommodations.

Dates: Year round. Cost: $749-$2,695. Contact: Backroads, Trip Planning Dept., 801 Cedar St., Berkeley, CA 94710-1800.

Earthwise Journeys. Earthwise Journeys is a resource for socially responsible travel worldwide. Our focus is cross-cultural exchange, nature, wildlife, adventure, volunteering, and women's programs. We link travelers to rewarding journeys to renew mind, body, and spirit. Earthwise provides a variety of resources to the caring travel adventurer: research, travel alternatives, and trip coordination.

Dates: Year round. Cost: Vary. Contact: Barbara Canavan, Earthwise Journeys, P.O. Box 42584, Portland, OR 97242; (800) 344-5309 or (503) 736-3364; earthwyz@teleport.com, / www.teleport.com/~earthwyz/.

Jewish Volunteer Corps. The Jewish Volunteer Corps of AJWS sends skilled adult volunteers to work with grassroots organizations throughout Africa, Latin America, Asia and Russia for up to 9 months. Projects range from assisting project staff in developing community health or education programs to teaching business skills to members of cooperatives, to helping design a soil conservation plan.

Dates: Year round. Cost: Varies with placements. Stipends, and scholarships available. Contact: Manager, Jewish Volunteer Corps, American Jewish World Service, 989 Avenue of the Americas, New York, NY 10018; (800) 889-7146 or (212) 736-AJWS, fax (212) 736-3463; jvcvol@jws.org.

Journeys of Discovery. Ecosummer Expeditions offers spectacular eco-adventure expeditions to the world's most pristine areas. Sea kayaking, canoeing, sailing, rafting, trekking, wildlife viewing, and photography. Combining education with vacation. Professional guides and naturalists. All levels of experience. Superior Journeys of Discovery since 1976.

Cost: $205-$7,495. Contact: Ecosummer Expeditions, 1516 Duranleau St., Vancouver, BC V6H 3S4, Canada; (800) 465-8884, fax (604) 669-3244; trips@ecosummer.com.

Moon Travel Handbooks. Founded in 1973, Moon Publications publishes award-winning, comprehensive travel handbooks to distinct destinations in North America and Hawaii, Mexico, Central America, the Caribbean, Asia, and the Pacific. Environmental and cultural sensitivity set these guides apart from the rest.

Dates: Ongoing publishing schedule includes new editions and titles. Cost: $11.95-$30. Contact: Moon Publications, P.O. Box 3040, Chico, CA 95927-3040; (800) 345-5473, fax (916) 345-6751; travel@moon.com, www.moon.com.

Project Ecotourism. Ecological tourism is promoted through trips to various countries worldwide. Guidelines provided on how to be a responsible and environmentally aware tourist and tour operator. Special emphasis on Suriname's Amazon rainforest.

Dates: Continuous. Cost: Varies. Contact: Nancy Pearlman, Educational Communications, P.O. Box 351419, Los Angeles, CA 90035; (310) 559-9160; ECNP@aol.com.

Reality Tours. Participate in one of our socially responsible, culturally focused (alternative) travel experiences and gain a first-hand perspective on what is truly happening in countries like: Cuba, Haiti, Guatemala, Mexico, Chile, Vietnam, the Philippines, Mongolia, Ireland, Senegal, South Africa, and Nicaragua. Learn about indigenous cultures, changing environments, art and crafts, public health and women issues; monitor human rights or observe presidential elections. We will try to arrange personal meetings to suit your particular interests.

Dates: Monthly throughout the year. Cost: Depending upon the trip—range is from $700 for a 7-day trip to Mexico to $3,000 for a trip to Vietnam or South Africa. Costs include roundtrip airfare (please call for more details). Contact: Reality Tours Department, Global Exchange, 2017 Mission St., Suite #303, San Francisco, CA 94110; (415) 255-7296 or (800) 497-1994, fax (415) 255-7498; globalexch@ igc.apc.org.

Servas International. Servas is an international cooperative system of hosts and travelers established to help build world peace, good will, and understanding by providing opportunities for deeper, more personal contacts among people of diverse cultures and backgrounds. Approved travelers are invited to share life in the home and community of their host for short-term home stays.

Dates: On-going. Cost: $55 per year traveler fee, $25 refundable deposit for the use of host listings (up to 5 countries), $25 suggested host contribution. Contact: U.S. Servas, 11 John St., #407, New York, NY 10038; (212) 267-0252, fax (212) 267-0292; usservas@igc.apc.org.

The Partnership for Service-Learning. Service learning in international and intercultural settings as offered by The Partnership combines formal studies for academic credit with extensive community service to those in need. Program locations include the Czech Repub-

lic, Ecuador, England, France, India, Israel, Jamaica, the Philippines, Scotland, and South Dakota (with Native Americans). Students from over 250 U.S. colleges and universities have participated in these unique opportunities.

Dates: Summer, semester, year, or January intersession. Cost: Vary—depending upon location. Contact: Howard Berry, President, The Partnership for Service-Learning, 815 2nd Ave., Suite 315, New York, NY 10017-4594.

Travel Beyond the End of the Road. World Neighbors organizes trips to various countries to meet people working to improve their lives through self-help activities. Trips are designed to provide a unique educational experience combined with limited tourism.

Dates: Monthly. Cost: Vary. Contact: World Neighbors, Education and Outreach Dept., 4127 NW 122nd St., Oklahoma City, OK 73120-8869; (800) 242-6387, fax (405) 752-9393; Kelly@wn.org.

Travel Study Tours. Each year, UCLA Extension offers a variety of one-time-only travel study tours to destinations around the world. In 1996, itineraries included Thailand, Peru, Egypt, Israel, Jordan, and Mexico. Call or write UCLA Extension's John Watson for details on 1997 tours to Mongolia (winter) and southern Africa (spring), among other destinations.

Dates: Vary. Cost: Vary. Contact: John Watson, UCLA Extension, 10995 LeConte Ave., #320, Los Angeles, CA 90024; (310) 825-1901, fax (310) 206-7878; jwatson@unex.ucla. edu.

STUDY

*Education abroad programming has never been
so diverse in its forms, locations, and approaches.*
—WILLIAM HOFFA, PAGE 90

Education Abroad
Present Constraints and Future Challenges

By William Hoffa

In the 20 years since Clay Hubbs founded *Transitions Abroad,* the number of travel-study programs for adults looking to combine a trip abroad with a structured learning experience has rapidly and steadily increased. By 1989, as Hubbs points out in the introduction to this volume, a Lou Harris survey of thousands of traveling Americans revealed that fully three-quarters of them took their last trip "to improve their minds, to gain new perspectives, and to meet new people."

As the average age of educated Americans grows ever more rapidly, so do the ranks of learning travelers. In only one year, the number of education abroad programs listed in this directory grew by 25 percent.

What about programs for enrolled students? As evidenced in the student program listings below, education abroad programming has never been so diverse in its forms, locations, and approaches. *The New York Times* for December 1, 1996, citing figures released that day by the Institute of International Education, reports the number of American students abroad rose 10.6 percent, to 84,403, in 1994-95, continuing a 10-year upward trend. But while progress toward achieving the national mandate for much greater expansion is being made, numerous factors limit its pace. They also define future challenges.

Economic Constraints. Meeting the national goal to more than double the number of undergraduates having a significant overseas educational experience by the year 2000 would require students, parents, and institutions to find new ways to pay for this expanded exodus. Yet private institutions are increasingly concerned over tuition drain, and public universities lack sufficient financial support for program development and financial aid. The hope that the federal government and private industry will contribute enough resources to make a major difference has all but faded. Furthermore, in this conservative economic climate it is likely that institutions and agencies will become increasingly protective of their own markets. This could mean decreasing program options for students as academic and financial disincentives are applied.

Increased competition may lead to the cloning of successful models and an even greater reliance on market-driven economics in program planning and assessment. Such competition favors big operations that can promote themselves nationally and works against smaller, equally worthy programs.

Parents and students, the consumers, with many options to choose from, are becoming ever more demanding. Among their demands are assurances of safety and security, e-mail communications, and often the creature comforts of home and a quick resolution of all adjustment problems. In addition, they want their daughters and sons to have specialized training courses related to career paths, which many see as a return on their investment. In this situation, program quality is being judged to mean not just intellectual rigor, but "good service" and "practical benefits" as well.

As students increasingly rely on telecommunications to find out about overseas opportunities, more are likely to enroll directly in overseas institutions, rather than relying on U.S. campus-sponsored programs or intermediating agencies. This trend will be reinforced as the marketing savvy of foreign institutions grows and they take advantage of the prevalence of English as the standard language of instruction. Most appealing to U.S. students, foreign institutions offer overseas education at a lower cost than American island programs or enrollment via U.S. agencies. (See Hoffa and Nolting, "Patterns in Direct Enrollment," in the September/October 1996 issue of *Transitions Abroad.*)

Cultural Immersion and the Emerging Global Culture. English is assuredly not the world's language, but English is indisputably the language of the global movers and shakers. Convincing today's students that proficiency in a foreign language—one traditional justification for study or work abroad programming—is truly important is likely to be an ever more daunting challenge. Employers themselves are giving very mixed signals. Enrollments in most language courses are either steady or plummeting. There are few reasons to think that this trend, which reinforces American monolingualism, will be reversed in the near future.

Similarly, the bicultural rationale for study abroad—that it allows students to "acquire a second culture"—is becoming increasingly difficult to defend. Such assimilation takes time. With only 16 percent of students now studying abroad doing so for an academic year, achieving this immersion goal is hard to imagine.

In this first-ever truly Global Culture, "here" and "there" as distinct cultural entities are increasingly hard to distinguish, given the rapid transport of ideas, goods, and services across national and cultural boundaries. However strong the traditional national culture is in a given country, the university culture—which dominates the experience of U.S. students—is likely to be more cosmopolitan.

Many students returning from overseas study say their most powerful lessons came through living and learning with students from all corners of the world, comparing and contrasting cultural differences with universal commonalities. Such lessons, they assert, opened their eyes to the internationalized lives and careers which lie ahead. Programs that provide a truly "globalizing" experience are likely to continue to attract students. Those that don't, won't.

Career Preparation. The academic rationale for overseas study is increasingly being challenged by a career-preparation rationale. More students every year are seeking practical training and work experience as an investment in their future job prospects. With the costs of higher education escalating, institutions may no longer be able to emphasize classroom academic studies over career-related, experiential education. Merely having studied abroad for a summer or semester will increasingly be seen as insufficient preparation for what employers are seeking.

International students with undergraduate, graduate, and professional degrees from U.S. campuses are now more likely to qualify for the plum jobs in the global job market. They know their own language and have become proficient in English and in telecommunications. They have U.S. academic degrees in the technical areas multi-national corporations are seeking. And they are used to functioning in the global arena.

Certain types of overseas living and learning are clearly superior to others in their immediate potential to enhance a career. Programs offering hands-on training, workplace experience, and problem-solving projects count more with most employers than classroom-only programs which merely mimic U.S. campus instruction.

As in higher education generally, success in overseas programming comes about when liberal education is combined with an informed and practical awareness of the real world. In the resources and programs that follow students and their advisers will find a truly impressive compendium of ways and means to help them toward this goal.

STUDY ABROAD RESOURCES

Whether you're a student or adviser looking for the right international study program or someone who has the time for a long stay abroad and wants to combine the least expense with the most reward, you will find the information you need in the resources described below.

Much of the material is free for the asking. Books that are too expensive to buy can be found at good public libraires and college and university study abroad offices. We have arranged the listings by country and region and marked those of widest interest—and thus essential to a basic resource library—with an asterisk.

Ordering information for key study abroad publishers and organizations is on page 151.

Asia

ABC's of Study in Japan. Association of International Education. Free from the Embassy of Japan, 2520 Massachusetts Ave., NW, Washington, DC 20008. Information on study and research at Japanese universities and graduate schools.

* **China Bound (Revised): A Guide to Life in the PRC** by Anne Thurston. National Academy of Sciences. 1994. 252 pp. $24.95 plus $4 shipping from National Academy Press, 2101 Constitution Ave., NW, Lockbox 285, Washington, DC 20055; (800) 624-6242. Updated classic on studying or teaching in the People's Republic of China. Invaluable for university students, researchers, and teachers.

Chinese Universities and Colleges. Chinese Education Association for International Exchange. 2nd edition, 1994. 760 pages. $75 plus $4 shipping from IIE. Profiles 1,062 higher education institutes in Peoples' Rep. of China with contact information.

Directory of Japan Specialists and Japanese Studies Institutions in the U.S. and Canada. Patricia G. Steinhoff, ed. The Japan Foundation. 1995. $50 plus $8 shipping ($12 non-U.S.) from The Association for Asian Studies, 1 Lane Hall, Univ. of Michigan, Ann Arbor, MI 48109; (313) 665-2490, fax (313) 665-3801; postmaster@aasianst.org.

* Japanese Colleges and Universities, 1995-97 (also Scholarships For International Students). 1995. Available from the Association of International Education, 4-5-29 Komba, Meguro-ku, Tokyo 153 Japan; fax (011) 81-3-5454-5236 for ordering information.

* Japan: Exploring Your Options—A Guide to Work, Study, and Research in Japan. Gateway Japan. 1995. 437 pp. $20 ($15 students) plus $5 shipping (checks payable to National Planning Association) from Gateway Japan, NPA, 1424 16th St., NW, Suite 700, Washington, DC 20036-2211; (202) 884-7642, fax (202) 797-5516; http://www.gw.japan.org. Study, cultural, and homestay programs; fellowships and research; English teaching.

Living in China: A Guide to Studying, Teaching, and Working in the PRC and Taiwan. Rebecca Weiner, Margaret Murphy, and Albert Li. China Books. 1991 (new edition February 1997). $16.95 from China Books and Periodicals, Inc., 2929 24th St., San Francisco, CA 94110. Contains directories of universities in China and Taiwan that offer study abroad or teaching placement. Revised edition due in 1997.

Studying in India. Published by Indian Council for Cultural Relations. Free from Indian consulates and embassies. Basic information and advice on studies or research in India's numerous educational and scientific institutions.

Universities Handbook (India). Published bi-annually. Available from: Association of Indian Universities, AIU House, 16 Kotla Marg, New Delhi 110002. Overview of courses of studies, faculty members, degrees, library and research facilities.

Yale-China Guide to Living, Studying, and Working in the People's Republic of China, Hong Kong, and Taiwan. 1996. The Yale-China Association, Inc., Box 208223, New Haven, CT 06520-8223; ycaffoc@minerva.cis.yale.edu.

Australia

A Guide to Australian Universities: A Directory of Programs Offered by Australian Universities for International Students. Magabook Pty. Ltd., 1995. P.O. Box 522, Randwick, NSW Australia 2031; (011) 61-2-398-2-5555, fax (011) 62-2-399-9465; info@magabook.com.au, http://www.magabook.com.au. Free. 1995. Highlights of Australian higher education and university profiles; listings far from complete.

Study Abroad in Australia: A Handbook for North American Students, Guidance Counsellors, Financial Aid Advisors and Study Abroad Staff. Annual. Free 30-page booklet from IDP Education Australia (North American Office), 5722 S. Flamingo Rd., #303, Cooper City, FL 33330; (954) 424-9255, fax (954) 424-9315; auststudy@aol.com. Guide to study abroad published by a consortium of 33 Australian universities

Studies in Australia: A Guide to Australian Study Abroad Programs. Magabook Pty. Ltd., 1995. Free from Magabook (above). Details on institutions and the courses they offer to North American students (including summer, recreational, and vocational programs) plus practical information on living in Australia.

Studies in Australia: A Guide for North American Students. 1996. Free from Australian Education Office, Australian Embassy, 1601 Massachusetts Ave., NW, Washington, DC 20036; (800) 245-2575. Information on year, semester, and summer progams; undergraduate, graduate, medical, and law degrees; scholarships and financial aid information (for both U.S. and Canadian citizens); internships.

Study and Travel in Australia: A Directory of Educational Opportunities in Australia for International Students. 1995. Free from Magabook (above). Overview of Australian education system, profiles secondary and vocational schools. Also available on CD-ROM.

Universities in Australia: The Complete Students Guide. Michael Dwyer and Kate Marshall. 1993. $17.95 from Financial Review, 201 Sussex St., Sydney NSW 2000, Australia; afr@afr.com.au. Indepth university profiles.

Canada

Awards for Study in Canada. Free from Canadian Bureau for International Education (CBIE), 220 Laurier Ave. W., Suite 1100, Ottawa, Ontario K1P 5Z9; (613) 237-4820. Awards and traineeships open to foreign nationals.

Destination Canada: Information for International Students. Free from CBIE (above). General information on Canadian education system and tuition fees.

Directory of Canadian Universities. Biennial. Free from the Association of Universities and Colleges of Canada (AUCC), Publications Office, 151 Slater St., Ottawa, Ontario, Canada K1P 5N1. Details on Canadian universities and program offerings.

International Student's Handbook. 6th edition, 1995. 60 pages. CAN$12 postpaid in U.S. funds. Order from CBIE (above). Overview for students new to Canada.

Study Tours '96: The Canadian Guide to Learning Vacations Around the World. CAN$18.95 from Study Tours, Public Affairs, Athabasca Univ., Athabasca, AB T9S 1A1, Canada; (403) 675-6109, fax (403) 675-6467. Over 100 educational travel tours for students, seniors, teachers, professionals, couples, singles.

European Continent

Academic Studies in the Federal Republic of Germany. Free from German Academic Exchange Service (DAAD).

Austria: Information for Foreign Students; Summer Language Courses for Foreign Students; Summer Courses in Austria. Annual. Free from the Austrian Cultural Institute, 950 3rd Ave., 20th Fl., New York, NY 10022; (212) 759-5165. Information for foreign students intending to study at an Austrian institution of higher learning.

Compendium: U.S. Assistance to Central and Eastern Europe and the Newly-Independent States. Francis A. Luzzato, ed. 1993. 347 pp. $15 postpaid from Citizen's Democracy Corps, 1735 I St., NW, Suite 720, Washington, DC 20006; (800) 394-1945. Directory to 700 U.S. organizations providing voluntary assistance (everything from volunteer-sending to educational exchanges to scholarships) in Eastern Europe and Russia.

Courses for Foreigners in Spain Sponsored by Spanish Institutions; American Programs in Spain; Study in Spain (entering the Spanish university system). Available from the Education Office of Spain, 150 5th Ave., Suite 918, New York, NY 10011.

Denmark: Guide for Young Visitors. European Youth Information and Counseling Association. 1992. Free. Available from Danish tourist board. Information on living and studying in Denmark for young people.

Directory of French Schools and Universities. 1996. $19.95 postpaid from Michael Giammarella, P.O. Box 640713, Oakland Gardens, NY 11364-0713; (718) 631-0096, fax

(718) 631-0316. A collection of brochures describing language courses offered by over 50 schools and universities in France.

Directory of Programs in Russian, Eurasian, and East European Studies. AAASS, 8 Story St., Cambridge, MA 02138; (617) 495-0677, fax (617) 495-0680. The most comprehensive source of information available on U.S. university programs in Russian, Eurasian, and East European studies. Currently out of print. New edition available in 1997.

The EARLS Guide to Language Schools in Europe 1995. Jeremy J. Garson, ed. 312 pp., $23.95. Order from Cassell, P.O. Box 605, Herndon, VA 20172, fax (703) 661-1501. Covers the 14 most popular European languages, including Russian. The guide profiles selected schools for each major language and gives details of specialized and general courses for children (ages seven and up), teenagers, adults, and business people.

German Language Courses for Foreign Applicants and Students in Austria. Austrian Foreign Student Service (ÖAD). Annual. Free from Austrian Cultural Institute, 950 3rd Ave., 20th Fl., New York, NY 10022.

Higher Education in the European Community. Brigitte Mohr and Ines Liebig, eds. 6th edition, 1990. $32.50 plus $3.25 shipping from Oryx Press. Information on study in 12-member nations of EU. New edition planned.

International Research and Exchanges Board (IREX) Grant. Opportunities for U.S. Scholars. Annual. Free from International Research and Exchanges Board, 1616 H. St., NW, Washington, DC 20006; (202) 628-8188; irex@irex. org, www.irex.org/. Descriptions of academic exchange programs and special projects administered by IREX in the Baltic States, Central and Eastern Europe, Mongolia, and the successor states of the former Soviet Union.

Sommerkürse in Bundesrepublik Deutschland. Annual. Free from German Academic Exchange Service (DAAD). In German. List of summer university programs for foreign students, including descriptions, dates, costs, and application information. Also information on courses of Goethe Institute, which offers language courses at 16 locations in Germany as well as at 150 cultural centers worldwide.

Studies in France. Free from the French Cultural Services, 972 5th Ave., New York, NY 10021; (212) 439-1455. Basic document outlining various possibilities for study in France, including direct enrollment at French institutions. Also distributes *French Courses for Foreign Students* (annual list of French universities and language centers offering summer and year courses for foreigners) and *I Am Going to France* (extensive overview of university degree programs).

Study in Finland. Annual. Free from Information and Counseling Office, P.O. Box 3, FIN-00014, Univ. of Helsinki, Finland. English language programs and postgraduate studies in Finnish universities.

Study in Scandinavia 1996-97. Annual. Free from the American-Scandinavian Foundation, 725 Park Ave., New York, NY 10021. Summer and academic year programs offered to high school and college students and anyone interested in Scandinavia; (212) 879-9779.

Studying in Denmark. Annual. Free from Danish consulates and embassies. Guide for foreign students who wish to pursue further and higher education in Denmark.

*Studying and Working in France: A Student Guide. Russell Cousins, Ron Hallmark, and Ian Pickup. 1994. $17.95 from Manchester Univ. Press (U.S. distrib. St. Martin's Press). Useful, detailed information on directly enrolling in French universities and language courses; 1 brief chapter on working.

Summer Courses in Austria - "Campus Austria." Annual. Free from Austrian National Tourist Office, Travel Information Center, P.O. Box 1142, New York, NY 10108-1142; (212) 944-6880 and Austrian Cultural Institute, 950 3rd Ave., 20th Fl., New York, NY 10022; (212) 759-5165.

Latin America/Caribbean

After Latin American Studies. A Guide to Graduate Study and Employment for Latin Americanists. Revised edition, 1995. Shirley A. Kregar and Annabelle Conroy. $10 from Latin American Studies, 4E04 Forbes Quad, Univ. of Pittsburgh, Pittsburgh, PA 15260; (412) 648-2199, fax (212) 249-3444; clas+@ pitt.edu, www.pit.edu/~clas.

Guide to Financial Assistance for Students in Latin American Studies. Revised edition, 1996. Shirley A. Kregar and Silvia Lucrecia Del Cid. Free. Center for Latin American Studies (above). Fellowships, internships, doctoral dissertation research.

An International Students' Guide to Mexican Universities. Alan Adelman, ed. 1995. $19.95 plus $2 shipping from IIE. Profiles higher education institutions in Mexico.

Latin America Study Programs Course Guide. 1995. $35 postpaid from WorldStudy, 9841 S.W. 73rd Court, Miami, FL 33156; (305) 665-5004, fax (305) 665-7085; 74722.32@ compuserve.com. Detailed guide to courses offered at universities in Argentina, Belize, Chile, Columbia, Costa Rica and Ecuador. Enrollment possible through WorldStudy.

Travel Programs in Central America. Ann Salzarulo-McGuigan and Carolyn Martino, eds. 1996. 91 pp. $8 postpaid from San Diego Interfaith Task Force on Central America

(IFTF), c/o 56 Seaview Ave., North Kingston, RI 02852. Comprehensive guide to over 300 organizations for study, and short- and long-term service in all fields. Essential for finding options located in this region.

Middle East/Africa

Beyond Safaris: A Guide to Building People-to-People Ties with Africa. Kevin Danaher. Africa World Press, Inc. 1991. $14.90 postpaid from Global Exchange, 2017 Mission St., #303, San Francisco, CA 94110; (800) 497-1994. Handbook on how to help build and strengthen links between U.S. citizens and grassroots development efforts in Africa. Includes volunteering, studying, and socially responsible travel; annotated list of organizations.

Directory of Graduate and Undergraduate Programs and Courses in Middle East Studies in the U.S., Canada, and Abroad. Updated biannually. $20 for nonmembers, $10 for members. Published by Middle East Studies Association of North America, Univ. of Arizona, 1643 E. Helen St., P.O. Box 210410, Tuscon, AZ 85721; (520) 621-5850, fax (520) 626-9095.

A Guide to Israel Programs. Annual. $1.50 from World Zionist Organization, 110 E. St., 3rd Fl., New York, NY 10022; (800) 274-7723, fax (212) 755-4781; usd@netcom.com, www. wzo.org.il/. Information on summer study and volunteer work opportunities.

Opportunities in Africa. Interbook. 1993. 24 pages. $3 per copy. Interbook, 130 Cedar St., New York, NY 10006; (212) 566-1944, fax (212) 566-1807. Addresses for information on employment, study, and educational travel. Interbook also distributes Africa Report, a bi-monthly magazine published by the African American Institute. $7 per copy.

United Kingdom and Ireland

Graduate Study and Research in the U.K. The British Council (Education Information Service, 3100 Massachusetts Ave., NW, Washington, DC 20008-3600; fax 202-898-4612; study.uk@bc-washingtondc.sprint.com.) provides information on study opportunities in the U.K. at the graduate and research level, including program information, addresses, and funding.

The Guide to Postgraduate Study in Britain 1997. 1996. £15 plus £2.50 shipping from The Newpoint Publishing Col. Ltd., Windsor Court, East Grinstead House, East Grinstead, West Sussex RH19 1XA; fax (011) 441 1342 335785. A comprehensive guide including both taught and research degrees.

Study Abroad in Ireland. Annual. Free from Irish Tourist Board offices, (800) 223-6470. Academic programs and travel-study tours.

Study in Britain. Guide to undergraduate study and for visiting students. Free from British Information Services, 845 3rd Ave., New York, NY 10022; (212) 752-5747, fax (212) 758-5395, or from The British Council.

The Underground Guide to University Study in Britain and Ireland. Bill Griesar. 1992. $9.95 postpaid from Intercultural Press. Designed to guide the reader through the entire study abroad experience.

University Courses in Education Open to Students from Overseas 1996/97. £7.50 surface mail from Universities Council for the Education of Teachers, 58 Gordon Square, London WC1H ONT, England. Postgraduate courses in education at British universities open to foreigners.

Young Britain. Annual. Free from British Tourist Authority, 557 W. 57th St., New York, NY 10176-0799. Information on study, work, and accommodations.

Worldwide

* Academic Year Abroad 1996/97. Sara J. Steen, ed. $40.95 postpaid from IIE. Authoritative directory of over 2,300 semester and academic year programs offered by U.S. and foreign universities and private organizations. Indexed for internships, practical training, student teaching, adult courses, volunteer work, as well as fields of study.

The Advising Quarterly. Subscription: $40 ($50 overseas) from AMIDEAST. Quarterly dealing with trends and developments in international educational exchanges with the Middle East.

* Advisory List of International Educational Travel & Exchange Programs. Annual. Council on Standards for International Educational Travel, 3 Loudoun St. SE, Leesburg, VA 22075; (703) 771-2040, fax (703) 771-2046. $8.50. Lists programs for high school students which adhere to CSIET's standards and provides valuable information for prospective exchange students, host families, and schools.

AIFS Advisors' Guides. Various authors and dates. AIFS. Free. Published quarterly by AIFS; (800) 727-AIFS. Study abroad topics include political advocacy, nontraditional programs, promoting ethnic diversity, and reentry.

Archaeological Fieldwork Opportunities Bulletin. Annual in January. Archaeological Institute of America. $13 for AIA members, $15 non-members from Kendall/Hunt Publishing Co., Order Dept., 4050 Westmark Dr., Dubuque, IA 52002; (800) 228-0810. A comprehensive guide to excavations, field schools, and special programs with openings for volunteers, students, and staff worldwide.

Back in the USA: Reflecting on Your Study Abroad Experience and Putting It to Work. Dawn Kepets. NAFSA: Association of International Educators, 1995. $5 plus $2 shipping from NAFSA. A 34-page booklet which helps returning students put their cross-cultural experiences into perspective.

* Basic Facts on Study Abroad. IIE, NAFSA. Single copies free from IIE. Basic information for students interested in an educational experience abroad. New edition expected in 1996.

Black Students and Overseas Programs: Broadening the Base of Participation. Holly Carter, ed. 1991. $11.50 postpaid from Council. An 80-page collection of papers by faculty, administrators, and students.

* The Canadian Guide to Working and Living Overseas. Jean-Marc Hachey. 2nd edition, 1995. $37 postpaid ($41 airmail) from Intercultural Systems, P.O. Box 588, Station B, Ottawa, ON K1P 5P7, Canada; (800) 267-0105. The most comprehensive guide to overseas opportunities published in North Aamerica.

Commonwealth Universities Yearbook. Compiled by the Association of Commonwealth Universities. 71st edition, 1995. Two-volume set. $235 plus $6 shipping from Stockton Press. (Available in major libraries.) Detailed profiles of universities in all 34 of the Commonwealth countries, with comprehensive guide to degree programs and a register of 230,000 academic and administrative staff.

Culturgrams: The Nations Around Us. 1996-97. Brigham Young University, Kennedy Center for Interntional Studies. $75 postpaid. Culturgrams provide clear and concise information on customs and courtesies, lifestyles, the people, and the history and government of 153 nations, and provide a quick overview for prospective travelers.

* Directory of International Internships: A World of Opportunities. Compiled and edited by Charles A. Gliozzo, Vernieka K. Tyson, and Adela Peña. 3rd edition, 1994. Available for $25 postpaid from Michigan State Univ., Attn: International Placement, Career Services & Placement, 113 Student Services Bldg., East Lansing, MI 48824. Based on a survey of 4,000 organizations, this directory describes a variety of experiential educational opportunities—for academic credit, for pay, or simply for experience. Useful indexes. This is the only directory to internships entirely located abroad.

Educational Associate. IIE membership newsletter, published five times annually, provides a chronicle of trends and resources in international education.

The Exchange Student Survival Kit. Bettina Hansel. Intercultural Press. 1993. $12.95 plus $2 shipping. Practical guide for U.S. students going abroad or foreign students coming to the U.S.

Film and Video Resources for International Exchange. Lee Zeigler. 1992. NAFSA. Available for $6.50 plus $2 shipping from Intercultural Press. Details on over 300 documentary videos and films of interest to study abroad advisers, foreign student advisers, and ESL instructors on U.S. campuses.

Frontiers: The Interdisciplinary Journal of Study Abroad. Brian Whalen, ed. Annual. $12 per issue from: Frontiers, Boston Univ., International Programs, 232 Bay State Rd., Boston, MA 02215; fax (617) 353-5402; bwhalen@bu.edu. A forum for research-based articles on study abroad.

Guide to Careers and Graduate Education in Peace Studies. 1996. $4.50 from PAWSS, Hampshire College, Amherst, MA 01002. Includes information on internships, fellowships, and relevant organizations.

* **How to Read Study Abroad Literature.** Lily von Klemperer. Reprinted in IIE's Academic Year Abroad and Vacation Study Abroad and in NAFSA's Guide to Education Abroad. What to look for in ads for a study abroad program.

A Handbook for Creating Your Own Internship in International Development. Overseas Development Network. $7.95 plus $1.50 shipping. How to arrange a position with an international development organization; evaluate your skills, motivations, and learning objectives; practical advice on financing an internship, living overseas, and returning home.

Harvard Guide to International Experience by William Klingelhofer. 1989. 159 pp. $15 postpaid from Office of Career Services, 54 Dunster St., Harvard Univ., Cambridge, MA 02138; (617) 495-2595. Half of this book is devoted to working or volunteering abroad, with numerous reports by students.

The High School Student's Guide to Study, Travel, and Adventure Abroad. Council. 5th edition, 1995., 308 pp. St. Martin's Press. $13.95 from Council. Describes over 200 programs of all types for people aged 13-18.

Home from Home. Central Bureau for Educational Visits and Exchanges. 3rd edition, 1994. $22.95 postpaid from IIE. Compiled from a comprehensive database used by U.K. government agencies, this guide contains details on homestays, home exchanges, hospitality exchanges, and school exchanges worldwide. Includes profiles of organizations by country.

Including Women with Disabilities in International Development Programs. Cindy Lewis. MIUSA. 1996. Contact MIUSA for price. Describes the efforts and successes of women with disabilities in other countries.

* **Increasing Participation of Ethnic Minorities in Study Abroad.** 1991. Council. Free. A brochure prepared to assist advisers in increasing enrollments of underrepresented minorities.

International Educator. NAFSA. Quarterly magazine. $24 per year in U.S.; $36 Canada and Mexico; $48 elsewhere. Essays on major issues and trends in international education.

International Handbook of Universities. 14th edition, 1996. $245 plus $6 shipping. International Association of Universities. (Available in major libraries.) Distributed in U.S. and Canada by Stockton Press. Entries for more than 5,700 universities and other institutions of higher education in 170 countries and territories. Complements Commonwealth Universities Yearbook, 1995-96.

NAFSA Newsletter. NAFSA: Association of International Educators; included in annual membership fee. Published eight times per year, contains current information on international educational exchange and related topics.

* **NAFSA's Guide to Education Abroad.** William Hoffa, John Pearson, eds. 1996. NAFSA. An indispensable reference for education abroad offices providing both an overview of principles and practices and detailed information and advice for advisers. Includes bibliography on work, study, and travel.

New Manual for Inclusion of Persons with Disabilities in International Exchange Programs. MIUSA. 1996. Contact MIUSA for price. Information on accessibility, resource lists to recruit people with disabilities, and checklists to identify specific needs of participants with disabilities.

Planning Guides Catalog. Transitions Abroad Publishing, Inc., P.O. Box 1300, Amherst, MA 01004-1300. Free. Descriptive listing of planning guides on international work, study, living, educational and socially responsible travel.

Planning for Study Abroad. IIE. 1989. $53.95 (members $26.95) postpaid from IIE. Advising video that presents basic information on study abroad from students acting as peer counselors.

Smart Vacations. The Traveler's Guide to Learning. Council. 1993. 320 pp. $14.95 from Council. Adult traveler's guide to learning abroad includes, in addition to study tours, opportunities for voluntary service, field research and archaeological digs, environmental and professional projects, fine arts, and more.

Student Travels Magazine. Fall and spring. Free from Council. A magazine that covers rail passes, insurance, work and study opportunities abroad, airfares, car rentals, and other services offered by CIEE and Council Travel. Includes articles by students on their experiences abroad.

Students Abroad: Strangers at Home—Education for a Global Society. Norman Kauffmann, Judith Martin, and Henry Weaver. 1992. $19.95 plus $3 shipping from Intercultural Press. The study abroad experience examined from the student's viewpoint, followed by a theoretical framework for understanding the effects of study abroad and recommendations for increasing effectiveness of programs.

* **Study Abroad 1996: A Guide to Semester, Summer, and Year Abroad Academic Programs.** Peterson's Guides. 956 pages. $26.95 plus $6.75 shipping. Over 1,000 pages of detailed information on over 2,000 programs at more than 500 accredited institutions worldwide.

Study Abroad, 1996-1997. UNESCO. Vol. 29, 1995. $29.95 plus $4 shipping from UNIPUB. Describes approximately 4,000 international study programs and sources of financial assistance in more than 100 countries.

Study Abroad: The Astute Student's Guide. David Judkins. Williamson, 1989. $13.95 plus $3 shipping from Intercultural Press. Sound but dated advice on choosing a program abroad.

Study Tours '96: The Canadian Guide to Learning Vacations Around the World. CAN$18.95 from Study Tours, Public Affairs, Athabasca Univ., Athabasca, AB T9S 1A1, Canada; (403) 675-6109, fax (403) 675-6467. Over 100 educational travel tours for students, seniors, teachers, professionals, couples, singles.

***Survival Kit for Overseas Living: For Americans Planning to Live and Work Abroad.** L Robert Kohls, ed. 1996 (3rd ed). Intercultural Press. $11.95 plus shipping. Provides a series of practical, do-it-yourself exercises for Americans planning to live and work abroad.

***Taking Time Off: Inspiring Stories of Students Who Enjoyed Successful Breaks from College and How You Can Plan Your Own.** Colin Hall and Ron Lieber. 1996. The Noonday Press. $12 from Farrar, Strauss and Giroux, 19 Union Square West, New York, NY 10003. Thoughtful book gives reports of individuals who studied abroad or had internships, worked, volunteered, or traveled both abroad and in the U.S. Useful directories to other resources.

Teenager's Vacation Guide to Work, Study, and Adventure Abroad by Victoria Pybus. 1991. £6.95 plus £2.50 shipping or dollar equivalent from Vacation Work. Addressed to a British audience, it covers jobs, study courses, and adventure holidays available in Britain and abroad during school vacations.

The Directory of Work and Study in Developing Countries. David Leppard. 1997. Vacation Work. $14.95 from Ulysses Books. A comprehensive guide to employment, volunary work, and academic opportunities in developing countries worldwide. Intended for a British audience, it omits some organizations of interest to Americans.

Time Out: Taking a Break from School to Travel, Work, and Study in the U.S. and Abroad. Robert Gilpin with Caroline Fitzgibbons. 1992. $12. Simon and Schuster; (800) 223-2348. Describes over 350 programs in U.S. and abroad for high school students who want to travel and learn.

The Travel Journal: An Assessment Tool for Overseas Study. Nancy Taylor. Council. 1991. Occasional Paper on International Educational Exchange No. 27. $5 from Council. Practical guide to writing and evaluating student travel journals.

Update. Monthly. Free. Council's monthly newsletter reports on developments in the field of international educational exchange as well as programs and events organized by the Council.

* **Vacation Study Abroad 1996/97.** Sara J. Steen, ed. $40.95 postpaid from IIE. Authoritative guide to over 1,800 summer and short-term study programs sponsored by U.S. and foreign organizations and language schools in over 60 countries. Indexed for internships, practical training, student teaching, adult courses, volunteer service as well as fields of study.

What in the World is Going On? A Guide for Canadians Wishing to Work, Volunteer or Study in Other Countries by Alan Cumyn. 5th edition, 1996. CAN$20 including shipping from Canadian Bureau for International Education, 220 Laurier Ave., W., Suite 1100, Ottawa, Ontario K1P 5Z9, Canada; (613) 237-4820. Includes a comprehensive listing of work abroad possibilities. Some listings restricted to Canadian citizens. Indexed by country and field.

The Whole World Guide to Language Learning. Terry Marshall. 1990. $15.95 plus $2 shipping from Intercultural Press. Guidelines on how to learn a language while abroad.

Wilderness U. Opportunities for Outdoor Education in the U.S. and Abroad. Bill McMillon. 1992. Chicago Review Press. $12.95. A descriptive listing of educational organizations offering programs in and about the great outdoors.

* **Work, Study, Travel Abroad: The Whole World Handbook.** St. Martin's Press. 12th edition, 1994-95. $7.95 plus $1.50 book rate or $3 first class postage from Council. Travel, work, and study opportunities around the world.

* **World Academic Database CD-ROM.** 1996. $435 plus $6 shipping from Stockton Press. Combines the 14th edition of International Handbook of Universities, 20th edition of World List of Universities, with additional information from TRACE. Most complete source of information on education around the world. (This and the two publications following are available in major libraries.)

World List of Universities. 20th edition, 1995. $160 plus $6 shipping from Stockton Press. Addresses of over 9,000 institutions of higher education worldwide.

The World of Learning. 46th edition, 1996. Annual. $415 plus postage from International Publications Service, c/o Taylor & Francis Group, 1900 Frost Rd., Suite 101, Bristol, PA 19007. This authoritative guide lists over 26,000 institutions of higher education by country, gives names of staff and faculty, and includes information on international organizations involved in education throughout the world.

A World of Options: A Guide to International Exchange, Community Service and Travel for Persons with Disabilities. Christa Bucks, Mobility International USA. 3rd edition, 1996. Contact MIUSA for price. A comprehensive guide to international exchange, study, and volunteer opportunities for people with disabilities.

A Year Between. Central Bureau for Educational Visits and Exchanges. 2nd edition, 1994. $23.95 postpaid from IIE. Designed for young British adults who have a year between high school and college, or during college, and want to explore and learn. Volunteer work, internships service, and study options.

Funding for International Activities

Council Scholarships. ISIC Third World Grants cover transportation costs for undergraduates to study, work, or volunteer in developing countries. Available to Council member school students only. Bailey Minority Student Scholarships cover transportation costs for undergraduate students of color to study, work, or volunteer with any Council program. Contact Council at (888) 268-6245.

Fellowship Guide to Western Europe. Gina Bria Vescovi, ed. 7th edition, 1989. Available for $8 prepaid by check to "Columbia University-CES" from Council for European Studies, 808-809 International Affairs Bldg., Columbia Univ., New York, NY 10027. Mostly for graduate study.

Fellowships in International Affairs: A Guide to Opportunities in the U.S. and Abroad. Women International Security. 1994. 195 pp. $17.95 plus $3.50 shipping from Lynne Rienner Publishers, 1800 30th St., Suite #314, Boulder, CO 80301; (303) 444-6684. Well-researched directory to fellowships and grants for students, scholars, and practitioners (most are for graduate and postdoctoral students or professionals). Very useful indexes, including one for non-U.S. applicants.

* Financial Aid for Research and Creative Activities Abroad 1996-1998 by Gail Ann Schlachter and R. David Weber. 1996. 440 pp. $45 plus $4 shipping from: Reference Service Press, 1100 Industrial Rd., Suite 9, San Carlos, CA 94070; (415) 594-0743, fax (415) 594-0411. Lists over 1,300 funding sources that support research, professional development, teaching assignments, and creative activities. Sources mainly for graduate students, postdoctorates, professionals. Very useful indexes.

* Financial Aid for Study Abroad: A Manual for Advisers and Administrators. Stephen Cooper, William W. Cressey, and Nancy K. Stubbs, eds. 1989. $12 (nonmembers) $8 (members) plus $5 shipping from NAFSA. How to use primarily federal sources of financial aid for study abroad programs for undergraduate students and how to utilize this information to help shape institutional policies.

Financial Aid for Study and Training Abroad 1996-1998 by Gail Ann Schlachter and R. David Weber. 1996. 275 pp. $38.50 plus $4 shipping from Reference Service press (see above). Lists 1,000 funding sources that support formal educational programs such as study abroad, training, internships, workshops, and seminars. Sources mainly for undergraduate, high school and graduate students, as well as postdoctorates. Very useful indexes.

* Financial Resources for International Study. Sara J. Steen, ed. 1996. IIE. $43.95 postpaid from IIE. Lists funding sources available to support undergraduate, graduate, postdoctorate, and professional learning abroad, from study and research to internships and other work experiences. Very useful indexes, including field of study, internships/work abroad.

Foundation Center Publications Catalog. Free. Call (800) 424-9836. The Foundation Center maintains a comprehensive and up-to-date database on foundations and corporate giving programs.

Fulbright and Other Grants for Graduate Study Abroad. Annual. Free from IIE. Describes grants administered by IIE for study and research abroad.

The International Scholarship Book. Daniel J. Cassidy. 5th edition, 1996. $24.95 paper, $32.95 cloth plus $4 shipping from Prentice-Hall Publishers, 200 Old Tappan Rd., Old Tappan, NJ 07675; (201) 767-5937. Information on private sector funding sources for study abroad compiled by the National Scholarship Research Service.

Money for International Exchange in the Arts. Jane Gullong and Noreen Tomassi, ed. 1992. 126 pp. $16.95 postpaid from IIE. Lists grant sources, exchange programs, and artists residencies and colonies for individuals and organizations in the creative arts.

Resources for International Arts Exchange. National Endowment for the Arts, 1100 Pennsylvania Ave., Washington, DC 20506; (800) 727-6232 (orders only). Guide for the artists and organizations contemplating work abroad.

Key Publishers and Organizations

The African-American Institute, 833 U.N. Plaza, New York, NY 10017. Publications on Africa.

American-Scandinavian Foundation, Exchange Division, 725 Park Ave., New York, NY 10021. Free publications on study, work, and travel in Scandinavia. Offers scholarships.

AMIDEAST, 1730 M St., NW, Washington, DC 20036-4505; (202) 776-9600, fax (202) 822-6563; inquiries@amideast.org, www. amideast.org.

British Information Services, 845 3rd Ave., New York, NY 10022. Free fact sheets on study in Britain.

The Central Bureau, 10 Spring Gardens, London; (011) 44-171-389-4004, fax 389-4426. Publishes information for people of all ages on work, study, and travel abroad. Most books available from IIE or Seven Hills.

The Council on International Education Exchange (CIEE), Publication Dept., 205 E. 42nd St., New York, NY 10017-5706; (212) 888-COUNCIL, fax (212) 822-2699; info@ciee. org(800), www.ciee.org. Publishers of materials on study, job opportunities, and inexpensive travel abroad.

French Cultural Services, 972 5th Ave., New York, NY 10021. Free publications on French higher education and opportunities for U.S. students.

German Academic Exchange Service (DAAD), 950 3rd Ave., 19th Fl., New York, NY 10022; (212) 758-3223, fax (212) 755-5780; daad@daad.org, http://www.daad.org. Free materials on German education; offers scholarships.

Global Exchange, 2017 Mission St., #303, San Francisco, CA 94110; (800) 497-1994.

IIE Books, Institute of International Education, P.O. Box 371, Annapolis Junction, MD 20701-0371; (800) 445-0443, (301) 617-7804. Publishes guides to study and educational travel abroad for U.S. students and adult learners. Free catalog.

Intercultural Press, P.O. Box 700, Yarmouth, ME 04096; (207) 846-5168. Books on intercultural relations, crosscultural communications, and living and working abroad. Free quarterly catalog.

Mobility International USA (MIUSA), P.O. Box 10767, Eugene, OR 97440; (541) 343-1284 (voice and TDD), fax (541) 343-6812. Publications and videos on including persons with disabilities in international exchange and travel programs.

NAFSA Publications, P.O. Box 1020, Sewickley, PA 15143; fax (412) 741-0609. Free catalog. Publishers of informational materials, geared toward its professional membership, on study, work, and travel abroad opportunities as well as advising and admissions. To rush order publications: (800) 836-4994.

Oryx Press, 4041 N. Central Ave., #700, Phoenix, AZ 85012-5397; (800) 279-ORYX. Guides on higher education abroad.

Overseas Development Network, 333 Valencia St., Suite 330, San Francisco, CA 94103; (415) 431-4204, fax (415) 431-5953; odn@igc.org, http://www.igc.apc.org/odn/. Publishes material on work and internships in international development.

Peterson's Guides, 202 Carnagie Center, P.O. Box 2123, Princeton, NJ 08543-2123; (800) 338-3282. Guides to jobs and careers, study abroad. U.S. distributor for Vacation Work Publications.

Stockton Press, 345 Park Ave. S., 10th Fl., New York, NY 10010-1707; (800) 221-2123 or (212) 689-9200, fax (212) 689-9711.

Superintendent of Documents, U.S. Government Printing Office, Washington, DC 20402. A wide range of material, including country "Background Notes" series.

UNIPUB, 4611-F Assembly Dr., Lanham, MD 20706; (800) 274-4888. UNESCO publications

on higher education; distributes E.U. publications.

Vacation Work Publications, 9 Park End St., Oxford OX1 1HJ, England; (011) 44-1865-241978, fax 790885. Books on employment and budget travel abroad. Books without U.S. distribution can also be purchased from Ulysses Books & Maps, 4176 St. Denis, Montréal, Québec H2W 3M5, Canada; (514) 843-9882.

Williamson Publishing Co., Church Hill Rd., P.O. Box 185, Charlotte, VT 05445; (800) 234-8796. Books on study, careers, and alternative travel abroad.

Study Abroad Web Sites

These sites provide links and a vast variety of other information too recent to be found in books. All web site addresses begin with http://.

www.amideast.org. AMIDEAST's Guide to Study Abroad in the Middle East. Kate Archambault. Up-to-date information on study in Middle East and North Africa.

www.cie.uci.edu/~cie/. Univ. of California—Irvine, International Opportunities Program (IOP). Ruth Sylte. One of the most comprehensive sites on the web, with directories of U.S.- and non-U.S.-based study abroad programs. and extensive guides for working abroad. Also features a how-to Internet user manual for students and advisers, "The World at Your Fingertips."

www.ciee.org/. Council on International Educational Exchange (CIEE)/Council Travel. Information on study, work, and volunteer programs offered through CIEE only, as well as services offered by Council Travel (ISIC student IDs, etc.)

www.finaid.org/. Home page of the National

Association of Financial Aid Administrators includes sections on financial aid and scholarships for study abroad.

www.iie.org. Institute of International Education. Provides information about services and publications offered by the IIE, including Fulbright scholarships.

www.isp.acad.umn.edu/istc/istc.html. Univ. of Minnesota, International Study and Travel Center (ISTC). Richard Warzecha. Excellent searchable database for study abroad, low-cost-study abroad, scholarships, and Ann Halpin's volunteer abroad directory.

www.nafsa.org. NAFSA: Association of International Educators. NAFSA. Essential professional resources for advisers and administrators in international education, though not a directory of overseas programs.

www.peterson.com/. Peterson's Education Center, Study Abroad Sector. A commercial directory of study abroad programs.

www.pitt.edu/~cjp/rees.html. REESWeb: Russian and East European Studies, Univ. of Pittsburgh. Karen Rondestvedt. Click on "Academic Programs and Centers" for listings of language and study abroad programs. Links to other REES centers and information.

www.sas.upenn.edu/AfricanStudies/AS. html. African Studies WWW, Univ. of Pennsylvania. Prof. Sandra Barnes. A search using the phrase "study abroad" produces a list of study abroad programs. Outstanding links to African and African-American information.

www.studyabroad.com/. Studyabroad.com. Commercial directory of study and work abroad programs.

www.usc.edu/dept/overseas/links.html. Univ. of Southern California, Education Abroad Program Office. Gary Rhodes. Links to sites about study, work, and travel abroad. Also provides some links to overseas universities, and the publication "Research on U.S. Students Abroad: A Bibliography."

Transitions Abroad's Guide to Work, Study, and Travel Abroad. Jason Whitmarsh. Current educational travel and study resource and program information. Going online in January 1997. Contact Jason at (413) 256-3414 or trabroad@aol.com for URL.

WILLIAM NOLTING is Director of International Opportunities, Univ. of Michigan International Center, 603 E. Madison Street, Ann Arbor, MI 48109-1370; (313) 647-2299, fax (313) 647-2181; bnolting@umich.edu. He welcomes suggestions, updates, or questions. CLAY HUBBS is Director of International Studies at Hampshire College and founding editor and publisher of Transitions Abroad. *He can be reached at Transitions Abroad Publishing, Inc., P.O. Box 1300, Amherst, MA 01004-1300; trabroad@aol.com or cah00@hamp.hampshire. edu.*

CHAPTER 11

ADULT STUDY/TRAVEL PROGRAMS

The following listing of adult study/travel programs was supplied by the organizers. Contact the program directors to confirm costs, dates, and other details. If you do not see the program you want in the country of your choice, look in the "Worldwide" listings at the end of the section for programs located in several different regions.

Africa

African American Studies Program. Nonprofit trips to 30 African countries, as well as Brazil and Cuba. All trips are full day programs of education.

Dates: Jun, Jul, Aug every year. Cost: $1,400 to $6,000. Contact: Prof. Harold Rogers, 19 S. LaSalle St, #301, Chicago, IL 60603; (312) 443-0929, fax (312) 684-6967.

An Indepth Safari to Uganda. Led by ecologists Gail and Doug Cheeseman (in their 16th year of guiding in Africa), world renowned African ornithologist Terry Stevenson and 3 Ugandan drivers in 3 pop-top Land Cruisers, this safari concentrates on the premier wildlife in the national parks and reserves of Uganda. Trek for Mountain gorillas, float the Nile, bird in pristine forests, and much more.

For 15 people max. Only eligibility requirement is to agree with nonsmoking policy.

Dates: Jul 25-Aug 15, 1997. Cost: $5,730 plus airfare to Entebbe, Uganda on British Air (group rates). Contact: Gail Cheeseman, Cheesemans' Ecology Safaris, 20800 Kittredge Rd., Saratoga, CA 95070; (800) 527-5330; cheeseman@aol.com.

Bicycle Africa Tours. Village-based, cross-cultural bicycle tours to all parts of Africa. Cycling difficulty is moderate. Each program is different, but all focus on the diversity of the culture, social institutions, and environment, as well as the complexity of the history, economy, culture, and society. Programs are led by African studies specialists.

Dates: Jan (Uganda), Feb (Kenya/Tanzania), Apr (Tunisia), Jun-Aug (Zimbabwe), Oct-Nov (Senegal/Mali), Nov (Burkina Faso/Togo/

Benin). Cost: $990-$1,290 plus airfare for 2 weeks. Includes food, lodging, guides, and fees. Contact: David Mozer, Director, International Bicycle Fund/Bicycle Africa, 4887 Columbia Dr. S. #T-7, Seattle, WA 98108; Tel./fax (206) 767-0848; intlbike@scn.org; www.halcyon.com/fkroger/bike/bikeafr.html.

Travel/Study Seminars. Learn from Southern Africans of diverse backgrounds about their economic, political, and social realities. Emphasis on the views of the poor and oppressed. Programming in South Africa and Namibia. Call for a free listing of upcoming programs.
Dates: Ongoing. Cost: $3,500-$4,400 depending on length of trip. Contact: Center for Global Education, Augsburg College, 2211 Riverside Ave., Box 307TR, Minneapolis, MN 55454; (800) 299-8889, fax (612) 330-1695; globaled@augsburg.edu, www.augsburg.edu/global.

Volunteer in Zimbabwe, Angola, or Mozambique. In Zimbabwe you teach at a school for disadvantaged youth or work with families in a health project. In Angola you plant trees, organize health campaigns, and teach people of all ages. In Mozambique you teach at schools for street children or at vocational schools. The Zimbabwe and Angola programs are 12 months long and the Mozambique is a 20-month program. All include preparation and follow-up periods in the U.S. The programs are open to persons 18 years of age and older.
Dates: Zimbabwe and Angola: Feb 15, and Aug 15, 1997. Mozambique: Nov 1, 1996. Cost: $4,600. Includes training, room and board, airfare, international health insurance, and other direct program costs. Contact: Josefin Jonsson, Administrative Director, IICD, Institute for International Cooperation and Development, P.O. Box 103-T, Williamstown, MA 01267; (413) 458-9828, fax (413) 458-3323; iicd1@berkshire.net, www.berkshire.net/~iicd1.

Amazon

Amazon Jungle Safari. An 8-day, natural history adventure offering a valuable rainforest experience. Overnights in serene jungle lodges, located in remote reserves for great bird/wildlife viewing. The small group educational tour is escorted by a qualified U.S. biologist and expert resident guides. Also experience the only Treetop Canopy Walkway in the Americas, over 1,500 feet long and 115 feet high. Also available are Amazon riverboat cruises and extensions to Cuzco and Machu Picchu.
Dates: Monthly. Cost: $1,895 including air from Miami, lodging, all meals, excursions. Contact: Charlie Strader, Explorations Inc., 27655 Kent Rd., Bonita Springs, FL 34135; (800) 446-9660, fax (941) 992-7666; cesxplor@aol.com.

Argentina

Instituto de Lengua Española para Extranjeros (ILEE). Located downtown in the most European-like city in Latin America. Dedicated exclusively to teaching Spanish to foreigners. Small groups and private classes year round. All teachers hold a university degree. Method is intensive, conversation-based. Student body is international, mostly European. Highly recommended worldwide (all travel guides, British and German universities, etc.). Ask for individual references in U.S.
Dates: Year round. Cost: Four weeks intensive program (20 hours a week) including homestay $1,400; 2 weeks $700. Individual classes $19 per hour. Registration fee (includes books) $100. Contact: ILEE, Daniel Korman, Director, Lavalle 1619 7th C (1048), Buenos Aires, Argentina; (011) 54-1-375-0730, fax 864-4942; www.worldwide.edu/argentina/ilee/index.html. In U.S.: David Babbitz; (415) 431-8219, fax (415) 431-5306.

Asia

Cross-Cultural Travel. Meet people from very different cultures and explore natural environments beyond the reach of ordinary travel. Himalayan adventures in Nepal, Tibet, Ladakh, Bhutan. Central Asia trips in Pakistan, China. Combine with Southeast Asia explorations in Burma, Thailand, India, Laos, Cambodia, Vietnam. Also year-round departures for learning experiences in Africa and Latin America.

Dates: Year round. Cost: Varies. Contact: William Weber, President, Journeys International, 4011 Jackson Rd., Ann Arbor, MI 48103; (800) 255-8735 or (313) 665-4407, fax (313) 665-2945; journeysmi@aol.com, www. journeys-intl.com.

Escorted Tours, Independent Travel. Study abroad programs in China, student travel groups to Thailand, China, Korea, Nepal, Singapore, Vietnam. Tours are focused on custom and culture, religion, arts and crafts, and language. Individual travel can be arranged. Discounted international airfare to the Orient available.

Dates: Winter 1996/1997. Summer 1997. Cost: Call for information. Contact: Anthony Bowen, Director of Sales, EBM Tours, Inc., 566 7th Ave., Suite 9F, New York, NY 10018; (212) 302-0318 or (800) 234-3888, fax (212) 302-2852.

Orangutan Conservation. In cooperation with the Orangutan Foundation International, Bolder Adventures offers a series of orangutan research study tours. Participants support the work of Dr. Birute Galdikas, who has spent 25 years studying these endangered primates. The 10-day programs take place at Camp Leakey on the island of Borneo in Indonesia.

Dates: Sep 16, Oct 7, Nov 4, 1996; Jul 7, Jul 21, Aug 4, Aug 18, Sep 15, Oct 6, Nov 6, Nov 3, 1997. Cost: $2,100 land cost only. Contact: Bolder Adventures, Inc., Southeast Asia Travel Specialists, 3055 Center Green Dr., Boulder, CO 80306; (800) 642-2742, fax (303) 443-7078; bolder@southeastasia.com, www.south eastasia.com.

Summer in Vietnam. Students study Vietnamese language and culture at Dong Do Univ. in Hanoi. American students will be paired with Vietnamese students as conversation partners. Participants will be housed in a guesthouse located within walking distance of the campus. Students will experience a homestay weekend, participate in field trips and tours, and a 2-day visit to Ho Chi Minh City.

Dates: Jun 1-Jul 13, 1996. Cost: New York State resident undergraduate $3,641; graduate $4,021 (non-credit $3,300). Contact: SUNY at Buffalo, Study Abroad Programs, 210 Talbert Hall, Buffalo, NY 14260-1604; (716) 645-3912, fax (716) 645-6197; studyabroad@ acsu.buffalo. edu.

Travel-Study Seminars. Visit with Asians from China, Hong Kong and Indochina as their countries undergo profound economic changes. Pursue critical questions, such as: Do these changes also bring political pluralism? What impact do economic changes have on the education and outlook of youth? On the natural environment? Who benefits from economic restructuring? Call for more information on current trips.

Dates: Varies. Cost: Approx. $3,800-$4,300 depending on length and destinations. Contact: Center for Global Education, Augsburg College, 2211 Riverside Ave., Box 307TR, Minneapolis, MN 55454; (800) 299-8889, fax (612) 330-1695; globaled@augsburg.edu, www. augsburg.edu/global.

Australia

Special Interest and Study Tours. Personalized programs for individuals and groups of all ages. We combine education, recreation, accommodations (homestay available), and transportation. Based in tropical Cairns with coverage throughout Australia. Subject areas include: aboriginal dreamtime and culture, Great Barrier Reef, rainforest and savannah. Diving, environmental interpretation, flora and fauna, bird watching, tropical islands and wilderness, adventure safaris and farmstay.

Dates: Year round. Start any date. Cost: Prices and customized itineraries on application. Contact: Murray Simpson, Study Venture International, P.O. Box 229A, Stratford Qld., 4870 Australia; (011) 61-70-411622, fax 552044; svi@ozemail.com.au; www.ozemail. au/~svi.

Study Abroad. Study 1 semester in a wide range of courses including humanities, arts, social sciences, economics, education, science, Australian studies.

Dates: Feb-Jun or Jul-Nov. Cost: Approx. $5,500 Contact: International Office, Univ. of New England, Armidale, NSW Australia 2351.

WWOOFING. Work in exchange for keep while learning organic growing with a farmer or enjoy a cultural exchange with Australian small businesses including farms, working for your keep (state your interest).

Dates: Year round. Cost: $25 single, $30 double (includes insurance). Contact: WWOOF Australia, Buchan, Victoria 3885, Australia.

Austria

Deutsch-Institut Tirol. German language courses for foreigners. Schedule for the typical day: a) mornings: half-day intensive course, in classes of 6 students maximum. Conversation, TV, newspapers, tapes, books, grammar, pronunciation; b) afternoons: Four times at least per week diverse recreational programs in company of a teacher: skiing, hiking, swimming, excursions; c) evenings: Three times per week 2 lessons, 4 times social programs with teacher.

Dates: Year round. Start at any time. Course length optional. Cost: Course and programs: ATS4,900 per week. Room and breakfast: from ATS200 per day. Evening meal at ATS770 per week possible. Contact: Hans Ebenhöh, Director, Am Sandhügel 2, A-6370 Kitzbühel, Austria; (011) 43-5356-71274, fax 72363; dit@ kitz.netwing.at.

German Courses at the University. German for beginners and advanced students, perfectionist courses, courses for students of the German language and teachers of German in foreign countries (6 levels). Lectures on German and Austrian literature, music, Austria— the country, people, and language. Special courses: translation, commercial German, commercial correspondence, phonetics, language laboratory, choir singing. Excursions.

Dates: Three sessions: Jul 6-Aug 2, Aug 3-30, Aug 31-Sep 20, 1997. Cost: Course fee (4 weeks): approx. ATS4,300, accommodation: approx. ATS6,500. Contact: Magister Sigrun Inmann-Trojer, Wiener Internationale Hochschulkurse, Universität, Dr. Karl Lueger-Ring 1, A1010 Wien; (011) 43-405-12-54 or (011) 43-405-47-37, fax (011) 43- 405-12-54/ 10.

International German Language Courses. German language classes at all levels. Classes for beginners, intermediate, advanced, very advanced, seminars. Phonetics, cultural events, tours, all kinds of sports.

Dates: Sep 1-29, 1996, summer courses 1997. Cost: ATS5,700. Includes daily school lessons, accommodations, and half board with host family, diploma. Contact: Helmut Lerch, Director; Waltraud Ertl, Secretary, Interschool, Deutsch in Innsbruck, Kohlstattgasse 3, A-6020 Innsbruck, Tirol, Austria; (011) 43-0512-58-89-57.

International Workshops. Summer seminar for musicians and artists (strings, orchestral conducting, piano, general music, choral conducting, watercolor). World class faculty, outstanding concert series, excursions to local areas of interest. For all ages, both amateurs and professionals. Meet in a different city worldwide every summer. Academic credit available. May be tax deductible.

Cost: $1,595 includes tuition, 3-star hotel, double occupancy, breakfasts, all concerts, special events. Contact: Tori Hintz, Manager, 187 Aqua View Rd., Cedarburg, WI 53012; (414) 377-7062, fax (414) 377-7096.

Belize

Archaeological Expedition to Maya Belize. Here is a chance to join an archaeological dig in Maya ruins in Belize, Central America. The project is under the direction of Dr. Leslie Shaw. You will be staying in the fresh thatch roof cabana and eating native meals at the Rio Bravo Conservation Area Camp. Besides archaeology, it is a great area for birding.

Dates: Jul 7-21, 1996. Cost: $1,295 (tax deductible contribution), as well as your transportation costs, which you must arrange. Contact: Dr. Leslie Shaw, 7711 Vail Valley Dr., Austin, TX 78749; (512) 892-6857; or Dr. Richard S. MacNeish, AFAR, Box 83, Andover, MA 01810; (508) 470-0840.

CHAA Creek School of Caribbean Cookery. Our week-long culinary course combines half days of cooking classes with food-related touring to Mayan sites, local markets, and native kitchens. Special emphasis on tropical ingredients, the foods of Belize, and decadent desserts. Enjoy staying at a jungle lodge on the Macal River while learning how to create gourmet meals.

Dates: Jun 1-Dec 15, alternate weeks. Cost: $1,500 per person, based on double occupancy. Contact: Bill Altman, CHAA Creek, P.O. Box 53, San Ignacio, Cayo, Belize, Central America; (011) 501-92-2037, fax 92-2501; chaa_creek@btl.net.

Rainforest of the Maya Mountains. Explore this verdant tropical forest—home to mon-

keys, deer, tapirs and jaguars, to help ecologists better understand the role mammals play in this pristine ecosystem. No prior experience necessary. Costs are tax deductible.

Dates: Mar 22-Apr 4, 1997 and Apr 5-18, 1997. Cost: $1,185. Contact: Univ. of California Research Expeditions Program (UREP), Desk MO8, 2223 Fulton St., Berkeley, CA 94720-7050; (510) 642-6586, fax (510) 642-6791; urep@uclink.berkeley.edu.

The Maya and the Rainforest. Monthly educational workshops. Special dates for teachers and families. Guided exploration of major Mayan sites including Tikal. Visits in communities or modern-day Maya. Rainforest hiking and canoeing with naturalists. Time to explore and develop individual interests. Eight-day programs with optional extensions to Caribbean Reef.

Dates: Dec-Jul. Request 1997 dates. (April specially geared to families; Jun and Jul for teachers). Cost: Land cost approx. $1,250 per adult, twin-share $850 per child, sharing with 2 adults. Contact: Joan Weber or Michelle Gervais, Journeys International, 4011 Jackson Rd., Ann Arbor, MI 48103; (800) 255-8735 or (313) 665-4407, fax (313) 665-2945; journeys mi@aol.com, www.journeys-intl.com or www.gorp.com/journeys.htm.

Canada

Canadian Outdoor Leadership Training. Our wilderness-based experiential education program will develop your skills to a level required to lead/instruct wilderness and outdoor pursuits at a basic level. It is ideal for those participants anticipating a career in this field and also of great value to those individuals wanting to take time out to develop their own personal direction and potential.

Dates: Mar 23-Jul 6; Apr 18-Jul 31; Aug 14-Nov 26. Cost: 1997: $7,895. Contact: Strathcona Park Lodge C.O.L.T., P.O. Box 2160, Campbell River, BC V9W 5C9, Canada.

Columbia College ESL. Seven- and 14-week programs, 25 hours per week. Small classes. Organized activities. International college also offering Senior, Secondary, and University Transfer programs. Facilities include tutorial center, library, computer center, gymnasium, cafeteria, counseling. Located 20 minutes from downtown Vancouver, near major shopping center and on excellent public transit routes.

Dates: Sep 3-Dec 12, 1996; Jan 2-Apr 10, May 5-Aug 14, and Sep 2-Dec 11, 1997. Cost: Tuition (7 weeks) CAN$1,850, (14 weeks) CAN$3,500; application fee CAN$75. Contact: Mr. John Helm, Columbia College, 6037 Marlborough Ave., Barnaby (Greater Vancouver), BC V5H 3L6 Canada; (604) 430-6422, fax (604) 439-0548; columbia_college@mindlink.bc.ca.

Columbia College Senior Secondary. Grade 11 and 12 high school program conforms to Ministry of Education guidelines. Students completing program receive British Columbia high school graduation diploma and are eligible to apply to universities and colleges in North America.

Dates: Sep 3-Dec 12, 1996, Jan 2-Apr 10, 1997, May 5-Aug 14, and Sep 2-Dec 11, 1997. Cost: Tuition (8 months) CAN$7,600; application fee CAN$75. Contact: Mr. John Helm, Columbia College, 6037 Marlborough Ave., Barnaby (Greater Vancouver), BC V5H 3L6, Canada; (604) 430-6422, fax (604) 439-0548; columbia_college@mindlink.bc.ca.

Ecole de français, Université de Montreal. For the last 50 years, the Ecole de français has offered courses in French as a Second Language to students from around the world. On the educational forefront as a learning institution, the Ecole is continually improving its programs to meet the changing needs of its students. Choose from Oral and Written Communication French (beginner to advanced), Workshop on Teaching French as a Second Language (for teachers), Contemporary Québec Culture (for advanced students), Business French (intermediate to advanced students).

Dates: Summer 1: Jun 28-Jul 19; summer 2: Jul 22-Aug 9; fall 96: Sep 5-Dec 6; winter 97: Jan 10-Apr 15. Cost: Summer: (3 weeks, 60 hours) CAN$495; summer (3 weeks, 45 hours) CAN$390; fall and winter: (12 weeks, 240 hours) CAN$1,495 (subject to change). Contact: Serge Bienvenu, Coordinator, Ecole de français, Faculté de l'education permanente, Université de Montreal, C.P. 6128, succursale Centre-ville, Montréal, PQ, H3C 3J7, Canada; (514) 343-6990, fax (514) 343-2430; bienvens@ere.umontreal.ca.

English as a Second Language Centre. The ESL Programs has a variety of noncredit courses. English for Academic Purposes (EAP) teaches oral and written communication and study skills with cultural and academic orientation. English for Business and Communication (EAP/B) focus on listening, discussion, and writing for business purposes in the world of international business. Other courses include English for Specific Purposes (ESP).

Dates: Jun 28-Aug 23, 1996 (8 weeks), Sep 13-Dec 6, 1996 (12 weeks), Jan 10-Apr 3, 1997. Cost: $1,525 (8 weeks); $1,825 (12 weeks). Contact: Penthes Rubrecht, Director, ESL Programs, Univ. of Regina, Campion College, Regina, SK, Canada S4S 0A2; (306) 585-4585, fax (306) 585-4971; esl@max.cc.uregina.ca, http://leroy.cc.uregina.ca/~esl.

Language Studies Canada Montréal. Using a multi-skill approach in a relaxed classroom atmosphere, the Standard Group program ensures that students develop communicative competence in French. Six levels of 4 weeks each, 4 hours daily. Maximum of 14 students per class. Audio-visual equipment, Student Resource Center. Optional activity program. Homestay available.

Dates: Two-week courses begin any Monday from Jan 15, 1996 year round, one-to-one instruction. Group 5 executive courses, Jun-

Oct Summer Language Adventure (14 to 17-year-olds), Jul and Aug. Cost: Two weeks: $390 Standard Group tuition; $400 homestay. Cost of other services available upon request. Contact: Language Studies Canada Montréal, 1450 City Councillors, Montréal, PQ, H3A 2E6, Canada; (514) 499-9911, fax (514) 499-0332.

Mohawk, Cayuga, Onondaga Languages and Culture Program. Doctoral or Masters thesis in cultural anthropology or linguistic anthropology with the emphasis on education and learning styles may apply for a 2- or 3-year placement. Mohawk, Cayuga, Onondaga Languages and Culture Programs are given on a regularly cycled basis to promote Iroquoian heritage. The programs are rich in language acquisition and cultural knowledge which operate on the traditional ideas of sharing, caring, trust and respect for oneself and all other living and non-living elements. These teachings aid in building self-esteem, understanding, and pride in the First Nation heritage. The style of learning through the oral tradition and experiential base still affects how we as a First Nation develop and adapt to the changing world. To find out more about the types, times, and cost of workshop contact the executive director. Workshops can be conducted upon request by small groups, classes, and community interest.

Dates: Classes and workshops run every 3 months. Cost: Approx. $85-$150. Contact: Yvonne Thomas, Executive Director, Jake Thomas Learning Centre, R.R. 1, Wilsonville, ON N0E 1Z0, Canada; (519) 445-4230, fax (519) 445-0076.

Queen's Univ. School of English. The Queen's Univ. School of English offers 5- and 12-week courses year-round at one of Canada's oldest and best-known universities in an almost totally English-speaking community. Students have the option of living in a University residence with monitors, in a homestay or in University cooperative housing. The English Only Rule is strictly enforced.

Dates: Jan 8-Apr 11, May 12-Aug 8, May 19-Jun 20, July 7-Aug 8, Sep 15-Dec 12. Cost: International students: $2,425 12 weeks; $1,325 5 weeks, plus $100 refundable book deposit, mandatory health insurance (price varies). Contact: Mrs. Eleanor Rogers, Director, The School of English, Queen's Univ., Kingston, ON, K7L 3N6 Canada; (613) 545-2472, fax (613) 545-6809; soe@post.queensu.ca, www.queensu.ca/soe/.

Special Intensive French Program. McGill Univ. was founded in 1821 and is internationally renowned for its high academic standards. The Special Intensive French courses was offered at 5 levels and run for 9 weeks. Classes are limited to about 15 students per class. There are 4 sessions a year. Instructional methods include the use of a modern language laboratory, audio-visual equipment, and a wide range of activities stressing the communicative approach.

Dates: Spring: Apr 1-May 31, 1996; summer: Jun 25-Aug 23, 1996; fall Sep 23-Nov 22, 1996; winter: Jan 20-Mar 21, 1997. Cost: CAN$1,795 for international students, CAN$1,450 for Canadian citizens and permanent residents. Contact: Ms. M. Brettler, 770 Sherbrooke St. W., Montreal PQ, H3A 1G1 Canada; (514) 398-6160, fax (514) 398-4448; info@conted.lan.mcgill.ca.

Wilderness Guide Training. One-month to 1-week training programs for those wanting employment in guiding and outdoor adventure tourism, and/or adventure and personal growth. Programs include horse handling, mountain riding, horse packing and shoeing, guiding, horse logging, and back-country living. Acquire skills for pack horse trips, big game viewing, photo safaris, fishing, and hunting.

Dates: May-Oct. Cost: All-inclusive package from CAN$1,000-$4,000. Contact: Sylvia Waterer and/or Kevan Bracewell, Chilcotin Holidays Guest Ranch, Box 152 Whistler, BC V0N 1B0, Canada; Tel./fax (604) 238-2274.

Central America

International Travel Seminar. More than 20 trips are offered each year to Nicaragua, El Salvador, Guatemala, and Mexico to meet with the poor and disenfranchised, women's groups, cooperatives, and alternative political parties, as well as decision-makers from the government, businesses, and churches. Programs are designed to bring you face-to-face with Latin American people's struggle for freedom, justice, and human dignity.

Dates: Trips of 7-14 days throughout the year. Cost: From $1,300-$2,500 (includes airfare, food, lodging, and program). Contact: Travel Seminar Division, Center for Global Education, Augsburg College, 2211 Riverside Ave., Box 307TR, Minneapolis, MN 55454; (800) 299-8889, (612) 330-1159, fax (612) 330-1695; globaled@augsburg.edu, www.augsburg.edu/global.

Sisters Without Borders. Sisters Without Borders is an ongoing work exchange with counselors, health care providers, and students for short- and long-term residencies in Nicaragua, El Salvador, Guatemala, and Haiti. Participants specialize in: midwifery, nutrition, drug counseling (prevention and awareness), anti-violence training, herbal medicine, and stress management.

Dates: Vary according to the availability of the volunteer, services being offered, and the needs of the region. Cost: Travel, housing, and food. Contact: MADRE, c/o Liliana Cortés, Program Director, 121 W. 27th St., Rm. 301, New York, NY 10001.

Travel/Study Seminars. Learn from Central Americans of diverse backgrounds about their economic, political, and social realities. Emphasis on the views of the poor and oppressed. Programming in El Salvador, Guatemala, and Nicaragua. Call for a free listing of upcoming programs.

Dates: Ongoing. Cost: $1,500-$2,500 depending on length of trip. Contact: Center for Global Education, Augsburg College, 2211 Riverside Ave., Box 307TR, Minneapolis, MN 55454; (800) 299-8889, fax (612) 330-1695; globaled@augsburg.edu, www.augsburg.edu/global.

Central Europe

Vienna and Kaprun. Visit the imperial city of Vienna; then it's on to Kaprun, a skier's playground. Eleven days and 10 nights. Daily departures. Three nights Vienna at Hotel Biedermeier, 7 nights Kaprun at Pension Martin. Buffet breakfast daily in Vienna, Vienna city tour, breakfast and dinner daily in Kaprun, optional sightseeing.

Dates: Not available Dec 23-Jan 6, 1996. Cost: Includes roundtrip airport and hotel transfers. Package (double) $994, (single) $242; Vienna extra nights, double $60; single $42. Contact: Euro Lloyd Tours; (800) 334-2724, (516) 794-1253 (NY state), fax (516) 228-8258.

Chile

Rice Univ. One semester program held in conjunction with the Univ. of Chile in Santiago. Participants live with Chilean families and attend classes at UC, Santiago. Rice Univ. professor accompanies group and serves as resident director and also teaches 2 courses. Included in the program fee is a 3-day visit to Buenos Aires. Pre-requisite: 2 years college-level Spanish or equivalent proficiency.

Dates: Early Aug-mid-Dec 1996. Cost: $7,850 (Fall 1996). Contact: Beverly Konzem, Dept. Coordinator, Rice Univ., Dept. of Hispanic and Classical Studies, MS34, 6100 Main St., Houston, TX 77005-1892; span@rice.edu.

Study Abroad in Santiago. Study for a semester or an academic year at the Pontificia Universidad Católica de Chile (PUC), one of the most prestigious universities in South

America. For students with intermediate to advanced Spanish language ability. Intensive pre-semester language training and orientation. On-site resident director. Family homestay. Co-sponsored by Univ. of Wisconsin at Madison and the Univ. of Michigan.

Dates: Late Feb-late Jun (semester); late Feb-mid-Dec (academic year). Cost: Approx. $5,235 per semester (WI residents). Includes tuition, room and board, social and cultural program. Contact: Lawrence Roscioli, Director, L&S Overseas Programs, Univ. of Wisconsin at Milwaukee, P.O. Box 413, Milwaukee, WI 53201; (414) 229-5879, fax (414) 229-6827; overseas@csd.uwm.edu.

China

Sino-American Field School of Archaeology. Credit and noncredit courses: 1) Chinese Culture History, 2) Field Archaeology. The excavation will take place near Xian. The program is sponsored by Xian Jiajong Univ. and the local Archaeological Institute. Transferable 6 credits.

Dates: Jul-Aug, 1997 (exact date later announced) Cost: $3,950 (everything included). Contact: Dr. Alfonz Lengyel, 1522 Schoolhouse Rd., Ambler, PA 19002.

Costa Rica

Costa Rican Language Academy. Costa Rican owned and operated language school offers first-rate Spanish instruction in a warm and friendly environment. Teachers with university degrees. Small groups or private classes. Included free in the programs are airport transportation, coffee and natural refreshments, excursions and Latin dance, Costa Rican cooking, music and conversation classes to provide students with complete cultural immersion.

Dates: Year round (start anytime). Cost: $135 per week or $220 per week for program with homestay. All other activities and services included at no additional cost. Contact: Costa Rican Language Academy, P.O. Box 336-2070, San José, Costa Rica; (011) 506-221-1624 or 233-8914 or 233-8938, fax 233-8670; crlang@sol.racsa.co.cr. In the U.S. (800) 854-6057.

Multi Media Landscape Painting. Enjoy extensive on-location painting. Course content suitable for beginners and more advanced painters. Students may use medium of choice. Individual expression encouraged. Instructor: John Leonard.

Dates: Feb 2-9, 1997. Cost: $1,315 from San Jose. Contact: Haliburton School of Fine Art, Box 839, Haliburton, ON, Canada K0M 1S0; (705) 457-1680, fax (705) 457-2255.

N.S.U. in San Jose. Credit transferred nationwide, 1-step registration, lowest tuition anywhere, 3-30 hours of credit, no out-of-state fees, no g.p.a. or junior standing required, no registration or late fees, no transcripts or credentials required, 22nd year of offering programs, humanities and graduate credit available, no language knowledge necessary, Christmas programs available, and class size 3-6 students.

Dates: Year round, classes begin every Monday. Cost: Three-week program, 6 hours per day, with homestay, 2 meals per day: $967 Contact: Gary McCann or Cynthia Webb, Study Programs Abroad, Nicholls State Univ., P.O. Box 2080, Thibodaux, LA 70310; (504) 448-4440; fl-caw@nich-nsunet.nich.edu.

Spanish Immersion Program. The Institute for Central American Development Studies (ICADS) offers 30-day programs of Intensive Spanish Languages—4 1/2 hours daily, 5 days a week. Small classes (4 students or less) geared to individual needs. Extra lectures and activities emphasize environmental issues, women's studies, economic development, and human rights. ICADS offers optional afternoon internship placements in grassroots organizations. Supportive informal learning environment. Homestays and field trips. A great alternative for the socially conscious.

Dates: Programs begin first Monday of each month. Cost: One month $1,150 (includes airport pick-up, classes, books, homestay, meals, laundry, lectures, activities, field trips, and placement). Ten percent discount after first month. Contact: Sandra Kinghorn, PhD, Director, ICADS, Dept. 826, P.O. Box 025216, Miami, FL 33102-5216; (506) 225-0508, fax (506) 234-1337; icadscr@expreso.co.cr.

Spanish Language Program of the Instituto Britanico. The Instituto offers courses in Spanish as a Second Language in the capital city of San Jose and at its regional branch in Liberia, Guanacaste. Courses for beginners, intermediate, and advanced students are taught by highly qualified and experienced staff. Specialty courses focusing on specific professional areas, such as business, medicine, law, and science are also available. Family homestays or hotel referrals are arranged. Individual students or groups can be accommodated for short or long term courses.

Dates: New courses begin weekly. Cost: $350 for 45-hour course. Contact: Gabriela Garcia, Director of the Spanish Department, Instituto Britanico, Apdo. 8184, San Jose, Costa Rica; (506) 225-0256 or 234-9054, fax (506) 253-1894; www.westnet.com/costarica/edu/britanica.html.

The Birds of Costa Rica. A research participation study of the migrant and neotropical resident birds of Tortuguero. Participants will study birds by making observations in 3 integrated ways: 1) along transects, 2) within specific habitat types, and 3) by mist-netting. Tortugero is strategically situated along a migratory path between North and South America. In addition, close to 200 resident birds make their home in the forests and waterways of exotic Tortuguero.

Dates: Year round. Cost: Approx. $1,900 for 15 days, includes travel to Costa Rica, room and board. Contact: Program Coordinator, Caribbean Conservation Corporation, 4424 NW 13th St., Suite A-1, Gainesville, FL 32609; (352) 373-6441, fax (352) 375-2449; ccc@atlantic.net.

Total Immersion Spanish. Seven separate year-round language institutes to choose from. Live with a Costa Rican family while taking 3 to 6 hours of intense language classes a day. Length of program is up to you—from as little as 1 week to 6 months. Locations: cloud forest, beach, country, and San Jose.

Dates: Every Monday except national holidays. Cost: Four-week course with homestay $850 to $2,000. Contact: ISLS, Dana G. Garrison, 1011 E. Washington Blvd., Los Angeles, CA 90021; (800) 765-0025, fax (213) 765-0026.

Volunteer Turtle Tagging And Monitoring. Volunteers assist scientists with several important tasks: tagging turtles, recording morphological and behavioral data, and conducting beach surveys. Tortuguero Beach is one of the most important nesting beaches for Atlantic Green turtles in the Western Hemisphere. By tagging turtles, we can identify individual animals and learn more about their behavioral patterns and survivorship.

Dates: Leatherback program Mar-May; Green Turtle program Jul-Sep. Cost: Approx. $1,500 for 8 days and $1,900 for 15 days. Includes travel to Costa Rica, room and board. Contact: Program Coordinator, Caribbean Conservation Corporation, 4424 NW 13th St., Suite A-1, Gainesville, FL 32609; (352) 373-6441, fax (352) 375-2449; ccc@atlantic.net.

Watercolor Painting-Floral. Enjoy creativity and impressionism in flower painting. Learn wet-in-wet techniques, bold use of colors and how to solve background problems. Capture the spirit of a floral painting. Instructor: Pauline Holancin.

Dates: Feb 2-9, 1997. Cost: $1,315 from San

Jose. Contact: Haliburton School of Fine Art, Box 839, Haliburton, Ontario, Canada K0M 1S0; (705) 457-1680, fax (705) 457-2255.

Denmark

Courses at Folkehøjskoler. One- or 2-week courses for adults in arts, crafts, literature, history, painting, drawing, music.

Dates: Year round. Cost: Approx. $435 for 1 week, approx. $725 for 2 weeks. Contact: Højskolernes Sekretariat, Nytorv 7, 1450 København K. Copenhagen, Denmark; (011) 45-3313-9822, fax 3313-9870; hs@grundtvig. dk.

Højskolekurser. Non-formal, adult education in a residential school with many different subjects: liberal arts, creative subjects, sports, civics, literature, history, etc.

Dates: Year round. Cost: Approx. 6,000 krones per month (includes room and board and tuition). Contact: Højskolernes Sekretariat, Nytorv 7, 1450 Kobenhavn K. Copenhagen, Denmark; (011) 45-3313-9822, fax 3313-9870; hs@grundtvig.dk.

Dominican Republic

Spanish, Development, Culture. Individual and group programs focused on (1) learning Spanish as a Second Language, (2) adaptation into Hispanic culture, (3) development themes on poverty, migration, sustainability, health, environment. Individually designed programs can include urban/rural homestays, with different degrees of immersion. Fifteen years experience.

Dates: Designed according to participant's needs. Cost: Varies with program ($1,530 per month immersion). Contact: Rafael Paz or Sobeya Seibel, Entrena, EPS-P-4507, Box 02-5261, Miami, FL 33102-5261; (011) 809-567-8990 or 541-4283, fax 566-3492.

East Africa

East Africa with the Experts. Join America's most distinguished museums, zoological societies and wildlife organizations on safaris to East and South Africa. Trips are led by outstanding local naturalists and feature excellent accommodations in the best reserves for animal viewing. Park East Tours has been a leader in travel to East Africa for over 30 years and is the 1996 recipient of the Africa Travel Association Award for Outstanding Achievement in the Promotion of Responsible Tourism to Africa.

Dates: All of 1997. Cost: From $2,995 to $5,995 (depending on program, land and air from New York). Contact: Marcia Gordon, Park East Tours, 1841 Broadway, New York, NY 10023; (800) 223-6078 ext. 316 or (212) 765-4870 ext 316, fax (212) 265-8952.

Ecuador

Academia Latinoamericana de Español (Quito). Ecuador's number-one private Spanish language institute in former diplomat's mansion with swimming pool, hot tub, sauna, sport facilities. Instruction by university-trained teachers, all one-on-one. Customized study programs tailored to the individual. Select host family accommodations. Excursions to haciendas, Indian markets, etc. College credit available and internships.

Dates: Year round. Cost: One-week tuition, lodging, meals $294. Contact: Suzanne Bell, Admissions Director, U.S., 640 East 3990 South, Suite E, Salt Lake City, UT 84107; (801) 268-4608, fax (801) 265-9156; latinoa1@ spanish.com.ec, http://ecnct.cc/academia/ learnspa.htm.

Galapagos Islands. Sail these magical, volcanic islands in maximum comfort and safety aboard a 48-passenger expedition ship, the M/ V Corinthian, or a 20-passenger motor yacht, the M/Y Eric, Flamingo and Letty or a 10-passenger motor sailor, the M/S Sea Cloud.

Dates: Year-round departures. Cost: Three nights $600-$800; 4 nights $800-$1,050; 7 nights $1,500-$1,850. Contact: Galapagos Network, 7200 Corporate Center Dr., #309, Miami, FL 33126; (800) 633-7972 or (305) 592-2294, fax (305) 592-6394; gpsnet@aol.com.

Spanish for Foreigners. One-to-one instruction with well-trained teachers; luxury house with natural light, gardens, and terrace without noise or smog. All levels. Special programs: literature, fine arts, history, childrens: "Activo: Learn and Travel." Twice a week free city tours (in programs of 7 hours daily). Accommodations in nice Ecuadorian homestay (all services).

Dates: Year round. Cost: $7 per hour, $21 family day. Contact: Director Alcira Muñoz, Instituto de Español "El Quijote," Manuel Godoy #144 and Juan Ramirez St., P.O. Box 17 - 17 1419, Quito, Ecuador; (011) 593-2-455-256, fax 464-967.

Europe

Archaeological Summer Field. The project consists of researching and documenting engraved and painted rocks in Paspardo (Valcamonica) and in Grosio (Vatellina). Accommodations will be provided in houses with rooms, dormitories, showers, and kichen. During the summer school we will also visit other localities with rock engravings or museums.

Cost: Accommodations, food, publications, and working material will be provided at a cost of LIT60,000 per day. Contact: Dr. Angelo Fossati, Cooperativa Archeologica "Le Orme Dell'Umo," Piazzale Donatori di Sangue, No. 1, 25040 Cerveno (BS), Italy; (011) 39 364-433983, fax 434351; aarca@mailer.inrete.it.

En Route Travel Experiences. Affordable, engaging, off-the-beaten-path group tours with a wide variety of topics from aromatherapy and hiking to sailing and environmental studies and historic architecture and gardens. Destinations in 1996 included France's chateau region, Iceland, Copenhagen, Oslo, Stockholm, Norway's Jotunheimen Mountains, the Baltic Sea, Jewish Poland, Wales, England, Provence, and Budapest. Call for free catalog.

Dates: Trip season is Apr-Nov; program length varies, from 7-19 days. Cost: Start at $870. Contact: Scandinavian Seminar/En Route, 24 Dickinson St., Amherst, MA 01002; (800) 316-9833 or (413) 253-9736, fax (413) 253-5282; enroute.org.

Finnish/Estonian Walking Tour. Finnish/Estonian Active Walking Holiday: Midsummer's Eve tour to Lapland and Helsinki in Finland and to the Medieval Estonan city of Tallin before going to Lahemaa and Korvemaa to walk through primeval forest, glacial moraines, peat bogs, and birch-lined lakes. Lodging in inns, small hotels, and lodges.

Dates: Jun 14-Jun 29, 1997. Cost: Airfare from NY, lodging, transport, guides, meals, and sightseeing as indicated: $3,650. Contact: The Earth is Yours Walking Tours, Inc., 930 Washington #1E, Evanston, IL 60202-2272; (847) 869-5745, fax (847) 869-5002.

Imperial Encounter in Austria. Imperial private meeting with His Royal Highness, Johann S. von Habsburg-Lothringen, Archduke of Austria, Royal Prince of Both Sicilies, Bohemia, Moravia, Hungary, great-grandson of Emperor Franz Joseph T. and Empress Elisabeth (Sisi). Johann von Habsburg lectures on his imperial family, shows memorabilia, and private photos.

Dates: Upon request, only for groups. Cost: Free of charge, but package only applicable with other touristic services, like hotel reservation, coach, sightseeing tours, etc. Contact: Christine Jocher, Reisebüro Jocher, Offenseeneg 1, A-4802 Ebensee Austria-Europe; (011) 43-6133-6636, fax 6017.

International Programs. CMC offers customized study abroad trips to groups of business students, executive students, and educators. Through lectures, company visits, and panel discussions, participants are exposed to one of the fastest developing markets. A 5-week study abroad program (Jun and Jul) and a 14-week fall semester (Sep-Dec) with a focus on doing business in the region are also offered.

Dates: Year round. Cost: Costs vary according to length of stay. Call for details. Contact: Patrick Uram, Master of Business Administration and International Programs Office, nám. 5. kvena 2, 250 88 Celákovice, Czech Republic; (011) 42-202-892245, fax 891997; ipdoff@cmc.cz.

International Relations/Business. Topics will cover the business, political, and historical aspect of the current transformation of Western Europe. The course will strive to achieve a balanced understanding of business practices, political realities, and social and cultural sensitivities. Three to 6 hours of college credit is granted through the Univ. of Missouri at Kansas City in economics, business, or political science.

Dates: Summer 1997. Cost: Approx. $2,000 (does not include airfare). Contact: People to People International, Collegiate and Professional Studies Program, 501 E. Armour Blvd., Kansas City, MO 64109-2200; (816) 531-4701, fax (816) 561-7502; ptpi@cctr.umkc.edu, www.umkc.edu/cctr/dept/ptpi/homepage.html.

International Social Issues. Topics covered will bring you face to face with policy makers and professionals in the fields of substance abuse, healthcare policies, criminal justice, women's issues, and political policies. Three to 6 hours of college credit is granted through the Univ. of Missouri at Kansas City in sociology, education, or administration of justice.

Dates: Summer 1997. Cost: Approx. $2,000 (does not include airfare). Contact: People to People International, Collegiate and Professional Studies Program, 501 E. Armour Blvd.,

Kansas City, MO 64109-2200; (816) 531-4701, fax (816) 561-7502; ptpi@cctr.umkc.edu, www.umkc.edu/cctr/dept/ptpi/homepage.html.

Le Cordon Bleu Summer Semester Abroad in Paris and London. The International Culinary Hospitality Programs (ICHP) is an intense 10-week program in Paris and London designed for undergraduates or recent graduates of hospitality schools seeking to gain an edge in the culinary arts and earn academic credits at the same time. Complemented by cultural excursions, theory courses, wine and cheese, catering and a unique 2-week internships in a European hotel or restaurant.

Dates: Jun 9-Aug 14. Cost: $7,500 includes classes, excursions, uniform, equipment, and housing. Contact: Le Cordon Bleu, 8, rue Léon Delhomme, 75015 Paris; (011) 33-1-53-68-22-60, fax 48-56-03-97. Le Cordon Bleu, Inc., 404 Airport Executive Park, Nanuet, NY 10954; (914) 426-7400, or (800) 457-CHEF, fax (914) 426-0104.

Moscow and/or Paris Study Trips. Examine political, economic, and social conditions of transition in Russia and/or the European Union. All interested adults eligible. In Moscow, special topics (business, labor, education, etc.) possible according to group composition. No Russian/French necessary. Programs offered since 1976.

Dates: 1) Moscow May 9-Jun 7; 2) Paris Jun 6-22; 3) Moscow Jun 21-July 20. (1) + (2) or (2) + (3). Cost: Moscow: $1,450-$1,650 plus airfare ($860 est. from U.S.); Paris $1,000 plus airfare ($600 est. from U.S.). Includes lodging, meals, program, internal travel, fees, visa (Russia). Contact: Eric Fenster, 27150 Zeman Ave., Euclid, OH 44132; efenster@igc.org, www.ourworld:compuserve.com/homepages/efenster.

Self-Drive Boating in Europe. Skipper Travel has available to a 4- to 6-passenger boat on the Canal du Midi in France designed to accommodate a wheelchair with a hydraulic lift between cabins and a joystick as well as a wheel. The base is at Homps near the historic Roman city of Carcassone. In England there is a 4- to 5-passenger narrowboat with wide aisles and a lift available on the Kennet and Avon canal.

Dates: Cruises are 1 week each between Mar and Oct. Cost: England: $700-$1,150 per boat per week depending on the season; France: $1,000-$2,000 per boat per week depending on the season. Contact: Susan Anshen, Skipper Travel Services Ltd., 1500 41st Ave., #8-B, Capitola, CA 95010; (800) 631-1030 or (408) 462-5333, fax (408) 462-5178.

Summer in Poland. Students can study Polish history, culture, economics, religion, politics, and language in either a 4- or 6-week program hosted by Jagiellonian Univ. in Krakow. Participants are housed in suite-style rooms in a residence hall, which also serves 3 meals a day. The program includes tours to Krakow, Warsaw, the Tatra and Pieniny Mountains, and the Martyrdom Museum in Auschwitz-Birkenau.

Dates: Six week: Jul 3-Aug 15, 1996; 4-week: Jul 3- Aug 1, 1996. Cost: Non-credit option: 6-week $1,386; 4-week $1,233 (credit is available). Contact: SUNY at Buffalo, Study Abroad Programs, 210 Talbert Hall, Buffalo, NY 14260-1604; (716) 645-3912, fax (716) 645-6197; studyabroad@acsu.buffalo.edu.

Vienna and Salzburg. Combine your trip to the Imperial city of Vienna with a stay in the medieval city of Salzburg. Eight days and 7 nights. Daily departures. Four nights Vienna at Hotel Biedermeier, 3 nights Salzburg at Austrotel. Buffet breakfast daily, optional sightseeing.

Dates: Not available Dec 23-Jan 6, 1996. Cost: Includes roundtrip airport and hotel transfers. Package (double) $593, (single) $377; Vienna extra nights, double $60; single $42; Salzburg extra nights, double $57; single $33. Contact: Euro Lloyd Tours; (800) 334-2724, (516) 794-1253 (NY state), fax (516) 228-8258.

Finland

Environmental Risk Assessment and Technology. The program consists of the following courses: Environmental Project Management, Water Chemistry, Risk Analysis, Risk Communication, Water Supply and Sanitation, Advanced Water Chemistry and Treatment, Atmospheric Hygiene I, Atmospheric Chemistry, Health-related Environmental Microbiology. Students are allowed to take either the whole study or single courses.

Dates: Aug 1996-Apr 1997. Cost: Free. Contact: Univ. of Kuopio, Dept. of Environmental Sciences, Student Affairs Secretary Katarina Juhola; (011) 358-71-163200, fax (011) 358-71-163230.

France

Adults in Montpellier. Two-week intensive French study-travel program with the Univ. of New Orleans. Morning classes, afternoon sightseeing excursions on weekends to places such as Arles, Nîmes, Pont du Gard, Roquefort, Larzac.

Dates: Jul 2-15. Cost: $1,465. Contact: Marie Kaposchyn, Program Director, Univ. of New Orleans, P.O. Box 569, New Orleans, LA 70148; (504) 286-7455, fax (504) 286-7317.

Cooking with the Masters. A 1-week series of intensive hands-on culinary education in the kitchens of French master chefs, including professional visits to vineyards, markets, local artisans, etc.

Dates: Jan-Feb; Jun; Sep-Oct. Next series: Sep 20-29, 1996. Cost: Approx. $2,550 per person. Includes dbl. occupancy, airfare. Single supplement applies. Contact: Michel Bouit, President, MBI Inc., P.O. Box 1801, Chicago, IL 60690; (312) 663-5701, fax (312) 663-5702.

Culinary Adventures. Join MBI and French-born chef Michel Bouit as he leads chefs and gourmets on culinary adventures through various regions of France. The program includes professional visits to local artisans, markets, vineyards. Experience gastronomic pleasures of 4-star restaurants, degustations, and cultural visits.

Dates: Next tour: "Paris and Normandy, Romance and Conquest," Sep 12-21, 1996. Cost: Approx. $2,950 per person, dbl. occupancy. Includes airfare, hotel accommodations, most meals. Single supplement applies. Contact: Michel Bouit, President, MBI Inc., P.O. Box 1801, Chicago, IL 60690; (312) 663-5701, fax (312) 663-5702.

Enjoy French in a Chateau. Château de Mâtel (17th century) offers residential courses for adults in General French, Intensive French, Cooking. On 32 hectares of parkland near Roanne city center. Close to Burgundy, Beaujolais, and city of Lyons. Single, ensuite, and shared rooms available. One through 12-week courses. Tennis, pool, horse-riding, kayak.

Dates: Every Sunday Apr-Nov. Cost: From $999 full board and classes in Chateau. Contact: Dr. C. Roberts, 204 via Morella, Encinitas, CA 92024; (619) 632-1923 or (800) 484-1235 #0096 or Joe Davies, 3473 Camino Valencia, Carlsbad, CA 92009; Tel./fax (619) 591-4537 (modem) or Ecole des Trois Ponts, Chateau de Matel, 42300 Roanne, France; (011) 33-77-70-80-01, fax 77-71-53-00.

Language Study in Loire Valley. Intensive French language courses in a relaxed and friendly atmosphere, 130 miles southwest of Paris. Four- to 8-week courses for beginners. Or advanced studies. Twenty-five hours of lessons per week. Accommodations in a small castle with pool and numerous sport facilities.

Dates: From Feb to Nov. Cost: $2,200 for 4 weeks (25 hours of lessons per week, meals and accommodations). Contact: Mme. Tartière, Chateau Bois Minhy Chemery, 41700 Contres, Loir et Cher, France; (011) 33-54-79-51-01, fax (011) 33-54-79-06-26.

Le Cordon Bleu, L'Art Culinaire. Le Cordon Bleu in Paris offers the highest diploma in cu-

linary education in just 9 months. Cuisine and pastry classes begin every 10 weeks. Summer abroad program—I CHP—in Paris and London. Chef catering program for professionals.

Dates: Jun 10-Aug 17, 1996. Every 10 weeks. Cost: From $6,000 to $30,000 for cuisine and pastry in 9 months. Contact: In U.S. call (800) 457-CHEF or fax (914) 426-0104. Le Cordon Bleu, 8, rue Leon Delhomme, 75015 Paris, France.

Live and Learn French. Live with a carefully selected, welcoming French family in the Paris region. Learn from a family member/teacher who has a university degree and will tailor a private course to suit your needs. Share in a cultural and learning experience that will develop both your understanding of the language and the people who speak it. Minimum of 1 week stay. We also offer touristic stays conducted in English or French.

Dates: Year round. Cost: Fifteen hours of study per week $1,250; 20 hours of study per week $1,315. Two people coming together $1,800 per week. Prices include room, 3 meals a day, and instruction. Contact: Sara S. Monick, Live & Learn, 4215 Poplar Dr., Minneapolis, MN 55422; (612) 374-2444, fax (612) 374-3290.

Spring Semester in Paris. The Paris Program is designed to improve proficiency in French and to provide coursework in a variety of subjects related to France, some at the Cours de Civilisation française at the Université de Paris IV (Sorbonne). The courses provide exposure to French social and cultural issues, while the overall program is designed to offer a broad experience of contemporary life in France.

Dates: Mid-Jan-mid-May. Cost: $6,175 (WI residents). Includes tuition, room and basic board, excursions. Contact: Lawrence Roscioli, Director, L&S Off-Campus Programs, Univ. of Wisconsin at Milwaukee, P.O. Box 413, Milwaukee, WI 53201; (414) 229-5879, fax (414) 229-6827; overseas@csd.uwm.edu.

Summer Workshops in Painting and Draw-

ing, **French Language, and Photography (Auvergne).** Enjoy painting and drawing, French language, or photography workshops at Paul and Babette Deggan's Summer Centre for the Arts in Montaigut-le-Blanc, a medieval hill village in the ruggedly beautiful Auvergne region of France. Overlooking a panorama of orchards, vineyards, and fields of giant sunflowers, the center is a charming complex of restored buildings dating from the 17th century. An optional week in Paris is also available.

Dates: Jul 11-29. Cost: CAN$2,495 includes accommodations, most meals and beverages, tuition, and local excursions. Does not include airfare. Contact: Lauren Mulholland, Capilano College Extension Division, 2055 Purcell Way, North Vancouver, BC V7J 3H5, Canada; (604) 984-4907, fax (604) 983-7545; lmulholl@capcollege.bc.ca.

The Académie de Paris. A month-long introduction for students (grades 10-12) to Parisian culture, with classes taught in the city's museums, cathedrals, and historic sites. Courses include medicine, theater, studio art, and creative writing. Most classes are taught in English, with a special series of courses for those desiring immersion in French language.

Dates: Jul 7-Aug 3, 1996. Cost: $4,195. Contact: OxBridge Academic Programs, 601 W. 110th St., Suite 7-R, New York, NY 10025-1535; (800) 828-8349, fax (212) 663-8169.

The Paris Program. Participants live in Paris for 3 weeks and choose one of 4 courses: Art of the Impressionists, History of Paris Through Its Architecture, Photographing Paris, or Beginning French. All courses are taught in English (except Beginning French). Courses may be taken for credit.

Dates: Jul 6-26. Cost: $3,200. Contact: Elizabeth Newton, UC Berkeley Ext., 55 Laguna St., San Francisco, CA 94102; (415) 252-5230, fax (415) 552-4237; ejn@unx.berkeley.edu.

The Paris Teacher Seminar. A unique opportunity to combine professional development with a personal adventure in Paris for teachers of all subjects and grade levels. A series of lectures on many far-reaching subjects will blend with walking tours and museum visits to give participants a true insider's perspective on Parisian and French life.

Dates: Jul 9-20, 1996. Cost: $1,895. Contact: OxBridge Academic Programs, 601 W. 110th St., Suite 7-R, New York, NY 10025-1535; (800) 828-8349, fax (212) 663-8169.

Germany

German Language Courses in Munich. Group tuition available at all levels. Choose 20, 26, or 30 lessons a week or preparation for officially recognized exams. One-to-one tuition with 10, 20, 30, 40, or 50 lessons a week.

Dates: Every Monday, year round. Cost: Twenty lessons a week (group): DM720 (tuition only) (2 weeks); half board, single room DM367 per week. Contact: Inlingua School, Sendlinger-Tor-P 6, D-80336 Muenchen, Germany; (011) 49-89-2311530, fax 2609920.

Professionals and Agriculturists. The 1-year work-study program is a cultural exchange with three parts: German language study in Germany to develop the facility for successful participation (about two months); classroom instruction at a German technical school or other institute of higher education (about 4 months); and a 5- to 6-month position with a German company. The program is designed for technical, vocational, and business fields and is meant to give participants a taste of how their professional counterparts are trained and the opportunity to experience the German workplace.

Dates: Jul to Jul following year. Cost: Funding provided: International airfare and partial domestic costs, insurance, and host family compensation during study portion of program. Own spending ($350 per month). Contact: Beate Witzler, Program Director, CDS International, 330 7th Ave., 19th Fl., New York, NY 10001; (212) 760-1400; (212) 268-1288.

Greece

A Potter's Camp. Master classes in ceramics. Camp in traditional mountain village close to the sea. Fire Raku, pit, stoneware. Make paper clay. Beach project, murals, totems. Inside information on the best places to see the ceramics of ancient and modern Greece.

Dates: May-Oct, 1997. Cost: £350 per week. Contact: Alan Bain, Kalamoudi, 35004 Rovies, Evia, Greece.

Classic Theatre Study Abroad. Students, teachers, and professionals spend 3 weeks on an idyllic Greek island with classes mornings and rehearsal evenings. The fourth week they go on tour, presenting an ancient drama in classic and modern amphitheaters and visiting major classic sites.

Dates: Mid-Jun-mid-Jul. Cost: $3,500 participant or $4,500 with 6 hours credit. Contact: Dr. Arthur J. Beer, Univ. of Detroit Mercy, P.O. Box 19900, Detroit, MI 48219-0900.

Greek Folk Dances and Culture. Workshops on Greek dance (traditional and ancient) including general courses on Greek culture (music, costume, language, etc.).

Dates: Summer 1996. Cost: $200 a week. Contact: Alkis Raftis, Greek Dances Theatre, 8 Schouiou St., GR-10558, Plaka, Athens, Greece; (011) 30-1-3244395.

Greek Language and Culture. Summer intensive course of Greek language and culture held in the Thessaloniki. The course is complemented by lectures, excursions, guided tours, visits to museums, and archaeological sites.

Dates: Aug 16-Sep 13, 1996. Cost: 80,000 (65,000 for European union citizens). Contact: School of Modern Greek Language, Aristole Univ. of Thessaloniki, GR S4006, Thessaloniki, Greece; (011) 30-31-99751-72, fax 31-997573.

Modern Greek Language and Culture. Summer intensive course in Greek language and civilization held in the island of Alonnissos. The course is complemented by lectures, excursions, and guided tours. In this program accommodations and meals (breakfast and 1 meal) included in the price.

Dates: Jun 10-28, 1996. Cost: GDR 370,000. Contact: School of Modern Greek Language, Aristole Univ. of Thessaloniki, GR S4006, Thessaloniki, Greece; (011) 30-31-99751-72, fax 31-997573.

Tour of Ancient Greece. This trip will begin in the ancient city of Athens, continue on to visit Corinth, Mycenae, Nauplia, Epidaurus, Sparta, Mystra, the Olympic grounds, the Delphi grounds and Museum Patras, and the islands of Mykonos and Delos. Lectures on the remarkable history of Greece, its art, and its architecture, will be held throughout the tour and at the Archaeological Museum in Athens.

Dates: Jun 8-30, 1997. Cost: Three credits - $2,500. Includes roundtrip airfare, double occupancy rooms, breakfast daily, bus, ship and airport transfers. Contact: Joel Garrick, School of Visual Arts, 209 E. 23rd St., New York, NY 10010; (212) 592-2011.

Guatemala

Eco-Escuela de Español. The Eco-Escuela de Español offers a unique educational experience by combining intensive Spanish language instruction with volunteer opportunities in conservation and community development projects. Students are immersed in the language, culture, and ecology of the Petén, Guatemala—an area renowned for its tropical forests and ancient Maya ruins. Ecological activities integrate classroom with field-based experiences.

Dates: Every Monday year round. Cost: Classes $60 per week (based on 20 hours of individual instruction per week, Monday-Friday). Room and board with local families $50 per week. Registration fee $10. Contact: Eco-Escuela, Conservation International, 1015 18th St. NW, Suite 1000, Washington, DC 20036; (202) 973-2264, fax (202) 887-5188; m.sister@conservation.org.

Escuela de Español "Sakribal". Program provides one-on-one intensive language instruction while giving students the chance to volunteer on student-supported development projects in the surrounding community, working in organic gardens, and in the country's only women's shelter. Family stays, guest lecturers, group discussions, and cultural activities round out the immersion program.

Dates: Classes start every Monday year round. Cost: $120 per week (includes classes, family stay, project work, other school activities). Contact: U.S. Office: 550 Ferncroft Ct., Danville, CA 94526; (510) 820-3632, fax (510) 820-6658; sakribal2@aol.com, http://kcyb.com/sakribal.

Honduras

Spanish Language School. Spend a week or more in a spectacular setting—the magnificent Mayan ruins of Copan, or the tropical beaches of Trujillo while learning Spanish from your own private instructor. Programs include 4 hours of instruction daily (weekdays), and 7 nights room and board with a Honduran family. Hotel based stays also available. All levels of instruction. Small groups and student groups welcome.

Dates: Year round (advance reservations recommended for summer; closed Holy Week). Cost: Single: (7 nights) $235, (14 nights) $410, (21 nights) $615; 2 or more (7 nights) $205, (14 nights) $410, (21 nights) $615. Contact: Roatan Charter, Inc., P.O. Box 877, San Antonio, FL 33576; (800) 282-8932 or (904) 588-4132, fax (904) 588-4158.

Indonesia

Experiencing the Arts in Bali. Providing insight and practice into Bali's arts and crafts, and based in the cultural center, includes island tours, traditional dance performances, and 10 classes in gamelan music, dance, painting, batik, or mask carving, taught by Balinese artists in family compounds. A life-changing experience created by quality guides with 16-year track record. Daily classes in Iyengar Yoga with certified instructor.

Dates: Jul 1-21. Cost: $3,100. Contact: Danu Enterprises, P.O. Box 156, Capitola, CA 95010; Tel./fax (888) 476-0543.

Independent Travel in Asia. Intensive programs designed to provide beginner travelers with the knowledge, skills, and confidence needed to travel independently, safely, and responsibly through Asia. Small group tours (max. 8) emphasize simple living, cross-cultural communication skills (inc. language learning option), and awareness of global issues. Travel by public transport with the local people and their chickens and goats.

Dates: Feb 23-Apr 5, May 4-Jun 14, 1997 (6 weeks). Contact: Ed Kiefer, Independent Travel in Asia, Siddha Farm, Young Rd., Nimbin, NSW 2480, Australia; (011) 61-66-891-608; ekiefer@metz.une.edu.au.

Study in Bali. Join the Naropa Institute (NCA accredited) program introducing students to the living traditions of Bali. Courses offered are meditation, gamelan music, language, culture, dance, painting, and maskmaking taught by master Balinese artists and teachers as well as Naropa faculty. Develop a deeper appreciation of yourself and the world through study and practice of arts coupled with daily awareness practice. Independent study/research option (3 credits).

Dates: Mid-Feb-mid-Apr, 1997. Cost: $5,000 in 1996. Includes tuition (9 semester credits), room and partial board, program expenses. Airfare not included. Contact: Study Abroad Office, The Naropa Institute, 2130 Arapahoe Ave., Boulder, CO 80302; (303) 546-3594, fax (303) 444-0410.

The Healing Arts of Bali. Research Bali's traditional healing practices, observing the work of folk doctors, study herbal medicines, temple offerings, traditional massages, and herbal body revitalization experiences. Participants visit all Bali's top attractions on island tours, attend dance performances and trance rituals, visit artists, and enjoy expert seminars on Balinese culture and religion. Daily classes in Iyengar Yoga with certified instructor.

Dates: Mar 14-27, Jul 28-Aug 12. Cost: Mar $2,900. Contact: Danu Enterprises, P.O. Box 156, Capitola, CA 95010; Tel./fax (888) 476-0543.

Ireland

9th Achill Archaeological Field School. Survey and excavation of a post-medieval deserted village: Slievemore, Achill, Co. Mayo. Activities include: surveying, excavation procedure, recording geology and botany of island, field trips, lectures and seminars. No previous knowledge required. Maximum 6 credits.

Dates: Weekly Jul 15-Aug 30. Cost: Weekly: IR£85 p.p. $200 course fee plus accommodations. Contact: Theresa McDonald, M.A. Director, Achill Archaeological Field School, St. O'Hara's Hill, Tullamore, Co. Offaly; (011) 353-1-505-21627, fax 506-21627.

Celtic Journeys. Intimate, behind-the-scenes journeys through scenic western Ireland to sites not easily accessible to unguided tourists. Touch milestones in 6,000 years of uninterrupted cultural development from first stone-age settlers to present-day Gaeltacht life. Guides are young native Irish-speaking archaeologists and historians. Groups of 6-9 for 8 days. Also custom-designed tours.

Dates: Six itineraries available to groups Apr-Jun and Sep-Nov; other dates available on request. Individuals welcome on special women's tour in Jun; mixed group tour in Sep. Cost: $1,150-$1,300 per person ground costs only. Includes pickup from airport, ground transport, lodging, breakfasts, lunches, some dinners, museum and monument plus entry fees (if applicable), and ferry travel. Contact: Laurie McNeill-Leggett, Western Isle, 405 E. Magnolia, Suite 104, Angleton, TX 77515; (409) 848-8318, fax (800) 379-2482; westisle@tgn.net.

Celtic Journeys: Irish Backroads. Small-group archeological and cultural tours focusing on Ireland's West and North. Guided by Irish archaeologists and historians raised in the Gaeltachts. We cater to the inquisitive, thinking traveler, in groups or alone.

Dates: Mar, Jun and Sep, or by request of a group of 6-8. Cost: $1,065-$1,250 ground only. Contact: Laurie McNeill-Leggett, Western Isle, 4017 Case St., Houston, TX 77005; Tel./fax (800) 379-2482; westisle@tgn.net.

Ireland's Language and Culture. Oideas Gael is based in Glencolmcille, County Donegal, Ireland, and offers weekly courses for students and adult learners in Irish language (all learning levels), music, archaeology, painting, set dancing. Other modules offered as part of semester programs.

Dates: All programs offered year round. Cost: From $100 per program. Accommodations not included. Contact: Oideas Gael, Glencolmcille, County Donegal; tel (011) 353-73-30248, fax (011) 353-73-30348; oidsgael@iol.ie.

Irish Language and Culture. Irish language programs at all learning levels, as well as cultural activities. Language learning in hillwalking, dancing, music and archaeology.

Dates: From Easter until Sep (weekly). Cost: $200 including tuition and houseshare. Contact: Liam O'Cuinneagain, Oideas Gael, Gleann Cholm Cille, County Donegal; (011) 353-73-30248, fax 30348; ocdsgael@iol.ie.

Landscape Painting in the Burren. Professional art tutors take groups outdoors on location for sketching and painting in the famous Burren country of North Clare: rockscapes, seascapes, streetscapes. Media include oils, watercolors, pastel, gouache, acrylics. Accommodations in Irish Tourist Board approved town home. Studio, materials, and equipment available.

Dates: May-Oct weekly and weekends. Cost: $500 per week. Contact: Christine O'Neill, The Burren Painting Centre, Lisdoonvarna, Co. Claire, Ireland.

Walking and Trekking Holidays. Countryside Tours, set up in 1990, is the specialist in providing leisurely guided and more challenging self-guided hiking tours. A varied program includes all the major areas of interest such as Kerry, Connemara, Wicklow Mountains, and Ulster. Good food, comfortable accommodations in Irish guesthouses.

Dates: Please ask for brochure. Cost: IR£420 for guided tours, from IR£205 for self-guided tours. Contact: Nick Becker, Countryside Tours Ltd., Glencar House, Glencar, County Kerry, Ireland; (011) 353-66 60211, fax (011) 353 66 60217; country@iol.ie.

Israel

Kibbutz Volunteers. Experience the kibbutz way of life, while you make a unique contribution to Israel: share your strengths and skills as a kibbutz volunteer. Receive food and lodging, laundry services, and an allotment for personal needs. Eligibility—Ages 18-35, singles and couple without children.

Dates: Any time. A 2-month commitment required. Cost: $165 registration fee, airfare not included. Contact: Kibbutz Program Center, Attn: Alice Stern, Ulpan Coordinator, 110 E. 59th St., 4th Fl., New York, NY 10022; (800) 247-7852, fax (212) 318-6134; kibbutzdsk@aol.com.

Pastor-Parishioner Study Tour. A 2-week program in Israel with daily field trips that concentrate on the geography of Israel and archaeology as they relate to Biblical interpretation. Extensive field trips to Galilee, Dead Sea, Masada, Jerusalem region, including overnights on the Sea of Galilee.

Dates: Oct 28-Nov 10, 1996; Apr 14-Apr 27 and Oct 27-Nov 9, 1997. Cost: $1,260 includes room and board, field trips. Contact: Jerusalem University College, 4249 E. State St., Suite 203, Rockford, IL 61108; (815) 229-5900 or (800) 891-9408, fax (815) 229-5901.

Project Oren Kibbutz Programs. Kibbutzim

(collective settlements) as a home for 4-5-month programs in which participants study Hebrew, work, and live on a kibbutz, take part in lectures on Israel and Judaism, and travel throughout Israel. Participants do all of this while practicing a lifestyle based on social and economic equality. Four separate programs, which include all of the above elements (in addition to classes on a specialty area): Israel Through Drama, Creative Arts, Jerusalem Studies and Archaeology, In the Land of Israel: Politics, Culture, or Enrivronmental Ethics.

Dates: Each program runs twice a year; beginning once in the fall (Sep) and once in the spring (Jan). Specific dates vary by program. Cost: From $1,300-$1,600. This includes all registration and tuition fees, all touring costs, and room and board. Contact: Beth Leviss, Director of Admissions, Project Oren Kibbutz Programs, 110 E. 59th St., 4th Fl., New York, NY 10022; (800) 247-7852, fax (212) 318-6134; projoren@aol.com, www.webflex.com/kibbutz.htm.

Italy

Biking and Walking Tours. Specializing in Italy for over 10 years, Ciclismo Classico distills the "Best of Italy," offering more unique Italian destinations than any other active vacation company. Educational, active tours for all abilities in Umbria, Tuscany, Piedmont, the Dolomites, Puglia, Sicily, the Amalfi Coast, Cinque Terre, Sardegna, Abruzzo, Campania, Corsica, and Elba, and Ireland, too. Charming accommodations, expert bilingual guides, cooking demonstrations, wine tastings, support vehicle, detailed route instructions, visits to local festivals, countryside picnics—an unforgettable cultural indulgence.

Dates: Apr-Nov (70 departures). Call for specific dates. Costs $1,500 $3,000. Contact: Lauren Hefferon, Director, Ciclismo Classico, 13 Marathon St., Arlington, MA 02174; (800) 866-7314 or (617) 646-3377.

Centro di Cultura Italiana in Casentino

(CCIC). CCIC "Piero della Francesca," located in the Tuscan hill town of Poppi, offers 2- or 4-week sessions of intensive, low-pressure Italian language instruction. All classes are conducted in Italian, even for beginners. No tests (except for an initial diagnostic test for placement), no grades, no diploma. Plenty of grammar, conversation, reinforcement, satisfaction.

Dates: May through Oct. Cost: $1,000 all-inclusive for 2-week session. Contact: Stephen Casale, U.S. Agent, 1 University Pl., Apt. 17-R, New York, NY 10003-4522; (212) 228-9273, fax (212) 353-1942.

Cooking and Art in Tuscany. Workshops in the glorious Tuscan landscape surrounded by vineyards and olive groves. Classes include painting, glass beads, metals/jewelry-making, photography, ceramics and even cooking, combined with art history and field trips to hilltop villages, Florence and Siena.

Dates: Oct 5-12, 1996; May 7-24, 1997. Cost: Both programs $1,225. Contact: Horizons, Jane Sinauer, Director, 108 N. Main St.-1st, Sunderland, MA 01375; Tel./fax (413) 665-4141.

Fujistudio Jewelry and Textile School. Monthly and semester courses in jewelry making, jewelry design, casting, stonesetting. All levels. Screenprinting on textiles on paper. Batik and silkpainting, weaving, textile sculpture, sewing. Taught in both English and/or Italian.

Dates: Jan to end of Jul and Sep to mid-Dec. Cost: Varies according to number of months, hours, and courses chosen. Contact: Fujistudio, Via Guelfa 79A, 50129 Florence, Italy; (011) 39-55-216877, fax 55-215400.

Italian Cuisine in Florence. Weekly intensive culinary programs in regional Italian cuisine. Gourmet I: Regional. Gourmet II: Lighter Nouvelle. Shorter 3-day programs as well. Italian tradition complemented by historical and cultural anecdotes. Classes are full-participation and followed by lunch with wine.

Dates: For travel agencies with larger groups, 1-day demo classes. Year round various dates; not Jan or Aug. Cost: Gourmet I and II: LIT1,300,000; 3-day: LIT800,000. Contact: Mr. William Grossi, 182 Four-Corners Rd., Ancramdule, NY 12503; (518) 329-1141 or Masha Innocenti, Via Trieste I, Florence 50139, Italy; Tel./fax (011) 39-55-480041.

Italian for Foreigners. Centro Cultura Italiana Bologna is a small school in a nontouristic charming North Italian town recently moved to a medieval palace. Two-, 3-, 4-week courses, plus cultural program, certification of participation. Method: direct, student-centered, combination of conversation, grammar, lecture.

Dates: Every 2 weeks year round. Cost: LIT800,000 for 4 weeks, LIT450,000 for 2 weeks. Contact: Centro Cultura Italiana Bologna, Via Castiglione 4, 40124 Bologna, Italy; (011) 51-39-228003, fax 227675.

Italian for Foreigners. Centro di Cultura Italiana Maremma is a small school in a countryside village of South Tuscany. Two-, 3-, and 4-week intensive language courses plus activities and excursions. Method: direct, student-centered, combination of conversation, grammar, lecture.

Dates: Every 2 weeks from Mar to Dec. Cost: LIT800,000 for 4 weeks; LIT450,000 for 2 weeks. Contact: Centro di Cultura Italiana Maremma, Via XX Settembre 79, 58014 Manciano, Italy; (011) 39-564-629382, fax 51-227675.

Italian Language and Culture in Tuscany. Regular 2- and 4-week courses of Italian at all levels. Plus Italian for business, art history, drawing, opera, Dante, Tuscan cooking. Art history "mini-breaks" a specialty. Also university semesters and pre-university courses. August season with opera near the Tuscan coast. Comprehensive service with accommodations. Excellent library facilities. Florence city center location.

Dates: Year round. Cost: From $150, depending on choice of course. Contact: Gillian

Parker, The British Institute of Florence, Lungarno Guicciardini 9, 50125, Firenze, Italy; (011) 39-55-284031, fax 289557; british@fol.it.

Italian Language Courses. Institute Galilei specializes in one-to-one courses held in Florence, in the countryside, and the island of Elba with tailored programs to fit the needs of the student. Training in specific vocabularies (economics, law, art history, etc.). All courses are divided into 10 levels. The Institute also organizes small group courses in 3 levels lasting from 2 weeks on.

Dates: One-to-one courses start and end on any days requested; small group courses start every 2 weeks. Cost: Starting from $349 per week. Contact: Institute Galilei, Ms. Alexandra Schmitz, Via degli Alfani 68, 50121 Florence, Italy; (011) 39-55-294680, fax 283481; institute.galilei@agora.stm.it.

Learn Italian and Get to Know Italy. Language expresses the history and the culture of a people; hence the study of a nation is strongly related to the study of its language. Italian language courses and information about social and cultural aspects in groups or individually. Four hours per day of language lessons Monday through Friday for a total of 20 hours per week. Classes organized in small homogeneous groups from 4-12 participants. Six different ability levels. Cultural information programs.

Dates: 1996: Jul 8, 29, Aug 19, Sep 9, 30, Oct 28, Nov 25. 1997: Jan 5, Feb 2, Mar 2, 30, Apr 27, May 25, Jun 15, Jul 6, Aug 17, Sep 7 28, Oct 26, Nov 23. Cost: 1996: group course 2 weeks (56 hours) $315, 3 weeks (82 hours) $420, 4 weeks (96 hours) $475. Prices for 1996 are $345, $460, $525. Contact: Dr. Phil Andrea Moradei, Director, Ms. Anja Schultz and Ms. Linda Larsson, Koiné Center, Via de' Pandolfini 27, I.50122 Firenze, Italy; (011) 39-55-213881, fax 216949.

Learning Italian in Sicily. Language courses which take place directly on one of the most beautiful beaches of Sicily. Small groups or students, full-time qualified teachers. Various

cultural and spare time activities: visiting of the archaeological mountains of Sicily, mountain biking.

Dates: Courses starting every second Sunday from Mar to Nov. Cost: Two-week course and apartment LIT720,000. Contact: Solemar, Via F. Perez 85a, I-90010 Aspra (PA), Sicily, Italy; (011) 39-335-453310, fax 91-955561.

Lorenzo de'Medici. Art history, Italian history and culture, cooking programs for adults. All conducted in English. Semester-summer classes-short-term programs. Learn Italian art history, cooking, civilization and culture in the heart of the Renaissance.

Dates: Every month year round. Cost: Package from $1,600, includes hotel, accommodations, meals, lectures, visits, field trips. Tuition: from $150. Contact: Dott. Arch. Gabriella Ganugi, Director, Lorenzo de'Medici, Via Faenza, #43, 50123 Florence, Italy; (011) 39-55-287143, fax (011) 39-55-23989 20/287203; ldm@dada.it.

Lorenzo de'Medici Language, Art, Culture. Language courses from 1 week up to 7 months. Art semesters and summer classes in the following subjects: painting, drawing, sculpture, architecture, photography, jewelry, textiles, printmaking, restoration of paintings and frescoes, ceramics, video production, art history, and liberal arts, cooking and wine tasting.

Dates: Year round. Cost: Package from $1,500 includes accommodations, meals, lectures, museum visits. Courses from $100. Contact: Dott. Arch. Gabriella Ganugi, Director, Lorenzo de'Medici, Via Faenza, #43, 50123 Florence, Italy; (011) 39-55-287143, fax (011) 39-55-23989 20/287203; ldm@dada.it.

Painting in the Hilltowns of Italy. The 4 painting workshops are held at La Romita facilities in a 16th century remodeled monastery in Umbria. For all levels of experience; 29 years of experience.

Dates: May 30-Jun 21; Jun 24-Jul 17; Jul 19-Aug 3; Aug 19-Sep 3. Cost: Sessions 1 and 2: $2,300; sessions 3 and 4: $1,600. Contact:

Paola Quargnali, La Romita School of Art, Inc., 1712 Old Town Rd., NW, Albuquerque, NM 87104; Tel./fax (505) 243-1924; quargnali@apsicc.aps.edu.

Piero Della Francesca. This new tour focuses specifically on the 15th century Italian artist Piero Della Francesca, allowing us to appreciate his most important works of art at first hand in the unspoiled towns of Tuscany, Umbria, and the Marches where he was born and spent most of his life. Other cultural tours throughout the world.

Dates: Jun 9, 1997. Cost: TBA. Contact: Emily Stokely, Andante Travels, Grange Cottage, Winterbourne Dauntsey, Salisbury, Wilts SP4 6ER, U.K.; (011) 44-1980-610555, fax 610002.

Summer Studies at SACI. Summer studies at Studio Art Centers International (SACI) are open to students enrolled in U.S. institutions who are seeking accredited summer study, independent non-credit students, mature students, and international students interested in studio arts, art history, art conservation, and Italian language. The following classes are offered: Drawing, Printing, Printmaking Workshop, Ceramics, Sculpture, Photography, Design Workshop, Batik and Fabric Design, Weaving, Jewelry, Renaissance Art History, Art Conservation, Italian Language.

Dates: May 22-Jun 23, and Jun 26-Jul 28, 1997. Cost: Tuition: $2,600; housing $750, activity fee $125. Contact: Jill Wooley, SACI Coordinator, U.S. Student Programs, Institute of International Education, 809 UN Plaza, New York, NY 10017; (800) 344-9186, (212) 984-5548, fax (212) 984-5325; jwooley@iie.org.

Tech Rome. Tech Rome is a 6-week summer travel-study program based in Rome. It features hotel housing, 3 meals per day, tours, and traditional classroom courses combined with field travel for college credit. Up to 13 semester hours may be earned in a choice of over 10 courses in diverse subject areas. Courses are taught by American professors.

All disciplines are accredited.

Dates: May 27-Jul 4, 1997. Cost: $4,328 includes tuition, all housing for 6 weeks, 3 meals per day, tours. Group flights available. Optional travel available. Contact: Tech Rome, P.O. Box 3172, Ruston, LA 71272; (800) 346-8324.

Jamaica

Tropical Marine Biology. Twelve-day course in the biology of Caribbean seashores and coral reefs for persons with a serious interest in snorkeling, shelling and understanding the complex marine biology of the region. Explore sunken shipwreck, fringing and barrier coral reefs, mangrove swamps, rocky shores. Observe animals in our aquaria. Course at Hofstra Univ. Marine Laboratory.

Dates: Jul 10-21, 1997. Cost: $1,400 (no credit), $2,200 graduate or undergraduate credit (includes airfare, room and board at our own watefront hotel). Contact: Dr. E. Kaplan, Director, Hofstra Univ. Marine Lab, Gittelson Hall 114, Hempstead, NY 11550; (516) 463-5520, fax (516) 463-6010; bioehk@vaxc.hofst ra.edu.

Japan

Asian Studies Program. The program has a wide variety of course offerings in both language and non-language studies on Asia and Japan. All classes except Japanese language are conducted in English. Our successful homestay program has contributed to the rapid development of students' personal and intercultural growth as well as their language skills.

Dates: Fall semester: Aug 28-Dec 13, 1996; spring semester: Jan 29-May 24, 1997. Cost: For 1 semester: tuition $6,000, homestay ¥290,000, dormitory ¥170,000 (no meals). Contact: Center for International Education, Kansai Gadai Univ., 16-1 Kitakatahoko-cho, Hirakata City, Osaka 573 Japan; (011) 81-720-51-6751, fax 50-9011; i52419@sakura.kudpc. kyoto_u.ac.jp.

Lex Homestay Programs. Lex offers homestay programs in which participants, living as members of a Japanese family, absorb the customs and characteristics of their host culture by taking part in daily life activities. Participants may go sightseeing with their families, meet friends and relatives, and attend festivals. Japanese language ability is not a requirement. Host families are fully screened volunteer members of the Lex organization. Adults, students, and entire families are encouraged to apply.

Dates: Jul-Aug 2, 4- and 6-week programs. Spring, 2-week program. Custom programs year round. Cost: Varies. Four-week summer program is $3,030, includes airfare from West Coast port of departure. Contact: Steffi Samman, Program Manager, Lex America, 68 Leonard St., Belmont, MA 02178; (617) 489-5800, fax (617) 489-5898; exchange@lex lrf.com.

Latin America

Volunteer in Nicaragua or Brazil. In Nicaragua you help to construct a school and a water supply and assist in a pre-school. You travel and study in the country and in Central America. In Brazil you live in a rural community, work in construction, and travel and study throughout the country. The Nicaragua program lasts 11 months, and the Brazil program lasts 6 months. Both include preparation and follow-up periods in the U.S. The programs are open to persons 18 years of age and older.

Dates: Nicaragua: Sep 15, 1996, and 1997; Brazil: Jan 4, 1997. Cost: Nicaragua: $4,600; Brazil: $3,400. Includes training, room and board, airfare, health insurance, and other direct program costs. Contact: Josefin Jonsson, Administrative Director, IICD, Institute for International Cooperation and Development, P.O. Box 103-T, Williamstown, MA 01267; (413) 458-9828, fax (413) 458-3323; iicd1@ berkshire.net, www.berkshire.net/~iicd1.

Latvia

Latvian Summer Course. The University summer course comprises Latvian language (beginners and advanced) and background courses in English (History, Ethnography, Literature, Politics) as well as excursions and theater and museum visits.

Dates: Mid-Jul-mid-Aug. Cost: Full price $850 (includes accommodations). Contact: Andrejs Veisbergs, Univ. of Latvia, Visvalza 4a, Riga, LV-1011, Latvia; (011) 7-371-7228837, fax 7820113.

Luxembourg

Miami Univ.-Dolibois Euro Center. One semester or full academic year. Courses taught in English; collateral study in French or German required. Seminars, tutorials, research, field work also used for instruction. Students live with host families in the heart of Europe. Approximately 100 students a semester. Average class size is 20. Apply by Jan 24.

Dates: Sep 7-Dec 21 (fall), Jan 12-May 13 (spring). Cost: One semester (state resident): $7,507; out-of-state $9,894. Contact: Dr. Annette Tomarken, MUDEC Coordinator, Langstroth Cottage, Oxford, OH 45056; (513) 523-8603, fax (513) 529-5051; mudec oxford@ msmail.muohio.edu.

Malta

Escorted Explorations. Sunny Mediterranean island offers an amazing span of history that includes one of the earliest civilizations on earth. Lectures and expert presentations supplement a full schedule of intensive site visits. Unique 9-day focused programs include: Architectural Study, Romance of Baroque, Vanishing Ancients, Sacred Spaces, Women's Study.

Dates: Fall, Winter, Spring. Cost: From $1,687 plus air. Contact for details on specific special interest programs. Contact: The OTS Foundation, P.O. Box 214, Lincolnshire, IL 60069-0214; (847) 949-1940, fax (847) 949-7059; otsf@aol.com.

Mexico

Art and Archaeology of Oaxaca. Workshops in the Oaxaca Valley of Mexico, considered the folk art capital of Mexico and set in the midst of an archaeologist's dream. Classes include ceramics, hats and masks, metals/jewelry, baskets and paper, Mesoamerican archaeology. Fall program during Day of the Dead plus one week in Jan and Mexico City "Add-On" options.
Dates: Oct 27-Nov 4, 1996, Jan 2-10, and Mar 6-14, 1997. Cost: $995 (tuition, room, board, field trips). Contact: HORIZONS, Jane Sinauer, Director, 108 N. Main St.-1st, Sunderland, MA 01375; Tel./fax (413) 665-4141.

Copper Canyon. Outstanding cultural and natural history rail trips. The most dramatic train ride in the western hemisphere. Deeper, wider, greener canyons than Arizona's Grand Canyon. Tarahumara Indian culture, nature walks, birding, waterfalls, spectacular vistas. Historic tours, small groups, personal attention. In-depth interpretation of the Copper Canyon and its people.
Dates: Year round. Cost: $1,695 per person for 8-day trips. Contact: S&S Tours, 865 El Camino Real, Sierra Vista, AZ 85635; (800) 499-5685, fax (520) 458-5258; ss@theriver.com.

Educational Community. Cemanahuac offers intensive Spanish language instruction by native speakers: academic credit, graduate and undergraduate; Latin American studies classes, with emphasis on the social reality of Mexico; strong field study programs led by anthropologists; rural studies program in a Mexican village; summer programs for educators; volunteer opportunities near the school; family stay program; special classes for professionals.
Dates: Year round program. New classes begin every Mon. Group programs arranged at reduced fees. Cost: Registration fee $90 (one-time fee); weekly tuition $190; housing with 3 meals per day $17 (double), $23 (single). Contact: Vivian B. Harvey, Educational Programs Coordinator, Apartado 5-21, Cuernavaca, Morelos, Mexico; (011) 52-73-18-6407 or 73-12-6419, fax 73-12-5418; 74052.2570@compuserve.com.

El Bosque del Caribe, Cancun. Take a professional Spanish course, 25 hours per week and enjoy the Caribbean beaches. Relaxed family atmosphere. No more than 6 students per class. Special conversation program. Mexican cooking classes and excursions to the Mayan sites. Housing with Mexican families. College credit available.
Dates: Year round. New classes begin every Monday. Group programs arranged at reduced fees. Cost: Enrollment fees $75, $175 per week, 1 week with a Mexican family $150. Contact: Eduardo Sotelo, Director, Calle Piña 1, S.M. 25, 77500 Cancún, Mexico; (011) 52-98-84-10-38, fax 84-58-88; bcaribe@mail.interacces.com.mx.

I.L.E.M., Mazatlán Mexico. The program at Instituto de la Lengua Española de Mazatlán includes 5 hours of daily language instruction (M-F). Conducted solely in Spanish, accommodations with a Mexican family, 3 meals daily and transportation from the airport to Mazatlán. Educational tours, golf, tennis, sport fishing, and gorgeous beaches await.
Dates: Jan, Jun-Aug, Dec, 1996. Semester stays may be arranged. Classes begin every Monday. Cost: Two weeks $800, 4 weeks $1,200, $300 each additional week. Contact: The Enrollment Center, 35 Thurlow Ave., Revere, MA 02151; (617) 284-6973.

Instituto Cultural Oaxaca/Spanish. Seven hours daily of intensive Spanish instruction in a lovely Oaxacan estate. Grammar, conversation, workshops in cooking, weaving, and pottery, one-on-one native speaking conversation partners, lectures and films are all part of the total immersion process. Tours to archaeological sites, artisan villages, and indigenous marketplaces. Homestays available.

Dates: Year round monthly sessions. Write, call, or fax for specific dates and informative brochure. Cost: $50 registration fee and $400 per session or $105 per week. Contact: Lic Lucero Topete, Director, Instituto Cultural Oaxaca, Apartado Postal #340, Oaxaca, Oaxaca, C.P. 68000, Mexico; (011)-52-951-53404, fax (011) 52-951-53728; inscuoax@antequera.com, http://antequera.com/inscuoax/.

Intensive Spanish in Cuauhnahuac. Cuauhnahuac, founded in 1972, offers a variety of intensive and flexible programs geared to individual needs. Six hours of classes daily with no more than 4 students to a class. Housing with Mexican families who really care about you. Cultural conferences, excursions, and special classes for professionals. College credit available.

Dates: Year round. New classes begin every Monday. Cost: $70 registration fee; $600 4 weeks tuition, housing $16 per night. Contact: Marcia Snell, 519 Park Dr., Kenilworth, IL 60043; (800) 245-9335, fax (847) 256-9475; lankysam@aol.com..

Intensive Spanish in Yucatan. Centro de Idiomas del Sureste, A.C. (CIS), founded in 1974, offers 3-5 hours per day of intensive conversational Spanish classes with native-speaking, university-trained professors. Maximum 6 students per group, average 3. Program includes beginner courses to very advanced with related field trips and recommended optional homestay. Also special classes in business, legal, medical vocabulary, or Mayan studies.

Dates: Year round. Starts any Monday, except last 2 weeks in Dec. Cost: Tuition (three hours per day program): $330 first 2 weeks, $115 each additional week, tuition (5 hours per day program): $490 first 2 weeks, $195 each additional week. Contact: Chloe C. Pacheco, Director, Centro de Idiomas del Sureste, A.C., Calle 14 #106 x 25, col. Mexico, CP 97128, Mérida, Yucatán, México; (011) 52-99-26-11-55 or (011) 52-99-26-94-94, 20-28-10, fax 26-90-20; cis@yucatan.com.m.

Intensive Spanish Summer Program. The Intensive Spanish Summer Program is a language immersion program of 5 hours of instruction daily, Monday through Friday. Students may enroll for 6 semester credits for the 6-week program or 4 semester credits for the 4-week course.

Dates: Six-week: Jun 23-Aug 7, 1997; 4-week: Jun 23-Jul 24, 1997. Cost: Six week: $2,060; 4-week $1,716 (registration, tuition, housing, meals and services). Contact: Lic. Ma. Eugenia Castro-Septién, Universidad Iberoamericana, A.C. Prol. Paseo de la Reforma #880, Col. Lomas de Sante Fe, México, D.F. 01210; (011) 525-292-1883, fax 292-1266; ecastro@hermes.uia.mx.

Junior Year Abroad. Emphasis is on Spanish language and courses related to Mexico and Latin America, all of which are conducted in Spanish. Students with high enough level of Spanish can choose courses from the regular departments. A normal semester load is 4 or 5 courses which earn 12-15 semester credits.

Dates: Spring semester: Jan 10, 1997; fall semester: Aug 8, 1997. Cost: Spring semester: $3,495; fall semester: $3,550 (registration, tuition, housing, field trips and services). Contact: Lic. Ma. Eugenia Castro-Septién, Universidad Iberoamericana, A.C. Prol. Paseo de la Reforma #880, Col. Lomas de Sante Fe, México, D.F. 01210; (011) 525-292-1883, fax 292-1266; ecastro@hermes.uia.mx.

Language Institute of Colima. The Language Institute of Colima Mexico offers a system of total immersion with classes held throughout the year Monday-Friday. Students live with local host families and attend 6 hours of instruction daily; no more than 5 students per class. Many extras, including beach excursions, are included.

Dates: Year round, Monday-Friday. Cost: Registration $80; tuition $415 1st week, $345 after 1st week (for shared room), $445 1st week, $375 after 1st week (for private room). 10% discount for 6 or more. Contact: Dennis Bourassa, Language Institute of Colima, P.O. Box 827, Miranda, CA 95553; (800) 604-6579, fax (707) 923-4232; colima@northcoast.com, www.northcoast.com/~colima

Learn, Live, and Love Spanish in the Land of the Maya (Chiapas). Spanish lessons in private sessions or small groups (4 people max). Family stays available. School tours to Indian (Mayan) villages, jungle trips available. Extracurricular activities included: Mexican cooking, discussions, video showings. Teach English in exchange for Spanish lessons. Centro Cultural "El Puente" includes gallery weaver's cooperative, travel agency, cafe, restaurant, phone/fax service.

Dates: Year round. Cost: Highest $220 per week; lowest $75 per week. Contact: Roberto Rivas, Bastidas Centro Bilingüe de Chiapas, C. Real de Guadalupe 55, Centro Cultural "El Puente," San Cristóbal de Las Casas 29230, Chiapas, Mexico; (011) 52-967-8-41-57, fax 967-83723 or Tel./fax (800) 303-4983; cenbili@chisnet.com.mx, www.mexonline. com/centro1.htm.

Loyola Univ. in Mexico City. Loyola offers 17 Spanish courses as well as courses on Latin American studies, communications, economics, history, political science, philosophy, sociology, and visual arts at the Jesuit Universidad Iberoamericana in Mexico City. Financial aid available. Trips to Cuernavaca, Taxco, Teotihuacan, and Tula. Three summer sessions and semester and year abroad program available.

Dates: Jan 7-May 15; May 30-Jul 12; Jun 23-Jul 24; Jun 23-Aug 7; Aug 8-Dec 5 , 1997; Jan 9-May 14, 1998. Cost: $2,480 and $2,160 for 6- and 4-week sessions; $6,758 for 17-week semester program. Contact: Maurice P. Brungardt, Director, Mexico Program, Loyola Univ., New Orleans, LA 70118; (504) 865-3539 day, (504) 861-3402 evening, fax (504) 865-2010; brungard@beta.loyno.edu.

Mar de Jade. Tropical ocean-front retreat center in a beautiful unspoiled fishing village near Puerto Vallarta offers unique learning experiences. Study Spanish in small groups and enjoy great swimming, kayaking, hiking, massages, and stress-reduction meditation. Gain further insight into local culture by studying and working in a farmers' clinic, local construction, cottage industries, or teaching.

Dates: Year round. Cost: $865 for 21-day work/study. Includes room (shared occupancy), board, 12 hours per week of Spanish and 15 hours per week of work. Longer resident program available at lower cost. Vacation/ Spanish 1-week minimum $365 room, board, 12 hours of Spanish. Vacation only $45 per night for any length of time. Contact: In Mexico: Mar de Jade/Casa Clinica, A.P. 81, Las Varas, Nayarit, 63715, Mexico; Tel./fax (011) 52-327-20184; In U.S.: P.O. Box 423353, San Francisco, CA 94142; (415) 281-0164.

Retire in Mexico Program. Led by the publisher of Retire in Mexico Updates & Business News, this fully escorted, fun, educational experience explores Ajijic (Lake Chapala), the number one retirement haven outside the U.S. Exclusive seminar (Health Care, Immigration, Real Estate and more), fabulous meals, lakeside hotel, a chance to meet local retirees, and much more.

Dates: Sep and Nov 1996. Contact for 1997 schedule. Cost: $689 (double occupancy) land only. Contact: Retire in Mexico, 40 4th St., Suite 203, Petaluma, CA 94952; (707) 765-4573, fax (707) 778-1080.

Six-Week Summer Session. Students enroll in 2 courses which meet daily for 90 minutes each. Language and literature courses in Spanish and courses in English relating to Mexico and Latin America. Students can earn credits to be transferred to their university.

Dates: May 30-Jul 12, 1997. Cost: $1,920 (registration, tuition, housing, meals, 3 field trips and services). Contact: Lic. Ma. Eugenia Castro-Septién, Universidad Iberoamericana, A.C. Prol. Paseo de la Reforma #880, Col. Lomas de Sante Fe, México, D.F. 01210; (011) 525-292-1883, fax 292-1266; ecastro@hermes.uia.mx.

Spanish. Our time-tested total immersion program is an oral-based technique which is designed to encourage the practical use of the language skills through imitation, interaction, structured drills and dialogues in a role-playing environment.

Dates: Courses start every Monday. Cost: Registration $100; tuition per week $150; room and board $18 per night per person. Contact: Cuernavaca Language School, Apdo. 4-254, 62430 Cuernavaca, Mexico; Tel./fax (73) 17-5151. International Office: P.O. Box 4133, Windham, NH 03087-4133; (603) 437-9714, fax (603) 437-6412.

Spanish as a Second Language. SSL through total immersion is a unique course designed by the language department of the Universidad del Mayab and includes Spanish language study, lectures, and visits to archaeological sites and modern communities. A call option is offered to interested students and consists of an interactive, multimedia language experience.

Dates: Rolling admissions. New classes begin on Mondays. Cost: $480 for 2 weeks (individual); $400 per person in groups of 8 or more. Contact: Universidad del Mayab, Language Dept., Apdo. Postal 96, Cordemex, Yucatan, Mexico 97310; Fax (011) 52 99 22 00-06.

Spanish Language in Guanajuato. We work with our students one-on-one or in small groups (2 to 5 students), tailoring instruction to each student's needs. We teach people of all ages and from many nationalities. Highlights: homestays with families, sports, movies, field trips, hikes, cultural events—all this taking place in the most beautiful colonial setting of Mexico.

Dates: Year round. New classes begin every Monday. Cost: $925. Includes lifetime registration fee, group classes (5 sessions per day Monday-Friday), and a homestay with 3 meals daily for 4 weeks. Lower price for fewer weeks. Contact: Director Jorge Barroso, Instituto Falcon, A.C., Guanajuato, Gto. 36000 Mexico; Tel./fax (011) 52-473-2-36-94, www.infonet.com.mx/falcon.

Spanish Learning Adventure in the Land of the Maya. Centro Bilingue combines an intensive Spanish learning program—80 hours of instruction—with the adventure of exploring living Maya towns, ecological reserves, natural attractions, Maya ruins, and much more. In the heart of Chiapas, Mexico. Regular programs are also available.

Dates: Year round starting first Monday of each month, 4 weeks. Cost: $2,140. Includes tuition, registration, meals, lodging, transportation (not airfare), taxes. Contact: Roberto Rivas, Centro Bilingue, C. Real de Guadalupe 55, "El Puente," San Cristobal de Las Casas, Chiapas, Mexico; Tel./fax (011) 52-967-83723.

Third World Opportunities (TWO). TWO is an awareness-building program designed to utilize the border with Mexico as a classroom in teaching participants the realities of hunger, poverty, and border issues. It offers opportunities to serve in developmental kinds of response to need, such as the house-building program of Habitat for Humanity in Tecate.

Dates: Weekend awareness trips; 6-day work projects spring and summer. Cost: Weekends $20 per person plus transportation; 6 day $200 per person. Contact: M. Laurel Gray, Third World Opportunities, 1363 Somermont Dr., El Cajon, CA 92021; (619) 449-9381.

Travel/Study Seminars. Learn from Mexicans

of diverse backgrounds about their economic, political, and social realities. Emphasis on the views of the poor and oppressed. Programming in Cuernavaca, Mexico City, and Chiapas. Call for a free list of upcoming programs.

Dates: Ongoing. Cost: $800-$1,900 depending on package, destination, and length of trip. Contact: Center for Global Education, Augsburg College, 2211 Riverside Ave., Box 307TR, Minneapolis, MN 55454; (800) 299-8889, fax (612) 330-1695; globaled@augsburg.edu, www.augsburg.edu/global.

Univ. of St. Thomas in Merida. This is a 6-week academic program. During the Houston segment (2 weeks) the students will have an in-depth introduction to the history and culture of Mexico as well as daily Spanish language studies. In Merida (4 weeks) students will be required to speak Spanish. They will also participate in exciting field trips to archaeological sites outside of Merida, concerts, etc. The Progreso beach is only about 45 minutes away.

Dates: May 28-Jul 2, 1997. Cost: $2,399. Contact: Prof. Elsa Zambosco-Thomas, Univ. of St. Thomas, 3800 Montrose Blvd., Houston, TX 77006; (713) 525-3123, fax (713) 525-2125.

Wilderness: Alaska/Mexico. Backpack Copper Canyon and Baja, sea kayak Baja, raft and explore Mayan ruins in Chiapas. Providing ecologically and culturally sensitive trips in small groups. Led by owner with assistance by local guides. Over 20 years experience in Mexico.

Dates: Mid-Dec.-mid-Mar. Cost: $875-$1,275. Contact: Wilderness: Alaska/Mexico, 1231-TA Sundance Loop, Fairbanks, AK 99709; Tel./fax (907) 479-8203; http://ecotravel.com.wam.

Nepal

Ecosystems and Cultures of Nepal. Join U.S. and Nepali research specialists for an in-depth investigation of the remarkable environmental and cultural elements in the undisturbed ecosystems of Nepal. Engage in a first-hand exploration of Nepal's intertwined natural and human histories. Previous fieldwork experience not required. Projects earns 9 to 14 university credits. Application deadline: May 30, 1997 or until programs are full. Additional programs in Thailand, Russia, New Zealand, and Mexico.

Dates: Jul 1-Aug 18 (summer program); Oct 8-Nov 29 (fall program). Cost: $1,900 academic fee. Contact: Crandall Bay, Director, Wildlands Studies, 3 Mosswood Circle, Cazadero, CA 95421; (707) 632-5665.

Himalayan Health Expedition. Twenty-three day trip for medical professionals of all disciplines, students, anyone interested in public or international health. Led by Nepalese physician. Visits to modern facilities and 12-day trek to remote villages. See healing trances and rituals of shamans, pundits, and Tibetan healers in villages. Trek past famous Himalayan peaks. Maximum elevation about 12,000 feet.

Dates: Scheduled departures Oct and Jan. Other departures arranged for minimum of 4 participants. Cost: Land cost approx. $2,595. Contact: Lillian Jenkins, Coordinator, Journeys International, 4011 Jackson Rd., Ann Arbor, MI 48103; (800) 255-8735 or (313) 665-4407, fax (313) 665-2945; journeysmi@aol.com, www.journeys-intl.com or www.gorp.com/journeys.htm.

Placement for Volunteer Service. Provides opportunities to those interested in contributing their time and skills to worthwhile community groups throughout Nepal. We arrange a limited number of volunteer placements involving either teaching or working in various organizations.

Dates: Feb, Apr, and Aug 1997. Cost: $600 program fee and visa fee depending on length of stay. Contact: Naresh M. Shrestha, Director, Insight Nepal, P.O. Box 6760, Kathmandu, Nepal; (011) 977-1-418-964, fax 223515 or 416144.

Sojourn Nepal. Sojourn Nepal is a 12-week program comprised of language study, homestay, lectures, trekking, and opportunities for apprenticeships in a vast variety of areas. Cultural immersion at its finest.

Dates: Fall and spring semesters. Cost: $4,500 all inclusive. Airfare not included. Contact: Jennifer Warren, Sojourn Nepal, 2440 N. 56th St., Phoenix, AZ 85008; Tel./fax (602) 840-9197; snepal@aol.com.

Study Abroad in Nepal. Join the Naropa Institute (NCA accredited) program introducing students to the living traditions of Nepal. Develop a greater appreciation of yourself and the world through courses taught by Nepali scholars, artists, and Naropa faculty in meditation, Buddhist traditions, arts and culture, dance, music, language, and independent study/travel.

Dates: Early-Sep-mid-Dec, 1997 Cost: $6,500 (1996). Includes tuition (12 semester credits), room and board, program expenses. Airfare not included. Contact: Study Abroad Office, The Naropa Institute, 2130 Arapahoe Ave., Boulder, CO 80302; (303) 546-3594, fax (303) 444-0410.

Papua New Guinea

New Guinea Experience. Spend 8 days and 7 nights in a remote area of the Sepik Basin at Karawari Lodge in the middle of a lowland rainforest. Explore the many sites of the coastline north of Madang and stay at Malolo Plantation overlooking the Bismar Sea.

Dates: Every Friday. Cost: $1,654 per person on share basis (land only). Contact: C/ - UNIREP Ltd., 850 Colorado Blvd., #105, Los Angeles, CA 90041; (800) 521-7242 or (213) 256-1991, fax (213) 256-0647.

Peru

California Institute for Peruvian Studies (CIPS). CIPS, working under a special permit from the Peruvian government, is conducting archaeological expeditions in the Acari River Valley of south coastal Peru. Sites span from 1200 B.C. through the arrival of the Spaniards. Archaeological field schools, Feb-Aug 1997 will be taught by specially selected professionals and include excavation, textile and pottery analysis, field methods, cultural history, physical anthropology, museology, and more. To date over 100 sites have been located. Few sites have been collected, mapped, photographed, and documented. College credit is available. Flexible independent adventure travelers are encouraged to apply. Space is limited.

Dates: Mar-Sep 97. Cost: $800-$2,300 depending on time spent at sites. Machu Picchu, Colca Canyon, and the Amazon included in some field schools. Ask for details. Contact: CIPS, 45 Quakie Way, Bailey, CO 80421; (303) 838-1215 or (800) 444-1285 for application.

Rainforests of Peru. See the rainforest with International Expeditions. The world leader in nature travel, we offer small group, ecologically responsible expeditions to the Peruvian Amazon. Now there are 2 ways to enjoy the adventure: by land, in rustic but comfortable lodges, or by air-conditioned riverboat. Write or call for color brochures.

Cost: Eight-day programs, all-inclusive from Miami start at $1,798; optional Cusco and Machu Picchu Extension $1,098. Contact: International Expeditions Inc., One Environs Park, Helena, AL 35080; (800) 623-4734, fax (205) 428-1714.

Puerto Rico

Euskalduna Instituto Internacional. Comprehensive language learning and culture program on a beautiful Caribbean island. Travel with 2 weeks notice, no passport or visa needed. We offer: communicative, learner-centered classes with a maximum of 6 students. U.S. university credit; monthly calendar of events; classes at all levels; and an optional homestay program.

Dates: Classes begin first and third Monday of every month (except on Jan 6 and Sep 1, 1997). Cost: Starting at $555 per week (minimum 2-week stay); price includes accommodations, meals and class materials. Contact: Director of Study Abroad, NESOL/EII, Edif. Euskalduna, Calle Navarro #56, Hato Rey, PR 00918; (787) 281-8013, fax (787) 274-8291.

Russia and the NIS

Culture, History and Language. This international travel program provides an opportunity to participate in an exciting experience in Russia. General programs offer instruction in culture, history and language. In special programs participants select field study, research, environmental science, biology and ecology, and space science.

Dates: Jul-Aug (3 weeks). Cost: $2,495. Contact: Jack Scheckner, International Education Center, P.O. Box 843, Bowling Green Station, New York, NY 11274.

Sweep of Russian History: Up-Close. Bed and Breakfast stays with English-speaking Russian families provide a glimpse of Russian life today as it undergoes sweeping transformation. Ten-day program includes private guided tours of major museums and excursions to nearby villages. Cities of Moscow and St. Petersburg are favorites but program is tailor-made to suit individual interests.

Dates: Open. Cost: From $1,550 per person for 10 days based on double occupancy all-inclusive of air, transfers, B and B accommodations, professionally guided tours. Contact: IBV Bed & Breakfast Systems, 13113 Ideal Dr., Silver Spring, MD 20906; (301) 942-3770, fax (301) 933-0024.

South Seas

AFAR in the South Seas. Here is a once in a lifetime chance to join an archaeological expedition—excavating and mapping 1,000 year-old archaeological ruins in the Vallahu Valley on Marquesean Island, 600 miles northeast of Tahiti. Dr. Barry Rolett will be in charge and will arrange room and board near the site, as well as transportation (at your tax deductible expense) from Tahiti. You will also be responsible for transportation and overnighting in Tahiti (also a tax deductible donation).

Dates: Three groups of 4 to 6: Jun 30-Jul 14, Jul 14-28, Jul 28-Aug 11, 1996. Cost: $2,500 (tax deductible contribution). Contact: Dr. Barry V. Rolett, Dept. of Anthropology, Univ. of Hawaii, Honolulu, HI 96822; (808) 956-7546; or Dr. Richard S. MacNeish, AFAR, Box 83, Andover, MA 01810; (508) 470-0840.

Spain

Don Quijote (Barcelona, Granada, Salamanca). Don Quijote, Europe's largest specialist in in-country Spanish language courses, offers courses of 2-36 weeks in intensive Spanish, DELE (official diploma preparation), Spanish, plus specialization (business, tourism, international secretary), refresher courses for teachers of Spanish, flight attendance course, combination courses, tailor-made individual courses, summer and Christmas courses.

Dates: Year round. Cost: Depends on course, duration, and accommodations. Contact: Don Quijote, Central Promotion Office (Ref. USAS96), Ms. Elvira Zingone, Student Services, Apdo. de Correos 333, 37080 Salamanca; (011) 34-23-26-88-60, fax 23-26-88-15; donquijote@offcampus.es.

Language and Culture Courses (Madrid, Salamanca, Malaga). Escuela Internacional offers quality programs in Spanish language and culture with U.S. undergraduate credits. Our qualified teachers and small classes (maximum 12 students per class) guarantee you a successful program. Stay with a selected family or in a shared apartment. Enjoy our extensive afternoon activities and weekend excursions. Our professionalism, enthusiasm, and personal touch will make your experience in Spain memorable and fun.

Dates: Year round, 2-48 weeks. Cost: From PTS54,500 for 2 weeks (tuition 15 hours per week, room, books) to PTS107,500 (30 hours per week, room and full board, books, activities, excursion). Contact: Escuela Internacional, Midori Ishizaka, Director of Admissions, c/Talamanca 10, 28807 Alcalá de Henares, Madrid, Spain; (011) 34-1-8831264, fax (011) 34-1-8831301; escuelai@ergos.es, www.ergos.es/escuelai.

Learn Spanish in Spain. Language immersion courses in Spain (Barcelona, Canary Islands, Granada, Madrid, Malaga, San Sebastian, Seville, and Valencia). Private language schools centrally located, convenient to interesting places, cultural events, sports activities. Programs feature qualified teachers, small classes, attractive surroundings and facilities. Affordable prices for instruction. Accommodations with Spanish families with meals, student residences, apartments, and nearby hotels.

Dates: Year round. Two weeks or more. Cost: Two-week courses with or without accommodations range from $245-$865. Contact: Ms. Lorraine Haber, Study Abroad Coordinator, CES Study Abroad Program, The Center for English Studies, 330 7th Ave., 6th Floor, New York, NY 10001; (212) 629-7300, fax (212) 736-7950.

Painting in Barcelona. A celebrated Spanish faculty made up of Tom Carr and Carme Miquel will conduct a 3-week advanced painting workshop at the spacious studio of Escola d'Arts Plastiques i Disseny "Llotja." Included are 3 museum tours to the Antonio Tapies Foundation, the Miro Foundation, and the Picasso Museum. Three credits.

Dates: Jun 21-Jul 13, 1997. Cost: $2,230. Includes double occupancy rooms, continental breakfast daily, and 3 tours. Contact: Dora Riomayor, Director of International Studies, School of Visual Arts, 209 E. 23rd St., New York, NY 10010-3994; (212) 592-2543.

Semester in Spain. Semester, year, and summer programs for high school graduates, college students, and adult learners. Beginning, intermediate, and advanced Spanish language studies along with Spanish literature, culture, history, and art. All courses taught in Spanish by native Spaniards. Four courses per semester, 4 credits each. Homestays are arranged for all students. January term and summer terms also.

Dates: Fall: Aug 26-Dec 18; spring: Jan 27-May 22; summer: May 30-Jun 25 and/or Jun 30-Jul 23. Cost: Fall or spring $8,000; year approx. $16,000; summer and Jan term approx. $2,000 each term. Includes tuition, books, room and board, and airfare for spring and fall semesters. Contact: Debra Veenstra, U.S. Coordinator, Semester in Spain, 6001 W. College Dr., Palos Heights, IL 60463; (800) 748-0087 or (708) 239-4766, fax (708) 385-5665.

Spanish in Malaga, Andalucia. Frequently called Spain's leading school of Spanish, Malaca Instituto offers general Spanish courses in small groups year-round at all levels. We have many European and Japanese students but very few Americans. Facilities include: video rooms, cinema, language lab, study center, bar, restaurant, pool, and on-site residential accommodations. We organize a comprehensive program of cultural and social activities.

Dates: Every two weeks from Jan 8, 1996 and from Jan 6, 1997. Cost: Course: from PTS72,900; accommodations from PTS62,300. Contact: Bob Burger, Malaca Instituto, c/Cortada 6, Cerrado de Calderon, 29018 Malaga, Spain; (011) 34-5-229-32-42, fax 229-63-16.

Spanish Intensive Courses. Spanish courses all year round. Four levels, 4 hours per day, maximum 13 students. Also private lessons. Accommodations in students residence near the beach half-board.

Dates: Any Monday of the year. Cost: Tuition: PTS13,000 ($100). Accommodations:

PTS25,000 single room, PTS18,000 double room. Contact: Oliver Belz, Director; (011) 34-28-267971, fax 278980; geschool@intercom.es.

Summer Courses for Older Teenagers. Frequently called Spain's leading school of Spanish, Malaca Instituto has created a special program for young people. It combines serious study of Spanish with a program of sports and cultural activities. Accommodations in our on-site residence or with host families. Facilities include: video rooms, language lab, cinema, restaurant, pool, and sun terraces.

Dates: Jun 23; Jul 7; Jul 21; Aug 4; Aug 18, 1997. Cost: Course: from PTS40,000; accommodations from PTS32,540. Contact: Bob Burger, Malaca Instituto, c/Cortada 6, Cerrado de Calderon, 29018 Malaga, Spain; (011) 34-5-229-32-42, fax 229-63-16.

The Center for Cross-Cultural Study. Learn and live in the vibrant city of Seville. CC-CS, now in its 27th year, offers 2 3-1/2-week summer sessions and January term with intensive courses in language, civilization, and literature. Upper division academic year and semester programs with courses in liberal arts, social sciences, business, and current events. Intensive intermediate program offers language, literature, civilization, and current events. Homestay and study tours included.

Dates: Jun, Jul, Sep-Dec, Jan, Feb-May. Cost: Fall $7,440; academic year $14,770; Jan $1,910; spring $7,440; summer $1,755 per session. Includes tuition, room and board, study tours, fees, laundry, and orientation. Contact: In the U.S.: CC-CS, Dept. T, 446 Main St., Amherst, MA 01002; (413) 256-0011 or (800) ESPANA-1 [(800) 377-2621], fax (413) 256-1968. In Spain: CC-CS, Calle Harinas, 18, 41001 Sevilla, Spain; (011) 34-5-422-4107, fax (011) 34-5-422-9204; www.cccs.com.

Switzerland

Bookbinding and Book Restoration. Centro del bel libro is a professional school for artisanal bookbinding and book restoration. Courses are offered on the quarter system.

Dates: Call or write for information. Cost: Call or write for information. Contact: Christina Bordoli, Director, Centro del bel libro, Ascona, 6612 Ascona, via Collegio, Centro culturale B. Berno, Switzerland; (011) 41-91-791-72-36, fax 791-72-56.

United Kingdom

Acorn Cultural Courses in London. London cultural courses are designed for the discerning traveler who wishes to enhance their knowledge while on vacation in this wonderful city of culture. Courses are run fortnightly from May to Aug and are taught by specialists in a variety of fields, such as art, architecture and theater.

Cost: From $995 per course. Tuition fees, admission fees and accommodations in apartments all included. Contact: Mr. J. Watkins, Acorn Management Services Ltd., P.O. Box 3031, London NW7 H2A, U.K.; (011) 44-81-905-3525, fax 905-3429.

Basics to Bernaise. An intensive 4-week residential course, taking students through all the methods and principles more frequently covered in a much longer course. The course builds on knowledge gained, progressing from basic principles to complex techniques with the emphasis on practical hands-on cookery.

Dates: Jan-Nov. Cost: £1,590-£1,750. Contact: Jane Averill, Cookery at the Grange, Whatley, Frome, Somerset BA11 3LA, U.K.

Beginners' Hat Making. This practical course will give step-by-step instructions on how to make 1 or possibly 2 hats in straw or felt using traditional hand blocking and finishing techniques. All materials can be purchased from the tutor but students should expect to spend approximately £40. This course is suitable for beginners but basic sewing skills are necessary.

Dates: July-September. Cost: Approx. £275.

Contact: Dillington House, Ilminster, Somerset TA19 9DT, UK.

Bobbin Lacemaking. This is a practical course aimed to give lacemakers the confidence to try a different type of lace, or gain more experience in their favorites. Students will be able to make Torchon, Bedfordshire, Buckinghamsh ire, Bruges, Flanders, Paris or Binche laces. This course is for students with some experience who should be able to work the basic stitches.

Dates: July-September. Cost: Approx. £275. Contact: Dillington House, Ilminster, Somerset TA19 9DT, UK.

British Studies at Oxford. British Studies at Oxford is designed to give vital, first-hand exposure to the historical, artistic, political, cultural, and commercial milieu that informed literary and political works, business management, communication, educational theories, and fine arts studied in our courses. The participants live in private rooms tidied daily by the college staff, who also serve 3 bountiful and tasty meals a day in the Great Hall. Wednesdays are travel days—plays in Stratford and London.

Dates: Summer: Jun 29-Jul 19; Jul 20-Aug 9. Cost: $2,800 per session or $5,200 for 2 sessions. Contact: M.B. Pigott, Oakland Univ., Rochester, MI 48309; (810) 370-4131, fax (810) 650-9107; pigott@vela.acs.oakland.edu.

Classic Cycle. Classic French cuisine and patisserie taught by Le Cordon Bleu master chefs. Comprehensive programs with 3 levels, leading, after only 9 months to the internationally renowned "Grand Diplome Le Cordon Bleu."

Dates: Jan, Mar, Jun, Oct. Cost: Each level £2,470-£4,010. Full Classic Cycle £17,160. Contact: Le Cordon Bleu, 114 Marylebone Ln., WIM 6HH, London, UK.

Crafts and Arts Courses. Week and weekend courses in painting and drawing, black-smithing, calligraphy, gardening and garden design, glass engraving, photography, pottery, sculpture, silversmithing, soft furnishing, textiles, woodcarving and woodworking. Courses for different levels of ability, from complete beginners to master classes, run parallel to 7 full-time Diploma courses.

Dates: Year round. Cost: Short course (residential) 5 days £349; weekends £146; 7 days £469. Contact: Heather Way, Public Relations, West Dean College, West Dean, Chichester, W. Sussex PO18 0QZ, UK; (011) 44-1243-811301, fax 811343; westdean@pavilion.co.uk.

Creative Writing Courses. Short residential courses for those seriously interested in writing. Two published writers as tutors working with groups of up to 16: living and working alongside for the duration of the course. A third writer visits for 1 evening to read and talk about their work. Three centers: Devon, Yorkshire, and Inverness-Shire.

Dates: Five-day courses from Apr-Nov each year. Cost: £290 (covers full board, lodging, tuition). Contact: Julia Wheadon, Senior Administrator, Arvon Foundation Ltd., Totleigh Barton, Sheepwash, Beaworthy, Devon EX21 5NS, U.K.; (011) 44-1409-23-13-38, fax 23-11-44.

Croquet. This "croquet week" is divided into 2 modules which can be taken separately or together. The first will take students through stroke production, basic tactics and break-building, and game strategies. No prior experience is necessary. For those who attended the first module or who have previous experience the second module will have more emphasis on tactics, game-plans and whole/part games, including the use of bisques. Dillington House provides the idyllic setting for this intriguing game which can be played by people of all ages.

Dates: July-September. Cost: Approx. £275. Contact: Dillington House, Ilminster, Somerset TA19 9DT, UK.

Drawing and Painting. By covering the basic

concepts and aspects of painting in a step-by-step progression throughout the week, it seeks to lay the ground for a confident and soild start for the beginner, while at the same time providing support and reinforcement of theories to those with some experience. The program will include drawing, composition, tone and color, etc. Wherever appropriate slides and videos will be shown to illustrate points. Talks on artists of the past will be held in the evening sessions.

Dates: July-September. Cost: Approx. £275. Contact: Dillington House, Ilminster, Somerset TA19 9DT, UK.

Edinburgh Univ. Summer Courses. Scotland past and present: Art, Architecture, History, Literature, Archaeology, Gaelic, Music, Drama, Creative Writing, Film, Ecology, the Edinburgh Festival. Courses last 1-4 weeks each. Instruction by University professors: highest academic standards. Integral field trips; theatre/concert/cinema tickets provided. Social program. Choice of accommodations.

Dates: Jun-Sep. Contact: Elaine Mowat, Univ. of Edinburgh, Centre for Continuing Education, 11 Buccleuch Pl., Edinburgh EH8 9LW, U.K.; (011) 44-131-650-4400, fax 131-667-6097; CCE@ed.ac.uk.

England Afloat. England by canal boat. Historian-skipper, small parties, no fixed itinerary. Also special interest cruises for larger groups: theater, history, painting, etc. Henley for the Regatta? Llangollen for the Eisteddfodd? Two thousand miles of waterways give economic access to all central England. Full board or self-catered.

Dates: Apr-Oct. (by the week). Cost: $695 per week, full board. Camp boats as little as $80. Contact: Jeremy Scanlon, England Afloat, 66 Old Holyoke Rd., Westfield, MA 01085; Tel./fax (413) 572-9013.

Guitar Summer School. Led by Raymond Burley, Cornelius Bruinsma and Peter Rueffer, this course is suitable for classical guitarists of all abilities. Tuition will encompass all aspects of performance although special emphasis will be placed on ensemble playing including work in trios, quartets and a guitar orchestra. Please contact Helen Howe, the Booking Secretary, for a special course program and booking form.

Dates: July-September. Cost: Approx. £275. Contact: Dillington House, Ilminster, Somerset TA19 9DT, UK.

Historic Buildings of Wessex. This is an "out and about" course, touching on some aspects of the varied building heritage of the ancient area known as "Wessex." Visits will be made to grand country houses, small towns, the World Heritage of City of Bath, abbeys, castles, some unusual churches and the cathedral City of Wells.

Dates: July-September. Cost: Approx. £275. Contact: Dillington House, Ilminster, Somerset TA19 9DT, UK.

Introduction to Prehistoric Britain. This course will explore the amazing worlds of prehistoric Britain. Through illustrated lectures, seminars and site visits, it will look at how our ancestors may have lived their lives. The course will examine the Neolithic period, the Bronze Age and the Iron Age up to the Roman Conquests. Site visits will include trips to Dartmoor and Wessex. This course is suitable for the complete beginner and those with some previous knowledge who would like to catch up on some recent developments.

Dates: July-September. Cost: Approx. £275. Contact: Dillington House, Ilminster, Somerset TA19 9DT, UK.

Japanese Dyeing. This is essentially a practical course although there will be opportunities to explore the history, techniques (including making the traditional rice paste for resist dyeing) and meaning behind the many aspects of this extraordinary and beautiful Japanese artistic tradition. Using traditional forms such as flowers and sea waves, the student will be able to work with both stencils and brush painting. All-comers welcome.

Dates: July-September. Cost: Approx. £275. Contact: Dillington House, Ilminster, Somerset TA19 9DT, UK.

Japanese Patchwork. A practical needlework course with applique and Sashiko quilting using silver and gold threads, brocades, etc. This course is for all-comers and is designed to enable the student to master traditional and contemporary needle-working techniques. During the course of the week, and depending on your ability and speed, you will be able to produce several small items or work on a larger project such as the making of a kimono.

Dates: July-September. Cost: Approx. £275. Contact: Dillington House, Ilminster, Somerset TA19 9DT, UK.

Le Cordon Bleu, L'Art Culinaire. Le Cordon Bleu in London offers the highest diploma in culinary education in just 9 months. Cuisine and pastry classes begin every 10 weeks. Summer abroad program--ICHP--in Paris and London. Catering program for professionals.

Dates: Jun 10-Aug 17, 1996. Trimesters begin every 10 weeks. Cost: From $6,000 to $30,000 for cuisine and pastry 9-month diploma. Contact: In U.S. call (800) 457-CHEF or fax (914) 426-0104. Le Cordon Bleu, 114 Marylebone Ln., WIM 6HH, London, UK.

London Academy of Performing Arts. An internationally renowned drama academy, offering a classical acting training for students wishing to enter the professional performing arts. Full-time 1- and 2-year courses offered as well as summer schools and 12-week programs. Many graduates work in top theater, film, and T.V. productions.

Dates: Summer schools Jul-Aug. Full time courses from Sep. Auditions throughout the year. Cost: From £850. Contact: The Administrator, London Academy of Performing Arts, The Church, 2 Effie Rd., Fulham Broadway, London SW6 1TB, U.K; (011) 44-171-736-0121, fax 371-5624.

London Study Program. The London Program is a dynamic study abroad program that brings the city into the classroom and the classroom out into the city. Program facilities are centrally located in newly renovated historic buildings in the Bloomsbury district of London near the British Museum and the Univ. of London student union. Courses are taught in literature, history, culture, art, theater, and contemporary society of England. Cosponsored by Univ. of Wisconsin at Madison.

Dates: Early Sep-mid-Dec (fall), mid-Jan-late Apr (spring). Cost: $5,900 per semester (WI residents). Includes tuition, apartment, excursions. Contact: Lawrence Roscioli, Director, L&S Off-Campus Programs, Univ. of Wisconsin at Milwaukee, P.O. Box 413, Milwaukee, WI 53201; (414) 229-5879, fax (414) 229-6827; overseas@csd.uwm.edu.

Modern Calligraphy. The "layering of letters" having them advance and recede in the 2-dimensional plane, is perhaps the most important development in modern day calligraphy. It gives both scribe and a viewer a new and closer involvement with the words, image and mood, drawing us "into" and not simply "across" the page. By placing these now 3-dimensional letters onto an active background of color, tone and texture, we can truly "serve the words" with nuance, clairty and deeper interior intensity. All-comers welcome.

Dates: July-September. Cost: Approx. £275. Contact: Dillington House, Ilminster, Somerset TA19 9DT, UK.

Oxford/FSU Summer Program. From Tom Tower to Stratford-on-Avon, pave your own pilgrim's path in the land of Chaucer and Shakespeare. Experience Oxford's rich academic traditions with an intimacy few visitors enjoy as you live and study in prestigious Christ Church College

Dates: Jun 30-Jul 19 and Jul 21-Aug 9, 1997. Cost: $3,400 per person. Includes course fee, single room, and 3 meals per day. Contact: Carol Abel, Center for Professional Development, Florida State Univ., Tallahassee, FL

32306-2027; (904) 644-7551, fax (904) 644-2589; cabel@mailer.fsu.edu.

Photography. A practical monochrome workshop designed to help the more experienced photographer obtain the perfect negative and the perfect monochrome print. The workshop will be limited to 10 participants and will include practical darkroom work, lectures, demonstrations, excursions to local venues and appraisal of students' work. There will be a small charge toward model expenses and own cars will be used for transport. This course is offered in association with the Royal Photographic Society.

Dates: July-September. Cost: Approx. £275. Contact: Dillington House, Ilminster, Somerset TA19 9DT, UK.

Pottery Courses at Lacock Pottery. A week spent making your own ceramics, learning about clay, hand making, making pots on the wheel, decorating and glazing. On Saturday the pots are ready to take home. Accommodations are at the pottery in Lacock, a medieval, quaint, stone, national trust village. Good homemade food and home grown vegetables.

Dates: Summer and Easter. Cost: Approx. £360. Contact: Lacock Pottery, The Tanyard, Lacock, Chippenham, Wiltshire SN152LB, U.K.; (011) 44-1249-730-266.

Pottery Residential Short Courses. Five-day or weekend residential pottery/ceramic programs are running year round at Alan Baxter's Workshop, just one hour from London. Students include all levels from professionals to beginners. All courses are structured around the wishes of our potting guests. Prices are inclusive of practically all domestic and workshop needs.

Dates: Year round. Cost: £255. Contact: Alan or Patt Baxter, The White House Pottery Workshop, Somersham, Ipswich IP8 4QA, UK; Tel./fax (011) 44-1473-831256.

Rambles-Somerset. A series of rambles through the various classic landscapes of Somerset specially selected to add to your knowledge and appreciation of this unique country. Each day's walk will concentrate on a particular area, giving a chance to look at the geology, physique, villages, architecture, natural history, historical sites and associations, etc. The walks will be at a medium level of effort—there will be an emphasis upon looking and enjoying rather than on physical power.

Dates: July-September. Cost: Approx. £275. Contact: Dillington House, Ilminster, Somerset TA19 9DT, UK.

Silk Painting. This course is designed as pure luxury for all previous "Possi" students. Non-stop inspiration and practical silk-painting which will include an outdoor class (weather permitting) to be used in conjunction with a silk-painting project. Student numbers on this course are limited to 8 so early booking is advised.

Dates: July-September. Cost: Approx. £275. Contact: Dillington House, Ilminster, Somerset TA19 9DT, UK

The Cambridge Prep Experience. A unique opportunity for enterprising 9th graders to spend a month at Cambridge Univ. in a close, supporitve environment. An expert faculty teaches 11 different courses including medicine, journalism, creative writing, history, and drama. An introduction to English sports, field trips to London, museum tours, and theater visits are also arranged.

Dates: Jul 2-26, 1996. Cost: $3,895. Contact: OxBridge Academic Programs, 601 W. 110th St., Suite 7-R, New York, NY 10025-1535; (800) 828-8349, fax (212) 663-8169.

The Edinboro at Oxford Program. Edinboro Univ. of PA is offering a summer study abroad program for teachers, undergraduates, and travelers at Oxford Univ. in England. Undergraduate and graduate courses offered are: English Literature and Life and other relevant courses. Participants live and study at Exeter College, the fourth-oldest college at Oxford Univ.

Dates: Aug 9-23, 1997. Cost: $1,900. Contact: Ted Atkinson, Director, The Edinboro at Oxford Program, Earp Hall, Edinboro Univ. of PA, Edinboro, PA 16444; (814) 732-2981, fax (814) 732-2982.

The Oxford Teacher Seminar. Two weeks of intellectual stimulation, cultural enrichment, and academic immersion in the life of Oxford for teachers of all subjects and grade levels. Seminars include Comparative International Education, Arts in the classroom, and Western Civilization in the curriculum, led by English university professors and a distinguished series of guest lecturers.

Dates: Jun 30-Jul 13, 1996 and Jul 14-27, 1996 Cost: $1,895. Contact: OxBridge Academic Programs, 601 W. 110th St., Suite 7-R, New York, NY 10025-1535; (800) 828-8349, fax (212) 663-8169.

The Oxford Tradition. Students (grades 10-12) live in Oxford for a month of intensive study with an expert faculty in 25 different subjects. Housed in three colleges in the medieval town center, students also visit London and Stratford, play English sports, and go to the theater, choral concerts, and a series of special guest lectures.

Dates: Jun 29-Jul 28, 1996. Cost: $4,195. Contact: OxBridge Academic Programs, 601 W. 110th St., Suite 7-R, New York, NY 10025-1535; (800) 828-8349, fax (212) 663-8169.

The Oxford/Berkeley Program. In this residential program participants spend 3 or 6 weeks living and studying at Worcester College, one of the oldest and most beautiful of the Oxford colleges. Small-group seminars are taught by distinguished faculty from Oxford and other British universities. Twenty courses are offered from Shakespeare to English Country Houses. All courses may be taken for credit.

Dates: Jun 30-Jul 19, Jul 21-Aug 9. Cost: $3,400. Contact: Shirley Beeler, UC Berkeley Ext., 55 Laguna St., San Francisco, CA 94102;

(415) 252-5229, fax (415) 552-4237; smb@unx.berkeley.edu.

Univ. of Cambridge Summer Study. Spend 2 weeks of serious study at the Univ. of Cambridge Summer Study Program. All courses are taught by Cambridge faculty in small group seminars. Appropriate field trips are available with each course. Courses include: The English Country House, Life in the Middle Ages, British Secret Services, Shakespeare in Performance, and The British Landscape. Graduate and undergraduate credit is available.

Dates: Jul 6-19, 1997. Cost: $2,895 for tuition, room and board and field trips. Contact: Dr. Joann Painter, Univ. of Cambridge Summer Study Program, 714 Sassafras St., Erie, PA 16501; (814) 456-0757, fax (814) 453-5502.

Univ. of York Visiting Student Program. The York Visiting Student Program allows students to participate in regular classes for a period of up to 1 year. Students are fully integrated into the academic and social life of the University, and are given a transcript of record. Credits can normally be transferred to the home university.

Dates: Oct-Jun. Cost: Approx. £7,000 inclusive of tuition and room. Contact: The International Office, Univ. of York, Heslington, York YO1 5DD, UK; (011) 44-1904-433534, fax 433538; international@york.ac.uk.

University Stays. Over 60 universities provide accommodations for groups, families, or individuals on a bed and breakfast, full-board, or self-cater basis during the vacation. From single bedrooms (with no supplements) to en suite or family rooms. Leisure facilities, study and activity courses.

Dates: Year round. Cost: Vary. Contact: Carole Formon, BUAC, Box 1406, University Park, Nottingham NG7 2RD, UK; (011) 44-115-950-4571, fax 942-2505.

Variety of Short Courses. Wide variety of interesting short courses for adults in country Manor House in picturesque village.

Dates: Year round. Cost: Approx. £46 per 24 hours, full residential and tuition. Contact: Janet Hooper, Adult Ed. Course Administrator, Burton Manor College, Burton, S. Wirral, Cheshire L64 5SJ, U.K.; (011) 44-151-336-5172, fax 336-6586.

Whithorn - Cradle of Christianity. Established in 1986, Whithorn offers the visitor an interesting and hands-on experience in the Visitor Centre and Discovery Centre. Ten years of archaeological discovery is interpreted in exhibitions, displays of finds and in the amazing 3-D jigsaw, 2 meters x 2 meters, 5 layers deep which show the site as discovered. In addition the Museum of the Whithorn School of Crosses, the ruined 12th Century Priory and Crypts, guided tours of the excavation and audio visual presentation bring to life the life and times of the folk of Whithorn from 500AD, when Christianity came to Scotland—at least a half-day visit.

Dates: Apr 1-Oct 31 each year, 7 days per week, 10:30 a.m.-5 p.m. Cost: Adult £2.70, concession £1.50 Contact: Mrs. C.L. Wilson, The Whithorn Trust, 45/47 George St., Whithorn, Dumfries and Galloway, Scotland DG8 8NS.

World of Anglo Saxons. Where did English begin? This course will explore the legacy of the Anglo-Saxons, in their art, the archaeology, and most of all, in their language—much of which lives on today in our own. Through their poetry, stories, and other writings, we will examine their culture, history and beliefs. The course will also include outings to important Anglo-Saxon sites not far from Dillington. This course is suitable for beginners and those with previous knowledge of the period.

Dates: July-September. Cost: Approx. £275. Contact: Dillington House, Ilminster, Somerset TA19 9DT, UK.

World of Pharaohs. The civilization of Ancient Egypt spanned at least 4,000 years, leaving behind written and material evident that enables us to glimpse into a forgotten, exotic world. With the aid of slides, the course will examine the story of Ancient Egypt, the sites, the artifacts and the people. Some time will also be spent looking at Egyptian writing and drawing. No previous knowledge is necessary.

Dates: July-September. Cost: Approx. £275. Contact: Dillington House, Ilminster, Somerset TA19 9DT, UK.

Writing. Many aspiring writers find their work rejected by editors, publishers or agents and they are given no explanation as to why; they are left feeling both disappointed and frustrated. The focus of this course will be on taking a close look at some of the most common reasons for rejection, thus increasing the chances of success. This course is suitable for beginners and the more experienced.

Dates: July-September. Cost: Approx. £275. Contact: Dillington House, Ilminster, Somerset TA19 9DT, UK.

United States

American Language Academy. ALA provides English language training at university locations in Ashland (OR), Berkeley (CA), Boston, Chicago, Cleveland, Indianapolis, Lakeland (FL), Lawrenceville (NJ), Philadelphia, Portland (OR), Pueblo (CO), Tampa, and Thibodaux (LA), and at private boarding high schools in Lake Forest (IL) and Poughkeepsie (NY). Ten-, 5-, and 4-week intensive English courses, and English for Special Purposes.

Dates: Year round. Contact: William M. Fish, ALA Executive Offices, 1401 Rockville Pike, Suite 550, Rockville, MD 20852; (301) 309-1400, fax (301) 309-0202; amerlang@mci mail.com.

RSA/Univ. of Cambridge CTEFLA Course. The most widely recognized initial qualification for teaching English as a foreign language to adults, the CTEFLA is offered at both our Santa Monica and Portland centers year round. You need to be at least 20 years old, have a good standard of education and a recent foreign language learning experience to be qualified.

Dates: Jan-Nov year round. Cost: $2,150. Contact: John Myers, Coast Language Academy, International House, 200 SW Market St., Suite #111, Portland, OR 97201; (503) 224-1960, fax (503) 224-2041; lgalas@coastpdx.com.

Venezuela

One-on-One. Merida is the capital of the Venezuelan Andes—a clean, safe university town where the weather and people are always warm and the scenery is breathtaking. This intensive and highly individualized program offers 4 hours of instruction every weekday with a qualified teaching professional. Students and professors work together to tailor schedules, teaching styles, and course content to the specific needs of the student. Room and board with a Venezuelan family is optional, but highly recommended. Program participants and Venezuelan students of English are invited to social events and activities. Some day trips or outings are available for a small additional cost.

Dates: Program starts every Saturday of the year. Cost: Instruction $478 for 2 weeks (includes registration fee); room and board $75 per week. Discount available for stays of 3 weeks or more. Contact: VENUSA, 6342 Forest Hill Blvd., Suite 287, West Palm Beach, FL 33415; (407) 753-3761, fax (407) 753-3758; venusa@flinet.com.

Vietnam

Cross Cultural Travel Study Programs. Discover Vietnam—a country in transition. Program explores the country's rich history, diverse cultures, and dynamic economy while visiting major cities throughout the country.

An opportunity to interact with peers, visit universities, and teach an English class. Tour fully escorted by professors in the field. Programs range from 10-25 days.

Dates: Call for dates. Cost: From $2,995 (all inclusive, from West Coast). Contact: The Global Spectrum, 1901 Pennsylvania Ave., NW, Suite 204, Washington, DC 20006; (202) 293-2065, (800) 419-4446, fax (202) 296-0815; gaspectrum@idsonline.com.

Worldwide

Academic Credit for Travel. Independent study courses that provide academic credit for travel undertaken anywhere/anytime in the world. Open to high school and college students and post-graduate credit for teachers and professionals. Language (Spanish, Italian, French) credit also available. Suitable for study abroad, language immersion, short trips, and sabbaticals.

Dates: Year round. Cost: $50-$65 per credit. Contact: Professor Steve Tash, Travel Study, P.O. Box 16501, Irvine, CA 92623-6501; (800) 484-1081, ext. 7775 (9 a.m.-9 p.m. PST), fax (714) 552-0740; stash3@ix.netcom.com.

American-Int'l Homestays. Stay in English-speaking foreign homes in over 30 countries. Explore foreign cultures responsibly. Learn foreign languages. Perfect for families or seniors. Learn how other people live by living with them in their homes.

Dates: Year round. Cost: From $49 per night. Contact: Joe Kinczel, American-Int'l Homestays, P.O. Box 1754, Nederland, CO 80466; (303) 642-3088 or (800) 876-2048, fax (303) 642-3365; ash@igc.apc.org.

AuPair Homestay Abroad. Immerse yourself in the culture of your choice in Europe or Argentina. Develop language skills and earn a monthly stipend while caring for the children of your host family. This is AuPair Homestay Abroad, an innovative program of World

Learning, offering participants ages 18-29 the opportunity for experiential learning overseas within the comfort and security of a family setting.

Dates: Individual departure with stays from 3-12 months and extensions possible. Cost: $775. Includes interviewing, screening, matching with a host family, predeparture materials, program support in U.S. and while overseas. Contact: Imelda R. Farrell, Program Specialist, AuPair Homestay Abroad, 1015 15th St., NW, Washington, DC 20005; (202) 408-5380, fax (202) 408-5397; 708-4391@mcimail.com.

CES Study Abroad Program. "Learn The Language Where It Is Spoken": French in France or Monaco; German in Germany or Austria; Italian in Italy; Portuguese in Portugal or Brazil; Spanish in Spain or Mexico. Other languages and locations available. Adult and youth programs. Courses include group instruction at ability level; private instruction; business-language; teacher-refresher; cultural studies; cooking, music, wines, art, history, dance. Housing can be hosted bed and breakfast, homestay half-board or full board, student residences; pensiones, or small hotels. School organized excursions and activities.

Dates: Year round. Two-week minimum and no maximum. Group classes have a maximum of 5-15 students. Cost: With and without accommodations, from $265-$2,700 per 2 weeks. Contact: Ms. Lorraine Haber, CES Study Abroad Program, 330 7th Ave., 6th Fl., New York, NY 10001; (212) 629-7300, fax (212) 736-7950.

Cross Cultural Journeys. Our travel program encompasses journeys to remote or unusual areas of the globe to experience traditional healing practices and learn indigenous wisdom from ancient teachings. Our trips include a knowledegeable trip leader, with an average number of 15 travelers. We practice socially responsible ecotourism—leaving only positive reminders.

Dates: Year round. Cost: From $1,000-$6,000 all inclusive with attention to details and accommodations. Contact: Carole Angermeir, President, P.O. Box 1369, Sausalito, CA 94966; (800) 353-2276, fax (415) 332-0683.

Cross Cultural Studies. Topics covered will be the current political scene in Russia, the social issues affecting the people and culture of Spain; the educational systems in England, France, and Germany; and the historical literature of London and Dublin. Three to 6 hours of college credit is granted through the Univ. of Missouri at Kansas City.

Dates: Summer 1997. Cost: Approx. $2,000 (does not include airfare). Contact: People to People International, Collegiate and Professional Studies Program, 501 E. Armour Blvd., Kansas City, MO 64109-2200; (816) 531-4701, fax (816) 561-7502; ptpi@cctr.umkc.edu, www.umkc.edu/cctr/dept/ptpi/homepage.html.

Dialysis at Sea. Dialysis at Sea Cruises, the only complete medical and travel service of its kind anywhere, arranges cruises for dialysis patients on a large variety of cruise ships and destinations, offering the best group rates available (dialysis treatments additional). Each cruise sets sail with a licensed nephrologist and experienced staff of dialysis clinicians.

Dates: Four to 5 departures per month. Cost: $549 per person to over $10,000 per person. Contact: Loretta McCollum Powell, Dialysis at Sea, 107 13th Ave., P.O. Box 218, Indian Rocks Beach, FL 34635; (800) 544-7604 or (813) 596-7604, fax (813) 596-0203.

Earthwatch. Unique opportunities to work with leading scientists on 1- to 3-week field research projects worldwide. Earthwatch sponsors 160 expeditions in over 30 U.S. states and in 60 countries. Project disciplines include archaeology, wildlife management, ecology, ornithology and marine mammalogy. No special skills needed—all training is done in the field.

Dates: Year round. Cost: Tax deductible contributions ranging from $695-$2,800 support the research and cover food and lodging expenses. Airfare not included. Contact: Earthwatch, 680 Mt. Auburn St., P.O. Box 9104MA, Watertown, MA 02272; (800) 776-0188, (617) 926-8200; info@earthwatch.org, www.earthwatch.org.

Educational Adventures. Educational Travel off the beaten path in Asia and South America. Customized for individuals and small groups. "Classrooms without Walls" offer cultural, craft/art, religion, holy site, traditional healing and folk medicine, and natural history/environmental travel study programs, and "Trekking with a Mission" in the world's special and untouristed places.

Dates: Year round. Cost: Vary. See free catalog. Contact: Myths and Mountains, Inc., 976 Tee Court, Incline Village, NV 89451; (800) 670-MYTH (6984), (702) 834-4454; edutrav@sierra.net, www.mythsandmountains.com.

EduVacations. Pursue a special interest in sports or arts with optional instruction while studying a language. Or just pursue your special interest. Examples: Study French (or any language) and ski (or any sport or art), archaeological digs, restoration, motorcycle touring with training. EduVacations tailored to your individual or group's special interests. Let us know what your interest is and where you'd like to go.

Dates: Programs run from 1 week to months. Cost: Include room and board, tuition. Contact: Mary Ann Puglisi, EduVacations, 1431 21st St., NW, Suite 302, Washington, DC 20036; (202) 857-8384, fax (202) 835-3756.

Eurocentres Language Schools. Immersion course of 20-25 hours per week for beginners to advanced levels. Learn in small classes with students of all ages from around the world. Full organizational social calendar with extended excursions available to students. Homestay living is available, college credit option.

Dates: Begins monthly all year long. Cost: Depends on school and length of stay. Contact: Eurocentres, 101 N. Union St., Alexandria, VA 22314; (703) 684-1494 or (800) 648-4809, fax (703) 684-1495; 100632.141@compuserve.com, www.clark.net/pub/eurocent/home.htm.

Global Awareness Through Experience (GATE). GATE offers alternative tourism through programs in Mexico, Central America (Guatemala, El Salvador, Nicaragua), and Central Europe. Participants connect with Third World people in face-to-face dialogue to explore social, political, economic, religious, and cultural issues. Mutual learning happens between GATE participants and the indigenous people.

Dates: Various open groups. Special groups also welcome. Cost: Depends on program. Contact: Beverly Budelier, GATE, 912 Market St., La Crosse, WI 54601.

Global Ecology. Travel around the world for 8 months, meeting leading environmental activists and scholars, comparative international study of key issues in global ecology. 1997-98 itinerary: England, India, Philippines, New Zealand, and Mexico. Courses in cultural anthropology, biology, ecology, and sustainable development. Small group of 30 students, undergraduates and older, homestays with families. Perfect for teachers on sabbatical, working professionals. Receive 32 credits and transcript from Bard College. IHP founded in 1958.

Dates: Sep 1997-May 1998. Cost: $19,850 (1996-97). Includes tuition, accommodations, most meals, academic program, fees. Airfare not included. Contact: Joan Tiffany, Director, International Honors Program, 19 Braddock Pk., Boston, MA 02116; (617) 267-0026; info@ihp.edu, www.ihp.edu.

Graduate and Undergraduate Programs. European University offers undergraduate and graduate programs in Business Administration, International Hospitality and Tourism

Management, Business Communications and Public Relations, Information Systems, and European Languages.

Dates: Courses begin Oct, Jan, Mar. Cost: SF3,0850. Contact: Prof. D. Craen, European Univ. Les Bosquets, 1817 Montreaux, Switzerland; (011) 41-21-964-84-64, fax 964-84-68, eurmon@iprolink.ch.

Indepth Wildlife Tour. From the tip of York Peninsula to Kangaroo Island and Tasmania, join ecologists Gail and Doug Cheeseman (in their 14th year of guiding in Australia) and resident naturalists and biologists during the glorious Austral springtime. The Cheesemans offer top leadership and lodgings and as much field time as possible for 14 tour members max. Only eligibility requirement is to agree with nonsmoking policy.

Dates: Oct 12-Nov 5, 1997. Cost: $5,160 plus airfare. The Cheesemans assist with flight bookings. Contact: Gail and Doug Cheeseman, Cheesemans' Ecology Safaris, 20800 Kittredge Rd., Saratoga, CA 95070; (800) 527-5330; cheesemans@aol.com..

International Travel Study. Over 20 faculty-led programs each year range from 1 to 4 weeks in length and offer university credit. Locations include France, Italy, Greece, Australia, Africa, South America, Great Britain, and more. Programs focus on art, language, or geography, among a variety of specialties.

Dates: Summer programs May 30-Aug 30; programs in Jan, spring, and fall. Cost: From $2,300-$5,000. Contact: Mary Pieratt, Director, Travel Study Programs, San Francisco State Univ., College of Extended Learning, 22 Tapia, San Francisco, CA 94132; (415) 338-1533, fax (415) 585-7345.

Italian Language Lessons. Individual Italian language lessons. Accommodations provided by the school. With a family in hotel or apartment. Course levels: beginners, intermediate, advanced.

Dates: Year round. Cost: From LIT310,000 per week. Contact: Prof. Luigi Foschi, Isttituto Studium, Via Baldini 22, 47042 Cesenatico (FO), Italy; Tel./fax (011) 39-547-84442.

Lions Youth Exchange Program. Purpose is to develop and encourage a spirit of understanding among youth worldwide. Program emphasizes the value of sharing in family and community life in another country. Open to young persons ages 15-21. All participants must be screened and sponsored by their local Lions club.

Dates: Open. Cost: Participant responsible for roundtrip transportation, health and travel insurance, sufficient funds for personal expenditures. Contact: Youth Programs Dept., Lions Clubs International, 300 22nd St., Oak Brook, IL 60521-8842; (708) 571-5466, ext. 323, fax (708) 571-8890.

Michigan State Study-Travel Programs. Our idea of travel is a search for new knowledge and understanding. Those who go with us worldwide increase their knowledge of other cultures and their understanding of themselves as lifelong learners. Programs involve faculty leaders and guest experts from the locations visited (Costa Rica, New Zealand, Egypt, Italy, Arizona, Ireland, Switzerland, and Oxford Univ.). Any adult committed to the ideal of travel as study and lifelong learning is welcome.

Dates: Jan through Sep, 1997. Cost: Varies by program. Contact: Charles A. McKee, Director, Alumni Lifelong Education, Michigan State Univ., 8 Kellogg Ctr., E. Lansing, MI 48824-1022; (517) 355-4562, fax (517) 432-2526; ala22@msu.edu.

New Directions. New Directions provides vacation travel and special education exchange programs for over 350 children, adults, and seniors who have developmental, emotional, medical, and physical disabilities. Most have never had a real vacation. Many have not been away from their facilities overnight for 10 or more years.

Dates: Call program for details. Cost: Call

program for details. Contact: Dee Duncan, Executive Director, New Directions, Inc., 5276 Hollister Ave., Suite 207, Santa Barbara, CA 93111; (805) 967-2841

Offshore Sailing School. Learn to sail, bareboat cruising preparation, live aboard cruising. Courses meet the needs of varying sailing abilities from beginners to advanced. Offshore has awarded diplomas to over 78,000 successful sailors over 30 years.

Dates: Year round. Cost: Start at $895 including course and accommodations. Contact: Steve and Doris Colgate's Offshore Sailing School, 16731 McGregor Blvd., Ft. Myers, FL 33908; (800) 221-4326, fax (941) 454-1191; offshore@packet. net, www.offshor-sailing. com.

Penn Summer Abroad. Academic programs granting Univ. of Pennsylvania credits. Courses focusing on language, culture, economics, theater, anthropology, Jewish studies, cinema, art history, traditional folk medicine, performing arts, and religion. Several programs offer homestays, some offer internships.

Dates: Mid-May-late Aug (2-8 weeks). Cost: Tuition: $1,420 per course. Living costs vary. Contact: Elizabeth Sachs, Penn Summer Abroad, College of General Studies, Univ. of Pennsylvania, 3440 Market St., Suite 100, Philadelphia, PA 19104-3335; (215) 898-5738, fax (215) 573-2053.

Plantagenet Tours. Accompanied tours with qualified (university teacher) tour directors. Special attention to history and culture. Destinations in 1997 include Venice and the Veneto, Henry the Navigator Tour to Portugal, Isabel tour to Medieval Andalucia, Greater Gascony, Provence, Castile and Santiago de Compostela, Cesare Borgia Tour to Papal States, Elinor Tour to Medieval Aquitaine, Christian IV Tour to Renaissance Denmark.

Contact: Susan or Peter Gravgaard, Plantagenet Tours, 85 The Grove, Moordown, Bournemouth, BH9 2TY, UK; Tel./fax (011) 44 1202 521 895.

Purdue Educational Travel Programs. Six programs. First 3 programs are for credit option. London and Paris: International Retailing (2 weeks May); U.S. Northern Plains in Transition (2 weeks May); Rome (2 weeks July); Bolivia and Peru (12 days Mar); Germany: Castles and Inns (12 days Jun); Australia/New Zealand: (17 days Jun).

Dates: Mar-May 1997. Cost: $1,000-$4,000. Contact: Joann Chaney, Continuing Education, Purdue Univ., 1586 Stewart Ctr., Rm. 116, W. Lafayette, IN 47907-1586; (800) 359-2968, (317) 494-3894, fax (317) 494-0567; jjchaney@cea.purdue.edu.

Reality Tours. Participate in one of our socially responsible, culturally focused (alternative) travel experiences and gain a first-hand perspective on what is truly happening in countries like: Cuba, Haiti, Guatemala, Mexico, Chile, Vietnam, the Philippines, Mongolia, Ireland, Senegal, South Africa, and Nicaragua. Learn about indigenous cultures, changing environments, art and crafts, public health and women issues; monitor human rights or observe presidential elections. We will try to arrange personal meetings to suit your particular interests.

Dates: Monthly throughout the year. Cost: Depending upon the trip—range is from $700 for a 7-day trip to Mexico to $3,000 for a trip to Vietnam or South Africa. Costs include roundtrip airfare (please call for more details). Contact: Reality Tours Department, Global Exchange, 2017 Mission St., Suite #303, San Francisco, CA 94110; (415) 255-7296 or (800) 497-1994, fax (415) 255-7498; globalexch@ igc.apc.org.

Road Scholar Programs. Saga Holidays, a provider of quality affordable tours to mature travelers since 1952, offers enriching, interesting travel experiences with a specific educational theme, created with the assistance of respected academic or cultural partners, often a university, and including lectures and program-related excursions.

Dates: Year round. Cost: From $1,949. Includes airfare. Contact: Saga Holidays' Road Scholar Program, 222 Berkeley St., Boston, MA 02116; (800) 621-2151.

Smithsonian Odyssey Tours. The Smithsonian Institution, our nation's museum, and Saga Holidays, a leading provider of quality travel since 1952, have formed a unique partnership to offer affordable educational adventures that include stimulating lectures, guided tours, and exciting excursions.

Dates: Year round. Cost: From $1,149. Includes airfare. Contact: Call (800) 258-5885 for a free Smithsonian Odyssey Brochure (code: TRNS).

Smithsonian Study Tours and Seminars. Smithsonian Study Tours and Seminars offers trips to over 250 destinations worldwide, making it the largest and most diverse program of its kind in the U.S. Tours are designed to meet a variety of budgets and activity levels. All tours provide travelers with rewarding experiences that satisfy their thirst for knowledge and desire to learn. Tours focus on a broad range of interests such as natural history, history, art, architecture, archaeology, gardens, wildlife, and theater.

Dates: Year round. Cost: $895-$12,000. Contact: Smithsonian Study Tours and Seminars, 1100 Jefferson Dr. SW, MRC 702, Washington, DC 20560; (202) 357-4700, fax (202) 633-9250; TSA.Tours@IC.SI.EDU, www.siedu/tsa/sst, AOL keyword: Smithsonian Travel.

St Giles Language Teaching Center. Earn the Certificate in English Language Teaching to Adults (CELTA) approved by the Univ. of Cambridge and the California Council for Private Postsecondary and Vocational Education. The course focuses on practical training and teaching methodology. Includes access to international job postings, graduate contacts, and teaching opportunities abroad. Sessions include resume writing, and interviewing techniques. Part of a group of schools in England, Switzerland, and U.S. offering 40 years of EFL teaching and training. CELTA courses also offered in Brighton and London, England.

Dates: Four-week intensive courses begin 6 times yearly. Cost: $2,250 all inclusive. Contact: St Giles Language Teaching Center, 1 Hallidie Plaza, Suite 350-TA, San Francisco, CA 94102; (415) 788-3552, fax (415) 788-1923.

Study/Travel for Teachers and Retirees. Teachers and retirees travel overseas with professors from California, who lecture to them enroute. Tour directors are aboard too. Program is in its 13th year.

Dates: Christmas holidays, spring break, summer. Cost: Range from $1,500-$4,000 (includes airfare). Contact: Joseph Jeppson or Peggy Searle (800) 527-3137, or write: Community College Tours, P.O. Box 620620, Woodside, CA 94062.

The Lisle Fellowship. Intensive cultural immersion in the social and human development aspects of the host country. Group interaction and process are emphasized. All programs have a unique work component that varies with each such as Habitat for Humanity in Uganda, or repairing an ashram in Bali. The work is unpaid, but limited scholarships are available to defray the program cost. All programs are affiliated with the Univ. of Toledo, and credit is available.

Dates: Summer 1997. Programs are typically 3 to 4 weeks. Cost: $1,000 to $3,500. Includes room and board, and excursion while in host country. In some cases, transportation may be extra. Contact: The Lisle Fellowship, 433 W. Stearns Rd., Temperance, MI 48182; (313) 847-7126 or (800) 477-1538, or Dr. Mark B. Kinney, Executive Director, Univ. of Toledo; fax (419) 530-7719.

The World for Free. Host/Guest Exchange. Members provide accommodations for other traveling members. Membership includes directory and cheap travel informaton. Please write for application before sending money.

Dates: Year round. Cost: $25 per year. Contact: c/o Seidboard World Enterprises, The World For Free, P.O. Box 137-TA, Prince St. Station, New York, NY 10012; fax (212) 979-8167; mykel@wps.com.

Travel Arrangements. We help arrange individualized trips for everyone and specialize in special needs for travelers with disabilities.

Dates: Year round. Cost: Free. Contact: Heidi VanArnem, Travel Headquarters, 870 Bowers, Birmingham, MI 48009; (810) 647-1001, (800) 486-2215, fax (810) 647-1002.

Trent International. Trent's International study and exchange programs provide students with an opportunity to spend an academic study year abroad. Students from all academic disciplines may pursue one of a number of formalized exchange or study abroad or language programs. Some programs involve an international work placement component. Students take regular courses and examinations at a host university, and credits earned abroad are counted toward their undergraduate degree.

Dates: Full academic year (often Oct-Jun). Cost: Differs according to program but generally pay Trent's tuition and (often) residence fees. Contact: Cynthia Bennett Awe, Programs Administrator/Exchange Coordinator, Trent Univ., Peterborough, ON K9J 7B8, Canada; (705) 748-1280, fax (705) 748-1626; cawe@trentu.ca.

WorldTeach. WorldTeach is a nonprofit organization based at Harvard Univ. that contributes to educational development and cultural exchange by placing volunteers to teach in developing countries (Costa Rica, Ecuador, Namibia, Poland, South Africa, Thailand, and Vietnam). Teach English, math, science, and environmental education to students of all ages. All programs last for 1 academic year; academic subjects taught vary with assignment. Teachers must have a bachelor's degree and are required to complete 25 hours of TEFL experience before departure. There is a summer program in China for undergraduates.

Dates: Year round departures vary depending on the program. Cost: Range from $3,600-$4,500. Includes health insurance, airfare, field support, and training. Contact: Anthony Meyer, Director of Recruiting and Admissions Training, WorldTeach, Harvard Institute for International Development, 1 Eliot St., Cambridge, MA 02138-5705; (617) 495-5527, fax (617) 495-1599; ameyer@hiid.harvard.edu.

CHAPTER 12

LANGUAGE
SCHOOLS

The following listing of language schools was supplied by the organizers. Contact the program directors to confirm costs, dates, and other details. If you do not see the program you want in the country of your choice, look in the "Worldwide" listings at the end of the section for programs located in several different regions.

Argentina

"Albert Schweitzer" Studio of Education and Culture, International. Spanish for foreigners, English, and German. Expertise is teaching English-speaking expatriates and tourists.

Cost: Average price per classroom—Individual: $20; Group of 2 students $18; 3 students $16; 4 students $14; 5 students $12; 6 students $10. Price is per person. Contact: Albert Schweitzer Studio of Education and Culture International, Alvear 69, 2nd Fl., Martínez 1640, Buenos Aires, Argentina; (011) 54-1-792-6322/790-6245, fax 793-6888.

CEDIC (Spanish Language Centre). The CEDIC (Spanish Language Centre) offers a completely integrated program in the instruction of the Spanish language with various courses for different levels. Private and small group lessons are available with flexible schedules to meet the students' requirements. Social activities with Argentine students can also be arranged.

Dates: Year round. Cost: Individual classes $16 per hour; groups $11 (per student) per hour. Contact: Prof. Susana Bernardi or Prof. Martin Duh, Reconquista 719, 11º E, 1003 Buenos Aires, Argentina; Tel./fax (011) 54-1-315-1156; martinduh@act.net.ar.

Instituto de Lengua Española para Extranjeros (ILEE). Located downtown in the most European-like city in Latin America. Dedicated exclusively to teaching Spanish to foreigners. Small groups and private classes year round. All teachers hold a university degree. Method is intensive, conversation-based.

Student body is international, mostly European. Highly recommended worldwide (all travel guides, British and German universities, etc.). Ask for individual references in U.S.

Dates: Year round. Cost: Four weeks intensive program (20 hours a week) including homestay $1,400; 2 weeks $700. Individual classes $19 per hour. Registration fee (includes books) $100. Contact: ILEE, Daniel Korman, Director, Lavalle 1619 7th C (1048), Buenos Aires, Argentina; (011) 54-1-375-0730, fax 864-4942; www.worldwide.edu/argentina/ilee/index.html. In U.S.: David Babbitz; (415) 431-8219, fax (415) 431-5306.

Australia

General Studies in Victoria. Victoria offers nearly every discipline in undergraduate/graduate levels at 5 different university campus sites: Australian studies, art, journalism, performing arts, women's studies, biology, chemistry, math, business, computing, etc. Known as the Garden State, Victoria has some of the country's most beautiful mountain and coastal areas.

Dates: First semester: Feb-Jul; second semester: Jul-Nov. Cost: $4,290 per semester, $7,750 for 1 year. Contact: University Studies Abroad Consortium (USAC), Univ. of Nevada, Reno #323, Reno, NV 89557-0093; (702) 784-6569, fax (702) 784-6010; usac@equinox.unr.edu

Austria

Deutsch in Graz. Learning is experiencing. DiG offers German courses for all ages at all levels. Organized intensive courses, vacation courses, evening and morning classes, and special courses for school classes, German teachers, German for tourist industry. Leisure program, excursions and accommodations will be arranged.

Dates: Year round. Cost: Example: 3-week intensive course (90 teaching units) AS7,950.

Contact: Deutsch in Graz, Dr. Monika Schneeberger, (manager), Ms. Karin Breyer (administration), A-8010 Graz, Kalchberggasse 10, Austria; (011) 43-316-833900, fax 833900-6.

Deutsch-Institut Tirol. German lessons for adults (over 16). Any standard from beginner to far advanced. Classes of 1 to 6 (maximum) participants. Courses from 1 week onwards. Program per week: 5 mornings with 4 lessons of 45 minutes each; 4 afternoons and 4 evenings with programs in teacher's company (sports, excursions, social events, skiing in winter).

Dates: Year round. Cost: ATS4,900 per week per course. Room and breakfast per day from ATS200. Contact: Hans Ebenhöh, Director, Am Sandhügel 2, A-6370 Kitzbühel, Austria; (011) 43-5356-71274, fax 72363; dit@kitz.netwing.at.

Wiener Internationale Hochschulkurse. German courses at the University for beginners and advanced students, perfectionist courses (6 levels). Lectures on German and Austrian literature, music, linguistics, introduction to Austria. Special courses: translation into German, commercial correspondence, business German, medical terminology, communication, phonetics, Vienna waltz, choir singing. Language laboratory. Excursions.

Dates: Jul 6-Aug 2, Aug 3-30, Aug 31-Sep 20. Cost: Course fee (4 weeks): Approx. ATS4,300; accommodations: Approx. ATS6,000. Contact: Magister Sigrun Anmann-Trojer, Wiener Internationale Hochschulkurse, Universität, Dr. Karl Lueger-Ring 1, A1010 Wien, Austria; (011) 43-1-405-12-54 or 405-47-37, fax 405-12-5410.

Brazil

Portuguese as a Foreign Language. Portuguese language training is combined with complete cultural immersion aiming at maximizing students' language learning. Although the methodology is eclectic and the curriculum is flexible to allow for meeting specific needs, the main focus is on the development of learners' communicative competence.

Dates: As of May 20, 1996, new groups begin every 10 days. Cost: On average, $10 per hour. Contact: Prof. Denise Scheyerl, PhD, Rua Milton de Oliveira, 231, Barra, Salvador, Bahia 40140-100, Brazil; Tel./fax (011) 55-71-245866.

Canada

Columbia College ESL. Seven- and 14-week programs, 25 hours per week. Small classes. Organized activities. International college also offering Senior, Secondary, and University Transfer programs. Facilities include tutorial center, library, computer center, gymnasium, cafeteria, counseling. Located 20 minutes from downtown Vancouver, near major shopping center and on excellent public transit routes.

Dates: Jan 2-Apr 10, May 5-Aug 14, and Sep 2-Dec 11, 1997. Cost: Tuition (7 weeks) CAN$1,850, (14 weeks) CAN$3,500; application fee CAN$75. Contact: Mr. John Helm, Columbia College, 6037 Marlborough Ave., Barnaby (Greater Vancouver), BC V5H 3L6 Canada; (604) 430-6422, fax (604) 439-0548; columbia_college@mindlink.bc.ca.

Ecole de français, Université de Montreal. For the last 50 years, the Ecole de français has offered courses in French as a Second Language to students from around the world. On the educational forefront as a learning institution, the Ecole is continually improving its programs to meet the changing needs of its students. Choose from Oral and Written Communication French (beginner to advanced), Workshop on Teaching French as a Second Language (for teachers), Contemporary Québec Culture (for advanced students), Business French (intermediate to advanced students).

Dates: Summer 1: Jun 28-Jul 19; summer 2: Jul 22-Aug 9; fall 96: Sep 5-Dec 6; winter 97: Jan 10-Apr 15. Cost: Summer: (3 weeks, 60 hours) CAN$495; summer (3 weeks, 45 hours) CAN$390; fall and winter: (12 weeks, 240 hours) CAN$1,495 (subject to change). Contact: Serge Bienvenu, Coordinator, Ecole de français, Faculté de l'education permanente, Université de Montreal, C.P. 6128, succursale Centre-ville, Montréal, PQ, H3C 3J7, Canada; (514) 343-6990, fax (514) 343-2430; bien vens@ere.umontreal.ca.

École de langue française de Trois-Pistoles. The oldest university-sponsored French immersion school in Canada, our school offers two 5-week sessions each year. Credit courses are offered in the areas of French language, culture, theater, and political science. Guided by dynamic monitors, students participate in one of a variety of nondegree workshops daily. While in Trois-Pistoles, students stay with families who provide them with 3 meals each day as well as with an opportunity to practice French in an informal setting.

Dates: May 12-Jun 13, 1997 and Jul 7-Aug 8, 1997. Cost: Approx. $1,550 plus $200 program deposit ($100 refundable). Contact: Maryanne Giangregorio, Administrative Assistant, The Univ. of Western Ontario, École de langue française de Trois-Pistoles, Univ. College 219, London, ON, N6A 3K7, Canada; tp@courier.ptce.uwo.ca.

English as a Second Language Centre. The ESL Programs has a variety of noncredit courses. English for Academic Purposes (EAP) teaches oral and written communication and study skills with cultural and academic orientation. English for Business and Communication (EAP/B) focus on listening, discussion, and writing for business purposes in the world of international business. Other courses include English for Specific Purposes (ESP).

Dates: Jun 28-Aug 23, 1996 (8 weeks), Sep 13-Dec 6, 1996 (12 weeks), Jan 10-Apr 3, 1997. Cost: $1,525 (8 weeks); $1,825 (12 weeks).

Contact: Penthes Rubrecht, Director, ESL Programs, Univ. of Regina, Campion College, Regina, SK, Canada S4S 0A2; (306) 585-4585, fax (306) 585-4971; esl@ max.cc.uregina.ca, http://leroy.cc.uregina.ca/~esl.

English Language Centre, Univ. of Victoria. English Language Centre (ELC), Univ. of Victoria provides intensive (12-week) English language programs 3 times annually for intermediate and advanced international students. Students may choose an Academic Program to improve academic and study skills for future studies or a Communicative Program to improve conversational English language skills for professional or personal development. Short-term programs are available throughout the spring and summer.

Dates: Spring and summer 1997: Mar 31-May 9 ($1,925); May 26-Jun 27 ($1,585), Jul 7-Aug 15 ($1,925), Aug 4-29 ($1,295). 1998: Apr 10-Jul 2, Sept 11-Dec 3, Jan 8-Apr 1 (tuition $2,700 per term). Contact: Maxine Macgillivray, Program Coordinator, English Language Centre, Univ. of Victoria, P.O. Box 1700 MS8452, Victoria, BC, V8W 2Y2 Canada; (604) 721-8469, fax (604) 721-6276; mmac gillivray@uvcs.uvic.ca.

English Language Program. The Univ. College of the Cariboo (UCC) is a public institution. The English Language Program is designed for students who require English skills for advanced study, or for career or personal development. The program allows students the chance to build English skills, prepare for advanced study in Canada, and combine academic elective courses with required English language courses.

Dates: Winter semester 1996: Jan 5-Apr 20. Summer semester 1996: Apr 29-Aug 7. Fall semester 1996: Sep 3-Dec 15. Cost: Application fee CAN$75; general fees CAN$100 per semester; tuition fees CAN$3,250 per semester; homestay placement CAN$150; homestay fee CAN$500 per month (meals included); campus residence fee CAN$295 per month

(meals not included); student apartment housing CAN$300 per month (meals not included). Contact: Carol Kerr, International Admissions, Univ. College of Cariboo, P.O. Box 3010, Kamloops, BC, V2C 5N3, Canada; (604) 828-5252, fax (604) 371-5513; ckerr@cariboo.bc.

French as a Second Language. Using a multi-skill approach, the program ensures that students develop communicative competence in French from the most basic levels to the most advanced. The program is both challenging and enjoyable, providing students with a language learning experience that is fun and entertaining. The 4 basic language skills, listening, speaking, reading, and writing, make up the curriculum. Four 60-minute hours per day, 5 days a week, 6 levels guaranteed, throughout 12 months. Each level lasts 4 weeks. Maximum 12 per class, extracurricular activities (optional). Youth program ages 15-17 in Jul and Aug.

Dates: Twelve starting dates from Jan to Dec. Cost: Four weeks: CAN$750 (approx. $600) tuition; CAN$830 (approx. $660) homestay; CAN $710 (approx. $595) YMCA Contact: Marie-Claire Marti, Registrar, LSC Montréal (Ecole de Langues de Montréal), 1450 City Councillors #300, Montreal, PQ, H3A 2E6, Canada; (514) 499-9911, fax (514) 499-0332.

French Immersion in the Summer. Courses in all levels at Université Laval in Quebec City, Université de Québec à Chicoutimi in Chicoutimi and Université de Montréal in Montreal. Minimum age 18. the programs are designed for students with a minimal background in French as well as those seeking to improve their oral fluency and reading and writing skills. Cultural, social, and spring activities are organized for students which allow them to apply the skills they learn in class. In Chicoutimi, all students live with a French speaking family.

Dates: Three- or 5-week sessions during May, Jun, Jul, and Aug depending on the program. Cost: Université de Montréal tuition

(SUNY in-state 3 credits), program fees and room, $710; Université Laval tuition (SUNY in-state 7 credits), program fees and single room, $1,100; Chicoutimi tuition (SUNY in-state 7 credits), program fee, room and board, and cultural activities, $1,577. Contact: Dodie Giltz, Assistant Director, International Programs, SUNY Plattsburgh, 130 Court St., Plattsburgh, NY 12901; (518) 564-2086, fax (518) 564-2112; giltzdr@splava.cc.plattsburgh. edu.

Intensive English Second Language. Intensive training in speaking, listening, writing, and reading. Advanced level. Students may combine post-secondary courses and language study. Program open to students at basic, intermediate, and advanced language levels. Students may enhance their language studies through participation in extracurricular activities and homestay with Canadian families.

Dates: Sep-Dec, Jan-Apr. Cost: CAN$3,750 tuition only (for 1 semester). Contact: Ms. Suzanne Woods, International Project Officer/Advisor, Sir Sandford Fleming College, Brealey Dr., Peterborough, ON, Canada; (705) 749-5530 ext. 1262, fax (705) 749-5526; swoods@ flemingc.on.ca.

Language Studies Canada Montréal. Using a multi-skill approach in a relaxed classroom atmosphere, the Standard Group program ensures that students develop communicative competence in French. Six levels of 4 weeks each, 4 hours daily. Maximum of 14 students per class. Audio-visual equipment, Student Resource Center. Optional activity program. Homestay available.

Dates: Two-week courses begin any Monday from Jan 15, 1996 year round, one-to-one instruction. Group 5 executive courses, Jun-Oct Summer Language Adventure (14 to 17-year-olds), Jul and Aug. Cost: Two weeks: $390 Standard Group tuition; $400 homestay. Cost of other services available upon request. Contact: Language Studies Canada Montréal, 1450 City Councillors, Montréal, PQ, H3A 2E6, Canada; (514) 499-9911, fax (514) 499-0332.

Music and Language Skills at Banff. Designed for non-English speaking students who wish to pursue a professional music career. An average of 15 hours of English classes per week with an accredited English as a Second Language teacher and classes with internationally renowned musicians. English and music studies are enhanced by living within the rich artistic environment of the Music and Sound department at the Banff Centre for the Arts.

Dates: Two to 12 weeks, Jun-Jul or Sep-Dec. Cost: Application fee $48; program fee $500 per week plus $231 per week room and meals. Contact: Karen Harper, Office of the Registrar, Banff Centre for the Arts, Box 1020, Stn. 28, Banff, AB, Canada T0L 0C0; (403) 762-6180, fax (403) 762-6345; arts_info@banff centre. ab.ca.

Queen's Univ. School of English. The Queen's Univ. School of English offers 5- and 12-week courses year-round at one of Canada's oldest and best-known universities in an almost totally English-speaking community. Students have the option of living in a University residence with monitors, in a homestay or in University cooperative housing. The English Only Rule is strictly enforced.

Dates: Jan 8-Apr 11, May 12-Aug 8, May 19-Jun 20, July 7-Aug 8, Sep 15-Dec 12. Cost: International students: $2,425 12 weeks; $1,325 5 weeks, plus $100 refundable book deposit, mandatory health insurance (price varies). Contact: Mrs. Eleanor Rogers, Director, The School of English, Queen's Univ., Kingston, Ontario, K7L 3N6 Canada; (613) 545-2472, fax (613) 545-6809; soe@post.queensu.ca, www.queensu.ca/soe/.

Special Intensive English Program. McGill Univ. was founded in 1821 and is internationally renowned for its high academic standards. The Special Intensive English courses are offered at 6 levels and run for 9 weeks. Classes are limited to about 15 students per class. There are 4 sessions a year. Instructional methods include the use of a modern language laboratory, audio-visual equipment, and a wide-range of activities stressing the communicative approach.

Dates: Spring 1996: Apr 1-May 31. Summer 1996: Jun 25-Aug 23. Fall 1996: Sep 23-Nov 22. Winter 1997: Jan 20-Mar 21. Cost: CAN$1,795 for international students, CAN$1,450 for Canadian citizens and permanent residents. Contact: Ms. M. Brettler, 770 Sherbrooke St. W., Montreal, PQ, H3A 1G1 Canada; (514) 398-6160, fax (514) 398-4448; info@conted.lan.mcgill.ca.

Univ. of New Brunswick English Language Programme. Established in 1954 in eastern Canada; tradition of expertise with international clientele. Language contract base; courses designed for client needs; experienced staff; residential approach. Participants live in English while learning in immersion: nonstop weekday and weekend. Classes extend into the community. Extensive diagnosis, ongoing assessment, constant quality control.

Dates: Three-week format (monthly Sep-Apr) in homestay; 5-week format (May-Jun, Jul-Aug) in University residence. Cost: Three-week CAN$3,339; 5-week CAN$1,700. Includes tuition fees. Contact: Mrs. Mary E. Murray, Director, Univ. of NB, English Language Program, P.O. Box 4400, Fredericton, New Brunswick, E3B 5A3, Canada; (506) 453-3564, fax (506) 453-3578.

Vancouver Community College. Vancouver Community College, British Columbia's largest center for English as a Second Language programs, is opening a new summer English program in beginner, intermediate, and advance listening and speaking. During the 3-week session, students will focus on idioms and vocabulary, conversational skills, and pronunciation and fluency.

Dates: CAN$250 per 3 week session. Cost: Jul 2-8; Jul 22-Aug 8, Aug 12-29. Classes held Monday to Thursday. Contact: Admissions Dept., Vancouver Community College, King Edward Campus, 1155 E Broadway, Box No.

24620 Sta. "F," Vancouver, BC, V5N 5T9, Canada; fax (604) 871-7458

Chile

Spanish and Latin American Studies. Santiago offers intensive language studies fulfilling up to 2 years of university Spanish requirements in 1 semester, with additional courses in literature, business, teacher education, history, political science. Week-long program-oriented field trips to the south and north of Chile, homestays, and many university activities at Chilean university.

Dates: Fall semester: Aug 28-Dec 17, 1996; spring semester: Jan 8-May 6, 1997. Cost: One semester $3,542; fall and spring $5,950. Contact: University Studies Abroad Consortium (USAC), Univ. of Nevada, Reno #323, Reno, NV 89557-0093; (702) 784-6569, fax (702) 784-6010; usac@equinox.unr.edu.

Spanish and Latin American Studies (Santiago). Santiago offers intensive language studies fulfilling up to 2 years of university Spanish requirements in 1 semester, with additional courses in literature, business, teacher ed., history, political science. Week-long program-oriented field trips to the south and north of Chile, homestays, and many university activities at Chilean university.

Dates: Fall semester: Aug 27-Dec 16, 1997; spring semester: Jan 7-May 5, 1998. Cost: One semester: $3,542; fall and spring: $5,950. Contact: University Studies Abroad Consortium (USAC), Univ. of Nevada, Reno #323, Reno, NV 89557-0093; (702) 784-6569, fax (702) 784-6010; usac@admin.unr.edu, www.scs.unr.edu/~usac.

China

Mandarin Language Study. Study intensive Mandarin Chinese at Beijing Language and Culture Univ., the only university in China specializing in teaching Mandarin to foreigners. Classes are intensive with 20 hours of classroom instruction per week. Fees include tuition, textbooks, double-occupancy accommodations, sightseeing in Beijing, cultural activities, orientation, visa processing, and roundtrip airfare from San Francisco.

Dates: Spring, summer, and fall programs and 1-year program. Cost: Five weeks $3,110, 20 weeks $4,720, 8 weeks $3,420, 1 year $6,850. Contact: China Advocates, 1635 Irving St., San Francisco, CA 94122; (800) 333-6474, fax (415) 753-0412; chinaadv@aol.com.

Colombia

CEUCA Intensive Summer Session. Designed for both beginners and more advanced students, this session stresses total immersion. Students live with Colombian host families. Also, classes are small and taught by Colombian faculty. Students can register for Spanish, Latin American Culture, and Handcrafts, but independent studies can be arranged. The session also includes field trips within and outside of Bogota.

Dates: Jun 3-Aug 1. Cost: $3,200 (includes room, board, and all land transportation). Contact: CEUCA, Jennifer Jones, U.S. Program Coordinator, P.O. Box 14942, Gainesville, FL 32604; Tel./fax (352) 376-5515; 6802499@ mcimail.com.

Costa Rica

CCIS-Intensive Spanish. At Centro Linguistico Conversa, Santa Ana, students earn 6 to 8 credits per 1-month cycle and may complete more than 1 cycle for 12-16 credits, essentially a language semester abroad. Classes are small (4 students maximum), and methodology is used. Oral proficiency test at end of program, swimming pool, sports, excursions arranged.

Dates: One-month cycles throughout academic year. Consult sponsor. Cost: $2,240 per cycle. Includes Costa Rican homestay, meals, airport transfer. Contact: Dr. Robert Vitale, Director of International Education, Miami-Dade Community College, 11011 SW 104th St., Miami, FL 33176-3393; (305) 237-2535, fax (305) 237-2949.

Central American Institute for International Affairs-ICAI. Three total immersion Spanish language programs designed to teach participants conversational Spanish. Four hours of classes per day with a low student-to-teacher ratio. Students are placed with carefully selected host families with single or double accommodations and all meals. Cultural activities and excursions are offered with each program.

Dates: Year round. New classes begin every Monday, all levels. Cost: From $632 (2-week program) to $1,298 (4-week program). Contact: Bill Fagan, Director, Language Studies Enrollment Center, 13948 Hemlock Dr., Penn Valley, CA 95946; (916) 432-7690, fax (916) 432-7615; bfaglsec@nccn.net, www.expreso. co.cr/icai/index.htm.

Centro Panamericano de Idiomas. CPI specializes in teaching Spanish as a second language to foreigners through total immersion (maximum 4 students per class). CPI first opened its doors in 1991 in Heredia (30 minutes from the capital city, San José); based upon its excellent reputation and experience, CPI has opened a new location near one of the most famous cloud forest reserves in the world, CPI Monteverde. Largest class size is 4 students per class.

Dates: Year round. Begin on a Monday. Cost: Prices for 1996: 5 1/2 hours of class (Monday-Friday) Heredia location only with homestay: 4 weeks $1,200, 3 weeks $920, 2 weeks $630 (includes 3 meals, text books, e-mail access, airport transportation, daily transportation to and from the school and laundry service); 4 hours of class (Monday-Friday) both Heredia and Monteverde with homestay: 4 weeks

$1,030, 3 weeks $830, 2 weeks $570 (includes text books, e-mail access, breakfast, dinner, airport and daily transportation—Heredia only—and laundry service); 4 hours of class (Monday-Friday) both Heredia and Monteverde without homestay: 4 weeks $630, 3 weeks $480, 2 weeks $320 (includes text books). Contact: Carlos Najarro or Jonle Sedar, P.O. Box 151-3007, San Joaquín de Flores, Heredia, Costa Rica; (506) 265-6866, Tel./fax (506) 265-6213; anajarro@sol.racsa.co.cr, www.westnet.com/costarica/cpi.html.

Costa Rican Language Academy. Costa Rican owned and operated language school offers first-rate Spanish instruction in a warm and friendly environment. Teachers with university degrees. Small groups or private classes. Included free in the programs are airport transportation, coffee and natural refreshments, excursions and Latin dance, Costa Rican cooking, music and conversation classes to provide students with complete cultural immersion.

Dates: Year round (start anytime). Cost: $135 per week or $220 per week for program with homestay. All other activities and services included at no additional cost. Contact: Costa Rican Language Academy, P.O. Box 336-2070, San José, Costa Rica; (011) 506-221-1624 or 233-8914 or 233-8938, fax 233-8670; crlang@sol.racsa.co.cr. In the U.S. (800) 854-6057.

Enjoy Learning Spanish Faster. Techniques developed from our ongoing research enable students at Centro Linguistico Latino-americ ano to learn more, faster, in a comfortable environment. Classes are 2-5 students plus group learning activities; conversations with middle-class homestay families (1 student per family). Homestays are within walking distance of school in small town (14,000 population) near the capital, San Jose.

Dates: Year round. Classes begin every Monday, at all levels. Cost: $295 per week for 25 hours of classes. Includes tuition, all meals (7 days a week), homestay, laundry, all materi-als, Costa Rican dance and cooking classes, and airport transportation. $25 one-time registration. Contact: Susan Shores, Registrar, Latin American Language Center, 7485 Rush River Dr., Suite 710-123, Sacramento, CA 95831; (916) 447-0938, fax (916) 428-9542.

Instituto de Lenguaje "Pura Vida." Only minutes from the capitol in the fresh mountain air of Heredia. Intense total immersion methods of teaching. Morning classes and daily cultural activities all conducted in Spanish, maximum 5 students per class. Teachers hold university degrees. Latin music and dance lessons, tours, trips, parties. Learn Spanish fast.

Dates: Classes for all levels start every Monday year round. Cost: Language only, 20 hours per week $230; total immersion, 35 hours per week with homestay $370; children's classes with homestay $370 per week, daycare available. Contact: Instituto de Lenguaje "Pura Vida," P.O. Box 730, Garden Grove, CA 92642; (714) 534-0125, fax (714) 534-1201; BS7324@aol.com.

Intensive Spanish. In Santa Ana, about 10 km from San Jose, the campus is a 6-acre "finca" with sports facilities and swimming pool. Operates in 1-month cycles throughout the academic year. Earn 6-7 credits on 1 month, or do a "Language Semester" in 2 months and earn 12-14 credits while mastering Spanish, 110 hours per month, classes of 4 students each. Peace Corps-style techniques. Costa Rican homestay, all meals. Optional lodging on campus at extra cost.

Dates: Operates in 1-month cycles throughout the year. Cost: $2,240 per 1-month cycle. Contact: Reinaldo Changsut, Study Abroad Adviser, Miami-Dade Community College, 11011 SW 104th St., Miami, FL 33176-3393; (305) 237-2535, fax (305) 237-2949.

Intensive Spanish Semester. At Centro Linguistico Conversa, Santa Ana, about 10 km. from San Jose. Two-month program, 12-16 credits. Peace Corps-style methodology, small classes. Costa Rican homestay or lodge on campus. Instruction 5 1/2 hours per day. Swimming pool, sports. One-month program available for 6 to 8 credits.

Dates: One-month cycles throughout the academic year. Cost: $4,270 per 2 months. Includes Costa Rican homestay, meals, airport transfer. Contact: Dr. Robert Vitale, Director of International Education, Miami-Dade Community College, 11011 SW 104th St., Miami, FL 33176-3393; (305) 237-2533 or (305) 237-2535, fax (305) 237-2949.

IPEE Total Immersion Spanish. The finest Spanish language school with the most friendly and qualified staff. All levels. Excellent upscale location, home stays, cultural events and excursions, student-centered attitude. Group rates. Professional, intensive, Spanish teacher, and private classes. Our attitude toward service and quality separates us from the rest.

Dates: Year round. Cost: One week plus homestay $305, 7-week class plus homestay $1,731. Contact: Robert Levy, Director, IPEE, 16057 Tampa Palms Blvd., Suite 158, Tampa, FL 33647; Tel./fax (813) 988-3916; ipee@gate. net, www.gate.net/~ipee/.

Spanish at Universal de Idiomas. Our international Spanish programs are designed to provide students with total immersion in the Spanish language. Classes are fun and our homestay program provides a natural setting in which to practice Spanish. Our 15-year experience in language teaching is a definite plus to learning Spanish and meeting friendly Costa Ricans.

Dates: Year round. Two- to 4-week courses. Cost: Economical Global Package: 4-week tuition room and board $890. Contact: Vilma de Castro, Instituto Universal de Idiomas, Spanish Department, P.O. Box 751-2150, Moravia, Costa Rica; (011) 506-257-0441, fax 223-9917; www.westnet.com/costarica/edu/universal.html.

Spanish Immersion Program. The Institute for Central American Development Studies (ICADS) offers 30-day programs of Intensive Spanish Languages—4 1/2 hours daily, 5 days a week. Small classes (4 students or less) geared to individual needs. Extra lectures and activities emphasize environmental issues, women's studies, economic development, and human rights. ICADS offers optional afternoon internship placements in grassroots organizations. Supportive informal learning environment. Homestays and field trips. A great alternative for the socially conscious.

Dates: Programs begin first Monday of each month. Cost: One month $1,150 (includes airport pick-up, classes, books, homestay, meals, laundry, lectures, activities, field trips, and placement). Ten percent discount after first month. Contact: Sandra Kinghorn, PhD, Director, ICADS, Dept. 826, P.O. Box 025216, Miami, FL 33102-5216; (506) 225-0508, fax (506) 234-1337; icadscr@expreso.co.cr.

Spanish Immersion Program. Nestled in colonial Barva, equidistant from Heredia's National Univ. and surrounding mountains, Escuela Latina offers an intensive, experience-based Spanish language and culture program. Students live in nearby homestays. Classes (max. 6 students) are taught entirely in Spanish. Tuition includes: 20 hours of Spanish; 1 hour of cooking; 4 hours of Latin dance, and 1 hour of music each week.

Dates: Classes begin every Monday. Cost: $875 for 4 weeks including homestay. Contact: In Costa Rica: Jill Dewey, Apdo 203-3000, Heredia, Costa Rica; (011) 506-237-5709, fax 506-237-2545 or in the U.S.: Roger Dewey (520) 776-7189, fax (520) 445-2546

Spanish Language. Intercultura Language Institute offers intensive Spanish and homestays in selected Costa Rican families. Academic credit available (with prior notice). Additional free activities: dance, music, theater, cinema, cooking. Weekend excursions to volcanoes, beaches, rainforest. Volunteer opportunities in social, environmental, and political organizations. Beach campus: optional 1 week per month, study on Pacific coast.

Dates: Year round. Cost: $960 per month (shorter stays available). Contact: Laura Ellington, Director, Intercultura Costa Rica, Apdo. 1952-3000, Heredia, Costa Rica; (011) 506-260-8480, Tel./fax (011) 506-260-9243.

Spanish, Ecology, and Latin American Studies (Heredia). Heredia offers intensive language studies which fulfills up to 2-year university Spanish requirements in a semester or 1 year in the 8-week summer program. Additional courses offered in political science, history, biology, teacher education, business, literature, etc. Program organized week-long and weekend field trips, homestays, and many local university activities.

Dates: Summer sessions: May 23-Jun 28 and Jun 23-Jul 28, 1996; fall term: Aug 28-Dec 20, 1996; spring term: Jan 9-May 11, 1997. Cost: One semester $3,542; 2 semesters $5,950; summer $1,360 per session; $2,275 both sessions. Contact: University Studies Abroad Consortium (USAC), Univ. of Nevada, Reno #323, Reno, NV 89557-0093; (702) 784-6569, fax (702) 784-6010; usac@equinox.unr.edu.

Spanish, Ecology, and Latin American Studies (Heredia). Heredia offers intensive language studies which fulfills up to 2-year university Spanish requirements in a semester or 1 year in the 8-week summer program. Additional courses offered in political science, history, biology, teacher ed., business, literature, etc. Program organized week-long and weekend field trips, homestays, and many local university activities.

Dates: Summer sessions: May 22-Jun 27, and Jun 22-Jul 27, 1997; fall term: Aug 27-Dec 19, 1997; spring term: Jan 8-May 10, 1998. Cost: One semester: $3,542; year: $5,950; summer: $1,360 per session; $2,275 both sessions. Contact: University Studies Abroad Consortium (USAC), Univ. of Nevada, Reno #323, Reno, NV 89557-0093; (702) 784-6569, fax (702) 784-6010; usac@admin.unr.edu, www.scs.unr.edu/~usac.

Summer Study Program in Costa Rica. The purpose of this program is to study Spanish and gain an appreciation for the people and culture of Costa Rica. Participants live with Costa Rican families and are provided 2 meals per day as well as laundry service. Excursions to Orosi Valley, Arenal Volcano, and Manuel Antonio National Park and Beach.

Dates: Jun 28-Jul 26. Cost: $1,750. Contact: Dr. Bill Hart, Compton Community College, 1111 E. Artesia Blvd., Compton, CA 90221-5393; (310) 637-2660, ext. 2545, fax (310) 608-3721.

Cuba

Cuba Language School. Global Exchange offers a rare and alternative opportunity to learn Spanish and understand Cuba's rich culture and complex political life. Study Spanish throughout the week at the Univ. of Havana and then sharpen your conversational skills with weekly meetings with Cuban experts. During these visits, learn about Alternative Energy, Sustainable Agriculture, Public Health, Women's Issues, and Art and Culture. Additional weekend excursions take you to rural areas, beaches and salsa dancing. Spanish classes are 5 days a week, 4-5 hours per day. Begining, intermediate and advanced students are welcome. Study Spanish, fine-tune your conversational abilities, and see Cuba for yourself.

Dates: Summer sessions: Jun 1-15; Jun 15-29; Jun 29-Jul 13; Jul 13-27; Jul 27-Aug 10; Aug 10-24. Cost: Two-week program is $1,200 from Cancuñ, México. Program includes roundtrip airfare from Cancuñ to Havana, visa fees, double room accommodations at a guest house, airport transfer in/out, transportation for day trips, language instruction, meals, cultural program, optional bicycle rental. Four-week program is $1,900; 6-week program is

$2,600. For optional hotel accommodations, add $400. Contact: Jennifer Cariño, Co-Director, Reality Tours Program, 2017 Mission St., #303, San Francisco, CA 94110; (415) 255-7296, fax (415) 255-7498; globalexch@igc.apc.org.

Denmark

Danish Language. Special course for foreigners in Danish language, culture, and society. Intensive language instruction, 40-55 hours per week at 8 levels. Lectures and study circles on Danish culture and society. Excursions.

Dates: Jul 21-Aug 3 and Aug 4-24, 1996. Cost: Two weeks DKK4,500; 3 weeks DKK6,500. Contact: The International People's College, Montebello Alle 1, DK-3000, Helsingør, Denmark; (011) 45-4921-33-61, fax 21-28.

Dominican Republic

Spanish, Development, Culture. Individual and group programs focused on (1) learning Spanish as a Second Language, (2) adaptation into Hispanic culture, (3) development themes on poverty, migration, sustainability, health, environment. Individually designed programs can include urban/rural homestays, with different degrees of immersion. Fifteen years experience.

Dates: Designed according to participant's needs. Cost: Varies with program ($1,530 per month immersion). Contact: Rafael Paz or Sobeya Seibel, Entrena, EPS-P-4507, Box 02-5261, Miami, FL 33102-5261; (011) 809-567-8990 or 541-4283, fax 566-3492.

Ecuador

Academia Latinoamericana de Español (Quito). Ecuador's number-one private Spanish language institute in former diplomat's mansion with swimming pool, hot tub, sauna, sport facilities. Instruction by university-trained teachers, all one-on-one. Customized study programs tailored to the individual. Select host family accommodations. Excursions to haciendas, Indian markets, etc. College credit available and internships.

Dates: Year round. Cost: One-week tuition, lodging, meals $294. Contact: Suzanne Bell, Admissions Director, U.S., 640 East 3990 South, Suite E, Salt Lake City, UT 84107; (801) 268-4608, fax (801) 265-9156; latinoa1@spanish.com.ec, http://ecnct.cc/academia/learnspa.htm.

Intensive Spanish Language. Specially designed programs for foreign students. Individual (one-to-one) instruction, up to 7 hours daily. Courses based on conversation, vocabulary, and grammar at all levels. Cultural and social activities provided weekly. The system is self-paced and it is possible to start at any time. Live with an Ecuadorian family, 1 student per family.

Dates: Year round. Cost: $1,430 for 4 weeks. Includes tuition, meals, housing, fees, airport transfer. Contact: Edgar J. Alvarez, Director, Academia de Español, Quito, P.O. Box 17-15-0039-C, Quito, Ecuador; (011) 593-2-553647 or 554811, fax 506474.

Spanish for Foreigners. One-to-one instruction with well-trained teachers; luxury house with natural light, gardens, and terrace without noise or smog; all levels. Special programs: Literature, Fine Arts, History, Commercial: "Activo," "Learn and Travel." Twice a week free city tours (in programs of 7 hours daily). Accommodations in nice Ecuadorian homestay near the school (3 meals, laundry, bed and bath private). Free services: airport pickup, cafeteria, mail and exchange service.

Dates: Year round. Cost: $7 per hour, $21 per day of family. No registration fee. Contact: Instituto de Español "El Quijote," Director Julio Cesar Muñoz Garay, P.O. Box 17 - 17 1419, Quito, Ecuador; (011) 593-2-455-256, fax 464-967 or 501-155 or 461-597.

Egypt

The American Univ. in Cairo. The Arabic Language Institute at the American Univ. in Cairo offers full-time Arabic language study in Egyptian colloquial and Modern Standard Arabic at elementary, intermediate, and advanced levels. Full use is made of the Arabic speaking environment and classes are enhanced by study-related field trips.

Dates: Sep-Jan; Feb-Jun; Jun-Aug. Cost: Approx. $4,600 per semester for tuition and academic fees. Contact: Mary Davidson, American Univ. in Cairo, 866 United Nations Plaza, Box 519, New York, NY 10017-1889.

El Salvador

Melida Anaya Montes Language School. Teach small-size English classes, all levels offered. Training provided. Students are adults working in the Salvadoran opposition who need to increase their capacity for their work and/or complete their studies. CIS also seeks volunteers for their human rights work. Volunteers can receive half-price Spanish classes.

Dates: Three-month sessions beginning mid-Jan, Apr, and Aug. Mini-sessions offered Jul and Nov. Cost: No fee. Must pay living costs ($250-$400 per month). Contact: CIS MAM Language School, Urb. Padilla Cuellar, Pasaje Los Pinos #17, San Salvador, El Salvador, Centro America; Tel./fax (011) 503-225-0076; cis@nicarao.apc.org, or Language School, c/o CISPES, P.O. Box 1801, New York, NY 10159; (212) 229-1290, fax (212) 645-7280.

Europe

Ceran Lingua Language Courses. Intensive residential language courses with programs offered in French, Spanish, German, Dutch, Japanese. All levels accepted. Classes combine group lessons (maximum 4 students), workshops, private lessons, and language laboratory. Full-time professional teaching staff with focus on verbal communication.

Dates: Year round. Cost: From $1,240 per week including accommodations, meals, and material. Contact: Elizabeth Bigwood, Languagency, P.O. Box 149, Northampton, MA 01060; (413) 584-0334, fax (413) 584-3046.

Language and Culture Immersion. By choosing one of our schools in France (17 different locations), Italy (Firenze, Roma, Siena), or Spain (Barcelona, Granada, Malaga, Salmanca), you are choosing the guarantee of quality. We have the support of the European Commission (Program Lingua-Socrates) and offer intensive courses for all levels and all ages: general language and specialty courses and methodology classes for teachers. All types of accommodations are available: family-stay, apartment, hotel. Remarkable equipment in a great atmosphere. You will speak the language of the country all day long thanks to continuous contact with native people.

Dates: Year round, beginning every Monday. Cost: From $400 per week (including course, accommodations, meals and extracurriculum activities). Contact: Promotion-Marketing-International, Pascale Mora, Director, 919 N. Kenmore St., Arlington, VA 22201; (703) 528-5300 or (703) 534-0668, fax (703) 528-5316; pascalem@aol.com, www.studyoverseas.com.

Language and Culture Programs. All-inclusive programs for high school seniors to senior citizens during the summer and year round. ICCE plans and arranges a complete learning vacation package including airfare, transfers, accommodations at a beach, resort, or similar homestay, student residence or hotel, meals, tuition, and class fees. Also spring painting workshop and summer opera festivals in Italy, Eastern Europe, and other adult programs. More than language programs.

Dates: Varied. Cost: Two weeks start at $2,499. Contact: Stanley Gochman, PhD, ICCE Program Coordinator, 352 Hungerford Dr., Rockville, MD 20850; (301) 983-9479.

Language Immersion Programs. Learn a language in the country where it's spoken. Intensive foreign language training offered in Spain, France, Italy, Germany, and Ecuador for students aged 16 and older. Classes are taught in up to 8 different proficiency levels and are suitable for beginners as well as people with advanced linguistic skills. All courses include accommodations and meals. Lots of extracurricular activities available. Students can earn college credit through Providence College.

Dates: Courses start every second Monday year round. Year programs commence in Sept., semester programs in Jan. Cost: Varies with program, approx. $950 per 2-week course. Contact: Kari Larsen, Admissions Coordinator, EF International Language Schools, 204 Lake St., Boston, MA 02135; (800) 992-1892, (617) 746-1700, fax (617) 746-1800; ils@ef.com.

France

Centre Int'l. D'Etudes Françaises. Levels: beginner, elementary, intermediate, advanced, session for teachers (July). Accommodations: single room either at the Foyer International d'Etudiants or on the campus. Numerous cultural activities are offered: shows, festivities, parties, homestays, trips (to Paris, the Châteaux de la Loire, Provence and in Burgundy), lectures, art, translation, dancing, singing, drama, sports.

Dates: Summer session: Jul 7-Aug 31, 1996; school year: Sep 1, 1996-Jun 7, 1997. Cost: Summer FF2,950 (4 weeks); winter FF5,350 (1 semester). Contact: Centre International d'Etudes Françaises, de l'Université de Bourgogne, 36 rue Chabot Charny, F-21000 Dijon, France; (011) 33-80-30-50-20, fax 30-13-08.

Domaine D'Esperance Cooking School. Six times a year, 1-week seminars are held in the spacious kitchen. Enrollment maximum is 9. Each morning is devoted to theoretical instruction, in the afternoon you gain practical experience, preparing the evening meal under the supervision of the chef. The D'Esperance is located in Gascony.

Dates: Oct, Dec, Jan, May, Jun. Cost: FF8,500 per week (10 percent discount for 2 enrollments). Includes full board, lessons. Contact: Claire de Montesquiou, Domaine D'Esperance, 40240 Mauvezin, D'Armagnac, France; (011) 33-5-58-44-68-33, fax 44-85-93.

Enjoy French in a Chateau. Château de Mâtel (17th century) offers residential courses for adults in General French, Intensive French, Cooking. On 32 hectares of parkland near Roanne city center. Close to Burgundy, Beaujolais, and city of Lyons. Single, en suite, and shared rooms available. One through 12-week courses. Tennis, pool, horse-riding, kayak.

Dates: Every Sunday Apr-Nov. Cost: From $999 full board and classes in Chateau. Contact: Dr. C. Roberts, 204 via Morella, Encinitas, CA 92024; (619) 632-1923 or (800) 484-1235 #0096 or Joe Davies, 3473 Camino Valencia, Carlsbad, CA 92009; Tel./fax (619) 591-4537 (modem) or Ecole des Trois Ponts, Chateau de Matel, 42300 Roanne, France; (011) 33-77-70-80-01, fax 77-71-53-00.

French in France. Total immersion is the most pleasant and the most effective way to learn a language. We have been doing it for 20 years in a small historical city located in Normandy (west of Paris, close to the seaside). We welcome people at any age, any level from 1- to 10-week programs, intensive or vacation type, from mid-March to mid-November.

Dates: Spring: Mar 25-Jun 1; summer: Jun 17-Aug 31; fall: Sep 9-Nov 16, 1996. Cost: From $524 per week (tuition, room and board, and excursions). Contact: Dr. Almeras, Chairman, French American Study Center, 12, 14, Blvd. Carnot, B.P. 176, 14104 Lisieux Cedex, France (011) 33-31-31-22-01, fax 31-22-21.

French Language and Culture. Intensive

French program. Classes at all levels from beginning to advanced. Placement tests determine language ability. A wide choice of cultural courses plus Business French. Progress monitored with graded exercises, assignments, midterm and final examinations. Credits transferred. Cultural activities and excursions, board and lodging (several solutions), sessions for teachers of French.

Dates: Jul 2-27, Sep 2-28; Academic year: Sep-Dec, Feb-Jun. Cost: Tuition and fees: Jul 3,500FF, Sep 4,100FF, 1 semester 7,600FF Contact: Renée Cochin, Directrice, 3, place André Leroy, BP 808, 49008 Angers Cedex 01, France; (011) 33-41-88-30-15, fax 87-71-67.

French Language Courses. La Ferme is a residential school of French for adults operating since 1978 in 2 restored 18th century manor houses near the South Atlantic coast. Courses for individuals or small groups include Intensive French, Business French, and French Language Marathons. See La Ferme's Internet pages at http://www.edunet.com/laferme.

Dates: Apr-Nov. Cost: From FF4,850-FF11,200 per week and per person including instruction, lodging, and most food. Contact: Mireille or Farrar Richardson, owners and managers, La Ferme, La Petite Eguille, 17600 Saujon, France; (011) 33-46-22-84-31, fax 22-91-38; fer@filnet.fr.

French Studies (Pau). Pau offers intensive language studies—up to 4 semesters of university language courses in 1 semester, 1 year in the 8-week summer program, in addition to art, political science, history, literature, second language teaching methods, etc. Program organized week-long field trips to Paris, homestay or student residence, and many activities at the French university.

Dates: Summer sessions: May 26-Jun 30, 1997 and Jun 24-Aug 1, 1997; fall semester: Sep 2-Dec 19, 1997; spring semester: Jan 3-May 1, 1998. Cost: One semester: $3,975; 2 semesters: $6,980; summer: $1,770 per session; $3,380 both sessions. Contact: University

Studies Abroad Consortium (USAC), Univ. of Nevada, Reno #323, Reno, NV 89557-0093; (702) 784-6569, fax (702) 784-6010; usac@admin.unr.edu, www.scs.unr.edu/~usac.

French-American Exchange. Learn French in the quaint city of Montpellier, just 10 kilometers off the sandy beaches of the Mediterranean. Programs offered during the summer, semester, and academic year. Housing is arranged with families, in apartments, dormitories, or hotels. Program cost includes introductory weekend in Paris, roundtrip transportation, housing and meals, and is tailored to the independent traveler.

Dates: Summer: Jun, Jul, Aug, Sep; semester: Sep-Jan, Feb-Jun; year: Sep-Jun. Cost: (1996) summer $2,455 (4 weeks); semester $6,149; year $11,288. Contact: Jim Pondolfino, Director, 111 Roberts Ct., Box 7, Alexandria, VA 22314; (703) 549-5087, fax (202) 337-1118.

Immersion Course in French. Intensive 2- to 4-week course for professional adults in picturesque Villefranche overlooking the French Riviera's most beautiful bay, 8 1/2 hours a day with 2 meals. Audio-visual classes, language lab, practice sessions, discussion-lunch. Evening film showings with discussions, evening outings with teachers, excursions to cultural and scenic landmarks. Accommodations provided in comfortable private apartments.

Dates: Courses start May 6, Jun 3, Jul 1, Aug 5, Sep 2, etc. (year round). Cost: May-Nov 1996: FF16,700 for 4 weeks. Accommodations from FF2,300 to FF5,800 for 4 weeks, depending on type of lodging. Contact: Sabine Letellier, Institut de Francais, 23 ave. Général Leclerc, 06230 Villefranche/Mer TR6, France.

Le Cordon Bleu, L'Art Culinaire. Le Cordon Bleu in Paris offers the highest diploma in culinary education in just 9 months. Cuisine and pastry classes begin every 10 weeks. Summer abroad program—I CHP—in Paris and London. Chef catering program for professionals.

Dates: Jun 10-Aug 17, 1996. Every 10 weeks. Cost: From $6,000 to $30,000 for cuisine and pastry in 9 months. Contact: In U.S. call (800) 457-CHEF or fax (914) 426-0104. Le Cordon Bleu, 8, rue Leon Delhomme, 75015 Paris, France.

Learn French in France. Language immersion courses in France (Paris, Nice, Antibes, Bordeaux, Cannes, Monaco, Aix-en-Provence, Tours). Private language schools centrally located, convenient to interesting places, cultural events, sports activities. Programs feature qualified teachers, small classes, attractive surroundings and facilities. Affordable prices for instruction. Accommodations with French families with meals, student residences, apartments, and nearby hotels.

Dates: Year round. Two weeks or more. Cost: Two-week courses with or without accommodations range from $605-$2,260. Contact: Ms. Lorraine Haber, Study Abroad Coordinator, CES Study Abroad Program, The Center for English Studies, 330 7th Ave., 6th Floor, New York, NY 10001; (212) 629-7300, fax (212) 736-7950.

Live and Learn French. Live with a carefully selected, welcoming French family in the Paris region. Learn from a family member/teacher who has a university degree and will tailor a private course to suit your needs. Share in a cultural and learning experience that will develop both your understanding of the language and the people who speak it. Minimum of 1 week stay. We also offer touristic stays conducted in English or French.

Dates: Year round. Cost: Fifteen hours of study per week $1,250; 20 hours of study per week $1,315. Two people coming together $1,800 per week. Prices include room, 3 meals a day, and instruction. Contact: Sara S. Monick, Live & Learn, 4215 Poplar Dr., Minneapolis, MN 55422; (612) 374-2444, fax (612) 374-3290.

Major in French Studies. The American Univ. of Paris offers a 4-year BA in French Studies, with concentrations in either French Literature or French with Business Applications; in addition, AUP has an exchange program with La Sorbonne, offering majors the chance to study there.

Dates: Fall application deadline May 1, spring application deadline Dec 1. Cost: Estimated total costs: $12,785 for 1 semester; $25,210 for 1 year. Contact: The American Univ. of Paris, U.S. Office, 80 E. 11th St., Suite 434, New York, NY 10003-6000; (212) 677-4870, fax (212) 475-5205; nyoffice@aup.fr, www.aup.fr.

Penn-in-Tours. For students interested in French language, literature, art, and civilization. Penn-in-Tours also offers various cultural opportunities and excursions in the beautiful Loire Valley. Students live with local families.

Dates: May 27-Jul 10. Cost: Tuition $2,840; family lodging $1,350; excursion and activity fee $250. Contact: Penn Summer Abroad, College of General Studies, Univ. of Pennsylvania, 3440 Market St., Suite 100, Philadelphia, PA 19104-3335; (215) 898-5738, fax (215) 573-2053.

USL/France. Five weeks in Paris and 1 week in London. For 3 weeks, the class is taught Monday to Thursday, leaving a 3-day weekend for travel. Courses offered, according to enrollment, in Management, Economics, Marketing, Humanities, Art History, History, Drawing, Photography, English Geology, Product Design, Communication, and French. All, except French, taught in English by American professors. Many field trips. Six credits.

Dates: Jun 1-Jul 14. Cost: $4,350. Includes airfare, tuition, transfers, room, breakfast, 1 meal a day, museum fees, and field trips. Contact: Gil Carner, Chairman, USL/France, USL Box 43850, Lafayette, LA 70504; (318) 482-5913 or (318) 482-5440, fax (318) 482-5907 or (318) 482-5446.

French West Indies

Le Français en Guadeloupe. An intensive French immersion course on the Caribbean island of Guadeloupe for adults with intermediate to advanced French skills. This is a total immersion in French language and Caribbean French culture on a beautiful tropical island. Our Guadeloupian friends provide instruction, local cuisine, excursions, and homestays—all in nonstop French.

Dates: Jan 3-20, 1997. Cost: $1,450 includes everything except airfare. Contact: Julia Schulz, President, Penobscot School, 28 Gay St., Rockland, ME 04841; (207) 594-1084, fax (207) 594-1067; penobscot@midcoast.com.

Germany

Collegium Palatinum. A German language institute located downtown Heidelberg offering German at all levels from beginner to advanced. Two-, 4-, and 8-week courses year round. Combination courses, one-on-one, and customized courses for groups. Recreational and cultural program. Accommodations: residential, guest family, private arrangement, or hotel.

Dates: Year round. Cost: Eight weeks DM2,730; 4 weeks DM1,370. Activity program DM50. Contact: Martine Berthet-Richter, PR Director, Adenauerplatz 8, D-69115 Heidelberg, Germany; (011) 49-06221-46289, fax (011) 49-06221-192023.

Europa-Kolleg Kassel. Language, culture, life in the heart of Germany. Study German in international classes of approximately 15 students at Kassel, in the center of Germany. Classes, afternoon activities, field trips, discussions with host families, and other students. Immerse yourself. Participants live in single rooms in German homes. College credit available.

Dates: Students with previous knowledge of German register for any 2-week period or more; 4 weeks required for programs bearing credit. Complete beginners begin on Jun 6, Jun 30, Jul 28. Call for other dates year round. Cost: DM665 per week for instruction, single room, full board, extracurricular activities. Pay with U.S. personal check. College program costs $2,100 for 6 hours of CUNY tuition and includes transportation and health insurance. Contact: Prof. K.E. Kuhn-Osius, 238 W. 106th St., Apt. 4A, New York, NY 10025; Tel./fax (212) 865-7332; ekuhnos@shiva.hunter. cuny. edu.

German as a Foreign Language. Students from all over the world are taught in small groups or on an individual basis. The school accepts all levels from total beginner to advanced, prepares for official examinations, offers courses for specific purposes, etc. Part of all courses: transmission of German culture, history, and news. The variety of art, culture and leisure activities in and around Munich provides each student endless possibilities. Baviera even has a Travel Service offering flights, tours, etc.

Dates: Year round except Christmas. Courses start every Monday. Cost: Small group: DM506 per week. Accommodations extra. Contact: Baviera, Nymphenburger Str. 154, 80634 Munich, Germany; (011) 49-89-1665599, fax 1665530.

German as a Foreign Language. We offer the following educational programs: various levels of German year round; intensive, crash, and long-term courses, individual tuition; special feature: German and Theatre, special programs: business German for professionals, German for teachers, German in a teacher's home, German for special purposes. Academic year, international study year, work placement, internship, guest studentship, homestays for groups, courses for firms and other institutions (banking, insurance, doctors, lawyers, etc.). Various types of accommodations. Full range of activities. Language tours worldwide.

Dates: Year round. Contact: GLS-Sprachenzentrum, Christina Langost, Director of Studies, Kolonnenstrasse 26, 10829 Berlin, Germany; (011) 49-30-787-41-52; fax 41-92.

German in Berlin. Intensive, crash, and long-term courses, individual tuition and small groups, busines German for professionals, German for teachers, German in the teacher's home. Homestays for groups; accommodations with guest families, in shared student apartments, or in hotels. Activity program; academic year or semester in Germany; guest studentship; university application help; work placement/internship. Special: German and theatre.

Dates: Start every week, year round. Cost: Prices from DM1205 for a 2-week standard course, including accommodations. Contact: Barbara Jaeschke, Managing Director, or Beate Gürtler, Course Counsellors, GLS Sprachenzentrum, Kolonnenstr 26, 10829 Berlin, Germany; (011) 49-30-787-4152, fax 787-4192.

German Studies. Intensive language study—up to 2 years of university language requirements in 1 semester. Additional courses in history, political science, culture, literature, etc. Program-organized field trips and housing. Beautiful city only 30 minutes from Hamburg.

Dates: Summer: May 23-Jun 27, 1997 and Jun 22-Jul 27, 1997; fall semester: Aug 26-Dec 16, 1997; spring semester: Jan 6-May 19, 1998. Cost: One semester: $3,575; fall and spring: $5,575; summer: $1,385 per session; $2,385 both sessions. Contact: University Studies Abroad Consortium (USAC), Univ. of Nevada, Reno #323, Reno, NV 89557-0093; (702) 784-6569, fax (702) 784-6010; usac@admin. unr. edu, www.scs.unr.edu/~usac.

Int'l. Univ. Language Summer Course. Language courses in German for students of the German language, prospective teachers of German, and teachers of German.

Dates: Three weeks in Jul and Aug. Cost: $583 includes course fees, accommodations, living expenses, some field trips. Contact: Dr. Steinicke, Sprachenzentrum der Otto-von-Guericke, Universität Magdeburg, Virchowstraße, Lehrgebäude IV, 39104 MD, Germany; (011) 49 391 67 16 51 6.

Learn German in Germany or Austria. Language immersion courses in Germany (Berlin, Freiburg, Stuttgart, Munich, Hamburg, Frankfurt) or Austria (Vienna). Private language schools centrally located, convenient to interesting places, cultural events, sports activities. Programs feature qualified teachers, small classes, attractive surroundings and facilities. Affordable prices for instruction. Accommodations with German or Austrian families with meals, student residences, apartments, and nearby hotels.

Dates: Year round. Two weeks or more. Cost: Two-week courses with or without accommodations range from $465-$1,355. Contact: Ms. Lorraine Haber, Study Abroad Coordinator, CES Study Abroad Program, The Center for English Studies, 330 7th Ave., 6th Floor, New York, NY 10001; (212) 629-7300, fax (212) 736-7950.

Penn-in-Freiburg. For students interested in coursework in intensive intermediate German. This program offers German language students an opportunity to gain proficiency skills and cultural insight while studying in the center of Renaissance Germany.

Dates: Jul 15-Aug 21. Cost: Tuition $2,840; housing and activities $600. Contact: Penn Summer Abroad, College of General Studies, Univ. of Pennsylvania, 3440 Market St., Suite 100, Philadelphia, PA 19104-3335; (215) 898-5738, fax (215) 573-2053.

Summer School for German Language. Language instruction on all levels (mornings); seminars and lectures on German literature, society, culture (afternoons); excursions, parties, concerts, theater (evenings).

Cost: DM750 (does not include room and board). Contact: Gisela Plock, Internationaler

Ferienkurs, Seminarstr. 2, D-69117 Heidelberg, Germany; (011) 49-6221-54-23-38, fax 54-23-32.

Greece

Intensive Modern Greek Language. Beginning, intermediate, and advanced levels of modern Greek classes meet for a total of 60 hours of intensive exercises and instruction in speaking, vocabulary, role-playing, grammar, reading, and writing. Held on the island of Paros.

Dates: Jun 30-Jul 18, 1997. Cost: $1,750. Includes tuition, course materials, housing. Contact: College Year in Athens, North American Office, Dept. T, P.O. Box 390890, Cambridge, MA 02139-0010; (617) 547-6141, fax (617) 547-6413; CYAthens@aol.com.

Modern Greek Language. The modern Greek language program is a comprehensive, integrated approach to learning modern Greek. Courses are year round, and include beginning through advanced proficiency levels. The syllabus has been created to teach the language to adults of all nationalities, using textbooks developed at the Center. Classes are small, with an average of 8-12 participants in each course.

Dates: Year round, new courses begin every month. Cost: $390 per 60-hour course. Contact: Rosemary Donnelly, Program Director, 48 Archimidous St., Athens 116 36, Greece; (011) 301-701-5242, fax 701-8603.

Guatemala

Academia de Español "Fundacion 23". The aim of the courses at "Fundacion 23" is to offer the students a conversation based approach to Spanish in the classroom from the very first day. Our program emphasizes personal attention as 1 teacher works with only 1 student. "Fundacion 23" is approved by the Ministry of Education and Tourism.

Dates: Year round. Cost: One week $125, 2 weeks $240, 3 weeks $365, 4 weeks $475. Contact: Cory de Herrera, Academia de Español "Fundacion 23," 6a. Av. 6-126 Zona 1, Huehuetenango, 13001, Guatemala, Central America; (011) 502-9-641478.

Casa de Español Xelajú (CEX). CEX offers the highest academic Spanish immersion program in the beautiful and nontouristed city of Quetzlatenango. It includes 5 hours of individual instruction daily, 3 hours of social and cultural activities. Homestay. Undergraduate credits transferable nationwide. Volunteer and internship positions available through our social programs. Children and high school students are welcome.

Dates: Year round. Classes begin every Monday. Cost: From Sep-May $140, summer $165. Contact: Julio E. Batres, 2206 Falcon Hill, Austin, TX 78745; (512) 416-6991, fax (512) 416-8965; cexspanish@aol.com, http://users.aol.com/cexspanish/casa.html.

Centro de Estudios de Español Pop Wuj. This school is a teacher-owned cooperative that donates its profits to projects that combat the problems of poverty and environmental degradation in Guatemala. Students receive 5 hours of one-on-one classes, live with a Guatemalan family, and take part in daily extracurricular activities such as community service work projects, conferences, films, and trips.

Dates: Year round, classes begin every Monday. Cost: $125 per week includes homestay (room and meals) with Guatemalan family. $20 registration fee additional. Contact: Centro de Estudios de Español Pop Wuj, P.O. Box 158, Sandstone, WV 25985-0158; (304) 466-2685; popwuj@aol.com. In Guatemala: Apdo. Postal 68, Quetzaltenango, Guatemala; Tel./fax (011) 502-9-61-82-86.

Eco-Escuela de Español. The Eco-Escuela de Español offers a unique educational experience by combining intensive Spanish language instruction with volunteer opportunities in conservation and community development projects. Students are immersed in the language, culture, and ecology of the Petén, Guatemala—an area renowned for its tropical forests and ancient Maya ruins. Ecological activities integrate classroom with field-based experiences.

Dates: Every Monday year round. Cost: Classes $60 per week (based on 20 hours of individual instruction per week, Monday-Friday). Room and board with local families $50 per week. Registration fee $10. Contact: Eco-Escuela, Conservation International, 1015 18th St. NW, Suite 1000, Washington, DC 20036; (202) 973-2264, fax (202) 887-5188; m.sister@conservation.org.

Escuela de Español "Sakribal". Program provides one-on-one intensive language instruction while giving students the chance to volunteer on student-supported development projects in the surrounding community, working in organic gardens, and in the country's only women's shelter. Family stays, guest lecturers, group discussions, and cultural activities round out the immersion program.

Dates: Classes start every Monday year round. Cost: $120 per week (includes classes, family stay, project work, other school activities). Contact: U.S. Office: 550 Ferncroft Ct., Danville, CA 94526; (510) 820-3632, fax (510) 820-6658; sakribal2@aol.com, http://kcyb.com/sakribal.

ICA Spanish Language/Guatemalan Culture Program. Our complete immersion program consists of one-on-one personalized language instruction 5 hours per day, 5 days per week, living with a Guatemalan family, and daily cultural activities include visits to surrounding villages, markets, cultural conferences, etc. It is also possible to do volunteer work for projects that help benefit the community.

Dates: Year round, 1-week classes. Cost: $120 per week Sep-May, $130 per week Jun-Aug. Contact: Bonnie and Dale Barth, U.S. Con-tacts, RR #2, Box 101, Stanton, NE 68779; Tel./fax (402) 439-2943, or Enrique Diaz, Director, la Calle 16-93, Zona 1, 09001 Quetzaltenango, Guatemala, C.A.; Tel./fax (011) 502-763-1871; icaxela13@pronet.net.gt or ICA c/o 5406 12 Ave., Edson, AB, T7E 1J8, Canada; (403) 723-6983, fax (403) 723-2017.

Proyecto Linguistico Francisco Marroquin. The Proyecto Linguistico Francisco Marroquin offers intensive Spanish language programs in the charming colonial city of Antigua, Guatemala. The program includes 7 hours daily or private, one-on-one instruction. Professional adults, students, retirees, and families at all Spanish levels are accommodated in this nonprofit school, dedicated to the preservation of the Mayan languages as well as to teaching Spanish. PLFM is authorized to administer the Foreign Service Institute exam to evaluate Spanish competency. Homestays in private room with local families are available. Programs of 1 to 12 weeks. The school has an international reputation for quality. Our U.S. office allows easy and convenient communication and registration and airport pickups can be easily arranged through our toll-free phone.

Dates: Year round. New classes begin every Monday. Summer months fill very early. Cost: $35 registration fee, $135 per week tuition, $65 per week homestay including all meals (except Sundays). Contact: Kay G. Rafool, Language Link Inc. (U.S. Office for Proyecto Linguistico, Francisco Marroquin), P.O. Box 3006, Peoria, IL 61512; (800) 552-2051, fax (309) 673-5537; info@langlink.com, www.langlink.com.

Spanish La Paz. Non-profit Spanish language and cultural immersion program. Weekly price includes 25 hours private instruction, family homestay, meals, educational/recreational activities. Volunteer possibilities on projects emphasizing education, natural health, womens' empowerment. Quality, well-trained teachers and friendly, helpful staff. Activities include conferences, videos, hikes, field trips. Peaceful, heart-centered setting.

Dates: Year round. Cost: $100 ($125 Jun-Aug). Room and board, activities, private instruction. Contact: Roy Holman, 5762 26th Ave. NE, Seattle, WA 98105; (206) 781-3676.

Spanish School "Juan Sisay". This language school formed by a collective of university-trained teachers focuses on Guatemalan culture. The school's small size provides personal instruction at all levels. The school also supports community projects in which the students learn about current issues as well as immerse themselves in the language.

Dates: Monday-Friday. Cost: $110 per week ($135 per week from Jun 1-Aug 15). Contact: Escuela de español "Juan Sisay," 3465 Cedar Valley Ct., Smyrna, GA 30080; (770) 436-6283.

Spanish School San Jose el Viejo. One teacher to 1 student, 32 1/2 hours per week. Spanish language, culture, and conversation, and live in a Guatemalan home. Other languages available. Easy transport from Guatemala International Airport.

Dates: Every Monday year round. Cost: $175 per week. Includes private tutor, homestay and meals in a Guatemalan home. School only: full day $90 per week, 32 1/2 hours per week; 4 hours a.m. or p.m. $65; 2 hours p.m. $40. Registration fee $10. Contact: Joan Ashton, P.O. Box 1218, Crystal Bay, NV 89402-1218; Tel./fax (702) 832-5678 or (800) JOAN ASH (562-6274), or (allow 2 months for reply if writing to Guatemala) Spanish School San Jose el Viejo, 5a Avenida Sur 34, Antigua, Guatemala, Central America; (011) 502-832-3028, fax 832-3029. Allow 3 weeks if writing to Miami mail drop: Spanish School San Jose el Viejo, Sec. 544, Box 02-5289, Miami, FL 33102; e-mail USA: joanash@aol.com; e-mail to Guatemala: spanish@guate.net.

Honduras

Centro Internacional de Idiomas. Learn Spanish on the Caribbean in historic Trujillo, Honduras, Central America. Students learn Spanish in a relaxed, tropical atmosphere with a one-on-one student to teacher ratio. Our program emphasizes intensive conversation, survival skills, grammar, and vocabulary. All teachers are university graduates in Spanish and linguistics; most of them are bilingual.

Dates: Year round. Cost: $175 for 4-hour classes, 5 days per week, 7 days homestay. Contact: Belinda Linton, Director, Centro Internacional de Idiomas, TGU 00068, P.O. Box 025387, Miami, FL 33102-5387; Tel./fax (011) 504-44-4777.

Ixbalanque Escuela de Español. Study just 1 km from the ruins or 2 km from the beach. We now have 2 campuses, one next to the Mayan Ruins of Copan and the other in Trujillo, located on the northcoast of Honduras. We offer one-to-one student/teacher ratio, a library with games, and study areas. All teachers are Honduran and are trained and certified to teach.

Dates: Closed during the week of Easter, Mar 24-28, 1997. Cost: $155 per week for 4 hours of class, 5 days per week, 7 nights of room and board with local family; $105 for classes only. Contact: Darla Brown de Hernández, Ixbalanque Escuela de Español, Copán Ruinas, Honduras, C.A.; (011) 504-98-3432, fax 57-6215.

Spanish Language School. Spend a week or more in a spectacular setting—the magnificent Mayan ruins of Copan, or the tropical beaches of Trujillo while learning Spanish from your own private instructor. Programs include 4 hours of instruction daily (weekdays), and 7 nights room and board with a Honduran family. Hotel based stays also available. All levels of instruction. Small groups and student groups welcome.

Dates: Year round (advance reservations recommended for summer; closed Holy Week). Cost: Single: (7 nights) $235, (14 nights) $410, (21 nights) $615; 2 or more (7 nights) $205, (14 nights) $410, (21 nights) $615. Contact:

Roatan Charter, Inc., P.O. Box 877, San Antonio, FL 33576; (800) 282-8932 or (904) 588-4132, fax (904) 588-4158.

Ireland

9th Achill Archaeological Field School. Survey and excavation of a post-medieval deserted village: Slievemore, Achill, Co. Mayo. Activities include: surveying, excavation procedure, recording geology and botany of island, field trips, lectures and seminars. No previous knowledge required. Maximum 6 credits.

Dates: Weekly Jul 15-Aug 30. Cost: Weekly: IR£85 p.p. $200 course fee plus accommodations. Contact: Theresa McDonald, M.A. Director, Achill Archaeological Field School, St. O'Hara's Hill, Tullamore, Co. Offaly; (011) 353-1-505-21627, fax 506-21627.

English as a Foreign Language/Teaching English as a Foreign Language. DAELS: 1-year full-time post-graduate Diploma in Advanced English Language Studies: English language, linguistics, one other academic subject; Summer school: 15-23 hours per week, 1- to 10-week stay. Levels from elementary to advanced. Options in English for language teachers, business English. Cambridge CTEFLA/DTEFLA teacher training.

Dates: DTEFLA, DAELS Oct-Jun; summer school Jul-Sep. (TEFLA at intervals throughout the year.) Cost: Tuition fees DAELS: IR£1,781 per year, DTEFLA IR£1,600, CTEFLA IR£850; summer school: IR£90 to IR£165 per week. Contact: Steven Dodd/Vivienne Lordan, Language Centre, Univ. College Cork, Republic of Ireland; (011) 353-21-904090 or 904102.

Irish Language and Cultural Programs. Irish language programs at all learning levels for adults are offered by Oideas Gael, which also offers cultural activity learning programs in hillwalking, dances of Ireland, painting, tapestry weaving, Raku-Celtic pottery, and archaeology.

Dates: Apr-Sep, 1997 (weekly). Cost: $140 plus accommodations (from $80 per week). Contact: Liam O'Cuinneagain, Director, Oideas Gael, Gleann Chohm Cille, County Donegal, Ireland.

Israel

Master of Arts in Hebrew Language. A 2-year program studying modern and Biblical Hebrew in Israel. The institute is an evangelical Christian university located on Mt. Zion, Jerusalem with 40 years experience in Hebrew language and Hebrew Bible translation. Other programs also available.

Dates: MA programs begin every fall semester. Cost: Approx. $7,000 per semester. Includes tuition, room and board, fees. Contact: Jerusalem University College, Amelia Nakai, Program Coordinator, 4249 E. State St., Suite 203, Rockford, IL 61108; (800) 891-9408 or (815) 229-5900.

Italy

Business, Economics, Italian Studies (Turin). Turin offers a diversified curriculum in English and in business and economics, plus intensive courses in Italian language and culture, literature, etc., at the foot of the majestic Alps. Program-organized housing and field trips and many Italian university activities.

Dates: Summer sessions: Jun 5-Jul 6, 1997 and Jun 30-Jul 25, 1998; fall semester: Aug 29-Dec 17, 1997; spring semester: Jan 4-Apr 30, 1998. Cost: $3,975 per semester, $6,980 fall and spring semesters; summer: $1,570 per session; $2,900 both sessions. Contact: University Studies Abroad Consortium (USAC), Univ. of Nevada, Reno #323, Reno, NV 89557-0093; (702) 784-6569, fax (702) 784-6010; usac@admin.unr.edu, www.scs.unr.edu/~usac.

Centro di Cultura Italiana in Casentino (CCIC). CCIC "Piero della Francesca," located in the Tuscan hill town of Poppi, offers 2- or 4-week sessions of intensive, low-pressure Italian language instruction. All classes are conducted in Italian, even for beginners. No tests (except for an initial diagnostic test for placement), no grades, no diploma. Plenty of grammar, conversation, reinforcement, satisfaction.

Dates: May through Oct. Cost: $1,000 all-inclusive for 2-week session. Contact: Stephen Casale, U.S. Agent, 1 University Pl., Apt. 17-R, New York, NY 10003-4522; (212) 228-9273, fax (212) 353-1942.

Centro Linguistico Sperimentale. Open year round (from a minimum stay of 2 weeks to maximum 5 months), small classes, open to all levels including total beginners, intensive individual courses, excursions, eating out, guided visits to museums, assistance in finding lodging (families, apartment, hotels).

Dates: From Jan to Dec. Cost: Two-week class course (4 hours a day) LIT420,000; 4 weeks, 4 hours a day LIT710,000. Contact: Danielle Lauber, Centro Linguistico Sperimentale, via del Corso, 50122 Florence, Italy; (011) 39-055-210592, fax (011) 39-055-289817.

Comitato Linguistico. School founded in 1986 situated in the old city center of Perugia. Professional teaching in friendly environment. Standard courses (20 hours per week), intensive courses, 5 levels including total beginners, Italian for translators and interpreters, business Italian, Italian for motel industry. Small groups. Students from many nations.

Dates: Jan 6-Dec 13. Cost: Enrollment fee: LIT100,000, standard course 2 weeks LIT300,000. Contact: Mrs. Christa Kernberger, Director, via del Conventuccio 13, 06121 Perugia, Italy; (011) 39-75-572147, fax 5734258; ctlingua@m.box.vol.it.

Italiaidea. Italiaidea is a center for comprehensive Italian instruction. We offer every level and format of Italian study from intensive short-term "survival Italian courses" to advanced semester-long courses meeting once or twice a week. We offer on-site lectures and visits to historic sites in Italian, conversation, and flexible scheduling. For over 10 years we have been offering college credit courses at numerous U.S. college and university programs in Italy; we now offer both academic assistance and travel/study assistance to our client institutions. Homestays are offered as well as accommodations in sharing apartments.

Dates: Year round. Cost: Sixty hours group course LIT720,000; 25 hours one-on-one program LIT1,170,000; 15 hours specific purposes or culture LIT1,150,000 (taxes not included). Contact: Carolina Ciampaglia, Co-Director, Piazza della Cancelleria 5, 00186 Roma, Italy; (011) 39-6-68307620, fax (011) 39-6-6892997.

Italian in Rome. Located a few minutes walk from the Colosseum, the school offers intensive and non-intensive, group and individual courses at all levels. A rich extracurricular program includes guided tours, excursions, seminars on art history, architecture, literature, and cinema. Accommodations with family or apartments with cooking facilities.

Dates: Year round, begins every 2 weeks. Cost: One-month course: LIT750,000, 3-month course: LIT1,850,000. Contact: Pier Luigi Arri, Director, via Bixio, 74 - 00185, Rome, Italy; (011) 39-6-7008434 or 70474976, fax 70497150; (temporary) www.nube.com/babele.

Italian Language and Culture. The school is centrally located only a few minutes walk from the Colosseum. Historical sites, shops, and entertainment facilities within easy reach. Courses year round 2-12 weeks (20 hours per week). Cultural program: guided tours, art history and architecture itineraries, seminars. Accommodation in private homes with cooking facilities.

Dates: 1996: Jan 8, 27; Feb 5, 19; Mar 4, 18; Apr 1, 15, 22; May 6, 20, Jun 3, 17; Jul 1, 15, 29; Aug 12, 26; Sep 9, 23; Oct 7, 21; Nov 4, 18; Dec 2, 9. Cost: Two weeks LIT500,000; 4 weeks LIT850,000; 8 weeks LIT1,550,000; 12 weeks

LIT2,240,000. Contact: Enzo Cosentino, Director, Torre de Babele Language Study Link, via Bixio, 74-00185 Rome, Italy; (011) 39-6-700-84-34, fax 70-49-71-50; babele@ flashnet. it, www.nube.com/babele.

Italian Language and Culture in Tuscany. Regular 2- and 4-week courses of Italian at all levels. Plus Italian for business, art history, drawing, opera, Dante, Tuscan cooking. Art history "mini-breaks" a specialty. Also university semesters and pre-university courses. August season with opera near the Tuscan coast. Comprehensive service with accommodations. Excellent library facilities. Florence city center location.

Dates: Year round. Cost: From $150, depending on choice of course. Contact: Gillian Parker, The British Institute of Florence, Lungarno Guicciardini 9, 50125, Firenze, Italy; (011) 39-55-284031, fax 289557; british@fol.it.

Italian Language Courses. Intensive group courses at 9 linguistic levels (from beginners to advanced), 4 lessons per day, Monday-Friday, year round. Combined courses: Intensive group course (see above) plus 2 hours private tuition per day. Intensive individual courses: 4-6-8 hours per day, general language and Italian for Business, Fashion, Design, Architecture. Business Italian Course: 4 hours per day for 2 weeks.

Dates: Jan 8, Feb 5, Mar 4, Apr 1, 29, May 27, Jun 24, Jul 22, Sep 2, 29, Oct 28, Nov 25, 1996. Cost: From LIT800,000 (1996). Contact: Linguadue, Mrs. Marialuisa Comini, Corso Buenos Aires, 43, 20124 Milano, Italy; (011) 39-2-2951-9972 or 2940-3544, fax 2951-9973.

Italian Language Courses. Group and individual Italian language courses (6 levels). Cultural courses (literature, art history, history of Florence, history of opera, operatic Italian and libretti), conversation courses, written expression, Italian politics, geography, Italian for business and commerce, Italian for tourism, wine course, cooking course.

Dates: Call or write for details. Cost: Call or write for details. Contact: Dr. Stefano Burbi, Director, Istituto Parola, Corso del Tintori 8, 50122 Florence, Italy; (011) 39-055-24-21-82, fax (055) 39-055-24-19-14; lstituto.parola@ agora.stm.it, /www.alba.fi.it/parola.

Italian Language Courses in Florence. Intensive group courses at 9 linguistic levels (from beginners to advanced), 4 lessons per day, Monday-Friday, year round. Combined courses: Intensive group courses (see above) plus 2 hours private tuition per day. Intensive individual courses: 4-6-8 hours per day. Conversations courses: 6 hours per day for 2 weeks.

Dates: Every second Monday starting from Jan 8, 1996. Cost: From LIT500,000 (1996). Contact: Linguaviva, Dr. Alessandro Vidoni, Via Fiume, 17, 50123 Florence, Italy; (011) 39-55-294359 or 280016, fax 283667.

Italian Language Courses in Milano. Intensive group courses at 9 linguistic levels (from beginners to advanced) 4 lessons per day, Monday-Friday, year round. Combined courses: Intensive group course (see above) plus 2 hours private tuition per day. Intensive individual courses: 4-6-8 hours per day, general language and Italian for Business, Fashion, Design, and Architecture. Business Italian Course: 4 hours per day for 2 weeks.

Dates: Jan 8, Feb 5, Mar 4, Apr 1, 29, May 27, Jun 24, Jul 22, Sep 2, 29, Oct 28, Nov 25, 1996. Cost: From LIT800,000 (1996). Contact: Mrs. Marialuisa Comini, Linguadue, Corso Buenos Aires, 43, 20124 Milano, Italy; (011) 39-2-2951-9972 or 2940-3544, fax 2951-9973.

Italian Language for Foreigners. The Univ. of Bergamo organizes a range of courses in Italian for foreigners.

Dates: Feb-Jul and Oct-Jan. Cost: From LIT650,000 for 3 weeks-LIT800,000 for 4 weeks. Contact: Corsi di Italiano per Stranieri, Universita degli Studi di Bergamo, Piazza Vecchia, 8, 24129 Bergamo, Italy; Tel./fax (011) 39-35-277407, 10-12 a.m. Monday-Friday.

Italian Language in Florence. Courses all year round (4 hours per day for 2, 4, 8 weeks, 3 and 6 months). Seven different levels from beginners to advanced. Maximum 8 people per class. Innovative teaching techniques like reading papers, organizing party games, singing Italian songs, etc. Visits to museums and churches, shows of Italian films.

Dates: Beginning of each month. Cost: From LIT530,000-LIT3,880,000. Free books. Contact: Franca Attendoli, Academia del Giglio, Via Ghibellina 116, 50122 Firenze, Italy; (011) 39-55-2302467, fax (011) 39-55-2302467

Italian Studies Summer Institute in Florence. For students interested in intensive beginning and intermediate language courses and cultural studies in literature, cinema, and art history taught in one of the world's most beautiful cities. Numerous cultural opportunities and field trips offer a valuable supplement to class work.

Dates: Jun 3-Jul 12. Cost: Tuition $2,700; housing $1,250-$1,800; travel $800. Contact: Penn Summer Abroad, College of General Studies, Univ. of Pennsylvania, 3440 Market St., Suite 100, Philadelphia, PA 19104-3335; (215) 898-5738, fax (215) 573-2053.

Learn Italian and Get to Know Italy. Language expresses the history and the culture of a people; hence the study of a nation is strongly related to the study of its language. Italian language courses and information about social and cultural aspects in groups or individually. Four hours per day of language lessons Monday through Friday for a total of 20 hours per week. Classes organized in small homogeneous groups from 4-12 participants. Six different ability levels. Cultural information programs.

Dates: 1996: Jul 8, 29, Aug 19, Sep 9, 30, Oct 28, Nov 25. 1997: Jan 5, Feb 2, Mar 2, 30, Apr 27, May 25, Jun 15, Jul 6, Aug 17, Sep 7 28, Oct 26, Nov 23. Cost: 1996: group course 2 weeks (56 hours) $315, 3 weeks (82 hours) $420, 4 weeks (96 hours) $475. Prices for 1996 are $345, $460, $525. Contact: Dr. Phil Andrea Moradei, Director, Ms. Anja Schultz and Ms. Linda Larsson, Koiné Center, Via de' Pandolfini 27, I.50122 Firenze, Italy; (011) 39-55-213881, fax 216949.

Learn Italian in Italy. Language immersion courses in Italy (Rome, Florence, Siena, Viareggio, Rimini, Bologna, Portico, Milan). Private language schools centrally located, convenient to interesting places, cultural events, sports activities. Programs feature qualified teachers, small classes, attractive surroundings and facilities. Affordable prices for instruction. Accommodations with Italian families with meals, student residences, apartments, and nearby hotels.

Dates: Year round. Two weeks or more. Cost: Two-week courses with or without accommodations range from $295-$905. Contact: Ms. Lorraine Haber, Study Abroad Coordinator, CES Study Abroad Program, The Center for English Studies, 330 7th Ave., 6th Floor, New York, NY 10001; (212) 629-7300, fax (212) 736-7950.

Lorenzo de Medici Language Art Culture. Italian language taught in the heart of Florence. The method is the total immersion in the culture. Additional seminars, museum visits, field trips, excursions. Tutor available for extra help at no charge.

Dates: Every Monday (beginners only the first Monday of each month). Cost: From $120. Contact: Dr. Gabriella Ganugi, Lorenzo de'Medici, Via Faenza, #43, 50123 Florence, Italy; (011) 39-55-287360, fax (011) 39-55-23989 20; ldm@dada.it.

Percorsi Italiani. School Locations: Florence, Milan, Rome, Siena and Elba (summer only). Italian taught at 9 levels, in groups or individually. Special classes for commercial and business. Italian, Italian Culture and Art, preparatory course for CILS examinations. Course duration 2 weeks minimum. Various activities for free time and weekends.

Dates: Beginning of month, year round.

Cost: $450-$570 depending on course and school chosen. Contact: Vera Dickson Frumkes, CONNECT, 28 Garey Dr., Chappaqua, NY 10514; (914) 242-8223, fax (914) 666-8160.

Japan

Intensive Japanese Language and Culture. This program has been created through the collaboration of Western Washington Univ. and KCP International Language Institute, Tokyo, Japan. Earn 1 year of Japanese language credit in 1 quarter at KCP (15 quarter credit hours). Study at the beautiful KCP campus in the heart of the Shinjuku district, Tokyo. Homestay or private dormitory room provided. Special features include: culture class for an additional 3 quarter credit hours, company visits, multicultural meetings with local Japanese university students, and KCP students from around the world. Educational excursions include trips to many cultural, historical and political sites around Tokyo.
Dates: Jul 3-Sep 13 (summer 96); Oct 3-Dec 11 (fall 96); Jan 7-Mar 17 (winter 97); Apr 3-Jun 16 (spring 97); Jul 2-Sep 12 (summer 97). Cost: Total package includes tuition and fees, housing, transportation pass, excursions, seminars: $4,500. Contact: Dr. Arthur S. Kimmel, Director, International Programs and Exchanges, Western Washington Univ., Old Main 530B, Bellingham, WA 98225-9046; (360) 650-3298, fax (360) 650-6572; kcp@kcp-usa.com, kcp-usa.com/~kcp.

Japanese as a Second Language. IEC Technical College of International Foreign Language offers 2 distinct avenues for overseas students: The first is a fun summer program, 5 1/2 weeks with credits applicable to the second trimester program where students study for 3 months. Prices include homestay or shared residence, accommodations, rural/urban location, small class size.

Dates: Start: Jul (1st week), Sep 15. Cost: Summer: ¥170,000; 2nd trimester: ¥360,000. Contact: Floyd Hodgins, IEC Technical College of International Foreign Language, 651-1 Hioki-Machi, Yatsushiro City, Kumamoto Ken, 866 Japan; (011) 81-096-535-5430, fax 532-0232.

Lex Homestay Programs. Lex offers homestay programs in which participants, living as members of a Japanese family, absorb the customs and characteristics of their host culture by taking part in daily life activities. Participants may go sightseeing with their families, meet friends and relatives, and attend festivals. Japanese language ability is not a requirement. Host families are fully screened volunteer members of the Lex organization. Adults, students, and entire families are encouraged to apply.
Dates: Jul-Aug 2, 4- and 6-week programs. Spring, 2-week program. Custom programs year round. Cost: Varies. Four-week summer program is $3,030, includes airfare from West Coast port of departure. Contact: Steffi Samman, Program Manager, Lex America, 68 Leonard St., Belmont, MA 02178; (617) 489-5800, fax (617) 489-5898; exchange@lexlrf.com.

Latin America

Academia Hispano Americana. The Academia Hispano Americana offers a completely integrated program of instruction in the fields of Spanish language and Latin American studies. The aim of the school is to make available to serious students a complete preparation for future life among the people of Latin America, with special emphasis on Mexico.
Dates: Jan 8, Feb 6, Mar 4, Apr 1, 29, May 6, Jun 3, Jul 1, 29, Aug 26, Sep 23, Oct 21, Nov 18, 1996. Jan 6, 1997. Cost: Intensive course: 2 weeks $250, 1 month $400; one-on-one $10 per hour. Family stay: private room $18 per day, double room $15 per day. Includes 3

meals. Contact: Academia Hispano Americano, Mesones #4, 37700 San Miguel de Allende, Gto. Mexico; (011) 52-415-2-03-49 or (011) 52-415-2-43-49, fax (011) 52-415-2-23-33.

Mexico

Center for Bilingual Multicultural Studies. The Center's total immersion Spanish program, designed to develop conversational fluency in the shortest possible time, combines daily classroom study and seminars on Mexico's history with living in a Mexican home and field trips to historical sites. No more than 5 students assigned to one professor. College accredited.

Dates: Year round. New classes begin every Monday. Two-week minimum study. Cost: Two-week program at $15 per day is $660; 2-week program at $22 per day is $758; 2-week program at $30 per day is $870. Includes 3 meals per day, registration fee, tuition and accommodations. Contact: U.S. Office, 3133 Lake Hollywood Dr., P.O. Box #1860, Los Angeles, CA 90078; (800) 466-4660 or (213) 851-3403, fax (213) 851-3684.

Centro de Servicios Lingüísticos. C.S.L. provides intensive Spanish language instruction by native-speaking professors at all levels, individually or in small groups. High school students, adults, professionals, or retired. Walk to the beach in your spare time or take our exclusive regional excursions. Group discounts. Room and meals available. Learn Spanish quickly and enjoyable.

Dates: Year round. New classes begin every Friday. Cost: No registration fee. Four hours of classes daily from Monday to Friday. Weekly tuition $200, 4 weeks $700. Double tuition for individual instruction. Room and all meals $200 per week, 4 weeks $700. Daily excursions and weekend trips to Huatulco or Oaxaca City $200 per week all expenses included. Four weeks $700. Form a group of 10 in any single

program and your program is free. Contact: Adam W. Armour, Director, Centro de Servicios Lingüísticos, Apartado Postal #307, Salina Cruz, Oaxaca, Mexico. Telegraph or mail.

Educational Community. Cemanahuac offers intensive Spanish language instruction by native speakers: academic credit, graduate and undergraduate; Latin American studies classes, with emphasis on the social reality of Mexico; strong field study programs led by anthropologists; rural studies program in a Mexican village; summer programs for educators; volunteer opportunities near the school; family stay program; special classes for professionals.

Dates: Year round program. New classes begin every Mon. Group programs arranged at reduced fees. Cost: Registration fee $90 (one-time fee); weekly tuition $190; housing with 3 meals per day $17 (double), $23 (single). Contact: Vivian B. Harvey, Educational Programs Coordinator, Apartado 5-21, Cuernavaca, Morelos, Mexico; (011) 52-73-18-6407 or 73-12-6419, fax 73-12-5418; 74052.2570@compuserve.com.

El Bosque del Caribe, Cancun. Take a professional Spanish course, 25 hours per week and enjoy the Caribbean beaches. Relaxed family atmosphere. No more than 6 students per class. Special conversation program. Mexican cooking classes and excursions to the Mayan sites. Housing with Mexican families. College credit available.

Dates: Year round. New classes begin every Monday. Group programs arranged at reduced fees. Cost: Enrollment fees $75, $175 per week, 1 week with a Mexican family $150. Contact: Eduardo Sotelo, Director, Calle Piña 1, S.M. 25, 77500 Cancún, Mexico; (011) 52-98 84 10 38, fax 84-58-88; bcaribe mail, inter acces.com.mx.

Instituto Allende. Arts and crafts, Spanish at all levels, Mexican studies, field trips, lectures.

BFA, MFA programs. College transfer credit. Incorporated with the Univ. of Guanajuato since 1953. Noncredit students of all ages also welcome. Campus is the 18th century hacienda of the Counts of Canal.

Dates: Year round. Cost: Tuition, Spanish $150-$420 per 4 weeks, depending on hours. Contact: Robert Somerlott, Academic Director, Instituto Allende, San Miguel de Allende, Guanajuato, Mexico 37700; (011) 52-415-2-01-90, fax 2-45-38; ferr@abasolo.ugto.mx.

Instituto Cultural Oaxaca/Spanish. Seven hours daily of intensive Spanish instruction in a lovely Oaxacan estate. Grammar, conversation, workshops in cooking, weaving, and pottery, one-on-one native speaking conversation partners, lectures and films are all part of the total immersion process. Tours to archaeological sites, artisan villages, and indigenous marketplaces. Homestays available.

Dates: Year round monthly sessions. Write, call, or fax for specific dates and informative brochure. Cost: $50 registration fee and $400 per session or $105 per week. Contact: Lic Lucero Topete, Director, Instituto Cultural Oaxaca, Apartado Postal #340, Oaxaca, Oaxaca, C.P. 68000, Mexico; (011)-52-951-53404, fax (011) 52-951-53728; inscuoax@antequera.com, http://antequera.com/inscuoax/.

Intensive Spanish Course. The Academia Hispano Americana, the oldest full-time specialized Spanish language program in Mexico, offers students 35 hours per week of activities in the Spanish language. Courses are held year round and start almost every 4 weeks. San Miguel is a pleasant mountain community with clear air and many cultural opportunities.

Dates: Jan 6, Feb 3, Mar 3, Mar 31, May 5, Jun 2 and 30, Jul 28, Aug 25, Sep 22, Oct 20, Nov 17, 1997. Cost: Tuition $400 per session, discounts after first full session. Room and board from $15 per day. Contact: Gary De Mirjyn, Director, Academia Hispano Americana, Mesones 4, San Miguel de Allende, Gto., Mexico; (011) 52-415-2-0349 or 2-43-49, fax 22333.

Intensive Spanish in Cuauhnahuac. Cuauhnahuac, founded in 1972, offers a variety of intensive and flexible programs geared to individual needs. Six hours of classes daily with no more than 4 students to a class. Housing with Mexican families who really care about you. Cultural conferences, excursions, and special classes for professionals. College credit available.

Dates: Year round. New classes begin every Monday. Cost: $70 registration fee; $600 4 weeks tuition, housing $16 per night. Contact: Marcia Snell, 519 Park Dr., Kenilworth, IL 60043; (800) 245-9335, fax (847) 256-9475; lankysam@aol.com.

Intensive Spanish in Yucatan. Centro de Idiomas del Sureste, A.C. (CIS), founded in 1974, offers 3-5 hours per day of intensive conversational Spanish classes with native-speaking, university-trained professors. Maximum 6 students per group, average 3. Program includes beginner courses to very advanced with related field trips and recommended optional homestay. Also special classes in business, legal, medical vocabulary, or Mayan studies.

Dates: Year round. Starts any Monday, except last 2 weeks in Dec. Cost: Tuition (3 hours per day program: $330 first 2 weeks, $115 each additional week); tuition 5 hours per day programs $490 first 2 weeks, $195 each additional week. Contact: Chloe C. Pacheco, Director, Centro de Idiomas del Sureste, A.C., Calle 14 #106 X25, col. Mexico, CP 97128, Mérida, Yucatán, México; (011) 52-99-26-11-55 or (011) 52-99-26-94-94, 20-28-10, fax (011) 52-99-26-90-20.

Language Institute of Colima. The Language Institute of Colima Mexico offers a system of total immersion with classes held throughout the year Monday-Friday. Students live with local host families and attend 6 hours of instruction daily; no more than 5 students per class. Many extras, including beach excursions, are included.

Dates: Year round, Monday-Friday. Cost: Registration $80; tuition $415 1st week, $345 after 1st week (for shared room), $445 1st week, $375 after 1st week (for private room). 10% discount for 6 or more. Contact: Dennis Bourassa, Language Institute of Colima, P.O. Box 827, Miranda, CA 95553; (800) 604-6579, fax (707) 923-4232; colima@northcoast.com, www.northcoast.com/~colima.

Learn, Live, and Love Spanish in the Land of the Maya (Chiapas). Spanish lessons in private sessions or small groups (4 people max). Family stays available. School tours to Indian (Mayan) villages, jungle trips available. Extracurricular activities included: Mexican cooking, discussions, video showings. Teach English in exchange for Spanish lessons. Centro Cultural "El Puente" includes gallery weaver's cooperative, travel agency, cafe, restaurant, phone/fax service.

Dates: Year round. Cost: Highest $220 per week; lowest $75 per week. Contact: Roberto Rivas, Bastidas Centro Bilingüe de Chiapas, C. Real de Guadalupe 55, Centro Cultural "El Puente," San Cristóbal de Las Casas 29230, Chiapas, Mexico; (011) 52-967-8-41-57, fax 967-83723 or Tel./fax (800) 303-4983; cenbili@chisnet.com.mx,www.mexonline.com/centro1.htm.

Loyola Univ. in Mexico City. Loyola offers 17 Spanish courses as well as courses on Latin American studies, communications, economics, history, political science, philosophy, sociology, and visual arts at the Jesuit Universidad Iberoamericana in Mexico City. Financial aid available. Trips to Cuernavaca, Taxco, Teotihuacan, and Tula. Three summer sessions and semester and year abroad program available.

Dates: Jan 7-May 15, 1997; May 30-Jul 12, 1997; Jun 23-Jul 24, 1997; Jun 23-Aug 7, 1997;

Aug 8-Dec 5, 1997; Jan 9-May 14, 1998. Cost: $2,480 and $2,160 for 6- and 4-week sessions; $6,758 for 17-week semester program. Contact: Maurice P. Brungardt, Director, Mexico Program, Loyola Univ., New Orleans, LA 70118; (504) 865-3539 day, (504) 861-3402 evening, fax (504) 865-2010; brungard@beta.loyno.edu.

Mar de Jade, Mexico. Tropical ocean-front responsible tourism center in a beautiful unspoiled fishing village near Puerto Vallarta offers unique study options. Learn Spanish in small groups and enjoy great swimming, kayaking, hiking, horseback riding, and meditation. Gain insight into rural culture by studying and working in a farmers' clinic, local construction, cottage industries, or teaching.

Dates: Year round. Cost: $865 for 21-day work/study. Includes room (shared occupancy), board, 12 hours per week of Spanish and 15 hours per week of work. Longer resident program available at lower cost. Vacation/Spanish 1-week minimum $365 room, board, 12 hours of Spanish. Vacation only $45 per night for any length of time. Contact: In Mexico: Mar de Jade/Casa Clinica, A.P. 81, Las Varas, Nayarit, 63715, Mexico; Tel./fax (011) 52-327-20184; In U.S.: P.O. Box 423353, San Francisco, CA 94142; (415) 281-0164.

School for Foreign Students-Taxco. Sixteenth century-founded refurbished hacienda in the colonial village of Taxco. Belongs to the oldest university in the Americas (National Autonomous University of Mexico). Six-week intensive courses. Five levels of Spanish, Mexican and Latin American Art, History, Literature, Social studies.

Dates: Fall: Aug, Oct, Dec. Spring: Jan, Mar, May. Summer: mid-Jun. Cost: Spring and fall: registration $25, tuition $240; summer: registration $25, tuition $485. Contact: Mr. Pena, Director, Apartado Postal 70, Taxco, Guerrero, Mexico 40220; Tel./fax (011) 52-20-124.

Spanish Education for Women. Spanish Education for Women offers 6 weeks of intensive Spanish for women committed to social justice who need Spanish in their roles as teachers, social workers, health care providers, etc. SEW offers: 4 hours of small group instruction daily, 6 hours of individual tutoring weekly, field trips and housing with a working-class family in Guadalajara, Mexico.

Dates: Jun 25-Aug 2, 1996. Cost: Tuition is $1,350. Room and board are $115 weekly. Contact: Debbie Polhemus, Summer Program Director, Spanish Education for Women, P.O. Box 29338, Washington, DC 20017; (202) 635-3118.

Spanish in Southeast Mexico. Centro Bilingue offers one-on-one or small group instruction, family stays. Group instruction begins the first and third Mondays of each month. Jungle trips and Mayan towns trips.

Dates: One-on-one, year round. Group classes begin first and third Mondays of each month. Cost: Most expensive $200 per week; lowest $115 per week. Contact: Roberto Rivas-Bastidas, C. Real de Guadalupe 55, Centro Cultural "El Puente," San Cristobal de Las Casas, Chiapas, Mexico, 29230; (011) 52-967-84157; Tel./fax (011) 52-967-83723. In U.S. (800) 303-49-83.

Spanish Language in Guanajuato. We work with our students one-on-one or in small groups (2 to 5 students), tailoring instruction to each student's needs. We teach people of all ages and from many nationalities. Highlights: homestays with families, sports, movies, field trips, hikes, cultural events—all this taking place in the most beautiful colonial setting of Mexico.

Dates: Year round. New classes begin every Monday. Cost: $925. Includes lifetime registration fee, group classes (5 sessions per day Monday-Friday), and a homestay with 3 meals daily for 4 weeks. Lower price for fewer weeks. Contact: Director Jorge Barroso, Instituto Falcon, A.C., Guanajuato, Gto. 36000 Mexico;

Tel./fax (011) 52-473-2-36-94, www.infonet.com.mx/falcon.

Spanish Language Institute. The Institute offers a complete immersion Spanish program. Maximum 5 students per class. Cultural courses cover politics, economics, art, history, Mexico today. The Institute offers an 8-hour executive program with a private instructor, with a field trip related to her/his area of interest; semi private with 8-hour program, 3 with private instructor. The programs are complemented with host Mexican families and excursions.

Dates: Year round. Classes begin every Monday. Cost: Registration fee $100. Regular program $150. Housing with 3 meals per day $15/$22. Contact: Francisco Ramos, Spanish Language Institute, Apartado Postal 2-3, Cuernavaca, Morelos 62191, Mexico.

Study in Mexico. A complete immersion program with homestays and internships. University credits are available. No previous knowledge of Spanish required. Extensive traveling available.

Dates: Year round and 4-week special programs May 24-Jun 23 and Jul 12-Aug 11. Cost: $1,795 (4 weeks). Scholarships and special discounts available. Contact: Dr. Rámon Magráns, Professor of Spanish, Austin Peay State Univ., Box 4487, Clarksville, TN 37044; (615) 648-7847 or (800) 747-1894.

Universal Centro de Lengua. Universal offers Spanish language programs specifically tailored to meet the needs of each student. Spanish courses are offered at all levels, individually or in groups, and are complemented by diverse lectures. Classes range from 2 to 5 students and meet 5 hours daily with hourly breaks of 10 minutes.

Dates: Year round. Cost: Normal $140 per week, advanced $180 per week, professional $200 per week. Contact: Ramiro Cuellar Hernandez, Universal Centro de Lengua,

J.H. Preciado #171, Col. San Anton, Cuernavaca, Morelos, Mexico; (011) 52-73-18-29-04 or 12-49-02, fax 18-29-10; univ ersa@laneta.apc.org.

New Zealand

Marlborough Sounds, "The Travelling Classroom." A 7-day English and Adventure course in the Marlborough Sounds (South Island). Morning class in the classroom in Picton or on the sailing yacht and afternoon activities, such as sailing, visiting historic places, meeting New Zealand indigenous people, the Maori, horse riding, kayaking, visiting vineyards in the Bleuheim area.

Dates: Feb 26, 1996, Mar 25, 1996. Cost: $1,100. Contact: Capital Language Academic, 57 Manners Mall, Box 1100, Wellington, New Zealand; (011) 64-04-4727557, fax 4725285; 100245.13@compuserve.com, http//nz.com/commerce/cla.html.

Poland

Polish Language and Culture. Jagiellonian Univ. (founded in 1364) offers intensive and non-intensive Polish language courses; 8 levels; academic methods. Courses on Polish history, literature, art, economy, politics, folklore, etc. Cultural program; trips to places of interest. Up to 8 credits for the language and/or 6 credits for other programs (transcripts of studies issued).

Dates: Four weeks: Jul 4-Aug 31; 6 weeks: Jul 4-Aug 14; 3 weeks: Jul 4-24, Jul 28-Aug 17. Cost: Four weeks $940 plus $30 registration fee; 6 weeks $1,220 plus $30; 3 weeks $690 plus $30. Room, board and tourist program included. Contact: Ewa Nowakowska, Program Director, Summer School, ul. Garbarska 7a, 31-131, Krakow, Poland; (011) 48-12-213692, fax 227701; uknowako@cyf-kr.edu.pl, www.if.uj.edu.pl/uj/sl.

Portugal

Portuguese Courses in Lisbon. Intensive Portuguese courses of 60 hours per month. Small groups with an average of 6 students. Portuguese is taught in a fully communicative context. Courses start every 4 weeks. A cultural program of visits included. Accommodation arranged.

Dates: Jul 7, Aug 4, Sep 1, Oct 6, Nov 3, Dec 2, Jan 5, Feb 2, Mar 3, Apr 2, May 5, June 2. Cost: From $600 for 4 weeks intensive (3 hours per day) group course. Contact: Resgate Bertardo da Costa, International House, Rua Marqués Sá Da Bandeira 16, 1050 Lisbon, Portugal; (011) 351-3151496, fax 3530081; imlisbon@mai.telepac.pt.

Spain

Collegium Palatinum (Madrid). CP offers an intesive Spanish program at all levels from beginners to advanced. Two- to 8-week courses year round. Small classes guarantee a great deal of individual attention to the student. Recreational and cultural program provided. Prime location in the town center. Accommodations: guest family, private arrangement, or hotel.

Dates: Year round.. Cost: PTS21000 per week (20 hours of 60 minutes). Activity program extra. Contact: Maria Dolores Romero, Director, Collegium Palatinum, c/o Schiller International Univ., Calle San Bernado 97/99, 28015 Madrid, Spain; (011) 34-01-448-2488, fax 445-2110.

Commercial Course, Chamber of Commerce and Industry. Thirty hours of classes per week in groups of 3-6 students. Two-week course. Basic and advanced levels. Certificates and examinations in our center. Recognized by Chamber of Commerce and Industry. All course materials. Activities and visits organized by the school are optional. Telefax facilities. Diploma. Exam dates: Mar 15, May 31, Jul 12, Nov 1.

Dates: Mar 3, May 19, Jun 30, Oct 20. Cost: Two weeks: PTS85,000; inscrip. for exam: PTS12,000. Contact: Mrs. Renate Urban, Director, Escuela de Idiomas "Nerja," C Almirante Ferrándiz, 73-29780 Nerja, Málaga, Spain; (011) 34-5-252-16-87, fax 252-21-19; idnerja@gandalf.leader.es.

Group 5 Course on Costa del Sol. Thirty hours of classes per week in groups of 4-6 students. Courses from 2-16 weeks. All course materials. Activities and excursions organized by the school are optional. Telefax facilities. Certificate/diploma. Intermediate and advanced students: any Monday.

Dates: Jan 7, Feb 3, Mar 3, 31, May 5, Jun 2, 30, Jul 14, Aug 4, 18, Sep 1, 15, Oct 6, Nov 3, Dec 1. Cost: Two weeks PTS80,000; 4 weeks PTS145,000. Contact: Mrs. Renate Urban, Director, Escuela de Idiomas "Nerja," C Almirante Ferrándiz, 73-29780 Nerja, Málaga, Spain; (011) 34-5-252-16-87, fax 252-21-19; idnerja@gandalf.leader.es.

Hispalengua Spanish for Foreigners. Small groups with qualified teachers, intensive courses from 2 weeks in selected homestays or hotels. We specialize in Spanish for young American students and provide personal escorts and introductions to local young people.

Dates: Year round. Cost: PTS170,000 for 4 weeks tuition and full board. Contact: Hispalengua, Julio Lalmolda, San Miguel 16, 500 001 Zaragoza, Spain; (011) 34-76-221810 or 211120, fax 212010.

In-Country Language Courses. The courses of Don Quijote, Europe's largest specialist in in-country Spanish language courses, vary from 2-36 weeks intensive Spanish, DELE (official diploma preparation), Spanish plus specialization (business, tourism, international secretary), refresher courses for teachers of

Spanish, flight attendant course, combination courses, tailor-made individual courses, summer and Christmas courses.

Dates: Year round. Cost: Depends on course, duration, and accommodations. Contact: Don Quijote, Central Promotion Office, Ref. USLS96, Ms. Elvira Zingone, Student Services, Apdo. de correos 333, 37080 Salamanca, Spain; (011) 34-23-268860, fax 268815; donquijote@offcampus.es.

Intensive Course on Costa del Sol. Twenty hours of classes per week in groups of 5-10 students. From 2-24 weeks. Registration and all course materials. Activities and visits organized by the school are optional. Continuous progress testing. Certificate of attendance/diploma. Intermediate and advanced students: any Monday.

Dates: Jan 7, Feb 3, Mar 3, 31, May 5, Jun 2, 30, Jul 14, Aug 4, 18, Sep 1, 15, Oct 6, Nov 3, Dec 1. Cost: Two weeks: PTS46,000; 4 weeks: PTS68,000. Contact: Mrs. Renate Urban, Director, Escuela de Idiomas "Nerja," C Almirante Ferrándiz, 73-29780 Nerja, Málaga, Spain; (011) 34-5-252-16-87, fax 252-21-19; idnerja@gandalf.leader.es.

Intensive Spanish Courses. CLIC offers intensive Spanish courses for all levels of learning, courses for teachers, as well as summer courses in Isla Cristina on the Costa de la Luz. Accommodations are carefully selected and we have a varied cultural program and exchanges with Spanish students. The CLIC Centre occupies 2 stately houses in the old part of the city and combines professionalism and a friendly atmosphere. The CLIC program is approved for academic credits.

Dates: Year round. Cost: Approx. $900 for a 4-week course (include 4 weeks Spanish course, plus homestay, individual room, daily breakfast and lunch). Contact: CLIC, Bernhard Roters, Manager, c/o Santa Ana 11, 41002, Sevilla, Spain; (011) 34-5-4374500, fax 4371806.

Language and Culture Courses (Madrid, Salamanca, Malaga). Escuela Internacional offers quality programs in Spanish language and culture with U.S. undergraduate credits. Our qualified teachers and small classes (maximum 12 students per class) guarantee you a successful program. Stay with a selected family or in a shared apartment. Enjoy our extensive afternoon activities and weekend excursions. Our professionalism, enthusiasm, and personal touch will make your experience in Spain memorable and fun.

Dates: Year round, 2-48 weeks. Cost: From PTS54,500 for 2 weeks (tuition 15 hours per week, room, books) to PTS107,500 (30 hours per week, room and full board, books, activities, excursion). Contact: Escuela Internacional, Midori Ishizaka, Director of Admissions, c/Talamanca 10, 28807 Alcalá de Henares, Madrid, Spain; (011) 34-1-8831264, fax (011) 34-1-8831301; escuelai@ergos.es, www.ergos.es/escuelai.

Learn Spanish in Spain. Language immersion courses in Spain (Barcelona, Canary Islands, Granada, Madrid, Malaga, San Sebastian, Seville, and Valencia). Private language schools centrally located, convenient to interesting places, cultural events, sports activities. Programs feature qualified teachers, small classes, attractive surroundings and facilities. Affordable prices for instruction. Accommodations with Spanish families with meals, student residences, apartments, and nearby hotels.

Dates: Year round. Two weeks or more. Cost: Two-week courses with or without accommodations range from $245-$865. Contact: Ms. Lorraine Haber, Study Abroad Coordinator, CES Study Abroad Program, The Center for English Studies, 330 7th Ave., 6th Floor, New York, NY 10001; (212) 629-7300, fax (212) 736-7950.

One-to-One, A, B, C Courses. A: 8 hours per day; B: 6 hours per day; C: 4 hours per day. In course A, the student lunches with one of the teachers (meals excluded). Classes Monday-Friday. All course materials. Activities and excursions organized by the school are optional. Telefax facilities. Met at the airport and transported to your accommodations. Certificate and diploma.

Dates: Any Monday. Cost: Two weeks A: PTS320,000; 2 weeks B: PTS240,000; 2 weeks C: PTS160,000. Contact: Mrs. Renate Urban, Director, Escuela de Idiomas "Nerja," C Almirante Ferrándiz, 73-29780 Nerja, Málaga, Spain; (011) 34-5-252-16-87, fax 252-21-19; idnerja@gandalf.leader.es.

Penn-in-Alicante. For students interested in the language, literature, and culture of Spain, this program combines classroom instruction with visits to points of cultural and historical interest, including Madrid and Toledo. Students live with local families.

Dates: Jun 25-Jul 26. Cost: Tuition $2,840; room and board $1,500; travel $890. Contact: Penn Summer Abroad, College of General Studies, Univ. of Pennsylvania, 3440 Market St., Suite 100, Philadelphia, PA 19104-3335; (215) 898-5738, fax (215) 573-2053.

RSA/UCLES Certificate in ELT. CELTA is the most widely recognized course in teaching English to adults. The course provides initial training for those without previous experience or training in this field. The course is based on daily teaching practice and evaluation of lessons. Highly regarded by employers.

Dates: Twelve 4-week courses per year. Cost: PTS140,000. Contact: Jenny Johnson, Courses Administrator, International House, d-Trafalgar 14 entlo, 08010 Barcelona, Spain; (011) 34-3-268-4511, 268-0239; ih_barcelona@msn.com.

Semester in Spain. Study Spanish in Seville for a semester, a year, a summer term, or our new January term. Earn 12-16 credits per semester, 4-8 for summer terms or January term. Classes are offered for beginning, intermediate, and advanced Spanish language students. Students live with Spanish families. Outstanding professors, small classes, and lots of fun. Approximately 50 students each semester.

Dates: Fall: Aug 27-Dec 18, spring: Jan 29-May 22, summer: May 28-Jun 19 and/or Jun 30-Jul 23, Jan 7-25. Cost: Fall or spring: $7,500. Includes room and board, tuition, books. Summer and Jan: $2,000 (1 term), $4,000 (2 terms). Airfare not included. Contact: Debra Veenstra, U.S. Coordinator, Semester in Spain, 6601 W. College Dr., Dept. TA, Palos Heights, IL 60463; (800) 748-0087 or (708) 396-7440, fax (708) 385-5665; spain@trnty.edu.

Spanish and Basque Studies (Bilbao). Bilbao offers intensive language studies (Spanish or Basque) fulfilling up to 2 years of university language requirements in 1 semester, plus courses in history, political science, art, culture, economics, teacher education, literature, etc. Program organized field trips to several provinces in the Basque country and a tour of Madrid. Students live with local families or share apartment with other students.

Dates: Fall semester: Aug 26-Dec 13, 1996; spring semester: Jan 7-May 14, 1997. Cost: One semester $3,950; 2 semesters $6,450. Contact: University Studies Abroad Consortium (USAC), Univ. of Nevada, Reno #323, Reno, NV 89557-0093; (702) 784-6569, fax (702) 784-6010; usac@equinox.unr.edu.

Spanish and Basque Studies (San Sebastian). San Sebastian offers intensive language (Spanish or Basque): Up to 2 years of university language requirements may be met in 1 semester plus courses in history, literature, political science, economics, art, teacher education, etc. Program organized field trips to Madrid and elsewhere, housing, and many local university activities in this beautiful seaside resort.

Dates: Summer sessions: May 27-Jul 1 and Jun 27-Jul 30 and Jul 30-Aug 28, 1997; fall semester: Aug 26-Dec 12, 1997; spring semester: Jan 7-May 13, 1998. Cost: Each summer session: $1,770; fall or spring semester: $5,690;

year: $8,870; $3,380 both sessions. Contact: University Studies Abroad Consortium (USAC), Univ. of Nevada, Reno #323, Reno, NV 89557-0093; (702) 784-6569, fax (702) 784-6010; usac@admin.unr.edu, www.scs.unr.edu/~usac.

Spanish and Hispanic Studies. Frequently called Spain's leading school of Spanish, Malaca Instituto has a special program combining Spanish from beginner to advanced level with study of Spanish culture, politics, and way of life. Divided in two terms: Term I: general Spanish. Term II: advanced Spanish and Hispanic studies. All accommodations, options, and comprehensive activities program.

Dates: Term I: 16 weeks from Sep 2, 1996, term II: 20 weeks from Jan 6, 1997. Cost: Course: Term I PTS247,900, term II PTS350,000, Accommodations: residence, host families, student apartments: from PTS 62,300 for 4 weeks. Contact: Bob Burger, Marketing Director, Malaca Instituto, c/Cortada 6, Cerrado de Calderon, 29018 Malaga, Spain; (011) 34-5-229-32-42, fax 229-63-16.

Spanish Courses in Malaga. Spanish courses in Malaga, Spain. All grades, small groups, 4 hours daily, courses commencing each month. Living with Spanish families (families or in small apartment in center).

Contact: F. Marin Fernandez, Director, Centro de Estudios de Castellano, Ave. Juan Sebastian Elcano, 120, 29017 Málaga, Spain; 34-5-2290551, fax 2290551.

Spanish for Corporate Executives. Frequently called Spain's leading school of Spanish, Malaca Instituto has courses that meet the varied needs of business executives. Programs are all very inexpensive, taking account of the need to make rapid progress in limited time. General or Commercial Spanish can be studied in small groups or one-on-one, and Spanish for business, technical, or other professional specialties can be taught one-on-one.

Dates: 1996: General Spanish "Minigroup": every 2 weeks from Jan 8; Commercial Spanish: Sep 30, Oct 28, Nov 25; one-on-one every Monday. 1997: General Spanish "Mini-Group": every 2 weeks from Jan 6; commercial Spanish: Jan 20, Feb 17, Mar 17, Apr 14, May 12, Sep 29, Oct 27, Nov 24; one-on-one every Monday. Cost: Course: Minigroup from PTS80,900 for 2 weeks; Commercial from PTS78,700 for 2 weeks; one-on-one from PTS4,200 per lesson. Accommodations: From PTS19,700 per week. On-site residence (Club Hispanico) recommended. Also host families. Contact: Bob Burger, Marketing Director, Malaca Instituto, c/Cortada 6, Cerrado de Calderon, 29018 Malaga, Spain; (011) 34-5-229-32-42, fax 63-16.

Spanish for Foreigners. Executive Programs: Individual, Intensive Combination, minigroup course. Adults and young adults programs. Children in Spanish. Summer seminars for teachers in Spanish. Total immersion courses.

Dates: Year round. Cost: Contact SLA for information. Contact: Natividad Mancebo, General Manager, Iñico Saez Azcona, International Marketing, Egña, 6, 2º C, 48010, Bilbao (Vizcaya), Spain; (011) 34-4-444 8062 or 66, fax 8066.

Spanish for Older Teenagers. Frequently called Spain's leading school of Spanish, Malaca Instituto offers a special program designed specifically for young people (16-22 years). It combines serious study of Spanish with a program of sports and cultural activities. Accommodations in our on-site residence or with host families. Facilities include: video rooms, cinema, language lab, self-access study center, bar, restaurant, and pool.

Dates: Jun 24, Jul 8, Jul 22, Aug 5, Aug 19, 1996; Jun 23, 1997, Jul 7, Jul 21, Aug 4, Aug 18, 1997. Cost: Course: from PTS40,000 for 2 weeks. Accommodations (residence, host families, student apartments): from PTS32,540 for 2 weeks. Contact: Bob Burger, Marketing Director, Malaca Instituto, c/

Cortada 6, Cerrado de Calderon, 29018 Malaga, Spain; (011) 34-5-229-32-42, fax 63-16.

Spanish for Senior Citizens. Frequently called Spain's leading school of Spanish, Malaca Instituto has designed a course for senior citizens. Offered at levels from beginner to advanced, the program combines studying highly practical everyday Spanish (for the market, restaurant, booking hotels, etc.) with a program of cultural and social activities. On-site residential accommodations are recommended.

Dates: Oct 14, 28; Nov 11, 25; Dec 9, 1996. Feb 3, 17; Mar 3, 17, 31; Apr 14, 28; May 12, 26; Oct 13, 27; Nov 10, 24, 1997. Cost: Course: from PTS55,000 (2 weeks); accommodations from PTS32,540 (2 weeks). On-site residence (Club Hispanico) recommended. Contact: Bob Burger, Malaca Instituto, c/Cortada 6, Cerrado de Calderon, 29018 Malaga, Spain; (011) 34-5-229-32-42, fax 63-16.

Spanish in Malaga, Andalucia. Frequently called Spain's leading school of Spanish, Malaca Instituto offers general Spanish courses in small groups year round at all levels. We have many European and Japanese students but very few Americans. Facilities include: video rooms, cinema, language lab, self-access study center, bar, restaurant, pool, and on-site residential accommodation. We organize a comprehensive program of cultural and social activities.

Dates: Every 2 weeks from Jan 8, 1996 and Jan 6, 1997. Cost: Course: from PTS72,900 for 4 weeks. Accommodations: residence, host families, student apartments: from PTS62,300 for 4 weeks. Contact: Bob Burger, Marketing Director, Malaca Instituto, c/Cortada 6, Cerrado de Calderon, 29018 Malaga, Spain; (011) 34-5-229-32-42, fax 63 16.

Spanish Language and Culture. Spanish language, all levels, at the Univ. of Grenada. Studies include literature, history, economics, politics, and sociology. The city of Granada is half

Moorish, half Christian. Participants live with Spanish families. Three meals provided daily. Excursions available to local and surrounding areas.

Dates: Intensive Spanish, 8-week sessions: Jan-Nov; summer, 4 weeks: Jun-Sep. Hispanic studies spring semester: Feb 15-May 31; fall: Oct 11-Feb 13, academic year: Oct 11-May 31. Cost: Intensive Spanish $2,995; Summer $1,795; Hispanic Studies $4,295 fall or spring, academic year $8,395. Contact: Program Director, Center for Study Abroad, 2802 E. Madison St., MS-#160, Seattle, WA 98112; (206) 726-1498; (206) 285-9197; virtuecsa@aol.com.

Spanish Language Courses. Raising Language Academy classes are designed for all levels. Lodging provided close to the academy, with easy access to beach, shopping, sports, and nightlife. Excursions to "white villages," Granada, Sevilla, and Cordoba.

Dates: Year-round. For 2 weeks, 1 month, or more. Cost: Varies according to length of stay and kind of accommodations. Contact: Ellen Solomon, Director, Sales and Marketing, USA, 107 W. 82nd St., New York, NY 10024; (212) 362-0709, fax (212) 595-2225; skph48c@prodigy.com.

Univ. of Leon. Our courses include Spanish language and Spanish culture (history, literature, art, etc.). Our students receive diploma awarded by Spanish Higher Education Institution. Courses at 3 levels: elementary, intermediate, and advanced. Small groups (about 15 students). Students can choose from university residence, living with a family, and flats shared with Spanish students. An attractive cultural-touristic option is also available.

Dates: Summer courses: first session Jul 1997, second Aug 1997. Permanent courses: first session Oct 1997-Jan 1998, second session Feb-Jun 1998. Cost: Summer courses: 1-month PTS65,000, 2-month PTS85,000; Permanent courses: One 4-month session PTS95,000; Two 4-month sessions PTS180,000. Contact: Rafael de Paz Ureña, Secretary of International Relations, Avda. de la Facultad, 25, E-24071, Léon, Spain; (011) 34-87-291646 or 291650, fax 291693; gerd mc@unileón.es.

URI Summer Study Program. Spend over 4 weeks in Spain studying Spanish language, literature, and culture at the prestigious Colegio de España in Salamanca. The program is designed for college students, graduates, and teachers, as well as for college-bound high school students. Program A: Intensive Undergraduate Language and Culture. Up to 7 credits. Program B: Literature, Language, and Culture, and Business Spanish. Six graduate or advanced undergraduate credits.

Dates: Jul 1-Jul 31, 1996. Cost: Program A $1,725; Program B $1,925. Contact: Mario F. Trubiano, Director, Summer Program in Spain, Dept. of Languages, Univ. of Rhode Island, Kingston, RI 02881-0812; (401) 792-4717 or (401) 792-5911 (after 5 p.m. 401-789-9501, fax 401-792-4694).

Sweden

Uppsala Univ. International Summer Session (UISS). Sweden's oldest academic summer program focuses on learning the Swedish language. All levels from beginners to advanced. Additional courses in Swedish history, social institutions, arts in Sweden, Swedish film. Excursions every Friday. Extensive evening program includes both lectures and entertainment. Single rooms in dormitories or apartments. Open to both students and adults. Credit possible.

Dates: Jun 22-Aug 15; Jun 22-Jul 18; Jul 20-Aug 15, 1997. Cost: SEK21,000 (approx. $3,000) for the 8-week session, SEK12,000 (approx. $1,715) for the 4-week session. Includes room, some meals, all classes, evening and excursion program. Contact: Dr. Nelleke Dorrestÿn, Uppsala Univ. Int. Summer Session, Box 513, 751 20 Uppsala, Sweden; (011) 31-71-541 4955, fax 71-5417705; nduiss@ worldaccess.nl.

Switzerland

Collegium Palatinum. Collegium Palatinum is an intensive French and English program which offers French and English at all levels, from beginning to advanced. Classes are Monday-Friday 8:30 a.m.-noon. Course covers conversation, grammar, vocabulary exercises, idioms, and culture. Classes are small and thus offer a great deal of individual attention to the student. Course can be taken in combination with university courses at the American College of Switzerland.

Dates: As advertised. Cost: Per week: Tuition SFR 377.50, room and board SFR 300, activities SFR 25, municipal tax SFR 25, liability deposit SFR 150 (refundable). Contact: Françoise Bailey, Director Collegium Palatinum c/o American College of Switzerland, CH-1854 Leysin, Switzerland; (011) 41-25-342223, fax 341346.

French as a Foreign Language. Situated in one of the most pleasant cities in the French-speaking part of Switzerland, the Institute Richelieu specializes in teaching French to foreigners. It offers a tradition of high-quality tuition as well as up-to-date methods. Holiday courses in summer. Diplomas of the Alliance Française. Optional excursions.

Dates: Month or term courses year-round. Cost: CHF1,180 per month or CHF3,050 per term. Contact: Institute Richelieu, École de français, 7, rue du Clos-de-Bulle, CH-1000, Lausanne 17, Switzerland; (011) 41-21-323-27-18 or (011) 41-21-311-05-19.

French Courses. All the teaching is in French. Courses are given in 4 series of 3 weeks each; but for beginners courses are given at least for 6 weeks. One series or more may be attended.

Dates: Jul 7-25, 1997; Jul 28-Aug 15, 1997; Aug 18-Sep 5, 1997; Sep 8-26, 1997. Cost: CHF470 for 3 weeks; CHF1050 for beginner (6 weeks). Contact: Université de Lausanne, Cours de Vacances, BFSH2, CH-1015 Lausanne, Switzerland; (011) 41-21-692-3090, fax 21-692-30-85.

Intensive French. Founded in 1908, Lemania College is located in the wonderful city of Lausanne in a peaceful setting on the shore of Lake Geneva. The professional team of experienced teachers, the individual syllabuses, the computer assisted language learning method, and the French speaking area will bring students to their expected level on official examinations. Leisure activities, sports, and excursions available.

Dates: Year round including summer. Cost: Per week: tuition $450; lodging with board $800; in family $400; in apartment $170. Contact: Lemania College, Miss E. Perni, International Admissions Office, Ch. de Préville 3, 1001 Lausanne, Switzerland; (011) 41-21-320-15-01, fax 312-67-00; hirtlemania@fasnetch.

International Language and Finishing School. Languages, finishing, art, business, hotel management and tourism.

Dates: Entries in Jan, Apr, and Sep. Cost: SF12,950 per term. Contact: Surval Mont-Fleuri, Mr. Fritz Sidler, Director, Route de Glion 56, 1820 Montreux, Switzerland; Tel./ fax (011) 41-21-963-86-63.

Univ. of Geneva Summer Courses. French language and civilization at all levels, beginners to advanced. All instructors have a university diploma. Excursions and visits to Geneva and its surroundings. Class of 15 to 20 students. Minimum age 17.

Dates: Jul 14-31; Aug 4-22; Aug 25-Sep 12; Sep 15-Oct 3. Cost: SF470 for 3 weeks (tuition). Contact: Mr. Gérard Benz, Univ. of Geneva, Summer Courses, rue de Candolle 3, CH-1211 Geneva 4, Switzerland; (011) 41-22-

750-74-34, fax 750-74-39; <bisatti@uni2a. unige.ch>.

Thailand

Southeast Asian Studies (Bangkok). Offers intensive language study of Thai and a variety of courses (taught in English or Thai) at undergraduate or graduate level at Rangsit Univ. Program-organized field trips, student residence halls, and many university activities.

Dates: Summer session: Jun 6-Aug 6, 1996; fall semester: Aug 30-Dec 20, 1996; spring semester: Jan 11-Apr 14, 1997. Cost: One semester $2,450; 2 semesters $4,100; summer session $1,100. Contact: University Studies Abroad Consortium (USAC), Univ. of Nevada, Reno #323, Reno, NV 89557-0093; (702) 784-6569, fax (702) 784-6010; usac@equinox.unr. edu.

Southeast Asian Studies (Bangkok). Diverse courses in culture, language, economics, business, society, and religions provide a fascinating, well-balanced approach to Southeast Asia. Program-organized field trips, student residence halls, and many university activities at one of Thailand's most modern universities.

Dates: Summer session: Jun 6-Jul 30, 1997; fall semester: Aug 20-Dec 23, 1997; spring semester: Jan 9-May 12, 1998. Cost: One semester: $2,450; year: $4,100; summer session: $1,100. Contact: University Studies Abroad Consortium (USAC), Univ. of Nevada, Reno #323, Reno, NV 89557-0093; (702) 784-6569, fax (702) 784-6010; usac@admin.unr.edu, www.scs.unr.edu/~usac.

United Kingdom

General Studies (Brighton). Brighton offers courses in many disciplines: art, business, sports science, engineering, computing, geography, design, education, math, etc. Organized

field trips, housing in student residence halls. Summer graduate program in teacher education. Only 45 minutes from London.

Dates: Summer: Jun 28-Aug 4, 1996; fall semester: Sep 1-Dec 15, 1996; spring: Jan 5-May 16, 1997. Cost: Fall or spring $2,290; year $5,225; summer $1,250. Contact: University Studies Abroad Consortium (USAC), Univ. of Nevada, Reno #323, Reno, NV 89557-0093; (702) 784-6569, fax (702) 784-6010; usac@ equinox.unr.edu.

General Studies (Reading). Reading offers courses in nearly every academic discipline: art, business, literature, performing arts, engineering, computing, geography, education, agriculture, etc. Housing in student residence halls. Only 25 minutes from London.

Dates: Fall semester: Sep 12-Dec 13, 1996; winter: Jan 7-Apr 27, 1997; spring quarter: Apr 28-Jul 3, 1997. Cost: Fall semester $3,450; winter or spring quarter $2,950; year $7,450. Contact: University Studies Abroad Consortium (USAC), Univ. of Nevada, Reno #323, Reno, NV 89557-0093; (702) 784-6569, fax (702) 784-6010; usac@equinox.unr.edu.

Le Cordon Bleu, L'Art Culinaire. Le Cordon Bleu in London offers the highest diploma in culinary education in just 9 months. Cuisine and pastry classes begin every 10 weeks. Summer abroad program--ICHP--in Paris and London. Catering program for professionals.

Dates: Jun 10-Aug 17, 1996. Trimesters begin every 10 weeks. Cost: From $6,000 to $30,000 for cuisine and pastry 9-month diploma. Contact: In U.S. call (800) 457-CHEF or fax (914) 426-0104. Le Cordon Bleu, 114 Marylebone Ln., WIM 6HH, London, England.

UCLES RSA CTEFLA. This is the most widely recognized introductory course to the TEFL profession allowing successful participants to work worldwide. The course is extremely practical, develops classroom skills and language awareness as well as dealing comprehensively with methodology, thus providing a sound basis in all aspects of TEFL teaching. Dates: Oct-Nov, Apr-Jun, Jan-May. Cost: £832. Contact: Guidance Centre, Thames Valley Univ., 18-22 Bond St., Ealing, London W5 5AA, U.K.; (011) 44-181-579-5000, fax 181-231-2900.

United States

Danish Language Intensive Semester. While this program was designed to prepare U.S. students selected to participate in an exchange with a Danish university, the program is open to students who wish to study Danish for other reasons. Daily intensive language classes, taught by KU faculty and native Danish-speaking graduate teaching assistant, are supplemented by excursions and enhanced by living in a Danish-speaking residence hall wing. Students receive 16 hours of KU credit. Dates: Approx. Jan 3-May 9, 1997. Students will be free during spring break. Cost: Approx. $7,400 (non-KU students). Includes tuition, room and board, cultural excursions, instructional materials, and all program administrative costs. Contact: Nancy Mitchell, Assistant Director/Adviser, Office of Study Abroad, 203 Lippincott, The Univ. of Kansas, Lawrence, KS 66045; (913) 864-3742, fax (913) 864-5040; osa@falcon.cc.ukans.edu.

Language Education. Language training in English and all other languages. Flexible schedules by the week or by the month. Individual and group classes. Special programs available in accent reduction and writing skills. Dates: Year round. Cost: Variable—depends on program length and intensity. Contact: Kelly Keclan, Director, InLingua School of Languages, 200 W. Madison, Suite 1835, Chicago, IL 60606; (312) 641-0488 or (800) 755-8753, fax (312) 641-1724.

Nova Intercultural Institute. One of the largest private language schools in Japan, Nova employs 1,800 teachers at over 180 locations throughout the islands. We offer a fixed schedule, a guaranteed monthly salary, paid training, assistance with housing, and an extensive support network. Lessons are taught at a variety of levels, ranging from beginner to advanced, and are 40-45 minutes in length. Classes are limited to a size of 3 or 4 students, depending on location. Dates: Continuous hiring year round. Cost: No application or processing fees. Contact: Trevor Phillips, Interact Nova Group, 2 Oliver St., 7th Fl., Boston, MA 02109; (617) 542-5027, fax (617) 542-3115.

Transworld English. Transworld English offers programs for everyone, from intensive language classes to TOEFL preparation. Emphasizing a communicative approach, classes focus on all aspects of English language acquisition, including grammar, reading, writing, listening and pronunciation. Class-sizes are small and progress is continuously monitored to ensure that students maximize their learning experience. Dates: Continuous enrollment; classes begin every Monday. Cost: $200 per week; $690 4 weeks; $1,000 6 weeks; $1,300 8 weeks; $1,590 10 weeks; $1,850 12 weeks. Contact: Admissions Office, Transworld English, 683 Sutter St., San Francisco, CA 94102; (800) 241-8071 or (415) 776-8071, fax (415) 441-1326; transworld@aol.com.

Univ. of Cambridge Certificate in English Language Teaching to Adults (CELTA). St Giles Colleges (established 1955 in London) offer 4-week intensive teacher training programs approved by the Royal Society of Arts/ University of Cambridge Examination Syndicate and, in San Francisco, the California State Department of Postsecondary Education. Program focuses on practical training, teaching methodology. Information on jobs, conditions in specific countries, resume writing, interviewing included. EFL school on site for observation.

Dates: Jan 27-Feb 21, Mar 24-Apr 18, May 5-30, Jun 16-Jul 11, Sep 8-Oct 3, Oct 27-Nov 2. Cost: $2,250. Contact: Teacher Training Coordinator, St Giles Language Teaching Center, 1 Hallidie Plaza, Third Floor, San Francisco, CA 94102; (415) 788-3552; (415) 788-1923.

Venezuela

Spanish as a Second Language. Beginners, intermediate, advanced, and conversation. Grammar-based program encourages the 4 skills: reading, writing, speaking, and listening. Lead students toward communicative competence in Spanish, 20 hours per level.

Dates: Classes begin every Monday. Cost: $147.50 per level. Contact: Carmen Montilla, Instituto Latinoamericano de Idiomas, Avenida las Américas C.C. Mamayeya, 4th Piso, Merida, Venezuela; Tel./fax (011) 58-74-447808.

Spanish in the Andes. Merida is the capital of the Venezuelan Andes—a clean, safe university town where the weather and people are always warm and the scenery is breathtaking. VENUSA specializes in offering North American students intensive Spanish classes and a variety of other courses. Credit is granted through the Univ. of Minnesota. Participants live with local families, who provide a vital link to the language and culture of Venezuela. VENUSA also operates an English institute for Venezuelans. Americans and Venezuelans alike are invited to social events and activities. Some day trips are also included. Individual language instruction is also available.

Dates: 1996 summer: May 18-Jun 29, Jun 29-Aug 10; 1996 fall: Aug 24-Dec 7; 1997 spring: Jan 11-Apr 29. Cost: $5,500 for semester and $3,000 for summer. Contact: VENUSA, 6342 Forest Hill Blvd., Suite 287, West Palm Beach, FL 33415; (407) 753-3761, fax (407) 753-3758.

Worldwide

AIYSEP. American International Youth Student Exchange Program (AIYSEP) is a nonprofit high school foreign exchange program based in the U.S. which establishes exchange programs for students in Europe, America, and many other foreign countries. Area counselors are located in Europe, U.S., Australia, New Zealand, Canada, and Japan. AIYSEP believes a greater international understanding is accomplished among people and countries through cultural and homestay programs.

Dates: Offers year, semester, and summer homestay programs. Cost: Year $3,895-$6,000; semester $3,395-$4,400; summer $1,900-$3,000. Contact: American International Youth Student Exchange, 200 Round Hill Rd., Tiburon, CA 94920; (800) 347-7575 or (415) 435-4049, fax (415) 499-5651.

American-Int'l Homestays. Stay in English-speaking foreign homes in over 30 countries. Explore foreign cultures responsibly. Learn foreign languages. Perfect for families or seniors. Learn how other people live by living with them in their homes.

Dates: Year round. Cost: From $49 per night. Contact: Joe Kinczel, American-Int'l Homestays, P.O. Box 1754, Nederland, CO 80466; (303) 642-3088 or (800) 876-2048, fax (303) 642-3365; ash@igc.apc.org.

Center for Language Studies. The CLS offers intensive instruction in beginning, intermediate, and advanced Russian, Chinese, and Japanese; beginning and intermediate Czech, Hungarian, Turkish, and Portuguese; and advanced English as a Second Language. Teaching certification minors are also offered in Russian and Japanese. Students receive 270 hours of instruction, earn 12 semester hours of credit, and complete the equivalent of 1 year of language study. Admission is open to undergraduate, graduate, and nondegree students. Financial aid is available.

Dates: Jun 9-Aug 9, 1996. Cost: Tuition, room and board $4,700 (double room). Contact: Dr. Terance W. Bigalke, Director, Center for Language Studies, Beloit College, 700 College St., Beloit, WI 53511; (608) 363-2269, fax (608) 363-2689; cls@beloit.edu.

Diploma Program in Teaching English as a Second or Foreign Language. The Diploma Program is a noncredit, intensive, 8-week professional training program offered in summers for teachers and prospective teachers of English as a Second or Foreign Language. It covers all essential aspects of English language teaching from a practical classroom perspective. Totals 210 hours of instruction, including practicum.

Dates: Mid-Jun-mid-Aug. Cost: $2,300 tuition (plus room and board, and materials). Contact: Daniel W. Evans, PhD, Acting Director, TESL Graduate Programs, School of International Studies, Saint Michael's College, Colchester, VT 05439; (802) 654-2684, fax (802) 654-2595; sis@smcvt.edu.

ELS Language Courses. ELS Language Centers has programs in English for adults, teenagers, and children in the following countries: Argentina, Australia, Brazil, Chile, China, Colombia, England, Indonesia, Korea, Malaysia, Saudi Arabia, Thailand, Taiwan, UAE.

Dates: Year round. Cost: Varies according to location. Contact: For teaching opportunities apply to ELS Language Centers, Attn: Gina Pilic, Director of Field Operations, 5761 Buckingham Pkwy., Culver City, CA 90230.

English Language Programs. The School of International Studies offers 5 levels of intensive English language instruction. Small classes in oral and written communication. Afternoon electives. Activities program. Twenty-five hours per week. Openings every 4 weeks. We also offer a semester program in University Academic Preparation (UAP).

Dates: Intensive English Program (IEP) openings every 4 weeks year round except closed Dec 21-Jan 9, 1998. UAP semester program: Jan 12-May 11-Aug 8, and Aug 28-Dec 20. Cost: IEP: room and board, tuition, infirmary $1,222 for 4 weeks; UAP: room and board, tuition, infirmary $9,324.33. Contact: Sheena Blodgett, Assistant Director of English Programs, Saint Michael's College, Winooski Park, Colchester, VT 05439; (802) 654-2355, fax (802) 654-2595; sis@smcvt.edu.

Eurocentres Language Schools. Immersion course of 20-25 hours per week for beginners to advanced levels. Learn in small classes with students of all ages from around the world. Full organizational social calendar with extended excursions available to students. Homestay living is available, college credit option.

Dates: Begins monthly all year long. Cost: Depends on school and length of stay. Contact: Eurocentres, 101 N. Union St., Alexandria, VA 22314; (703) 684-1494 or (800) 648-4809, fax (703) 684-1495; 100632.141@ compuserve.com, www.clark.net/pub/euro cent/home.htm.

Home Language International. A unique opportunity for a full immersion experience, living with and being taught by your own private teacher, ensuring rapid progress. Most languages offered by qualified, experienced teachers in homes that have been thoroughly inspected by our local organizers.

Dates: Year round. Cost: From £450 per week: course, accommodations, and full board. Contact: Sarah Amerena, Reservations Office, Home Language International, 17 Royal Crescent, Ramsgate, Kent CT11 9PE, UK; (011) 44-84-38-51-116,

International Cooperative Education. Paid employment and internships for college and university students for a period of 8-12 weeks in 8 European and 1 Asian country. Employment depends on foreign language knowledge, major, and previous work experience. Work permits and housing are provided.

Dates: From Jun-Sep. Cost: Students must pay for air transportation and have a reserve of at least $800 for initial expenses. Contact: Gunter Seefeldt, PhD., Director, International Cooperative Education Program, 15 Spiros Way, Menlo Park, CA 94025; (415) 323-4944, fax (415) 323-1104.

ISOK Katwijk Zh Holland. Teaching languages there where they are spoken; i.e., Dutch in the Netherlands (stay with host family, group lessons or private lessons), German in Graz, Austria (various accommodations, lessons as in Holland).

Dates: Year round. Cost: Holland: group lessons DFL15 per session (2 hours), private lessons DFL25 per hour. Contact: ISOK, "Voor een vreemde taal naar het vreemde land" Jan-Tooropstr. 4, 2225 XT, Katwijk, Holland; (011) 71-40-13533.

Italian Language Lessons. Individual Italian language lessons. Accommodations provided by the school. With a family in hotel or apartment. Course levels: beginners, intermediate, advanced.

Dates: Year round. Cost: From LIT310,000 per week. Contact: Prof. Luigi Foschi, Isttituto Studium, Via Baldini 22, 47042 Cesenatico (FO), Italy; Tel./fax (011) 39-547-84442.

Master of Arts in Teaching English as a Second Language (MATESL). The MATESL Program is a 36-credit program (39 credits with thesis option) designed for both prospective and experienced techers. Theoretical and methodological training is integrated with practical coursework to prepare graduates for professional roles in TESL/TEFL or continued graduate study. A variety of practicum experiences are offered both domestically and abroad.

Dates: Begin in Sep, Jan, or Jun. Cost: $260 per credit. Contact: Daniel W. Evans, PhD, Acting Director, TESL Graduate Programs, School of International Studies, Saint Michael's College, Colchester, VT 05439; (802) 654-2684, fax (802) 654-2595; sis@smcvt.edu.

Peace Corps Volunteer Opportunities. Since 1961, more than 140,000 Americans have joined the Peace Corps. Assignments are 27 months long. Volunteers must be U.S. citizens, at least 18 years old, and in good health. Peace Corps has volunteer programs in education, business, agriculture, the environment, and health.

Dates: Apply 9 to 12 months prior to availability. Cost: Volunteers receive transportation to and from assignment, a stipend, complete health care, and $5,400 after 27 months of service. Contact: Peace Corps, Room 8506, 1990 K St., NW, Washington, DC 20526; (800) 424-8580; www.peacecorps.gov.

St Giles Language Teaching Center. Earn the Certificate in English Language Teaching to Adults (CELTA) approved by the Univ. of Cambridge and the California Council for Private Postsecondary and Vocational Education. The course focuses on practical training and teaching methodology. Includes access to international job postings, graduate contacts, and teaching opportunities abroad. Sessions include resume writing, and interviewing techniques. Part of a group of schools in England, Switzerland, and U.S. offering 40 years of EFL teaching and training. CELTA courses also offered in Brighton and London, England.

Dates: Four-week intensive courses begin 6 times yearly. Cost: $2,250 all inclusive. Contact: St Giles Language Teaching Center, 1 Hallidie Plaza, Suite 350-TA, San Francisco, CA 94102; (415) 788-3552, fax (415) 788-1923.

Total Immersion Language Study. Learn a language and immerse yourself in an exciting program of social and cultural experiences. Programs year round at all levels in Spain, Mexico, Costa Rica, Brazil, Latin America, Portugal, France, Italy, Germany, Greece, Japan, Taiwan, and more. Homestays. Courses for students, professionals, executives, teachers. College credit available.

Dates: Year round. Cost: Varies with program. Contact: Nancy Forman, Language Liaison Inc., 20533 Biscayne Blvd., Suite. 2-164, Miami, FL 33180; (305) 682-9909 or (800) 284-4448, fax (305) 682-9907.

Reach your goal.
Study abroad.

The choices you make today build your prospects for tomorrow. Choose to study abroad. An experience in another country will help you to visualize, define and reach your goals. Take the first step and call for our free catalogs today. Specify Australia, Great Britain, Greece, Ireland, Austria, Mexico, Peace Studies or Summer Study Abroad.

1.888.BEAVER-9
http://www.beaver.edu/cea/
cea@beaver.edu

BeaverCollege
Center for Education Abroad

CHAPTER 13

UNDERGRADUATE STUDY PROGRAMS

The following listing of undergraduate study programs was supplied by the organizers. Contact the program directors to confirm costs, dates, and other details. If you do not see the program you want in the country of your choice, look in the "Worldwide" listings at the end of the section for programs located in several different regions.

Africa

Kalamazoo in Senegal, Kenya, or Zimbabwe. Programs combine academics and experiential learning. Course work in a host-country setting, often with local students and specially arranged courses give participants a broad overview of the host country. Instruction in the local language as well as internships or independent projects provide opportunities for greater understanding of the host culture.

Dates: Senegal and Kenya: early Sep-early Jun; Zimbabwe: mid-Aug-late May. Cost: (1995-1996) $19,113. Includes roundtrip international transportation, tuition and fees, room and board, and some excursions. Contact: Dr. Michael Vande Berg, Director of the Center for International Programs, Kalamazoo College, 1200 Academy, Kalamazoo, MI 49006; (616) 337-7133, fax (616) 337-7400; cip@ kzoo.edu.

Univ. of Wisconsin-Madison's College Year Program in West Africa. Study abroad in Francophone Africa at the Université de Saint Louis in Saint Louis, Senegal. Students experience a blend of Africa, French, and Muslim traditions while they live in dorms with Senegalese roommates. Classes taught in French in a variety of humanities and social sciences. Includes a year-long course in Wolof, the most widely spoken Senegalese language, and an independent fieldwork project. Orientation including an introduction to Wolof and local culture, includes several days in Madison and 2 weeks in Dakar, Senegal. Four semesters of French or equivalent language capability required. Application deadline: first

Friday in Feb. Late applications considered on a space-available basis.

Dates: Mid-Sep-mid-Jun. Cost: Call for current information. Contact: Office of International Studies and Programs, 261 Bascom Hall, Univ. of Wisconsin, 500 Lincoln Dr., Madison, WI 53706; (608) 262-2851, fax (608) 262-6998; abroad@macc.wisc.edu.

Work in Zimbabwe, Angola, and Mozambique. In Zimbabwe you will teach at a school for disadvantaged youth or at a rural health and education project. The Angola project focuses on tree-planting and community work with people of all ages. In Mozambique you will teach street children or at vocational schools. Families in rural areas learn to take part in a program to improve the health and living conditions. Zimbabwe and Angola are 12-month programs, Mozambique is an 18-month program. Open to students and adults and includes preparation and follow-up periods in the U.S.

Dates: Zimbabwe and Angola: Feb 15 and Aug 15, 1996. Mozambique: Nov 1, 1996. Cost: $4,600. Includes training, room and board, airfare, health insurance, and other direct program costs. Contact: Josefin Jonsson, Administrative Director, P.O. Box 103-T, Williamstown, MA 01267; (413) 458-9828, fax (413) 458-3323.

Argentina

Argentina Universities Program. A loosely structured integrated program based in Buenos Aires. Courses available at 3 universities: Univ. del Salvador, Univ. Torcuato Di Tella, and Univ. de Buenos Aires. Participants can also take program-sponsored courses in Argentine society and Latin American literature. Six-week summer language and culture program is also available.

Dates: Fall semester: Jul-Dec; Spring semester: Mar-Jul; summer program: Jun-mid-Jul. Cost: $4,800 includes tuition, registration fees,

excursions, orientation, and partial insurance, site director, support services. Contact: IPA, Univ. of Illinois at Urbana-Champaign, 115 International Studies Bldg., 910 S. 5th St., Champaign, IL 61820; (800) 531-4404, fax (217) 244-0249; ipa@uiuc.edu.

Instituto de Lengua Española par Extranjeros (ILEE). Located downtown. Dedicated exclusively to teaching Spanish to foreigners. Small groups and private classes year round. All teachers hold a university degree. Method is intensive, conversation-based. Student body is international, mostly European. Highly recommended worldwide (all travel guides, Univ. of Cambridge, etc.). Ask for individual recommendations in U.S.

Dates: Year round. Cost: Four weeks intensive program (20 hours a week) including homestay $1,400; 2 weeks $700. Individual classes: $17 per hour. Registration fee (includes books) $100. Contact: ILEE, Daniel Korman, Director, Lavalle 1619, 7º C, (1048) Buenos Aires, Argentina; (011) 54-1-375-0730, fax 864-4942.

Australia

Advanced Diploma in Hospitality (Management). This 3-year program prepares students for careers at middle and senior management levels in the hospitality industry. After 2 years students can graduate with a Diploma in Hospitality (Management) with the skills to operate as a manager. After 1 year, students can graduate with a Certificate in Hospitality with supervisor skills.

Dates: Feb 12, Jul 15, 1996; Feb 10, Jul 14, 1997. Cost: $3,145 tuition per semester plus living expenses approx. $7,500 per year, ($145 per week). Contact: Mr. Vernon Bruce, Manager, International Education, William Angliss Institute of TAFE, 555 La Trobe St., Melbourne, 3000 Australia; (011) 61-3-96062139, fax 9670-9348; international@angliss.vic.edu.au.

Advanced Diploma in Tourism. This 3-year program prepares students for careers at middle and senior management levels in marketing, sales, and related administrative areas in the travel and tourism industry. After 2 years students can graduate with a Diploma in Tourism with the skills to operate as area marketing officers, information center managers, section managers in tour operations, branch managers in retail travel, or venue managers in meetings agencies. After 1 year, students can graduate with a Certificate in Tourism with supervisor skills, coordinating, or tour planning skills.

Dates: Feb 12, Jul 15, 1996; Feb 10, Jul 14, 1997. Cost: $2,960 tuition per semester plus living expenses approx. $7,500 per year ($145 per week). Contact: Mr. Vernon Bruce, Manager, International Education, William Angliss Institute of TAFE, 555 La Trobe St., Melbourne, 3000 Australia; (011) 61-3-96062139, fax 9670-9348; international@ angliss.vic.edu.au.

Associate Diploma of Applied Science in Food Technology (Manufacturing and Processing). This 2-year course provides a broad-based qualification in food technology for paraprofessional staff in the food industry. The course develops the ability to identify, analyze, and resolve food processing problems; leadership and communication skills; an innovative approach to support the development and implementation of company policies and practices; and a commitment to total quality management.

Dates: Feb 12, Jul 15, 1996; Feb 10, Jul 14, 1997. Cost: $2,960 tuition per semester plus living expenses approx. $7,500 per year ($145 per week). Contact: Mr. Vernon Bruce, Manager, International Education, William Angliss Institute of TAFE, 555 La Trobe St., Melbourne, 3000 Australia; (011) 61-3-96062139, fax 9670-9348; international@ angliss.vic.edu.au.

AustraLearn: Study in Australia. AustraLearn is the most comprehensive Australian study abroad program for U.S. students. You can choose from universities throughout Australia (Queensland, Victoria, Western Australia, New South Wales, Australian capital Territory, South Australia, Tasmania, and the Northern Territory). Semester, year, graduate, short-term experiential, and internship programs are available. Pre-trip orientation.

Dates: Semester/year (Feb or Jul admit), summer or winter abroad short courses. Cost: Semester: $6,500-$9,500, short-term internship: $3,500-$4,200. Contact: Ms. Cynthia Flannery-Banks, Director, AustraLearn, 110 16th St., CSU Denver Center, Denver, CO 80202; (800) 980-0033, fax (303) 446-5955; cflannery@vines.colostate.edu.

Certificate in Breadmaking, Pastrycooking, and Baking. This 6-month course provides basic skills in breadmaking, pastrycooking, and baking. Graduates are eligible to apply for employment in the baking/pastrycooking industry.

Dates: Feb 12, Jul 15, 1996; Feb 10, Jul 14, 1997. Cost: $2,960 plus living expenses approx. $7,500 per year ($145 per week). Contact: Mr. Vernon Bruce, Manager, International Education, William Angliss Institute of TAFE, 555 La Trobe St., Melbourne, 3000 Australia; (011) 61-3-96062139, fax 9670-9348; international@ angliss.vic.edu.au.

Certificate in Butchery and Smallgoods. This 8-week course is designed to provide students with off-the-job training for the butchery and smallgoods industry. It is an excellent course for those students currently working in this industry with no formal training.

Dates: Feb 12, Jul 15, 1996; Feb 10, Jul 14, 1997. Cost: $2,810 tuition plus living expenses approx. $7,500 per year ($145 per week). Contact: Mr. Vernon Bruce, Manager, International Education, William Angliss Institute of TAFE, 555 La Trobe St., Melbourne, 3000 Australia; (011) 61-3-96062139, fax 9670-9348; international @angliss.vic.edu.au.

Certificate in Chinese and Southeast Asian Cookery. This 15-week program provides students with industry-recognized qualifications in Asian cookery, covering the cuisines of regional China and Southeast Asia such as Cantonese, Sichuan, Chui Chow, Northern Chinese, Thai, Vietnamese, Malaysian, Indonesian, and Nonya.

Dates: Feb 12, Jul 15, 1996; Feb 10, Jul 14, 1997. Cost: $2,775 tuition plus living expenses approx. $7,500 per year ($145 per week). Contact: Mr. Vernon Bruce, Manager, International Education, William Angliss Institute of TAFE, 555 La Trobe St., Melbourne, 3000 Australia; (011) 61-3-96062139, fax 9670-9348; international@angliss.vic.edu.au.

Certificate in Practical Confectionery. This 17-day course is designed to introduce students to a range of confectionery ingredients and processes. It is a practical course with theoretical support. The course is supported by the Confectionery Manufacturers of Australasia.

Dates: Feb 12, Jul 15, 1996; Feb 10, Jul 14, 1997. Cost: $1,295 tuition plus living expenses approx. $7,500 per year ($145 per week). Contact: Mr. Vernon Bruce, Manager, International Education, William Angliss Institute of TAFE, 555 La Trobe St., Melbourne, 3000 Australia; (011) 61-3-96062139, fax 9670-9348; international@angliss.vic.edu.au.

Certificate in Professional Cookery. This 6-month course provides students with industry-recognized qualifications in cookery. Graduates are eligible to seek employment as cooks in clubs, restaurants, casinos, motels, reception rooms, hospitals, employee food services, institutions, commercial venues, and private catering businesses.

Dates: Feb 12, Jul 15, 1996; Feb 10, Jul 14, 1997. Cost: $5,000 tuition plus living expenses approx. $7,500 per year ($145 per week). Contact: Mr. Vernon Bruce, Manager, International Education, William Angliss Institute of TAFE, 555 La Trobe St., Melbourne, 3000 Australia; (011) 61-3-96062139, fax 9670-9348; international@angliss.vic.edu.au.

ECU Study Abroad Program. ECU is a multi-campus institution within the metropolitan area of Perth with 21,000 students, including over 1,000 international students from 58 different countries. Two hundred courses are offered at both undergraduate and post-graduate level through 6 faculties: Arts, Business, Health and Human Services, Education, Science, Technology and Engineering, and the Academic of Performing Arts.

Dates: Feb-late Jun (Sem I); late Jul-late Nov (Sem II). Cost: AUS$5,500 per semester plus AUS$188 medical insurance. Contact: Joan Wurm, Coordinator, Study Abroad Programme, Edith Cowan Univ., Pearson St., Churchlands, W. Australia 6018; (011) 619-273-8240, fax 273-8732.

Education Australia. Study abroad for a semester or a year at Australian National Univ. (Canberra), Deakin Univ. (Victoria), Univ. of Ballarat (Victoria), Univ. of Tasmania (Tasmania), Univ. of Wollongong (New South Wales), or the Australian Catholic Univ. (several states). In New Zealand courses are offered at the Univ. of Canterbury and Lincoln Univ. (Christchurch). Liberal arts, science, business, biology, psychology, education, Australian studies, etc. Customized internships in all fields are also available. See our web page www. javanet.com/~ edaust.

Dates: Mid-Jul-mid-Nov, mid-Feb-late Jun. Cost: Tuition approx. $4,000, accommodations approx. $2,250. Airfare. Contact: Dr. Maurice A. Howe, Executive Director, Education Australia, P.O. Box 2233, Amherst, MA 01004; (800) 344-6741, fax (413) 549-0741; mauriehowe@aol.com.

General Studies in Australia (Victoria). Victoria offers nearly every discipline in undergraduate/graduate levels at 5 different university campus sites: Australian studies, art, journalism, performing arts, women's studies, biology, chemistry, math, business, computing, etc. Known as the Garden State, Victoria has some of the country's most beautiful mountain and coastal areas.

Dates: First semester: Jul 12-Nov 14, 1997; second semester: Feb 20-Jun 27, 1998. Cost: $4,290 per semester, $7,750 for 1 year. Contact: University Studies Abroad Consortium (USAC), Univ. of Nevada, Reno #323, Reno, NV 89557-0093; (702) 784-6569, fax (702) 784-6010; usac@admin.unr.edu, www.scs.unr. edu/~usac.

Griffith Univ. Study Abroad. Griffith Univ. is ideally located in Brisbane on the Gold Coast, the east coast of Australia. It has a perfect climate of mild winters and warm summers. International students in the Study Abroad Program can take courses for 1 or 2 semesters for either credit at their home institution or their own interest. Participation in internship programs may also be arranged.

Dates: Semester 1: Feb-Jun; Semester 2: Jul-Nov. Cost: AUS$5,250 per semester. Contact: Study Abroad and Exchanges Officer, Griffith Univ. International Centre, Nathan, Queensland 4111, Australia; (011) 61-7-3875-7200, fax 5280; guic@ic.gu.edu.au.

Institute for Study Abroad. The ISA cooperates with 15 universities in Australia to provide high quality academic programs (academic year, calendar year, and semester) for U.S. undergraduates. The ISA guarantees housing, aims to achieve full integration whenever possible, and offers a wide variety of student services during all phases of the study abroad experience.

Dates: Semester (Feb-Jul, Jul-Nov), academic year (Feb-Nov), calendar year (Jul-Jul). Deadlines: fall semester and academic year Mar 15, spring semester and calendar year Nov 15. Cost: Begins at $7,895 and $12,995 for semester and year programs respectively. Includes tuition, housing, predeparture preparation, ISIC, overseas orientation, domestic and overseas student services, farm visit, excursions, and transcript translation. Competitive roundtrip group flight fares arranged for all program participants. Some travel grants and scholarships available. Contact: Institute for Study Abroad, Butler Univ., 4600 Sunset Ave., Indianapolis, IN 46208; (800) 858-0229, fax (317) 940-9704; study-abroad@butler.edu.

Rollins in Sydney. Students choose from Australian studies courses in history, literature, economics, politics, Aboriginal studies, flora and fauna, environmental studies, and art. Courses are taught by Australian faculty on the campus of the Univ. of Sydney. Students live with Australian families. Many field trips and excursions enhance the academic work.

Dates: Jul-Nov. Cost: 1996 program: $9,050. Includes tuition, room and board, roundtrip airfare, excursions connected with classes. Contact: Donna O'Connor, Director of International Programs, Rollins College-2759, 1000 Holt Ave., Winter Park, FL 32789-4499; (407) 646-2466, fax (407) 646-2595; intprog@ rollins.edu.

Special Interest and Study Tours. Personalized programs for individuals and groups of all ages. We combine education, recreation, accommodations (homestay available), and transportation. Based in tropical Cairns with coverage throughout Australia. Subject areas include: aboriginal dreamtime and culture, Great Barrier Reef, rainforest and savannah. Diving, environmental interpretation, flora and fauna, bird watching, tropical islands and wilderness, adventure safaris and farmstay.

Dates: Year round. Start any date. Cost: Prices and customized itineraries on application. Contact: Murray Simpson, Study Venture International, P.O. Box 229A, Stratford Qld., 4870 Australia; (011) 61-70-411622, fax 552044; svi@ozemail.com.au; www.ozemail. au/~svi.

Study Abroad. Study 1 semester in a wide range of courses including humanities, arts, social sciences, economics, education, science, Australian studies.

Dates: Feb-Jun or Jul-Nov. Cost: Approx. $5,500 Contact: International Office, Univ. of New England, Armidale, NSW Australia 2351.

Study in Australia. Seven programs available

in Sydney, Melbourne, Brisbane and Gold Coast, including summer opportunities in co-operation with the National Institute of Dramatic Art and the Univ. of New South Wales. Full range of program services. Need-based scholarships available.

Dates: Fall, Spring, Academic Year, Summer. Cost: Varies. Call for current fees. Contact: Christopher Hennessy, Beaver College CEA, 450 S. Easton Rd., Glenside, PA 19038-3295; (888) BEAVER-9, fax (215) 572-2174; cea@beaver.edu, www.beaver.edu.cea.

Univ. of South Australia. The Univ. of South Australia hosts study abroad programs for university students wishing to undertake a semester (or 2) of their studies overseas and have the credits transferred to their home institution. U-SA offers many field-based units, giving the students the opportunity to study in different environments and to learn about something unavailable at home: Aboriginal culture, Australia's environmental settings, South Australian history.

Dates: Semester 2: Jul 29-Nov 30, 1996; Semester 1: (Mar-Jun) dates for 1997 not yet available. Cost: Call for details. Contact: Study Abroad Adviser, Int'l. Students Office, Univ. of South Australia, GPO Box 2471, Adelaide, South Australia 5001; (011) 618-302-2169, fax 302-2233; chris.haas@unisa.edu.au. For students in the U.S. and Canada: American Univ. Int'l. Program, 246 Forestry Bldg., Colorado State Univ., Ft. Collins, CO 80523; (970) 491-5511, fax (970) 491-2255; aukerman@crn.colstate.edu or Australearn, 315 Aylesworth Hall, Colorado State Univ., Ft. Collins, CO 80523; (970) 491-0228, fax (970) 491-5501; cflannery@vines.colstate.edu.

Austria

Austria-Illinois Exchange Program. Full curriculum in humanities, business, sciences, music, and arts. Program bases in Vienna, excursions to selected sites, ski week mid-year.

Resident director assists with cultural adjustment and course selection. Housing in dormitories. Internships possible following program. At least sophomore standing and 4 semesters German required. More information on http:/www.wu-wien.ac.at/aiep/aiep.html. Also summer intensive German 103.

Dates: Sep 20, 1996-Jun 30, 1997; May-Jun 1996. Cost: $15,000. Includes tuition, room and board, transportation, theater, concerts, excursions, ski week, insurance. $2,500 summer program. Contact: Prof. John F. Lalande II, Director, Dept. of Germanic Langs. and Lits., Univ. of Illinois, 3072 FLB, 707 S. Mathews Ave., Urbana, IL 61801; (217) 333-1288, fax (217) 244-0190; lalande@uiuc.edu.

Bregenz Program. The program in Bregenz will last 5 weeks. During the week, students attend classes in the Studenzentrum located near the center of town. Several 3-day weekends have been scheduled into the programs to permit students sufficient time for independent travel. In Bregenz, the institute sponsors numerous opportunities to visit important cultural sites and events. (Other programs in Europe and Latin America.)

Dates: May 28-Jul 1 (tentative). Cost: $3,080. Contact: J. Milton Grimes, KIIS, Murray State Univ., P.O. Box 9, Murray, KY 42071-0009; (502) 762-3091, fax (502) 762-3434; kiismsu@msumusik.mursuky.edu, www.berea.edu/kiis/kiis.html.

European Studies in Vienna. Semester program with 3 distinct tracks of study: Central European Studies (Fall), European Integration: European Union (spring), and Hungary, Romania, Bulgaria, and Former Yugoslavia Studies (spring). No knowledge of German required, study of German during program. Extensive field study trips.

Dates: Fall, spring, academic year. Pre-sessions in Intensive German Language. Cost: Varies. Call for current fees. Contact: Beaver College Center for Education Abroad, 450 S. Easton Rd., Glenside, PA 19038-3295; (800)

755-5607, fax (215) 572-2174; cea@ beaver. edu, www.beaver.edu/cea/.

Learn German—Experience Vienna. Year round German courses for adults in our modern school in the heart of Vienna. Courses from 1-48 weeks, specialization in tourism and business possible. Cultural activities included. Accommodations in families, apartments, or residences. Junior courses in July and August.

Dates: Adults: starting dates every Monday, beginners every 4 weeks. Cost: Two weeks: approx. $800; 4 weeks: approx. $1,300; 12 weeks: approx. $2,800. Includes accommodations. Contact: Actilingua Academy, 1130 Vienna, Gloriettegasse 8, Austria; (011) 43-1-8776701, fax 877603.

Slippery Rock Univ. (Vienna Semester). Students can spend a semester or year in Vienna earning 15 credits per semester (9-12 in language and 3 taught in English).

Dates: Fall 1996: Sep 9-Dec 6 with 2-week holiday Sep 28-Oct 13; winter 1997: Jan 7-Apr 4; spring 1997: Apr 23-Jul 1 with 11-day Easter holiday. Cost: $3,350. Includes tuition and room. Contact: Stan Kendziorski, Director of International Studies, Slippery Rock Univ., Slippery Rock, PA 16057; (412) 738-2603, fax (412) 738-2959; sjk@sruvm.sru.edu.

Vienna Master Courses for Music. Two-week courses in singing, opera, musical, piano, violin, cello, guitar, chamber music, conducting, for students, young artists (as active members), and anyone who is interested (as auditors). Twenty lessons per week, final concert, diploma and certificate.

Dates: Jul 1-Aug 10, 1997. Cost: Registration fee AS1,500, active participation AS5,200, auditors AS2,700. Contact: Elisabeth Keschmann, Vienna Master Courses, Reisnerstrasse 3, A 1030 Vienna; (011) 43-1-0222-714-88-22, fax 714-88-21.

Vienna Program. Subject areas include business, economics, literature, history, politics, cultural, music, art history, and psychology. All courses, other than German language, are conducted in English. No German language experience required for admission. Full academic year or individual semesters.

Dates: Sep-Dec (fall) and Jan-Apr (winter). Cost: Approx. $6,500 per semester. Includes tuition, housing, some meals, international student identity card, texts, local transportation, excursions, and insurance. Financial aid accepted. Contact: Gail Lavin, Assoc. Director for Univ. Programs, American Heritage Association, 741 SW Lincoln St., Portland, OR 97201-3178; (800) 654-2051 or (503) 295-7730, fax (503) 295-5969; 96trab@am heritage.org.

Vienna Summer School. Annual program in art history, music history, German and Austrian literature, Eastern European literature, modern Austrian history, international communication, German I and II. Vienna: Values in Transit seminar, side trips to Amsterdam and The Hague, Venice, Prague, Salzburg, Austrian Alps.

Dates: May 26-Jul 10, 1996. Cost: $3,400 includes 6 credit hours, housing, 2 meals per day, transportation, 4 weekend trips. Contact: Dr. Stephen I. Hemenway, English Dept., Hope College, Holland, MI 49422-9000; (616) 395-7616, fax (616) 395-7134.

Webster Univ. in Vienna. Webster Univ. in Vienna has more than 400 students from 59 countries. Students may pursue a degree program leading to a BA, MA, or MBA. In addition, students may enroll for a study abroad semester or year (summer session and other short-term options also available). All courses are taught in English and are fully accredited. Major areas of study include: business, Central and Eastern European studies, computer science, economics, psychology, international relations, management, and marketing. A complete range of electives is also offered.

Dates: Five entry terms: late Aug, mid-Oct, mid-Jan, mid-Mar, late May. Cost: $20,000

(1996-97 academic year), $10,000 (1996-97 semester). Estimate includes tuition, room and board, books, local transportation, social activities. Contact: Study Abroad Office, Webster Univ., 470 E. Lockwood, St. Louis, MO 63119; (314) 968-6988 or (800) 984-6857, fax (314) 968-7119; brunote@websteruniv.edu. Visit our website http://webster2.websteruniv.edu.

Wiener Internationale Hochschulkurse. German courses at the University for beginners and advanced students, perfectionist courses (6 levels). Lectures on German and Austrian literature, music, linguistics, introduction to Austria. Special courses: translation into German, commercial correspondence, business German, medical terminology, communication, phonetics, Vienna waltz, choir singing. Language laboratory. Excursions.

Dates: Jul 6-Aug 2, Aug 3-30, Aug 31-Sep 20. Cost: Course fee (4 weeks): Approx. ATS4,300; accommodations: Approx. ATS6,000. Contact: Magister Sigrun Anmann-Trojer, Wiener Internationale Hochschulkurse, Universität, Dr. Karl Lueger-Ring 1, A1010 Wien, Austria; (011) 43-1-405-12-54 or 405-47-37, fax 405-12-5410.

Belgium

BA and BBA in Business. The 4-year bachelor programs cover all aspects of international business and marketing with a special focus on finance, management, marketing, information systems, law, and foreign languages. BA students first establish a firm basis in business subjects and, during the last 2 years, follow the same path as the BBA students in marketing while specializing in communications and public relations.

Dates: Early Oct through end Jan, early Feb through mid-Jun, and mid-Jun through mid-Sep. Cost: Tuition BEF285,000 per year. Contact: Dr. Ludo Lambrechts, Dean, Rue de Livourne 116-120, 1050 Brussels, Belgium; (011) 32-2-648-67-81, fax (011) 32-2-648-59-68.

Environmental Information Centre. Minimum 2 weeks assistance in technical management of Environmental Information Centre for Young People (library with books, magazines, reports, etc. on nature conservation).

Dates: Spring, summer, fall. Cost: $100 per week for accommodations and food. Contact: NATUUR 2000, Bervoetstraat 33, 2000 Antwerpen, Belgium; (011) 32-3-2312604, fax 2336499.

International Program in Philosophy. The Institute of Philosophy offers programs in English at all levels. We have both a 1-year and a 2-year BA program, a 2-year MA program, a doctoral preparatory year (equivalent to the second year of the MA), and a full doctoral program.

Dates: Academic year starts in the last week of Sep, and ends either in Jun (the first exam session) or Sep (the second exam session). Cost: Junior Year: Approx. $4,000; Belgian registration: BF17,600; tuition waivers are possible. Contact: Brendan Maloney, Assistant Academic Secretary, Int'l. Program in Philosophy, Univ. of Louvain, Kardinaal Mercierplein 2, B-3000, Leuven, Belgium; (011) 32-16-32-63-02, fax (011) 32-16-32-63-11.

MA in Business. The MA program combines several key courses from the MBA program with subjects concerning the theory and implementation of communication and public relations. European Univ. graduates are prepared for careers in public relations, human resources, and training development and organizational consulting. A full-time student can complete the program in 1 academic year.

Dates: Early Oct through Dec, early Jan through mid-Mar, and mid-Mar through mid-Jun. Cost: Tuition BEF345,000 per program (full-time or part-time). Contact: Dr. Ludo Lambrechts, Dean, Rue de Livourne 116-120, 1050 Brussels, Belgium; (011) 32-2-648-67-81, fax (011) 32-2-648-59-68.

MBA. The MBA program covers many aspects

of international operations. The emphasis is on international finance and marketing as well as strategic management; it includes a solid foundation in the traditional management disciplines. A full-time student can complete the program in one academic year.

Dates: Early Oct to Dec, early Jan to mid-Mar, and mid-Mar to mid-Jun. Cost: Tuition BEF345,000 per program (full-time or part-time). Contact: Dr. Ludo Lambrechts, Dean, Rue de Livourne 116-120, 1050 Brussels, Belgium; (011) 32-2-648-67-81, fax (011) 32-2-648-59-68.

Vesalius College, Vrije Univ. Brussel (VUB). Founded by the Vrije Univ. Brussel and Boston Univ., Vesalius offers an American-style undergraduate university education in Europe (BA's in arts, science, or engineering science). Choice of 16 majors including languages, engineering, computer science, international affairs, business, economics, and communications studies. About 430 students representing over 60 nationalities. Study abroad students live with a Belgian host family and enjoy full use of campus facilities.

Dates: Aug-Dec (fall), Jan-May (spring), Jun-Jul (summer). Cost: Approx. $4,500 per semester (tuition). Contact: Mr. E. Amrhein, Head of Admissions, Vesalius College-VUB, Pleinlaan 2, B-1050 Brussels, Belgium; (011) 32-2-629-36-26, fax (011) 32-2-629-36-37; vesalius@vnet3.vub.ac.be.

Brazil

Beloit College Brazil Exchange. Located in southeastern Brazil, the Federal Univ. of Ouro Preto offers exchange students a flexible curriculum involving Portuguese language, Brazilian art history, Brazilian society and culture, and other options in the social sciences, humanities, or geology. Students live in university-owned houses with 12-15 Brazilian students, thereby gaining instant access to true Brazilian student life.

Dates: Approx. Aug 1-Dec 20. Cost: Tuition $8,672, room and board $1,923. Contact: Dr. Terance W. Bigalke, Director, World Affairs Center, Beloit College, 700 College St., Beloit, WI 53511; (608) 363-2269, fax (608) 363-2689; bigalket@beloit.edu.

Brazil's Economy and Business Environment. Study and observe the business climate and process of economic development in Brazil. Open to students of all majors. Lasts 6 weeks: early Jun to mid-Jul. Seminars taught in English by faculty from the Univ. of Sao Paulo a series of field trips allow students to observe first-hand the process of economic development in an emerging market. All students take intensive language course. No knowledge of Portuguese necessary. Housing with local families.

Dates: Early Jun-mid-Jul. Cost: $3,100 includes tuition, registration fees, room and board, field trips, and partial insurance coverage. Contact: IPA, Univ. of Illinois at Urbana-Champaign, 115 International Studies Bldg., 910 S. 5th St., Champaign, IL 61820; (800) 531-4404, fax (217) 244-0249; ipa@uiuc.edu.

Canada

Audubon Expedition Institute (AEI). One of 8 semester options available, AEI's Canadian Maritime semester program focuses on the natural and cultural history of the region through an intensive, experiential approach to environmental education. Undergraduate and graduate students visit people and places at the forefront of today's most pressing environmental issues, learning firsthand about the complexity involved, and gaining a unique perspective unavailable in a traditional classroom setting.

Dates: Sep-Dec. Cost: $8,822 tuition per semester. Contact: Melanie West, Admissions Coordinator, Audubon Expedition Institute, P.O. Box 365, Belfast, ME 04915; (207) 338-

5859, fax (207) 338-1037; smckim@audubon. org, www.audubon.org/audubon/aei.html.

Comparative Health Care Systems. Compare U.S. and Canadian systems of health care through lectures, panel presentations and visits to health care facilities, and meetings with administrators of hospitals, nursing homes, health centers, etc. On-campus housing at Ryerson Institute in Toronto. Three graduate credits.

Dates: Jul 24-30, 1996. Cost: Approx. $1,300. Includes airfare, room and board, and tuition. Contact: SUNY Brockport, Office of International Education, 350 New Campus Dr., Brockport, NY 14420; (716) 395-2119, fax (716) 395-2606.

English Language Centre, Univ. of Victoria. The English Language Centre is known throughout the world for its high standards of English language instruction. Established in 1970, the ELC offers quality language programs aimed at international and Canadian students wishing to improve their English language and cross-cultural skills for personal, professional, and academic purposes. Students from all over the world have attended the ELC. The 12-week Intensive English Language Program is offered 3 times each year, and a series of spring and summer programs are available. UVic is a mid-sized university with 17,000 students and is a friendly and comfortable place to study. It was rated the #1 Comprehensive Univ. in Canada for the second year in a row.

Dates: Apr 10-1-Jul 2; Sep 11-Nov 3; Jan 8-Apr 1, 1998 (tuition $2,700 per term). Cost: Spring and summer 1997: Mar 31-May 9, ($1,925); May 26-Jun 27 ($1,585); Jul 7-Aug 15 ($1,925); Aug 4-29 ($1,295). Contact: Bronwyn Jenkins or Maxine Macgillivray, Program Coordinators, English Language Centre, Univ. of Victoria, P.O. Box 1700, Victoria, BC V8W 2Y2, Canada; (604) 721-8469, fax (604) 721-6276; mmcagillivray@uvcs.uvic.ca.

Language Studies Canada Montréal. Using a multi-skill approach in a relaxed classroom atmosphere, the Standard Group program ensures that students develop communicative competence in French. Six levels of 4 weeks each, 4 hours daily. Maximum of 14 students per class. Audio-visual equipment, Student Resource Center. Optional activity program. Homestay available.

Dates: Two-week courses begin any Monday from Jan 15, 1996 year round, one-to-one instruction. Group 5 executive courses, Jun-Oct. Summer Language Adventure (14 to 17 year-olds), Jul and Aug. Cost: Two weeks: $390 Standard Group tuition; $400 homestay. Cost of other services available upon request. Contact: Language Studies Canada Montréal, 1450 City Councillors, Montréal H3A 2E6, Canada; (514) 499-9911, fax (514) 499-0332.

Univ. of New Brunswick English Language Programme. Established in 1954 in eastern Canada, tradition of expertise with international clientele. Language contract base; courses designed for client needs; experienced staff; residential approach. Participants live in English while learning in immersion: nonstop weekday and weekend. Classes extend into the community. Extensive diagnosis, ongoing assessment, constant quality control.

Dates: Three-week format (monthly Sep-Apr) in homestay; 5-week format (May-Jun, Jul-Aug) in university residence. Cost: Three-week CAN$3,339; 5-week CAN$1,700. Includes tuition fees. Contact: Mrs. Mary E. Murray, Director, Univ. of New Brunswick, English Language Programme, P.O. Box 4400, Fredericton, New Brunswick, E3B 5A3, Canada; (506) 453-3564, fax (506) 453-3578.

Univ. of Regina Language Institute. A variety of non-credit programs are offered in 3 streams: English for Academic Purposes (EA), which prepares students for attending university; English for Business (EB) which focuses on increasing students' understanding and use of of business vocabulary and concepts; and English for Communication (EC) which focuses on increasing students' oral communication. Evening courses, conversation partners, and short-term customized courses are also available.

Dates: 1997: Jan 10-Apr 4 (12 weeks); Apr 18-Jun 13 (8 weeks); Jun 27-Aug 22 (8 weeks); Sep 12-Dec 5 (12 weeks). Cost: Winter 1997: $1,825. Spring/summer 1997: $1,625. Fall 1997: $1,945. Conversation partners: $110 per semester. Placement fee for housing: $160. Plus rent, security, and telephone deposits. Contact: Penthes Rubrecht, English as a Second Language Centre, Univ. of Regina, Rm. 211, Language Institute, Regina, Saskatchewan, Canada S4S 0A2; (306) 585-4585, fax (306) 585-4971; esl@max.cc.uregina.ca, www.uregina.ca/~esl.

Central America

Semester Internship and Research Program. The Institute for Central American Development Studies (ICADS) offers a semester abroad study program, including coursework and structured internship opportunities in Costa Rica, Nicaragua, and Belize in the following areas: women's studies, environment/ecology, public health, agriculture, human rights, and many others. The program is progressive and aimed at students who wish to work on social justice issues and on behalf of the poor, women, and the oppressed in Central America. Fall and spring with academic credit, summer noncredit internship-only program.

Dates: Fall, spring, and summer semesters. Cost: $6,900 per semester. Includes all travel (except from U.S.), housing, food, books, classes and study tour to Nicaragua or Panama. Contact: Sandra Kinghorn, PhD, Director, ICADS, Dept. 826, P.O. Box 025216, Miami, FL 33102-5216, or ICADS, Apartado 3-2070, Sabanilla, San Jose, Costa Rica; (011) 506-225-0508, fax (011) 506-234-1337; icadscr@ expreso.co.cr.

Chile

CWU Semester Program in Chile. Semester abroad program hosted by the Universidad Autral de Chile (Valdivia) that combines intensive language training, core electives in Latin American politics, history and literature, direct enrollment courses, and field research/independent study. Participants enjoy cross-cultural learning experience in the beautiful lake region of southern Chile.

Dates: Spring semester: Mar 15-Jul 6 (approx.); fall: Aug. 15-Dec. 15. Cost: $3,500 (tuition, housing and meals). Contact: Stacia Zukroff, Study Abroad/Exchange Advisor, Central Washington Univ., Office of International Studies and Programs, 400 E. 8th Ave., Ellensburg, WA 98926-7408; (509) 963-3615, fax (509) 963-1558; zukroff@cwu.edu.

Public Policy Semester/Summer Language and Culture. The Public Policy Semester offers students the opportunity to conduct an in-depth research policy on issues facing Chilean government and society. Research preceded by intensive courses on contemporary economcs, history, and politics. Housing with local families. Graduate and undergraduate credit available. A summer language and cultuer program is also available.

Dates: Spring semester: Mar-Jul; fall semester: Jul-Dec; summer: Jun-mid-Jul. Cost: $5,800 (spring 1997 fee) includes tuition, room and board, registration fees, excursions, orientation, site director, partial insurance coverage. Contact: IPA, Univ. of Illinois at Urbana-Champaign, 115 International Studies Bldg., 910 S. 5th St., Champaign, IL 61820; (800) 531-4404, fax (217) 244-0249; ipa@uiuc.edu.

Spanish and Latin American Studies (Santiago). Santiago offers intensive language studies fulfilling up to 2 years of university Spanish requirements in 1 semester, with additional courses in literature, business, teacher ed., history, political science. Week-long program-oriented field trips to the south and north of Chile, homestays, and many university activities at Chilean university.

Dates: Fall semester: Aug 27-Dec 16, 1997; spring semester: Jan 7-May 5, 1998. Cost: One semester: $3,542; fall and spring: $5,950. Contact: University Studies Abroad Consortium (USAC), Univ. of Nevada, Reno #323, Reno, NV 89557-0093; (702) 784-6569, fax (702) 784-6010; usac@admin.unr.edu, www.scs.unr.edu/~usac.

Study Abroad in Santiago. Study for a semester or an academic year at the Pontificia Universidad Católica de Chile (PUC), one of the most prestigious universities in South America. For students with intermediate to advanced Spanish language ability. Intensive pre-semester language training and orientation. On-site resident director. Family homestay. Co-sponsored by Univ. of Wisconsin at Madison and the Univ. of Michigan.

Dates: Late Feb-late Jun (semester); late Feb-mid-Dec (academic year). Cost: Approx. $5,235 per semester (WI residents). Includes tuition, room and board, social and cultural program. Contact: Lawrence Roscioli, Director, L&S Overseas Programs, Univ. of Wisconsin at Milwaukee, P.O. Box 413, Milwaukee, WI 53201; (414) 229-5879, fax (414) 229-6827; overseas@csd.uwm.edu.

China

BCA Program in Dalian. Earn 16-20 credits per semester at the Dalian Univ. of Foreign Languages in China, with a 1-week orientation period, field trips, and extended study tours through Beijing and northern or southern China. Year students could study second semester in Sapporo, Japan. Tamula Drumm is BCA Director in Residence. Students from all U.S. colleges and universities accepted. No foreign language prerequisite. All levels of Chinese language available plus Russian and Japanese.

Dates: Aug 25-Jan 20 (fall), Feb 10-Jul 15 (spring), Aug 25-Jul 15 (year). Cost: $12,545 (academic year 1996-1997); $7,245 (semester 1996-1997) includes international transportation, tuition, room and board, insurance, group in-country travel. Contact: Beverly S.

Eikenberry, Box 184, Manchester College, North Manchester, IN 46962; (219) 982-5238, fax (219) 982-7755; bca@manchester.edu, http://studyabroad.com/bca.

Chinese Language Program. This language program available at 70 major universities in China offers tailored programs from 4 weeks to 1 year. Study is in an integrated environment with other foreign students. Courses are taught at 4 different levels, based on the students' previous language skills. Courses meet 20 hours per week.

Dates: Application deadlines vary. Cost: Cost varies depending on length of course. Tuition lodging, meals, books, and materials approximate $1,100 for 4 weeks. Contact: Cascade Huan, Assoc. Director for Program Development, American Heritage Association, 741 SW Lincoln St., Portland, OR 97201-3178; (800) 654-2051, fax (503) 295-5969; chuan@amheritage.org.

Friends World Program. A semester or year program at Zhejiang Univ. in Hangzhou, including Chinese language instruction. Classes include Chinese culture, customs, Chinese arts or calligraphy. Students also have their own research projects which may include the study of Chinese medicine, gender issues, religion, or environmental issues. Students may earn 12-18 credits per semester.

Dates: Fall: mid-Oct-end of Jan; spring: beg. of Mar-beg of Jul. Cost: $10,185 per semester in 1996/1997. Includes tuition, travel, room and board, fees, and books. Contact: James Howard, Friends World Program, 239 Montauk Highway, Southampton, NY 11968; (516) 287-8475; jhoward@sand.liunet.edu.

Mandarin Language Study. Study intensive Mandarin Chinese at Beijing Language and Culture Univ., the only university in China specializing in teaching Mandarin to foreigners. Classes are intensive with 20 hours of classroom instruction per week. Fees include tuition, textbooks, double-occupancy accommodations, sightseeing in Beijing, cultural activities, orientation, visa processing, and roundtrip airfare from San Francisco.

Dates: Spring, summer, fall programs and 1-year program. Cost: Five weeks $3,110, 20 weeks $4,720, 8 weeks $3,420, 1 year $6,850. Contact: China Advocates, 1635 Irving St., San Francisco, CA 94122; (800) 333-6474, fax (415) 753-0412; chinaadv@aol.com.

Colombia

Community Internships in Latin America. Emphasis on community participation for social change. Students work 3 days a week in an internship, meet together for core seminar and internship seminar, and carry out independent study project. Wide range of internship opportunities in community development and related activities. Based in Bogotá. Family homestay. Latin American faculty. Full semester's credit, U.S. transcript provided. All majors.

Dates: Early Feb-mid-May. Cost: $8,100 (1997-98). Includes tuition, room and board, field trips. Contact: Elizabeth Andress, Assistant Director, HECUA, Mail #36, Hamline Univ., 1536 Hewitt Ave., St. Paul, MN 55104-1284; (612) 646-8832 or (800) 554-9421, fax (612) 659-9421; hecua@hamline.edu, www.hamline.edu/~hecua.

Culture and Society in Latin America. Innovative approach combines classroom experience with extensive field work. Courses include ideologies of social change, Latin American arts and society, Latin American literature's perspectives on social change, and independent study. Based in Bogotá, with field study and travel in Colombia, Guatemala, and the Caribbean. Family homestay. Latin American faculty. Full semester's credit, U.S. transcript provided. All majors.

Dates: Early Feb-mid-May. Cost: $8,100 (1997-98). Includes tuition, room and board, field trips. Contact: Elizabeth Andress, Assis-

tant Director, HECUA, Mail #36, Hamline Univ., 1536 Hewitt Ave., St. Paul, MN 55104-1284; (612) 646-8832 or (800) 554-1089), fax (612) 659-9421; hecua@hamline.edu, www.hamline.edu/~hecua.

South American Urban Semester. Innovative approach combines classroom experience with extensive field work. Courses include introduction to Latin America, urbanization and development in Latin America, Spanish language, and independent study. Based in Bogotá, with field study and travel in Colombia, Guatemala, and Ecuador. Family homestay. Latin American faculty. Full semester's credit, U.S. transcript provided. All majors.

Dates: Late Aug-early Dec. Cost: $8,100 (1997-98). Includes tuition, room and board, field trips. Contact: Elizabeth Andress, Assistant Director, HECUA, Mail #36, Hamline Univ., 1536 Hewitt Ave., St. Paul, MN 55104-1284; (612) 646-8832 or (800) 554-1089, fax (612) 659-9421; hecua@hamline.edu; www.hamline.edu/~hecua.

Costa Rica

Central American Institute for International Affairs-ICAI. Three total immersion Spanish language programs designed to teach participants conversational Spanish. Four hours of classes per day with a low student-to-teacher ratio. Students are placed with carefully selected host families with single or double accommodations and all meals. Cultural activities and excursions are offered with each program.

Dates: Year round. New classes begin every Monday, all levels. Cost: From $632 (2-week program) to $1,298 (4-week program). Contact: Bill Fagan, Director, Language Studies Enrollment Center, 13948 Hemlock Dr., Penn Valley, CA 95946; (916) 432-7690, fax (916) 432-7615; bfaglsec@nccn.net, http: www.expreso.co.cr/icai/index.htm.

Contemporary Issues in Central America. Contemporary Issues in Central America is a 21-day university credit program (in English) based in San Jose, Costa Rica, that provides an anaytical overview of the development of contemporary society through seminars with social and political leaders, homestays with 2 meals per day with private room and bath, walking and city tours, trips to Arenal Volcano Park and the Pacific Coast.

Dates: Jun 23-Jul 11, 1997. Cost: Program: $1,350, university tuition $396. Airfare not included. Contact: Dr. Marjorie Bray, Director, Latin American Studies Program, California State Univ., Los Angeles, 5151 University Dr., Los Angeles, CA 90032-8619; (213) 343-2180, fax (213) 935-3975; psimun@calstatela.edu.

Costa Rican Language Academy. Costa Rican owned and operated language school offers first-rate Spanish instruction in a warm and friendly environment. Teachers with university degrees. Small groups or private classes. Included free in the programs are airport transportation, coffee and natural refreshments, excursions and Latin dance, Costa Rican cooking, music and conversation classes to provide students with complete cultural immersion.

Dates: Year round (start anytime). Cost: $135 per week or $220 per week for program with homestay. All other activities and services included at no additional cost. Contact: Costa Rican Language Academy, P.O. Box 336-2070, San José, Costa Rica; (011) 506-221-1624 or 233-8914 or 233-8938, fax 233-8670; crlang@sol.racsa.co.cr. In the U.S. (800) 854-6057.

Education and Society in Costa Rica. Education and Society in Costa Rica is a 21-day university credit program (in English) based in San Jose that includes preschool through higher education observations, seminars with education and political leaders, homestays with two meals per day with private room and bath, walking and city tours, a 2-day trip to Arenal Volcano Park, and a 3-day trip to the Pacific Coast.

Dates: Jun 23-Jul 11, 1997. Cost: Program $1,355; university tuition $396. Airfare not included. Contact: Patricia Bates Simun, Ph.D., Prof. of Education, California State Univ., Los Angeles, 1019 Longwood Ave., Los Angeles, CA 90019-1755; (213) 936-3938, fax (213) 935-5975; psimun@calstatela.edu.

Enjoy Learning Spanish Faster. Techniques developed from our ongoing research enable students at Centro Linguistico Latinoamericano to learn more, faster, in a comfortable environment. Classes are 2-5 students plus group learning activities; conversations with middle-class homestay families (1 student per family). Homestays are within walking distance of school in small town (14,000 population) near the capital, San Jose.

Dates: Year round. Classes begin every Monday, at all levels. Cost: $295 per week for 25 hours of classes. Includes tuition, all meals (7 days a week), homestay, laundry, all materials, Costa Rican dance and cooking classes, and airport transportation. $25 one-time registration. Contact: Susan Shores, Registrar, Latin American Language Center, 7485 Rush River Dr., Suite 710-123, Sacramento, CA 95831; (916) 447-0938, fax (916) 428-9542.

ILISA and Language Link. ILISA offers intensive Spanish language programs with a professional emphasis in the quiet university area of San Pedro, a suburb of San Jose, Costa Rica. Your choice of either 4 hours daily of small classes (never more than 4), a combination of 4 hours group and 2 hours private, or completely private. Professional adults, college students, and all Spanish levels accommodated in a very well-organized school in a beautiful mountain setting. Programs of 2 to12 weeks starting on any Monday. U.S. graduate and undergraduate credit. Earn 6 credits in 3 weeks. Homestays and 3 additional weekly activities included, such as videos, cultural lectures, and dance classes. Great excursion program. A well-developed program is available for families.

Dates: Year round. New classes begin every Monday. Summer months fill very early. Cost: Four hours daily of group classes and homestay: 2 weeks $725, 4 weeks $1,295. Includes registration, insurance, tuition, materials, airport pickup, private room, and 2 meals daily. Contact: Kay G. Rafool, Language Link Inc. (U.S. Office for ILISA), P.O. Box 3006, Peoria, IL 61612; (800) 552-2051, fax (309) 673-5537; info@langlink.com; www.langlink.com.

Intensive Spanish. In Santa Ana, about 10 km from San Jose, the campus is a 6-acre "finca" with sports facilities and swimming pool. Operates in 1-month cycles throughout the academic year. Earn 6-7 credits on 1 month, or do a "Language Semester" in 2 months and earn 12-14 credits while mastering Spanish, 110 hours per month, classes of 4 students each. Peace-Corps-style techniques. Costa Rican homestay, all meals. Optional lodging on campus at extra cost.

Dates: Operates in 1-month cycles throughout the year. Cost: $2,240 per 1-month cycle. Contact: Reinaldo Changsut, Study Abroad Adviser, Miami-Dade Community College, 11011 SW 104th St., Miami, FL 33176-3393; (305) 237-2535, fax (305) 237-2949.

Intensive Spanish Immersion Program. The Institute for Central American Development Studies (ICADS) offers 30-day programs of intensive Spanish languages—4 1/2 hours daily, 5 days a week. Small classes (4 students or less) geared to individual needs. Extra lectures and activities emphasize environmental issues, women's studies, economic development, and human rights. ICADS offers optional afternoon internship placements in grassroots organizations. Supportive informal learning environment. Homestays and field trips.

Dates: Programs begin first day Monday of each month. Cost: One month $1,100. Includes airport pick-up, classes, books, homestay, meals, laundry, lectures, activities, field trips, and internship placements. (10% discount after first month.) Contact: Sandra Kinghorn, Ph.D., Director, ICADS, Dept. 826, P.O. Box 025216, Miami, FL 33102-5216; or ICADS, Apartado 3-2070, Sabanilla, San Jose, Costa Rica; (011) 506-225-0508, fax (011) 506-234-1337; icadscr@expreso.co.ro.

Intercultura and Language Link. Intercultura offers intensive Spanish language programs in peaceful Costa Rica. Your choice of either 4 hours daily of small classes (never more than 6, often less), a combination of 4 hours group and 2 hours private, or completely private. Professional adults, college students, and all Spanish levels accommodated. Programs of 1 to 12 weeks starting on any Monday. U.S. graduate and undergraduate credit. Earn 6 credits in 3 weeks. Caring homestays and excursions. A smaller school with a dynamic, professional staff dedicated to personal attention. Located in Heredia, a small university town, just 30 minutes outside the busy capital city. Option of a week's stay at our beach campus.

Dates: Year round. New classes begin every Monday. Summer months fill very early. Cost: Four hours daily of group classes and homestay: 2 weeks $495, 4 weeks $875. Includes registration, insurance, tuition, materials, airport pickup, private room, and 2 meals daily. Contact: Kay G. Rafool, Language Link Inc. (U.S. Office for Intercultura), P.O. Box 3006, Peoria, IL 61612; (800) 552-2051, fax (309) 673-5537; info@langlink.com; www.langlink.com.

IPEE Spanish Language School. IPEE is Costa Rica's premiere total immersion language school. Our direct personal service and commitment to quality is what separates us from the rest. All levels starts every week. Homestays and excursions. Student discounts.

Dates: Year round. Cost: One week with homestay $305, 1 month with homestay

$1,020. Contact: Robert Levy, IPEE, 16057 Tampa Palms Blvd., Suite 158, Tampa, FL 33647; (813) 988-3916; ipee@gate.net, www.gate.net.~ipee.

Outward Bound Costa Rica. Save the Rainforest Adventures. Outward Bound Costa Rica (CRROBS) creates courses that help your rainforest experience endure beyond the canopy of Latin America. We offer year round, multi-element (rafting, kayaking, canopy or rock climbing, hiking, and homestays). Costa Rica courses for any age group or individual. We also offer an 85-day tri-country (Costa Rica, Ecuador, and Peru) semester course (biology, anthropology, Spanish credit). Spanish/biology emphasis are available on all courses. For adventurers who want a less physically demanding experience than CRROBS offers, Save the Rainforest Adventures offers excursions catered to the needs and interests of each group or individual.

Dates: Year round 8-, 10-, 12-, 15-, 25-, 30-, and 85-day courses. Cost: $1,000-$2,600 for multi-day; $6,800 for 85 tri-country semester. Scholarships available. Contact: Outward Bound Costa Rica and Save the Rainforest Adventures, P.O. Box 243, Quepos, Costa Rica; (800) 676-2018, fax (011) 506-777-1222; crrobs@sol.racsa.co.cr, www.centralamerica.com/cr/crrobs.

Spanish Language. Intercultura Language Institute offers intensive Spanish and homestays in selected Costa Rican families. Academic credit available (with prior notice). Additional free activities: dance, music, theater, cinema, cooking. Weekend excursions to volcanoes, beaches, rainforest. Volunteer opportunities in social, environmental, and political organizations. Beach campus: optional 1 week per month, study on Pacific coast.

Dates: Year round. Cost: $875 per month (shorter stays available). Contact: Laura Ellington, Codirector, Intercultura Costa Rica, Apdo. 1952-3000, Heredia, Costa Rica; (011) 506-260-8480, Tel./fax (011) 506-260-9243.

Spanish Language Immersion. Intensive Spanish language immersion program for all levels of Spanish speakers at the Spanish Language Institute in San Jose. Language courses taught by native speakers with no more than 5 students per class. Housing with Coasta Rican families. Field trips and on-site residential director. Fall, spring, summer.

Dates: Sep 5-Dec 20 (fall); Jan 21-May 25 (spring); Jun 30-Aug 6 (summer). Cost: Semester: Approx. $3,300; summer: approx. $1,800. Includes tuition, room and board. Contact: SUNY Brockport, Office of International Education, 350 New Campus Dr., Brockport, NY 14420; (716) 395-2119, fax (716) 395-2606.

Spanish Language Immersion. Intensive Spanish language immersion program for students with 2 years of Spanish language or the equivalent at the Spanish Language Institute in San Jose. Language courses taught by native speakers with no more than 5 students per class. Housing with Costa Rican families. Field trips and on-site resident director. Six credits: graduate, undergraduate.

Dates: Jun 30-Aug 6. Cost: Approx. $1,100. Includes tuition, insurance, room and board. Contact: SUNY Brockport, Office of International Education, 350 New Campus Dr., Brockport, NY 14420; (716) 395-2119, fax (716) 395-2606.

Spanish, Ecology, and Latin American Studies (Heredia). Heredia offers intensive language studies which fulfills up to 2-year university Spanish requirements in a semester or 1 year in the 8-week summer program. Additional courses offered in political science, history, biology, teacher ed., business, literature, etc. Program organized week-long and weekend field trips, homestays, and many local university activities.

Dates: Summer sessions: May 22-Jun 27, and Jun 22-Jul 27, 1997; fall term: Aug 27-Dec 19, 1997; spring term: Jan 8-May 10, 1998. Cost: One semester: $3,542; year: $5,950; summer: $1,360 per session; $2,275 both sessions. Contact: University Studies Abroad Consortium (USAC), Univ. of Nevada, Reno #323, Reno, NV 89557-0093; (702) 784-6569, fax (702) 784-6010; usac@admin.unr.edu, www.scs.unr.edu/~usac.

Summer-Semester Programs at Universidad de Costa Rica. A graduate and undergraduate program at the Universidad de Costa Rica for students interested in studying courses in language, literature, culture and civilization, composition, and history of Costa Rica. All courses are taught by full-time faculty members from the Univ. of Costa Rica, the most prestigious university in Costa Rica. A lot of extra activities and excursions are organized for students. Students stay with Costa Rican families.

Dates: Summer: Jun-Jul; semester: fall and winter. Cost: Total cost from $1,885 including airfare. Contact: Modern Language Studies Abroad, P.O. Box 623, Griffith, IN 46319; Tel./fax (219) 838-9460.

Tropical Studies in Golfito. Study for a semester in the port town of Golfito on the southern Pacific coast of Costa Rica. This program is designed for today's independent, environmentally and socially conscious student interested in contemporary issues of Latin America. Earn up to 15 credit hours in the fields of anthropology, ecology, biology, and Spanish language and contemporary culture. Four semesters Spanish and 2.75 GPA required.

Dates: Early Aug-mid-Dec or early Jan-mid-May. Six-week summer program also available. Cost: Approx. $5,000. Includes tuition, on-site orientation, room and board, and all program administrative costs. Contact: Ellen Hart Strubert, Program Coordinator, Office of Study Abroad, The Univ. of Kansas, Lawrence, KS 66045; (913) 864-3742, fax (913) 864-5040.

Czech Republic

Penn-in-Prague. For students interested in Jewish studies and Czech culture, this program, located amidst the fairy tale beauty of Prague and affiliated with Charles Univ. and the Jewish Museum of Prague, offers an insight into the rich history and urgent contemporary problems of this important region, as well as an opportunity to learn beginning and intermediate Czech. Some internships can be arranged with the Jewish Museum.

Dates: Jul 8-Aug 16. Cost: Tuition $2,840; housing and excursion $750. Contact: Penn Summer Abroad, College of General Studies, Univ. of Pennsylvania, 3440 Market St., Suite 100, Philadelphia, PA 19104-3335; (215) 898-5738, fax (215) 573-2053.

The Magic of Prague. The lovely Eastern European city of Prague will be a source of ideas for a 3-unit writing workshop offered by Professor Bernard Goldberg of West Los Angeles College. Required reading will be Kafka's "The Trial," Rilke's "Letters to a Young Poet," and "The Hunger Wall" by Ragan.

Dates: Jul 8-30, 1996. Cost: $1,624, plus $39 class fee for California residents. Nonresidents pay $138 per unit. Contact: International Education Program, Los Angeles Community College District, 770 Wilshire Blvd., Los Angeles, CA 90017; (213) 891-2282, fax (213) 891-2150; intered@laccd.cc.ca.us.

Denmark

Danish Language Intensive Semester. This program, to be held at the Univ. of Kansas in Lawrence, offers 16 semester credit hours of Danish language and culture supplemented by group excursions and activities, and the opportunity to live in a Danish-speaking residence hall wing. Classes are taught by KU faculty and a native Danish-speaking graduate teaching assistant from Aarhus Univ., Denmark.

Dates: Spring semester, approx. Jan. 3-May 9, 1997. Cost: Approx. $7,400 (non-KU students). Includes KU tuition, room, meal plan, group cultural activities and excursions, instructional materials, administrative costs. Contact: Nancy Mitchell, Office of Study Abroad, 203-T Lippincott, The Univ. of Kansas, Lawrence, KS 66045.

Ecuador

Academia de Español Quito. The Academia de Español Quito offers intensive Spanish language programs in the exciting capital of Ecuador, Quito. Your choice of 4 to 7 hours daily of one-on-one instruction. Professional adults, college students, and all Spanish levels accommodated in a very well-organized school. Programs of 1 to 12 weeks starting on any Monday. U.S. graduate and undergraduate credit. Earn 6 credits in 3 weeks. Caring homestays and many additional weekly activities included, such as videos, cultural lectures and excursions. Also offered is the Activo program, in which students study 4 hours in the morning in the classroom and in the afternoon explore Quito and surrounding area with their teacher, using the city as an expanded classroom. Ages are 16 and up, and student evaluations are consistently superior.

Dates: Year round. New classes begin every Monday. Summer months fill very early. Cost: Four hours daily private classes and homestay: $260 per week; 7 hours daily Activo program (includes all transportation, entry fees, etc.): $350 per week. Includes tuition, materials, insurance, airport pickup, private room, 3 meals daily, and laundry. Contact: Kay G. Rafool, Language Link Inc., P.O. Box 3006, Peoria, IL 61612; (800) 552-2051, fax (309) 673-5537; info@langlink.com; www.langlink.com.

Academia Latinoamericana de Español (Quito). Ecuador's number-one private Spanish language institute in former diplomat's mansion with swimming pool, hot tub, sauna, sport facilities. Instruction by university-trained teachers, all one-on-one. Customized study programs tailored to the individual. Select host family accommodations. Excursions to haciendas, Indian markets, etc. College credit available and internships.

Dates: Year round. Cost: One-week tuition, lodging, meals $294. Contact: Suzanne Bell, Admissions Director, U.S., 640 East 3990 South, Suite E, Salt Lake City, UT 84107; (801) 268-4608, fax (801) 265-9156; latinoa1@spanish.com.ec, http://ecnct.cc/academia/learnspa.htm.

BCA Program in Quito. Earn 13-17 credits per semester at Universidad San Francisco de Quito, with a 4-week intensive language and orientation, homestay with Ecuadoran families, field trips, extended study tour to Amazon headwaters and Galápagos Islands. Students from all U.S. colleges and universities accepted. Intermediate level college Spanish required.

Dates: Aug 20-Dec 15 (fall), Mar 1-Jul 6 (spring), Aug 20-Mar 31 (year). Cost: $17,345 (1996-1997 academic year); $9,645 (1996-1997 semester). Includes international transportation, room and board, tuition, insurance, group travel in country. Contact: Beverly S. Eikenberry, Box 184, Manchester College, North Manchester, IN 46962; (219) 982-5238, fax (219) 982-7755; bca@manchester.edu, http://studyabroad.com/bca.

Beloit College Ecuador Seminar. Pre-term classes in Spanish conversation and Ecuadoran culture ready students for a course on 20th-century Latin American issues and 2 courses chosen from the regular offerings of the Universidad Catolica in Quito. Students gain additional language practice by living with Ecuadoran families. Group excursions include a trip to the Galápagos islands and the Amazon rainforest.

Dates: Approx. Aug 26-Dec 20. Cost: Tuition $8,672, room and board $1,923 Contact: Dr. Terance W. Bigalke, Director, World Affairs Center, Beloit College, 700 College St., Beloit, WI 53511; (608) 363-2269, fax (608) 363-2689; bigalket@beloit.edu.

Environmental Studies in Ecuador. The program focuses on the growing conflict between the development of Ecuador's economy and the preservation of its ecological resources. Program includes course work in Spanish with Ecuadoran students at the Universidad San Francisco de Quito, field study trips to several regions of the country, and an independent research project. Minimum 2 years college Spanish and strong background in biology required.

Dates: Jan-mid-May. Cost: (1995-1996) $11,788 includes roundtrip international transportation, tuition and fees, field study trips, room and board, and some excursions. Contact: Dr. Michael Vande Berg, Director of the Center for International Programs, Kalamazoo College, 1200 Academy, Kalamazoo, MI 49006; (616) 337-7133, fax (616) 337-7400; cip@kzoo.edu.

Golondrinas Cloudforest Project. We welcome students to assist in or carry out research concerning sustainable agriculture (agroforestry) and forest resource management. Fluency in Spanish is necessary. The reserve spans 3 different ecosystems, lending to great biodiversity, making it a fascinating area for study. If interested, request list of studies to be conducted.

Dates: Year round. Cost: Depending on duration of stay between $95 and $180 per month. Contact: Fundación Golondrinas, Attn: Piet T. Sabbe, c/o Calle Isabel la Católica, 1559, Quito, Ecuador.

Spanish for Foreigners in Quito. One-to-one instruction with well-trained teachers; luxury house with natural light, gardens, and terrace without noise or smog, all levels. Special programs: literature, fine arts, history, commercial, children's (8+ years old) activities, learning and travel. Twice weekly free guided tours (in programs of 7 hours daily). Accommodations in nice Ecuadorian homestay, near the school (3 meals, laundry, bed and bath private), airport pickup free. Cafeteria, mail.

Dates: Year round. Cost: $7 per class hour, $21 family per day (full room and board). Contact: Instituto de Español "El Quijote," Director Julio Cesar Muñoz Garay, Pasaue

Manuel Godoy Nº 144 and Juan Ramirez St., P.O. Box 17-17-1419, Quito, Ecuador; (011) 593-2-455256, fax 464967.

Univ. of San Francisco de Quito. Students take courses with Ecuadorian students at the Univ. of San Francisco de Quito. Courses are available in a variety of subject areas for semester or year. Housing arranged in local homes. Resident director conducts orientation and excursions. Courses taught in Spanish; 4 semesters of college-level Spanish required.

Dates: Fall semester: Aug-Dec; spring semester: Jan-May; year: Aug-May. Cost: $5,850 (spring 1997 fee) includes: tuition, registration, excursions, orientation, room and board, support services, on-site director, partial ins. Contact: IPA, Univ. of Illinois at Urbana-Champaign, 115 International Studies Bldg., 910 S. 5th St., Champaign, IL 61820; (800) 531-4404, fax (217) 244-0249; ipa@uiuc.edu.

Egypt

The American Univ. in Cairo. Study for 1 or 2 semesters with Egyptian students at an American-style liberal arts university in the heart of Cairo. Study abroad students may elect courses from the general course offerings; most popular are those dealing with Middle East, Egyptian, and Arab history, politics, culture, Egyptology, Islamic studies, Arabic language. Language of instruction is English.

Dates: Sep-Jan, Feb-Jun, Jun-Aug. Cost: Approx. $4,500 per semester for tuition and fees. Contact: Mary Davidson, American Univ. in Cairo, 866 United Nations Plaza, Box 519, New York, NY 10017-1889.

Europe

ACCELS Programs. ACCELS offers summer, semester, and academic year language study and research programs in the Czech and Slovak republics and Hungary. All programs require some prior knowledge of Czech, Slovak, or Hungarian and are affiliated with universities in the host country. Need-based financial aid will be available, pending grant approval.

Dates: Summer, year, fall, and spring. Cost: Vary according to program and length of stay. Contact: ACCELS (American Council for Collaboration in Education and Language Study), 1776 Massachusetts Ave., NW, Suite 700, Washington, DC 20036; (202) 833-7522, fax (202) 833-7523; kuban@actr.org.

Art Under One Roof. Live the arts in Florence at Art Under One Roof. Study for a month, a semester, or academic year. With over 30 applied art programs we're sure to satisfy you. Enrollments in all courses are limited to 10 to ensure the maximum amount of attention to each student's individual needs.

Dates: Year round. Cost: From $400-$6,000. Contact: Art Under One Roof, Admissions, Borgo dei Greci, 14, 50122 Florence, Italy; Tel./fax (011) 39-55-239-6821; berarducci@iol.it.

AuPair Homestay Abroad. Immerse yourself in the culture of your choice. Develop language skills and earn a monthly stipend while caring for the children of your host family. This is AuPair Homestay Abroad, an innovative program of World Learning, offering participants ages 18-29 the opportunity for experiential learning overseas within the comfort and security of a family setting. Placement in Europe and Argentina also.

Dates: Individual departure with stays from 3 to 12 months and extensions possible. Cost: $775. Includes interviewing, screening, matching with a host family, predeparture materials, program support in U.S. and while overseas. Contact: Imelda R. Farrell, Program Specialist, AuPair Homestay Abroad, 1015 15th St., NW, Washington, DC 20005; (202) 408-5380, fax (202) 408-5397; imelda.farrell@worldlearning.org.

Business/Liberal Arts Abroad. Undergraduate and graduate business programs located in Brussels, Paris, Madrid, Maastricht, Tartu and Florence. Semester, year long and short-term programs available. Bentley is AACSB accredited. Coursework offered primarily in English; collateral study of native language required. Beginner-advanced instruction offered.

Dates: Year: Sep-May, semester: Sep-Dec, Jan-May. Cost: Varies. Includes tuition, room and board, orientation, ISIC. Contact: Jennifer Scully, Director of Study Abroad, Bentley College, 175 Forest St., Waltham, MA 02154, (617) 891-3474, fax (617) 891-2819; inprinfo@bentley.edu, www.bentley.edu.

Comparative Criminal Justice: Europe and the U.S. This 6-credit traveling seminar follows the process the criminal follows, from apprehension to confinement, asking many questions along the way and observing criminal justice institutions in operation. The ports of call are Amsterdam, Strasbourg, France, London, and New York City. Participants arrange and pay for their own transatlantic flights. Air travel and ground transportation in Europe and housing in hotels or pensions during seminars are arranged and covered by the program fee.

Dates: Jun 16-Jul 17, 1996. Cost: Undergraduate tuition for 6 credits: $2,766; graduate tuition for 6 credits: $3,000; program fee: $2,820. Contact: Daisy Fried, Syracuse Summer Abroad, Syracuse Univ., 119 Euclid Ave., Syracuse, NY 13244-4170; (315) 443-9419, fax (315) 443-4593; dsfried@suadmin.syr.edu.

Comparative Education Abroad. Educators will participate for 3 weeks in their professional fields in English-speaking schools overseas. Your unique program will be established by a native site coordinator, usually a headmaster. You will interact with teachers and administrators as well as observe/interact in classrooms of varied schools.

Dates: Late Sep-Jul; prime time late Jun-early Jul. Cost: $1,512 includes tuition (3 graduate credits), private room, and 2 meals per day. Non-Pennsylvania resident cost is

$1,941. Contact: Dr. Donald R. Bortz, Chair, Professional and Secondary Education Department, East Stroudsburgh Univ., East Stroudsburgh, PA 18301-2999; (717) 424-3680 or (717) 424-3363, fax (717) 424-3777.

Friends World Program. A semester or year program in Europe at Friends World Center in London includes an intensive introduction into European culture and history. The program offers seminars, field study, travel, and independent work. The center serves as a base to explore all regions and cultures in the European continent. Field studies in literature, politics, arts, history, peace studies, theater, education, and community development are all available. Students may earn 12-18 credits per semester.

Dates: Fall: mid-Sep-mid-Dec; spring: mid-Jan-mid-May. Cost: $11,600 per semester in 1996/1997. Includes tuition, travel, room and board, fees and books. Contact: James Howard, Friends World Program, 239 Montauk Hwy., Southampton, NY 11968; (516) 287-8475; jhoward@sand.liunet.edu.

ICCE-International Council for Cultural Exchange. Enjoy an affordable all-inclusive top-quality academic learning vacation package—French and Italian on the Riviera, Spanish on the Costa del Sol, or German in Austria or Germany. All levels. Also painting workshop and summer opera festivals in Italy and Eastern Europe. Absorb the culture and atmosphere of your host country.

Dates: Summer and all year. Cost: $2,989 up, all inclusive (air, room, and board). Contact: Dr. Stanley I. Gochman, Program Coordinator, ICCE, 5 Bellport Ln., Bellport, NY 11713; (516) 286-5228.

International Relations/Business. Topics will cover the business, political, and historical aspect of the current transformation of Western Europe. The course will strive to achieve a balanced understanding of business practices, political realities, and social and cultural

sensitivities. Three to 6 hours of college credit is granted through the Univ. of Missouri at Kansas City in economics, business, or political science.

Dates: Summer 1997. Cost: Approx. $2,000 (does not include airfare). Contact: People to People International, Collegiate and Professional Studies Program, 501 E. Armour Blvd., Kansas City, MO 64109-2200; (816) 531-4701, fax (816) 561-7502; ptpi@cctr.umkc.edu, www.umkc.edu/cctr/dept/ptpi/homepage.html.

International Social Issues. Topics covered will bring you face to face with policy makers and professionals in the fields of substance abuse, healthcare policies, criminal justice, women's issues, and political policies. Three to 6 hours of college credit is granted through the Univ. of Missouri at Kansas City in sociology, education, or administration of justice.

Dates: Summer 1997. Cost: Approx. $2,000 (does not include airfare). Contact: People to People International, Collegiate and Professional Studies Program, 501 E. Armour Blvd., Kansas City, MO 64109-2200; (816) 531-4701, fax (816) 561-7502; ptpi@cctr.umkc.edu, www.umkc.edu/cctr/dept/ptpi/homepage.html.

Language and Culture Immersion. By choosing one of our schools in France (17 different locations), Italy (Firenze, Roma, Siena), or Spain (Barcelona, Granada, Malaga, Salmanca), you are choosing the guarantee of quality. We have the support of the European Commission (Program Lingua-Socrates) and offer intensive courses for all levels and all ages: general language and specialty courses and methodology classes for teachers. All types of accommodations are available: family-stay, apartment, hotel. Remarkable equipment in a great atmosphere. You will speak the language of the country all day long thanks to continuous contact with native people.

Dates: Year round, beginning every Monday. Cost: From $400 per week (including course, accommodations, meals and extracurriculum activities). Contact: Promotion-Marketing-International, Pascale Mora, Director, 919 N. Kenmore St., Arlington, VA 22201; (703) 528-5300 or (703) 534-0668, fax (703) 528-5316; pascalem@aol.com, www.studyoverseas.com..

Language Immersion Programs. Learn a language in the country where it's spoken. Intensive foreign language training offered in Spain, France, Italy, Germany, and Ecuador for students aged 16 and older. Classes are taught in up to 8 different proficiency levels and are suitable for beginners as well as people with advanced linguistic skills. All courses include accommodations and meals. Lots of extracurricular activities available. Students can earn college credit through Providence College.

Dates: Courses start every second Monday year round. Year programs commence in Sept., semester programs in January. Cost: Varies with program, approx. $950 per 2-week course. Contact: Kari Larsen, Admissions Coordinator, EF International Language Schools, 204 Lake St., Boston, MA 02135; (800) 992-1892, (617) 746-1700, fax (617) 746-1800; ils@ef.com.

France

A French Experience in Strasbourg. This 6-credit summer program in Strasbourg, France, places students in the Council of Europe. Students work in areas such as political research, human rights, European cultural and educational policies, public health policies, and youth policies. In addition, they take a course on the Council of Europe and European Parliament or a language course. Ground transportation and housing in private homes are arranged and covered by the program fee.

Dates: Jun 3-Jul 12, 1996. Cost: Undergraduate tuition for 6 credits: $2,766; program fee: $2,220. Contact: Daisy Fried, Syracuse Summer Abroad, Syracuse Univ., 119 Euclid Ave.,

Syracuse, NY 13244-4170; (315) 443-9419, fax (315) 443-4593; dsfried@suadmin.syr.edu.

American Univ. Center of Provence. In coordination with the Kalamazoo College Center for International Programs, the AUCP accepts motivated students of advanced French level for a semester/year of serious college-credit course work and intensive cultural involvement. French homestay, French university course, unique "French Practicum" core class with weekly community service requirement. Consistent focus upon integration into French culture.

Dates: Sep 9, 1996-May 4, 1997 (semester or year). Cost: Semester: $8,800; year: $16,200. Includes tuition, demi-pension housing, book fees, activities and excursion program. Contact: John Engle, President, American Univ. Center of Provence, c/o Center for International Programs, Kalamazoo College, Kalamazoo, MI 49006-3295; (616) 337-7133, fax (616) 337-7400.

AUP Summer Programs. The programs are uniquely designed for students seeking to acquire a real knowledge of Europe and an understanding of today's international environment. Two 5-week sessions are offered (12-16 credits) each summer. There is also an intensive 3-week French immersion program, a fine arts/art history program, and a high school program.

Dates: Jun 3-Jul 4, 1996, Jul 9 to Aug 9, 1996. Cost: $1,320 (FF7,260). Contact: The American Univ. of Paris Summer Programs Office, 31 ave. Bosquet, 75343 Paris Cedex 07, France; (011) 33-1-40-62-06-00, U.S. Office (212) 677-4870; summer@aup.fr.

Avignon Program. Courses are tailored to the needs of American students and are designed to take advantage of the Avignon setting. Language classes are available for nearly every level of French proficiency. Excursions are an important part of the program.

Dates: Sep-Dec (fall); Jan-Mar (winter);

Mar-Jun (spring). Cost: $5,300 per term. Includes tuition, housing, meals, international student identity card, texts, local transportation, excursions, and insurance. Financial aid accepted. Contact: Nancy Murray, Assoc. Director for Univ. Programs, American Heritage Association, 741 SW Lincoln St., Portland, OR 97201-3178; (800) 654-2051 or (503) 295-7730, fax (503) 295-5969; taa@amheritage.org.

BCA in Strasbourg or Nancy. Earn 14-16 credits per semester at either the Université de Nancy or the Université de Strasbourg, with a 4-week intensive language training and orientation plus field trips and extended study tour to Paris and/or Provence. Selective Honors Program offered in both universities. Internships available. Students accepted from all U.S. colleges and universities. Intermediate level college French required.

Dates: Sep 1-Jan 20 (fall), Jan 18-Jun 10 (spring), Sep 1-Jun 10 (year). Cost: $17,345 (1996-1997 academic year), $9,645 (1996-1997 semester). Includes international transportation, room and board, tuition, insurance, group travel in country. Contact: Beverly S. Eikenberry, Box 184, Manchester College, North Manchester, IN 46962; (219) 982-5238, fax (219) 982-7755; bca@manchester.edu, http://studyabroad.com/bca.

CCIS Semester in France. In Aix-en-Provence at the Institute for American Universities. Courses in French language (all levels), literature and civilization. Many courses taught in English: humanities, art history, history, geography, psychology, international relations, international business. Homestay with half-board. A College Consortium for International Studies program. All courses carry upper-division (junior-senior level) credit.

Dates: Mid-Sep-Dec/Jan-end May. Cost: Consult sponsor. Contact: Reinaldo Changsut, Study Abroad Adviser, Miami-Dade Community College, 11011 SW 104th St., Miami, FL 33176-3393; (305) 237-2535, fax (305) 237-2949.

Cooking with the Masters. A 1-week series of intensive hands-on culinary education in the kitchens of French master chefs, including professional visits to vineyards, markets, local artisans, etc.

Dates: Jan-Feb; Jun; Sep-Oct. Next series: Sep 20-29, 1996. Cost: Approx. $2,550 per person. Includes dbl. occupancy, airfare. Single supplement applies. Contact: Michel Bouit, President, MBI Inc., P.O. Box 1801, Chicago, IL 60690; (312) 663-5701, fax (312) 663-5702.

Cornell in Paris (EDUCO). Spend a semester or year studying at leading universities of Paris: Paris I (Pantheon-Sorbonne), Paris VII, and Institut d'Etudes Politiques (Sciences Po). Extensive orientation, language preparation, and special coursework at the Cornell-Duke (EDUCO) Center on rue Montparnasse. Housing arranged in private residences or apartments. Four semesters of university-level French required.

Dates: Mid-Sep-late Jan and late Jan-mid-Jun. Cost: $13,300 per semester (1996-1997). Includes tuition and fees, housing, some meals, orientation, language instruction, field trips, and excursions. Contact: Cornell Abroad, 474 Uris Hall, Ithaca, NY 14853-7601; (607) 255-6224, fax (607) 255-8700; CUAbroad@cornell.edu.

En Famille Overseas. En Famille Overseas arranges stays for students of all ages with French families to improve their knowledge of the French language. Visits can be arranged for any period from 1 week to 1 year. Stays combined with language courses for all standards are available also in Paris, Tours, or on the West coast of France.

Dates: Year-round. Cost: From FF225 per week, full board upwards. Contact: En Famille Overseas, 60b Maltravers St., Arundel, W. Sussex BN18 9BG, U.K.; (011) 44-903-883266, fax 903-883582.

English as a Second Language. The ESL Program at the American Univ. of Paris is designed for intermediate to advanced level students to prepare them for integration into the University's regular undergraduate program. Students take 1-3 courses, depending on level, stressing writing, reading and literary analysis, and aural/oral skills. Small classes and close contact with teachers insure rapid progress.

Dates: Fall application deadline May 1, spring application deadline Dec 1. Cost: Approx. $12,785 for 1 semester; $25,210 for 1 year. Contact: The American Univ. of Paris, U.S. Office, 80 E. 11th St., Suite 434, New York, NY 10003-6000; (212) 677-4870, fax (212) 475-5205; nyoffice@aup.fr, www.aup.fr.

French as a Second Language. Semester or year intensive program. Four-week intensive program in summer. Short sessions. All levels of French, open to everyone. DEFL, DALF "Credits." Optional day trips to Châteaux de la Loire, Anjou, Normandie, Bretagne.... Accommodations guaranteed with a French family. Great atmosphere. Attractive surroundings. Angers is located in the Loire Valley (90 minutes from Paris).

Dates: Jul 1-30, Sep 2-28, Oct 2-Feb 1, Feb 6-Jun 7. Cost: Tuition and fees: Jul FF3,650, Sep FF4,250, 1 semester FF7,600. Contact: Renée Cochin, CIDEF, Université Catholique de l'ouest, 3, place André Leroy, BP 808, 49008 Angers Cedex 01, France; (011) 33-41-88-30-15, fax 87-71-67.

French Immersion Semester in Tours. Intensive immersion program for French speakers of all levels. Language courses taught by native speakers. Designed for French and non-French majors with studies concentrating on language and culture. Housing with French families. Fifteen undergraduate credits.

Dates: Sep 28-Dec 16 (fall); Jan 4-May 9 (spring). Cost: Approx. $7,000. Includes room and board, airfare, local transportation, books, tuition, and miscellaneous expenses. Contact: SUNY Brockport, Office of International Education, 350 New Campus Dr., Brockport, NY 14420; (716) 395-2119, fax (716) 395-2606.

French in Normandy. For 20 years, we have been teaching French to American people (any age, any level) via immersion. We are located in one of the most picturesque parts of Normandy, near Deauville. Participants live in a 150-year-old renovated mansion in historic Lisieux or with a French family. Intensive or vacation programs. Programs for groups and individuals, 1 to 10 weeks long.

Dates: Spring: Mar 25-Jun 1, summer: Jun 17-Aug 31, fall: Sep 9-Nov 16. Cost: From $524 per week (tuition, room, board, and excursions). Contact: Dr. Alméras, Chairman, French American Study Center, 12, 14, Blvd. Carnot, B.P. 176, 14104 Lisieux Cedex, France (011) 33-31-31-22-01, fax (011) 33-31-31-22-21.

French Language and Culture. Intensive French program. Classes at all levels from beginning to advanced. Placement tests determine language ability. A wide choice of cultural courses plus Business French. Progress monitored with graded exercises, assignments, midterm and final examinations. Credits transferred. Cultural activities and excursions, board and lodging (several solutions), sessions for teachers of French.

Dates: Jul 2-27, Sep 2-28; Academic year: Sep-Dec, Feb-Jun. Cost: Tuition and fees: Jul 3,500FF, Sep 4,100FF, 1 semester 7,600FF Contact: Renée Cochin, Directrice, 3, place André Leroy, BP 808, 49008 Angers Cedex 01, France; (011) 33-41-88-30-15, fax 87-71-67.

French Language Sessions. An intensive immersion program, linking daily French classes in small groups with a large variety of activities, and with the daily life of French residents in a beautiful southern French village; an authentic and personalized (only 12 participants per session) experience of language and culture.

Dates: Feb 15-May 9 and Sep 14-Dec 7, 1997. Cost: $5,100 includes tuition, room and full board, all activities and excursions. Contact: La Sabranenque, Jacqueline C. Simon, 217

High Park Blvd., Buffalo, NY 14226; (716) 836-8698.

French Language Studies. Five-week intensive program in Paris, emphasizing language proficiency, culture and civilization, and contemporary French literature. Open to all students with at least 2 semesters of college-level French or equivalent. Field trips. Six credit hours: undergraduate, graduate.

Dates: Late Jun-early Aug. Cost: Approx. $2,800. Airfare not included. Contact: Office of International Education, SUNY New Paltz, HAB 33, New Paltz, NY 12561; (914) 257-3125, fax (914) 257-3129; international@ newpaltz.edu, www.newpaltz.edu/oie.

French Studies (Pau). Pau offers intensive language studies—up to 4 semesters of university language courses in 1 semester, 1 year in the 8-week summer program, in addition to art, political science, history, literature, second language teaching methods, etc. Program organized week-long field trips to Paris, homestay or student residence, and many activities at the French university.

Dates: Summer sessions: May 26-Jun 30, 1997 and Jun 24-Aug 1, 1997; fall semester: Sep 2-Dec 19, 1997; spring semester: Jan 3-May 1, 1998. Cost: One semester: $3,975; 2 semesters: $6,980; summer: $1,770 per session; $3,380 both sessions. Contact: University Studies Abroad Consortium (USAC), Univ. of Nevada, Reno #323, Reno, NV 89557-0093; (702) 784-6569, fax (702) 784-6010; usac@ admin.unr.edu, www.scs.unr.edu/~usac.

Homestays with Families. A nonprofit organization founded in 1978 arranging homestays and language course in southwest of France. Accommodations with carefully selected families of similar backgrounds and intersts with children of same age where appropriate.

Dates: Year round. Cost: Full board: FF1,490 per week; courses: FF800 for 10 courses. Contact: Aquitaine Service Linguistique (ASL), 15 rue Guénard, 33200 Bordeaux, France; (011) 33-5-56-08-33-23, fax 08-32-74.

Institute for American Universities. The Institute for American Universities, established in 1957 under the auspices of the Université d'Aix-Marseille, offers full-year, semester, and summer programs with centers in Aix-en-Provence and Avignon. IAU's general studies programs include the specialized areas of French language and literature, studio art and art history, political science, international relations, international business, archaeology and ancient history, and pre-law.

Dates: Summer 1996: Jun 10-Jul 19; 1996-97: Sep 2-Dec 21, and Jan 13-May 28. Cost: Summer 1996: $2,910. Includes tuition, books, site visits, insurance, room and half-board; 1996-1997: semester $8,740. Includes tuition, books, insurance, room and half-board, activity deposit, damage deposit. Contact: Institute for American Universities, U.S. Office, 711 Lake Ave., Wilmette, IL 60091-1723; Tel./fax (800) 221-2051; iauadm@univ-aix.fr.

Intensive French in the Loire Valley. All levels, all ages: intensive courses to develop students' accuracy in listening, speaking, reading, and writing French language, business French; courses of civilization, literature, history of France, music, arts, philosophy. Jul-Sep (1); Jul-Sep academic year (1 and 2). Credits, accommodations, cultural visits, activities. Univ. in town, 90 minutes from Paris.

Dates: Oct 2, 1996-Jun 6, 1997 FF14,800; Jul 1-30, 1997 FF3,650; Sep 2-28, 1997 FF4,250. Contact: Madame Renée Cochin, Directrice, CIDEF, 3, place André Leroy, BP 808, 49008 Angers Cedex 01, France; (011) 33-0141-88-30-15, fax (011) 33-0141-87-71-67.

Internships in Francophone Europe. IFE is an academic internship program—accredited at a number of schools—that places student interns in mid- to high-levels of French public life including government, politics, the press, social institutions, NGOs, etc. IFE is a selective admissions program for highly-motivated students, already proficient in French, who are interested in immersion in the working life of a French institution. The program includes, as well, course work in French history and politics, high-level language training, and the completion of a research project related to the internship.

Dates: May 1 deadline for fall semester (Aug 21-Dec 22); Nov 1 deadline for spring semester (Jan 22-May 24). Cost: $5,950 (tuition only); tuition plus housing $7,660. Contact: Bernard Riviere Platt, Director, Internships in Francophone Europe, Reid Hall, 4, rue de Chevreuse, 75006 Paris, France; (011) 33-1-43-21-78-07, fax (011) 33-1-42-79-94-13.

Le Cordon Bleu, L'Art Culinaire. Le Cordon Bleu in Paris offers the highest diploma in culinary education in just 9 months. Cuisine and pastry classes begin every 10 weeks. Summer abroad program—ICHP—in Paris and London. Chef catering program for professionals.

Dates: Jun 10-Aug 17, 1996. Every 10 weeks. Cost: From $6,000 to $30,000 for cuisine and pastry in 9 months. Contact: In U.S. call (800) 457-CHEF or fax (914) 426-0104. Le Cordon Bleu, 8, rue Leon Delhomme, 75015 Paris, France.

Paris Orientation Program. This 3-week program is a language and cultural orientation for students who will study at a French university during the regular academic year. Students earn 3 hours of upper-level French language and civilization credit from the Univ. of Kansas. This program provides a review of French grammar and practical vocabulary; discussions on how to take notes and write French exams; lectures on French civilization; and an introduction to the extensive cultural resources of Paris.

Dates: Approx. Sep 2-24. Cost: Approx. $1,675. Includes all educational and administrative costs, lodging and most meals, group entries to cultural events and activities, ground transportation in France. Contact:

Laura Leonard, Office of Study Abroad, 203-T Lippincott, The Univ. of Kansas, Lawrence, KS 66045.

Penn-in-Bordeaux. For students interested in anthropology, archaeology, and the origins of humankind. This program is located near Lascaux and Cro-Magnon, areas where anthropologists have unearthed much of our knowledge about the beginnings of modern humankind. It will center on the issue of what makes us human and how this quality evolved. Lectures will be augmented with the examination of artifacts and fossils as well as visits to important sites.

Dates: Jun 17-Jul 4. Cost: Tuition $1,420; housing and excursions $450. Contact: Penn Summer Abroad, College of General Studies, Univ. of Pennsylvania, 3440 Market St., Suite 100, Philadelphia, PA 19104-3335; (215) 898-5738, fax (215) 573-2053.

Penn-in-Compiegne. For students with some proficiency in French who are interested in international relations, economics, or business. The program, affiliated with The Universite de Technologie de Compiegne, also offers a 2-week internship in a French enterprise. Students live with local families.

Dates: May 28-Jul 4; with internship: May 28-Jul 20. Cost: Tuition $2,840; room and board, and activities $900 (study only) or $1,200 (full program). Contact: Penn Summer Abroad, College of General Studies, Univ. of Pennsylvania, 3440 Market St., Suite 100, Philadelphia, PA 19104-3335; (215) 898-5738, fax (215) 573-2053.

Penn-in-Tours. For students interested in French language, literature, art, and civilization. Penn-in-Tours also offers various cultural opportunities and excursions in the beautiful Loire Valley. Students live with local families.

Dates: May 27-Jul 10. Cost: Tuition $2,840; family lodging $1,350; excursion and activity fee $250. Contact: Penn Summer Abroad, College of General Studies, Univ. of Pennsylvania, 3440 Market St., Suite 100, Philadelphia, PA 19104-3335; (215) 898-5738, fax (215) 573-2053.

Semester in Avignon. French language and literature at the Centre d'Etudes Françaises. Complementary courses in international business, art history, history and international relations. All courses taught in French. Homestay with half-board. Full college credit (upper division). A College Consortium for International Studies program.

Dates: Mid-Sep-Dec/Jan-end May. Cost: Consult sponsor. Contact: Reinaldo Changsut, Study Abroad Adviser, Miami-Dade Community College, 11011 SW 104th St., Miami, FL 33176-3393; (305) 237-2535, fax (305) 237-2949.

Semester in Paris. Study French language, social sciences, and European studies at Reid Hall. Language courses taught by native speakers; social science courses taught by Brockport faculty. Extensive field trips and opportunity for travel. Housing in apartments. Resident director on site. Fifteen undergraduate credits.

Dates: Sep 5-Dec 20 (fall); Jan 12-May 9 (spring). Cost: Approx. $8,500. Includes room and board, airfare, local transportation, books, tuition, and miscellaneous expenses. Contact: SUNY Brockport, Office of International Education, 350 New Campus Dr., Brockport, NY 14420; (716) 395-2119, fax (716) 395-2606.

Spéos Paris Photographic Institute. Spéos is a meeting place for participants to develop all aspects of photography from fine art to computer imaging. Most of the professors work in the artistic, photojournalistic, or advertising worlds in Paris, thereby involving participants in professional activity. Spéos has formal arrangements with the Rhode Island School of Design, Rochester Institute of Technology, the Univ. of Hartford, and the School of the Art Institute of Chicago.

Dates: Sep 30, 1996-Jan 24, 1997; Jan 27-May 23, 1997. Cost: $6,500 per semester. Contact:

Spéos Admissions, Spéos Paris Photographic Institute, 8 rue Jules Valles, 75011 Paris, France; (011) 33-1-40-09-18-58, fax (011) 33-1-40-09-84-97; www.rever.fr/speos/.

Spring Semester in Paris. The Paris Program is designed to improve proficiency in French and to provide coursework in a variety of subjects related to France, some at the Cours de Civilisation française at the Université de Paris IV (Sorbonne). The courses provide exposure to French social and cultural issues, while the overall program is designed to offer a broad experience of contemporary life in France.

Dates: Mid-Jan-mid-May. Cost: $6,175 (WI residents). Includes tuition, room and basic board, excursions. Contact: Lawrence Roscioli, Director, L&S Off-Campus Programs, Univ. of Wisconsin at Milwaukee, P.O. Box 413, Milwaukee, WI 53201; (414) 229-5879, fax (414) 229-6827; overseas@csd.uwm.edu.

SRU/College International de Cannes. Students can spend a semester or year in Cannes earning 15 credits per semester (9 in language and 6 from selected courses taught in English).

Dates: Sep 29-Dec 21, 1996; Mar 2-Jun 1, 1997. Cost: $5,510. Includes tuition, meals, and room. Contact: Stan Kendziorski, Director of International Studies, Slippery Rock Univ., Slippery Rock, PA 16057; (412) 738-2603, fax (412) 738-2959; sjk@sruvm.sru.edu.

Studio Art in Provence. At the Marchutz School of Drawing and Painting of the Institute for American Universities. Full college credit. Courses taught in English. Homestay with half board. Atelier in Le Tholonet, Aix-en-Provence. Courses in French language available. A College Consortium for International Studies program.

Dates: Mid-Sep-Dec/Jan-end May. Cost: Consult sponsor. Contact: Reinaldo Changsut, Study Abroad Adviser, Miami-Dade Community College, 11011 SW 104th St., Miami, FL 33176-3393; (305) 237-2535, fax (305) 237-2949.

Study in Besancon. Fall, spring, or academic year programs in French language, culture, and civilization at the Univ. of Franche-Comte Center for Applied Linguistics, one of the top language schools of Europe. Dormitory housing, native resident director, field trips, on-site orientation, 12-18 undergraduate credits per semester. Requires a minimum of 3 semesters college-level French or the equivalent.

Dates: Fall: early Oct-late Jan; spring: late Jan-late May. Cost: Approx. $5,100 fall, $5,300 spring. Includes tuition, fees, orientation, room and board, and insurance. (Non-New York state residents add $2,100 per semester.) Contact: Office of International Education, SUNY New Paltz, HAB 33, New Paltz, NY 12561; (914) 257-3125, fax (914) 257-3129; international@newpaltz.edu, www.newpaltz.edu/oie.

Study Programs in France. Four majors: fine arts, fashion, interior design, and language.

Dates: Throughout year. Cost: One month $2,700 (includes lodging), academic year $9,500 (tuition only). Contact: Richard Roy, Paris American Academy, 9, rue des Ursulines, 75005 Paris, France; (011) 44-41-99-20, fax 41-99-29.

Summer in France. Five weeks in Aix-en-Provence and 1 week in Paris. French homestay, breakfast and evening meal on class days in Aix, field trips. In Paris, hotel with breakfast, half-day city tour, Louvre and Orsay museum visits, Metropass. Six-9 credits. A College Consortium for International Studies program.

Dates: Mid-Jun-end Jul. Cost: $3,095. Contact: Reinaldo Changsut, Study Abroad Adviser, Miami-Dade Community College, 11011 SW 104th St., Miami, FL 33176-3393; (305) 237-2535, fax (305) 237-2949.

Sweet Briar Junior Year in France. September pre-session in Tours, academic year in Paris. Enrollment in regular university courses at Sorbonne Nouvelle, Paris-Sorbonne or Université Denis Diderot, and public and private institutions of higher learning such as Institut d'Etudes Politiques, Institut Catholique de Paris, art studios. Live with selected families, foyers or pensions de famille. Now in its 49th year.

Dates: Sep-May. Cost: $20,150 (1995-1996). Includes airfare, tuition, housing, most meals, medical and liability insurance, excursions, etc. Contact: Prof. Emile A. Langlois, Director, Junior Year in France, Sweet Briar College, Sweet Briar, VA 24595; (804) 381-6109, fax (804) 381-6283; jyf@sbc.edu.

Tapestry (Gobelins Techniques). Our training is highly personalized. Limited to 4 students: initiation course, advanced course, all levels: choice of a pattern. Preparing the warp, connecting the warp. Heddles sampling, tracing, interpretation of the tapestry with study of basic classical and modern techniques. Working out personal answers. We are located in a 14th-century Cevenuf farmhouse.

Dates: Jun 29-Jul 12, Jul 13-26 (30 hours teaching per week). Cost: One course: FF9,400; 2 courses FF17,200 (accommodations, full board, course, supplies). Contact: Mesnage, Mas de Casty, 30500 Allegre, France; (011) 33-66-29-82-33.

The American Univ. of Paris. Within the context of a changing Europe, the University continues to offer a full range of courses for 4-year students and semester or 1-year visitors. Academic offerings, especially in art history, European studies, and international affairs, are enriched by integrating classwork with study trips that capitalize on the university's central location.

Dates: Fall application deadline May 1, spring application deadline Dec 1. Cost: Estimated total costs: $12,785 for 1 semester; $25,210 for 1 year. Contact: The American Univ. of Paris, U.S. Office, 80 E. 11th St., Suite 434, New York, NY 10003-6000; (212) 677-4870, fax (212) 475-5205; nyoffice@aup.fr, www.aup.fr.

The American Univ. of Paris Summer Programs. Two summer sessions, a High School College Preview program and French Immersion Programs. Summer in Paris offers not only cultural excursions to historic regions of Europe, but an academic challenge one can only find at the oldest American Univ. in Europe. AUP's 80 courses are offered for credit or noncredit.

Dates: Session I: Jun 3-Jul 4, 1996; Session II: Jul 9-Aug 9, 1996. Contact: The American Univ. of Paris, U.S. Office, 80 E. 11th St., Suite 434, New York, NY 10003-6000; (212) 677-4870, fax (212) 475-5205.

UNC-Chapel Hill Paris Summer Program. Earn 6 credit hours in one of Europe's most exciting and beautiful cities. Dynamic resident director teaches course on History of Paris with many field trips, and students attend language classes at the Sorbonne. Two previous semesters of French language study minimum. The June schedule leaves students with plenty of summer.

Dates: May 30-Jun 30 (approx.). Cost: Approx. $2,600. Includes fees, room and board, excursions. Contact: Study Abroad Office, Dept. T, CB #3130, 12 Caldwell Hall, Univ. of North Carolina, Chapel Hill, NC 27599-3130; (919) 962-7001, fax (919) 962-2262; abroad@unc.edu.

Germany

BCA Program in Marburg. Earn 14-16 credits per semester at Phillipps-Universität in Marburg, with a 4-week intensive language training and orientation, field trips, and an extended study tour to Eastern Germany or Prague. Internships available. Students accepted from all U.S. colleges and universities. Intermediate level college German required.

Dates: Sep 10-Feb 15 (fall); Feb 25-Jul 15 (spring); Sep 10-Jul 15 (year). Cost: $17,345 (1996-1997 academic year), $9,645 (1996-1997 semester). Includes international transportation, room and board, tuition, insurance, group travel in country. Contact: Beverly S. Eikenberry, Box 184, Manchester College, North Manchester, IN 46962; (219) 982-5238, fax (219) 982-7755; bca@manchester.edu, http://studyabroad.com/bca.

Business Studies. Four years of study in courses covering all aspects of business management. Practical placements in industry, studies abroad, opportunities for specialization (e.g., in marketing).

Dates: Oct 1-Feb 14, Mar 15-Jul 31. Contact: Fachhochschule Rosenheim, Business Studies Faculty, Marienberger Strasse 26, D-83024 Rosenheim; Fax (011) 49-8031-890-445, or (011) 49-8035-1246.

Cologne Program. Subject areas include business, German language, art, business, economics, history, literature, political science. All courses, other than German language, are conducted in English. Fall term is 12-week business and humanities program, consisting of 2-week intensive German language study, followed by 10 weeks of business, humanities, and German language. No German language experience required for admission. Spring term is 11-week liberal arts curriculum, 2 terms or 1 semester of German language required.

Dates: Sep-Dec (fall); Apr-Jun (spring). Cost: Approx. $5,200 per term. Includes tuition, housing, meals, excursions, texts, international student identity card, local transportation, insurance. Financial aid accepted. Contact: Gail Lavin, Assoc. Director, Univ. Programs, American Heritage Association, 741 SW Lincoln St., Portland, OR 97201-3178; (800) 654-2051, fax (503) 295-5969; 96trab@amheritage.org.

Europa-Kolleg Kassel. Study German language, culture, and life in the heart of united Germany. Participants live with German families and attend international language classes in the morning and cultural or social activities in the afternoon. Kassel is the city where the brothers Grimm collected their fairy tales. It is a medium-sized city with a wide range of activities and in an area where people (host families) speak standard German. Kassel's central location makes travel easy.

Dates: Year round operation, summer courses Jun 9, Jun 30, Jul 28, Aug 25. Cost: DM665 per week (approx. $450). Includes tuition, materials, room, full board, excursions, activities. Contact: Prof. K.E. Kuhn-Osius, 238 W. 106th St., Apt. 4A, New York, NY 10025; Tel./fax (212) 865-7332; ekuhnos@shiva.hunter.cuny.edu.

German Language Courses in Munich. Group tuition available at all levels. Choose 20, 26, or 30 lessons a week or preparation for officially recognized exams. One-to-one tuition with 10, 20, 30, 40, or 50 lessons a week.

Dates: Every Monday, year round. Cost: Twenty lessons a week (group): DM720 (tuition only) (2 weeks); half board, single room DM367 per week. Contact: Inlingua School, Sendlinger-Tor-P 6, D-80336 Muenchen, Germany; (011) 49-89-2311530, fax 2609920.

German Language Studies. Seven weeks of intensive instruction in intermediate and advanced German and contemporary German civilization. Three weeks of classes in and family stay in Stade, 3 weeks of classes in Hamburg, and a 1-week field trip to Berlin, as well as other excursions. Nine undergraduate credit hours.

Dates: Jun-early Aug. Cost: Approx. $3,300. Airfare not included. Contact: Office of International Education, SUNY New Paltz, HAB 33, New Paltz, NY 12561; (914) 257-3125, fax (914) 257-3129; international@newpaltz.edu, www.newpaltz.edu/oie.

German Studies. Intensive language study—up to 2 years of university language requirements in 1 semester. Additional courses in history, political science, culture, literature, etc. Program-organized field trips and housing. Beautiful city only 30 minutes from Hamburg.

Dates: Summer: May 23-Jun 27, 1997 and Jun 22-Jul 27, 1997; fall semester: Aug 26-Dec 16, 1997; spring semester: Jan 6-May 19, 1998. Cost: One semester: $3,575; fall and spring: $5,575; summer: $1,385 per session; $2,385 both sessions. Contact: University Studies Abroad Consortium (USAC), Univ. of Nevada, Reno #323, Reno, NV 89557-0093; (702) 784-6569, fax (702) 784-6010; usac@admin.unr.edu, www.scs.unr.edu/~usac.

International Summer Univ. Five-week intensive courses (20 hours per week, different levels, no beginners) of German language, literature, and socio-cultural studies for students and other interested persons. Qualified university teachers. Accommodations in student dormitories or guest families. Fees include: cultural and social activities, public transportation and 5 day-trips (admission fees and meals) to Cologne, Weimar, etc.

Dates: Jul 22-Aug 25, 1996. Cost: $1,070 (course fees) plus $495 (dormitories, lunch included) or $990 (guest family/full board). Contact: Universität Gesamthochschule Kassel, Sprachenzentrum, Mönchebergstrasse 7, D-34109 Kassel, Germany; (011) 49-561-804-2020, fax (011) 49-561-804-3815; sz@hrz.uni-kassel.de.

Junior Year in Heidelberg Univ. Sponsored by Heidelberg College since 1958, the program provides an immersion experience in German language and culture. Students are enrolled at Germany's oldest university, the Univ. of Heidelberg. Living with German students, participating in various community activities, and meeting regularly with a language exchange partner, students become quickly integrated into German student life.

Dates: Late Aug-mid-Jul (full year); late Aug-late Dec (fall); late Feb-mid-Jul (spring). Cost: General fee for 1996-97: Full year $12,290; fall $5,880; spring $6,020. Contact: Dr. Raymond Wise, Registrar, Heidelberg College, Tiffin, OH 44883; (419) 448-2256, fax (419) 448-2124; rwise@prime.heidelberg.edu.

Kalamazoo in Erlangen. This university-integrated program begins with a 5-6-week intensive German course. Participants then enroll in regular courses at the Univ. of Erlangen-Nuernberg. All participants complete an independent cultural research project or internship of personal interest under the guidance of a local mentor. Minimum of 2 years of college German required.

Dates: Mid-Sep-late Jul (academic year); mid-Sep-late Feb (fall); Apr-late-Jul (spring). Cost: (1995-96) Academic year: $19,113; one semester $11,788 includes roundtrip international transportation, tuition and fees, room and board, and some excursions. Contact: Dr. Michael Vande Berg, Director of the Center for International Programs, Kalamazoo College, 1200 Academy, Kalamazoo, MI 49006; (616) 337-7133, fax (616) 337-7400; cip@kzoo.edu.

Penn-in-Freiburg. For students interested in coursework in intensive intermediate German. This program offers German language students an opportunity to gain proficiency skills and cultural insight while studying in the center of Renaissance Germany.

Dates: Jul 15-Aug 21. Cost: Tuition $2,840; housing and activities $600. Contact: Penn Summer Abroad, College of General Studies, Univ. of Pennsylvania, 3440 Market St., Suite 100, Philadelphia, PA 19104-3335; (215) 898-5738, fax (215) 573-2053.

Schiller International Univ. at Heidelberg. Schiller International Univ. is an American-style university with all courses except language classes taught in English. Schiller's particular strengths are in international business and international relations but it offers courses in the humanities and social sciences as well. Students may take German at Schiller or intensive German at the Collegium Palatinum, a specialized language division. One semester college German or equivalent is required.

Dates: Fall: end-Aug-Dec 17; spring: mid-Jan-mid-May. Cost: Fall 1996 estimate $6,279 (somewhat higher for homestays); spring 1997: $6,379 (somewhat higher for homestays). Estimates include full-day orientation before departure, application fee, room and food allowance in residence hall, mandatory German insurance, airfare, books and supplies, health and accident insurance, German Residence Permit, administrative fees. SUNY tuition not included. Contact: Dr. John Ogden, Director, Office of International Programs, Box 2000, SUNY at Cortland, Cortland, NY 13045; (607) 753-2209, fax (607) 753-5989; tonerp@snycorva.cortland.edu.

Semester in Regensburg. This program combines German language courses at the beginning and intermediate levels with a range of courses in humanities, German culture, finance, and international business taught in English. Language courses are taught by Univ. of Regensburg faculty and others by Murray State Univ. faculty. No prior knowledge of German is required.

Dates: Aug 27-Dec 10, 1997. Cost: $2,895 program fee, MSU tuition ($1,030 for KY residents, $2,770 others), airfare. Contact: Dr. Fred Miller, Regensburg Program Director, Murray State Univ., P.O. Box 9, Murray, KY 42071; (502) 762-6206, fax (502) 762-3740; flmiller@msumusikmursuky.edu, or Ms. Linda Bartnik, Center for International Programs, P.O. Box 9, Murray State Univ., Murray, KY 42071; (502) 752-4152, fax (502) 762-3237; lbartnik@msumusik.mursuky.edu, www.mursuky.edu/qacd/cip/sirprog.htm

UNC-Chapel Hill Berlin Semester. Designed for intermediate level language and culture study, this program includes intensive language as well as German studies courses taught in English, and independent study option. Students live with families; program affiliation with Freie Universität Berlin provides student privileges. Advanced students should inquire about our year-long programs in Germany and Austria.

Dates: Sep-Dec. Cost: $6,400 includes tuition, fees, excursions, room. Contact: Study

Abroad Office, Dept. T, CB # 3130, 12 Caldwell Hall, Univ. of North Carolina, Chapel Hill, NC 27599-3130; (919) 962-7001, fax (919) 962-2262; abroad@unc.edu.

Univ. of Maryland Univ. College at Schwäbisch Gmünd. UMUC at Schwäbisch Gmünd is a 4-year residential campus located 33 km from Stuttgart in scenic southern Germany. Through classes taught in English, individualized attention, and an international student body, UMUC provides an ideal environment for academic achievement and cultural enrichment. Applications are invited from potential freshman, transfer, and semester or academic year abroad students.

Dates: Semesters run from Aug-Dec and Jan-May. Cost: Approx. $13,000 per year for tuition, approx. $5,500 for double room with full board. For Maryland residents, tuition is $5,700 per year for tuition. Contact: Allison Roach, International Admissions Counselor, UMUC-International Programs, University Blvd. at Adelphi Rd., College Park, MD 20742-1644; (301) 985-7442, fax (301) 985-7959; aroach@nova.umc.edu or Admissions Office, UMUC, Universitätspark, 73525 Schwäbisch Gmünd, Germany; (011) 49-7171-18070, fax (011) 49-7171-180732; tshea@admin.sg. umuc.edu.

Wayne State Univ.'s Junior Year. The full university curriculum in arts and sciences at the Univ. of Munich or Freiburg will be open to you, plus German studies courses through the program itself. All instruction is in German, taught by German faculty. A 6-week orientation period of intensive language preparation precedes the beginning of university classes. Juniors, seniors, and graduate students with 2 years of college German and an overall "B" average are eligible.

Dates: Sep 9-Jul 31. Includes a 2-month semester break. Cost: $6,400 for tuition and fees. Scholarships and financial aid available. Contact: Junior Year in Germany, Wayne State Univ., Detroit, MI 48202; (313) 577-4605, fax (313) 577-3266; junyear@cms.cc.wayne.edu.

Ghana

Semester/Year in Ghana. Exchange program at the Univ. of Ghana. Choose from courses regularly offered by the university. All instruction in English. Housing is in the university residence halls. Fifteen undergraduate credits per semester.

Dates: Sep 27-Dec 20 (fall); Feb 12-Jun 14 (spring). Cost: Semester: $6,000; year: $9,000. Includes tuition, room and board, airfare, local transportation, books, tuition, and miscellaneous expenses. Contact: SUNY Brockport, Office of International Education, 350 New Campus Dr., Brockport, NY 14420; (716) 395-2119, fax (716) 395-2606.

Greece

An Archaeological Tour of Ancient Greece. Obtain first-hand knowledge of the art and architecture of ancient Greece through on-site archaeological visits and museum tours. This is the only course of its kind in which students are invited to have one of their lectures inside the Parthenon. Other highlights include visits to Sparta, Corinth, Mycenae, the Olympia Grounds, Delphi, Thermopylae, and Mystra, the world's best-preserved medieval city. The trip ends with 4 days on the island of Mykonos and a visit to the "birthplace" of Apollo.

Dates: Jun 12-Jul 1. Cost: $2,500 (3 credits) includes roundtrip airfare, double occupancy rooms, breakfast daily, bus, ship, and airport transfers. Contact: Dora Riomayor, Director of International Studies, School of Visual Arts, 209 E. 23rd St., New York, NY 10010-3994; (212) 592-2543, fax (212) 592-2545.

Ancient and Modern Greece. Nine days unique experience: Athens (2 nights) and the Greek islands by private 115-foot air-conditioned yacht for 7 nights: Tinos-Delos-Naxos-Ios-Santorini (the volcano isle)-Paros-Mykonos. Exploration trips to sites and villages. Greek dancing. Large sun deck, swimming, outside cabins with shower. Air from U.S. from $600 roundtrip.

Dates: Every Wednesday Apr-Oct 1996. Cost: $995 per person in 3/4 berth cabins, $1,195 from Athens per person in 2-bedded cabins, breakfast daily, 7 lunches or dinners onboard plus 2 overnights Athens, transfers, and port taxes. Contact: Thalia Cocconi, Sales Manager, Educational Tours and Cruises, 14(R) Wyman St., Medford, MA 02155; (800) 275-4109, fax (617) 396-3096.

BCA Program in Athens. Earn 15-16 credits per semester at the Univ. of La Verne Athens, with a 1-week orientation and survival Greek training. Field trips and an extended study tour to Cairo or Istanbul. All classes taught in English by international faculty. No foreign language prerequisite. Graduate courses in business and education. Students from all U.S. colleges and universities accepted.

Dates: Aug 28-Dec 15 (fall), Mar 8-Jun 15 (spring), Aug 28-Jun 15 (year). Cost: $17,345 (1996-1997 academic year), $9,645 (1996-1997 semester). Includes international transportation, room and board, tuition, insurance, group travel in country, and 1 travel tour. Contact: Beverly S. Eikenberry, Box 184, Manchester College, North Manchester, IN 46962; (219) 982-5238, fax (219) 982-7755; bca@manchester.edu, http://studyabroad.com/bca.

Beaver College Study in Greece. An individualized opportunity to learn about Greece, its people and its heritage. Courses available in classical, byzantine, and modern Greek studies, with required study of modern Greek language (no prior knowledge of Greek required). On-site resident director and expert specialist faculty. Field trips. Full range of program services. Need-based scholarships available.

Dates: Fall, Spring, Full year and summer.

Cost: Summer (1996): $3,300; Full year: (1996-97) $15,500; fall or spring semester: $8,000. Contact: Audrianna Jones, Beaver College CEA, 450 S. Easton Rd., Glenside, PA 19038-3295; (888) BEAVER-9, fax (215) 572-2174; cea@beaver.edu, www.beaver.edu.cea.

Classic Theatre Study Abroad. Students, teachers, and professionals spend 3 weeks on an idyllic Greek island with classes mornings and rehearsal evenings. The fourth week they go on tour, presenting an ancient drama in classic and modern amphitheaters and visiting major classic sites.

Dates: Mid-Jun-mid-Jul. Cost: $3,500 participant or $4,500 with 6 hours credit. Contact: Dr. Arthur J. Beer, Univ. of Detroit Mercy, P.O. Box 19900, Detroit, MI 48219-0900.

College Year in Athens. One- or 2-semester programs during the academic year. The 2-track curriculum offers a focus on either Ancient Greek Civilization or Mediterranean Studies and is supplemented by at least 10 days each semester of study and travel within Greece. Instruction is in English. Credit is granted by prearrangement with the home institution.

Dates: Sep 1-Dec 19, 1997; Jan 12-May 16, 1998. Cost: Semester fee of $9.900 includes tuition, housing, partial board, study, travel, most course materials, $100 refundable damage deposit. Contact: College Year in Athens, North American Office, Dept. T, P.O. Box 390890, Cambridge, MA 02139-0010; (617) 494-1008, fax (617) 494-1662; CYAthens@aol.com.

Ithaka Cultural Study Program in Crete. The Ithaka Semester combines intensive study of ancient and modern Greek culture with cultural immersion on Crete. Good writing, wide reading emphasized. Required local internships, frequent field trips. Warm, dynamic learning community with 5 tutors to 15 students in traditional neighborhood. Challenging program is superb preparation for college;

restores vigor, excitement to learning for college students.

Dates: Spring semester: Feb 10-May 15, 1997; fall semester: Sep 10-Dec 15. Cost: $10,500. Includes tuition, room, board, field trips, and overnight excursions. Partial financial assistance available. Contact: Alice Brown, U.S. Director, Ithaka Cultural Study Program in Greece, 1692 Massachusetts Ave., Cambridge, MA 02138; (617) 868-4547, fax (617) 661-1904.

Mythology in Greece. Study tour of mythological Greece. Lectures will cover Mycenaean, Classical, and Byzantine sites including visits to Athens, Peloponnesus, Crete, and several archaeological museums. Three credits; graduate, undergraduate, non-credit.

Dates: Jun 25-Jul 15. Cost: Approx. $3,000. Includes airfare, local transportation, room and board. Contact: SUNY Brockport, Office of International Education, 350 New Campus Dr., Brockport, NY 14420; (716) 395-2119, fax (716) 395-2606.

Summer 1997. Three- and 6-week programs on Ancient Greek Civilization, Modern Greek Language (4 levels).

Dates: Jun 11-Aug 10. Cost: $3,400 (Jun 11-Jul 19, including study-travel); $1,650 (Jun 30-Jul 20 on island of Paros); $1,500 (Jul 22-Aug 10 in Athens). Covers tuition, housing, and course materials. Contact: College Year in Athens, North American Office, Dept. T, P.O. Box 390890, Cambridge, MA 02139-0010; (617) 547-6141, fax (617) 547-6413; CYAthens@aol.com.

The Aegean School of Classical Studies and Philosophy. This course focuses on the ancient Greek idea of the structure of society and its culture as the highest form of art (techne) starting with the art and mythology of the pre-Classical periods through the Classical and Hellenistic periods to Byzantine times. Members explore the ways in which varying philosophies, mythology, literature, drama, and art and architecture contributed to ancient Greek and Byzantine life. Most major archaeological sites and museums throughout Greece are visited and studied; lessons and seminars in modern Greek language and culture are presented. The program is rigorous and each applicant should be in good physical condition.

Dates: Jun 24-Jul 27, 1996. Cost: $1,900. Tuition includes all intra-Greece travel, taxes, and transfer fees; room and board averages $40 per day. Airfare fluctuates with prevailing seasonal rates. Contact: Professor Philip Drew, Aegean School of Classical Studies and Philosophy, P.O. Box 3602, Arlington, VA 22203.

Tour of Ancient Greece. This trip will begin in the ancient city of Athens, continue on to visit Corinth, Mycenae, Nauplia, Epidaurus, Sparta, Mystra, the Olympic grounds, the Delphi grounds and Museum Patras, and the islands of Mykonos and Delos. Lectures on the remarkable history of Greece, its art, and its architecture, will be held throughout the tour and at the Archaeological Museum in Athens.

Dates: Jun 8-30, 1997. Cost: Three credits - $2,500. Includes roundtrip airfare, double occupancy rooms, breakfast daily, bus, ship and airport transfers. Contact: Joel Garrick, School of Visual Arts, 209 E. 23rd St., New York, NY 10010; (212) 592-2011.

Guatemala

Centro de Estudios de Español Pop Wuj. This school is a teacher-owned cooperative that donates its profits to community projects that combat the problems of poverty in Guatemala. Students receive 5 hours of one-on-one instruction, live with a Guatemalan family, and take part in daily extracurricular activities such as community service work projects, conferences, films, and day-trips to surrounding areas.

Cost: $125 per week plus $20 registration fee; includes 5 days of classes and 7 days of homestay with a Guatemalan family. Contact:

In U.S.: Centro Pop Wuj, P.O. Box 158, Sandstone, WV 25985-0158; (304) 466-2685; popwuj@aol.com. In Guatemala: Pop Wuj, A.P. 68, Quetzaltenango, Guatemala; Tel./fax (in Guatemala): (011) 502-9-61-82-86.

Eco-Escuela de Español. The Eco-Escuela de Español offers a unique educational experience by combining intensive Spanish language instruction with volunteer opportunities in conservation and community development projects. Students are immersed in the language, culture, and ecology of the Petén, Guatemala—an area renowned for its tropical forests and ancient Maya ruins. Ecological activities integrate classroom with field-based experiences.

Dates: Every Monday year round. Cost: Classes $60 per week (based on 20 hours of individual instruction per week, Monday-Friday). Room and board with local families $50 per week. Registration fee $10. Contact: Eco-Escuela, Conservation International, 1015 18th St. NW, Suite 1000, Washington, DC 20036; (202) 973-2264, fax (202) 887-5188; m.sister@conservation.org.

Kie-Balam Spanish Language School. The school features one-on-one instruction with university-degreed teachers. Special rate programs for high school teachers and students; programs for bilingual teachers, social workers, medical personnel. Course work transfers to degree programs. School starts rural lending libraries, help at a battered women's shelter, and works with a special education school.

Dates: Year round, classes start Mondays. Cost: Application fee: $50; tuition: $100 per week, includes room and board. Contact: Martha Weese, 1007 Duncan Ave., Elgin, IL 60120; (708) 888-2514 (U.S.), (011) 502-9-611636 (Guatemala from U.S.); moebius@super-highway.net.

La Hermandad Educativa. The nonprofit network of language schools (Proyecto Lingüístico Quezalteco de Español, Proyecto Lingüístico de Español "Educación para Todos," and Proyecto Lingüístico de Español Todos Santos/Mam) is a sisterhood of 3 nonprofit educational collectives in Quetzaltenango and Todos Santos, Guatemala. All offer 5 hours per day, one-on-one instruction with experienced Spanish teachers and room and board with local families. Daily activities include conferences, field trips, films, and discussions about the culture, history, and political and social reality of Guatemala.

Dates: Classes begin every Monday. Cost: $120 per week Sep-May and $150 per week Jun, Jul, and Aug, $100 per week year round in Todos Santos. Contact: La Hermandad Educativa, 915 Cole St., #363, San Francisco, CA 94117; (800) 963-9889.

Honduras

Centro Internacional de Idiomas. Learn Spanish on the Caribbean in historic Trujillo, Honduras, Central America. Students learn Spanish in a relaxed, tropical atmosphere with a one-on-one student to teacher ratio. Our program emphasizes intensive conversation, survival skills, grammar, and vocabulary. All teachers are university graduates in Spanish and linguistics; most of them are bilingual.

Dates: Year round. Cost: $175 for 4-hour classes, 5 days per week, 7 days homestay. Contact: Belinda Linton, Director, Centro Internacional de Idiomas, TGU 00068, P.O. Box 025387, Miami, FL 33102-5387; Tel./fax (011) 504-44-4777.

Hong Kong

Syracuse Univ. Focus on international business and economy in Asia. Courses on business, economics, political science, history, Chinese language, sociology. Internships in Hong Kong, field trips to Beijing, Shanghai, elsewhere. Based at Univ. of Hong Kong. Housing in residence halls, apartments.

Dates: Aug-Dec 1996 and Jan-May 1997. Cost: $7,995 tuition (1995-96); $5,985 includes housing, excursions, roundtrip travel. Contact: James Buschman, Associate Director, Syracuse Univ., 119 Euclid Ave., Syracuse, NY 13244-4170; (800) 235-3472, fax (315) 443-4593; dipa@suadmin.syr.edu.

Hungary

Beloit College Hungary Exchange Program. Focusing on aspects of Hungarian culture, students study at Eotvos Collegium in Budapest. Conducted in English, courses equal 16 semester hours of credit and include: Hungarian language, Hungarian culture, and elective courses in the social sciences, economics, and communications. Students live in the Collegium's residence hall with Hungarian students.

Dates: Approx. Feb 1-May 30. Cost: Tuition $8,672, room and board $1,923. Contact: Dr. Terance W. Bigalke, Director, World Affairs Center, Beloit College, 700 College St., Beloit, WI 53511; (608) 363-2269, fax (608) 363-2689; bigalket@beloit.edu.

Graduate Degree Program. The 2-year graduate program is offered in English in 4 specializations: International Economics, International Business, Social and Political Studies, and Business Administration. Students completing the program are awarded an MS degree by the BUES. The credits and degrees obtained are internationally recognized, which facilitates transfers and exchange programs.

Dates: Sep 8, 1997-May 14, 1998 (preliminary dates). Cost: $2,500 per semester (4 semesters for the whole program) tuition plus about $200 for books and $300-$400 per month for living costs. Contact: Budapest Univ. of Economic Sciences (BUES), International Studies Center (ISC), H-1093 Budapest, Fövám tér 8, Budapest, Hungary; (011) 36-1-217-1153 or (011) 36-1-217-0608, fax 217-0608; isc@cleo.bke.hu, gopher-isc.bke.hu.

Summer Univ. Program. Three-week accred-ited courses (3 credits each) offered in English. The subjects (5 or 6 altogether) are taught in 2 different time slots by reputed professors, with the involvement of guest experts. They provide interested students with a comprehensive view of Hungary and the region, including the economic, political, social, and cultural aspects.

Dates: First: Mid-Jun-early Jul; second: Jul. Cost: $450 per course plus about $50 for books and $300-$400 per month for living costs (places in the dormitory might be offered for $180 per 3 weeks). Contact: Budapest Univ. of Economic Sciences (BUES), International Studies Center (ISC), H-1093 Budapest, Fövám tér 8, Budapest, Hungary; (011) 36-1-217-1153 or (011) 36-1-217-0608, fax 217-0608; isc@cleo.bke.hu, gopher-isc.bke.hu.

Undergraduate Degree Program. The 4-year undergraduate program is offered in English in 2 specializations: International Economics and Business Administration. Students completing the program are awarded a BA degree by Budapest Univ. of Economic Sciences. The credits and degrees obtained are internationally recognized, which facilitates transfers and exchange programs.

Dates: Sep 8, 1997-May 14, 1998 (preliminary dates). Cost: $2,100 per semester (8 semesters for the whole program) tuition plus about $200 for books and $300-$400 per month for living costs. Contact: Budapest Univ. of Economic Sciences (BUES), International Studies Center (ISC), H-1093 Budapest, Fövám tér 8, Budapest, Hungary; (011) 36-1-217-1153 or (011) 36-1-217-0608, fax 217-0608; isc@cleo.bke.hu, gopher-isc.bke.hu.

India

Community Development. This study/travel course based in rural India, offers intensive study of 3 connected issues: community development at the village and city street level, the environment, and the roles of women in balancing the demands of the community.

Each of the 4 sequential courses begins with an orientation; students then visit development projects where they observe and are taught by development professionals. Appropriate for students from many majors. While the program introduces the religions and cultures of India to students as essential to understanding and learning, the focus of the course is on current issues of development in India.

Dates: Sep-Dec. Contact: Ruth S. Mason, Director of International Education, Gustavus Adolphus College, St. Peter, MN 56082; (507) 933-7545, fax (507) 933-6277.

Friends World Program. A semester or year program in India at the Friends World Center in Bangalore includes orientation, intensive seminars, field studies, travel, and independent work. The core curriculum serves as an introduction to India's complex cultures. Independent study sample topics include: Gandhian studies, sustainable development, Buddhist studies in Nepal, dance, women's studies, philosophy, and traditional medicine. Students may earn 12-18 credits per semester.

Dates: Fall: mid-Sep-mid-Dec; spring: mid-Jan-mid-May. Cost: $10,000 per semester in 1996/1997. Includes tuition, travel, room and board, fees, and books. Contact: James Howard, Friends World Program, 239 Montauk Hwy., Southampton, NY 11968; (516) 287-8475; jhoward@sand.liunet.edu.

Penn-in-India. For students interested in South Asian studies, performing arts, religion, economics, and traditional medicine, PSA's newest program offers students a survey of both India's rich cultural history and its burgeoning industrial life. The program is located in Pune, a cosmopolitan city of 4,000,000 which is a thriving arts center, a hub of scholarship, and a growing economic presence. Students will live with Indian families in the area and be involved in community projects.

Dates: Jun 28-Aug 9. Cost: Tuition $2,840; program cost $1,860. Contact: Penn Summer Abroad, College of General Studies, Univ. of Pennsylvania, 3440 Market St., Suite 100, Philadelphia, PA 19104-3335; (215) 898-5738, fax (215) 573-2053.

Univ. of Wisconsin-Madison's College Year in India. The program provides integrated language training, tutorial instruction, and independent fieldwork projects, beginning with summer school in the U.S. The 4 program sites are at Banaras Hindu Univ. (for Hindu-Urdu students); Hyderabad Univ., Hyderabad, A.P. (for Telugu students); Madurai Kamaraj Univ. (for Tamil students), and Kerala Univ., Thiruvananthapuram, Kerala (for Malayalam students).

Dates: Summer in Madison: early Jun-mid-Aug; academic program abroad: late Aug-Apr. Cost: Call for current information. Contact: Office of International Studies and Programs, 261 Bascom Hall, 500 Lincoln Dr., Madison, WI 53706; (608) 262-2851, fax (608) 262-6998; abroad@macc.wisc.edu.

Indonesia

Beloit College Indonesia Exchange Program. Students arrive at Satya Wacana Univ. in Salatiga, Central Java, in late June for a 6-week intensive introduction to Indonesian language and culture. During the fall semester students study in the arts and humanities, pursue 1 or 2 directed studies, and continue to study Indonesian language for a total of 16 semester hours of credit.

Dates: Approx. Jun 28-Dec 20. Cost: Tuition $8,672, room and board $1,923. Contact: Dr. Terance W. Bigalke, Director, World Affairs Center, Beloit College, 700 College St., Beloit, WI 53511; (608) 363-2269, fax (608) 363-2689; bigalket@beloit.edu.

Ireland

9th Achill Archaeological Field School. Survey and excavation of a post-medieval deserted village: Slievemore, Achill, Co. Mayo.

Activities include: surveying, excavation procedure, recording geology and botany of island, field trips, lectures and seminars. No previous knowledge required. Maximum 6 credits. Dates: Weekly Jul 15-Aug 30. Cost: Weekly: IR£85 p.p. $200 course fee plus accommodations. Contact: Theresa McDonald, M.A. Director, Achill Archaeological Field School, St. O'Hara's Hill, Tullamore, Co. Offaly; (011) 353-1-505-21627, fax 506-21627.

Burren College of Art. The Burren College of Art is located on the west coast of Ireland. It offers studio art courses in a variety of media for year, semester, and 4- and 8-week summer sessions. Students will find the setting and environment of the College conducive to individual growth and self expression, with ample contact between students, teaching staff, and visiting artists. Housing in shared cottages.

Dates: Sep-Dec, Jan-Jun; 4- and 8-week summer programs available as well. Cost: Semester: $8,000; summer: $2,200-$4,000. Includes tuition, housing, some art materials, support services, excursions, partial insurance coverage. Contact: IPA, Univ. of Illinois at Urbana-Champaign, 115 International Studies Bldg., 910 S. 5th St., Champaign, IL 61820; (800) 531-4404, fax (217) 244-0249; ipa@uiuc.edu.

Dublin Parliamentary Internship. Twelve program opportunities in the Republic and the North. University study and special subject area programs including internships in the Irish parliament. Program provides a full range of services including a full-time resident director and staff in Dublin, orientation, homestay, and guaranteed housing.

Dates: Fall, spring, academic year, and summer. semestes and terms. Cost: Varies. Call for current fees. Contact: Meghan Mazick, Beaver College Center for Education Abroad, 450 S. Easton Rd., Glenside, PA 19038-3295; (800) 755-5607, fax (215) 572-2174; cea@beaver.edu, www.beaver.edu/cea/.

Institute for Study Abroad. The ISA cooper-ates with 6 universities in Ireland to provide high quality academic year, semester, and term programs for U.S. undergraduates. The ISA guarantees housing, aims to achieve full integration whenever possible, and offers a wide variety of student services during all phases of the study abroad experience.

Dates: Semester/term/2-term (Sep-Dec, Jan-late Jun), academic year (Sep-late Jun). Deadlines: fall and year programs Apr 15, spring programs Oct 15. Cost: Begins at $6,975 and $10,775 (1995-96 fees) for semester and year programs respectively. Includes tuition, housing, predeparture preparation, ISIC, one-way airfare, overseas orientation, domestic and overseas student services, family visit, excursions, and transcript translation. Some scholarships available. Contact: Institute for Study Abroad, Butler Univ., 4600 Sunset Ave., Indianapolis, IN 46208; (800) 858-0229, fax (317) 940-9704; study-abroad@butler.edu.

Lynn Univ. in Ireland. Earn college credits while enjoying old world Dublin, a friendly city of young people. Students from all over the world come to this center of learning for cultural and social activities. Programs for college students in summer, fall, and spring. Year round English Language Studies and special summer schedule for high school students.

Dates: College: Jun 17-Jul 26, 1996; high school: Jul 1-26, 1996. Cost: College: $3,825; high school: $2,825. Contact: Lee Ross, Lynn Univ., 3601 N. Military Trail, Boca Raton, FL 33431; (407) 994-0770, (800) 453-8306; luadmiss@igc.net.

North American Institute for Study Abroad. Semester, academic year, or summer term. Two to 6 courses per semester. Graduate credit available. Courses taught in English. Typical class size 25. Less than 25 percent of each class are program participants. Other students are from host institution, host country, other programs. Seminars and tutorials also used for instruction. Unstructured time each week to be used at students' leisure.

Dates: Sep 22-Dec 18 (fall), Jan 9-May 20 (spring). Approx. dates. Apply by Jul 1 for fall year, by Oct 1 for spring, and by Apr 1 for summer. Cost: 1996-1997: semester $6,000-$8,500, year $11,500-$16,500, summer $1,000-$2,950. Contact: Elizabeth Strauss, Office Manager, or Amy Armstrong, Operations Manager, North American Institute for Study Abroad, P.O. Box 279, Riverside, PA 17868 ; (717) 275-5099, fax (717) 275-1644.

Univ. College Cork. First opened in 1849, the Univ. College Cork (UCC) is 1 of 3 constituent colleges of the National Univ. of Ireland. Eight faculties comprise the educational offerings of UCC: Arts, Celtic Studies, Commerce, Law, Science, Food Science and Technology, Engineering and Medicine. Enrollment in regular UCC classes with Irish language, history, and culture, but other courses may be available. Housing arranged prior to departure from U.S. in apartments near campus. Fall, spring, summer, academic year.

Dates: Fall: Early Sep-mid-Dec:, spring: mid-Jan-early Jun; summer: early Jul-end of Jul. Cost: Fall 1996 estimate $5,995; spring 1997: $6,366; summer: $2,570; academic year: $12,026. Estimates include full-day orientation before departure, application fee, apartment rental (including utilities), food allowance, health and accident insurance, airfare from NY, books and supplies. SUNY tuition not included. Contact: Dr. John Ogden, Director, Office of International Programs, Box 2000, SUNY Cortland, Cortland, NY 13045; (607) 753-2209, fax (607) 753-5989; tonerp@snycorva.cortland.edu.

Israel

Bar-Ilan Univ. Junior Year. A special year of Jewish heritage combining classic study abroad with an accent on Jewish heritage and culture. No religious requirements, 19 credits per semester. Off-campus housing. Communal service. Home hospitality. Tours. All courses in English. Offered in conjunction with the Boston Univ. International Programs Office. Dates: Sep 1996-Jun 1997. Year or semester. Cost: $12,000 per year includes tuition, housing, tours. Scholarships available. Contact: Office of Academic Affairs, Bar-Ilan Univ., 91 5th Ave., New York, NY 10003; (212) 337-1286, fax (212) 337-1274; tobiu@village.ios.com.

Ben Gurion Univ. The Overseas Student Program at BGU provides a unique and challenging semester or year abroad for qualified students. Located in Beer-Sheva, BGU offers the opportunity to live with Israelis, learn Hebrew, and be truly immersed in Israeli culture and society. Students can participate in community internships or conduct individual research in university departments. Courses are taught in English in such areas as anthropology, archaeology, economics, ecology, Judaic studies, political science, and women's studies. Program includes optional kibbutz stay and archaeological dig. Financial aid available. Dates: Aug 4-Dec 26, 1996 (fall); Jan 5-Jun 5, 1997 (spring). Cost: Semester: $5,580; year: $8,770. Includes tuition, room, health insurance, Hebrew ulpan, activity fee (trips). Contact: Caroline Fox, Associate Director, 342 Madison Ave., Suite 1224, New York, NY 10173; (212) 687-7721, fax (212) 370-0805; outside NY (800) 962-2248; bguosp@haven.ios.com, www.bgu.ac.il/osp.

Field Study Internship Program. Designed for students with an interest in policy applications of social science research and/or area studies interest in Israel, this semester program gives students the opportunity to carry out an individual research project on an aspect of Israel's socio-economic development. Also included are instruction in research methods, a background course on Israel's development and instruction in basic conversational Hebrew. Study tours and field trips are important components in this program. Dates: Aug 20-Dec 18, 1996; Jan 14-May 13, 1997. Cost: Tuition: $4,700 fall, spring. Room

$150 per month, board $400 per month (optional). Contact: Dr. Aliza Fleischer, Field Study Program Coordinator, Development Study Center, P.O. Box 2355, Rehovot 76122, Israel; fax (972) 8-9475884; xsvinn@weizmann.weizmann.ac.il.

Geographical and Historical Settings—Short-Term Program. A 3-week program (4 semester hours of graduate/undergraduate credit) with extensive field trips throughout the region. Introduces the student to the geography, history, and archaeology of Israel and Trans-Jordan as they relate to Biblical studies.

Dates: Call for dates, programs run year round. Cost: $1,625 on campus; $1,775 off campus. Contact: Jerusalem University College, 4249 E. State St., Suite 203, Rockford, IL 61108; (815) 229-5900 or (800) 891-9408, fax (815) 229-5901.

Hebrew Univ. of Jerusalem. Programs in English are offered for both undergraduate and graduate students. They vary in length from 2 years to 1 semester and include summer courses. Areas of specialization include Israel Studies, Jewish Studies, International Relations, and Hebrew and Arabic.

Dates: Vary according to program. Cost: Vary according to program. Contact: The Hebrew Univ. of Jerusalem, Office of Academic Affairs, 11 E. 69th St., New York, NY 10021; (800) 4040-8622, fax (212) 517-4548; 74542.340@compuserve.com.

Jesus and His Times—Short-Term Program. A 2-week (2-semester hour) program of studies related to the geography, history, culture, and archaeology of the Second Temple period (time of Christ). Concentrations in the Jerusalem and Galilee regions.

Dates: Jul each year. Cost: $1,050 on campus; $1,260 off campus. Contact: Jerusalem University College, 4249 E. State St., Suite 203, Rockford, IL 61108; (815) 229-5900 or (800) 891-9408, fax (815) 229-5901.

Long-Term Study Programs. Two-year master of arts degrees in the history of Syro-Palestine; Middle Eastern studies; Hebrew language; Hebrew Bible translation; New Testament backgrounds. Also 1-year graduate studies certificates and semester abroad for undergraduates.

Dates: Year round. Cost: Approx. $7,000 per semester. Includes tuition and room and board. Contact: Jerusalem University College, 4249 E. State St., Suite 203, Rockford, IL 61108; (815) 229-5900 or (800) 891-9408, fax (815) 229-5901.

Master of Arts Degree. Ancient History of Syro-Palestine, Middle Eastern Studies, Hebrew Language, Hebrew Bible Translation. Two-year MA degrees. Extensive fieldwork and study in the languages, geography, history, culture, social, and religious aspects of Israel and the Middle East.

Dates: Sep-May every year. Cost: Approx. $7,000 per semester. Includes tuition, room and board, fees. Contact: Jerusalem University College, Amelia Nakai, Program Coordinator, 4249 E. State St., Suite 203, Rockford, IL 61108; (815) 229-5900 or (800) 891-9408, fax (815) 229-5901.

Short-Term Program. Two- and 3-week academic study program with intensive field trips and investigation of historical geography of Israel. Tour the land of the Bible while receiving lectures from resident scholars specially trained in the geography of Israel as it relates to biblical interpretation.

Dates: Jan-Dec every year. Cost: Approx. $1,700 for 3 weeks, $1,100 for 2 weeks. Contact: Institute of Holy Land Studies, Amelia Nakai, Program Coordinator, 4249 E. State St., Suite 203, Rockford, IL 61108; (815) 229-5900 or (800) 891-9408, fax (815) 229-5901.

Summer in Jerusalem. This 7-week, 6-credit program, hosted by Hebrew Univ., combines intensive language study with an overview of contemporary Israeli poetry, drama, painting, and music. Writers and artists will present their work to the group. Students will go on an extended field trip to the Galilee and participate in the Klezmer Music Festival. Participants arrange and pay for their own transatlantic flights. Ground transportation in private buses and housing throughout the seminar are arranged and covered by the program fee.

Dates: Jun 30-Aug 15, 1996. Cost: Undergraduate tuition for 6 credits: $2,766; program fee: $2,550. Contact: Daisy Fried, Syracuse Summer Abroad, Syracuse Univ., 119 Euclid Ave., Syracuse, NY 13244-4170; (315) 443-9419, fax (315) 443-4593; dsfried@suadmin.syr.edu.

The Israel Archaeological Society. The Israel Archaeological Society's Expedition 1997, invites the participation of students, seniors, and families at archaeological digs in Israel and Jordan; work hard, but sleep in comfortable hotels. We will also visit archaeological and historical sites in Israel, Jordan, Syria, and Egypt with a cruise on the Nile. From 1-7 weeks. University students may earn from 4-6 credits from Hebrew Univ.

Dates: Jun 13-Aug 1, 1997. Cost: $1,095-$4,995 land only plus roundtrip airfare. Contact: Arthur D. Greenberg, Israel Archaeological Society, 467 Levering Ave., Los Angeles, CA 90024; (800) 477-2358, fax (310) 476-6259.

Italy

American Univ. of Rome. Programs for students of international business, international relations, Italian civilization and culture, Italian studies. Credits fully transferable through affiliations with U.S. institutions. Housing in studio apartments. All courses (except language classes) in English. All programs are designed to provide students with studies of immediate relevance in a highly competitive job market.

Dates: Fall and Spring semesters plus May/Jun summer sessions. Cost: $4,475 per semester, tuition/housing $2,350. Contact: Mary B. Handley, Dean of Administration, American Univ. of Rome, Via Pietro Roselli 4, Rome 00153, Italy; (011) 39-6-58330919, fax 583-30992.

Art Under One Roof. Study over 40 applied art programs in Florence with The Applied Arts Institute of Florence. Study monthly, semester, or summer and experience Italy: painting, fresco, jewelry making and design, interior design, fashion design, sculpture, restoration .

Dates: Jan, Mar, Jun, Jul, Sep, Oct, Nov. Cost: From $400-$5,000 (monthly to 1 year). Contact: Arte Sotto un Tetto, Admissions Office, Borgo dei Greci, 14, 50122 Florence, Italy; Tel./fax (011) 39-55-239-6821.

Business, Economics, Italian Studies (Turin). Turin offers a diversified curriculum in English and in business and economics, plus intensive courses in Italian language and culture, literature, etc., at the foot of the majestic Alps. Program-organized housing and field trips and many Italian university activities.

Dates: Summer sessions: Jun 5-Jul 6, 1997 and Jun 30-Jul 25, 1998; fall semester: Aug 29-Dec 17, 1997; spring semester: Jan 4-Apr 30, 1998. Cost: $3,975 per semester, $6,980 fall and spring semesters; summer: $1,570 per session; $2,900 both sessions. Contact: University Studies Abroad Consortium (USAC), Univ. of Nevada, Reno #323, Reno, NV 89557-0093; (702) 784-6569, fax (702) 784-6010; usac@admin.unr.edu, www.scs.unr.edu/~usac.

Ceramics and Art History (Faenza). Hosted by the Istituto Statale d'Arte per la Ceramica. The Istituto is an internationally known ceramics schools that draws upon a tradition dating back to the middle ages. Program consists of 2 courses (ceramics and art history) Ceramics instruction will be tailored to the individual student. Art history will explore Medieval and Renaissance art. Six credits: graduate, undergraduate.

Dates: Jun 20-Jul 8. Cost: Approx. $2,800. Includes airfare, local transportation, room, 1 meal per day, insurance and tuition. Contact: SUNY Brockport, Office of International Education, 350 New Campus Dr., Brockport, NY 14420; (716) 395-2119, fax (716) 395-2606.

Dance in Italy. Located in the Renaissance city of Urbino, this 3-week intensive modern dance workshop will include daily technique class, development of performance skills, and on-site performance. Three undergraduate credits.

Dates: Early Jul-late Jul. Cost: Approx. $1,500. Airfare not included. Contact: Office of International Education, SUNY New Paltz, HAB 33, New Paltz, NY 12561; (914) 257-3125, fax (914) 257-3129; international@ newpaltz.edu, www.newpaltz.edu/oie.

Italian in Rome. Located a few minutes walk from the Colosseum, the school offers intensive and non-intensive, group and individual courses at all levels. A rich extracurricular program includes guided tours, excursions, seminars on art history, architecture, literature, and cinema. Accommodations with family or apartments with cooking facilities.

Dates: Year round, begins every 2 weeks. Cost: One-month course: 750,000 Lire, 3-month course: 1,850,000 Lire. Contact: Pier Luigi Arri, Director, via Bixio, 74 - 00185, Rome, Italy; (011) 39-6-7008434, 70474976, fax 70497150; (temporary) www.nube.com/babele.

Italian Language (Florence). Intensive courses of Italian language and culture in small groups with maximum of 8 students per class. Four or 6 lesson a day, 5 days per week. Duration: From 2 weeks to 6 months. Full leisure time program. Accommodation facilities: family/half board, rooms with Italians/use of kitchen, holidays apartments.

Dates: New courses start every 2 weeks. Cost: Two weeks, 4 lessons per day Lit460,000; 4 weeks Lit700,000. Contact: CLIC, Centro Lingua Italiana Calvino, Viale Fratelli Roselli 76, 50123 Florence, Italy; (011) 39-55-288081, fax 288125.

Italian Language Courses. Group and individual Italian language courses (6 levels). Cultural courses (literature, art history, history of Florence, history of opera, operatic Italian and libretti), conversation courses, written expression, Italian politics, geography, Italian for business and commerce, Italian for tourism, wine course, cooking course.

Dates: Call or write for details. Cost: Call or write for details. Contact: Dr. Stefano Burbi, Director, Istituto Parola, Corso del Tintori 8, 50122 Florence, Italy; (011) 39-055-24-21-82, fax (055) 39-055-24-19-14; lstituto.parola@ agora.stm.it, www.alba.fi.it/parola.

Italian Language Studies. Four-week intensive program in Urbino, emphasizing language proficiency, culture and civilization, and contemporary Italian literature. Open to all students at all levels. Field trips. Six credit hours: undergraduate, graduate.

Dates: Late Jun-early Aug. Cost: Approx. $3,200. Airfare not included. Contact: Office of International Education, SUNY New Paltz, HAB 33, New Paltz, NY 12561; (914) 257-3125, fax (914) 257-3129; international@ newpaltz.edu, www.newpaltz.edu/oie.

Italian Studies Summer Institute in Florence. For students interested in intensive beginning and intermediate language courses and cultural studies in literature, cinema, and art history taught in one of the world's most beautiful cities. Numerous cultural opportunities and field trips offer a valuable supplement to class work.

Dates: Jun 3-Jul 12. Cost: Tuition $2,700; housing $1,250-$1,800; travel $800. Contact: Penn Summer Abroad, College of General Studies, Univ. of Pennsylvania, 3440 Market St., Suite 100, Philadelphia, PA 19104-3335; (215) 898-5738, fax (215) 573-2053.

Language Art Culture in Florence. A) Italian

language year round; B) Drawing, history of art, cinema, literature, music; C) A special preparatory course for students asking for admission to Italian academies of fine arts (4 weeks in Jul and Sep only).

Dates: Start every month (except course C), 2 weeks-6 months. Cost: A) LIR 530,000-3,800,000; B) LIR 220,000-1,500,000. Contact: Lucia Erbori, c/o Academia del Giglio, Via Ghibellina 116, 50122 Firenze, Italy; Tel./fax (011) 39-55-2302467; www.leonet.it/bol/AccademiaDelGiglio/.

Lorenzo de' Medici. Art history, Italian history and culture, studio art, business and economics. All conducted in English. Semester, summer classes, short-term programs. Learn Italian art history, cooking, civilization, and culture in the heart of the Renaissance. U.S. credits available.

Dates: Sep/Dec-Jan-Apr. Summer: May, Jun, Jul, Aug. Cost: Tuition: Semester $3,500, summer: approx. $1,100. Contact: Dott. Arch. Gabriella Ganugi, Director, Lorenzo de'Medici, Via Faenza, #43, 50123 Florence, Italy; (011) 39-55-287143, fax (011) 39-55-23989 20/287203; ldm@dada.it.

Louisiana Tech Rome. Tech Rome is a 6-week summer travel-study program based in Rome. It features hotel housing, 3 meals per day, tours, and traditional classroom courses combined with field travel for college credit. Up to 13 semester hours may be earned in a choice of over 40 courses in diverse subject areas. Courses are taught by American professors. All disciplines are accredited.

Dates: May 27-Jul 4. Cost: $4,328 includes tuition, all housing for 6 weeks, all meals, tours. Contact: Tech Rome, P.O. Box 3172, Ruston, LA 71272; (800) 346-8324.

Macerata Program. Subject areas include Italian language, architecture, art history, civilization and culture, economics, history, literature, politics. All courses other than Italian language are conducted in English. No Italian

language experience required for admission. Full academic year or individual semesters, fall, winter.

Dates: Sep-Dec (fall), Jan-Apr (winter). Cost: Approx. $6,500 per semester. Includes tuition, housing, some meals, excursions, texts, international student identity card, local transportation, insurance. Financial aid accepted. Contact: Gail Lavin, Assoc. Director, Univ. Programs, American Heritage Association, 741 SW Lincoln St., Portland, OR 97201-3178; (800) 654-2051, fax (503) 295-5969; 96trab@amheritage.org.

On-Site Studies in Art History. Topics and locations vary from year to year. In 1996 the program will focus on "Ancient Roman Houses, Villas and Gardens," with on-site studies in and around Rome, Ostia, Pompeii, Herculaneum, Boscoreale, and Oplontis. Three credit hours: undergraduate, graduate.

Dates: Approx. Jun 29-Jul 19, 1996. Cost: Approx. $2,400. Airfare not included. Contact: Office of International Education, HAB 33, SUNY New Paltz, New Paltz, NY 12561; (914) 257-3125, fax (914) 257-3129.

Siena Program. Subject areas include Italian language, architecture, art history, civilization and culture, classical studies, economics, history, political science. All courses other than Italian language are conducted in English. No Italian language experience required for admissions. Full academic year or individual 10-week terms, fall, winter, spring.

Dates: Sep-Dec (fall), Jan-Mar (winter), Apr-Jun (spring). Cost: Approx. $5,200 per term. Includes tuition, housing, some meals, excursions, texts, international student identity card, local transportation, insurance. Financial aid accepted. Contact: Gail Lavin, Assoc. Director, Univ. Programs, American Heritage Association, 741 SW Lincoln St., Portland, OR 97201-3178; (800) 654-2051, fax (503) 295-5969; 96trab@amheritage.org.

Study in Urbino. An academic year program

in the Renaissance city of Urbino, offering intensive Italian language and regular university courses at the Univ. of Urbino. Dormitory housing, native resident director, field trips, 12-18 undergraduate credits per semester. Qualifications: junior or above; minimum of 2 years college-level Italian or the equivalent. Qualified applicant may be considered for spring-only program.

Dates: Late Sep-early Jun. Cost: Approx. $10,100. Includes tuition, fees, room and board, and insurance (non-New York state residents add $4,900). Contact: Office of International Education, SUNY New Paltz, HAB 33, New Paltz, NY 12561; (914) 257-3125, fax (914) 257-3129; international@newpaltz.edu, www.newpaltz.edu/oie.

Summer in Rome. The program is open to high school seniors and college students at any accredited university or college in the U.S., and to secondary school teachers. No previous knowledge of Italian is required since the program offers language courses at the elementary, intermediate, and advanced levels, and the art and culture courses are conducted in English. Double occupancy and 3 meals a day are provided at the designated residence in Rome. Participants must register for 6 credits.

Dates: Jun 27-Jul 25, 1997. Cost: $2,100 includes room and board, excursions. Airfare and tuition additional. Contact: Study Abroad Office, Univ. at Stony Brook, Melville Library E5340, Stony Brook, NY 11794-3397; (516) 632-7030, fax (516) 632-6544; bgilkes@ccmail.sunysb.edu.

Tech Rome. A comprehensive resident program based in Rome offering up to 13 semester hours credit in a choice of over 40 courses taught by American faculty. Travel in Italy and to other countries. Financial aid available.

Dates: May 28-Jul 5, 1996. Cost: $4,328 (hotel housing, 3 meals per day, travel). Contact: Tech Rome, P.O. Box 3172, Ruston, LA 71272; (800) 346-8324.

The American Univ. of Rome. BBA: International business, BA programs in international relations, Italian studies, interdisciplinary studies. Semester and year study abroad programs.

Dates: Summer sessions May, Jun, Jul. Semesters: (fall) Aug-Dec, (spring) Jan-Apr. Cost: $1,036 per course or full-time $4,200 per semester. Contact: Mary B. Handley, Dean of Administration, The American Univ. of Rome, Via Pietro Roselli 4, Rome 00153, Italy; (011) 39-6-58330919, fax (011) 39-6-58330992.

UGA Studies Abroad at Cortona. Studio art (ceramics, drawing, book arts, fabric design [tapestry weaving], interior design, jewelry and metalworking, painting, papermaking, printmaking, photography, sculpture, and watercolor), art history, beginning Italian, Italian culture, architecture, and landscape architecture courses for undergraduate and graduate university credit. Courses vary each quarter. Deadlines: Jan 10 spring; Apr 10 summer; and Jun 10 fall.

Dates: 1996: Mar 26-Jun 1 (spring); Jun 17-Aug 23 (summer); Sep 6-Nov 11 (fall). Cost: $5,880. Includes tuition for 2 courses, lodging and 2 meals per day, airfare, and land travel with the program. $125 out-of-state fee. Contact: Larry Millard, Director, UGA Studies Abroad, School of Art, Visual Arts Building, Univ. of Georgia, Athens, GA 30602-4102; (706) 542-7011, fax (706) 542-2467.

Univ. of Wisconsin-Madison's Summer in Perugia. This intensive Italian language program gives students an opportunity to study at the Universitá Italiana per Stranieri in Perugia, a train-ride away from Florence and Rome. Students take courses in Italian language, at any level, and a 1-credit cultural survey, taught in English. No previous knowledge of Italian required. Application deadline: First Friday in Mar. Late applications considered on a space-available basis.

Dates: Late May through Jul (8 weeks). Cost: Call for current information. Contact: Office of International Studies and Programs, 261 Bascom Hall, Univ. of Wisconsin, 500 Lincoln Dr., Madison, WI 53706; (608) 262-2851, fax (608) 262-6998; abroad@macc.wisc.edu.

Jamaica

East/West Marine Biology Program. The East/West Program allows advanced undergraduate and beginning graduate students to spend a year taking field marine science courses in 3 diverse environments. Twenty students live in the environment that they are studying for 3 quarters, beginning with fall in Washington, followed by winter in Jamaica, and ending with spring in Massachusetts.

Dates: Sep-Jun annually. Cost: $21,700 includes tuition, room and board, lab, and dive fees. Contact: Sarah Jordan, Coordinator, Northeastern Univ., Marine Science Center, East Point, Nahant, MA 01908; (617) 595-5597, fax (617) 581-6076; eastwest@lynx.neu.edu.

Performing Arts in Jamaica. Semester program at the Cultural Training Center in Kingston. Provides participants the opportunity to study dance, theater, music, and/or art. Housing in on-campus dorms. Fifteen undergraduate credits.

Dates: Sep 15-Dec 19 (fall); Feb 6-May 31 (spring). Cost: Approx. $5,200. Includes room and board, airfare, local transportation, books, tuition, and miscellaneous expenses. Contact: SUNY Brockport, Office of International Education, 350 New Campus Dr., Brockport, NY 14420; (716) 395-2119, fax (716) 395-2606.

Japan

Asian Studies Exchange in Osaka. Academic year exchange program at Kansai Gaidai Univ. Study Japanese language and Asian studies. All instruction in English except language courses. Besides language courses choose 3 or 4 courses from all those offered at the university. Housing with families. Thirty undergraduate credits.

Dates: Early Sep-mid-May. Cost: Approx. $9,000. Includes room, board, airfare, books, tuition. Contact: SUNY Brockport, Office of International Education, 350 New Campus Dr., Brockport, NY 14420; (716) 395-2119, fax (716) 395-2606.

BCA Program in Sapporo. Earn 15-18 credits per semester at Hokusei Gakuen Univ. in Sapporo, with a 1-week orientation, homestay with Japanese families, field trips, and extended study tour through Honshu. Year program could include first semester or 2-month interterm in Dalian, China. Students accepted from all U.S. colleges and universities. No foreign language prerequisite. All levels of Japanese language study available. Practica and internships available.

Dates: Aug 16-Dec 19 (fall), Mar 21-Jul 23 (spring), Aug-Jul or Mar-Dec (year). Cost: $17,345 (academic year 1996-1997); $9,645 (semester 1996-1997). Includes international transportation, room and board, tuition, insurance, group travel in country. Contact: Beverly S. Eikenberry, Box 184, Manchester College, North Manchester, IN 46962; (219) 982-5238, fax (219) 982-7755; bca@manchester.edu, http://studyabroad.com/bca.

Friends World Program. A semester or year program at the Friends World Center in Kyoto includes intensive seminars focused on Japanese culture, language, and the arts. Writing workshops are also offered. Students design internships and independent research projects. Sample topics include: traditional medicine, education, Buddhism, gender studies, peace movements, and environmental policy. Student may earn 12-18 credits per semester.

Dates: Fall: mid-Sep-mid-Dec; spring: mid-Jan-mid-May. Cost: $11,875 per semester in 1996/1997. Includes tuition, travel, room and board, fees, and books. Contact: James Howard, Friends World Program, 239 Montauk Hwy., Southampton, NY 11968; (516) 287-8475; jhoward@sand.liunet.edu.

Kenya

Friends World Program. A semester or year program in Kenya at Friends World Center in Machakos. Includes intensive seminars, field study, homestays, travel, and independent study. Seminars are offered in historical and contemporary East Africa and Swahili language. Field projects have been done in the areas of sustainable development, education, traditional medicine, agroforestry, marine ecology, wildlife studies, and music. Students may earn 12-18 credits per semester.

Dates: Fall: mid-Sep-mid-Dec.; spring: mid-Jan-mid-May. Cost: $10,600 per semester in 1996/1997. Includes tuition, travel, room and board, fees, and books. Contact: James Howard, Friends World Program, 239 Montauk Hwy., Southampton, NY 11968; (516) 287-8475; jhoward@sand.liunet.edu.

Korea

Penn-in-Seoul. For students interested in East Asia, Korea, international relations and other business disciplines. This program, offered in conjunction with Kyung Hee Univ., includes courses in the area of international relations as well as internships with multinational corporations, government agencies, and think tanks. Field trips exploring Korean history and culture are integral to the program.

Dates: Jun 14-Aug 17. Cost: Tuition $2,840; housing $850. Contact: Penn Summer Abroad, College of General Studies, Univ. of Pennsylvania, 3440 Market St., Suite 100, Philadelphia, PA 19104-3335; (215) 898-5738, fax (215) 573-2053.

Latin America

Development Work. Programs in Nicaragua and Brazil. In the 11-month Nicaragua program you do construction work in a rural co-operative and travel and study in countries in Central America. In the 6-month program in Brazil you live and work in a rural cooperative and travel throughout the country. Both programs are open to students and non-students and include preparation and follow-up in the U.S.

Dates: Nicaragua: Sep 15, 1996; Brazil: Jan 4, 1997. Cost: Nicaragua: $4,600; Brazil: $3,400. Includes training, room and board, airfare, health insurance, and other direct program costs. Contact: Josefin Jonsson, Administrative Director, P.O. Box 103-T, Williamstown, MA 01267; (413) 458-9828, fax (413) 458-3323.

Friends World Program. A semester or year in Latin America at Friends World Center in San José, Costa Rica, incorporates seminars, field study, travel, and independent projects. Seminars to introduce students into Latin America and its culture include Central America today, intensive Spanish for any level student, ecology and development, women's studies in Latin America. Independent work has included: ecology, community development, peace studies, health and refugee studies. Students may earn 12-18 credits per semester.

Dates: Fall: mid-Sep-mid-Dec; spring: mid-Jan-mid-May. Cost: $10,010 per semester in 1996/1997. Includes tuition, travel, room and board, fees and books. Contact: James Howard, Friends World Program, 239 Montauk Hwy., Southampton, NY 11968; (516) 287-8475; jhoward@sand.liunet.edu.

Mexico

BCA Program in Xalapa. Earn 15-18 credits per semester at Univ. Veracruzana with a 4-week intensive language and orientation period, homestay with families, field trips, and extended study tour. Intermediate college level Spanish required for regular university courses. Students with lower level Spanish accepted for language and culture study only.

Dates: Aug 15-Jan 20 (fall), Feb 15-Jul 11 (spring), Aug 15-Jul 11 (year). Cost: $12,545 (academic year 1996-1997); $7,245 (semester 1996-1997). Includes international transportation, room and board, tuition, insurance, group travel in country. Contact: Beverly S. Eikenberry, Box 184, Manchester College, North Manchester, IN 46962; (219) 982-5238, fax (219) 982-7755; bca@manchester.edu, http://studyabroad.com/bca.

Center for Bilingual Multicultural Studies. The center's total immersion Spanish program, designed to develop conversational fluency in the shortest possible time, combines daily classroom study and seminars on Mexico's history with living in a Mexican home and field trips to historical sites. No more than 5 students assigned to 1 professor. College accredited.

Dates: Year round. New classes begin every Monday. Two-week minimum study. Cost: Two-week program at $15 per day is $660; 2-week program at $22 per day is $758; 2-week program at $30 per day is $870; includes 3 meals per day, registration fee, tuition and accommodations. Contact: U.S. Office, 3133 Lake Hollywood Dr., P.O. Box #1860, Los Angeles, CA 90078; (800) 426-4660 or (213) 851-3403, fax (213) 851-3684.

Center for Wetland Studies. You will assist local residents and scientists in understanding the critical impacts of exploiting the unique coastal wetland ecosystems in Baja California Sur. In addition, you will develop environmentally sound, culturally sensitive, and economically feasible recommendations for sustainable resource management and employment alternatives for resources dependent local communities. Here, you will live in a small fishing community on Magdalena Bay and split your time between classroom study and wetlands field research.

Dates: Sep 4-Dec 7 (fall); Jan 31-May 6 (winter); and 2 1-month summer sessions. Cost: Semester: $11,200. Includes tuition, room and board. Summer approx. $3,000. Contact: Admissions Office, The School for Field Studies, 16 Broadway, Box 3, Beverly, MA 01915; (508) 927-7777.

El Bosque del Caribe. The International Language Center El Bosque del Caribe specializes in teaching Spanish to adult students, 25 hours per week, in the morning. Experienced instructors teach in a relaxed and pleasant atmosphere. Afternoons are devoted to cultural and recreational activities (excursions, cooking classes, dance classes).

Dates: Year round. Cost: $175 per week; enrollment fees $75. Contact: Mr. Eduardo Sotelo, Academic Director, Calle Pina 1, S.M. 25. M. 11, Apartado Postal 1082, 77599 Cancun, Q. Roo, Mexico; Tel./fax (011) 52-98-84-10-38.

Guadalajara Summer School. For the 45th year, the Univ. of Arizona Guadalajara Summer School will offer intensive Spanish in the 6-week session, intensive Spanish in the 3-week session, and upper-division Spanish and Mexico-related courses in the 5-week session. Courses may be taken for credit or audit.

Dates: Jul 7-Aug 15. Cost: $1,024-$1,872 includes tuition and host family housing with meals. Contact: Dr. Macario Saldate IV, Director, Guadalajara Summer School, The Univ. of Arizona, P.O. Box 40966, Tucson, AZ 85717; (520) 621-5137, fax (520) 621-8141.

Intensive Spanish at the Autonomous Univ. of Guadalajara. Innovative teaching methods combine with cultural immersion and a specialized Beaver-taught class in English, culminating in an extensive field study trip. Full range of program services. On-site representative. Need-based scholarships available.

Dates: Fall, Spring, Full Year. Summer. Cost: Full year: $9,900; Semester: $5,800; Summer:

$1,350. Contact: Meredith Chamorro, Beaver College Center for Education Abroad, 450 S. Easton Rd., Glenside, PA 19038-3295; (800) 755-5607, fax (215) 572-2174; cea@beaver. edu, www.beaver.edu/cea/.

Intensive Spanish in Cuauhnahuac. Cuauhnahuac, founded in 1972, offers a variety of intensive and flexible programs geared to individual needs. Six hours of classes daily with no more than 4 students to a class. Housing with Mexican families who really care about you. Cultural conferences, excursions, and special classes for professionals. College credit available.

Dates: Year round. New classes begin every Monday. Cost: $70 registration fee; $600 4 weeks tuition, housing $16 per night. Contact: Marcia Snell, 519 Park Dr., Kenilworth, IL 60043; (800) 245-9335, fax (847) 256-9475; lankysam@aol.com.

Language Institute of Colima. The Language Institute of Colima Mexico offers a system of total immersion with classes held throughout the year Monday-Friday. Students live with local host families and attend 6 hours of instruction daily; no more than 5 students per class. Many extras, including beach excursions.

Dates: Year round, Monday-Friday. Cost: Registration $80; tuition $415 1st week, $345 after 1st week (for shared room), $445 1st week, $375 after 1st week (for private room). 10% discount for 6 or more. Contact: Dennis Bourassa, Language Institute of Colima, P.O. Box 827, Miranda, CA 95553; (800) 604-6579, fax (707) 923-4232; colima@northcoast.com, www.northcoast.com/~colima.

Learn, Live, and Love Spanish in the Land of the Maya (Chiapas). Spanish lessons in private sessions or small groups (4 people max). Family stays available. School tours to Indian (Mayan) villages, jungle trips available. Extracurricular activities included: Mexican cooking, discussions, video showings. Teach English in exchange for Spanish lessons. Centro Cultural "El Puente" includes gallery weaver's cooperative, travel agency, cafe, restaurant, phone/fax service.

Dates: Year round. Cost: Highest $220 per week; lowest $75 per week. Contact: Roberto Rivas, Bastidas Centro Bilingüe de Chiapas, C. Real de Guadalupe 55, Centro Cultural "El Puente," San Cristóbal de Las Casas 29230, Chiapas, Mexico; (011) 52-967-8-41-57, fax 967-83723 or Tel./fax (800) 303-4983; cenbili@chisnet.com.mx, www.mexonline. com/centro1.htm.

Loyola Univ. in Mexico City. Loyola offers 17 Spanish courses as well as courses on Latin American studies, communications, economics, history, political science, philosophy, sociology, and visual arts at the Jesuit Universidad Iberoamericana in Mexico City. Financial aid available. Trips to Cuernavaca, Taxco, Teotihuacan, and Tula. Three summer sessions and semester and year abroad program available.

Dates: Jan 7-May 15, 1997; May 30-Jul 12, 1997; Jun 23-Jul 24, 1997; Jun 23-Aug 7, 1997; Aug 8-Dec 5, 1997; Jan 9-May 14, 1998. Cost: $2,480 and $2,160 for 6- and 4-week sessions; $6,758 for 17-week semester program. Contact: Maurice P. Brungardt, Director, Mexico Program, Loyola Univ., New Orleans, LA 70118; (504) 865-3539 day, (504) 861-3402 evening, fax (504) 865-2010; brungard@ beta.loyno.edu.

Many Mexicos. The 6-credit traveling seminar provides an in-depth perspective on the current political and socio-economic situation in Mexico by means of a cross-country trip. Ports of call are the Yucatan peninsula, Mexico City, Cuernavaca, and Taxco, the villages of Michoacan, Colima, and the Guadalajara. Ground transportation in private buses and housing in hotels are arranged and covered by the program fee.

Dates: Jun 2-Jul 7, 1996. Cost: Undergraduate tuition for 6 credits: $2,766; program fee: $2,220. Contact: Daisy Fried, Syracuse Summer Abroad, Syracuse Univ., 119 Euclid Ave., Syracuse, NY 13244-4170; (315) 443-9419, fax (315) 443-4593; dsfried@suadmin.syr.edu.

Morelia. Semester weeks. Courses are taught at the Centro Mexicano Internacional (CMI). Intensive Spanish classes, history, politics, art, literature, business, and field study.

Dates: Jan-Dec 12, intensive Spanish in the summer. Cost: Univ. programs approx. $5,200 semester. Intensive Spanish approx. $245 first week, $195 subsequent weeks. Housing and meals $12 per day double occupancy. Contact: Linda Kopfer, Assoc. Director of Univ. Programs, American Heritage Association, 741 SW Lincoln St., Portland, OR 97201-3178; (503) 295-7730 or (800) 654-2051, fax (503) 295-5969; 96trab@ amheritage.org.

Rollins in Mexico. One year of college-level Spanish language or equivalent required. Courses available in history, art and architecture, literature, environmental studies, anthropology, and Spanish taught by faculty from the Univ. of the Yucatan. Housing is with families. Excursions to Mexico City, Guatemala, and historical and cultural sites included.

Dates: Jan-Apr. Cost: Spring 1996: $8,250. Includes tuition, room and partial board, excursions connected with classes, roundtrip airfare Miami-Merida. Contact: Donna O'Connor, Director of International Programs, Rollins College-2759, 1000 Holt Ave., Winter Park, FL 32789-4499; (407) 646-2466, fax (407) 646-2595; kaziz@rollins.edu.

Semester in Mexico. At the American International College of Mexico, Queretaro, operating under the auspices of the Universidad del Valle de Mexico. Spanish language, Mexico colloquium, government and politics of Mexico, history of Mexico. Courses taught in English. Also, students may select from courses offered in regular program of Americom. Mexican homestay. Upper division credit

(junior-senior). A College Consortium for International Studies Program.

Dates: Mid-Sep-Dec/Jan-May. Cost: Approx. $4,000 per semester. Contact: Reinaldo Changsut, Study Abroad Adviser, Miami-Dade Community College, 11011 SW 104th St., Miami, FL 33176-3393; (305) 237-2535, fax (305) 237-2949.

Spanish in Southeast Mexico. Centro Bilingue offers one-on-one or small group instruction, family stays. Group instruction begins the first and third Mondays of each month. Jungle trips and Mayan towns trips.

Dates: One-on-one, year round. Group classes begin first and third Mondays of each month. Cost: Most expensive $200 per week; lowest $115 per week. Contact: Roberto Rivas-Bastidas, C. Real de Guadalupe 55, Centro Cultural "El Puente," San Cristobal de Las Casas, Chiapas, Mexico, 29230; (011) 52-967-84157; Tel./fax (011) 52-967-83723.

Spanish Language and Cultural Immersion. Intensive Spanish language immersion program for all levels of Spanish speakers at the Center for Bilingual and Multicultural Studies in Cuernavaca. Language courses taught by native speakers with no more than 5 students per class. Housing with Mexican families. Field trips and on-site Resident Director. Six credits: graduate, undergraduate.

Dates: May 28-Jun 28, 1996. Cost: Approx. $3,000. Includes airfare, room and board, local transportation, tuition, books, health insurance, and miscellaneous expenses. Contact: SUNY Brockport, Office of International Education, 350 New Campus Dr., Brockport, NY 14420; (716) 395-2119, fax (716) 395-2606.

Spanish Language and Latin American Studies. Intensive Spanish language immersion program for all levels of Spanish speakers at the Center for Bilingual and Multicultural Studies in Cueranvaca. Language classes taught by native speakers with no more than 5 students per class. Housing with Mexican families. Field trips and on-site resident director. Fall, spring, and summer.

Dates: Sep 2-Dec 10 (fall); Jan (winter); Jan 12-May 1 (spring); Jun 30-Aug 6 (summer). Cost: Semester: Approx. $5,500; summer: Approx. $3,000. Includes tuition, airfare, room and board. Contact: SUNY Brockport, Office of International Education, 350 New Campus Dr., Brockport, NY 14420; (716) 395-2119, fax (716) 395-2606.

Spanish Language in Guanajuato. We work with our students one-on-one or in small groups (2 to 5 students), tailoring instruction to each student's needs. We teach people of all ages and from many nationalities. Highlights: homestays with families, sports, movies, field trips, hikes, cultural events—all this taking place in the most beautiful colonial setting of Mexico.

Dates: Year round. New classes begin every Monday. Cost: $925. Includes lifetime registration fee, group classes (5 sessions per day Monday-Friday), and a homestay with 3 meals daily for 4 weeks. Lower price for fewer weeks. Contact: Director Jorge Barroso, Instituto Falcon, A.C., Guanajuato, Gto. 36000 Mexico; Tel./fax (011) 52-473-2-36-94, www.infonet. com.mx/falcon.

Spanish Language Institute. Become a participant in the Mexican culture by studying Spanish in Cuernavaca at the Spanish Language Institute as an independent student on the dates of your choice or in a 23-day escorted group. Students and professionals from ages 18 to 80 at all language levels study 6 hours daily in classes of 5 students in a small school of excellent reputation dedicated to personal attention and professionalism. U.S. graduate and undergraduate credit (6 credits in 3 weeks) available. Caring family stays and full excursion program. Longer stays and additional credits also possible.

Dates: Escorted group: May 17, Jul 12, Dec 20 and 27, 1996. Independents can begin any Monday. Year round. Cost: $100 registration (insurance included), $150 per week tuition, $105-$154 per week for homestay, all meals, school transportation. Form a group of 12 and your trip is complimentary. Contact: Kay G. Rafool, Language Link Inc., P.O. Box 3006, Peoria, IL 61612; (800) 552-2051, fax (309) 673-5537; info@langlink.com, www.langlink. com.

UNC-Chapel Hill Semester/Year in Mexico. Study Spanish and Latin American studies in Mexico City at any language level. On-site orientation and outstanding civilization course with guest lecturers who are the academic and political leaders of the country. Excellent excursions available. Classes held at Universidad Nacional Autonoma de Mexico (UNAM) and Centro de Investigacion y Docencia Economicas (CIDE).

Dates: Mid-Aug-Dec, Jan-May. Cost: $3,100 per semester includes tuition and fees, orientation. Room and board approx. $2,500 per semester. Contact: Study Abroad Office, Dept. T, CB# 3130, 12 Caldwell Hall, Univ. of North Carolina, Chapel Hill, NC 27599-3130; (919) 962-7001, fax (919) 962-2262; abroad@unc. edu.

Univ. of Wisconsin-Madison's Summer in Oaxaca. Students live in a beautiful and historic setting with local families while they study Spanish language and Latin American literature and culture. All classes are taught in Spanish by local instructors under the direction of a Univ. of Wisconsin director. Includes excursions to local Indian villages and pre-Columbian ruins. Intermediate Spanish language ability required. Application deadline: First Friday in Mar. Late applications considered on a space-available basis.

Dates: Approx. late May-mid-Jul. Cost: Call for current information. Contact: Office of International Studies and Programs, 261 Bascom Hall, Univ. of Wisconsin, 500 Lincoln Dr., Madison, WI 53706; (608) 262-

2851, fax (608) 262-6998; abroad@macc. wisc.edu.

Universal Centro de Lengua. Universal offers Spanish language programs specifically tailored to meet the needs of each student. Spanish courses are offered at all levels, individually or in groups, and are complemented by diverse lectures. Classes range from 2 to 5 students and meet 5 hours daily with hourly breaks of 10 minutes.

Dates: Year round. Cost: Normal $140 per week, advanced $180 per week, professional $200 per week. Contact: Ramiro Cuellar Hernandez, Universal Centro de Lengua, J.H. Preciado #171, Col. San Anton, Cuernavaca, Morelos, Mexico; (011) 52-73-18-29-04 or 12-49-02, fax 18-29-10; universa@laneta.apc.org.

WSU Puebla Summer Program. The WSU Summer Program in Puebla provides an outstanding opportunity for students, teachers, and other interested individuals to study the Spanish language, gain the invaluable experience of living in another country, and earn college credit toward a degree or teaching certification. Students in the program spend 6 weeks in Puebla, either in the Hotel Colonial or in a private home with a Mexican family or both.

Dates: Jun 23-Aug 1, 1997. Cost: $1,600. Contact: John H. Koppenhaver, Wichita State Univ., Wichita, KS 67260-0005; (316) 978-3100, fax (316) 978-3234; koppenha@twsuvm.uc.twsu.edu.

Middle East

Friends World Program. A semester or year program in the Middle East at Friends World Center in Jerusalem consists of intensive seminars that introduce students to the culture of the Middle East. Field work, travel, and independent research are also offered. Sample topics include desert agriculture, archaeology, anthropology, journalism, public health, conflict resolution, religious studies. Fieldwork can be conducted in Israel, Jordan, and other countries and may earn 12-18 credits per semester.

Dates: Fall: mid-Sep-mid-Dec; spring: mid-Jan-mid-May. Cost: $10,770 per semester in 1996/1997. Includes tuition, travel, room and board, fees and books. Contact: James Howard, Friends World Program, 239 Montauk Hwy., Southampton, NY 11968; (516) 287-8475; jhoward@sand.liunet.edu.

Peace and Conflict in the Middle East. This 4-week, 6-credit traveling seminar is given in Jordan, the West Bank, Israel, and Egypt. The focus is on the intricate nature of the Arab-Israeli conflict and on the views of the four parties who entered into negotiations for peace. Participants arrange and pay for their own transatlantic flights. Ground transportation in private buses and housing in hotels throughout the seminar are arranged and covered by the program fee.

Dates: Jun 1-Jun 30, 1996. Cost: Undergraduate tuition for 6 credits: $2,766; graduate tuition for 6 credits: $3,000; program fee: $2,925. Contact: Daisy Fried, Syracuse Summer Abroad, Syracuse Univ., 119 Euclid Ave., Syracuse, NY 13244-4170; (315) 443-9419, fax (315) 443-4593; dsfried@suadmin.syr.edu.

Seminar in the Middle East. The Seminar in the Middle East includes 4 weeks of intensive study on the Baldwin Wallace College campus followed by a 6-week tour through Egypt, Jordan, Israel, and Turkey. The focus will be on the religious and cultural heritage of the Middle East and will include visits to historical sites in all 4 countries, with significant exposure to modern cultures as well.

Dates: Apr 1-Apr 24 (on campus), Apr 27-Jun 8 (overseas). Contact: Dorothy Hunter, Coordinator, The Study Abroad Center, Baldwin-Wallace College, 275 Eastland Rd.,

Berea, OH 44017; (216) 826-2231, fax (216) 826-3021; dhunter@rs6000.baldwin.edu.

The American Univ. in Dubai. Situated on the southern shore of the Arabian Gulf, AUD offers a comprehensive program in Middle Eastern Studies in one of the key commercial centers of the Middle East. The program opened in fall, 1996. Among the courses to be offered are: Arabic, Islamic Art and Architecture, Modern Middle Eastern History, Arabic Literature, Comparative Middle Eastern Cultures, Comparative Politics, Islam and Middle Eastern Culture, International Business.

Dates: Fall, winter, and spring terms. Ten-week programs. Cost: $4,560 includes tuition and fees, activities, textbooks, and housing. Contact: Office of International Programs, The American Univ. in Dubai, 3330 Peachtree Rd., NE, Atlanta, GA 30326; (800) 255-6839, fax (404) 364-6611.

Morocco

Arabic Language Institute in Fez. ALIF offers 3- and 6-week intensive courses in Modern Standard Arabic and Colloquial Moroccan Arabic throughout the year. All courses meet approx. 20 hours per week. Private and specialized courses can be arranged. Students may live with a Moroccan family or in a student residence.

Cost: 6,200 Moroccan Dirhams per 6-week course; 3,300 DH for 3-week course. Contact: Assistant to the Director, ALIF, B.D. 2136, Fez 3000, Morocco; alif@mbox.azure.net, www.zure.net/alif.

Univ. of Wisconsin-Madison's Summer in Morocco. Study at the Mohammed V Univ., the most prestigious institution of higher education in Morocco. Primary courses are taught in English on Moroccan history, culture, and society. Additional Moroccan Arabic course, and 1-week educational excursions. Initial 1-week family homestay, then stay with the family or live in university dormitories. Co-spon-

sored with Univ. of Wisconsin at Milwaukee. Application deadline: First Friday in Feb. Late applications considered on a space-available basis.

Dates: Late May-mid-Jul. Cost: Call for current information. Contact: Office of International Studies and Programs, 261 Bascom Hall, Univ. of Wisconsin, 500 Lincoln Dr., Madison, WI 53706; (608) 262-2851, fax (608) 262-6998; abroad@macc.wisc.edu.

Nepal

Cornell/Nepal Study Program. Join the first study abroad program in Nepal with courses taught by faculty of Tribhuvan National Univ., located in the medieval hill town of Kirtipur. Coursework includes Nepali language and the cultural and biological diversity of the Kathmandu Valley, culminating in a 1-month independent field study. Special program houses shared with Nepali students.

Dates: Aug-Dec or Jan-Jun. Cost: $13,300 per semester (1996-1997). Includes 3-week orientation, 2-week study tour/trek, tuition, fees, room and board, cultural and social activities. Airfare ($2,500), personal expenses (approx. $500) not included. Contact: Cornell Abroad, 474 Uris Hall, Cornell Univ., Ithaca, NY 14853-7601; (607) 255-6224, fax (607) 255-8700; CUAbroad@cornell.edu.

Sojourn Nepal. Sojourn Nepal is a 12-week program consisting of homestay, language study, apprenticeship, and trekking. Students are immersed in the culture of Nepal and learn a lot about themselves as they get to know their host country.

Dates: Fall and spring semesters. Cost: $4,500. Airfare not included. Contact: Jennifer Warren, American Director, Sojourn Nepal, 2440 N. 56th St., Phoenix, AZ 85008; Tel./fax (602) 840-9197.

Univ. of Wisconsin-Madison's College Year in Nepal. The program provides integrated language training, tutorial instruction, and inpendent fieldwork projects. Participants attend summer school in U.S. prior to the term abroad for intensive language study and orientation to South Asian life and cultures. The first semester begins with a homestay period, in a 1-month village-study tour. The entire second semester is devoted to fieldwork projects.

Dates: Summer school in Madison: early Jun-mid-Aug; academic program abroad: late Aug-Apr. Cost: One-way airfare from the U.S. West Coast to Nepal, room, board and pocket money while abroad. Summer school and related expenses additional. Call for current information. Contact: Office of International Studies and Programs, 261 Bascom Hall, Univ. of Wisconsin, 500 Lincoln Dr., Madison, WI 53706; (608) 262-2851, fax (608) 262-6998; abroad@macc.wisc.edu.

Netherlands

Comparative Health Care Systems. One-week intensive examination of the Netherlands health care system including lectures, site visits, panel discussions, and seminars. Focus on long-term care and chronic care including euthanasia as practiced in the Netherlands. Three graduate credits.

Dates: Jun 3-12, 1996. Cost: Approx. $2,300. Includes airfare, room, and breakfasts. Contact: SUNY Brockport, Office of International Education, 350 New Campus Dr., Brockport, NY 14420; (716) 395-2119, fax (716) 395-2606.

Leiden Univ. Language of instruction is English. Undergraduate program streams include Dutch culture and government, European politics and administration, global studies, elective program. Electives in the field of law, philosophy, social sciences and public administration, environmental studies, liberal arts; excursions, and guest lectures. Complete program information available through WWW.

Dates: Aug-late Jun. Cost: NGL12,000 (year), NGL6,000 (semester). Includes tuition fee, courses, electives, guest lectures, excursions, museum pass. Contact: Mrs. Els Bogaerts, MA, Coordinator, Study Abroad Program, Leiden Univ., P.N. van Eyckhof 3, P.O. Box 9515, 2300 RA Leiden, The Netherlands; (011) 31-71-527-2048 or (011) 31-71-527-7256, fax 527-26-15; elsbogaerts@rullet.leidenuniv.nl, www.leiden univ.nl.

MSC Program. This program offers agricultural economics and marketing, agricultural engineering, animal science, aquaculture, biotechnology, crop science, ecological agriculture, environmental sciences, geographic information systems, management of agricultural knowledge systems, soil and water, tropical forestry, urban environmental management.

Dates: Starts Sep, lasts 17 months. Cost: NLG12,000-NLG16,000 plus research costs NLG1,000-NLG5,000. Contact: Wageningen Agricultural Univ., Dean's Office for International Students, P.O. Box 453, 6700 AL Wageningen, The Netherlands; (011) 31-317-482680 or (011) 31-317-483618, fax (011) 31-317-484464, telex NL45854 luwag; jeanine hermans@doffs@sz.wau.nl., www.wau.nl/.

Netherlandic Studies Program in Contemporary Europe. This program offers students a unique opportunity to spend the spring semester in Amsterdam. Netherlands-SPICE is an area studies program focusing on the arts, history, culture, and language of the Netherlands. Students will also be able to take a course in European business.

Dates: Feb 19-Jun 8, 1996. Cost: Approx. $7,285. Includes board and room (not travel). Contact: Dr. K.J. Boot, Director, Dordt College, Sioux Center, IA 51250-1697; (712) 722-6263, fax (712) 722-1967; kboot@dordt.edu.

School of Child Neuropsychology. Advanced training for graduate students from all countries. Classes (Thursdays and Fridays) are taught in English. Requirement to apply: Master's degree in psychology, medicine, special education, speech pathology, or equivalent qualification. Module A: basics and child neuropsychological syndromes. Module B: child neuropsychological assessment and treatment. Diploma: Satisfactory standards in exams.

Dates: A: Sep-early Nov; B: Jan-early Mar. Cost: A: DFL4,300; B: DFL4,300; A and B: DFL7,800. Contact: Professor Dirk J. Bakker, Ph.D., Director, Paedological Institute, P.O. Box 303, 1115 ZG Duivendrecht, Netherlands; (Tuesday, Thursday, Friday) (011) 31-20-6982131, fax 31-20-6952541.

New Zealand

Foundation Cookery Skills. A 15-week intensive program taking students through the basics of French cuisine. Based on the text book of the Leith's School, London. The New Zealand certificate of wine also available as part of this program. Students also complete menu project and costings, hygiene, nutrition, and service culture components.

Dates: May 6, 1996; Aug 26, 1996; Jan 22, 1997. Cost: NZ$4,220 (includes tax). Contact: Celia Hay, Director, New Zealand School of Food and Wine, Box 25217, Christchurch, New Zealand; Tel./fax (011) 64-3-379-7501.

Institute for Study Abroad. The ISA cooperates with 3 universities in New Zealand to provide high quality academic programs (academic year, calendar year, and semester) for U.S. undergraduates. The ISA guarantees housing, aims to achieve full integration whenever possible, and offers a wide variety of student services during all phases of the study abroad experience.

Dates: Semester (Feb-Jul, Jul-Nov), academic year (Feb-Nov), calendar year (Jul-Jul). Deadlines: fall semester and academic year Mar 15, spring semester and calendar year Nov 15. Cost: Begins at $7,300 and $12,200 for semester and year programs respectively. Includes tuition, housing, predeparture preparation, ISIC, overseas orientation, domestic and overseas student services, farm visit, excursions, and transcript translation. Competitive roundtrip group flight fares arranged for all program participants. Some scholarships available. Contact: Institute for Study Abroad, Butler Univ., 4600 Sunset Ave., Indianapolis, IN 46208; (800) 858-0229, fax (317) 940-9704; study-abroad@butler.edu.

Norway

Camp Norway. Camp Norway is an innovative summer program combining fast-paced learning with the direct experience of living in Norway. Enjoy the majestic scenery of the western fjord district, the warmth and closeness of a small community, the hospitality of local Norwegians, and excellent education with individual attention. Field trips and other activities let you discover and explore many aspects of the Norwegian lifestyle. College and high school credit available.

Dates: Jul 2-Aug 1, 1996, Jul 1-Jul 31, 1997. Cost: $2,495 for Sons of Norway members, $2,595 for nonmembers. Scholarships available. (Prices subject to change if significant fluctuations in the exchange rate occur.) Contact: Liv Dahl, Sons of Norway, 1455 W. Lake St., Minneapolis, MN 55408; (800) 945-8851.

Norwegian Nature and Culture at Telemark College. Semester or year programs at Telemark College focus on the interaction of humans with their environment from a Scandinavian perspective. Classes consists of both Norwegians and non-Norwegians. The program focuses on the thoughts and attitudes of Norwegians regarding their cultural and environmental heritage and the way environmental protection and management are implemented in public, institutional, and private sectors. Courses include Norwegian Language and Culture, the Environment in Norway, Environmental Management, and in-depth field studies.

Dates: Aug 13-Dec 20 (fall); Jan 6-Jun 20

(spring). Cost: Approx. $4,260 (fall), $4,560 (spring), $8,820 (full year). These costs do not include airfare, food, books and materials, or personal expenses. Contact: Scandinavian Seminar, 24 Dickinson St., Amherst, MA 01002; (413) 253-9736, fax (413) 253-5282.

Scandinavian Urban Studies Term. Explore the values, culture, and history that shape Scandinavia's innovative strategies for social change. Courses include urbanization and development in Scandinavia, Scandinavia in the world, art and literature/perspectives on social change, and Norwegian language. Offered in cooperation with Univ. of Oslo, housing in student village with field study-travel to Stockholm, Sweden, and Tallin, Estonia, plus 2 weekend homestays in Norway. Full semester's credit. All majors. No language requirement.

Dates: Mid-Aug-late Nov. Cost: $9,400 (1997-98). Includes tuition, room and board, field trips. Contact: Elizabeth Andress, Assistant Director, HECUA, Mail #36, Hamline Univ., 1536 Hewitt Ave., St. Paul, MN 55104-1284; (612) 646-8832 or (800) 554-1089, fax (612) 659-9421; hecua@hamline.edu, www.hamline.edu/~hecua.

Univ. of Oslo International Summer School. The International Summer School of the Univ. of Oslo in Norway welcomes qualified participants from all parts of the world from late Jun-early Aug. The ISS is a center for learning in an international context, offering courses in the humanities, social sciences, and environmental protection to more than 500 students from over 80 nations every summer.

Dates: Jun 28-Aug 8, 1997. Cost: Approx. $2,400 (basic fees, room and board). Contact: JoAnn Kleber, Administrator, Univ. of Oslo, International Summer School, North American Admissions-A, St. Olaf College, 1520 St. Olaf Ave., Northfield, MN 55057-1098; (800) 639-0058 or (507) 646-3269, fax (507) 646-3549; iss@stolaf.edu.

Poland

Penn-in-Warsaw. For students interested in Polish history and culture, as well as international relations, economics, and other business disciplines. Taught in English, this program will acquaint students with the political and economic changes occurring in Poland and provide insight into the conditions for doing business in a changing economy. Short-term internships with Polish or joint-venture institutions will complement class instruction.

Dates: Jun 21-Jul 30. Cost: Tuition $3,250; housing $400. Contact: Penn Summer Abroad, College of General Studies, Univ. of Pennsylvania, 3440 Market St., Suite 100, Philadelphia, PA 19104-3335; (215) 898-5738, fax (215) 573-2053.

Polish Language and Culture. Jagiellonian Univ. (founded in 1364) offers intensive and non-intensive Polish language courses; 8 levels; academic methods. Courses on Polish history, literature, art, economy, politics, folklore, etc. Cultural program; trips to places of interest. Up to 8 credits for the language and/or 6 credits for other programs (transcripts of studies issued).

Dates: Four weeks: Jul 4-Aug 31; 6 weeks: Jul 4-Aug 14; 3 weeks: Jul 4-24, Jul 28-Aug 17. Cost: Four weeks $940 plus $30 registration fee; 6 weeks $1,220 plus $30; 3 weeks $690 plus $30. Room, board and tourist program included. Contact: Ewa Nowakowska, Program Director, Summer School, ul. Garbarska 7a, 31-131, Krakow, Poland; (011) 48-12-213692, fax 227701; uknowako@cyf-kr.edu.pl, www.if.uj.edu.pl/uj/sl.

Portugal

Univ. of Wisconsin-Madison's Study Abroad in Portugal. Study at the Univ. of Coimbra, one of the world's oldest universities, founded in 1285. Students enroll in the Portuguese Language and Culture course for international students in the Faculty of Arts. Courses in Portuguese grammar, conversation, composition, history, art, geography. Advanced study includes linguistics and literature. Students with advanced language skills may register for regular university courses. Application deadline: Second Friday in Oct for spring, first Friday in Feb for fall or year.

Dates: Mid-Oct-mid-Jun. Semester or year option. Cost: Call for current information. Contact: Office of International Studies and Programs, 261 Bascom Hall, Univ. of Wisconsin, 500 Lincoln Dr., Madison, WI 53706; (608) 262-2851, fax (608) 262-6998; abroad@macc.wisc.edu.

Russia

OSU-Purdue-Emory Pushkin Program. Semester and 10-month programs. Russian language study at the Pushkin Institute in Moscow, the premier educational facility of its kind in Russia. Group travel in and outside Moscow (including St. Petersburg) complements excellent instruction at the institute. Flexible homestay/dormitory living arrangement. Full-time on-site resident director oversees all aspects of program. Accredited and affordable.

Dates: Autumn 1996: Sep 1-Dec 23; spring 1997: Feb 1-May 23; 10-month: Sep 1, 1996-May 23, 1997. Cost: Semester programs: Approx. $3,600 plus OSU tuition (undergraduate $1,028; graduate $1,494), and an OSU admission fee ($30). Does not include transatlantic transportation, insurance, or personal expenses. Ten-month program: Approx. $6,500 plus OSU tuition for 3 quarters ($4,482), and a $30 OSU admission fee. Does not include transatlantic transportation, insurance, or personal expenses. All costs include meal and hotel expenses for group orientation in New York and subsequent transport to the Pushkin Institute, all costs (room and meals) in and around Russia (excluding personal costs), excursions in

Moscow, 1-week travel in Russia, and departure from Russia. Contact: Gail E. Lewis, Dept. of Slavic and East European Languages and Literatures, The Ohio State Univ., 232 Cunz Hall, 1841 Millikin Rd., Columbus, OH 43210; (800) 678-6139, fax (614) 688-3107; glewis.-13@magnus.acs.ohio-state.edu.

St. Petersburg State Univ. Designed to meet the needs of students with as little as 2 semesters of college-level Russian. The curriculum focuses on contemporary Russian language, culture, and politics. All courses taught at St. Petersburg State Univ. Resident director arranges excursions and volunteer/internship assignments for students. Housing in the Chaika, an apartment complex on the beach of the Gulf of Finland. Semester and summer program available.

Dates: Fall semester: Aug-Dec; spring semester: Feb-mid-May; summer program: late May-mid-Jul. Cost: $6,700 (spring 1997 fee) includes tuition, registration fees, houisng, excursions, visa, ISIC card, airfare, partial insurance coverage. Contact: IPA, Univ. of Illinois at Urbana-Champaign, 115 International Studies Bldg., 910 S. 5th St., Champaign, IL 61820; (800) 531-4404, fax (217) 244-0249; ipa@uiuc.edu.

UNC-Chapel Hill Semester in Rostov. Rostov-on-Don, 500 miles south of Moscow, is in an agricultural and relatively apolitical region of Russia. For intensive language and culture study, Rostov State Univ. provides an excellent teaching faculty, small classes, and comfortable accommodations for advanced students of Russian language. Four previous semesters of study required. Juniors, seniors, and grads preferred.

Dates: Sep-Dec, late Jan-mid-May, summer program Jun-mid-Jul. Cost: $3,100 includes tuition, fees, room, excursions. Contact: Study Abroad Office, Dept. T, CB# 3130, 12 Caldwell Hall, Univ. of North Carolina, Chapel Hill, NC 27599-3130; (919) 962-7001, fax (919) 962-2262; abroad@unc.edu.

Slovak Republic

European Studies. One-year program consisting of 3 separate but overlapping and complementary modules taught over 3 semesters: 1) European Cultural and Social History , 2) European Political Culture, 3) European Cooperation and Integration. The modules can be taken separately. Applicants for the program must have completed undergraduate university education. The program is conducted in English. Each academic year starts with an orientation week.

Dates: Module 1: Oct-Dec, Module 2: Jan-Mar, Module 3: Apr-Jun. Cost: $1,500 for 1 module, $4,000 for 3 modules (whole academic year). Contact: Barbara Jakubíková, Program Assistant, Academia Istropolitana, Hanulova 5/B P.O. Box 92, 840 02 Bratislava, Slovak Republic; (011) 42-7-785117, fax (011) 42-7-785341, 785117; eurost@acadistr.sk.

South Africa

Post-Apartheid South Africa. The program focuses on the politics, economics, ecology, history, and geography of post-apartheid South Africa. Participants will visit Johannesburg, Peoria, Durban, Cape Town, and the Pilanesberg Game Reserve. The program will be led by Dr. Donald N. Rallis, a South African geographer who has led 4 previous study tours in Southern Africa.

Dates: May 12-Jun 3, 1997 (subject to confirmation). Cost: $3,800 per person, double occupancy. Includes transportation from Washington, DC, accommodations, tours, and breakfasts. Contact: Dr. Donald N. Rallis, Dept. of Geography, Mary Washington College, Fredericksburg, VA 22401; (540) 654-1491; drallis@mwc.edu.

Spain

BCA Program in Barcelona. Earn 14-16 credits per semester at Universidad de Barcelona, with a 4-week intensive language training and orientation, field trips, and an extended study tour to Madrid and Toledo or Andulcía. Internships and practica available. Students from all U.S. colleges and universities accepted. Intermediate level college Spanish required. Courses in all academic disciplines taught by university professors. Cost includes international transportation, room and board, tuition, insurance, group travel in country.

Dates: Sep 8-Jan 25 (fall), Jan 18-Jun 5 (spring), Sep 8-Jun 5 (year). Cost: $17,345 (academic year 1996-1997); $9,645 (semester 1996-1997). Includes international transportation, room and board, tuition, insurance, group travel in country. Contact: Beverly S. Eikenberry, Box 184, Manchester College, North Manchester, IN 46962; (219) 982-5238, fax (219) 982-7755; bca@manchester.edu, http://studyabroad.com/bca.

Hispalengua Spanish for Foreigners. Small groups with qualified teachers, intensive courses from 2 weeks in selected homestays or hotels. We specialize in Spanish for young American students and provide personal escorts and introductions to local young people.

Dates: Year round. Cost: PTS170,000 for 4 weeks tuition and full board. Contact: Hispalengua, Julio Lalmolda, San Miguel 16, 500 001 Zaragoza, Spain; (011) 34-76-221810 or 211120, fax 212010.

Hispanic Studies Program. Collaboration of the Univ. of Virginia and Valencia, offering summer, fall, spring, and year programs for undergraduates; summer only for teachers of high school Spanish. Located in Valencia, on the Mediterranean coast of Spain, we offer homestays, and classes taught by Spanish professors in language, literature, history, art, and culture.

Cost: Summer: $3,330; fall $5,525; spring $6,035; year $9,725 includes roundtrip from NY, room and board, tuition, insurance, and use of Univ. of Valencia facilities. Contact: F. Operé, Univ. of Virginia, 115 Wilson Hall,

Charlottesville, VA 22903; (804) 924-7155; aam4s@faraday.clas.virginia.edu.

In-Country Language Courses. The courses of Don Quijote, Europe's largest specialist in in-country Spanish language courses, vary from 2-36 weeks intensive Spanish, DELE (official diploma preparation), Spanish plus specialization (business, tourism, international secretary), refresher courses for teachers of Spanish, flight attendant course, combination courses, tailor-made individual courses, summer and Christmas courses.

Dates: Year round. Cost: Depends upon course, duration, and accommodations. Contact: Don Quijote, Central Promotion Office, Ref. USTA96, Ms. Elvira Zingone, Student Services, Apdo. de correos 333, 37080 Salamanca, Spain; (011) 34-23-268860, fax 268815; don quijote@offcampus.es.

International Program in Toledo. Participants with 2 years of Spanish select courses to suit individual needs from a wide spectrum of the humanities taught in Spanish. Summer term requires only 1 year of Spanish. Monday-Thursday courses are enhanced by excursions. Housing available in an historic residence or with Spanish host families. Univ. of Minnesota accredited.

Dates: 1997-98 fall and/or spring semesters, summer term. Cost: $8,250 (fall or spring), $3,400 (summer). Includes tuition, study abroad and registration fees, room and board, and one-day excursions. Contact: The Global Campus, Univ. of Minnesota, 102T Nicholson Hall, 216 Pillsbury Dr. SE, Minneapolis, MN 55455-0138; (612) 625-3379, fax (612) 626-8009; globalc@tc.umn.edu, www.isp.umn.edu.

La Coruna Summer Program. Intensive language program providing participants with opportunity to study Spanish language, civilization, and culture in one of the most beautiful regions in Spain. Cultural immersion is further achieved through homestays with Spanish families. Cultural excursions include

Madrid and nearby Santiago de Compostela, site of the famous pilgrimage of Saint James.

Dates: Approx. Jul 1-31. Cost: $1,700 (tuition, room and board). Contact: Stacia Zukroff, Study Abroad/Exchange Advisor, Central Washington Univ., Office of International Studies and Programs, 400 E. 8th Ave., Ellensburg, WA 98926-7408; (509) 963-3615, fax (509) 963-1558; zukroff@cwu.edu.

Painting in Barcelona. A celebrated Spanish faculty made up of Tom Carr and Carme Miquel will conduct a 3-week advanced painting workshop at the spacious studio of Escola d'Arts Plastiques i Disseny "Llotja." Included are 3 museum tours to the Antonio Tapies Foundation, the Miro Foundation, and the Picasso Museum. Three credits.

Dates: Jun 21-Jul 13, 1997. Cost: $2,250. Includes double occupancy rooms, continental breakfast daily, and 3 tours. Contact: Dora Riomayor, Director of International Studies, School of Visual Arts, 209 E. 23rd St., New York, NY 10010-3994; (212) 592-2543.

Penn-in-Alicante. For students interested in the language, literature, and culture of Spain, this program combines classroom instruction with visits to points of cultural and historical interest, including Madrid and Toledo. Students live with local families.

Dates: Jun 25-Jul 26. Cost: Tuition $2,840; room and board $1,500; travel $890. Contact: Penn Summer Abroad, College of General Studies, Univ. of Pennsylvania, 3440 Market St., Suite 100, Philadelphia, PA 19104-3335; (215) 898-5738, fax (215) 573-2053.

Semester in Spain. Study Spanish in Seville for a semester, a year, a summer term, or our new January term. Earn 12-16 credits per semester, 4-8 for summer terms or January term. Classes are offered for beginning, intermediate, and advanced Spanish language students. Students live with Spanish families. Outstanding professors, small classes, and lots of fun. Approximately 50 students each semester.

Dates: Fall: Aug 27-Dec 18, spring: Jan 29-May 22, summer: May 28-Jun 19 and/or Jun 30-Jul 23, Jan 7-25. Cost: Fall or spring: $7,500. Includes room and board, tuition, books. Summer and Jan: $2,000 (1 term), $4,000 (2 terms). Airfare not included. Contact: Debra Veenstra, U.S. Coordinator, Semester in Spain, 6601 W. College Dr., Dept. TA, Palos Heights, IL 60463; (800) 748-0087 or (708) 396-7440, fax (708) 385-5665; spain@trnty.edu.

Simmons College in Córdoba. The Simmons in Córdoba Program, sponsored by Simmons College, offers students the opportunity to live and study—for either a semester or an academic year—in one of Spain's oldest and historically most important cities. Open to undergraduates and MA students. Fields: (Spanish) Foreign Language. Internships available for undergraduates.

Dates: Fall: Sep 3-Dec 18, 1997. Spring: Jan 12-Apr 30, 1998. Application deadline: Mar 30 (Fall); Oct 15 (Spring). Late applications are considered on a space available basis. Cost: $12,174 per semester (1996-1997). Contact: Professor Susan Keane, Foreign Study Advisor, or Racquel María Halty, Program Director, Simmons College, Foreign Languages and Literatures, Boston, MA 02115; fax (617) 521-3199; swilliams2@vmsvaxsimmons.edu.

Spanish and Basque Studies (Bilbao). Bilbao offers intensive language studies (Spanish or Basque) fulfilling up to 2 years of university language requirements in 1 semester, plus courses in history, political science, art, culture, economics, teacher education, literature, etc. Program organized field trips, housing, and many local university activities at this seaside city.

Dates: Fall semester: Aug 26-Dec 12, 1997; spring semester: Jan 7-May 13, 1998. Cost: Fall or spring semester: $3,950; year: $6,450. Contact: University Studies Abroad Consortium (USAC), Univ. of Nevada, Reno #323, Reno, NV 89557-0093; (702) 784-6569, fax (702) 784-6010; usac@admin.unr.edu, www.scs.unr.edu/~usac.

Spanish and Basque Studies (San Sebastian). San Sebastian offers intensive language (Spanish or Basque): Up to 2 years of university language requirements may be met in 1 semester plus courses in history, literature, political science, economics, art, teacher education, etc. Program organized field trips to Madrid and elsewhere, housing, and many local university activities in this beautiful seaside resort.

Dates: Summer sessions: May 27-Jul 1 and Jun 27-Jul 30 and Jul 30-Aug 28, 1997; fall semester: Aug 26-Dec 12, 1997; spring semester: Jan 7-May 13, 1998. Cost: Each summer session: $1,770; fall or spring semester: $5,690; year: $8,870; $3,380 both sessions. Contact: University Studies Abroad Consortium (USAC), Univ. of Nevada, Reno #323, Reno, NV 89557-0093; (702) 784-6569, fax (702) 784-6010; usac@admin.unr.edu, www.scs.unr.edu/~usac.

Spanish and Hispanic Studies. Frequently called Spain's leading school of Spanish, Malaca Instituto has a special program combining Spanish from beginner to advanced level with study of Spanish culture, politics, and way of life. Term I: General Spanish. Term II: Advanced Spanish and Hispanic Studies. All accommodation options and comprehensive activities program.

Dates: Term I: 16 weeks from Sep 2, 1996, term II: 20 weeks from Jan 6, 1997. Cost: Course: Term I Pts247,900, term II Pts350,000, Accommodations: residence, host families, student apartments: from Pts 62,300 for 4 weeks. Contact: Bob Burger, Marketing Director, Malaca Instituto, c/Cortada 6, Cerrado de Calderon, 29018 Malaga, Spain; (011) 34-5-229-32-42, fax (011) 34-5-229-63-16.

Spanish in Malaga. Frequently called Spain's leading school of Spanish, Malaca Instituto offers general Spanish courses in small groups year round at all levels. We have many European and Japanese students but very few Americans. Facilities include video rooms, cinema, language lab, self-access study center, bar, restaurant, pool, and on-site center, bar, restaurant, pool, and on-site residential accommodations. We organize a comprehensive program of cultural and social activities.

Dates: Every 2 weeks from Jan 8, 1996 and Jan 6, 1997. Cost: Course: from Pts72,900 for 4 weeks, Accommodations: residence, host families, student apartments: from Pts62,300 for 4 weeks. Contact: Bob Burger, Marketing Director, Malaca Instituto, c/Cortada 6, Cerrado de Calderon, 29018 Malaga, Spain; (011) 34-5-229-32-42, fax (011) 34-5-229-63-16.

Spanish Language Studies. Four-week intensive language and culture studies program in Asturias and Andalusia, Spain. Open to students at all levels. Field trips. Six credit hours: undergraduate, graduate.

Dates: Late Jun-late Jul. Cost: Approx. $2,700. Airfare not included. Contact: Office of International Education, SUNY New Paltz, HAB 33, New Paltz, NY 12561; (914) 257-3125, fax (914) 257-3129; international@ newpaltz.edu, www.newpaltz.edu/oie.

Students in Spain. Bravo Tours is a tour operator specializing in programs to Spain for high school and college students organized and chaperoned by your own school's teachers. Our programs cover Madrid, Barcelona, Mallorca, Toldeo, Avila, Segovia, Tenerife, Santiago, Sevilla, Granada, and more.

Contact: See our website at www. bravotours.com or call us at (800) 272-8674.

Study in Oviedo. Fall or spring programs in Spanish language, culture, and civilization at the Universidad de Oviedo Cursos Para Extranjeros. Students share apartments and prepare their own meals, 12-15 undergraduate credits per semester. Qualifications: Junior or above; 2 or more years college-level Spanish or the equivalent.

Dates: Fall: mid-Sep-late Dec; spring: mid-Jan-late May. Cost: Approx. $4,700 per semester. Includes tuition, fees, room and board, and insurance. (Non-New York state residents add $2,450.) Contact: Office of International Education, SUNY New Paltz, HAB 33, New Paltz, NY 12561; (914) 257-3125, fax (914) 257-3129; international@newpaltz.edu, www.new paltz.edu/oie.

Study in Seville. Fall, spring, or academic year programs in Spanish language, culture, and civilization at the Universidad de Sevilla Cursos Para Extranjeros. Family owned student housing, native resident director, field trips, on-site orientation, 12-18 undergraduate credits per semester. Qualifications: junior or above; 5 semesters college-level Spanish or equivalent.

Dates: Fall: late Sep-late Dec; spring: mid-Jan-early Jun. Cost: Approx. $5,400 (fall); $6,000 (spring). Includes tuition, fees, orientation, room and board, and insurance. (Non-New York residents add $2,450 per semester.) Contact: Office of International Education, SUNY New Paltz, New Paltz, HAB 33, New Paltz, NY 12561; (914) 257-3125, fax (914) 257-3129; international@newpaltz.edu, www.newpaltz.edu/oie.

Summer Spanish Courses for Older Teenagers. Frequently called Spain's leading school of Spanish, Malaca Instituto offers a special program designed specifically for young people (16-22 years). It combines serious study of Spanish with sports and cultural activities. Accommodations in our on-site residence or host families. Facilities include: video rooms, cinema, language lab, self-access study center, bar, restaurant, and pool.

Dates: Jun 24, Jul 8, Jul 22, Aug 5, Aug 19, 1996; Jun 23, 1997, Jul 7, Jul 21, Aug 4, Aug 18. Cost: Course: from Pts40,000 for 2 weeks, Accommodations: residence, host families, student apartments: from Pts32,540 for 2 weeks. Contact: Bob Burger, Marketing Director, Malaca Instituto, c/Cortada 6, Cerrado de Calderon, 29018 Malaga, Spain; (011) 34-5-229-32-42, fax (011) 34-5-229-63-16.

Summer, Semester and Year Programs. A graduate and undergraduate program at the

Universidad Compultense de Madrid for students interested in studying courses in language, literature, culture and civilization, composition, art history, philosophy of Spain. Students are taught by full-time faculty members from the Universidad Compultense de Madrid, the most prestigious university in Spain. A lot of extra activities and excursions are organized for students.

Dates: Summer program: Jul; semester: fall, winter, spring. Cost: Summer: total cost from $1,985 including airfare; year: $10,250 total cost including airfare. Contact: Modern Language Studies Abroad, P.O. Box 623, Griffith, IN 46319; Tel./fax (219) 838-9460.

The Center for Cross-Cultural Study. Since 1969, CC-CS has offered quality summer, semester, January, and academic-year study abroad programs in the vibrant city of Seville. All levels of Spanish offered during 3 1/2-week summer sessions; intermediate and advanced levels during the academic year. All courses taught in Spanish: language, literature, civilization, history, art, politics, sociology, business, economics, marketing, and current events. Internships, independent research, or university study for qualified students. Homestay and study tours included. Credits transferable. Financial aid available.

Dates: Jun, Jul, Sep-Dec, Jan, Feb-May. Cost: Fall: $7,300; spring: $7,395; academic year: $14,660; Jan: $1,865; summer: $1,755 per session or $3,380 for both sessions. Includes tuition, room and board, laundry, study tours, activity fees. Contact: In the U.S.: CC-CS, Dept. T, 446 Main St., Amherst, MA 01002; (413) 256-0011 or (800) ESPANA-1, fax (413) 256-1968. In Spain: CC-CS, Calle Harinas, 18, 41001 Sevilla, Spain; (011) 34-5-422-4107, fax (011) 34-5-422-9204; www.cccs.com.

The Ecology of Spain. This 6-credit program allows students to examine and photograph the Atlantic and Mediterranean ecosystems in northern Spain. The program is for students who enjoy engaging in challenging, outdoor physical activities and are able to take an ecol-ogy course taught in Spanish. Intermediate and advanced language courses complement the ecology course. Participants arrange and pay for their own transatlantic flights. Ground transportation in private buses and housing throughout the traveling seminar are arranged and covered by the program fee.

Dates: May 26-Jul 5, 1996. Cost: Undergraduate tuition for 6 credits: $2,766; program fee: $2,540. Contact: Daisy Fried, Syracuse Summer Abroad, Syracuse Univ., 119 Euclid Ave., Syracuse, NY 13244-4170; (315) 443-9419, fax (315) 443-4593; dsfried@suadmin.syr.edu.

UNC-Chapel Hill Summer in Madrid. This summer session will offer beginning and intermediate intensive language and culture study at the Center for International Studies, Madrid. Students will spend the first week in Sitges on the Mediterranean Coast, then proceed to Madrid where they live with host families for the next 5 weeks. Excellent excursions are included as part of the culture and civilization course.

Dates: Late May-Jun. Cost: Approx. $3,700 for tuition, fees, room and board, excursions. Contact: Study Abroad Office, Dept. T, CB# 3130, 12 Caldwell Hall, Univ. of North Carolina, Chapel Hill, NC 27599-3130; (919) 962-7001, fax (919) 962-2262; abroad@unc.edu.

Univ. of Salamanca. Founded in the 13th century, the Univ. of Salamanca is one of the most distinguished centers of learning in Europe. SUNY Cortland is celebrating the 30th consecutive year in this "City of the Golden Stones." The lives of Cervantes, Lope de Vega, Santa Teresa, and Miguel de Unamuno were all linked to the Univ. of Salamanca. Fields of study include Spanish language and literature, humanities, social sciences. Upper division and some qualified sophomores may apply. Requires at least 4 semesters college-level Spanish for fall, 6 semesters for spring. Homestays.

Dates: Fall: early Sep-mid-Dec; spring: early Jan-mid-Jun. Cost: Fall 1996 estimate: $4,007, spring 1997 $4,716. Includes full-day orientation before departure, application fee, room and food allowance, mandatory Spanish insurance, airfare, transportation from Madrid to Salamanca, books and supplies, repatriation, insurance, walking tour of Salamanca, 2 excursions, administrative fees. SUNY tuition additional. Contact: Dr. John Ogden, Director, Office of International Programs, Box 2000, SUNY at Cortland, Cortland, NY 13045; (607) 753-2209, fax (607) 753-5989; tonerp@snycorva.cortland.edu.

Sweden

Uppsala Univ. International Summer Session (UISS). Sweden's oldest academic summer program focuses on learning the Swedish language. All levels from beginners to advanced. Additional courses in Swedish history, social institutions, arts in Sweden, Swedish film. Excursions every Friday. Extensive evening program includes both lectures and entertainment. Single rooms in dormitories or apartments. Open to both students and adults. Credit possible.

Dates: Jun 22-Aug 15; Jun 22-Jul 18; Jul 20-Aug 15, 1997. Cost: SEK21,000 (approx. $3,000) for the 8-week session, SEK12,000 (approx. $1,715) for the 4-week session. Includes room, some meals, all classes, evening and excursion program. Contact: Dr. Nelleke Dorrestÿn, Uppsala Univ. Int. Summer Session, Box 513, 751 20 Uppsala, Sweden; (011) 31-71-541 4955, fax 71-5417705; nduiss@worldaccess.nl.

Switzerland

American Studies. Five months of studies at the undergraduate level recognized by American accredited universities as one academic year in terms of transfer credits (up to 36). Learn French or a get a European background in an international environment.

Dates: End of Jan-Jun or Aug-Dec. Cost: Tuition approx. $8,000. Various lodgings available. Contact: Lemania College, Miss E. Perni, International Admissions Office, Chemin de Préville 3, 1001 Lausanne, Switzerland; (011) 41-21-320-15-01, fax (011) 41-21-312-67-00; hirtlemania@fasnet.ch.

Bookbinding and Book Restoration. Centro del bel libro is a professional school for artisanal bookbinding and book restoration. Courses are offered on the quarter system.

Dates: Call or write for information. Cost: Call or write for information. Contact: Christina Bordoli, Director, Centro del bel libro, Ascona, 6612 Ascona, via Collegio, Centro culturale B. Berno, Switzerland; (011) 41-91-791-72-36, fax 791-72-56.

Cornell in Geneva. Spend a full academic year studying at the Univ. of Geneva through Cornell. Three-week intensive language and culture orientation, full university curriculum of study, field trips, excursions. Harvard Model United Nations participation, non-credit internships with international agencies. Housing at international student village. Four semesters of university-level French required.

Dates: Mid-Sep-mid-Jul. Cost: $26,600 (1996-1997). Includes tuition and fees, housing, health insurance, field trips, excursions, orientation, instruction, and activities. Contact: Cornell Abroad, 474 Uris Hall, Cornell Univ., Ithaca, NY 14853-7601; (607) 255-6224, fax (607) 255-8700; CUAbroad@cornell.edu.

Franklin College—Switzerland. Opportunities for study abroad for year, semester, and summer. Transfer opportunities available. Subjects available: Art, Art History, Communications, French Language, German Language, History, International Business, International Relations, Italian Language, Literature, Music, Political Science, Social Sciences. Middle states accredited.

Dates: Summer session I: May 20-Jun 20; Summer session II: Jun 24-Jul 25; fall 1996: Aug 26-Dec 20; spring 1997: Jan 14-May 9. Cost: Tuition: $7,620 per semester; residence: $2,800 per semester; academic travel: $1,600 per semester. Contact: James O'Hara, Associate Director of Admission, Franklin College-Switzerland, 135 E. 65th St., New York, NY 10021; (212) 772-2090, fax (212) 772-2718.

Intensive French. Founded in 1908, Lemania College is located in the city of Lausanne in a peaceful setting on the shore of Lake Geneva. The professional team of experienced teachers, the individual syllabuses, the computer-assisted language learning method, and the French-speaking area will bring students up to their expected level for official examinations. Leisure activities, sports, and excursions available.

Dates: Year round. Cost: Per week: tuition $450; lodging in boarding house $800, with family: $400; in apartment $170. Contact: Lemania College, Miss E. Perni, International Admissions Office, Chemin de Préville 3, 1001 Lausanne, Switzerland; (011) 41-21-320-15-01, fax (011) 41-21-312-67-00; hirtlemania@fasnet.ch.

Leysin American School in Switzerland. Leysin American School in Switzerland is a coeducational boarding school for grades 9-13. It offers a challenging curricula leading to the U.S. high school diploma, with Advanced Placement courses in all major subject areas, as well as the International Baccalaureate Diploma. The school has an excellent college placement record. Located in the Swiss Alps above Lake Geneva, LAS offers a balanced program of sports, activities, and excursions throughout Europe. There is a ski program in the winter. The 280 students represent 40 nationalities. Year-abroad students welcome.

Dates: Beg Sep-mid Jun. Cost: $22,640. Includes room and board, activities, excursions. Contact: Mrs. Carol Moore, Director of Admissions, Leysin American School, CH-1854 Leysin, Switzerland; (011) 41-25-34-15-85.

Univ. of Geneva Summer Courses. French language and civilization at all levels, beginners to advanced. All instructors have a university diploma. Excursions and visits to Geneva and its surroundings. Class of 15 to 20 students. Minimum age 17.

Dates: Jul 14-31; Aug 4-22; Aug 25-Sep 12; Sep 15-Oct 3. Cost: SF470 for 3 weeks (tuition). Contact: Mr. Gérard Benz, Univ. of Geneva, Summer Courses, rue de Candolle 3, CH-1211 Geneva 4, Switzerland; (011) 41-22-750-74-34, fax 750-74-39; bisatti@uni2a.unige.ch.

Webster Univ. in Geneva. Webster Univ. in Geneva has more than 400 students from 65 countries. Students may pursue a degree program leading to a BA, MA, or MBA. In addition, students may enroll for a study abroad semester or a year (summer session and some short-term options also available). All courses are taught in English and are fully accredited. Major areas of study include: business, computer science, economics, human resources management, psychology, sociology, international relations, refugee studies, management, marketing. A complete range of electives is also offered.

Dates: Five entry terms: late Aug, mid-Oct, mid-Jan, mid-Mar, late May. Cost: $20,000 (1996-97 academic year), $10,000 (semester 1996-97). Estimate includes tuition, room and board, books, local transportation, social activities. Contact: Study Abroad Office, Webster Univ., 470 E. Lockwood, St. Louis, MO 63119; (314) 968-6988 or (800) 984-6857, fax (314) 968-7119; brunote@websteruniv.edu. Visit our website at http://webster2.websteruniv.edu.

Thailand

College Year in Thailand. The program at Chiang Mai Univ. features Thai language study, subject tutorials, and a fieldwork project. Students attend summer school in Madison before the term abroad for intensive Thai language study as well as cultural and academic orientation. Application deadline: Second Friday in Feb. Late applications are considered on a space-available basis.

Dates: Summer school in Madison Jun-mid-

Aug; academic year abroad late Aug-May. Cost: Call for current information. Contact: Office of International Studies and Programs, 261 Bascom Hall, Univ. of Wisconsin, 500 Lincoln Dr., Madison, WI 53706; (608) 262-2851, fax (608) 262-6998; abroad@macc.wisc.edu.

Southeast Asian Studies (Bangkok). Diverse courses in culture, language, economics, business, society, and religions provide a fascinating, well-balanced approach to Southeast Asia. Program-organized field trips, student residence halls, and many university activities at one of Thailand's most modern universities.

Dates: Summer session: Jun 6-Jul 30, 1997; fall semester: Aug 20-Dec 23, 1997; spring semester: Jan 9-May 12, 1998. Cost: One semester: $2,450; year: $4,100; summer session: $1,100. Contact: University Studies Abroad Consortium (USAC), Univ. of Nevada, Reno #323, Reno, NV 89557-0093; (702) 784-6569, fax (702) 784-6010; usac@admin.unr.edu, www.scs.unr.edu/~usac.

Turkey

Beloit College Exchange Program in Turkey. The meeting place of Asia, the Middle East, and Europe, Istanbul is a vibrant city where a vast array of experiences can be found. Courses for exchange students at Marmara Univ. include Turkish language, a seminar on Modern Turkish society, and 2 elective courses from economics, international relations, business, studio art, anthropology, sociology, and other social sciences.

Dates: Approx. Feb 5-Jun 12. Cost: Tuition $8,672, room and board $1,923. Contact: Dr. Terance W. Bigalke, Director, World Affairs Center, Beloit College, 700 College St., Beloit, WI 53511; (608) 363-2269, fax (608) 363-2689; bigalket@beloit.edu.

Live and Study in Istanbul. Here is your chance to live in Istanbul for 7 weeks while studying at Bogaziçi Univ. All courses taught in English by Bogaziçi faculty; a wide variety of courses are available. Resident director arranges orientation program and excursions. Housing in residence hall with full board plan. No knowledge of Turkish necessary.

Dates: Late Jun-mid-Aug. Cost: $2,800 includes tuition, registration, room and board, orientation, excursion, partial insurance coverage, support services. Contact: IPA, Univ. of Illinois at Urbana-Champaign, 115 International Studies Bldg., 910 S. 5th St., Champaign, IL 61820; (800) 531-4404, fax (217) 244-0249; ipa@uiuc.edu.

Uganda

Workcamps and Developmental Activities. Workcamps aim to: assist needy communities, bind communities together in all apects of life, create common understanding people to people, work for the welfare of African society and the world at large, and link an experience with comparible organizations in the world.

Dates: May, Sep, Dec. Cost: $200 per workcamp, lasts 14 days each. Contact: Mr. G. Stuart Semakula, National Chairman, Uganda Voluntary Workcamps Association, P.O. Box 3367, Kampala, Uganda; Fax (011) 256-41-234168/250668.

United Kingdom

Art and Design in Britain. Studio Art (including painting, sculpture, graphic and industrial design, ceramics, printmaking, film, etc.) programs offered at 5 British universities: Chelsea College of Art, De Montford Univ., Norwich School of Art, Univ. of Northumbria, and Univ. of Wolverhampton. Courses integrated with British students. Housing in university residence halls or shared apartments. Resident director organizes orientation program, monitors students' academic progress.

Dates: Sep-Dec, Jan-Jun. Cost: Varies by programs: semester $5,580-$9,880; year $12,300-$14,300. Contact: IPA, Univ. of Illinois at Urbana-Champaign, 115 International Studies Bldg., 910 S. 5th St., Champaign, IL 61820; (800) 531-4404, fax (217) 244-0249; ipa@uiuc.edu.

BA (Hons) Fine and Decorative Arts. A 3-year program validated by the Univ. of Manchester combining the teaching of the history of fine and decorative art. Theoretical and practical approaches are combined with the wealth of one of the great art capitals of the world and Sotheby's auction rooms to develop a range of academic and professional transferable skills.

Dates: Sep or Feb. Cost: $4,450 per module, 6 modules in total. Contact: Sotheby's Institute, 30 Oxford St., London W1N 9FL, England; (011) 44-171-323-5775, fax 171-580-8160; sothses@ibm.com.

BCA Program in Cheltenham. Earn 15-16 credits per semester at the Cheltenham and Gloucester College of Higher Learning, with a 2-week orientation in country, field trips, and an extended study tour to Wales or Kent. Courses in all academic disciplines including women's studies. Internships and practica available. Students accepted from all U.S. colleges and universities.

Dates: Sep 15-Dec 20 (fall), Feb 8-May 20 (spring), Sep 15-May 20 (year). Cost: $17,345 (academic year 1996-1997); $9,645 (semester 1996-1997). Includes international transportation, room and board, tuition, insurance, group travel in country. Contact: Beverly S. Eikenberry, Box 184, Manchester College, North Manchester, IN 46962; (219) 982-5238, fax (219) 982-7755; bca@manchester.edu, http://studyabroad.com/bca.

Binghamton Semester in London. An integrated study experience in which courses in literature, theater, art history, and English history are enriched by theater performances, in-city excursions, and out of town trips. An internship option provides career-related placements in British businesses and agencies. Apartments provided. Spring-only program, 4-credit courses.

Dates: Mid-Jan-early May. Cost: Approx.

$7,000. Includes tuition, airfare, housing, food, books, in-city transportation. Contact: Frank Newman, Director, English Dept., Binghamton Univ., P.O. Box 6000, Binghamton, NY 13902-6000; (607) 777-2087, fax (607) 777-2408; london@bingsuns.cc.binghamton.edu.

British Orientation Program. This 5-day program in London is a cultural orientation for students who will study at a university in Great Britain or Ireland during the regular academic year. The program introduces students to various aspects of the British culture through a series of lectures and activities that utilize the cultural resources of London. Class lectures and discussion will address cultural assumptions and misperceptions and will compare the U.S. and U.K. educational systems.

Dates: Approx. Sep 2-24. Cost: Approx. $795. Includes all educational and administrative costs, lodging and breakfast, and group cultural activities. Contact: Nancy Mitchell, Office of Study Abroad, 203-T Lippincott, The Univ. of Kansas, Lawrence, KS 66045.

British Studies at Oxford. A program at Corpus Christi College, Oxford Univ., offering graduate and undergraduate courses in art history, business, communication, education, English literature, drama, history, and political science. The program includes private room and board, theater and excursions.

Dates: Jun 30-Aug 10, 1996 or Jun 30-Jul 20; Jul 21-Aug 10. Cost: $2,800 for 3 weeks, 5,200 for 6 weeks. Contact: Margaret B. Pigott, Oakland Univ., 322 Wilson Hall, Rochester, MI 48309-4401; (810) 370-4131 or (810) 652-3405, fax (810) 650-9107; pigott@oakland.edu.

Crafts and Arts Courses. Week and weekend courses. Summer schools in art, ceramics, woodworking, textiles, sculpture, silver smithing, music, and art appreciation. One-, 2-, and 3-year diploma courses in conservation and restoration of antique furniture, clocks, ceramics, fine metalwork, and rare books and manuscripts; tapestry weaving (also 6-week modules); making early stringed musical instruments. Validation at postgraduate level is by the Univ. of Sussex.

Dates: Diploma courses start each year and end in July. Short courses year round. Cost: Diploma courses £6,498 per annum. Residential accommodations £2,802 per annum. Short courses (residential) 5 days £349, weekends £146, 7 days £469. Contact: Heather Way, Public Relations, West Dean College, West Dean, Chichester, W. Sussex PO18 0QZ, England; (011) 44-1243-811301, fax 811343; westdean@pavilion.co.uk.

Criminal Justice/Program in London. At Brunel Univ. in Northwest London: The English Criminal Justice System (4 credits), Criminal Justice Agency visitations and seminars (5 credits), and British Culture and Institutions (6 credits). Extensive field trips and full-time resident director. Off-campus housing. Fifteen undergraduate credits.

Dates: Sep 5-Dec 20 (fall); Jan 11-May 5 (spring). Cost: Approx. $7,500. Includes room and board, airfare and local transportation, books, tuition and miscellaneous expenses. Contact: SUNY Brockport, Office of International Education, 350 New Campus Dr., Brockport, NY 14420; (716) 395-2119, fax (716) 395-2606.

Cultural-Literary Tour to Scotland/England. Visit several locations throughout Scotland and England including Edinburgh, York Univ., Oxford Univ. (Mansfield College), and Imperial College. Courses in 19th- and 20th-century British writers. Three credits: graduate, undergraduate.

Dates: Jun 30-Jul 15, 1996. Cost: Approx. $2,600. Includes airfare and bus transportation, housing, site admission, plays, tours, and some meals. Contact: SUNY Brockport, Office of International Education, 350 New Campus Dr., Brockport, NY 14420; (716) 395-2119, fax (716) 395-2606.

Diploma of Higher Education in the Fine and

Decorative Arts. A 2-year program made up of 4 15-week semesters intended for future art world professionals. Modules are: Styles in Art, 17th- and 18th-Century Decorative Arts, 19th- and 20th-Century Decorative Arts, 19th- and 20th-Century Fine Art. It is possible and very common to take an individual module for credit.

Dates: A 2-year program starts in early Sep and mid-Feb each year. Cost: £4,450 per module. Includes tuition, field trips, sale catalogs. Accommodations and daily travel not included. Contact: Sotheby's Institute, 30 Oxford St., London W1N 9FL, England; (011) 44-171-323-5775, fax (011) 44-171-580-8160 for a copy of the current academic prospectus.

European Studies at Brunel Univ. Study British Society and the European Community as well as courses in a wide variety of disciplines such as business, government, psychology, and history at Brunel Univ. in Northwest London. Field trips and resident director. Off-campus housing. Fifteen undergraduate credits.

Dates: Sep 5-Dec 20 (fall); Jan 11-May 5 (spring). Cost: Approx. $7,000. Includes room and board, airfare, local transportation, tuition, and books. Contact: SUNY Brockport, Office of International Education, 350 New Campus Dr., Brockport, NY 14420; (716) 395-2119, fax (716) 395-2606.

Fashion Design/Fashion Merchandising and Communications. London College of Fashion is the only College in the British university sector to specialize in fashion. Located in the center of London, we offer you: a choice of 2 specialist programs, each covering seven subject areas; 16 credits per program; further courses from our range of 20 professional evening courses; internship opportunities, plus optional Paris field trip.

Dates: Fall semester: Sep 23-Dec 12, 1996; spring semester: Jan 6-Mar 27, 1997. Cost: 1996/1997 tuition fees £2,195 per 12-week semester. Airfare and accommodations not included. Contact: Jan Miller, Business Manager, DALI at London College of Fashion, 20 John

Princes St., London W1M 0BJ, England; (011) 44-171-514-7400, ext. 7411, fax (011) 44-171-514-7490.

General Studies (Brighton). Brighton offers courses in many disciplines: art, business, sports science, engineering, computing, geography, design, education, math, etc. Organized field trips, housing in student residence halls. Summer graduate program in teacher education. Only 45 minutes from London.

Dates: Summer: Jun 29-Aug 2, 1997; fall semester: Aug 31-Dec 14, 1997; spring: Jan 4-May 15, 1998. Cost: Fall or spring: $2,290; year: $5,225; summer: $1,250. Contact: University Studies Abroad Consortium (USAC), Univ. of Nevada, Reno #323, Reno, NV 89557-0093; (702) 784-6569, fax (702) 784-6010; usac@admin.unr.edu, www.scs.unr.edu/~usac.

General Studies (Reading). Reading offers courses in nearly every academic disciplines: art, business, literature, performing arts, engineering, computing, geography, education, agriculture, etc. Housing in student residence halls. Only 25 minutes from London.

Dates: Fall semester: Sep 11-Dec 12, 1997; winter: Jan 6-Mar 20, 1998; Apr 27-Jul 2, 1998. Cost: Fall semester: $3,450; winter or spring quarter: $2,950; year: $7,450. Contact: University Studies Abroad Consortium (USAC), Univ. of Nevada, Reno #323, Reno, NV 89557-0093; (702) 784-6569, fax (702) 784-6010; usac@admin.unr.edu, www.scs.unr.edu/~usac.

Harlaxton College. Harlaxton College is owned and operated by the Univ. of Evansville in Indiana. Therefore, all courses are U.S. accredited and usually transfer easily. Students live and study in a magnificent 19th-century Victorian manor house in the English Midlands. Assistance is available with air arrangements and airport pickup; optional field trips are available throughout England, Ireland, Scotland, Wales, and the Continent. Harlaxton is a full-service study abroad program with help every step of the way.

Dates: Fall 1996: Aug 30-Dec 12; spring 1997: Jan 10-Apr 24. Cost: $8,760 per semester (1995-96). Includes tuition, room and board. Contact: Suzy Lantz, Harlaxton Coordinator, Univ. of Evansville, 1800 Lincoln Ave., Evansville, IN 47722; (800) UKMANOR or (812) 479-2146; lw23@evansville.edu.

Institute for Study Abroad. The ISA cooperates with 30 universities in the U.K. to provide high quality academic year, semester, and term programs for U.S. undergraduates. The ISA guarantees housing, aims to achieve full integration whenever possible, and offers a wide variety of student services during all phases of the study abroad experience.

Dates: Semester/term/2-term (Sep-Dec, Jan-late Jun); academic year (Sep-late Jun). Deadlines: fall and year programs Apr 15, spring programs Oct 15. Cost: Begins at $6,495 and $11,995 (1995-96 fees) for term and year programs respectively. Includes tuition, housing, predeparture preparation, ISIC, one-way airfare, overseas orientation, domestic and overseas student services, family visit, excursions, and transcript translation. Some scholarships available. Contact: Institute for Study Abroad, Butler Univ., 4600 Sunset Ave., Indianapolis, IN 46208; (800) 858-0229, fax (317) 940-9704; study-abroad@butler.edu.

Ithaca College London Center. British and international faculty teach undergraduate courses in business, communications, humanities, music, social sciences, and theater. Field trips and excursions to various sites throughout London and the U.K. are an integral part of the curriculum. Internships are available to juniors and seniors majoring in art history, business, communications, economics, English, history, politics, psychology, sociology, and theater arts. A special intensive drama program is offered in the spring semester.

Dates: Aug 20-Dec 13, 1996 and/or Jan 7-May 1, 1997. Cost: Approx. $13,600 per semester. Includes tuition, fees, books, room and board, college-sponsored excursions, and airfare. Costs may vary depending on students' lifestyles and spending habits. Contact: Amy Sonnenfeld Teel, Assistant Director, International Programs, Ithaca College, 214 Muller Ctr., Ithaca, NY 14850-7150; (607) 274-3306, fax (607) 274-1515.

Lancaster Univ. Beautiful northern location near Lake District. Full year, fall, spring, pre-sessions options. Integration into academic, residential, sports, social life. Collegiate campus university. Housing guaranteed. Full range of arts, humanities, business, social and natural (including pre-med) science courses, women's studies, independent study, creative writing. Diverse student body, minority and disabled students welcome. Comprehensive orientation and support services. Alumni contacts, video available.

Dates: 1996-97 academic year: Jul 18-Aug 17 or Aug 22-Sep 21 (pre-sessional); Oct 1-Jun 27 (full year); Oct 1-Dec 13 (fall, 1 term); Jan 8-Jun 27 (spring, 2 terms). Cost: 1996-97 academic year: Approx. £875 (pre-sessional. Includes orientation, tuition, housing, meals, local transfers, excursions. Approx. £7,220 (full year), £3,000 (fall), £4,900 (spring). Includes orientation, tuition, housing, and meals. Contact: Ethel Sussman, North American Officer, 111 E. 10th St., New York, NY 10003; (212) 228-0321; 74544.1273@compuserve.com.

Le Cordon Bleu, L'Art Culinaire. Le Cordon Bleu in London offers the highest diploma in culinary education in just 9 months. Cuisine and pastry classes begin every 10 weeks. Summer abroad program—ICHP—in Paris and London. Catering program for professionals.

Dates: Jun 10-Aug 17, 1996. Trimesters begin every 10 weeks. Cost: From $6,000 to $30,000 for cuisine and pastry 9-month diploma. Contact: In U.S. call (800) 457-CHEF or fax (914) 426-0104. Le Cordon Bleu, 114 Marylebone Ln., WIM 6HH, London, England.

London. Full academic year or one trimester.

Courses are tailored for American students and are designed to take advantage of the London setting. Classes meet 3 or 4 times per week and students generally enroll in 3 or 4 courses. Academic focus is theater, literature, history, economics, and art.

Dates: Sep-Dec, 1996; Jan-Mar, 1997; Mar-Jun, 1997. Cost: Approx. $5,300 per term. Includes tuition, books, housing, meals, international student identity card, excursions, insurance, all-London transportation pass. Financial aid accepted. Contact: Linda Kopfer, Assoc. Director of Univ. Programs, American Heritage Association, 741 SW Lincoln St., Portland, OR 97201-3178; (800) 654-2051, fax (503) 295-5969; 96trab@amheritage.org.

London Study Program. The London Program is a dynamic study abroad program that brings the city into the classroom and the classroom out into the city. Program facilities are centrally located in newly renovated historic buildings in the Bloomsbury district of London near the British Museum and the Univ. of London student union. Courses are taught in literature, history, culture, art, theater, and contemporary society of England. Cosponsored by Univ. of Wisconsin at Madison.

Dates: Early Sep-mid-Dec (fall), mid-Jan-late Apr (spring). Cost: $5,900 per semester (WI residents). Includes tuition, apartment, excursions. Contact: Lawrence Roscioli, Director, L&S Off-Campus Programs, Univ. of Wisconsin at Milwaukee, P.O. Box 413, Milwaukee, WI 53201; (414) 229-5879, fax (414) 229-6827; overseas@csd.uwm.edu.

LSE International Summer Programs. The programs consist of 18 undergraduate-level courses in the areas of management, international relations, finance, and criminology. These are suitable for people wishing to broaden or update their knowledge of particular areas and graduates who wish to embark upon the study of a new or related field. There are also advanced executive seminars in health and management that are suitable for executives and graduates who already have some academic or practical experience in the field.

Dates: Various times between Jun 24 and Sep 6, 1996. Cost: £900 for one 3-week session; £1,400 for 2 sessions. Presessional English £300; advanced executive seminars £1,850; International Pharmaceutical Regulation and Business £2,000; Options for Financing Health in Developing Countries £1,950; Economic Evaluation of Medical Therapies and Other Healthcare Technologies £2,680. Contact: Continuing and Professional Unit, LSE, Houghton St., London WC2A 2AE, England; (011) 44-171-955-7227; p.myrmus@lse.ac.uk.

MA in Fine and Decorative Art. A 15-month master's degree combining academic and practical approaches to the study of the fine and decorative arts—a unique combination at this level. The timetable is structured around an active weekly program of lectures, seminars, and tutored visits to museums, galleries, and historic houses in London and beyond. It is an ideal way to prepare for a research-based career in the art world.

Dates: Late Sep-early Dec the following year. Cost: £8,600. Includes tuition, field trips, sale catalogs. Accommodations and daily travel not included. Contact: Sotheby's Institute, 30 Oxford St., London W1N 9FL, England; (011) 44-171-323-5775, fax 580-8160 for a copy of the current academic prospectus.

MA in Post-War and Contemporary Art. A unique and highly specialized 14-month master's degree combining academic and practical approaches to the study of recent art. Contact with artists, galleries, curators, editors, and Sotheby's specialists complement an integrated program of lectures, seminars, and visits including 2 1-week tours: one to Germany and another to Holland and Belgium.

Dates: Early Sep-late Oct the following year. Cost: £8,800. Includes tuition, field trips (to Germany, Holland, and Belgium), sale catalogs. Accommodations and daily travel not included. Contact: Sotheby's Institute, 30 Oxford St., London W1N 9FL, England; (011) 44-

171-323-5775, fax 171-580-8160 for a copy of the current academic prospectus.

Oxford Advanced Studies Program. The program is an academic and cultural summer course held at Magdalen College, one of Oxford's oldest and most famous colleges. Students select 2 or 3 subjects from a wide choice; teaching is in a combination of small seminar groups and individual tutorials. The social and cultural program is packed with a variety of exciting experiences.

Dates: Jun 30-Jul 25, 1997; Jun 29-Jul 24, 1998. Cost: $4,700. Contact: Mrs. J. Ives, U.S. Registrar, Oxford Advanced Studies Program, P.O. Box 2043, Darien, CT 06820; (203) 966-2886, fax (203) 972-3083.

Oxford/FSU Summer Program. From Tom Tower to Stratford-on-Avon, pave your own pilgrim's path in the land of Chaucer and Shakespeare. Experience Oxford's rich academic traditions with an intimacy few visitors enjoy as you live and study in prestigious Christ Church College.

Dates: Jul 1-20, 1996 and Jul 22-Aug 10, 1996; Jun 30-Jul 19, 1997 and Jul 21-Aug 9, 1997. Cost: $3,400 per person. Includes course fee, single room, and 3 meals per day. Contact: Carol Abel, Center for Professional Development, Florida State Univ., Tallahassee, FL 32306-2027; (904) 644-7551, fax (904) 644-2589; cabel@mailer.fsu.edu.

Penn-in-London. For students interested in theater and literature, this program offers first-hand opportunities to experience the best in traditional and contemporary British theater, from page to footlights.

Dates: Jun 29-Aug 2. Cost: Tuition $2,840; theater tickets $450; housing $750. Contact: Penn Summer Abroad, College of General Studies, Univ. of Pennsylvania, 3440 Market St., Suite 100, Philadelphia, PA 19104-3335; (215) 898-5738, fax (215) 573-2053.

Postgraduate Diploma in Asian Arts. A 1-year program taught in association with the

School of Oriental and African Studies, Univ. of London. Students take 3 out of 5 possible options in the arts: India and South Asia, China, South East Asia and Oceania, Japan and Korea, Middle and Near East to be awarded the diploma. It is possible and very common for students to take any of the modules individually.

Dates: Starts in Sep, Jan, and Apr. Cost: £3,250 per term. Includes tuition, field trips, sale catalogs. Accommodations and daily travel not included. Contact: Sotheby's Institute, 30 Oxford St., London W1N 9FL, England; (011) 44-171-323-5775, fax 171-580-8160 for a copy of the current academic prospectus.

Royal Holloway, Univ. of London. Royal Holloway's visiting student program offers students an opportunity to spend the full academic year, fall semester, or spring semester/summer term in the U.K. Royal Holloway is a college of the Univ. of London but is located 30 km to the west of Central London.

Dates: Full year: Sep 23, 1996-Jun 20, 1997; fall semester Sep 23-Dec 18, 1996; spring semester/summer term: Jan 13-Apr 11, 1997. Cost: (1995 costs) full year: £6,625 (arts), £7,970 (science); fall semester: £3,050 (arts), £3,665 (science); spring semester/summer term: £3,840 (arts), £4,620 (science). Contact: Robert Walls, Head of Schools and International Liaison, Royal Holloway, Univ. of London, Egham, Surrey TW20 0EX, U.K.; (011) 44-1784-443025, fax 437520; liaison-office@ rhbnc.ac.ur.

Semester or Year. Each semester program equals 3 U.S. credits: business and marketing, communications and media, hotel and tourism, food and nutrition, health care, drama studies, health sciences, information management, social science and health.

Dates: Semester 1: Sep 23, 1996-Jan 24, 1997; semester 2: Feb 3, 1997-Jun 13, 1997. Cost: Academic tuition per semester $4,530 plus housing. Contact: Dr. J.G. Duncan, Queen Margaret College, Edinburgh EH12 8TS, U.K.; (011) 44-131-317-3000, fax 3256; etdunc@ main.qmced.ac.uk.

Semester/Year at Middlesex Univ. Study at Middlesex Univ. in Northeast London and choose from more than 900 courses in arts and sciences, business, computer science, fine arts, languages, law, liberal arts, literature, math, natural and social sciences, philosophy, and psychology. Full integration and Student Union privileges. On-campus housing. Fifteen undergraduate credits per semester.

Dates: Sep 28-Dec 20 (fall); Feb 12-Jun 5 (spring). Cost: Approx. $9,000. Includes room and board, airfare, local transportation, books, tuition, and miscellaneous expenses. Contact: SUNY Brockport, Office of International Education, 350 New Campus Dr., Brockport, NY 14420; (716) 395-2119, fax (716) 395-2606.

Semester/Year at the Univ. of Leeds. Study at Leeds Univ. (2 hours north of London) and choose from any course offered in arts and sciences, business, computer science, law, liberal arts, literature, mathematics, philosophy, psychology, and social sciences—more than 1,100 courses to choose from. Participate in all student union privileges. On-campus housing. Fifteen undergraduate credits per semester.

Dates: Sep 27-Dec 10 (fall); Feb 15-Jun 28 (spring). Cost: Semester: $7,000; year: $12,600. Includes room and board, airfare, local transportation, books, tuition, and miscellaneous expenses. Contact: SUNY Brockport, Office of International Education, 350 New Campus Dr., Brockport, NY 14420; (716) 395-2119, fax (716) 395-2606.

Study Abroad. The Univ. of Westminster offers a program tailor made for visiting international students. Study Abroad offers you the chance to study at the Univ. alongside students from all over the world for either 6 months or a year in the modules of your choice. The classes we offer encompass a wide variety of fields and interests, from Shakespeare to Sociology.

Dates: Fall semester, spring semester, or academic year. Cost: Approx. £2,340 per semester. Contact: Andrea Toyias, Univ. of Westminster, 74A Great Portland St., London

W1N 5AL, England; (011) 44-171-911-5136, fax 911-5873; a.r.toyias@wmin.ac.uk.

Study Abroad and Internships. Undergraduate degree classes in all subjects fully integrated with British students. One or 2 semesters of full 3- and 4-year degrees. Twelve to 15 credits per semester. Transcript provided. Internships for academic credit.

Dates: Sep-Jun. Cost: On application. Contact: International Education Office, The Nottingham Trent Univ., Clifton, Nottingham NG11 8NS, U.K.; (011) 44-5948-6688, fax (011) 44-5948-6615; ine4globe@ntu.ac.uk.

Study Abroad in Northern Ireland. The Queen's Univ. of Belfast offers study abroad opportunities in all subject areas except medicine. Attendance can be for 1 or 2 semesters; students usually take 3 modules per semester.

Dates: First semester: Sep 23, 1996-Jan 24, 1997; second semester: Feb 3-Jun 13, 1997 (3 weeks vacation at Christmas and Easter). Cost: Tuition fee for 1995-96 was £2,100 for 1 semester, £4,200 for 2 semesters (rate for 1996-97 not available at press time). Accommodations range from £40-£55 per week. Contact: Mrs. C. McEachern, Administrative Officer, International Liaison Office, The Queen's Univ. of Belfast, Belfast BT7 1NN, Northern Ireland, U.K; (011) 44-1232-335415, fax (011) 44-1232-687297; ilo@qub.ac.uk.

Study in Great Britain. Thirty-eight program opportunities in England, Scotland, and Wales. University study and special subject area programs, including internships, for fall, spring, academic year and summer program provides a full range of services including predeparture advising, orientation, homestay, and guaranteed housing. Need-based scholarships available.

Dates: Fall, spring, acdemic year. Summer semester and terms. Cost: Varies. Call for current fees. Contact: Beaver College Center for Education Abroad, 450 S. Easton Rd., Glenside, PA 19038-3295; (800) 755-5607, fax (215) 572-2174; cea@beaver.edu, www.beaver. edu/cea//.

Study in London. Four-week program offering a wide selection of regular university courses at Middlesex Univ. University housing, field trips and cultural activities. Six credit hours, undergraduate

Dates: Mid-Jul-mid-aug. Cost: Approx. $3,100. Airfare not included. Contact: Office of International Education, SUNY New Paltz, HAB 33, New Paltz, NY 12561; (914) 257-3125, fax (914) 257-3129; international@ newpaltz.edu, www.newpaltz.edu/oie.

Study in Wales. Opportunities for either year-long or semester study abroad at the Univ. of Wales Swansea (8,500 students, located by the sea) in fully integrated programs. Host family and summer internship programs are available. University housing, orientation, and cultural events are integral to all programs. Swansea is a lively maritime city with great social life and numerous outdoor activities.

Dates: Sep-Dec/Jan-May/May-Jul. Cost: From $4,500. Contact: Emma Frearson, Study Abroad Swansea, American Studies Centre, Univ. of Wales Swansea, Singleton Park, Swansea SA2 8PP, Wales, U.K.; (011) 44-1-792-295135, fax 295719; e.frearson@swansea.ac.uk, www.swan. ac.uk/sao/saohp/html.

Summer Academy. Summer Academy offers study holidays at 13 British and Irish universities. The course fee includes full board accommodations for 6 to 7 nights. Tuition fees and course related excursions. Study topics inlcude: heritage, the arts, countryside and creative writing. Accommodations are in single rooms in university halls of residence. Locations include: Aberystwyth, Ambleside, Canterbury, Cork (Ireland), Durham, Exeter, Lancaster, Maynooth (Ireland), Norwich, Oxford, Sheffield, Southampton, Stirling, and Swansea.

Dates: Jun 21-Aug 23, 1997. Cost: £355-£440 (see above for what fee includes). Contact: Andrea Nicholaides, Marketing and Reservations Coordinator, Summer Academy, Keynes College, The Univ., Canterbury, Kent CT2 7NP; (011) 44-1227-470402/823473, fax 784338; a.m.nicholaides@ukc.ac.uk.

The American College in London. Located in central London, ACL offers 300 courses in international business, communications, video, fashion design/marketing, interior design, commercial art, and liberal arts. Internships are also available. Students attend classes with an international student body and faculty represented by over 100 countries. Travel programs within England and throughout Europe are offered each term.

Dates: Regular terms beginning each Oct, Jan, Mar, Jun, and Aug, 4-week summer sessions in Jun and Jul. Cost: $5,500 (regular terms); $3,085 (4-week sessions). Contact: Office of International Programs, The American College in London, 3330 Peachtree Rd., NE, Atlanta, GA 30326; (800) 255-6839, fax (404) 364-6611.

The European Fashion Industry. London College of Fashion is the only college in the British university sector to specialize in fashion. Unique 4-credit summer program; specialist courses in design, marketing and merchandising, cosmetics and beauty; historical and cultural studies; Paris field trip; plus optional 4-week internship.

Dates: Jun 24-Jul 19, 1996. Cost: £1,255 for 4 weeks. Includes airfare and accommodations for Paris field trip. London accommodations not included. Contact: Jan Miller, Business Manager, DALI at London College of Fashion, 20 John Princes St., London W1M 0BJ, England; (011) 44-171-514-7400, ext. 7411, fax (011) 44-171-514-7490; lcfdali@london-fashion.ac.uk.

The Univ. of Reading. Students are fully integrated into regular university classes, studying for credit in one or more of 46 departments. One year or 1 or 2 terms. Campus accommodations. Reading, an international university, is situated on a beautiful campus just west of London.

Dates: Oct 1-Dec 13, Jan 13-Mar 21, Apr 28-Jul 3. Cost: (1995) one term: £1,950; two terms: £3,700; year: £5,350. Room and board approx. £75 per week. Contact: Tony Hassan, Visiting Students Office, The Univ. of Reading, Whiteknights, Reading RG6 6AH, England; (011) 44-1734-318323, fax 750046; n.hamilton@reading.ac.uk.

UCLES RSA CTEFLA. This is the most widely recognized introductory course to the TEFL profession allowing successful participants to work worldwide. The course is extremely practical, develops classroom skills and language awareness as well as dealing comprehensively with methodology, thus providing a sound basis in all aspects of TEFL teaching.

Dates: Oct-Nov, Apr-Jun, Jan-May. Cost: £832. Contact: Guidance Centre, Thames Valley Univ., 18-22 Bond St., Ealing, London W5 5AA, U.K.; (011) 44-181-579-5000, fax 181-231-2900.

UNH Cambridge Summer Program. This program's outstanding reputation rests in its balance between offerings of challenging courses in literature, and history taught by primarily Cambridge Univ. professors and a wealth of activities including fine theater, excursions, lectures, readings, and socializing, all in traditional English style. Courses in creative writing have joined the exciting possibilities offered in 1997.

Dates: Jul 7-Aug 15. Cost: $4,475. Contact: Romana Huk, Director, UNH Cambridge Summer Program, 95 Main St., Durham, NH 03824; Tel./fax (603) 862-3962; cambridge.program@unh.edu.

Univ. of Cambridge International Summer Programs. Largest and longest-established program of summer schools in the U.K. Intensive study in Cambridge as part of an international community. Term I (6 weeks) and Term II (2 weeks) of the International Summer School offer over 60 different courses. Three-week specialist programs: Art history, Medieval Studies, History, English Literature, and Shakespeare. Wide range of classes on all programs. Participants must have sufficient knowledge of English to study at university level. U.S. and other overseas institutions grant credit for study at the Univ. of Cambridge Summer School. Guidelines available.

Dates: Jul 7-Aug 16, 1997. Cost: Tuition from £445-£650 (2 to 4 weeks), accommodations from £225-£896 (2 to 4 weeks). Six-week period of study also possible by combining 2 summer schools. Contact: Sarah Ormrod, Director, International Division, Univ. of Cambridge Board of Continuing Education, Madingley Hall, Madingley, Cambridge CB3 8AQ, England; (011) 44-1954-210636, fax (011) 44-1954-210677; rdi1000@cam.ac.uk.

Univ. of Essex. Undergraduates (sophomores, juniors, or seniors) can normally select 4 courses from all regular undergraduate courses in the Univ. (subject to prerequisites, schedules, and space). Guaranteed single occupancy, fully integrated with British students. On-campus accommodations are less than 1 hour from London. Full support services including transcripts of credit and grades. Students can come for full year or autumn term or spring and summer terms.

Dates: Academic year: Oct 3, 1996-Jun 28, 1997; autumn term: Oct 3-Dec 14, 1996; spring and summer terms: Jan 13-Jun 28, 1997. Cost: 1995-96: full year £5,945; spring and summer terms £3,585; autumn term £2,390 (costs for tuition only). Contact: Mrs. Gloria Vicary, Coordinator of International Programmes, Univ. of Essex, Wivenhoe Park, Colchester CO4 3SQ, England.

Univ. of North London. SUNY Cortland celebrates its 22nd consecutive year at UNL, the prestigious public university formerly known as London Polytechnic. Over 400 courses are offered. Fields of study include education, natural sciences, humanities, communications, social sciences, business, health, theater arts. Credits per semester: 12-16. Pre-arranged housing in flats in the Bayswater district. Internships available.

Dates: Fall: mid-Sep-mid-Dec:, spring: end-Jan-mid-May. Cost: Fall 1996 estimate $4,259, spring 1997 $4,784. Estimates include full-day orientation in the U.S., application fee, apartment rental, meals, transportation in London, London tour and Thames cruise, insurance, airfare, transportation from airport to downtown London upon arrival, books and supplies, administrative fees. SUNY tuition not included. Contact: Dr. John Ogden, Director, Office of International Programs, Box 2000, SUNY at Cortland, Cortland, NY 13045; (607) 753-2209, fax (607) 753-5989; tonerp@snycorva.cortland.edu.

Webster Univ. in London. Webster Univ. in London, located on the campus of Regent's College, has students from more than 50 countries. Students may pursue a degree program leading to a BA, MA, or MBA. In addition, students may enroll for a study abroad semester or year (summer session and other short-term options also available). Each semester more than 70 courses are available in 15 different disciplines. Major areas of study include: business, computer science, economics, psychology, international relations, management, marketing.

Dates: Five entry terms: late Aug, mid-Oct, mid-Jan, mid-Mar, late May. Cost: $20,000 (1996-97 academic year); $10,000 (semester 1996-97). Estimate includes tuition, room and board, books, local transportation, social activities. Contact: Teresa Bruno, Study Abroad Office, Webster Univ., 470 E. Lockwood Ave., St. Louis, MO 63119-3194; (314) 968-6988 or (800) 984-6857, fax (314) 963-6051. Visit our website at http://webster2.websteruniv.edu.

Wroxton College of Fairleigh Dickinson Univ. Wroxton College in Oxfordshire, England, has been owned and operated by Fairleigh Dickinson Univ. since 1965. The College offers students a unique but affordable study-abroad educational experience with high academic standards plus the advantages and rewards of the opportunities to travel within the British Isles and throughout the European continent. Undergraduate and graduate courses in literature, history, political science, fine arts, economics, business, and sociology. Students can enroll for a semester or full-year or 4-week summer program.

Dates: Jun 23-Jul 19, 1996 (summer); Aug 30-Dec 16, 1996 (fall); Jan 31-May 18, 1997 (spring). Cost: $8,941 per semester (1995-96), $2,491 (summer). Includes undergraduate tuition, room and board, tour program. Contact: Prof. Albert D. Schielke, Director of the Study Abroad Office, 1000 River Rd., Teaneck, NJ 07666; (800) 338-8803, fax (201) 692-7309.

United States

Master's Program in Intercultural Management. The School for International Training's Master's Program in Intercultural Management offers concentrations in sustainable development, international education and training and human resource development in a 1 academic-year program.

Dates: Aug 28, 1996-Jun 2, 1997. Cost: $16,000 (1996-97 tuition). Contact: Marshall Brewer, Admissions Counselor, School for International Learning, P.O. Box 676, Kipling Rd., Brattleboro, VT 05302; (802) 257-7751, fax (802) 258-3500; csa@sit@worldlearning. org, www. worldlearning.org/sit.html.

Vietnam

Vietnam Program (Ho Chi Minh City). Includes Vietnamese language, business economics, political science, history, geography, and Vietnamese literature course. All courses taught in English except literature, which has a language proficiency pre-requisite. Spring and fall terms are 11-week programs including a 3-day excursion to Hanoi. Accreditation from Western Washington Univ.

Dates: Spring: Apr 8-Jun 10; fall: Sep 17-Dec 2. Cost: $5,500 per term includes tuition, housing, meals. Contact: Cheryl Brown, Program Coordinator or Roger Edginton, Senior Director, American Heritage Association, 741 SW Lincoln St., Portland, OR 97201-3178; (800) 654-2051, fax (503) 295-5969; vn@am heritage.org.

Worldwide

Career Development Exchanges. The Career Development Exchanges Program, one of 3 exchange programs operated by the Association for International Practical Training (AIPT), helps individuals arrange training programs in nearly any career field. Individuals wishing to participate in this program must find an employer to provide them with training before the Career Development Exchanges Program can assist them with visa and other arrangements.

Dates: Year round. Cost: $150 application fee. Program fees vary according to the type of training program. Contact: Career Development Exchanges Program, AIPT, 10400 Little Patuxent Pkwy., Suite 250-M, Columbia, MD 21044-3510; (410) 997-2886, fax (410) 992-3924; cd@aipt.org, www.softaid. net/aipt/aipt.html.

Center for Global Education. The center facilitates cross-cultural learning experiences that prepare students to think more critically about global issues and to work toward a more just and sustainable world. Programs include homestays, community learning, and regional travel. Students explore women's issues and issues of social change, sustainable development, and human rights. Programs in Mexico, Central America, and Namibia/South Africa.

Dates: Semesters (Sep-Dec or Feb-May). Cost: Contact the Center for current costs. Contact: Academic Programs Abroad, Center for Global Education, Augsburg College, 2211 Riverside Ave., Box 307TR, Minneapolis, MN 55454; (800) 299-8889, fax (612) 330-1695; globaled@augsburg.edu, www.augsburg.edu/global.

College Semester Abroad. Through College Semester Abroad (CSA) you have the opportunity to learn firsthand about our interdependent world and its diversity through interdisciplinary study in more than 40 countries worldwide. The structure of each program provides you with the best possible opportunity to immerse yourself into the culture of the host country.

Dates: Fall and spring semesters (vary). Cost: Average $9,700 (room and board, tuition, international travel, insurance, excursions). Contact: Admissions College Semester Abroad, SIT, P.O. Box 676, Kipling Rd., Brattleboro, VT 05302; (802) 257-7751, fax (802) 258-3500; csa@sit@worldlearning.org, www.worldlearning.org/csa.html.

Cross Cultural Studies. Topics covered will be the current political scene in Russia, the social issues affecting the people and culture of Spain; the educational systems in England, France, and Germany; and the historical literature of London and Dublin. Three to 6 hours of college credit is granted through the Univ. of Missouri at Kansas City.

Dates: Summer 1997. Cost: Approx. $2,000 (does not include airfare). Contact: People to People International, Collegiate and Professional Studies Program, 501 E. Armour Blvd., Kansas City, MO 64109-2200; (816) 531-4701, fax (816) 561-7502; ptpi@cctr.umkc.edu, www.umkc.edu/cctr/dept/ptpi/homepage.html.

Friends World Program. A full year program in comparative religion and culture. Students will study for three 10-week terms in Japan, India, and Israel. The field course will be based on experiential approaches, emphasizing participation, observation, and involvement in local religious life. Culture's relation to religion will be emphasized.

Dates: Mid-Sep-mid-May. Cost: $23,500 for year (1996/1997). Includes tuition, travel, room and board, fees and books. Contact: James Howard, Friends World Program, 239 Montauk Hwy., Southampton, NY 11968; (516) 287-8475; jhoward@sand.liunet.edu.

Global Ecology. Travel around the world for 8 months, meeting leading environmental activists and scholars, comparative international study of key issues in global ecology. 1997-98 itinerary: England, India, Philippines, New Zealand, and Mexico. Courses in cultural anthropology, biology, ecology, and sustainable development. Small group of 30 students, undergraduates and older, homestays with families. Perfect for teachers on sabbatical, working professionals. Receive 32 credits and transcript from Bard College. IHP founded in 1958.

Dates: Sep 1997-May 1998. Cost: $19,850 (1996-97). Includes tuition, accommodations, most meals, academic program, fees. Airfare not included. Contact: Joan Tiffany, Director, International Honors Program, 19 Braddock Pk., Boston, MA 02116; (617) 267-0026; info@ihp.edu, www.ihp.edu.

Global Routes: Internship Program. Global Routes interns are assigned in pairs to remote villages where they teach in local schools and complete at least 1 community service project. Each intern lives separately with a local family in a simple, traditional home. Training, support, and adventure travel are an integral part of the programs. Programs offered in Costa Rica, Ecuador, Kenya, Thailand, Navajo Nation.

Dates: Year round in 3-month sessions. Cost: $3,550 summer, $3,950 during year. Includes all expenses (room, board, adventure travel) except airfare to and from country. Scholarships and fundraising information available. Contact: Global Routes, 1814 7th St., Suite A, Berkeley, CA 94710; (510) 848-4800, fax (510) 848-4801; mail@globalroutes.org, www.lanka. net.globali ts.

Graduate and Undergraduate Programs. European University offers undergraduate and graduate programs in Business Administration, International Hospitality and Tourism Management, Business Communications and Public Relations, Information Systems, and European Languages.

Dates: Courses begin Oct, Jan, Mar. Cost: SF3,0850. Contact: Prof. D. Craen, European Univ. Les Bosquets, 1817 Montreaux, Switzerland; (011) 41-21-964-84-64, fax 964-84-68, eurmon@iprolink.ch.

Hospitality/Tourism Exchanges. The Hospitality/Tourism Exchanges Program, 1 of 3 exchange programs operated by the Association for International Practical Training (AIPT), assists young people beginning a career in the hotel and culinary, food service, and travel/tourism fields by helping them arrange practical training experience abroad. Participants must be currently enrolled in or be a graduate of a university or vocational school in the hospitality and tourism fields or have substantial career experience in those areas.

Dates: Year round. Cost: $75 for students, $150 for nonstudents. Program fees vary depending on the country in which the training will take place. Contact: Susan-Ellis Dougherty, Program Director, Hospitality Tourism Exchanges, AIPT, 10400 Little Patuxent Pkwy., Suite 250-M, Columbia, MD 21044-3510; (410) 997-2883, fax (410) 992-3924; ht@aipt.org, www.softaid.net/aipt/aipt.html.

Illinois Programs Abroad. Argentina, Brazil, Chile, Ecuador, Great Britain, Ireland, Turkey, and Russia. Summer: language, literature, culture, social sciences, art and design (Ireland only), business (Brazil only). Semester/year: Full university curriculum. Political/congressional internship: Chile (spring only). Art and design: Great Britain and Ireland only. Russian language, literature, social sciences: Russia.

Dates: Summer, fall, spring, and year. Cost: Varies by program. Contact: Illinois Programs Abroad, Univ. of Illinois, 115 International Studies Bldg., 910 S. 5th St., Champaign, IL 61820; (800) 531-4404 or (217) 333-6168, fax (217) 244-0249; ipa@uiuc.edu.

International Cooperative Education Program. Paid employment and internships for college and university students for a period of 8-12 weeks in 8 European and one Asian country. Employment depends on foreign language knowledge, major, and previous work experience. Work permits and housing are provided.

Dates: From Jun-Sep. Cost: Students must pay for air transportation and have a reserve of at least $800 for initial expenses. Contact: Günter Seefeldt, PhD, Director, International Cooperative Education Program, 15 Spiros Way, Menlo Park, CA 94025; (415) 323-4944, fax (415) 323-1104.

International Internships. Working for-credit internships available in a wide variety of areas including placement with governmental, educational, public, and private businesses. Placement depends upon student's qualifications and interests. Some areas require previous language knowledge. Available all semester, including summers; 12-15 undergraduate credits.

Dates: Varies by country, call for information. Cost: Varies by country, call for information. Contact: SUNY Brockport, Office of International Education, 350 New Campus Dr., Brockport, NY 14420; (716) 395-2119, fax (716) 395-2606.

Internships. Internships for credit available in a wide variety of areas including placement with governmental, educational, public, and private organizations. Placement depends upon student's specific interests and qualifications. Three to 15 credits: graduate, undergraduate.

Dates: Varies by country; call for specific information. Cost: Varies by country; call for specific information. Contact: SUNY Brockport, Office of International Education, 350 New Campus Dr., Brockport, NY 14420; (716) 395-2119, fax (716) 395-2606.

Jewish Volunteer Corps.-JVC Summer. JVC Summer Program is an active volunteering and learning experience for Jewish college students that offer a unique opportunity to study issues of global and community development and a means to express commitment to community service. Participants will spend 3 weeks in 1 country in either Latin America or Africa doing volunteer work in a rural community, followed by 3 weeks in Israel studying issues of development with top experts at Israel's leading international development training institutes. Participants will also have the opportunity to volunteer in communities in Israel.

Dates: Jun 5-Jul 17, 1997. Cost: Up to $3,000. Contact: JVC Summer Program, American Jewish World Service, 989 Avenue of the Americas, New York, NY 10018; (800) 889-7146 or (212) 736-AJWS, fax (212) 736-3463; jvcvol@jws.org.

Joe Mooney Summer School of Music. Traditional Irish music classes in flute, tin whistle, fiddle, button accordion, concertina, piano accordion, harp, banjo, pipes, traditional singing and set dancing (daily). Evening lectures, nightly recitals, and concerts.

Dates: Jul 19-26. Cost: £30 for classes. Lectures and recitals not included. Contact: Nancy Woods, Joe Mooney Summer School, Drumshanbo, Co. Leitrin, Ireland; (011) 353-78-41213.

Marymount Study Abroad. Opportunities for direct enrollment in foreign universities in Australia, England, Ireland, and Scotland, with undergraduate courses available in all fields of study; pre-professional programs in London in fashion design, fashion merchandising, interior design, and drama. General information and guidance available through campus office. Transcript of credits earned overseas issued by Marymount College.

Dates: Fall semester, spring semester, and academic year. Cost: Varies by program. Price listing available upon request. Contact: Rita Arthur, Ph.D., Director, Office of Study

Abroad, Marymount College, Tarrytown, NY 10591; (914) 332-8222, fax (914) 631-8586; studyab@mmc.marymt.edu.

Michigan State Univ. Michigan State Univ. offers over 80 overseas study program opportunities around the world throughout the year for academic credit. Scholarships available.

Dates: Write for details. Cost: Write for details. Contact: Brenda Sprite, Acting Director of Overseas Study, 109 International Center, Michigan State Univ., E. Lansing, MI 48823-1035; (517) 353-8920, fax (517) 432-2082.

Partnerships International. A short-term, school-to-school pairing program designed to foster long-term academic and cultural partnerships between secondary schools in the U.S. and other countries. Once schools are linked, a group of 6-15 students, accompanied by a faculty member, visits their partner school for approximately 3 weeks. During this time, students live in the homes of host students, attend classes, participate in another way of life, and discover local points of interest.

Dates: Vary with academic year. Cost: Range $800-$1,900 depending on country of destination. Partnership International/NASSP, 1904 Association Dr., Reston, VA 22091; (800) 253-7746, fax (703) 476-6319.

Peace and Conflict Studies at the European Peace Univ. (EPU). A unique opportunity to study with the world's foremost experts in the areas of peace, conflict, and deveopment. Campuses in Spain, Austria, and Ireland. Full range of program services. Need-based scholarships available.

Dates: Fall, winter, and spring semesters. Full academic year. Cost: Semesters $7,400. Contact: Beaver College Center for Education Abroad, 450 S. Easton Rd., Glenside, PA 19038-3295, (800) 755-5607, fax (215) 572 2174; cea@beaver.edu, www.beaver.edu/cea/.

Penn Summer Abroad. Academic programs granting Univ. of Pennsylvania credits.

Courses focusing on language, culture, economics, theater, anthropology, Jewish studies, cinema, art history, traditional folk medicine, performing arts, and religion. Several programs offer homestays, some offer internships. Dates: Mid-May-late Aug (2-8 weeks). Cost: Tuition: $1,420 per course. Living costs vary. Contact: Elizabeth Sachs, Penn Summer Abroad, College of General Studies, Univ. of Pennsylvania, 3440 Market St., Suite 100, Philadelphia, PA 19104-3335; (215) 898-5738, fax (215) 573-2053.

Rutgers Study Abroad. Exciting study abroad programs offered in Britain, France, Germany, Ireland, Israel, Italy, Mexico, and Spain. All programs are fully integrated with host universities. There are no language requirements for Britain, Ireland, or Israel; others require 2 college level years. All majors and disciplines are available.
Dates: Year, semester, and summer programs. Cost: $5,000-$12,000. Contact: Seth Gopin, Director, Rutgers Study Abroad, Milledoler Hall, Rm. 205, Rutgers Univ., New Brunswick, NJ 08903; (908) 932-7787, fax (908) 932-8659; ru.abroad@email.rutgers.edu.

Semester and Academic Year Abroad. NIU has study abroad programs in Salzburg, Austria; Aix-en-Provence, France; Avignon, France; Guadalajara, Mexico; Mexico City, Mexico; and Segovia, Spain. Internships are available in Melbourne, Australia; Salzburg, Austria; Brussels, Belgium; Bonn/Cologne, Germany; Madrid, Spain; and London, England. Academic credit. Financial aid available.
Dates: Fall or spring semester or academic year. Cost: Varies by program. Contact: The Foreign Study Office, Williston Hall #100, Northern Illinois Univ., DeKalb, IL 60115; (815) 753-0304 or (815) 753-0420, fax (815) 753-0825; acoyle@niu.edu.

Summer and Short-Term Programs. NIU has study abroad programs in Austria, Bahamas, Chile, China, Costa Rica, Egypt, England, France, Greece, Ireland, Italy, Korea, Russia, Spain, and Thailand. Internships are available in London, student teaching opportunities in Australia.
Dates: Summer or winter breaks. Cost: Varies by program. Contact: International Programs Office, Northern Illinois Univ., Williston Hall #405, DeKalb, IL 60115; (815) 753-0700, fax (815) 753-1488; acoyle@ niu.edu.

Summer Study Abroad. Summer opportunities in Australia, Austria, England, Ireland, Mexico, and Scotland, including internships, fine arts, drama, history, literature, environmental studies, psychology and languages. Full range of program services. Guaranteed housing.
Dates: Vary. Call for tentative dates. Cost: Varies. Call for fees. Contact: Beaver College Center for Education Abroad, 450 S. Easton Rd., Glenside, PA 19038-3295; (800) 755-5607, fax (215) 572-2174; cea@beaver.edu, www. beaver.edu/cea/.

SUNY Plattsburgh Programs. Exciting study abroad opportunities for a semester, academic year, or summer at major universities in Australia, Argentina, Canada, Chile, England, and Uruguay. Summer French immersion programs in Quebec from beginning to advanced levels are available. Spanish is necessary for Latin American programs. Internships are available in Chile and Latin America. No language requirements for Canada, England, and Australia programs.
Dates: Year round. Varies by program. Cost: Program fees vary depending on the country and semester attending. Contact: Mrs. Dodie Giltz, Center for International Programs, SUNY Plattsburgh, Plattsburgh, NY 12901; (518) 564-2086, fax (518) 564-2112; giltzdr@splava.cc.plattsburgh.edu.

Teaching Internship Program. Global Routes interns are assigned in pairs to remote villages where they teach in local schools and complete at least 1 community service project. Each intern lives separately with a local family in a simple, traditional home. Training, support, and adventure travel are an integral part of the programs. Programs offered in Costa Rica, Ecuador, Kenya, Thailand, Navajo Nation.

Dates: Year round in 3-month session. Cost: $3,550 summer, $3,950 during year. Incluldes all expenses (room, board, adventure travel) except airfare to and from country. Scholarships and fundraising information available. Contact: Global Routes, 1814 7th St., Suite A, Berkeley, CA 94710; (510) 848-4800, fax (510) 848-4801; mail@globalroutes.org, www.lanka.net/gloalrts.

The Global Campus. Choose from 30 programs featuring language, theme, area studies, integrated classroom and field study. Program courses include language, culture, humanities, internships, and international relations. Destinations range from Austria to Venezuela with Third World internship programs in Ecuador, India, Kenya, and Senegal. Open to all students and professionals.

Dates: Quarter, semester, summer, and academic year options. Cost: From $2,600-$14,000 (most $3,800). Contact: The Global Campus, Univ. of Minnesota, 102T Nicholson Hall, 216 Pillsbury Dr. SE, Minneapolis, MN 55455-0138; (612) 625-3379, fax (612) 626-8009; globalc@tc.umn.edu, www.isp.umn.edu.

The Institute of European and Asian Studies (IES/IAS). IES/IAS is an independent, not-for-profit educational institution offering study abroad programs in 11 countries with programs in Adelaide, Berlin, Beijing, Canberra, Dijon, Durham, European Union, Freiburg, London, Madrid, Milan, Moscow, Nagoya, Nantes, Paris, Salamanca, Singapore, Tokyo, and Vienna. A wide range of courses, internships, housing, and field trips are available.

Dates: Semester, full year, and summer. Cost: Varies by program. Contact: IES/IAS Admissions, 223 W. Ohio St., Chicago, IL 60610, (800) 995-2300, fax (312) 944-1448; iesrecrt@mcs.net.

Total Immersion Study. Learn a language and immerse yourself in an exciting program of social and cultural experiences. New programs start year round for all ages and levels throughout Europe, Asia Central, and South America. Homestays, activities, excursions, specialized courses, courses for professionals and teachers. Don't just learn a language—live it.

Dates: Year round. Cost: Varies with program. Contact: Nancy Forman, Director, Melodie E. Rodriguez, Program Coordinator, Language Liaison, 20533 Biscayne Blvd., Suite 4-162, Miami, FL 33180; (305) 682-9909 or (800) 284-4448, fax (305) 682-9907.

Trent International. Trent's International study and exchange programs provide students with an opportunity to spend an academic study year abroad. Students from all academic disciplines may pursue one of a number of formalized exchange or study abroad or language programs. Some programs involve an international work placement component. Students take regular courses and examinations at a host university, and credits earned abroad are counted toward their undergraduate degree.

Dates: Full academic year (often Oct-Jun). Cost: Differs according to program but generally pay Trent's tuition and (often) residence fees. Contact: Cynthia Bennett Awe, Programs Administrator/Exchange Coordinator, Trent Univ., Peterborough, ON K9J 7B8, Canada; (705) 748-1280, fax (705) 748-1626; cawe@trentu.ca.

World Experience Student Exchange Program. World Experience offers an opportunity to have an experience of a lifetime. Learn another language while living with a host family from 1 of 25 countries for a semester or school year. Attend school locally. Add a new dimension to your life. Eligibility: 15-18 years. 3.0 GPA.

Dates: Aug or Jan departure for 1 to 2 semesters. Cost: $2,600 plus individual country fees for 1 year; $2,265 plus individual country fees for 1 semester. Contact: World Experience, 2440 Hacienda Blvd #116, Hacienda Heights, CA 91745; (800) 633-6653, fax (818) 333-4914; weworld@aol.com.

CHAPTER 14

High School Exchange Resources

Whether you're a student or adviser looking for the right international study program or someone who has the time for a long stay abroad and wants to combine the least expense with the most reward, you will find the information you need in the resources described below.

The Advisory List of International Educational Travel & Exchange Programs, published annually by the Council on Standards for International Educational Travel (CSIET) (3 Loudon St. SE, Suite 3, Leesburg, VA 22075; 703-771-2040, fax 703-771-2046; $8.50) lists programs for high school students which adhere to CSIET's standards and provides valuable information for prospective exchange students, host families, and schools.

The CSIET is a nonprofit organization committed to quality international educational travel and exchange. It establishes standards for organizations operating international educational travel and exchange programs at the high school level and monitors compliance with those standards by annually reviewing those programs that submit themselves for evaluation. It also disseminates information on international educational travel organizations. CSIET's advisory list provides the best available information on many of the best exchange programs available to young people.

The following resource materials and organizations are recommended by CSIET for those seeking additional information on travel and study abroad for high-school age students.

Organizations

American Association of School Administrators (AASA), 1801 N. Moore St., Arlington, VA 22209; (703) 528-0700. Publications include: Development Education: Building a Better World, a guidebook for integrating Third World issues and ideas into school curricula.

Council on International Educational Exchange (Council), 205 E. 42nd St., New York, NY 10017; (212) 882-2600. Organizes and administers a variety of international study, work, and travel programs at the secondary and post-secondary levels.

Institute of International Education (IIE), Publications Service, 809 United Nations Plaza, New York, NY 10017; (212) 984-5412.

Intercultural Press, P.O. Box 700, Yarmouth, ME 04096; (207) 846-5168. Intercultural Press publishes numerous books on international living, travel, study, and cross-cultural experiences. Titles include: Host Family Survival Kit: A Guide for American Host Families, Orientation Handbook for Youth Exchange Programs, Survival Kit for Overseas Living, Exchange Student Survival Kit.

International Youth Exchange Staff (USIA), 301 4th St., Room 314, SW, Washington, DC 20547; (202) 619-6299. The International Youth Exchange Staff of USIA oversees activities initiated under the President's International Youth Exchange Initiative and works closely with other organizations involved in international educational exchange activities.

NAFSA: Association of International Educators, 1875 Connecticut Ave., Suite 1000, NW, Washington, DC 20009-5728; (202) 462-4811, (800) 836-4994 (orders only). Provides training, information, and other educational services to professionals in international educational exchange.

U.S. Information Agency (USIA), Exchange Visitor Program Services, 301 4th St., (FEMA Room 200), SW, Washington, DC 20547; (202) 475-2389. The USIA evaluates not-for-profit organizations to determine whether they meet Criteria for Teenage Visitor Programs. It grants authorization to issue Forms IAP-66 for securing J-1 visas to enter the U.S.

CHAPTER 15

HIGH SCHOOL EXCHANGE PROGRAMS

The following listing of high school exchange programs was supplied by the organizers. Contact the program directors to confirm costs, dates, and other details. If you do not see the program you want in the country of your choice, look in the "Worldwide" listings at the end of the section for programs located in several different regions.

Australia

Custom Designed Professional Development Internships. Upon application, participants are asked to describe their internship needs, after which the placement service in Australia locates suitable programs. Responsibilities vary by placement. Excellent professional development and career building opportunities. Opportunities to travel in Australia before and after the placement. Flexible duration and start dates. Interns are not usually placed as a group. On-call support service, airport transfers, academic or professional supervisor provided in Australia. Pre-trip support for air travel, visas and orientation.

Fields: Management, Marketing, Finance and Accounting, Communications (radio, television, newspaper, public relations), Law,

Politics, The Arts, Social Work, Biology, Wildlife Management, Natural Resources, and Marine Science. Academic credit can be arranged through home university. One-hundred-200 internships per year. Prerequisites: Pursuing or have obtained a university/college degree. Application materials: application and transcript(s).

Dates: Six, 8, 10, 12, 16 weeks or more (52 weeks maximum) placements. Year-round start dates. Sign up at least 4 months prior to intended departure. Cost: $3,240 (6 weeks) to $4,480 (16 weeks). Includes room, 2 meals per day in homestay (or no meals in an apartment), internship placement, liaison service in Australia, airport transfers. Compensation: placements are typically unpaid due to immigration rules. Application fee: $500 deposit with application. Eighty percent refundable for cancellation after placement is found. Contact: AustraLearn, U.S. Center for Australian Universities, 110 16th St., CSU Denver Center, Denver, CO 80202; (800) 980-0033, fax (303) 446-5955; cflannery@vines.colostate.edu.

Special Interest and Study Tours. Personalized programs for individuals and groups of all ages. We combine education, recreation, accommodations (homestay available), and transportation. Based in tropical Cairns with coverage throughout Australia. Subject areas include: aboriginal dreamtime and culture, Great Barrier Reef, rainforest and savannah. Diving, environmental interpretation, flora and fauna, bird watching, tropical islands and wilderness, adventure safaris and farmstay.

Dates: Year round. Start any date. Cost: Prices and customized itineraries on application. Contact: Murray Simpson, Study Venture International, P.O. Box 229A, Stratford Qld., 4870 Australia; (011) 61-70-411622, fax 552044; svi@ozemail.com.au; www.ozemail. au/~svi.

Canada

Columbia College ESL. Seven- and 14-week programs, 25 hours per week. Small classes. Organized activities. International college also offering Senior, Secondary, and University Transfer programs. Facilities include tutorial center, library, computer center, gymnasium, cafeteria, counseling. Located 20 minutes from downtown Vancouver, near major shopping center and on excellent public transit routes.

Dates: Sep 3-Dec 12, 1996; Jan 2-Apr 10, May 5-Aug 14, and Sep 2-Dec 11, 1997. Cost: Tuition (7 weeks) CAN$1,850, (14 weeks) CAN$3,500; application fee CAN$75. Contact: Mr. John Helm, Columbia College, 6037 Marlborough Ave., Barnaby (Greater Vancouver), BC V5H 3L6 Canada; (604) 430-6422, fax (604) 439-0548; columbia_ college@ mindlink.bc.ca.

Columbia College Senior Secondary. Grade 11 and 12 high school program conforms to Ministry of Education guidelines. Students completing program receive British Columbia high school graduation diploma and are eligible to apply to universities and colleges in North America.

Dates: Sep 3-Dec 12, 1996, Jan 2-Apr 10, 1997, May 5-Aug 14, and Sep 2-Dec 11, 1997. Cost: Tuition (8 months) CAN$7,600; application fee CAN$75. Contact: Mr. John Helm, Columbia College, 6037 Marlborough Ave., Barnaby (Greater Vancouver), BC V5H 3L6, Canada; (604) 430-6422, fax (604) 439-0548; columbia_college@ mindlink.bc.ca.

Costa Rica

Costa Rican Language Academy. Costa Rican owned and operated language school offers first-rate Spanish instruction in a warm and friendly environment. Teachers with university degrees. Small groups or private classes. Included free in the programs are airport transportation, coffee and natural refreshments, excursions and Latin dance, Costa Rican cooking, music and conversation classes to provide students with complete cultural immersion.

Dates: Year round (start anytime). Cost: $135 per week or $220 per week for program with homestay. All other activities and services included at no additional cost. Contact: Costa Rican Language Academy, P.O. Box 336-2070, San José, Costa Rica; (011) 506-221-1624 or 233-8914 or 233-8938, fax 233-8670; crlang@ sol.racsa.co.cr. In the U.S. (800) 854-6057.

Outward Bound Costa Rica. Save the Rainforest Adventures. Outward Bound Costa Rica (CRROBS) creates courses that help your rainforest experience endure beyond the canopy of Latin America. We offer year round, multi-element (rafting, kayaking, canopy or rock climbing, hiking, and homestays). Costa Rica courses for any age group or individual. We also offer an 85-day tri-country (Costa Rica, Ecuador, and Peru) semester course (biology, anthropology, Spanish credit). Spanish/biology emphasis are available on all courses. For adventurers who want a less physically demanding experience than CRROBS offers, Save the Rainforest Adventures offers excursions catered to the needs and interests of each group or individual.

Dates: Year round 8-, 10-, 12-, 15-, 25-, 30-, and 85-day courses. Cost: $1,000-$2,600 for multi-day; $6,800 for 85 tri-country semester. Scholarships available. Contact: Outward Bound Costa Rica and Save the Rainforest Adventures, P.O. Box 243, Quepos, Costa Rica; (800) 676-2018, fax (011) 506-777-1222; crrobs@sol.racsa.co.cr, www.centralamerica.com/cr/crrobs.

Spanish Language Training. Nonprofit organization. Program includes intensive Spanish language training, optional excursions, lodging with a Costa Rican host family or hotel, introductory orientation, WEF certificates.

Dates: Four-week programs start any Monday of the year. Cost: $825 includes room and food. Contact: José O. Arauz, Executive Director, World Education Forum, P.O. Box 383-4005, San Antonio de Belén, Heredia, Costa Rica; Fax (506) 239-2254.

Spanish Language, Secondary School. Nonprofit organization. Program includes private or public high school attendance, elective curriculum in Spanish or English language, intensive Spanish language training, extra-curricular activities, excursions, lodging with a host family, introductory orientation.

Dates: Mar 1-Nov 30 (1 academic year). Cost: $5,964 includes room and board and local transport. Contact: José O. Arauz, Executive Director, World Education Forum, P.O. Box 383-4005, San Antonio de Belén, Heredia, Costa Rica; Fax (506) 239-2254.

Total Immersion Spanish. Seven separate year-round language institutes to choose from. Live with a Costa Rican family while taking 3 to 6 hours of intense language classes a day. Length of program is up to you—from as little as 1 week to 6 months. Locations: cloud forest, beach, country, and San Jose.

Dates: Every Monday except national holidays. Cost: Four-week course with homestay $850 to $2,000. Contact: ISLS, Dana G. Garrison, 1011 E. Washington Blvd., Los Angeles, CA 90021; (800) 765-0025, fax (213) 765-0026.

France

The Académie de Paris. A month-long introduction for students (grades 10-12) to Parisian culture, with classes taught in the city's museums, cathedrals, and historic sites. Courses include medicine, theater, studio art, and creative writing. Most classes are taught in English, with a special series of courses for those desiring immersion in French language.

Dates: Jul 7-Aug 3, 1996. Cost: $4,195. Contact: OxBridge Academic Programs, 601 W. 110th St., Suite 7-R, New York, NY 10025-1535; (800) 828-8349, fax (212) 663-8169.

Germany

German as a Foreign Language. We offer the following educational programs: various levels of German year round; intensive, crash, and long-term courses, individual tuition; special feature: German and Theatre, special programs: business German for professionals, German for teachers, German in a teacher's home, German for special purposes. Academic year, international study year, work placement, internship, guest studentship, homestays for groups, courses for firms and other institutions (banking, insurance, doctors, lawyers, etc.). Various types of accommodations. Full range of activities. Language tours worldwide.

Dates: Year round. Contact: GLS-Sprachenzentrum, Christina Langost, Director of Studies, Kolonnenstrasse 26, 10829 Berlin, Germany; (011) 49-30-787-41-52; fax 41-92.

Greece

Greek Summer. Greek Summer promotes intercultural exchange between Americans and Greeks under the sponsorhip of the American Farm School. It serves high school students who are enthusiastic about living in a rural Greek village and completing a beneficial work project. Nine days are spent touring Greece and 2 days climbing Mount Olympus.

Dates: Jun 23-Jul 31. Cost: $500 (tax deductible) to A.F.S., plus $2,350 fee. Airfare not included. Contact: Gemina Gianino, Program Coordinator, American Farm School and Greek Summer, 1133 Broadway, New York, NY 10010; (212) 463-8434, fax (212) 463-8208; gemina@amerfarm.com.

Guatemala

Kie-Balam Spanish Language School. The school features one-on-one instruction with university-degreed teachers. Special rate programs for high school teachers and students; programs for bilingual teachers, social workers, medical personnel. Course work transfers to degree programs. School starts rural lending libraries, help at a battered women's shelter, and works with a special education school.

Dates: Year round, classes start Mondays. Cost: Application fee: $50; tuition: $100 per week, includes room and board. Contact: Martha Weese, 1007 Duncan Ave., Elgin, IL 60120; (708) 888-2514 (U.S.), (011) 502-9-611636 (Guatemala from U.S.); moebius@ super-highway.net.

India

Studies Abroad for Global Education. Year-abroad program in India for high school students in grades 10-12 at accredited international schools offering college preparatory courses and many extracurricular activities. Includes a winter tour of India and volunteer opportunities between semesters.

Cost: Fee $9,000. Does not include travel to and from India. Contact: Jane Cummings, KWI, 159 Ralph McGill Blvd., #408, NE, Atlanta, GA 30308; (404) 524-0988, fax (404) 523-5420.

Italy

UGA Studies Abroad at Cortona. Studio art (ceramics, drawing, book arts, design, interior design, jewelry and metalworking, painting, papermaking, printmaking, photography, sculpture, and watercolor), art history, beginning Italian, Italian culture, landscape architecture, and women studies for undergraduate and graduate university credit. Courses vary each quarter. Deadlines: Jan 10, spring; Apr 10, summer; and Jun, 10 fall.

Dates: 1997: Mar 31-Jun 5 (spring); Jun 16-Aug 20 (summer); Sep 7-Nov 11 (fall). Cost: $6,300. Includes tuition for 2 courses, lodging and 2 meals per day, airfare, and land travel with the program. $125 out-of-state fee. Contact: Larry Millard, Director, UGA Studies Abroad, Visual Arts Building, Univ. of Georgia, Athens, GA 30602-4102; (706) 542-7011, fax (706) 542-2467; cortona@uga.cc.uga.edu.

Japan

Lex Homestay Programs. Lex offers homestay programs in which participants, living as members of a Japanese family, absorb the customs and characteristics of their host culture by taking part in daily life activities. Participants may go sightseeing with their families, meet friends and relatives, and attend festivals. Japanese language ability is not a requirement. Host families are fully screened volunteer members of the Lex organization. Adults, students, and entire families are encouraged to apply.

Dates: Jul-Aug 2, 4- and 6-week programs. Spring, 2-week program. Custom programs year round. Cost: Varies. Four-week summer program is $3,030, includes airfare from West

Coast port of departure. Contact: Steffi Samman, Program Manager, Lex America, 68 Leonard St., Belmont, MA 02178; (617) 489-5800, fax (617) 489-5898; exchange@lexlrf.com.

Latin America

Iberoamerican Cultural Exchange Program. U.S. Spanish students live as a member of a foreign host family for periods of 6 weeks, 3 months, 1 semester, or 1 school year. The program includes pre-experience orientation, local supervision, and—depending on time of year—school attendance. Participants must be 15 to 18 years of age and have studied a minimum of 2 years of Spanish. Applications due 3 months prior to start of program.

Dates: Programs begin Aug, Jan, and Jun. Cost: Six weeks $825, 3 months $925; semester $1,250; school year $2,500. Does not include airfare and insurance. Contact: Bonnie P. Mortell, 13920 93rd Ave., NE, Kirkland, WA 98034; (206) 821-1463, fax (206) 821-1849.

Mexico

Intensive Spanish in Cuauhnahuac. Cuauhnahuac, founded in 1972, offers a variety of intensive and flexible programs geared to individual needs. Six hours of classes daily with no more than 4 students to a class. Housing with Mexican families who really care about you. Cultural conferences, excursions, and special classes for professionals. College credit available.

Dates: Year round. New classes begin every Monday. Cost: $70 registration fee; $600 4 weeks tuition, housing $16 per night. Contact: Marcia Snell, 519 Park Dr., Kenilworth, IL 60043; (800) 245-9335, fax (847) 256-9475; lankysam@aol.com..

Spanish Language in Guanajuato. We work with our students one-on-one or in small groups (2 to 5 students), tailoring instruction

to each student's needs. We teach people of all ages and from many nationalities. Highlights: homestays with families, sports, movies, field trips, hikes, cultural events—all this taking place in the most beautiful colonial setting of Mexico.

Dates: Year round. New classes begin every Monday. Cost: $925. Includes lifetime registration fee, group classes (5 sessions per day Monday-Friday), and a homestay with 3 meals daily for 4 weeks. Lower price for fewer weeks. Contact: Director Jorge Barroso, Instituto Falcon, A.C., Guanajuato, Gto. 36000 Mexico; Tel./fax (011) 52-473-2-36-94, www.infonet.com.mx/falcon.

Spain

High School Exchange Programs. Locations of the programs include Alicante, Castellon, Barcelona, Tarragona, Lerida, Tervel, Zaragoza, Bilbao, San Sebastian, Vitoria. Students can participate in short-term programs during the summer (2, 4, or 6 weeks) or in semester/academic year programs. Students my live with families only, or they may take academic courses. Boarding school option is also available.

Dates: Year round. Cost: Varies by program. Contact: Ann Marie Coyle, FEYDA, 1670 Sheffield Ct., Aurora, IL 60504; (630) 978-4223; amcoyle@aol.com.

Students in Spain. Bravo Tours is a tour operator specializing in programs to Spain for high school and college students organized and chaperoned by your own school's teachers. Our programs cover Madrid, Barcelona, Mallorca, Toldeo, Avila, Segovia, Tenerife, Santiago, Sevilla, Granada, and more.

Contact: See our website at www.bravotours.com or call us at (800) 272-8674.

The Center for Cross-Cultural Study. Learn and live in the vibrant city of Seville. CC-CS, now in its 27th year, offers 2, 3 1/2-week summer sessions and Jan term with intensive courses in language civilization and literature. Upper division academic year and semester programs with courses in liberal arts, social sciences, business, and current events. Intensive intermediate program offers language, literature, civilization, and current events. Homestay and study tours included.

Dates: Jun, Jul, Sep-Dec, Jan, Feb-May. Cost: Fall: $7,440; academic year: $14,770; Jan: $1,910; spring: $7,440; summer: $1,755 per session. Includes tuition, room and board, study tours, fees, laundry. Contact: In the U.S.: CC-CS, Dept. T, 446 Main St., Amherst, MA 01002; (413) 256-0011 or (800) ESPANA-1, fax (413) 256-1968. In Spain: CC-CS, Calle Harinas 18, 41001 Sevilla, Spain; (011) 34-5-422-4107, fax (011) 34-5-422-9204; www.cccs.com.

Switzerland

Bookbinding and Book Restoration. Centro del bel libro is a professional school for artisanal bookbinding and book restoration. Courses are offered on the quarter system.

Dates: Call or write for information. Cost: Call or write for information. Contact: Christina Bordoli, Director, Centro del bel libro, Ascona, 6612 Ascona, via Collegio, Centro culturale B. Berno, Switzerland; (011) 41-91-791-72-36, fax 791-72-56.

United Kingdom

Summer Discovery at Cambridge. Summer Discovery at Cambridge Univ., England is a pre-college study-enrichment experience for high school students currently in grades 10 to 12. College credit, enrichment classes, Princeton Review SAT prep, community service, day and evening activities, sports, exciting excursions to London, trips, and fun. We have a 30-year commitment to the finest student programs.

Dates: Jun 28-Jul 27, 1997; Paris extension: Jul 28-Aug 1, 1996. Cost: $4,199; Paris extension $995. Contact: Lewis Biblowitz, c/o Summer Discovery Educational Programs, 1326 Old Northern Blvd., Roslyn, NY 11576; (800) 645-6611, in NY (516) 621-3939, fax (516) 625-3438; sdiscovery@aol.com.

The Cambridge Prep Experience. A unique opportunity for enterprising 9th graders to spend a month at Cambridge Univ. in a close, supporitve environment. An expert faculty teach 11 different courses including medicine, journalism, creative writing, history, and drama. An introduction to English sports, field trips to London, museum tours, and theater visits are also arranged.

Dates: Jul 2-26, 1996. Cost: $3,895. Contact: OxBridge Academic Programs, 601 W. 110th St., Suite 7-R, New York, NY 10025-1535; (800) 828-8349, fax (212) 663-8169.

The Oxford Tradition. Students (grades 10-12) live in Oxford for a month of intensive study with an expert faculty in 25 different subjects. Housed in 3 colleges in the medieval town center, students also visit London and Stratford, play English sports, and go to the theater, choral concerts, and a series of special guest lectures.

Dates: Jun 29-Jul 28, 1996. Cost: $4,195. Contact: OxBridge Academic Programs, 601 W. 110th St., Suite 7-R, New York, NY 10025-1535; (800) 828-8349, fax (212) 663-8169.

United States

The Williston Northampton School. The Williston Northampton School welcomes high school age applicants who seek a challenging academic-year program in an American boarding school. Students take a full academic schedule and participate actively in extracurricular areas—sports, music, clubs. Intermediate and advanced ESL available. Excellent facilities and faculty.

Dates: Sep-Jun. Cost: $22,700. Contact: Ann C. Pickrell, Director of Admissions, The Williston Northampton School, 19 Payson Ave., Easthampton, MA 01027; (413) 527-1520, fax (413) 527-9494.

Worldwide

American Int'l. Youth Student. American International Youth Student Exchange Program is a nonprofit high school foreign exchange program in the U.S. and other foreign countries. The purpose of AIYSEP is to establish exchange programs for students in Europe, America, and many other foreign countries. AIYSEP's international office is in Tirubon, CA; area counselors are in Europe, U.S., Australia, New Zealand, Canada, and Japan. AIYSEP believes a greater international understanding is accomplished among people and countries through cultural and homestay programs.

Dates: Offers year, semester, and summer homestay programs. Cost: Year $3,895-$6,000, semester $3,395-$4,400, summer $1,900-$3,000. Contact: American International Youth Student Exchange, 200 Round Hill Rd., Tiburon, CA 94920; (800) 347-7575 or (415) 435-4049, fax (415) 499-5651.

English Course. This course consists of general class, conversation, TOEFL, G-MAT, SAT, and private tutoring. We recruit English teachers with BA degrees and TESL/TEFL/RSA certification, preferably those who have teaching experience in Asian countries.

Dates: Year round. Contact: Triad English Centre, JL. Purnawarman, No. 76, Bandung 40116, Indonesia; (011) 6222 431309, fax (011) 6222 431149; triad09@ibm.net.

Group Travel Abroad—Exchanges and Performances. Groups of 20 or larger with artistic and cultural exchange and performance interests are invited to apply or nominate others for travel and performance opportunities abroad. Homestays and direct exchanges available, performance tours, and institutional services are provided linking educational organizations. No deadlines or eligibility requirements.

Dates: Year long. Cost: Varies by group. FAF seeks subsidies and discounts. Average cost $2,500; grants not available. Contact: Daniel Forté, Friendship Ambassadors Foundation, 31 Park St., Montclair, NJ 07042.

Intercambio Internacional De Estudiantes, A.C. Intercambio is a short-term inbound and outbound cultural exchange program. Students 11-16 years of age are placed with volunteer host families who have a same-gender child similar in age with similar interests.

Dates: Exchanges are during students' summer break and last 7-9 weeks. Cost: $1,700-$2,500, including international transportation and insurance. Contact: Cathy Taxis, Intercambio Internacional De Estudiantes, A.C., 16 Broadway, Suite 107, Fargo, ND 58103; (701) 232-1176 or (800) 437-4170, fax (701) 232-1670.

Legacy International. Summer program brings together in U.S. young people ages 11-18 from over 20 countries. Workshops in leadership, global issues, diplomacy, environment. Join 1,700 alumni from more than 83 countries in a worldwide network of friends. Visit our homepage http://www.infi.net/—legacy.

Dates: Jul 1-21; Jul 27-Aug 16. Cost: $1,700-$2,000. Contact: Mary Helmig, Route 4, Box 265, Bedford, VA 24523; (540) 297-5982, fax (540) 297-1860; legacy@infi.net.

Partnerships International. A short-term, school-to-school pairing program designed to foster long-term academic and cultural partnerships between secondary schools in the U.S. and other countries. Once schools are linked, a group of 6-15 students, accompanied by a faculty member, visits their partner school for approximately 3 weeks. During this time, students live in the homes of host students, attend classes, participate in another way of life, and discover local points of interest.

Dates: Vary with academic year. Cost: Range $800-$1,900 depending on country of destination. Contact: Partnership International/NASSP, 1904 Association Dr., Reston, VA 22091; (800) 253-7746, fax (703) 476-6319.

People to People Student Ambassador Program. The People to People Student Ambassador Program selects high school and junior high school students to participate in 2- to 4-

week educational programs in Eastern and Western Europe, Australia, New Zealand, China, and South Africa. Participants live with families for periods of 2 to 5 days in several of the countries visited. High school and university credits are available.

Dates: Students depart mid-Jun to mid-Jul. Cost: Tuition ranges from $2,175 to $3,990. Includes transportation. Contact: Paul Watson, People to People Student Ambassador Program, South 110 Ferrall, Spokane, WA 99202-4861; (509) 534-0430 or (509) 534-5245.

Phenix International Campuses, Inc. Spring and summer language programs to Germany, France, Spain, Mexico, Costa Rica. Combination of homestay and travel. Small groups with teacher chaperones. Individualized programs possible with your itinerary. Recommendations from former students and teachers. All inclusive prices. Twenty-eight years experience.

Dates: Spring and summer vacation times. Cost: Each program individually priced. Contact: Nellie Jackson, Director, Phenix International Campuses, 7651 N. Carolyn Dr., Castle Rock, CO 80104; (303) 688-9397, fax (303) 688-6543.

Putney Student Travel, Inc. Putney Student Travel offers 5 categories of programs offering a variety of small group trips: Wilderness, Adventure Travel, Language Learning, Community Service, and Pre-College Programs. Travel programs to Europe, China, Australia, and New Zealand allow the students to experience the true country. Language programs in France and Spain emphasis acquiring conversational fluency in fun and active settings. Community Service programs (Eastern Europe, Central America, Africa, the Caribbean, and the U.S.) emphasize helping those in need.

Dates: Jun-Aug; 4-, 5-, and 6-week programs. Cost: $3,390-$7,590. Contact: Jeffrey Shumlin and Peter Shumlin, Directors, Putney Student Travel, Inc., P.O. Box 707, Putney, VT 05346; (802) 387-5885, fax (802) 387-4276; pst@sover.net.

Sport For Understanding. Sport For Understanding (SFU) is an international exchange program for 14- to 19-year-old student athletes of average to better ability who wish to pursue their interests in sport, travel, and culture for 4 weeks during the summer. SFU is a summer program of Youth For Understanding (YFU) International Exchange, a private, nonprofit, educational organization dedicated to international understanding and world peace.

Dates: Summer programs of 3 to 4 weeks. Cost: Program fees for athletes range from $2,800 to $3,100 depending on the sport and destination. Contact: Sport For Understanding, International Center, 3501 Newark St., NW, Washington, DC 20016-3199; (800) 424-3691, fax (202) 895-1104.

The U.S. Experiment in International Living. High school students can choose from programs in 19 countries, concentrating on language, study, adventure travel, community or homestay, and travel. Each program also includes an in-country orientation, usually in the capital city, and a homestay with a family.

Dates: Summer—starting late Jun. Cost: From $1,900-$5,000. Contact: The U.S. Experiment in International Living, P.O. Box 676, Kipling Rd., Brattleboro, VT 05302-0676; (800) 345-2929, fax (802) 258-3428.

World Experience Student Exchange Program. World Experience offers an opportunity to have an experience of a lifetime. Learn another language while living with a host family from one of 25 countries for a semester or school year. Attend school locally. Add a new dimension to your life. Eligibility: 15-18 years. 3.0 GPA.

Dates: Aug or Jan departure for 1 to 2 semesters. Cost: $2,600 plus individual country fees for 1 year; $2,265 plus individual country fees for 1 semester. Contact: World Experience, 2440 Hacienda Blvd #116, Hacienda Heights, CA 91745; (800) 633-6653, fax (818) 333-4914; weworld@aol.com.

WORK

Any individual with guts and gusto,
from students to grandmothers,
has the potential for funding themselves
as they travel to the corners of the globe.
—SUSAN GRIFFITH, PAGE 289

Working Abroad

Experiencing a Foreign Culture from the Inside

By Susan Griffith

We look for alternatives to the conventional two-week vacation for a multitude of reasons: traveling in out-of-the-ordinary ways or to out-of-the-ordinary places is, by definition, one of the best ways to shake off the boredom which comes with routine. Other reasons are more positive: to experience a foreign culture from the inside rather than as an onlooker, to fill a gap of time in our life (perhaps between graduation and the working world or one job and another) in a productive way, to improve our knowledge of foreign languages and cultures, to gain practical skills.

Underlying all these worthy motives for shunning mass market tourism is a belief that the experience of doing it our way and traveling outside the safe parameters will be more rewarding and even more fun. Experiences which require some personal input are potentially more valuable than those purchased off the peg.

Working abroad for an extended period gives us the chance to absorb a foreign culture, to meet foreign people on their own terms. The kind of job we find obviously determines the stratum of society in which we will mix and therefore the content of the experience. The traveler who spends a few weeks picking olives for a Cretan farmer will get very different insights and have more culturally worthwhile experiences than the traveler who settles for working at a beach cafe frequented only by partying foreigners.

Generalizations about the valuable cultural insights afforded by working in a foreign land should be tempered with a careful consideration of the reality of doing a job abroad. True "working holidays" are rare, though they do exist. Traveling Americans have exchanged their labor for a free trip with an outback Australian camping tour operator or on a cruise to the midnight sun. But jobs tend to be jobs wherever you do them. There is little scope for visiting historic sights or even making friends if you are stranded in an obscure industrial town teaching English six days a week or cooped up in a damp caravan which serves as an office for a camping holiday operator.

Yet those who have shed their unrealistic expectations are normally exhilarated by the novelty and challenge of working abroad. Any individual with guts and gusto, from students to grandmothers, has the potential for funding themselves as they travel to the corners of the globe. In hopes of soothing the minds of the irresolute, here are some general guidelines to preface the specific information and contact addresses included in this *Alternative Travel Directory*.

Motives. Some travelers have future career prospects in view when they go abroad; a few go in search of highly paid jobs. Success is easier for people with acknowledged qualifications such as nurses and pipe-fitters, though cherry pickers and pot washers have been known to earn and save substantial sums. Those on open-ended trips may decide to postpone cashing their last traveler's check by looking around for ways of boosting their travel fund. They may find paid work, or they may decide to volunteer their labor in exchange for a bed and board.

Advance Planning. The aspiring working traveler either arranges a definite job before leaving home or gambles on finding something on the spot. There is a lot to recommend prior planning, especially for people who have never traveled abroad and who feel some trepidation at the prospect. Jobs can be pre-arranged either through private contacts or with the help of a mediating organization.

A range of organizations, both public and private, can offer advice and practical assistance to those who wish to arrange a job before leaving home. Some accept a tiny handful of individuals who satisfy stringent requirements; others accept almost anyone who can pay the required fee. Many work schemes and official exchanges require a lot of advance planning since it is not unusual for an application deadline to fall six or nine months before departure.

While it's easy to arrange a job to teach English in the former Soviet Union or work on an Israeli kibbutz, the price you pay for this security is that you commit yourself to a new life, however temporary, sight unseen. Furthermore, a participation fee in some cases can be as expensive as booking a conventional holiday.

The alternative to these packaged arrangements is to wait until after arrival at your destination to explore local job possibilities. In the course of research for my book *Work Your Way Around the World*, I have come across many examples of fearless travelers who are prepared to arrive in a foreign city with very little money, confident that a means by which they can earn money will present itself. In most cases it does, but not without a few moments of panic and desperation.

Like job-hunting in any context, it will be much easier to contend with the inevitable competition if prospective employers can meet you in the flesh and be assured that you are available to start work the minute a vacancy crops up. For casual work on farms or arranging a passage on a transatlantic yacht, a visit to a village pub frequented by farmers or yachties is worth dozens of speculative applications from home.

The more unusual and interesting the job the more competition it will attract. Only a small percentage of applicants for advertised jobs actually get the chance to work as underwater models in the Caribbean. Other, less glamorous, options can absorb an almost unlimited number of people. International workcamps, for example, mobilize thousands of volunteers from many countries every year to build footpaths, work with disabled persons, etc.

Red Tape. Work permits and residence visas are not readily available in many countries and for many kinds of jobs. In most cases, job-seekers from overseas must find an employer willing to apply to the immigration authorities on their behalf well in advance of the job's starting date, while they are still in their home country. This is easier for nuclear physicists and foreign correspondents than for mere mortals, though in certain countries English teachers are welcomed by the authorities. In an organized exchange program like the ones administered by Council on International Educational Exchange and InterExchange the red tape is taken care of by the sponsoring organization.

Temporary jobs like apple picking and burger flipping will never qualify for a work permit, and unofficial employment can quite often lead to exploitative working conditions.

Improving Your Chances. Preparation will improve your chances either of being accepted on an organized work scheme or convincing a potential employer of your superiority to the competition. For example, before leaving home you might take a short course in teaching English as a foreign language, cooking, word processing, or sailing—all skills which have been put to good us by working travelers. If you are serious, you might learn or improve your knowledge of a foreign language.

Even if you are not lucky enough to have friends and family scattered strategically throughout the world, it is always worth broadcasting your intentions to third cousins, pen friends, and visiting Oriental professors. The more widely publicized your travel plans, the better your chance of a lead.

Even if you set off without an address book full of contacts, your fellow travelers are undoubtedly the best source of information on job prospects; most are surprisingly generous with their information and assistance. Youth hostels can be a gold mine for the job seeker. Jobs may even be advertised on the notice board. Any locals or expatriates you meet are a potential source of help. Any skill or hobby, from jazz music to motor car racing, can become the basis for pursuing contacts.

Local English language newspapers like Mexico City's *The News*, the *Bangkok Post*, or *Cairo Today* may carry job advertisements appropriate to your situation, or may be a good place for you to advertise your services. The most effective method of finding a job overseas is to walk in and ask. As in any job hunt, it helps to have a neat appearance and show a keenness and persistence. If you want a job for which there appear to be no openings, volunteer. If you prove yourself competent, you will have an excellent chance of filling a vacancy if one does occur.

Seasonal Jobs are the ones most likely to go to itinerant foreigners. In times of recession the number of temporary jobs available may even increase since employers are not eager to expand their permanent staff but will need extra help at busy times.

Farmers and hotel/restaurant managers are the best potential sources of employment, and, in most cases, one setback leads to a success once you are on the track.

English teaching normally requires some experience and a nine-month commitment, though many travelers from Bangkok to Buenos Aires have used the Yellow Pages to direct them to local language schools willing to employ native speakers of English as conversational assistants.

Young women and (increasingly) young men who want the security of a family placement and who may also wish to learn a European language, may choose to live with a family helping to look after the children in exchange for pocket money. Such positions can be found on the spot by means of advertisement or in advance through agencies, like AuPair Homestay.

Volunteering. Paid work in developing nations is rarely available, yet many travelers arrange to live for next to nothing doing something positive. Charities and aid organizations offer a range of volunteer opportunities around the world. Many volunteer agencies require more than a curiosity about a country; they require a strong wish to become involved in a specific project and in many cases an ideological commitment to a cause. Almost without exception, volunteers must be self-funding.

For anyone with a green conscience, conservation organizations throughout the world welcome volunteers for short or long periods in projects ranging from tree planting to gibbon counting. Unfortunately, the more glamorous projects, such as helping accompanying scientific research expeditions into wild and woolly places, charge volunteers a great deal of money for the privilege of helping.

Whether you set off to work abroad with the help of a mediating organization or with the intention of living by your wits, you are bound to encounter interesting characters and lifestyles, collect a wealth of anecdotes, increase your self-reliance, and feel that you have achieved something. Inevitably there will be some surprises along the way.

CHAPTER 16

WORK
ABROAD
RESOURCES

Looking for international work, whether abroad or in the U.S. with an international organization, can be daunting—and downright frustrating without good resources. Fortunately, there are now useful guides for almost any field in almost any country.

But you won't find many in your bookstore. Some of the best guides, published by small organizations, lack retail distribution. Even books by major publishers may not be stocked. To help you in your search, we provide complete contact information (if no address is given, see the last section, Key Publishers and Organizations).

The best resource is useless if it's not appropriate for what you want:

Worldwide Overviews and Overviews by Geographic Area (page 294) include information about work, study, and travel options, either worldwide or for a specific region.

Short-Term Paid Work Abroad Resources (page 298) are for casual work abroad, often—though not always—for students or recent graduates, and generally not career-related. The positions last from a summer to 6 months. Typical location: Western Europe. Look into

these a few months before going.

International Internships (page 299), like the international careers they can help open up, may be either located in the U.S. with international organizations, or overseas. They are often unpaid. Start your search early, as applications can be due three to nine months in advance.

Teaching English (page 301) may not require any special credentials other than having English as your native language and a year's commitment (and usually a college degree). Typical locations: Eastern Europe and Asia. Apply as early as December prior to the fall you want to start.

Teaching K-12/University Level (page 304) includes resources for teachers with credentials. Typical locations: worldwide. Major K-12 job fairs are in February (apply in November).

Volunteer Options (page 305) are the best choice for working in developing countries or for social causes anywhere. Many do "pay," at least room and board, and it may be possible to defer educational loans during the volunteer assignment. Typical locations: Africa, Eastern and Western Europe, Latin America, and North America (with international volunteer organizations). For summer workcamps apply March-May. For long-term options like the Peace Corps, apply six to nine months in advance.

International Careers (page 308) resources offer help in planning for a "global" lifetime, which more often than not develops in several stages. Typical home-base location for American citizens: U.S.

International Job Listings (page 312) include newsletters specializing in international job openings in all sectors, but advertised jobs tend to be only a fraction of those actually available.

Internet Resources (page 313) lists some of the most useful e-mail discussion groups and World Wide Web sites for work abroad and international careers.

* **Resources of broadest interest**—and thus essential for libraries—are marked with an asterisk.

** **Best resources to start with,** or for a small library, are marked with two asterisks.

The reviews indicate other outstanding resources whose focus is more specialized. As information of this type becomes dated quickly, I have made every possible attempt to ascertain the latest edition of each resource. Please send updates to me at the address indicated at the end of this section.

Worldwide Overviews

** **Academic Year Abroad / Vacation Study Abroad,** edited by Sara Steen. 1996 (revised annually). 650/432 pp. $42.95/$36.95 from Institute of International Education. Authoritative and comprehensive directories of over 4,150 study and work abroad programs of-fered by U.S. and foreign universities and private organizations (semester/summer). Indexes for internships, practical training, student teaching, volunteer/service, professional and adult courses, as well as fields of study and location. Can be found in most college libraries and study abroad offices.

* **Council Scholarships.** (1) ISIC Travel Grants for Educational Programs in Developing Countries cover transportation costs for undergraduates to study, work or volunteer in developing countries. (2) Bailey Minority Student Scholarships cover transportation costs for undergraduate students of color to study, work, or volunteer with any Council program. Contact Council toll-free at (888) COUNCIL for applications.

* **Fellowships in International Affairs: A Guide to Opportunities in the United States and Abroad,** edited by Gale Mattox. 1994. 195 pp. Women in International Security. $17.95 plus $3 shipping from Lynne Rienner Publishers, 1800 30th St., Suite 314, Boulder CO 80301; (303) 444-6684. Well-researched directory of fellowships and grants for students, scholars and practitioners (most are for graduate and postdoctoral students or professionals). Indexes for level of study and geographic specialization.

* **Financial Aid for Research and Creative Activities Abroad 1996-1998,** edited by Gail Ann Schlachter and R. David Weber. 1996. 440 pp. $45 plus $4 shipping from Reference Service Press, 1100 Industrial Rd., Suite 9, San Carlos, CA 94070; (415) 594-0743, fax (415) 594-0411. Lists over 1,300 funding sources available to support research, professional development, teaching assignments, or creative activities. Sources mainly for graduate students, postdoctorates, and professionals. Indexes for level of study, location, and subject.

* **Financial Aid for Study and Training Abroad 1994-1996,** edited by Gail Ann Schlachter and R. David Weber. 1996. 275 pp.

$38.50 plus $4 shipping from Reference Service Press (see above). Lists 1,000 funding sources available to support formal educational programs such as study abroad, training, internships, workshops, or seminars. Sources for high school, undergraduate and graduate students, postdoctorates; some for professionals. Indexes for level of study, location, and subject.

** **Financial Resources for International Study: A Guide for US Nationals,** edited by Sara Steen. 1996. $39.95 from IIE. Authoritative and comprehensive directory based on a survey of over 5,000 organizations and universities in the U.S. and abroad. Lists funding sources available to support undergraduate, graduate, post-doctorate, and professional learning abroad, from study and research to internships and other work experiences. Indexes for level of study, subject, and organization.

Harvard Guide to International Experience by William Klingelhofer. 1989. 159 pp. $15 postpaid from Office of Career Services, 54 Dunster St., Harvard Univ., Cambridge, MA 02138; (617) 495-2595. Half of this book is devoted to working or volunteering abroad, with numerous insightful reports by students.

* **The High-School Student's Guide to Study, Travel, and Adventure Abroad,** edited by Richard Christiano. 1995. 308 pp. St. Martins. $13.95 from Council. Describes over 200 programs for high-school students, including language programs, summer camps, homestays, study tours, and work and volunteer opportunities. Indexes for program type and location.

** **Intercultural Press Catalog.** Updated quarterly. Free from Intercultural Press, Inc., or see http://www.bookmasters.com/intercelt.htm. Catalog of practical books on international cross-cultural issues in settings ranging from academic to business.

** **International Job, Career, and Travel Re-**sources for the 1990s. Free from Impact Publications, or see www.impactpublications.com. Catalog of hard-to-find books on international jobs and careers which can be ordered from Impact.

* **Money for International Exchange in the Arts,** edited by Jane Gullong and Noreen Tomassi. 1992. 126 pp. $14.95 from Institute of International Education. Lists grant sources, exchange programs, artists' residencies and colonies for individuals and organizations in the creative arts.

* **NAFSA's Guide to Education Abroad for Advisers and Administrators,** edited by William Hoffa, John Pearson, Marvin Slind. 1993 (new edition, 1996). 313 pp. $20 (members) or $30 (non-members) plus $4.50 shipping from NAFSA Publications. A indispensable reference for education abroad offices, providing an overview of principles and practices, and detailed information for advisers; not a directory of programs. Includes one chapter on advising for work abroad and international careers.

* **Peterson's Study Abroad 1996: A Guide to Semester, Summer and Year Abroad Academic Programs.** 1996 (revised annually). 955 pp. $26.95 plus $6.75 shipping from Peterson's Guides. Detailed information on over 2,000 study abroad programs worldwide. Includes essays on credit, financial aid, nontraditional destinations, internships and volunteering, and travelling (also for those with disabilities). Indexes for field of study, location, host institutions, and internships.

Smart Vacations: The Traveler's Guide to Learning Abroad. 1993. 320 pp. St. Martin's Press. $14.95 from Council. Guide to programs for adults lists study tours, opportunities for voluntary service, field research and archaeological digs, environmental and professional projects, fine arts, and more.

Teenager's Vacation Guide to Work, Study,

and **Adventure Abroad** by Victoria Pybus. 1992. Vacation Work. $16.95 from Ulysses Books. Addressed to a British audience, this guide covers jobs, study courses, and adventure holidays available for teenagers in Britain and abroad during school vacations.

** **Transitions Abroad.** Available from Transitions Abroad, P.O. Box 1300, Amherst, MA 01004-1300, (800) 293-0373; trabroad@aol.com. $24.95/6 issues, $44/12 issues. Also available in bulk for educators. Published 6 times a year, this is the only U.S. periodical which gives extensive coverage to work abroad options, in addition to all other varieties of education abroad.

What in the World is Going On? A Guide for Canadians Wishing to Work, Volunteer or Study in Other Countries by Alan Cumyn. 1995. CAN$20 postpaid from Canadian Bureau for International Education, 220 Laurier Ave. W., Suite 1100, Ottawa, Ontario K1P 5Z9, Canada; (613) 237-4820. Includes a comprehensive listing of work abroad possibilities, organized according to skills required and location. Invaluable for Canadians.

* **Work, Study, Travel Abroad: The Whole World Handbook 1994-1995,** edited by Lazar Hernandez and Max Terry. 1994. 605 pp. St. Martin's Press. $13.95 from Council. Overview of opportunities around the world for college students. Lists only programs of Council members. Indexes for country and field.

* **A World of Options: A Guide to International Exchange, Community Service and Travel for Persons with Disabilities** by Christa Bucks. 1996. 659 pp. Mobility International USA (MIUSA). For price and to order new edition, contact: MIUSA, Box 10767, Eugene, OR 97440; Tel./TDD (503) 343-1284; miusa@igc.apc.org. Comprehensive guide to international educational exchange, volunteer service, and travel for persons with disabilities.

Overviews By Geographic Area

** **After Latin American Studies: A Guide to Graduate Study and Fellowships, Internships, and Employment** by Shirley A. Kregar and Annabel Conroy. 1995. $10 (check payable to Univ. of Pittsburgh) postpaid from: Center for Latin American Studies, 4E04 Forbes Quad, Univ. of Pittsburgh, Pittsburgh, PA 15260; (412) 648-7392, fax (412) 648-2199; clas+@pitt.edu, http://www.pitt.edu/~clas. The essential resource for anyone with career or scholarly interests in this region—an information-packed bargain. Most listings not overseas. Extensive bibliography. Also available, free: ** **A Guide to Financial Assistance for Graduate Study, Dissertation Research and Internships for Students in Latin American Studies.** 1996.

Beyond Safaris: A Guide to Building People-to-People Ties with Africa by Kevin Danaher. Africa World Press, Inc. 1991. 193 pp. $12.95 from Global Exchange. Tells how to build links between U.S. citizens and grassroots development efforts in Africa; one brief chapter on volunteering and studying abroad.

Bridging the Global Gap: A Handbook to Linking Citizens of the First and Third Worlds by Medea Benjamin and Andrea Freedman. 1989. 338 pp. Seven Locks Press. $12.95 from Global Exchange. Information on ending hunger and poverty and building peaceful international ties through direct action. For overseas options see The Peace Corps and More (below).

** **China Bound (Revised): A Guide to Life in the PRC** by Anne Thurston. 1994. 252 pp. National Academy of Sciences. $24.95 plus $4 shipping from National Academy Press, 2101 Constitution Ave. NW, Lockbox 285, Washington, DC 20055; (800) 624-6242. Updated classic on studying or teaching in the People's

Republic of China. Invaluable for university students, researchers, and teachers.

Compendium: U.S. Assistance to Central and Eastern Europe and the Newly-Independent States, edited by Francis A. Luzzato. 1993 (no revision planned). 347 pp. $15 postpaid from Citizen's Democracy Corps, 1735 I St. NW, Suite 720, Washington, DC 20006; (800) 394-1945. Directory of 700 U.S. organizations providing voluntary assistance (everything from volunteer-sending to educational exchanges to scholarships) in Eastern Europe and Russia. See also Post-Soviet Handbook (below).

The Directory of Work and Study In Developing Countries by David Leppard. 1990 (new edition, 1997). 222 pp. Vacation Work. $14.95 from Ulysses Books. Comprehensive guide to employment, voluntary work, and academic opportunities in developing countries.

** Japan: Exploring Your Options—A Guide to Work, Study and Research in Japan, edited by Gretchen Shinoda and Nicholas Namba. 1995. 437 pp. $20 ($15 students) plus $5 shipping (checks payable to National Planning Association) from Gateway Japan, NPA, 1424 16th St. NW, Suite 700, Washington, DC 20036; (202) 884-7646, fax (202) 265-4673. Comprehensive directory of study, cultural, and homestay programs; fellowships and research; and teaching opportunities. A must for anyone interested in Japan.

* Living in China: A Guide to Teaching and Studying in China Including Taiwan by R. Weiner, M. Murphy, and A. Li. 1991 (new edition, Feb 1997). $16.95 from China Books and Periodicals, Inc., 2929 24th St., San Francisco, CA 94110; (415) 282-2994, fax (415) 282-0994; chinabks@slip.net. Practical advice with extensive directories of schools and colleges as well as organizations which offer study abroad or teacher placement.

Opportunities in Africa. 1993. 24 pp. The African-American Institute. $3 postpaid from Interbook, 131 Varick St., New York, NY 10013; (212) 566-1944. Booklet lists resources for students and professionals for teaching, working, visiting, or doing business in Africa.

* Studying and Working in France: A Student Guide by Russell Cousins, Ron Hallmark, and Ian Pickup. 1994. 314 pp. $17.95 from Manchester Univ. Press (U.S. distributor St. Martin's Press). Very useful information for directly enrolling in French universities or language courses; one brief chapter on working.

* The Peace Corps and More: 120 Ways to Work, Study, and Travel in the Third World by Medea Benjamin. 1993 (new edition, 1996). 107 pp. Seven Locks Press. $6.95 from Global Exchange. Describes 120 programs that allow anyone to gain Third World experience while promoting the ideals of social justice and sustainable development. Lacks indexes.

* The Post-Soviet Handbook: A Guide to Grassroots Organizations and Internet Resources in the Newly Independent States by M. Holt Ruffin, Joan McCarter, and Richard Upjohn. 1996. 393 pp. Univ. of Washington Press. $19.95 plus $4 shipping from Center for Civil Society International, 2929 N.E. Blakely St., Seattle, WA 98105; (206)-523-4755, fax (206) 523-1974; ccsi@u.washington.edu, http://solar.rtd.utk.edu/~ccsi/ccsihome.html. The best guide to U.S. and host-country nongovernmental organizations involved in "institution building" in the former Soviet Union; many welcome volunteers.

** Travel Programs in Central America, 1995-96, edited by Kim Harley and Ann Salzarulo-McGuigan. 1995 (revised annually). 91 pp. $8 postpaid from San Diego Interfaith Task Force on Central America (IFTF), c/o Ann Salzarulo-McGuigan, 56 Seaview Ave., North Kingston, RI 02852 (written orders only). Comprehensive guide to 250 organizations for study, conferences, environmental projects, human rights, and short- and long-term service in all fields. Essential for finding options in this region.

Short-Term Paid Work Abroad

The Au Pair & Nanny's Guide to Working Abroad by Susan Griffith and Sharon Legg. 1993. 300 pp. Vacation Work. $16.95 from Ulysses Books. Practical, insightful advice on how to prepare for and find a child care job in another country. Lists agencies worldwide. Work Your Way Around the World (below) has some of this information.

** **Council Work Abroad.** Free brochure from Council Work Abroad, 205 E. 42nd St., New York, NY 10017-5706; (888)-COUNCIL; wabrochure@ciee.org. Application for paying work exchange programs through Council, a large non-profit organization, for college students and recent grads in Britain, Canada, Costa Rica, France, Germany, Ireland, Jamaica, and New Zealand. Approx. 6,000 U.S. participants annually.

** **Council Work Abroad Participant's Handbooks** can be requested from Council at (212) 822-2659 by college study abroad or career planning offices; otherwise for program participants only (not for sale).

* **The Directory of Overseas Summer Jobs,** edited by David Woodworth. Updated each Jan. 256 pp. Vacation Work. $15.95 from Peterson's Guides. More than 30,000 temporary jobs, paid and volunteer, in over 50 countries: who to contact, pay rates, how and when to apply. Valuable information on work permits required. Council (see above) and AIPT (see Internships section below) can assist Americans in obtaining work permits.

* **The Directory of Summer Jobs in Britain (1996),** edited by David Woodworth. Updated

each Jan. 255 pp. Vacation Work. $15.95 from Peterson's Guides. More than 30,000 jobs listed, ranging from internships, farming, and hotel work to volunteering. Listings include wages, qualifications, and contacts. Americans need a work permit—contact Council or AIPT.

Emplois d'Été en France (1996). Vac-Job, Paris. Updated annually. $14.95. Available from Ulysses Books. Lists temporary summer jobs in France, including names and addresses of employers. In French.

Employment in France for Students. 1991. Free from French Cultural Services, 972 5th Ave., New York NY 10021; (212) 439-1400, fax (212) 439-1455. Work regulations and work possibilities. Also free: Au Pair Work in France.

Le guide du Job-Trotter en France by Emmanuelle Rozenzweig. 1994. 204 pp. Dakota Editions (France). $18.95 from Ulysses Books. In French. Guide to temporary jobs in France.

Guide to Cruise Ship Jobs by George Reilly. 1994. 40 pp. $5.95 from Pilot Books. Step-by-step guidance.

How to Get a Job with a Cruise Line by Mary Fallon Miller. 1994. 191 pp. $17.95 from Ticket to Adventure, Inc., P.O. Box 41005, St. Petersburg, FL 33743; (800) 929-7447. Detailed information on how to apply plus tips from cruise line employees. Bibliography.

** **Work Your Way Around The World** by Susan Griffith. 1995 (new edition, Jan 1997). 512 pp. Vacation Work. $17.95 from Peterson's Guides. The authoritative (and only) guide to looking for short-term jobs while abroad. Extensive country-by-country narratives include first-hand reports.

* **Working Abroad (InterExchange).** Free brochure from InterExchange, Inc., 161 6th Ave., New York, NY 10013; (212) 924-0446, fax (212) 924-0575; interex@earthlink.net.

Non-profit program offers placements for paid work abroad, internships, English teaching, and au pair in Europe.

* Working Holidays 1996. Updated annually. 382 pp. Central Bureau (U.K.). $18.95 from IIE. Thoroughly researched information on 101,000 paid and voluntary work opportunities in over 70 countries. Written for a British audience, it sometimes omits relevant U.S. organizations.

Working in Ski Resorts—Europe and North America by Victoria Pybus and Charles James. 1993. Vacation Work. $14.95 from Ulysses Books. Available jobs plus reports from resorts.

* Worldwide Internships and Service Education (WISE). Free brochure from WISE, 303 S. Craig St., Suite 202, Pittsburgh, PA 15213; (412) 681-8120, fax (412) 681-8187; wise@unix.cls.pitt.edu. Non-profit program offers experiential learning placements for au pair (Europe), service and internships (U.K.), farm work (Norway), and low-cost language immersion programs.

International Internships

** Academic Year Abroad / Vacation Study Abroad. (See Worldwide Overviews section above.) Indexes for internships, practical training, volunteering, and student teaching list over 1,100 programs, most of which charge tuition and give academic credit.

** The ACCESS Guide to International Affairs Internships in the Washington, DC Area, edited by Bruce Seymore II and Susan D. Krutt. 1995. 157 pp. $19.95 plus $5 shipping from ACCESS, 1511 K St. NW, Suite 643, Washington, DC 20005; (202) 783-6050, fax (202) 783-4767. The most up-to-date directory for the city with the most internships in international affairs. Also: International Affairs Directory of Organizations, edited by

Bruce Seymore II. 1992. 326 pp. $30. Includes U.S. and overseas organizations.

* American-Scandinavian Foundation. Free brochure on study and scholarships (all fields) and work opportunities. This non-profit organization also offers paid internships in Scandinavia in engineering, horticultural, forestry, and agricultural fields. Apply for internships by late Dec. ASF also assists with obtaining work permits for Scandinavia. Contact ASF at 725 Park Ave., New York, NY 10021; (212) 879-9779, fax (212) 249-3444; asf@amscan.org.

** Association for International Practical Training (AIPT) / International Association for the Exchange of Students for Technical Experience (IAESTE). Free brochures. Non-profit organization provides paid internships in over 60 countries in engineering and science (apply by Dec 10), and in tourism and hotel and restaurant management. They can also assist in obtaining work permits for career-related practical training in other fields. Contact them at 10400 Little Patuxent Parkway, Suite 250, Columbia, MD 21044-3510; (410) 997-2200, fax (410) 992-3924; aipt@aipt.org; www.softaid.net/aipt/aipt.html.

* Center for Interim Programs. Free information from CIP, P.O. Box 2347, Cambridge, MA 02238; (617) 547-0980, fax (617) 661-2864; interimcip@aol.com. Organization provides placements in approx. 3,000 "non-academic but structured" opportunities, from internships to teaching, worldwide for people aged 16-70. Some provide room and board.

* CDS International, Inc. Non-profit organization offers several paying internship programs (deadlines as early as Dec) in Germany in fields ranging from business to engineering. Knowledge of German necessary. CDS also assists with obtaining work permits for Germany. Contact them at 330 Seventh Ave., New York, NY 10001; (212) 760-1400, fax (212) 268-1288; http://www.cdsintl.org.

* Development Opportunities Catalog: A Guide to Internships, Research, and Employment with Development Organizations, edited by Sri Indah Prihadi. 1993 (1996 insert, $5). 127 pp. $8.95 (students), $10 (individuals), $15 (institutions) plus $1.50 shipping from Overseas Development Network, 333 Valencia St., Suite 330, San Francisco, CA 94103; (415) 431-4204; odn@igc.org. Descriptions of 79 development organizations offering internships or staff positions in the U.S. (and a few abroad). Indexed by subject and location. Also available from ODN, a nationwide student organization for development issues: Career Opportunities in International Development in Washington, D.C.,edited by Brian Dunn. 1994. 98 pp. $6 (students), $9 (individuals), $12 (institutions). Opportunities in Grassroots Development in California, edited by Wesley Batten. 1994. 89 pp. $7 (students), $10 (individuals), $15 (institutions). Opportunities in International Development in New England, edited by Michelle Burts. 1993. $7 (students), $10 (individuals), $15 (institutions). Add $1.50 shipping for each book.

** Directory of International Internships: A World of Opportunities by Charles Gliozzo, Vernicka Tyson, Adela Pena, and Bob Dye. 1994. 168 pp. Michigan State University. $25 postpaid from Career Development and Placement Services, Attn: International Placement, MSU, 113 Student Services Bldg., East Lansing, MI 48824; (517) 355-9510 ext. 371. Describes experiential educational opportunities offered through educational institutions, government, and private organizations—for academic credit, for pay, or simply for experience. Indexed by subject and country, this is the only directory to both academic and non-academic internships located abroad.

* The Directory of Summer Jobs in Britain. Includes listings of internships in Britain ("traineeships"). The ** CIEE/BUNAC Work in Britain Participant's Handbook is an even better source. (See Short-Term Work section above.)

* Guide to Careers in World Affairs. (See Careers section below.) Lists internships with some 200 international organizations located in the U.S., most not found elsewhere.

* A Handbook for Creating Your Own Internship in International Development by Natalie Folster and Nicole Howell. 1994. 98 pp. $7.95 plus $1.50 shipping from Overseas Development Network (above). How to arrange a position; evaluate your skills, motivations and learning objectives. Not a directory of opportunities.

* International Cooperative Education Program. Free information from ICE, 15 Spiros Way, Menlo Park CA 94025; (415) 323-4944, fax (415) 323-1104; ICEmenlo@aol.com. Organization offers 450 paid summer internships for students with knowledge of foreign languages in Europe, Asia, and South Africa. U.S. or Canadian citizens only. Apply in fall or winter.

International Directory of Youth Internships by Michael Culligan and Cynthia T. Morehouse. 1993. 52 pp. $7.50 plus $3.50 shipping from Apex Press, Publications Office, P.O. Box 337, Croton-on-Hudson, NY 10520; Tel./fax (914) 271-6500. Comprehensive guide to U.N. agencies and U.N.-affiliated organizations that regularly use interns and volunteers. Most internships are in the U.S. and unpaid.

International Health Electives for Medical Students. 1993. American Medical Student Association. $31 ($21 members) for 4-volume set, also available separately, from AMSA Publications, 1890 Preston White Dr., Reston, VA 22091; (703) 620-6600, fax (703) 620-5873; amsatf@aol.com. Overseas internships for third- or fourth-year medical students. Related titles, A Student's Guide to International Health ($7.50/$5.50) and Cross-Cultural Medicine: What to Know Before You Go ($7/ $5), also available from AMSA.

* International Internships and Volunteer Programs by Will Cantrell and Francine Modderno. 1992. 233 pp. $18.95 postpaid

from Worldwise Books. Well-researched information, much of it not available elsewhere, on programs abroad and in the U.S. which can serve as "stepping stones" to international careers, for both students and professionals.

* **The Internship Bible** by Mark Oldman and Samer Hamadeh. 1995. 614 pp. $25 from Princeton Review—Random House; (800) REVIEW-6 or (212) 874-8282, fax (212) 874-0775; interninfo@aol.com. New directory describes in detail paid and unpaid internships offered by more than 900 mostly non-academic organizations. Around 120 of these may offer overseas internships, listed in an index for location. Other indexes for field, benefits, level of study, minority programs, and deadlines.

* **Internships International.** Free information from Judy Tilson, Director, 1116 Cowper Dr., Raleigh, NC 27608; Tel./fax (919) 832-1572; intinl@aol.com. Organization offers unpaid, not-for-credit internship placements in London, Paris, Stuttgart, Florence, Dublin, and Mexico City.

Mexico: Oportunidades de Empleo. 1996 (revised annually). Available from American Chamber of Commerce of Mexico, Lucerna 78, Col. Juárez, 06600 México, D.F.; (011) 52 724-3800, fax 703-3908 or 703-2911. Lists internships in Mexico for Mexican and U.S. students.

* **U.S. Department of State Student Intern Program.** Free brochure and application from U.S. Department of State, Student Intern Program, Recruitment Division, Box 9317, Arlington, VA 22219; (703) 875-4884; http://www.state.gov. Nearly 1,000 unpaid and paid internships annually in Washington and abroad. Only for currently-enrolled undergraduate and graduate students who will continue studies after the internship. Competitive. Deadlines: Nov 1 (summer), Mar 1 (fall), Jul 1 (spring).

* **Volunteer & Internship Possibilities in Israel** by Leon Dow. 1994. Guide is temporarily out-of-print, but information available from University Student Department, World Zionist Organization, 110 E. 59th St., 3rd Fl., New York, NY 10022; (800) 274-7723, fax 212-755-4781; usd@netcom.com.

* **A Year Between: The Complete International Guide to Work, Training, and Travel in a Year Out.** Central Bureau (U.K.). 1994 (new edition, 1997). 288 pp. $18.95 from IIE. Addressed to a British audience, this book describes over 100 internships, teaching, and volunteer possibilities of up to one year, primarily in Britain and Europe.

Teaching English Abroad

Asia Employment Program. (See Now Hiring! Jobs in Asia below.)

English in Asia: Teaching Tactics for the Classrooms of Japan, Korea, Taiwan by John Wharton. 1992. 214 pp. $12.95 plus $2 shipping ($4 first-class) from Global Press, 697 College Pkwy., Rockville, MD 20850; (202) 466-1663. Overview of teaching methodologies and practical details of living in Japan, Korea, and Taiwan. Extensive lists of schools.

* **Fulbright English Teaching Assistantships.** Applications free from USIA Fulbright, U.S. Student Program, 809 United Nations Plaza, New York, NY 10017-3580; (212) 984-5330. Enrolled students should apply through own college. English teaching options for graduates in Belgium/Luxembourg, France, Germany, Hungary, Korea, and Taiwan. Application deadline is Oct 23, 1996 (1 month earlier through campuses) for teaching in 1997-98.

** **Japan Exchange Teaching Program (JET).** FREE brochures. Office of the JET Program, Embassy of Japan, 2520 Massachusetts Ave. NW, Washington, DC 20008; (202) 939-6772 or (202) 939-6773 or (800) INFO-JET, or contact any Japanese embassy or consulate. The largest program for teaching English abroad, with more than 4,000 placements annually. Offers 2 types of positions in Japan: English-teaching assistantships in secondary schools or Coordinator for International Relations (latter requires Japanese proficiency). Application deadline early Dec.

** Japan: Exploring Your Options—A Guide to Work, Study and Research in Japan. (See Worldwide Overviews section above.) Detailed descriptions of English teaching possibilities, through both U.S.- and Japan-based organizations.

Jobs in Japan: The Complete Guide to Living and Working in the Land of Rising Opportunity by John Wharton. 1993. 270 pp. $14.95 plus $2 shipping ($4 first-class) from Global Press (above). More about the details of living in Japan than on teaching. Recent users say it makes the on-site job search sound easier than it now is.

The Korea Super Job Catalog by James F. Haddon. 1993. 215 pp. Bonus Books. $13 postpaid from Korea Services Group, 2950 S.E. Stark, Suite 200, Portland, OR 97214; (503) 230-6932, fax (503) 233-9966; ksg@teleport. com. Practical guide to jobs in Korea for non-Koreans; lists hundreds of employers in most fields. KSG also offers placements, primarily for English teachers.

* Living in China: A Guide to Teaching and Studying in China Including Taiwan. (See Geographic Overviews section above.) Useful tips and hundreds of addresses for anyone who wants to teach English in China or Taiwan; wait for new edition.

Make a Mil-¥en: Teaching English in Japan by Don Best. 1994. 176 pp. $14.95 plus $2 (book rate) or $3.50 (first-class) shipping from Stone Bridge Press, P.O. Box 8208, Berkeley, CA 94707; (800) 947-7271, fax (510) 524-8711. Guide has up-to-date information on everything from the job search to settling in.

* More Than a Native Speaker: An Introduction for Volunteers Teaching Abroad by Don Snow. 1996. 320 pp. $29.95 plus $3.50 shipping from TESOL (see below). Comprehensive source of English teaching ideas and techniques.

Native Speaker: Teach English and See the World by Elizabeth Reid. 1996. 93 pp. $7.95 plus $3 shipping from In One Ear Publications, 29481 Manzanita Dr., Campo, CA 91906-1128; (800) 356-9315. Guide by an American who taught English in Latin America; main focus on teaching tips.

* Now Hiring! Jobs in Asia by Jennifer Dubois, Steve Gutman, and Clarke Canfield. 1994. 289 pp. $17.95 from Perpetual Press, P.O. Box 45628, Seattle, WA 98145-0628; (800) 807-3036. Guide to finding an English teaching job in Japan, South Korea, or Taiwan. Lists U.S. placement organizations and overseas schools. Some information on living and teaching abroad. Similar Asia Employment Program, (several authors are the same) is direct-marketed for $50, supposedly with a guarantee of employment, by Progressive Media Inc., P.O. Box 45220, Seattle, WA 98145-0220; (206) 545-7950. Perpetual Press also publishes * **Now Hiring! Jobs in Eastern Europe** by Clarke Canfield. 1996. 330 pp. $14.95. Similar content to Now Hiring: Jobs in Asia.

* O-Hayo Sensei: The Newsletter of Teaching Jobs in Japan. edited by Lynn Cullivan. Bi-weekly listings by e-mail, $1 per issue or free on the Web. Contact: Editor, O-Hayo Sensei, 1032 Irving St., Suite 508, San Francisco, CA 94122; fax (415) 731-1113; editor@ohayo sensei, www.ohayosensei.com.

Opportunities in Teaching English to Speakers of Other Languages by Blyth Camenson. 1995. 143 pp. $10.95 from VGM Career Horizons. Overview of the professional field of Teaching English as a Foreign/Second Language.

Teach Central Europe by Stephanie Hinton and Judy Moore. 1995. 184 pp. $19.95 plus $4.75 shipping from Teach Central Europe, 536 Mosswood Shoals, Stone Mountain, GA 30087; outside U.S.: Teach Central Europe, Belgicka 36, 120 00 Praha 2, Czech Republic; (011) 422 2423-1730, fax 422 2423-1731. Over 400 addresses of schools and universities which supposedly offer English teaching positions; little information about living or teaching there.

Teach English in Japan by Charles Wordell and Greta Gorsuch. 1992. 212 pp. Japan Times. $18.25 plus $5 shipping from Kinokuniya Book Store, 10 W. 49th St., New York, NY 10020; (212) 765-1461. Valuable for its realistic reports by experienced American teachers; no job search information.

** **Teaching Abroad** by Sara Steen. Planned for 1997. IIE. New edition of this out-of-print directory will be the most authoritative U.S. guide to teaching opportunities worldwide for TESL, K-12, and university teaching.

** **Teaching English Abroad: First-Hand Reports and Resource Information.** 1996. 95 pp. $9.95 postpaid from *Transitions Abroad*. Describes teaching opportunities worldwide by region, legitimate placement organizations, training centers, resource books, first-hand reports. Especially useful for Americans. New edition April 1997.

** **Teaching English Abroad: Talk Your Way Around the World** by Susan Griffith. Vacation Work. 1994 (new edition Jan 1997). 368 pp. $16.95 from Peterson's Guides. The only guide with extensive worldwide coverage (including Western and Eastern Europe, the Middle East, and other regions ignored in other guides), this outstanding volume gives in depth information on everything from preparation to the job search. Extensive directories of schools.

* **Teaching English in Asia: Finding a Job and**

Doing it Well by Galen Harris Valle. 1995. 178 pp. $19.95 from Pacific View Press, P.O. Box 2657, Berkeley, CA 94702. Detailed yet lively overview of teaching English in East and S.E. Asia, with comprehensive teaching tips, by a professional teacher. Few contact addresses provided.

Teaching English Guides (Passport Books/In Print Publishing series). Books in this British series offer extensive advice by professional teachers on teaching and living abroad, tailored to the specific regions covered. All would be valuable for teachers headed abroad, but provide few job search addresses. Available in the U.S. from Passport Books (see NTC/VGM listing); elsewhere from In Print Publishing Ltd., 9 Beufort Terrace, Brighton BN2 2SU, U.K.; (011) 44 1273 682836, fax 1273 620958.

* **Teaching English in Asia** by Jerry and Nuala O'Sullivan. 1996. $14.95. Covers PR China, Hong Kong, India, Indonesia, Japan, South Korea, Malaysia, Philippines, Singapore, Taiwan, Thailand, and Vietnam.

Teaching English in Italy by Martin Penner. 1996. $14.95. Note that the job search in Italy will be extremely difficult for citizens of non-European-Union countries.

** **Teaching English in Eastern & Central Europe** by Robert Lynes. 1996. $14.95. The only book to date with extensive coverage of this region, including Bulgaria, the Czech and Slovak Republics, Hungary, Poland, and Romania.

* **Teaching English in Japan** by Jerry O'Sullivan. 1996. $14.95.

TESOL Placement Bulletin. $21/year (U.S., Canada, Mexico); $31/year (all other countries). Available only to members of TESOL, 1600 Cameron St., Suite 300, Alexandria, VA 22314; (703) 836-0774, fax (703) 518-2535; publ@tesol.edu. The best job bulletin for professionally qualified teachers of ESL/EFL. TESOL also publishes a Directory of U.S. schools providing TESOL training ($16.50 for members and $22.50 for nonmembers).

Teaching Abroad: K-12 And University-Level

** **China Bound (Revised): A Guide to Life in the PRC.** (See Worldwide Overviews section above.) Invaluable for university students, researchers and teachers.

* **College Teaching Abroad: A Handbook of Strategies for Successful Cross-Cultural Exchanges** by Pamela Gale George. 256 pp. Longwood (hardcover). $37.50 plus $5.99 shipping from Allyn and Bacon, 160 Gould St., Needham Heights, MA 02194; (800) 278-3525. Thought-provoking yet practical guide to the cross-cultural dimensions of teaching abroad, based on the reports of 700 Fulbright exchange participants. Essential reading for any teacher headed overseas.

* **Fulbright Scholar Awards Abroad: Grants for Faculty and Professionals.** Free information from Council for International Exchange of Scholars, 3007 Tilden St. NW, Suite 5M, Washington, DC 20008-3009; (202) 686-4000; info@ciesnet.cies.org. Information and application for university-level opportunities for lecturing and research abroad; most positions require doctoral degrees and/or 3 year's professional experience. 1996 deadlines for 1997-98: May 1 (Western Europe, Canada); Aug 1 (rest of world); Nov 1 (international education administrators); Jan 1, 1997 (NATO scholars).

* **Fulbright Teacher Exchange: Opportunities Abroad for Educators.** Free information from the U.S. Information Agency, Fulbright Teacher Exchange Program, 600 Maryland Ave. S.W., Room 235, Washington, DC 20024-2520; (800) 726-0479, fax (202) 401-1433; advise@usia.gov. Program descriptions and application for direct exchanges in over 30 countries for currently employed K-12 and community college faculty and administrators. Deadline for 1997-98: Oct 15.

Global Alternatives—World Learning/SIT. (See Job Listings section below.) Includes teaching positions.

International Educator. Published quarterly. $25 for non-members from International Educator's Institute, P.O. Box 513, Cummaquid, MA 02637; (508) 362-1414. Vacancies in overseas American and international schools plus news about English-speaking K-12 schools.

* **The ISS Directory of Overseas Schools,** edited by Gina Parziale. 1995. 530 pp. International Schools Services. $34.95 from Peterson's Guides, or ISS Inc., P.O. Box 5910, Princeton, NJ 08543; (609) 452-0990, fax (609) 452-2690; iss%iss@mcimail.com, http://www.iss.edu. The most comprehensive and up-to-date directory to overseas K-12 schools that hire qualified American teachers. Available FREE from ISS: NewsLinks, a bimonthly news magazine for the international school community; and Teaching and Administrative Opportunities Abroad, application to ISS job fairs (apply in Nov) for teaching overseas.

Overseas Academic Opportunities. Monthly bulletin. $38/year from Overseas Academic Opportunities, 72 Franklin Ave., Ocean Grove, NJ 07756; Tel./fax (908) 774-1040. Openings primarily for new teachers in all K-12 subject areas for jobs where the only language needed is English and state certification is not required.

Overseas American-Sponsored Elementary Schools Assisted by the U.S. Department of State. Free 30-page pamphlet available from the Office of Overseas Schools, Room 245, SA-29, U.S. Department of State, Washington, DC 20522-2902; (703) 875-7800. Information on private overseas K-12 schools. Fact Sheets, also free, provide more detailed information.

Overseas Employment Opportunities for Educators. Annual. Free from Department of

Defense Dependents Schools, Teacher Recruitment Section, 2461 Eisenhower Ave., Alexandria, VA 22331; (703) 696-3255. Application for K-12 employment opportunities in over 200 schools worldwide serving U.S. military bases. Minimum academic requirement is a baccalaureate degree with at least 18 hours of education courses.

* Overseas Placement Service for Educators. Description and application for one of the 2 largest U.S. placement fairs (the other is ISS, above) for certified K-12 teachers. Free from Overseas Placement Service for Educators, Univ. of Northern Iowa, Cedar Falls, IA 50615-0390; (319) 273-2083, fax (319) 273-3509. Apply by Nov. Job fair participants receive detailed descriptions of schools.

Overseas Teaching Opportunities. Friends of World Teaching. $20 for first three country lists, $4 for each additional country from Friends of World Teaching, P.O. Box 1049, San Diego, CA 92112-1049; (800) 503-7436. List of over 1,000 English-speaking schools in over 100 countries where educators may apply.

Schools Abroad of Interest to Americans. 1991 (new edition 1997). $35 plus $4.50 shipping from Porter Sargent Publishers, 11 Beacon St., Suite 1400, Boston, MA 02108. Descriptive listings of 800 elementary and secondary schools enrolling American and English-speaking students in 130 countries.

* Teach Abroad. 1993 (new edition 1997). 192 pp. £8.99 from the Central Bureau (U.K.). A comprehensive British survey of paid and volunteer teaching opportunities worldwide.

** Teaching Abroad by Sara Steen. Planned for 1997. IIE. New edition of this out-of-print directory will be the most authoritative U.S. guide to teaching opportunities worldwide for TESL, K-12, and university teaching.

Teaching Opportunities in the Middle East and North Africa. 1987. 222 pp. $18 from AMIDEAST, 1730 M St. N.W., Suite 1100, Washington, DC 20036-4045; (202) 776-9600, fax (202) 822-6563. Still-useful survey of 140 K-12 and postsecondary institutions.

Teaching Overseas: The Caribbean and Latin American Area, edited by Carlton H. Bowyer and Burton Fox. 1989. 106 pp. $4 from Inter-Regional Center for Curriculum and Materials Development, P.O. Box 013449, Tuscaloosa, AL 35403. Comprehensive handbook on teaching in 30 U.S.-sponsored schools in Latin America and the Caribbean.

Volunteer Abroad

** Alternatives to the Peace Corps: A Directory of Third World and U.S. Volunteer Opportunities by Phil Lowenthal, Stephanie Tarnoff, and Lisa David. 1996. 88 pp. $9.95 plus $4 shipping from Food First Books, 398 60th St., Oakland, CA 94618; (510) 654-4400 (book orders 800-274-7826); fax (510) 654-4551; foodfirst@igc.apc.org. Thoroughly researched guide to voluntary service, study, and alternative travel overseas and in the U.S. with organizations which "address the political and economic causes of poverty." Excellent bibliography.

Archaeological Fieldwork Opportunities Bulletin, compiled by Susanna Burns. 100 pp. Updated each Jan. Archaeological Institute of America. $13 for AIA members ($15 non-members) from Kendall/Hunt Publishing Co., Order Dept., 4050 West Mark Dr., Dubuque, IA 52002; (800) 228-0810. Comprehensive guide to excavations, field schools, and programs worldwide with openings for volunteers, students, and staff. AIA also publishes Archaeology magazine, which lists volunteer opportunities in the Old World (Mar/Apr) and the New World (May/Jun). For membership in AIA or subscriptions, call (617) 353-9361 or fax (617) 353-6550.

Archaeology Abroad, 31-34 Gordon Square, London WC1H OPY, U.K. Three annual bulletins (Mar, May, and Oct). Lists worldwide projects and provides details on staffing needs.

Directory of Volunteer Opportunities, edited by Kerry L. Mahoney. 1992. 90 pp. CAN$10 (Canadian residents $10.70) in advance from Volunteer Directory, Career Resource Centre, Univ. of Waterloo, Waterloo, Ontario N2L 3G1, Canada; (519) 885-1211 ext. 3001. Over 100 listings of part- and full-time volunteer opportunities in North America and overseas. Especially useful for Canadians.

From the Center of the Earth: Stories out of the Peace Corps, edited by Geraldine Kennedy. 1991. 223 pp. $12.95 from Clover Park Press, P.O. Box 5067, Santa Monica, CA 90409-5067. Interesting accounts by Peace Corps volunteers.

Going Places: A Catalog of Domestic and International Internship, Volunteer, Travel and Career Opportunities in the Fields of Hunger, Housing, Homelessness and Grassroots Development by Joanne Woods. 1991 (new edition, 1997). 63 pp. $6.25 postpaid from National Student Campaign Against Hunger and Homelessness, 11965 Venice Blvd., #408, Los Angeles, CA 90066; (800)-NOHUNGE or (310) 397-5270 ext. 324; fax (310) 391-0053. Well-researched descriptions of more than 90 organizations and selected graduate programs.

* How to Serve and Learn Effectively: Students Tell Students by Howard Berry and Linda Chisholm. 1992. 77 pp. $7.00 from Partnership for Service Learning, 815 2nd Ave., Suite 315, New York, NY 10017, (212) 986-0989, fax (212) 986-5039; pslny@aol.com. Reality-testing and exploration of motivations for students considering volunteering overseas. Not a directory of opportunities.

* InterAction Member Profiles 1995-1996. 1995. 350 pp. $40 ($20 members) from InterAction Publications, 1717 Massachusetts Ave. NW, Suite 801, Washington, DC 20036; (202) 667-8227, fax (202) 667-8236; iac@interaction.org. Up-to-date information on 150 U.S. private voluntary organizations in relief and development work. Details which agencies are doing what in which countries. Also by Interaction: Monday Developments. $65 per year (individuals); $275 per year (institutions). Biweekly job listing in this field. The Essential Internet. 47 pp. $12. Also see Internet Resources section below.

* The International Directory of Voluntary Work by David Woodworth. 1993 (new edition, Jan 1997). 264 pp. Vacation Work. $15.95 from Peterson's Guides. Directory of over 500 agencies offering volunteer jobs and how to apply. Most comprehensive listing of volunteer opportunities in Britain and Europe of any directory.

* International Voluntary Service Guide: Peace Through Deeds, Not Words. Updated each Apr. $3 postpaid from SCI-IVS, 5474 Walnut Level Rd., Crozet, VA 22932; (804) 823-1826, fax (804) 823-5027; sciivsusa@igc.apc.org. Describes short-term volunteer options in Europe, Africa, Asia, and North America available through SCI-IVS.

* International Workcamper (VFP). Free brochure available from Volunteers for Peace (VFP), International Workcamps, 43 Tiffany Rd., Belmont, VT 05730; (802) 259-2759, fax (802) 259-2922; vfp@vermontel.com, http://www.vermontel.com/vfp/home.htm. The VFP International Workcamp Directory (119 pp.), available each Apr for $12 from VFP, describes over 800 short-term service placements in over 40 countries available through VFP for the summer and fall of the year of publication.

* International Volunteer Projects (Council). Free brochure available from Council, 205 E. 42nd St., New York, NY 10017-5706; (888)-

COUNCIL or (212) 822-2695; IVPBrochure@ ciee.org, http://www.ciee.org. Describes over 600 short-term summer voluntary service options available through Council in 23 countries of Europe, Africa, and North America. The Council International Volunteer Projects Directory (82 pp.), available each Apr for $12 postpaid, describes the workcamps in depth.

* **Kibbutz Volunteer** by John Bedford. 1996. Vacation Work. $14.95 from Ulysses Books. Now the most up-to-date resource on volunteering in Israel. New edition lists over 200 kibbutzim at different sites in Israel; also includes information on work on a moshav and other employment opportunities in Israel.

** **Peace Corps Information Packet.** Free from Peace Corps, 1990 K St. NW, Room 9320, Washington, DC 20526; (800) 424-8580; http://www.peacecorps.gov/. The largest U.S. volunteer-sending organization, with approx. 3,000 placements annually. Two-year assignment. One of the best job opportunities (paid, too) in the developing world and Eastern Europe for Americans.

* **The Post-Soviet Handbook: A Guide to Grassroots Organizations and Internet Resources in the Newly Independent States.** (See Geographic Overviews section above.) Most up-to-date source for organizations which may welcome volunteers.

* **Response: Volunteer Opportunities Directory of the Catholic Network of Volunteer Service.** 1996. 90 pp. Free (donations accepted) from CNVS, 4121 Harewood Rd. NE, Washington, DC 20017; (800) 543-5046 or (202) 529-1100, fax (202) 526-1094; cnvs@ari.net. Directory also on-line at http://www2.ari.net/home3/cnvs/. Directory of lay mission opportunities in the U.S. and abroad. Indexes by type of placement, location, length of time, couples, parents, etc.

** **Travel Programs in Central America.** (See

Geographic Overview section above.) The most comprehensive listing of volunteer opportunities in this region.

** **Volunteer: The Comprehensive Guide to Voluntary Service in the U.S. and Abroad,** edited by Richard Christiano. 1995. 188 pp. $12.95 from Council. Detailed descriptions of nearly 200 voluntary service organizations recruiting volunteers for work in the U.S. and abroad. Organized by short- and long-term opportunities, with indexes by country and type of work. Absolutely the best place to start exploring volunteer options.

* **Volunteer & Internship Possibilities in Israel.** (See Internships section above.)

* **Volunteer Vacations: Short-Term Adventures That Will Benefit You and Others** by Bill McMillon. 1995 (new edition, 1997). 453 pp. $13.95 from Chicago Review Press, 814 N. Franklin St., Chicago, IL 60610; (312) 337-0747. Describes more than 250 organizations sponsoring projects in the U.S. and abroad. Indexed by cost, length of time, location, type of project, and season. Opportunities from 1 weekend to 6 weeks.

* **Volunteer Work: The Complete International Guide to Medium & Long-Term Voluntary Service.** Central Bureau (U.K.). 1995. 240 pp. Available for $18.95 from IIE. A thoroughly researched British survey of volunteer possibilities worldwide, with many listings not found elsewhere. Indexed by country and type of work.

International Careers

The Adventure Of Working Abroad: Hero Tales From The Global Frontier by Joyce Sautters Osland. 1995. 269 pp. Jossey-Bass. $25 from Intercultural Press. Thirty-five American expatriates assigned abroad tell the perils and opportunities of working in a new culture. Suggestions for employers and employees for preparation, support, and reentry.

** **The Almanac of International Jobs and Careers: A Guide to Over 1001 Employers** by Ronald Krannich and Caryl Krannich. 1994 (new edition, 1997). 334 pp. $19.95 from Impact Publications. Companion volume to The Complete Guide to International Jobs and Careers, this is a comprehensive source of hard-to-find information, tips on other resources, and trends in international employment for Americans.

* **American Jobs Abroad** by Victoria Harlow and Edward Knappman. 1994. 882 pp. $19.94 from Visible Ink Press, a division of Gale Research Inc., 835 Penobscot Bldg., Detroit, MI 48226-4094; (800) 776-6265, fax (313) 961-6083. The only directory listing the number of Americans working abroad for specific organizations; most employees worked in the U.S. before being assigned abroad. Gives contact information. Useful indexes by country and job category. Out-of-print but copies available from Gale or Impact Publications.

Building an Import/Export Business by Kenneth D. Weiss. 1991. $18.95 from John Wiley & Sons. Detailed guide to entering the import/export business.

* **The Canadian Guide to Working and Living Overseas** by Jean-Marc Hachey. 1995. 1,000 pp. $37 postpaid from Intercultural Systems, P.O. Box 588, Station B, Ottawa, ON K1P 5P7, Canada; (800) 267-0105 or (613) 238-6169, fax (613) 238-5274. The most comprehensive single volume on working and living abroad; listings emphasize Canadian organizations. Americans can benefit from the thorough overseas job-search advice, and from the most extensive bibliography anywhere—describing 550 publications.

Career Opportunities for Bilinguals and Multilinguals: A Directory of Resources in

Education, Employment, and Business by Vladmir Wertsman. 1994. 308 pp. $35 plus $3 shipping from Scarecrow Press, 4720 Boston Way, Lanham, MD 20706; (800) 462-6420. Lists thousands of local organizations across the U.S. that may need people with foreign language skills. Cross-indexed by location and language.

Careers for Foreign Language Aficionados and Other Multilingual Types by Ned Seelye and Laurence Day. 1992. 114 pp. $12.95 from VGM Career Horizons. Mainstream and offbeat jobs for those who want to use a foreign language. Includes profiles.

** **Careers in International Affairs,** edited by Maria Pinto Carland and Michael Trucano. 1996. 320 pp. $17.95 plus $4.75 shipping from Georgetown Univ. Press, P.O. Box 4866, Hampden Station, Baltimore, MD 21211-4866; (800) 246-9606, fax (410) 516-6998. New edition is the most up-to-date U.S. overview of international career fields; provides survey-based specifics on major organizations in all international sectors. Highly recommended.

Careers In International Business by Edward J. Halloran. 1995. 97 pp. $12.95 from VGM. Overview of education for international business and types of opportunities, from employment to entreprenuers.

Careers in International Law, edited by Mark W. Janis. 1993. 229 pp. $19.95 plus $3.95 shipping from American Bar Association, Attn: Financial Services, 9th Fl., 750 N. Lake Shore Dr., Chicago, IL 60611; (312) 988-5522. Essays on how to plan for a career in international law by lawyers in the field. Also lists ABA-approved study abroad programs.

** **The Complete Guide to International Jobs and Careers** by Ronald L. Krannich and Caryl R. Krannich. 1992. 306 pp. $13.95 from Impact Publications. The best introduction to strategies and skills for landing an international job in the 1990s, along with listings of resources for researching international employers.

Directory of American Firms Operating in Foreign Countries. 1996. $220 from Uniworld, 342 E. 51st St., New York, NY 10022; Tel./fax (212) 752-0329. Lists 3,000 American companies with subsidiaries and affiliates in 138 foreign countries. Check your local library for this and dozens of other expensive specialized international directories that are beyond the scope of this bibliography. Impact Publications also carries many of these.

* The Directory of Jobs and Careers Abroad, edited by André DeVries. 1993 (new edition, Jan 1997). 407 pp. Vacation Work Publications. $16.95 from Peterson's Guides. The only career guide with country-by-country coverage of everything from professional fields to short-term and volunteer possibilities. British publication, but usually includes relevant U.S. organizations.

Directory of Opportunities in International Law, edited by Paul Brinkman. 1992. 204 pp. $20 ($10 for students) from John Bassett Moore Society of International Law, Univ. of Virginia School of Law, Charlottesville, VA 22901; (804) 924-3087. Law firms, agencies, and organizations with international practices, and a partial list of U.S. law schools that provide international training.

* Directory of U.S. Based Agencies Involved in International Health Assistance. 1996. 254 pp. $65 ($35 members) postpaid from National Council for International Health, 1701 K St. NW, Suite 600, Washington, DC 20006; (202) 833-5900, fax (202) 833-0075; ncih@ncih.org. Lists organizations in international health fields by specialty and location. Career Network ($120 non-members, $60 members per year) is the NCIH job bulletin.

Employment Abroad: Facts and Fallacies, edited by Rachel Theus. 1993. $7.50 plus $3 shipping from the International Division of the U.S. Chamber of Commerce, 1615 H St. NW, Washington, DC 20062; (202) 463-5460, fax (202) 463-3114; http://www.uschamber.org/chamber. Booklet stresses the realities of international employment.

Evaluating an Overseas Job Opportunity by John Williams. 1992. 39 pp. $5.95 from Pilot Books. Booklet with good advice (career gamble, family, financial factors) for anyone considering an overseas assignment.

Flying High in Travel by Karen Rubin. 1992. 319 pp. John Wiley & Sons. $19.95 from Impact Publications. Surveys the travel industry and includes hundreds of jobs people outside the industry never hear about. Includes useful resources.

Getting Your Job in the Middle East by David Lay. 1992. 184 pp. DCL International. $19.95 from Impact Publications. An overview of career possibilities in the Middle East, along with information about Middle East history, culture, and recent events.

* Great Jobs for Foreign Language Majors by Julie DeGalan and Stephen Lambert. 1994. 242 pp. VGM Career Horizons. $11.95. Thorough book covers careers in all sectors which involve foreign languages, either directly or as an auxiliary skill, as well as career strategies.

** Guide to Careers in World Affairs, edited by Pamela Gerard. 1993. 421 pp. Foreign Policy Association. $14.95 from Impact Publications. Thoroughly researched information on careers with hundreds of U.S.-based international employers in business, law, journalism, consulting, nonprofit organizations, and the U.S. government. Gives specifics on entry-level qualifications, internships, etc. Excellent annotated bibliography. Highly recommended.

Guide to Careers, Internships & Graduate Education in Peace Studies. 1996. 71 pp. $4.50 from PAWSS Publications, Hampshire College, Amherst, MA 01002. Includes information on internships, fellowships, and relevant organizations.

How to Be an Importer and Pay for Your World Travel (Revised) by Mary Green and Stanley Gilmar. 1993. 215 pp. $9.95 plus $3.50 shipping from Ten Speed Press, P.O. Box 7123, Berkeley, CA 94707; (800) 841-BOOK.

* How to Find an Overseas Job with the U.S. Government by Will Cantrell and Francine Modderno. 1992. 421 pp. $28.95 postpaid from Worldwise Books. Comprehensive guide to finding work with the organization that hires the greatest number of Americans to work abroad.

* How to Get a Job in Europe: The Insider's Guide by Robert Sanborn. 1995. 546 pp. $17.95 plus $3 shipping from Surrey Books, Inc., 230 E. Ohio St., Suite 120, Chicago, IL 60611; (800) 326-4430. Good source for country-by-country employer addresses (otherwise found in expensive directories) and general suggestions for finding a job.

* How to Get a Job in the Pacific Rim by Robert Sanborn and Anderson Brandao. 1992. 425 pp. Surrey Books. Same concept, same price as above, for Asia.

How to Get the Job You Want Overseas by Arthur Liebers. 1990. 39 pp. $4.95 from Pilot Books. Sketchy advice on private industry and government opportunities.

The International Businesswoman of the 1990s: A Guide to Success in the Global Marketplace by Marlene Rossman. 1990. 171 pp. $19.95 plus $4 shipping from Praeger Publishers, 1 Madison Ave., New York, NY 10010; (212) 736-4444. One of the best descriptions to date of what it's like to work in international business.

* International Careers: An Insider's Guide by David Win. 1987. 222 pp. Williamson Publishing Co. Analyzes why international careers are different from domestic ones and suggests strategies for developing one. Out-of-print.

* International Education Career Information. NAFSA Working Paper #40. 1994. 45 pp. $10 postpaid from NAFSA Publications. Good overview of careers in international educational exchange.

* International Jobs: Where They Are and How to Get Them by Eric Kocher. 1993. 394 pp. $16 from Addison-Wesley; (800) 822-6339, fax (617) 944-4968. An overview of international career fields and how to prepare for them.

International Opportunities: A Career Guide for Students. 1993. 128 pp. David M. Kennedy International Center. $10.95 postpaid from Brigham Young Univ., Kennedy Center for International Studies, Publication Services, P.O. Box 24538, Provo, UT 84602; (800) 528-6279, fax (801) 378-5882; http://www.byu.edu/culturegrams. Useful guide for the student interested in international career opportunities.

The Job Hunter's Guide to Japan by Terra Brockman. 1990. 232 pp. Kodansha International. $12.95 from Impact Publications. Insightful first-hand interviews with Americans working in Japan in various professions.

* Jobs For People Who Love Travel by Ronald and Caryl Krannich. 1995. 304 pp. $15.95 from Impact Publications. Information for those who want to work the world before settling down, including but going far beyond the travel industry. Explores motivations; 50 myths about jobs involving travel.

* Jobs in Russia and the Newly Independent States by Moira Forbes. 1994. 228 pp. $15.95 from Impact Publications. Provides much-needed help in finding work opportunities, in this rapidly changing region.

* **Jobs Worldwide** by David Lay and Benedict Leerburger. 1996. 377 pp. $17.95 from Impact Publications. Country-by-country examination of employment opportunities; identifies key employers.

Journal of Career Planning and Employment. Periodical published by National Association of Colleges and Employers (formerly College Placement Council), 62 Highland Ave., Bethlehem, PA 18017, (800) 544-5272. Articles by career planning professionals. See especially "Student Dreams and the Real International Job Market," by Jeffrey B. Wood, and other articles on international jobs, in the Nov 1992 issue; see also the May 1994 issue.

The Korea Super Job Catalog. (See Teaching English Abroad section above.) Includes professional listings.

Live and Work in … (series): Australia & New Zealand (1996); Belgium, The Netherlands, and Luxembourg (1993); France (1994); Germany (1992); Italy (1992); Scandinavia (1995); Spain & Portugal (1991). Vacation Work. $18.95 each from Ulysses Books. Excellent British series for long-term stays. Information on employment, residence, home buying, daily life, retirement, and starting a business. More useful for those on overseas assignment than for those looking for a job.

Living and Working in … (series): Britain (1995), France (1996), Spain (1995) Switzerland (1996), USA (1995) by David Hampshire. Survival Books. $21.95 plus $3.50 shipping each from Seven Hills, 49 Central Ave., Cincinnati, OH 45202; (800) 545-2005, fax (513) 381-0753. Detailed information for long-term stays on everything from working to buying a house. More useful for those on overseas assignment than for those looking for a job.

* **Making It Abroad: The International Job Hunting Guide** by Howard Schuman. 1988. 168 pp. John Wiley & Sons. Positive insight into career patterns in various international career fields and employment sectors. Out-of-print, but available in libraries.

* **Opportunities in Foreign Languages Careers** by Wilga Rivers. 1993. 151 pp. $11.95 from VGM Career Books. Harvard professor emerita discusses the use of languages as an auxiliary skill; also covers teaching languages and working as a translator or interpreter.

Opportunities in International Business Careers by Jeffry Arpan. 1995. 150 pp. $11.95 from VGM Career Books. General overview of careers in international business, with discussion of types of international business degrees and specific business schools.

OPTIONS. Job opening newsletter available for $25 per year (6 issues) from Project Concern's OPTIONS/Service, 3550 Afton Rd., San Diego, CA 92123; (619) 279-9690. Places doctors, nurses, and other healthcare professionals in Third World countries and underserved areas of the U.S.

Special Career Opportunities for Linguists/ Translators/Interpreters. Free pamphlet from U.S. Department of State, Language Services Division, Room 2212, Washington, DC 20520; (202) 647-1528, fax (202) 647-0749.

Strategies for Getting an Overseas Job by Kenneth O. Parsons. 1989. 32 pp. $3.95 from Pilot Books. Booklet describes strategies and lists U.S. firms doing business abroad.

Tax Guide for U.S. Citizens Abroad (Publication 54). Free from Forms Distribution Center, P.O. Box 25866, Richmond, VA 23260.

Trade & Culture (magazine). $32.95 for 12 issues from Trade & Culture Inc., P.O Box 10988, Baltimore, MD 21734-9871; (800) 544-5684, fax (410) 342-8560. Focus on the cross-cultural aspects of doing business abroad.

* **U.S. Department of State Foreign Service Careers.** Free pamphlet available from Re-

cruitment Division, Department of State, Box 12226, Arlington, VA 22219; (703) 875-7490; http://www.state.gov. Application for the Foreign Service Officer Program. Available from above address (written requests only). Applications for 1996 exam must be postmarked by Oct 4 (overseas locations) or Oct 18 (U.S.). Study Guide to the Foreign Service Officer Written Examination and Assessment Procedure. $9.95 postpaid from FSO Study Guide, Educational Testing Service, Mail Stop 31-X, Princeton, NJ 08541-0001; (609) 921-9000. Invaluable preparation.

* **Working in France: The Ultimate Guide to Job Hunting and Career Success à la Française** by Carol Pineau and Maureen Kelly. 1991. 194 pp. Frank Books. Exceptionally useful guide to working in France, focusing on cross-cultural differences in the workplace, written by 2 Americans who live there. Out-of-print but well worth a search.

Working in the Persian Gulf by Blythe Camenson. 1993. 149 pp. $16.95 plus $3 shipping from Desert Diamond Books, P.O. Box 9580, Coral Springs, FL 33075. Subtitled "Survival Secrets," this useful book combines details on finding jobs with tips on what to expect when you do.

International Job Listings

Note: The majority of international jobs, like all jobs, are not advertised

* **Global Alternatives.** Monthly listing from the Professional Development Resource Center, School for International Training, Box 676, Kipling Rd., Brattleboro, VT 05302-0676; (802) 258-3397, fax (802) 258-3248. Subscriptions (within U.S.) $40/year non-alum, $30/year SIT alumni (pay by check or money order only). Each issue lists 80-100 domestic and overseas openings, mainly in the fields of administration, educational exchange, teaching, stu-

dent services, consulting, intercultural training, and refugee work. Internships listed as well.

International Career Employment Opportunities. Biweekly listings of 500-600 international job openings (about half located overseas) organized by career fields: international education, foreign policy, trade and finance, environment, development, program administration, health care. Main listings are for professionals, typically asking for 2 to 5 years or more experience. One section in each issue covers internships; these are nearly all in U.S. Subscriptions available from 2 months ($29 individuals, $35 institutions) to 2 years ($229/$350) from International Employment Opportunities, Rt. 2, Box 305, Stanardsville, VA 22973; (804) 985-6444, fax (804) 985-6828; intlcareers@internetmci.com.

International Employment Gazette. Each biweekly issue includes more than 400 overseas job openings by region and field. Good for private-sector business and technical jobs, although many of these require extensive experience, as well as teaching and volunteer positions. $35 for 3 months (6 issues); $55 for 6 months (13 issues); $95 for 1 year (26 issues) from International Employment Gazette, 220 N. Main St., Suite 100, Greenville, SC 29601; (800) 882-9188, fax (803) 235-3369.

** **International Employment Hotline,** edited by Will Cantrell. $39 for 12 issues from Worldwise Books, P.O. Box 3030, Oakton, VA 22124; (703) 620-1972, fax (703) 620-1973. Monthly reports by an international careers expert on who's hiring now in private companies, government, and nonprofit organizations. Lists overseas job openings, both entry-level and mid-career. Each issue has information-packed articles of lasting value on topics such as internships, organizations recruiting for teaching English abroad, and more. An outstanding bargain.

Job Registry, NAFSA: Association of Inter-

national Educators. 10 issues a year for $30 ($20 members) from NAFSA Job Registry, 1875 Connecticut Ave. NW, Suite 1000, Washington, DC 20009-5728; (202) 939-3131. The best job listing for those interested in the field of international educational exchange.

Internet Resources

E-mail discussion groups and World Wide Web sites on work abroad are free, but none of them displace print resources in terms of quality and quantity of useful information. You need access to the internet or other on-line service to use these.

E-MAIL DISCUSSION GROUPS ("lists"). To sign on to any e-mail list, send a message to the LISTSERV address where the group is based, along with a SUBSCRIBE command in the body of the message. For example: 1) Send e-mail message to: LISTSERV@cmuvm.csv. cmich.edu. 2) Leave subject blank, and in message section, type only: SUB PCORPS-L yourfirstname yourlastname. 3) Post the message, and you will shortly receive a confirmation message with information about the group. Save it for instructions!

* **PCORPS-L,** SUB request to: listserv@ cmuvm.csv.cmich.edu. Discussion by returned and potential Peace Corps volunteers, on the Peace Corps experience, developing countries, etc. Updates on positions. Very lively (a dozen messages daily) and very informative. Owner: Elliot Parker, Central Michigan Univ.

* **JET-L,** SUB request to: listserv@listserv. arizona.edu. Discussion by returned and prospective JET participants (teaching English in Japan); moderate activity. Owner: Michael McVey.

O-Hayo Sensei. Request subscription information from editor@ohayosensei.com (or see web site). Twice-monthly announcements of openings for teaching English in Japan.

CIE-NEWS, SUB request to: listserv@uci.edu. Twice-monthly announcements of overseas opportunities for study, work, and volunteering (or see web site). Owner: Ruth Sylte, Univ. of California-Irvine.

CIVILSOC, SUB request to: listproc@ solar.rtd.utk.edu (or see web site). Announcements about job openings and new developments in Russia, the Newly Independent States, and Eastern Europe. Owner: Center for Civil Society International, Seattle, WA.

ICEN-L, SUB request to: listserv@iubvm. indiana.edu. International job openings, various fields and locations. Owner: Susan Salmon, Indiana Univ. International Center.

ASPIRE-L, SUB request to: listserv@iubvm. ucs.indiana.edu (or see web site). Announcements for students from Asian nations studying in the U.S. to assist them in finding home-country employment; also for others interested in the region. Owner: NAFSA/Project ASPIRE.

INTER-L, SUB request to: listserv@vtvm1. cc.vt.edu. Essential for US university advisers working with foreign students; esoteric for anyone else. Owner: NAFSA.

SECUSS-L, SUB request to: listserv@ubvm. cc.buffalo.edu. Essential discussion group for university education abroad advisors. Owner: INTER-L and NAFSA.

WORLD WIDE WEB SITES. You'll have the best luck using standard search tools such as Infoseek or Yahoo and experimenting with key words such as TESL, TESOL, ESL or other fields and countries. Here are a few sites which are excellent places to start:

* **www.cie.uci.edu/~cic/cie.html.** Very useful information on study, work and travel abroad, with many links to other web sites. Also has a how-to guide for finding study and work abroad options on the web. From the Univ. of

California at Irvine's Center for International Education, Ruth Sylte.

* **www.isp.acad.umn.edu/istc/istc.html.** Searchable listings of scholarships, study abroad, internships, and Ann Halpin's volunteer directory. From Univ. of Minnesota's International Study & Travel Center, Richard Warzecha.

www.umich.edu/~icenter. Articles on working abroad, with links, from Univ. of Michigan's International Center, Bill Nolting.

www.ciee.org. Information on study, work, and travel abroad opportunities offered by Council. Lacks links.

www.indiana.edu/~intlcent/icen/index.html. Postings from ICEN-L and AS-PIRE-L (above).

www.vita.org/iaction/iaction.html. InterAction's clearinghouse of organizations and volunteer options in the relief and development field, found under "Alliance for a Global Community." Lists opportunities by type of activity and country.

www.pitt.edu/~ian/index.html. International Affairs Network Web provides information on graduate programs and careers in international relations.

www.wpi.edu/~mfriley/jobguide.html. Resources for International Opportunities, from the Riley Guide. Country-by-country lists of web and Gopher sites listing job opportunities. Best overview of online job services, but most postings are for experienced specialists in computers, engineering, and business.

Key Publishers And Organizations

Central Bureau For Educational Visits & Exchanges, 10 Spring Gardens, London, SW1A 2BN, U.K.; (011) (44) (171) 389-4004, fax (171) 389-4426. British non-profit organization and publisher of authoritative directories on working abroad; most publications distributed in the U.S. through IIE.

Council (Council on International Educational Exchange), Council-Pubs Dept., 205 E. 42nd St., New York, NY 10017-5706; (888)-COUNCIL, fax (212) 822-2699; info@ciee.org, www.ciee.org. Publishers of materials on work, study, and travel abroad, especially for students; also administers the Council Work Abroad Program and Council Workcamps. Add $1.50 (book rate) or $3 (first-class) shipping for each book.

Global Exchange, 2017 Mission St., Room 303, San Francisco, CA 94110; (415) 255-7296, fax (415) 255-7498; globalexch@igc.org. Distributes books on solidarity with developing countries; also organizes "reality tours." Add $1.75 ($3 first class) shipping for each book ordered.

Impact Publications, 9104-N Manassas Dr., Manassas Park, VA 22111; (703) 361-7300, fax (703) 335-9486; www.impactpublications.com. The best one-stop source for international career books published by Impact and many other publishers. Add $4 shipping for the first book ordered plus $1 for each additional one.

Institute of International Education (IIE), IIE Books, P.O. Box 371, Annapolis Junction, MD 20701-0371; (800) 445-0443, fax (301) 953-2838; iiebooks@iie.org; http://www.iie.org. Publisher of authoritative directories for study or teaching abroad and financial aid, and distributor of Central Bureau (U.K.) publications on working abroad. Add $2 each shipping for books under $25; $4 each for books over $25, or 10% for orders over $100.

Intercultural Press, P.O. Box 700, Yarmouth, ME 04096; (207) 846-5168, fax (207) 846-

5181; interculturalpress@ mcimail.com, www.bookmasters.com/interclt.htm. Numerous publications dealing with cross-cultural issues in settings ranging from academic to business.

John Wiley & Sons, 1 Wiley Dr., Summerset, NJ 08875; (908) 469-4400. Publications on careers.

NAFSA Publications, P.O. Box 1020, Sewickley, PA 15143; (800) 836-4994, fax (412) 741-0609. Essential publications for advisers and administrators in international educational exchange. For membership information, contact NAFSA: Association of International Educators, 1875 Connecticut Ave. NW, Suite 1000, Washington, DC 20009-5728, (202) 939-3103 or (202) 462-4811, fax (202) 667-3419; inbox@nafsa.org, www.nafsa.org.

Peterson's Guides, 202 Carnegie Center, P.O. Box 2123, Princeton, NJ 08543; (800) 338-3282. Guides to jobs and careers, study abroad. U.S. distributor for many of the Vacation Work Publications (U.K.). Add $4.75 shipping for each book or avoid this charge by ordering through a bookstore.

Pilot Books, 103 Cooper St., Babylon, NY 11702; (516) 422-2225, fax (516) 422-2227. Booklet-sized guides to international jobs and budget travel. Add $1.50 shipping for each book ordered.

Seven Locks Press, P.O. Box 68, Arlington, VA 22210; (800) 354-5348, fax (310) 834-2835. Books on social change. Add $3 for first book, $.75 for each additional title.

Transitions Abroad Publishing, Inc., P.O. Box 1300, Amherst, MA 01004-1300, (800) 293-0373; trabroad@ aol.com. Publisher of *Transitions Abroad* magazine ($24.95 per year, see Worldwide Overviews section); *Alternative Travel Directory* ($23.95 postpaid); *Teaching English Abroad* ($9.95 postpaid, see Teaching English Abroad section); and numerous Planning Guides devoted to overseas work, study, and travel. Call or write for free information flyer.

Vacation Work Publications, 9 Park End St., Oxford, OX1 1HJ, U.K.; (011) 44 1865 241978, fax 1865 790885. Publisher of numerous books on work abroad and international careers. Many are distributed in the U.S. by Peterson's Guides. Those which lack U.S. distribution can be purchased from Ulysses Books & Maps, 4176 Saint Denis, Montreal, Quebec H2W 3M5, Canada; (514) 843-9882 ext. 2232, fax (514) 843-9448; guiduly@ulysse.ca.

VGM Career Horizons, a division of NTC Publishing Group, 4255 West Touhy Ave., Lincolnwood, IL 60646-1975; (708) 679-5500 or (800) 679-5500. Books on careers. Available through bookstores.

Worldwise Books, P.O. Box 3030, Oakton, VA 22124; (703) 620-1972, fax (703) 620-1973. Publisher of books on international jobs and careers as well as the newsletter International Employment Hotline.

WILLIAM NOLTING *is Director of International Opportunities, Univ. of Michigan International Center, 603 E. Madison Street, Ann Arbor, MI 48109-1370; (313) 647-2299, fax (313) 647-2181; bnolting@umich.edu. He welcomes suggestions, updates, or questions.*

CHAPTER 17

Short-Term Jobs Abroad: The Key Employers

The major fields of temporary employment abroad are tourism and agriculture (both seasonal), au pairing (almost exclusively for women), English teaching (difficult for periods of less than nine months), and volunteer work.

Everyone will tell you that the more research you do before you go abroad the better. But the limited information available is often discouraging, misleading, or useless. Remain determined in the face of discouragement, and use the reliable resources in the Work Abroad Resources section to clarify what you want to do and determine what is possible.

As a first step in finding a short-term job, contact the embassy or consulate and the tourist office of the countries in which you want to work. Consult their telephone directories and yellow pages for addresses of companies in your field. If you don't have a field, look up English-language teaching institutes. Diplomatic missions should also have newspapers from which you can study the "situations vacant" columns.

Exchanging labor for room and board is an excellent way of gaining worthwhile experience while seeing another country. Be aware that most organizations that take on short-term volunteers look for people willing to finance themselves completely or perhaps even make a financial contribution.

If you are searching for a specific kind of job or are qualified in a certain field, you might get leads by consulting the specialist press. For example, you can find out about crewing or yacht delivery possibilities from yachting magazines like Cruising World.

Professionals should consult their own associations and journals.

Finally, when contacting agencies and potential employers, increase your chances of receiving a reply by enclosing several international reply coupons (IRCs), available from post offices.

International Organizations

Council, 205 E. 42nd St., New York, NY 10017-5706; (888) COUNCIL coordinates a working holiday program for U.S. college students to Britain, Ireland, France, Germany, Canada, New Zealand, Jamaica, and Costa Rica. The participation fee for all programs is $225. Participants receive work documentation and access to job-finding assistance in the destination country. The Canadian equivalent is the Student Work Abroad Program (SWAP) administered by the Canadian Federation of Students, 243 College St., Suite 500, Toronto, ON M5T 2TY, Canada; (416) 977-3703.

Alliances Abroad, 2830 Alameda, San Francisco, CA 94103; fax (415) 621-1609. Range of programs including au pair placement in Europe and volunteer work in Ecuador, Mexico, and Ghana.

InterExchange Program, 161 6th Ave., New York, NY 10013; (212) 924-0446. Work placements for students in Germany and anyone 18-30 in France, Scandinavia, Switzerland, and Eastern Europe. Also au pair placements in Europe.

Internships International, 1116 Cowper Dr., Raleigh, NC 27608; Tel./fax (919) 832-8980. Internships (i.e., unpaid work placements) arranged in London, Dublin, Paris, Stuttgart, Florence, Madrid, Budapest, Mexico City, and Santiago.

International Cooperative Education, 15 Spiros Way, Menlo Park, CA 94025; (415) 323-4944. Arranges paid summer work for 2-3 months in Germany, Switzerland, Belgium, Finland, and Japan. Jobs include retail sales, hotels and restaurants, agriculture, offices, etc.; most require knowledge of relevant language.

WISE (Worldwide Internships & Service Education), 303 S. Craig St., Suite 202, Pittsburg, PA 15213; (412) 681-8120. American liaison for European work placement programs—au pairing, farm work in Norway, internships in London, etc. Program fees from $475.

AIESEC (International Association for Students in Economics and Business Management), 135 W. 50th St., 20th Fl., New York, NY 10020; (212) 757-3774. Business-related jobs available in over 75 countries. Highly qualified interns must apply through an AIESEC chapter in the U.S.

Association for International Practical Training, 10400 Little Patuxent Parkway, Suite 250, Columbia, MD 21044-3510; (410) 997-3068 or 997-2886. Summer placements in over 59 countries through the International Association for the Exchange of Students for Technical Experience (IAESTE) available to students in science, engineering, math, agriculture, or architecture. Also runs hotel and culinary exchanges to Austria, Finland, France, Germany, Ireland, Netherlands, Switzerland, U.K., Australia, and Japan and Career Development Exchanges for candidates who can find their own employer overseas.

AIFS U.K. Ltd. (American Institute for Foreign Study), 15-17 Young St., London W8 5EH, England; (011) 44-171-376-0800. U.S. office: 102 Greenwich Ave., Greenwich, CT 06830. Tour directors needed to lead educational tours of Europe for North American students.

Interlocken International, RR 2, Box 165, Hillsboro, NH 03244; (603) 478-3166. Group leaders needed to escort high school students on tours worldwide.

Specialised Travel Ltd., 12-15 Hanger Green, London W5 3EL, England; (011) 44-181-991-2200. Couriers required to escort choirs and orchestras throughout Europe.

IAEA (International Agricultural Exchange Association), 1000 1st Ave. S, Great Falls, MT 59401; (406) 727-1999. Farm placements of agricultural trainees in many European countries plus Japan, Australia, and New Zealand. A separate agricultural and horticultural work exchange exists between the U.S. and most European countries (including Eastern Europe) and elsewhere; details from Communicating for Agriculture, 112 East Lincoln, Fergus Falls, MN 56538.

National Future Farmers of America (FFA), P.O. Box 15160, Alexandria, VA 22309. Arranges international farm exchanges in 35 countries.

AuPair Homestay, World Learning, Inc., 1015 15th St., Suite 750, NW, Washington, DC 20005; (202) 408-5380. Arranges for young Americans to spend 3-12 months as au pairs in France, Germany, Iceland, the Netherlands, Norway, Finland, Switzerland, U.K., and Argentina. Program fee is $775.

Au Pair in Europe, P.O. Box 68056, Blakely Postal Outlet, Hamilton, ON L8M 3M7, Canada; (905) 545-6305. Au pairs placed in 16 countries including South Africa.

Berlitz, 400 Alexander Park Dr., Princeton, NJ 08540; (609) 514-9650. Teacher vacancies often occur in Latin America, Korea, and Europe. Berlitz teachers must be university graduates and willing to be trained in the Berlitz method.

ELS International Inc., 5761 Buckingham Parkway, Culver City, CA 90230; (310) 642-0988. International chain of language schools. U.S. office handles the bulk of recruitment for ELS's overseas franchises. Also now runs its own TEFL training courses.

ISS, P.O. Box 5910, Princeton, NJ 08543; (609) 452-0990. Places state-certified U.S. teachers in international schools worldwide. Recruitment meetings in February, March, and June.

Wall Street Institute International, Torre Mapfre, Marina 16-18, 08005 Barcelona, Spain; (011) 34 3 225 45 55, fax 225 48 88.

Chain of 164 commercial language institutes for adults that employ approximately 350 full-time EFL teachers in Europe and Latin America. In some countries the "Master Center" acts as a clearinghouse for teacher vacancies; addresses from HQ.

Taking Off, P.O. Box 104, Newton Highlands, MA 02161; (617) 630-1606, and Center for Interim Programs, P.O. Box 2347, Cambridge, MA 02238. Consulting services aimed primarily at preuniversity and university students looking to arrange a worthwhile experience abroad, including paid and voluntary work. Flat fee of $895 and $1,500 respectively. Two similar companies are Time Out, 619 E. Blithedale Ave., Suite C, Mill Valley, CA 94941; and Time Out Associates, 94 Center St., Milton, MA 02186.

International House, 106 Piccadilly, London W1V 9FL, U.K.; (011) 44-171-491 2679. With 100 schools in 24 countries, IH is one of the largest English teaching organizations in the world. The Central Department (address above) does much of the hiring of teachers—who must have at least a Cambridge/RSA Certificate (Pass B).

Africa

Travelers sometimes negotiate teaching contracts in East Africa and casual tutoring in Cairo on the spot. It may also be possible to join conservation or scientific research trips for a fee. For example:

Foreign Placements cc, P.O. Box 912, Somerset West 7129, South Africa; (011) 27-4457 7677. Casual work arranged for short periods and also contracts for medical staff and tradesmen with skills.

Frontier Conservation Expeditions, 77 Leonard St., London EC2A 4QS, England; (011) 44-171-613-2422, carries out environmental surveys in Tanzania, Uganda, and

Mozambique that use paying volunteers for 10-12 weeks.

Global Citizens Network, 1931 Iglehart Ave., St. Paul, MN 55104; (612) 644-0960. Sends paying volunteers to rural Kenya.

International Language Institute, P.O. Box 13, Embaba, Cairo, Egypt. English teaching positions are available for people with some TEFL training. Also 10 American Language Centers throughout Morocco, including ALC, 4 Zankat Tanja, Rabat, 10000 Morocco.

Operation Crossroads Africa, 475 Riverside Dr., Suite 830, New York, NY 10027; (212) 870-2106. Runs 7-week projects in rural Africa staffed by self-financing volunteers. Canadian Cross International is at 31 Madison Ave., Toronto, ON MSR 252, Canada.

Overland Adventure Tours. A number of overland adventure tour operators require expedition leaders for at least 1 year. These include Guerba Expeditions, 40 Station Rd., Westbury, Wiltshire BA13 3QX, England; and Kumuka Africa, 40 Earls Court Rd., London W8 6EJ, England.

Pa Santigie Conteh Farmer's Association (Pasacofaas), 5A City Rd., Wellington, P.M.B. 686, Freetown, Sierra Leone. Sends volunteers to 26 villages in Northern Province to build, teach, plant, harvest, etc. Application fee is $50.

SCORE, South Africa Sports Coaching Program, c/o Netherlands Government representative Steffan Howells; howells@aztec.co.za. Summer program for self-funding volunteers.

Umzi Wabantu Inc., 555 Sparkman Drive, Suite 1602-F, Huntsville, AL 35818-3418. New project to build African-style kibbutz in Soweto near Johannesbury, South Africa, using volunteer labor.

Visions in Africa. 3637 Fulton St., NW, Washington, DC 20007; (202) 625-7403. Range of

volunteer projects in Kenya, Uganda, Zimbabwe, Burkina Faso, South Africa and Egypt. Volunteers must raise $5,000-$6,000 and commit themselves to stay for 1 year.

Workcamps in Africa. The following organizations arrange workcamps in Africa, though applications should normally be sent to the partner organization in the U.S. (See Voluntary Service below.) Chantiers Sociaux Marocains, P.O. Box 456, Rabat, Morocco; Tunisian Assoc. of Voluntary Work, Maison du RCD, Blvd. 9 Avril, 1938, 1002 Tunis, Tunisia; Africa Voluntary Service of Sierra Leone, Private Mail Bag 717, Freetown, Sierra Leone; Nigeria Voluntary Service Assoc., GPO Box 11837, Ibadan, Nigeria; Kenya Voluntary Development Assoc., P.O. Box 48902, Nairobi, Kenya; Lesotho Workcamps Assn., P.O. Box 6, Linare Rd., Maseru 100, Lesotho; Zimbabwe Workcamps Assoc., P.O. Box CY 2039, Causeway, Harare, Zimbabwe; Rainbow Relief Foundation, P.O. Box 673, Kaneshie-Accra, Ghana (organizes workcamps to help with community projects); and WWOOF-FIOH, P.O. Box 154, Trade Fair Site, La-Accra, Ghana (places volunteers in schools on traditional farms and bicycle workshops in Ghana). Also new WWOOF organization in Togo: c/o Prosper Agbeko, B.P. 25, Abou gare, Togo; (011) 228-47-1030.

WorldTeach (see Voluntary Service section). Recruits college graduates to teach science, English, etc., in Namibia.

Asia

AEON Intercultural USA, 9301 Wilshire Blvd., Suite 202, Beverly Hills, CA 90210; (310) 550-0940. Recruits university graduates to teach in their 450 language schools in Japan,

Bangladesh Workcamps Association, 289/2 Work Camps Rd., North Shahjahanpur, Dhaka 17, Bangladesh; fax (011)88-2-86- 37- 97. Attn: BWCA. Development workcamps of

7-10 days, and medium-term projects also. Participation fee $100 plus application fee $25.

China Teaching Program, Western Washington Univ., Old Main 530, Bellingham, WA 98225-9047; (360) 650-3753. Places teachers and teaching assistants in China.

Colorado China Council, 4556 Apple Way, Boulder, CO 80301; (303) 443-1108. Twenty-five ESL teachers placed at institutes throughout China, including Tibet and Mongolia from next year.

Council (see International Organizations). Small teaching in China program anticipated soon.

ELS International, 12 Kuling St., Taipei, Taiwan; (011) 886-2-321-9005. Nine schools needing 200 teachers in Taiwan.

English and Computer College (ECC), 430/17-24 Chula Soi 64, Siam Square, Bangkok 10330, Thailand; (011) 66-2-255-1856. English school with 60 branches in Thailand (half in Bangkok) that employs native-speaker teachers.

English Language Recruitment Center, Inc., 4344 South Archer Ave., Suite 131, Chicago, IL 60632-2827; (312) 843-9792 or 843-9723. Recruits instructors for language academies throughout South Korea. Minimum requirements: BA and clear speaking voice.

Grahung Kalika (Walling Village Development Committee), Bartung, Ward 2, Syngja, West Nepal. Community needs volunteers from 2 weeks to much longer to teach English. Details from recently returned volunteer Mark Scotton (125 Trowell Rd., Nottingham NG8 2EN, U.K.).

Hess Language Schools, 83 Po Ai Rd. 2F, Taipei, Taiwan. Recruits 200 teachers for 40 schools in Taiwan. Details from 4 Horicon Ave., Glens Falls, NY 12801; (518) 793-6183.

Insight Nepal, P.O. Box 6760, Kathmandu, Nepal; (011) 977-1-418964. Volunteer placements for 3-4 months in Nepali schools for $600 fee.

Interact Nova Group, 2 Oliver St., Suite 7, Boston, MA 02110; (617) 542-5027. Also 1881 Yonge St., Suite 700, Toronto, ON M4S 3C4, Canada. Hires native speaker teachers for its 120 institutes throughout Japan.

International Language Programs (ILP), ILP centre, J1. Raya Pasar Minggu, No. 39A, Jakarta, 12780, Indonesia; (011) 62-21-798-5210. Employs qualified instructors for various schools in Indonesia.

Jaffe International Education Service, Kunnuparambil Buildings, Kurichy, Kottayam 686549, India; Tel./fax (011) 91-481 430470. Places young foreign volunteer teachers in English high schools, vocational institutes, etc. in Kerala State, including 4-week summer schools (in April and May).

Japan Exchange and Teaching Programs (JET), c/o Japanese Embassy, 2520 Massachusetts Ave. NW, Washington, DC 20008; (202) 939-6772. Places English language teaching assistants in 1-year contracts throughout Japan.

Narayana Gurakula Botanical Sanctuary, Alattil, P.O., North Waynd, Kerala, India 670644. Rainforest research center welcomes self-funded volunteers; minimum donation $10 per day.

State Bureau of Foreign Experts, Friendship Hotel, 3 Bai Shi Qiao Rd., 100873 Beijing. Coordinates selection of foreign teachers and foreign experts.

The Japan Times and Korea Times. English-language newspapers that carry teaching advertisements.

YBM/ELSI and ECC Language Institutes and ECC Language Institutes. Recruits 400 teachers for language schools throughout Korea. Contact Sisa America, 17420 Carmenita Rd., Cerritos, CA 90703; (800) 501-SISA.

YMCA Overseas Service Corps., 101 North Wacker Dr., Chicago, IL 60606; (800) 872-9622 ext. 167. Twenty-five ESL teachers placed in 9 localities in Taiwan for 1 year.

Youth Charitable Organization, 20/14 Urban Bank St., Yellamanchili, 531055 Visakha-patnam District, Andhra Pradesh, India; (011) 91-8924-51122. Volunteers needed for local community and conservation work.

Australasia

Au Pair Australia, 6 Wilford St, Corrimal, NSW 2518, Australia. Places young women in live-in childcare positions for a minimum of 3 months.

Australian Trust for Conservation Volunteers, P.O. Box 423, Ballarat, Victoria 3350, Australia; (011) 61-53-331483. Organizes short- and long-term voluntary conservation projects throughout Australia. Overseas volunteers participate in a 6-week package costing from AUS$840.

Farm Helpers in New Zealand, Kumeroa Lodge, RD1, Woodville 5473; Tel./fax (011) 64-6-376-4582. NZ$20 membership to be put in touch with farmers looking for helpers in exchange for room and board.

Northern Victoria Fruitgrowers' Association, P.O. Box 394, Shepparton, Victoria 3630, Australia. Actively recruits fruit pickers in February and March. Also Victorian Peach and Apricot Growers' Association, 30A Bank St., Cobram, VIC 3644, Australia.

Stablemate, 156 Pitt Town Rd., Kenthurst, NSW 2156, Australia. Supply staff to the horse industry. Operates new exchange program with the U.S.

Student Travel Bureau, New Zealand Univ. Students Assoc., NZUSA, P.O. Box 6368, Te Aro, Wellington, New Zealand. Assists American students on the Council Work in New Zealand program find catering and agricultural jobs from May to October.

Wilderness Society, 1st Floor, 263 Broadway, Glebe, Sydney, NSW 2037, Australia. Casual work available as collectors dressed in koala suits.

WWOOF, Mt. Murrindal Cooperative, Buchan, Victoria 3885, Australia; (011) 61-51-550218. Issues a list of 400 member farms in Australia for $25. Also publishes worldwide list of farms and volunteer work opportunities for $15.

WWOOF, P.O. Box 1172, Nelson, New Zealand; (011) 64-25-345711. Provides a list of over 300 organic growers for $12.

Eastern and Central Europe

Many new opportunities, especially in English language teaching, have become available in the Baltic states and the Russian republics.

Albanian Youth Council, P.O. Box 1741, Tirana, Albania. Requesting volunteer teachers to tutor children and adults at English classes in Tirana, preferably in summer.

American Language Institute, City University Slovakia, 335 116th Ave. SE, Bellevue, WA 98004; (800) 426-5596, fax (206) 637-6989. Bratislava site: Drienova 34, P.O. Box 78, 820 09 Bratislava; Tel./fax 7-293 114. Trencin site: Bezrucova 64, 911 01 Trencin; Tel./fax 831-529337. Recruit 30-35 teachers (must have teaching experience) for Slovakia.

American Slavic Student Internship Service and Training Corporation (ASSIST), 1535 SW Upper Hall St., Portland, OR 97201; Tel./fax (503) 220-2535. Organizes fee-paying internships in Russia for students and graduates in relevant fields.

Avalon '92 Agency, Erzsebet Krt. 15, 1st Fl., #19, Budapest 1073, Hungary; (011) 36-1- 351 3010. Nanny positions available in Hungary year round. Also a few posts for English teachers and secretaries.

Belarusian Association of International Youth Workcamps (ATM), 220119 Minsk, p/b 64 Belarus. International youth workcamps lasting 3 weeks, organized as part of Anti-Chernobyl Project. Participants must know some Russian (Russian course can be arranged).

Brontosaurus Movement, Bubenská 6, 170 00 Prague 7, Czech Republic; (011) 42-2-6671-0245. Volunteers needed for environmental projects throughout the Czech Republic.

Caledonian School, Vlatavska 24, 150 00 Prague 5, Czech Republic; (011) 42-2 57 31 36 50. Employs 80 teachers with TEFL background to teach English in a large Prague language institute.

Central European Teaching Program, Beloit College, 700 College St., Beloit, WI 53511; (608) 363-2619. Supplies English teachers to Hungary and Romania. Placement fee of $750.

Czech Academic Information Agency, Dum Zahranicnich Sluzeb, Senovázné Námesti 26, 11121 Prague, Czech Republic; (011) 42-2-24-22-9698. Slovak AIA is at Na vrsku 8, P.O. Box 108, 81000 Bratislava, Slovakia; (011) 42-7-5333 010. Helps prospective English teachers find posts mainly in state schools but also in private institutes.

English for Everybody, 655 Powell St., Suite 505, San Francisco, CA 94108; (415) 789-7641. EFL teacher placement agency with office in Prague.

English School of Communication Skills

(ESCS), ul. sw. Agnieszki 2/Ip, 31-068 Kraków, Poland; Tel./fax (011) 48-12 22 85 83. Also at ul. Bernrdynska 15, 33-100 Tarnów. Fifteen EFL teachers for summer and winter language camps in Poland.

Foundation for a Civil Society, 1270 Avenue of the Americas, Suite 609, New York, NY 10020; (212) 332-2890. Two-month summer and year-round teaching placements in Czech and Slovak republics for ESL teachers.

International Exchange Center, 2 Republic Sq., LV-1010 Riga, Latvia; (011) 371-2-702 7476. Recruits English-speaking volunteers for summer projects in Latvia and Russia that may involve camp counseling, au pairing, etc.

International House maintains a large contingent of language schools in Poland employing many Certificate-qualified EFL teachers. IH Katowice (U1. Gliwicka 10, 40-079 Katowice), IH Kraków (ul. Pilsudskiego 6, Ip, 31-110 Kraków), IH Opole (U1. Kosciuszki 17, 45-062 Opole), IH Wroclaw, (U1. Ruska 46a, 50-079 Wroclaw) and IH Bielsko-Biala (U1. Karsinskiego 24, 43-300 Bielsko Biala).

Language Link Schools, Novoslobodskaya ul. 5 bld. 2, 101030 Moscow; Tel./fax (011) 95-973 2154. Forty native-English teachers for various schools.

Mir-V-Mig, P.O. Box 1085, 310168 Kharkov, Ukraine; (011) 7-0572 653141. Places native speaker teachers at secondary schools and universities in Kiev and Kharkov, Ukraine.

Pleiades, PPI 057, 208 E. 51st St., Box 295, New York, NY 10022. Interns needed for 1 year in Moscow as language editors of translated Russian journals (many of them scientific).

Project Harmony, 6 Irasville Common, Waitsfield, VT 05673; (802) 496-4545. Teaching Intern Program places teachers in Russia, the Baltics, central Asian republics, etc. Recent college graduates accepted.

Services for Open Learning, North Devon Professional Centre, Vicarage St., Barnstable, Devon EX32 7HB, U.K.; (011) 44 1271 327319. Recruits graduates to teach in schools in Belarus, Croatia, Czech Republic, Hungary, Romania, and Slovakia. Interviews in Eastern Central Europe or U.K.

Soros Professional English Language Teaching Program (SPELT), 888 7th Ave., 31st Fl., New York, NY 10106; (212) 757-2323. Teaching positions in most East European countries for trained, experienced English teachers.

Sunny School, P.O. Box 23, 125057 Moscow, Russia; (011) 7-95-151-2500. Hires university-educated Americans with some teaching experience.

Teachers for Central and Eastern Europe, 21 V 5 Rakovski Blvd., Dimitrovgrad 6400, Bulgaria; (011) 359-391 24787, fax 391 26218. Appoints native speakers to teach in English language secondary schools on behalf of the Ministry of Education in Bulgaria, and also in Czech Republic, Hungary, Poland, and Slovakia. Details available from Mr. Bill Morrow; (512) 494-0392; jbmorrow@mail.utexas.edu.

Teaching Abroad, 46 Beech Rd., Angmering, Sussex BN16 4DE, U.K.; (011) 44-1903 859911. Short- and long-term voluntary teaching positions in Lithuania, Ukraine, Moscow, and Siberia (also Ghana and India). Fees from about £500.

Travel Teach USA, P.O. Box 357, Rigby, ID 83442; Tel./fax (208) 745-7222. Working holiday opportunities teaching English in Russia, Ukraine, Moldova, Romania, and Lithuania. Placement fee from $325.

Ukrainian National Association, Inc., P.O. Box 17A, 30 Montgomery St., Jersey City, NJ 07303; (201) 451-2200. Sponsors an English-teaching program for volunteers who stay for a month in the summer.

UNIO Youth Workcamps Association, Nepszinhaz u. 24, 1081 Budapest, Hungary. Volunteers placed on range of summer workcamps in Hungary.

France

Acorn Venture Ltd., 137 Worcester Rd., Hagley, Stourbridge, West Midlands DY9 0NW, England. Activity holiday centers in France that need instructors and catering staff.

APARE, 41 cours Jean Jaurès, 84000 Avignon, France; (011) 33-490-85-51-15. Runs volunteer workcamps at historic sites in southern France.

Centres d'Information et de Documentation Jeunesse (CIDJ). Act as general advisory centers for young people. For leaflets about temporary work possibilities, send 4 IRCs to 101 Quai Branly, 75740, Cedex 15, Paris; Fax (011) 33-1-40-65-02-61. This main Paris branch has a useful notice board for job seekers.

Continental Waterways, 76 rue Balard, 75015 Paris, France; (011) 33-1-40 60 11 23. Employs deck hands on holiday barges on the inland waterways of France.

Fédération Unie des Auberges de Jeunesse, 27 rue Pajol, 75018 Paris, France. Short-term work (catering, reception, sports, instruction, etc.) at youth hostels throughout France. Applications must be sent to individual hostels. FUAJ also organizes voluntary workcamps to renovate hostels; volunteers pay FF350 per week.

Inter séjours, 179 rue de Courcelles, 75017 Paris, France; (011) 33-1-47-63-06-81. Places au pairs throughout France. Other agencies to approach include Accueil Familial des Jeunes Etrangers, 23 rue de Cherche-Midi,

75006 Paris, and SILC, 32 Rempart de l'Est, 16022 Angoulême Cedex, France.

Jeunesse et Réconstruction, 10 rue de Trévise, 75009 Paris, France; (011) 33-1-47-70-15-88. Arranges workcamps throughout France and recruits grapepickers.

La Sabranenque, Centre International, rue de la Tour de l'Oume, 30290 Saint Victor la Coste, France; (011) 33 466 50 05 05. Volunteers needed to help preserve and restore monuments in France and Italy. Inquiries to Jacqueline Simon, 217 High Park Blvd., Buffalo, NY 14226; (716) 836-8698.

Ministry of Culture, Sous-Direction de l'Archéologie, 4 rue d'Aboukir, 75002 Paris, France; (011) 33-1-40-15-73-00. Every year in May publishes a list of excavations throughout France that accept volunteers.

Nature et Progrès, 3 place Pasteur, 84000 Avignon, France. Sells "Les Bonnes Addresses de la Bio," a list of organic farmers who need temporary assistants, for FF60.

PGL Adventure (see United Kingdom section). Needs outdoor activity center staff for holiday centers in France.

REMPART, 1 rue des Guillemites, 75004 Paris, France; (011) 33-1-42-71-96-55. Needs volunteers to care for endangered monuments. Most projects charge FF45 a day, plus membership of FF200.

The French Embassy publishes the leaflets Employment in France for Students and Au Pair Positions in France which include agency addresses and information on red tape. Contact: Studies Office, Cultural Services, French Embassy, 972 5th Ave., New York, NY 10021. In Paris, look for the publications France-USA Contacts and J'Annonce, which carry job ads. Also, consult notice boards at American Church, 65 quai d'Orsay, Paris 7, France.

Germany, Switzerland, Austria

Au Pair in Germany/GIJK, Ubierstrasse 94, 53173 Bonn, Germany; (011) 49-228-95-73-00. Au pair placements for all nationalities under the age of 24.

CDS International, 330 7th Ave., 19th Fl., New York, NY 10001-5010; (212) 497-3500. Arranges 6-month paid internships in Germany for students or recent graduates in business, engineering, and other technical fields. Longer placements of 12-18 months also available.

English for Kids, A. Baumgartnerstr. 44, A/7042, 1230 Vienna, Austria; (011) 43-1-667 45 79. TEFL trained teachers needed for residential summer school.

FJM/Freundinnen Junger Mädchen, Zähringerstrasse 36, 8001 Zürich, Switzerland; (011) 41-1-252 38 40. Au pair placements throughout Switzerland.

German Academic Exchange Service/DAAD, 950 3rd Ave., 19th Fl., New York, NY 10022. May be able to advise on teaching opportunities in Germany.

IBG, Schlosserstrasse 28, D-70180 Stuttgart, Germany; (011) 49-711-649-11-28. Organizes voluntary workcamps throughout Germany.

Institut du Hau-Lau, 1831 Les Scierne d'Albeuve, Switzerland; (011) 41-26-928 4. 00. Teacher and monitors needed for summer and winter language programs.

International School Kaprun, Alpine Sport and Ski Racing Academy, Postfach 47, 571 Kaprun, Austria; Tel./fax (011) 43-6547 710(Young graduates needed to live in on low pay for a year; some teaching and pastoral duties

Internationale Umweltschutz Korps, P.C

Box 9101, Herisau, Switzerland; (011) 41-71 515103. Volunteers needed for conservation camps at Zermatt, Saas Fee, etc. Knowledge of German required.

Involvement Volunteers—Deutschland Giesbethweg 27, 91056 Erlangen, Germany; Tel./fax (011) 49-9135-8075. International conservation organization.

Okista, Türkenstrasse 8/11, 1090 Vienna, Austria; (011) 43-1-401-48/8827. Live-in childcare positions throughout Austria.

Österreichischer Bauorden, P.O. Box 149, Hornesgasse 3, 1031 Vienna, Austria. Organizes projects staffed by volunteers to help disadvantaged communities.

Pro Filia, 51 rue de Carouge, 1205 Geneva, Switzerland; (011) 41-22-329-84-62. Places live-in babysitters with French-speaking families for a minimum of 1 year; the office at Beckenhofstrasse 16, 8036 Zurich deals with German-speaking Switzerland.

Swiss Travel Service, Bridge House, 55-59 High Rd., Broxbourne, Hertfordshire EN10 7DT, England. Winter and summer resort representatives needed.

TASIS Summer Programs, The American School in Switzerland, CH-6926 Montagnola-Lugano, Switzerland; (011) 41-91-9946471. EFL teachers and sports monitors needed in the summer.

Travelbound/Skibound, Olivier House, 18 Marine Parade, Brighton, East Sussex BN2 1TL, U.K.; (011) 44-1273 677777. Domestic and kitchen staff needed to work summer or winter season for tour operator who runs hotels in Alpine resorts in Austria (and also France).

U.S. military bases throughout Germany have Civilian Personnel Offices (CPOs) that are responsible for recruiting auxiliary staff to work

in bars, shops, etc. on base. Fewer vacancies exist because of the scaling down of the U.S. military presence in Europe. The best bet is at Armed Forces Recreational Centers at Garmisch Partenkirchen, Berchtesgaden, and Chiemsee.

Village Camps S.A., c/o Chalet Seneca, 1854 Leysin, Switzerland; (011) 41-25-34-23-38. Recruits monitors and counselors to work for the summer or winter season at children's sports camps in several Swiss resorts and Zell-am-See, Austria.

WWOOF (Germany), Thalhauser Fussweg 30, D-85354 Freising, Germany. Volunteer openings on organic farms. Membership costs DM30.

WWOOF (Switzerland), Postfach 615, 9001 St. Gallen, Switzerland; fairtours@gn.apc.org. For details of working for your keep on an organic farm, send 2 IRCs.

Zentralstelle für Arbeitsvermittlung, Postfach 17 05 45, 60079 Frankfurt-am L-Main, Germany; (011) 49-69-71-11-0. This federal employment bureau handles student applications from abroad.

Latin America

American Friends Service Committee, 1501 Cherry St., Philadelphia, PA 19102; (215) 241-7000. Sends paying volunteers who speak Spanish to community projects in Mexico and Cuba during the summer.

Amigos de las Americas, 5618 Star Ln., Houston, TX 77057. Sends about 500 volunteers with some knowledge of Spanish to Caribbean islands and South and Central America. Participants pay $2,500-$3,000.

Artemis Cloudforest Preserve, Apdo. 937, 2050 San Pedro, Montes de Oca, Costa Rica; (011) 506-253-7243. Volunteers build trails, help with gardens, and plant trees. Participants pay $125 a week.

Bermuda Biological Station for Research, Inc., 17 Biological Ln., St. George's, GE01 Bermuda; (809) 297-1880. Volunteer interns help scientists conduct research for 4 months.

Casa de los Amigos, Ignacio Mariscal 132, 06030 Mexico, D.F., Mexico; Tel./fax (011) 52-5-705 0521. Quaker-run community center in Mexico City which assigns volunteers for at least 6 months to worthwhile social projects.

Casa Guatemala, 14th Calle 10-63, Zona 1, Guatemala City; (011) 502-2-1-25517. Runs orphanage in the Petén region that needs volunteer medical staff, teachers, and nannies.

Centro Cultural Colombo Americano, Carrera 43, 51-95 Barranquilla, Colombia. Recruits English teachers. Similar centers in Cali, Bogota, Medellin, etc.

ICADS (Institute for Central American Development Studies), Apartado 3, 2070 Sabanilla, San Jose, Costa Rica; (011) 506-225-0508. One month Spanish course combined with voluntary sevice. Cost is $1,100.

Latin Link, 325 Kennington Park Rd., London SE11 QE, England. Runs Short-Term Experience Projects (STEPs) in Argentina, Brazil, Bolivia, Peru, and Nicaragua for committed Christians.

Programa de Voluntariado Internacional, Servicio de Parques Nacionales, Apdo. 11384-1000, San Jose, Costa Rica; (011) 506-222-50-85. Spanish-speaking volunteers work in national parks for at least 2 months. Cost is $400 per month.

World Education Forum, P.O. Box 383-4005, San Antonio de Belen, Heredia, Costa Rica; (800) 689-1170. Sponsors exchange programs between U.S. and Costa Rica and Mexico. Volunteers teach English while learning Spanish.

Mediterranean

Greece, Italy, Spain, and Portugal. English-language newspapers such as the Athens-News, Greek News or the Anglo-Portuguese News are helpful sources of tutoring or au pair positions. Many people find work in language schools by applying in person to schools in Madrid, Barcelona, Oporto, Thessaloniki, Milan, etc. Lists of English language schools in Italy may be found in the Italian Yellow Pages under "Scuole di Lingua."

3 esse Agency, Via F. Baracca 18-1, 21013 Gallarate (VA), Italy; Tel./fax (011) 39-331-771065. Au pair positions available.

Acorn Venture Ltd. (see under France). Activity instructors and support staff for holiday center on the Costa Brava.

American Farm School, 1133 Broadway, New York, NY 10010; or Summer Work Activities Program, P.O. Box 23, 55 102 Kalamaria Thessaloniki, Greece. Young people needed in the summer for agricultural and maintenance programs on farms near Thessaloniki.

Centros Europeos, Calle Principe 12-6ºA 28012 Madrid, Spain. Au pair placements in Spain. Also vacancies for English teachers.

Club Paradisus, 8/9 Paradise, Coalbrookcale Telford, Shropshire TF8 7NR, U.K.; (011) 44 1952 432337. Conservation volunteers needed for 1-month stints mid-June to end of September to clean up beach and surrounding habitats of the loggerhead turtle near Koron on the Peloponnese.

Consolas Travel, 100 Eolou St., 10559 Athens Greece; (011) 30-1-325-4931. This travel agency hires office staff for its branches plus hostel staff for pensions in Athens and the islands.

Coordinatora d'Agricultura Ecològica, Apdo. de Correus 2580, 08080 Barcelona, Spain. Send 1 IRC for a list of organic farms.

Employment Agencies. Several employment agencies in Athens run a placement service for au pairs and may offer positions in the tourist industry, including: Au Pair Activities, P.O. Box 76080, 17110 Nea Smyrni, Athens, Greece; Tel./fax (011) 30-1-932-6016.

European Conservation Volunteers in Greece, 15 Omirou St., 14564 Kifissia, Greece. Voluntary projects to restore old buildings and maintain areas of natural beauty. Apply through a U.S. counterpart (e.g. CIEE, VFP).

GIC, Apartado 2008, 46080 Valencia, Spain; Tel./fax (011) 34-6 334 5744. Au pair agency and youth exchange organization.

Instituto da Juventude, Av. da Liberdade 194, 1200 Lisbon, Portugal. Arranges workcamps and archaeological digs throughout Portugal

International Intern Programme, 55 Monmouth St., Covent Garden, London WC2, England; (011) 44-171-240 5795. Volunteers needed to work 3-4 months in depopulated rural areas of Tenerife, Spain. Must contribute $75 per week to expenses.

Kursolan, S.A., Calle Sándalo 5, 28042, Madrid, Spain; (011) 34-91-320-7500. Runs 2 summer camps outside Madrid employing 40 teacher-counselors.

Language School Agencies. Teachers in Greece, 79 Taxilou St., 157 71 Zographou, Athens, Greece; (011) 30-1-779-2587 and English Studies Advisory Center [not Advisor], Cosmos Center, 125-127 Kifisias Ave., 11524 Athens; (011) 30-1-64 95 744.

Malta Youth Hostels Association, 17 Triq Tal-Borg, Pawla PLA 06, Malta; (011) 356-693957. Volunteers who spend 21 hours a week doing hostel maintenance and administration receive free bed and breakfast for 2 weeks to 3 months.

Mr. Panayotis Passalis, Stavros Kallas, Theologos 85106, Rhodes, Greece; (011) 30-241-41173. Volunteers with knowledge of farming can stay and work on his property which he wants to turn into an international community.

O'Neill School of English, Servicio Au Pair, Ibarluce 20, 48960 Galdakao, Spain; (011) 34-4-456 49 17. Demand for native speakers to live with families and help the children with conversational English.

Summer Camps, Via Roma 54, 18038 San Remo, Italy; Tel./fax (011) 39-184-506070. Need counselors for multi-activity and English-language camps in northern Italy.

Sunsail, The Port House, Port Solent, Portsmouth, Hampshire P06 4TH, England; (011) 44-1705-214330, hires sailors, hostesses, clubhouse staff, cooks, and nannies for Greece, Corsica, and Turkey.

Sunseed Trust, Eastside, Huntingdon, PE18 7BY, England; (011) 44-1480-411 784. Invites volunteers to help at a remote research project near Almeria on the south coast of Spain. Costs from £45-£96 per week.

Sunworld Sailing Ltd., 120 St. Georges Rd., Brighton, E. Sussex BN2 1EA, U.K. Employs instructors, maintenance staff, crew and other staff for sailing and windsurfing holidays in Turkey, Spain, Greece, and Turkey.

Trireme Trust, c/o 803 South Main St., Geneva, NY 14456. Volunteer crew members needed to row in a replica trireme in the Mediterranean. Must be fit.

Tutoring and Au Pair Positions. English-language newspapers such as the Athens News or the Anglo-Portuguese News are helpful sources for positions.

Unijet Travel Ltd., Sandrocks, Rocky Lane, Hayward Heath, Sussex RH16 4RH, U.K.; (011) 44-1444 417100. Resort representatives and children's monitors for holiday resorts along the Mediterranean.

Middle East

American Language Center Damascus, c/o USIS, P.O. Box 29, Damascus, Syria; (011) 963-11-332 7236, or c/o USIS, Department of State, Washington, DC 20521-6110. Forty native speaker teachers employed after interview and orientation/training session.

Anglo Nannies, 20 Beverley Ave., London SW20 0RL, England; (011) 44-181-944-6677. Places mother's helpers and nannies in wealthy Istanbul households.

Au Pair International, 2 Desler St., Bnei Brak 51507, Israel; (011) 972-3-619 0423. Places mother's helpers and nannies in Tel Aviv and elsewhere. Also try Mrs. Hilma Shmoshkovitz, Au Pair Intermedian, P.O. Box 91, Rishon-le-Zion, Israel; (011) 972-3-965 99 37.

Dogan International Organization (Au Pair and Employment Agency), Sehitmuhtar Caddesi 37/7, Taskim 80090, Istanbul, Turkey; (011) 90 216-235-1599. Places English-speaking au pairs, preferably after interview.

Eilat. This prospering and expanding Red Sea resort employs many passers-through in hotels, bars, marinas, etc. Inquire at the youth hostel or the Peace Cafe about work.

English Fast, Burhaniye Mah-Resmi Efendi Sok. No. 4, Beylerbeyi, Istanbul, Turkey; (011) 90-216-318-7018 or 7019. Openings for teachers in Istanbul, Ankara, and Izmir.

Gençtur, Istiklal Cad. Zambak Sok. 15/5, Taksim, 80080 Istanbul, Turkey; (011) 90-212-249-2515. A student travel organization that arranges international workcamps and English language summer camps for which ESL teachers and monitors are needed.

GSM Youth Activities Services, Bayindir Sokak No. 45/9, 06450 Kizilay, Ankara, Turkey; (011) 90-312-417-29-91. Arranges 2-week workcamps in Anatolia. Registration fee is $70.

Israel Antiquities Authority, P.O. Box 586, Jerusalem 91004, Israel; (011) 772-2-560 2607. Coordinates archaeological excavations throughout Israel. Publishes an annual listing of digs looking for paying volunteers.

Israel Youth Hostels Assoc., 1 Shezer St., P.O. Box 6001, Jerusalem 91060, Israel; (011) 972-2-558400. Volunteers needed for hostel work throughout Israel. Applications should be sent to individual hostels.

Kibbutz Program Center, 18 Frishman St., Cr. Ben Yehuda, 3rd Fl., Apt. 6, Tel Aviv 61030, Israel; (011) 972-3-527-8874. This office can place you on a kibbutz, although it is better to arrive with a letter of introduction from Kibbutz Program Center, 110 E. 59th St., 4th fl., New York, NY 10022; (800) 247-7852, a clearinghouse for American volunteers. Minimum stay 2 months. Registration fee $95. Summer is the busiest time.

Meira's Volunteers, 73 Ben Yehuda St., 1st Fl., Tel Aviv 63435, Israel; (011) 972-3-523-7369. Agent for kibbutzim and moshavim for volunteers already in Israel.

Noah's Ark International, 12 Broadlands, Brixworth, Northamptonshire NN6 9BH, U.K.; (011) 44-1604 881639. Places qualified TEFL teachers in public and private schools in Turkey.

Saday Educational Consultancy, Necatibey Caddesi 92/3, Karakoy, Istanbul, Turkey; (011) 90-212-243 2078. Supply English tutors to live in with Turkish families.

Transonic Travel, 3 Phoenix St., London WC2H 8PW, U.K.; (011) 44-171 240 8909. Agency which places volunteers on kibbutzim and moshavim for at least 2 months.

UNIPAL (Universities Educational Fund for Palestinian Refugees), c/o Centre for Middle Eastern and Islamic Studies, South Rd., Durham, DH1 3TG, U.K. Sends volunteers to teach English to Palestinians and help with handicapped children in the occupied territories and Jordan.

Netherlands, Belgium, Luxembourg

Aida Luxembourg, 70 Grand'rue, 1660 Luxembourg City, Luxembourg. Provides information to students already in Luxembourg who are looking for temporary work.

Archeolo-j, Avenue Paul Terlinden 23, 1330 Rixensart, Belgium; (011) 2-653 82 68. Residential archaeological digs require paying volunteers.

Au Pair and Activity International, P.O. Box 7097, 9701 JB Groningen, Netherlands; (011) 31-50-3130666. Au pair placements via Au Pair Homestay Program (see International Organizations section).

BLS (Brussels Language Studies), 8 rue du Marteau, 1210 Brussels, Belgium; (011) 32-2-217 23 73. Freelance English teachers needed to teach children and adults.

ICVD, MvB Bastiaan sestraat 56, 1054 SP Amsterdam, Netherlands. Volunteers needed for building restoration and other voluntary camps.

L'Administration de l'Emploi, 38a rue Philippe II, 3rd fl., L-2340 Luxembourg; (011) 352-47-68-55. Operates a Service Vacancies for students seeking summer jobs in warehouses, restaurants, etc. Non-European students must visit the office in person.

Natuur 2000, Bervoetstraat 33, 2000 Antwerp, Belgium; (011) 32-3-231-26-04. Organizes summer conservation workcamps and study projects throughout Belgium, which cost from BF1,000.

Phone Languages, 65 rue des Echevins, 1050 Brussels, Belgium; (011) 32-2-647-40-20. Telephone teachers recruited for clients throughout Belgium and Luxembourg.

Stufam V.Z.W., Vierwindenlaan 7, 1780 Wemmel, Belgium; (011) 32-2-460 3395. Places au pairs in Belgium for a fee of BF1,000.

The Bulletin. A weekly English-language magazine in Brussels which carries job ads.

Travel Active Programs, Postbus 107, 5800 AC Venray, Netherlands; (011) 31-478 58 80 74. Arranges 6-month live-in child care positions in the Netherlands. Applications should be made through partner agency InterExchange (see International Organizations section).

Scandinavia

APØG, Norsk Økologisk Landbrukslag, Langeveien 18, N-5003 Bergen, Norway; (011) 47-55 32 04 80. Service for volunteers who want to work on organic farms in Norway; send $8 or 10 IRCs for list of 50 plus farm addresses.

Atlantis (Norwegian Foundation for Youth Exchange), Rolf Hofmosgate 18, 0655 Oslo, Norway; (011) 47-2-67-00-43. Arranges summer working guest positions on farms for 1-3 months. Also recruits au pairs for a minimum of 6 months. Applications should be sent to InterExchange in New York (see International Organizations).

Center for International Mobility (CIMO), P.B. 343, 00531 Helsinki, Finland; (011) 358-0-7747-7033. Arranges family stays with participant teaching host family English. Also arranges internships for 2-18 months.

Exis, Rebslagergade 3, Postbox 291, 6400 Snderborg, Denmark; (011) 45-74-42-97-49. Au pair placements in Denmark, Norway, and Iceland.

IAL/Internationella Arbetslag, Barnängsgatan 23, 116 41 Stockholm, Sweden; (011) 46-8-643 08 89. Peace and conservation camps organized through the Swedish branch of Service Civil International (see U.S. address at end of Directory).

Icelandic Nature Conservation Volunteers,

SJA, P.O. Box 8468, 128 Reykjavik. Recruits volunteers for local short-term summer projects throughout Iceland.

MS/Mellemfolkeligt Samvirke, Studsgade 20, 8000 Aarhus C, Denmark. Two 4-week summer workcamps in Denmark and Greenland. Danish camp fee 885 kroner.

The American-Scandinavian Foundation (Exchange Division), 725 Park Ave., New York, NY 10021; (212) 879-9779. Places summer trainees in engineering, agriculture, chemistry, etc. throughout Scandinavia.

Use It, Youth Information Copenhagen, Radhusstraede 13, 1466 Copenhagen K, Denmark; (011) 45-1-33-15-65-18. Publishes English Language Guide to Copenhagen, Short Cuts, including short section on working, for 40 Danish kroner.

VHH, c/o Inga Nielsen, Asenvej 35, 9881 Bindslev, Denmark. For $10 publishes a list of English-speaking farmers looking for volunteers.

WOOF Finland, Luomu-Liiton talkoovälitys, Koiddalamylly, 51880 Koikkala, Finland; (011) 358-9-55 450 251. New Finnish organic farm organization. Send 2 IRCs to get list of 40 farmers looking for volunteers over the summer.

United Kingdom and Ireland

An Oige, 61 Mountjoy St., Dublin 1, Ireland. Irish Youth Hostels Association makes use of voluntary assistant wardens in the summer.

British Trust for Conservation Volunteers, 36 Saint Mary's St., Wallingford, Oxfordshire OX10 0EU, England; (011) 44-1491-839766. Organizes 1- or 2-week working breaks for environmentally concerned volunteers.

Community Service Volunteers, Overseas Programme, 237 Pentonville Rd., London N1 9NJ, England; (011) 44-1-71-278-6601. Places volunteers in socially worthwhile projects from 4 months to a year, throughout Britain. U.S. applicants should apply through WISE (see International Organizations).

Conservation Volunteers Ireland, P.O. Box 3836, Ballsbridge, Dublin 4, Ireland; (011) 353-1-668-1844. Coordinates unpaid environmental working holidays throughout Ireland. Membership is £15.

Council for British Archaeology, Bowes Morrell House, 111 Walmgate, York Y01 2UA, England. Publishes CBA Briefing 5 times a year with details of upcoming excavations in Britain. A subscription costs £18 (plus postage).

Council/CIEE (Work in Britain), 205 E. 42nd St., New York, NY 10017-5706; (888) COUNCIL. Runs the Work in Britain Program in conjunction with BUNAC (16 Bowling Green Ln., London EC1R 0BD, England) whereby students can obtain a 6-month work permit to do any job in the British Isles or a 4-month permit for Ireland.

Dublin Internships, 8 Orlagh Lawn, Scholarstown Rd., Dublin 16, Ireland; Tel./fax (011) 353-1 494 5277. Places American students in salaried internships of varying durations in Dublin. A placement fee is charged.

National Trust, Residential Holidays, P.O. Box 84, Cirencester, Glos. GL7 1ZP, England; (011) 44-1285 644727. One-week outdoor conservation camps throughout the U.K. year round. Volunteers pay £42-50 per week.

Nord-Anglia International Ltd., 10 Eden Pl., Cheadle, Stockport, Cheshire SK8 1AT, England; (011) 44-161-491-4191. Places over 500 young people in English-language summer schools in Britain and Ireland as language and sports instructors. Many positions are nonresidential.

People to People International, 501 E.

Armour Blvd., Kansas City, MO 64109-2200; (816) 531-4701. Two-month unpaid internships in London and Dublin.

PGL Adventure, Alton Court, Penyard Ln., Ross-on-Wye, Herefordshire HR9 5NR, England; (011) 44-1989-767833. Hires over 500 people as sports instructors, counselors, and general staff for activity centers throughout Britain. Other children's holiday companies include: Prime Leisure Activity Holidays, Ltd., The Manor Farm House, Dunstan Rd., Old Headington, Oxford OX3 9BY, England; Camp Beaumont, Worthington House, 203-205 Marylebone Rd., London NW1 5QP, England; EF Language Travel, 1-3 Farman St., Hove, Sussex BN3 1AL, England; and Action Holidays, Robinwood, Jumps Rd., Todmorden, Lancashire OL14 8HJ, England. All recruit large numbers of summer staff.

Programme of International Agricultural Workcamps in the U.K. Listing available from Concordia Youth Service Volunteers, 8 Brunswick Pl., Hove, Sussex BN3 1ET, England; (011) 44-1273-772086 in exchange for 2 IRCs. Recruits students aged 19-25 to pick fruit and hops at over 160 U.K. farms. Applications should be sent between September and December.

TASIS England American School, Cold-Harbour Ln., Thorpe, Surrey KT20 8TE, England; (011) 44-1932 565252. EFL teaching vacancies for qualified Americans and jobs for sports monitors at children's summer camp.

Thistle Camps, National Trust for Scotland, 5 Charlotte Sq., Edinburgh EH2 4DU, Scotland; (011) 44-131-243-9470. Similar to National Trust but in Scotland. Includes archaeological digs. Week-long projects cost from £40.

Trident Transnational, Saffron Court, 14B Saint Cross St., London EC1N 8XA, England; (011) 44-171-242-1515. Offers unpaid work placements lasting 3 weeks to 6 months in U.K. businesses. Participants aged 18-26. Fee of £200 for 2-month attachment.

USIT (Union of Students in Ireland Travel Service), 19 Aston Quay, Dublin 2, Ireland; (011) 353-1-677-8117. Advice on job opportunities for Council work abroad participants.

Winant & Clayton Volunteers, 109 E. 50th St., New York, NY 10022; (212) 751-1616 ext. 271, arranges for U.S. citizens to work 6-10 weeks during the summer in youth clubs, with the homeless, AIDS sufferers, etc. in Britain.

WWOOF (Working for Organic Growers), 19 Bradford Rd., Lewes, Sussex BN7 1RB, England. Connects members with organic farmers throughout Britain (annual membership £10). The Irish equivalent is WWOOF Ireland, Harpoonstown, Drinagh, Co. Wexford, Ireland (membership IR£5).

Voluntary Service

Archaeological Institute of America, in Boston; fax (617) 353-6550. Publishes each January the Archaeological Fieldwork Opportunities Bulletin listing digs and projects open to volunteers. The Bulletin costs $12.50 from Kendall Hunt Publishing, 4050 Westmark Dr., P.O. Box 1840, Dubuque, IA 52004-1840.

British Trust for Conservation Volunteers, 36 St. Mary's St., Wallingford, Oxfordshire OX10 0EU, U.K.; (011) 44-1491 839766. Conservation projects around the world.

Conservation International, 1015 18th St., #1000, NW, Washington, DC 20036; (202) 429-5660. Accepts volunteers to work with local people to help save rainforests in Brazil, Colombia, Costa Rica, Indonesia, Botswana, etc.

Europe Conservation, Via Fusetti 14, 20143 Milan, Italy. Volunteers help researchers with projects worldwide. Costs range from $200-$750.

Global Routes, 1814 7th St., Suite A, Berkeley, CA 94710; (510) 848-4800; mail@globalroutes.org. Sends interns in pairs to remote villages in Costa Rica, Ecuador, Thailand, Kenya, and Navajo Nation to teach in local schools and do community service.

Global Service Corps, 1272 Filbert St., #405, San Francisco, CA 94109. Cooperates with grassroots organizations in Kenya, Costa Rica, and Thailand. Sends volunteers for 2-3 weeks (fee $1,500-$1,700).

Global Volunteers, 375 E. Little Canada Rd., Little Canada, MN 55117. Sends volunteers to short-term community projects in selected countries.

Partnership for Service Learning, 815 2nd Ave., Suite 315, New York, NY 10017. Sends students to India, Philippines, Israel, Ecuador, Mexico, Jamaica, and Europe to teach, help care for disadvantaged people, etc.

Peace Corps, 1990 K St. NW, Washington, DC 20526. The main government agency that recruits volunteers to work in developing countries.

Raleigh International, Raleigh House, 27 Parsons Green Lane, London SW6 4HS, England. Selects young people aged 17 to 25 for 10-week expeditions to carry out scientific research and community aid in remote areas.

Scientific and Conservation Expeditions. Some organizations recruit paying volunteers to help staff scientific and conservation expeditions throughout the world. Examples are: Earthwatch, 680 Mt. Auburn St., P.O. Box 403, Watertown, MA 02272; and Univ. of California Research Expeditions (UREP), Univ. of California, Berkeley, CA 94720-7050.

Traveler's Earth Repair Network (TERN), c/o Michael Pilarski, P.O. Box 4469, Bellingham, WA 98227; (360) 738-4972. Supplies list of potential hosts worldwide involved in organic farming, tree planting, etc. A subscription costs $50.

Volunteers Exchange International, 134 W. 26th St., New York, NY 10001; (212) 206-7307. Exchanges with over 33 countries that involve voluntary service in the community.

Volunteers, P.O. Box 218, Port Melbourne, VIC 3207, Australia; Tel./fax (011) 61-3-9646 5504. Arranges short-term individual, group, and team voluntary placements in Australia, New Zealand, Fiji, Papua New Guinea, Thailand, India, Germany, Finland, Italy, and Latvia. Most projects involve conservation. Program fee is AUS$400.

Workcamp Organizations. The major workcamp organizations for American volunteers are: Council, 205 E. 42nd St., New York, NY 10017-5706; (888) COUNCIL. Service Civil International, 5474 Walnut Level Rd., Crozet, VA 22932; (804) 823-1826, and Volunteers for Peace, 43 Tiffany Rd., Belmont, VT 05730; (802) 259-2759.

World Challenge Expeditions Ltd., Black Arrow House, 2 Chandos Rd., London NW10 6NF, U.K.; (011) 44-181-961 1122. Expedition leaders for school groups to developing countries.

World Horizons International, P.O. Box 662, Bethlehem, CT 06751. Sends high school and college students on summer programs to Botswana, Namibia, and Costa Rica.

WorldTeach, Harvard Institute for International Development, 1 Eliot St., Cambridge, MA 02138; (617) 495-5527. Sends volunteers to teach English, and other subjects for one year in Ecuador, Costa Rica, Poland, Lithuania, Namibia, Vietnam, and Thailand. Also has summer program in China.

SUSAN GRIFFITH is the author of Work Your Way Around the World *and* Teaching English Abroad: Talking Your Way Around the World, *both available from Peterson's Guides (800-EDU-DATA).*

CHAPTER 18

VOLUNTEER PROGRAMS

The following listing of volunteer abroad programs was supplied by the organizers. Contact the program directors to confirm costs, dates, and other details. If you do not see the program you want in the country of your choice, look in the "Worldwide" listings at the end of the section for programs located in several different regions.

Africa

African Am. Studies Program. To educate the American public concerning social, cultural, political developments in Africa with educational trips to 25 African countries.

Dates: Feb, Jun, Jul, Aug. Cost: From $1,000 to $5,000. Contact: AASP, 19 S. La Salle, #301, Chicago, IL 60615; (312) 443-0929, fax (312) 684-6967.

Integrated Development Program. PASA-COFAAS Community Development Organization (NGO) invites volunteers to work on its programs. Applicants must pay $50 for processing applications. Programs for 18 to 65 years old. In operational villages lodging is provided. Program aids cultural understanding, farming (tree crops), animal husbandry, youth and women activities.

Dates: Year round. Contact: Mr. A.R.C. Conteh, Director, Private Mail Bag 686, 5A City Rd. Welling, Freetown, Sierra Leone, West Africa; (011) 22 232 224439.

Short Term Ministry in Africa. Africa Inland Mission (AIM) is a church-based agency sending qualified individuals to East Africa to work with church-based ministries (teaching in national schools, refugees, dental). A Christian commitment is an essential priority for ministry with AIM.

Dates: Jan-Dec. Cost: $4,000 (3 months); $7,000 (6 months); $10,000 (1 year). Contact: R. Cousins, Personnel Director, Africa Inland Mission, 1641 Victoria Pk. Ave., Scarborough, ON M1R 1P8, Canada; (416) 751-6077, fax (416) 751-3467.

Volunteer in Zimbabwe, Angola, or

Mozambique. In Zimbabwe you teach at a school for disadvantaged youth or work with families in a health project. In Angola you plant trees, organize health campaigns, and teach people of all ages. In Mozambique you teach at schools for street children or at vocational schools. The Zimbabwe and Angola programs are 12 months long and the Mozambique is a 20-month program. All include preparation and follow-up periods in the U.S. The programs are open to persons 18 years of age and older.

Dates: Zimbabwe and Angola: Feb 15 and Aug 15, 1997. Mozambique: Nov 1, 1996. Cost: $4,600. Includes training, room and board, airfare, international health insurance, and other direct program costs. Contact: Josefin Jonsson, Administrative Director, IICD, Institute for International Cooperation and Development, P.O. Box 103-T, Williamstown, MA 01267; (413) 458-9828, fax (413) 458-3323; iicd1@berkshire.net, www.berkshire.net/~iicd1.

Antarctica

Project Antarctica III. Volunteers will live aboard a former Russian research vessel, cruise to the South Shetland Islands, and weigh anchor off King George Island. Once on land, we will work in cooperation with scientists at the Bellingshausen Station to remove debris from nearby beaches, and continue our efforts to preserve this pristine environment. The VIEW Foundation (Volunteer International Environmental and Community Work Projects) is a nonprofit Canadian organization.

Dates: Feb 20-Mar 7, 1997. Cost: $4,550 plus port dues and taxes (includes air and 10 days on ship). Contact: Karin Chykaliuk, The VIEW Foundation, 13 Hazelton Ave., Toronto, ON M5R 2E1, Canada; (416) 964-1914, fax (416) 964-3416.

Australia

Australian Trust for Conservation Volunteers. ATCV is a national, nonprofit, nonpolitical organization undertaking practical conservation projects, including tree planting, seed collection, flora/fauna survey, habitat restoration, track construction, and weed eradication. Projects take place on private and public lands; rivers, creeks and coastal areas; national and state parks, including world heritage areas.

Dates: Year round. Cost: Six-week 'Echidna Package' AUS$840, including food, accommdations, and project-related travel. Contact: Colin Jackson, Executive Director, P.O. Box 423, Ballarat, VIC 3353, Australia (please inlcude an IRC); (011) 61-53-331-483, fax 332-290; atcv@netconnect.com.au.

Canada

Archaeology Field School. Hands-on experience in an archaeological excavation is provided, under professional supervision. Finds are typical of Northern Plains prehistoric hunter gatherers dating back as far as 10,000 years: pottery shards, stone working debitage and tools, butchered and charred bone, fire-broken rock. Accommodations and meals are on-site.

Dates: Jun 30-Jul 3 and Jul 4-7 (two 4-day sessions). Cost: Fees are $40 (individual), $50 (family). Daily food and lodging is $34-$40 per person. Contact: Tim Jones, Executive Director, Saskatchewan Archaeological Society, #5 - 816 1st Ave. N, Saskatoon, SK S7K 1Y3, Canada; (306) 664-4124, fax (306) 665-1928.

Old Fort Churchill Archaeology Project. Excavation of a Hudson's Bay Company fur trade post 1717-1933. Volunteers learn the techniques of archaeological excavation as well as exploring the historical record. Educational hikes to pre-Dorset and Dorset sites also included. Volunteers walk to site. Rustic lodge accommodations (hot and cold showers, etc.), whale watching, birding, plant identification, legends, etc.

Dates: Jul 9-Aug 29, 1997. Cost: $1,700 plus

transportation to Churchill. Contact: Virginia Petch, Northern Lights Heritage Services, 121 Cunnington Ave., Winnipeg, MB R2M OW6, Canada; Tel./fax (204) 231-8190.

Parks Canada Research Adventures. A Parks Canada Research Adventure is a unique opportunity for you to help protect Canada's National Parks. It is an exciting chance to work alongside researchers, park wardens, and environmental educators to meet nature face to face. Your personal contribution to science and education will lead to a better understanding of natural ecosystems and vulnerable wildlife.

Dates: Year round ranging from 2- to 10-day experiences. Cost: CAN$80 to CAN$170 per day (depending on program). Includes food and lodging. Contact: Donna Cook, Parks Canada Research Adventures, Yoho National Park, Box 99, Field, BC V0A 1G0, Canada; (604) 343-6324, fax (604) 343-6758; donna_ cook@pch.gc.ca.

Willing Workers on Organic Farms. WWOOF-Canada is an exchange venture. In exchange for your help on one of over 200 farms or homesteads (animal care, weeding, harvesting, construction projects) volunteers receive accommodations, 3 meals daily, and a wonderful learning experience.

Dates: Year round. Most opportunities spring-fall. Cost: $25 (single), $35 (couple) plus 2 IRCs. Contact: WWOOF-Canada, R.R. 2, S. 18, C. 9 Nelson, BC V1L 5P5, Canada; (604) 354-4417, fax (604) 352-3927.

WWOOF-Canada (Willing Workers on Organic Farms). A volunteer work exchange where you can choose from over 200 farms across Canada. You help with the work and the farm host provides accommodations, 3 meals, and a wonderful learning experience. Thousands have participated in this highly successful program.

Dates: Anytime. Best from early spring to late fall. Cost: $25 (single), $35 (couple), and 2 postal coupons. Contact: WWOOF-Canada,

R.R.2, S.18, C.9, Nelson, BC V1L 5P5, Canada; (604) 354-4417.

Caribbean

International Environmental Work Project. Volunteers from around the world will work in Dominica in partnership with the Springfield Centre for Enviornmental Protection, Research and Education (SCEPTRE) and the Dominica Conservation Association. Projects include soil survey, mapping, trail maintenance/construction, campground development, swimminghole improvements, and compact-soil structure construction.

Dates: Oct 28-Nov 6, 1996. Cost: $400 (tax deductible contribution, exclusive of airfare). Contact: International Volunteer Expeditions (IVEX), P.O. Box 13309, Oakland, CA 94661-0309; (510) 339-7770, fax (510) 339-3749; oakland2@ix.netcom.com.

Central America

Plenty Volunteer Program. Plenty places a limited number (approx. 15 per year) of volunteers to work on community-based development projects in food production, communications, crafts marketing, and other appropriate technologies related to increasing local self-sufficiency. Length of service varies per position, but is typically 1-6 months.

Dates: Ongoing. Cost: Volunteer pays travel and living expenses. Contact: Lisa Wartinger, Plenty West Coast, Dept. T, 22 Harper Canyon Rd., Salinas, CA 93908; (408) 484-5845; www.public.usit.net/plenty1/.

Sea Turtle Nesting Protection. Volunteers work with biologists to collect important information on nesting population. Volunteers count and tag turtles, learn about sea turtle conservation and biology, and visit nearby forests and local communities.

Dates: Summer and fall. Cost: Approx.

$1,000 per week. Contact: Randall Arauz, Sea Turtle Restoration Project, Earth Island Institute, P.O. Box 400, Forest Knolls, CA 94933; (415) 488-0370, fax (415) 488-0372; sea-turtles@earthisland.org.

Volunteers for TAU. Volunteers for TAU is a program sponsored by the School Sisters of St. Francis. It is an invitation to be a source of new life, new meaning, and new hope to women, men, and children throughout the U.S. and abroad. Volunteers for TAU and S.S.S.F. become partners in ministry as they share a communal lifestyle and empower others to live to the fullest. TAU volunteers and vowed members share common values as together they make Christ's mission their own. At least 1 year commitment.

Cost: Insurance, travel to site, and personal needs. Contact: School Sisters of St. Francis, Volunteers for TAU, Sister Rosemary Reier, OSF, 3545 N. Nora, Chicago, IL 60634; (312) 685-0187, fax (312) 685-0207.

Chile

Restoration in National Parks. This program, which will take place in the 10th region of Chile (South), principally includes environmental education and work with communities most in need. Spanish knowledge is required.

Contact: Rocio Gonzalez, Int. Officer, N.G.O. Usazul, Pio NoNo 53, Providencia, Santigao, Chile; Tel./fax (011) 56-2-7380883.

China

Human Rights and Economic Development. Hong Kong hosts will conduct a program to examine the ramifications of the June, 1997 return of Hong Kong to Chinese sovereignty. The cultural diversity of life in the former British colony, the center of capitalist-oriented trade with China and Asia, serves as contrast to life in China. In China the group will meet with religious, government, and education leaders in Shanghai, Beijing, and Nanjing. The delegation will also visit rural areas, an important difference from life in the principal cities. Unique to this seminar will be close personal contact with members and leaders of Christian churches in Hong Kong and the People's Republic of China.

Dates: Jun 2-16. Cost: $3,500 includes tuition, room and board, and travel from Los Angeles. Contact: Maralyn R. Lipner, Plowshares Institute, 809 Hopmeadow St., P.O. Box 243, Simsbury, CT 06070; (860) 651-4304, fax (860) 651-4305; evans@mstr.hgc.edu.

Overseas Service Corps YMCA (OSCY). Teach conversational English in community-based YMCAs in Taiwan for 1 year (minimum). Must have a 4-year degree, preferably in English or teaching-related field. Prior teaching experience is desired. Must reside in North America and be a citizen of an English-speaking country. Twenty to 30 openings.

Dates: Year round. Application deadline is Apr 15 for Sep placement. Cost: $25 application fee. Benefits for successful applicants include: Salary, return airfare, financial bonuses, paid vacation, health insurance, and more. Deferment of university loans. Contact: Janis Sterling, World Service/OSCY Manager, International Division, YMCA of the USA, 101 N. Wacker Dr., Chicago, IL 60606; (800) 872-9622.

Summer Field Work in Archaeology in Xian, China. Excavation practicum, lectures, museum visits, and 10-day study tour.

Dates: Jul 1-Aug 5. Cost: $4,100, includes roundtrip airfare from NY, tuition, room and board, and excursions. Contact: Dr. Alfonz Lengyel, Fudan Museum Foundation, 1522 Schoolhouse Rd., Ambler, PA 19002; Tel./fax (215) 699-6448.

Costa Rica

Casa Rio Blanco Rainforest Reserve. Volunteers maintain trails, map, develop educational materials, teach, garden, etc. Also available: 1 paid position in lodge helping with cooking and cleaning. Room, board, and $30 per week. Minimum of 3 months.

Dates: Four-week sessions throughout the year. Cost: $150 per week, includes room, food, laundry, materials. Contact: Thea Gaudette, Casa Rio Blanco, Apdo 241-7210, Guapiles, Pococi, Costa Rica.

Forest Conservation Project. Volunteers have the unique opportunity to live and work within a cloud forest. Under the direction of local staff, small groups construct trails and maintain pathways within the Monteverde Cloud Forest Reserve. Other projects include reforestation of farming pastures and maintenance of a field station within the Eternal Children's Rainforest. The VIEW Foundation (Volunteer International Environmental and Community Work Projects) is a nonprofit Canadian organization.

Dates: Youth (aged 15-18): Mar break 1997 (2 weeks); Jul 1997 (3 weeks). Adult: Jan, Mar, May, Jul, Sep, Nov 1997 (2-3 weeks). Cost: $2,000-$2,500 (includes air from Toronto or New York plus food, lodging, and excursions). Contact: Karin Chykaliuk, The VIEW Foundation, 13 Hazelton Ave., Toronto, ON M5R 2E1, Canada; (416) 964-1914, fax (416) 964-3416.

Genesis II Cloudforest Preserve. The main activity during the dry season (Jan to Jun) is trail maintenance and construction. In the rainy season (Jul to Dec) work is done on reforestation in a deforested area.

Dates: Jan 3-31, Feb 7-Mar 6, Mar 13-Apr 10, Apr 17-May 15, May 22-Jun 19, Jun 26-Jul 24, Jul 31-Aug 28, Sep 11-Oct 9, Oct 16-Nov 13. Cost: $600 per unit of 28 days. Inquiries should include 3 IRCs. Contact: Steve or Paula Friedman, Apdo. 655, 7,050 Cartago, Costa Rica.

Lyök Ami. Conservation and maintenance of the tropical cloudforest: reforestation and trailmaking, working with native species, En-

glish teaching in local schools, independent personal projects (e.g. research, studies) also welcome. Volunteers stay in Albergue in the reserve belonging to a Costa Rican family.

Dates: Any time of year, minimum stay 1 month. Cost: $500 per month of stay, includes food and laundry. Contact: Maureen Vargas, Iyök Ami, P.O. Box 335-2100, Guadalupe, San José, Costa Rica; (011) 506 285 2546, fax 223-1609.

The Birds of Costa Rica. A research participation study of the migrant and neotropical resident birds of Tortuguero. Participants will study birds by making observations in 3 integrated ways: 1) along transects, 2) within specific habitat types, and 3) by mist-netting. Tortugero is strategically situated along a migratory path between North and South America. In addition, close to 200 resident birds make their home in the forests and waterways of exotic Tortuguero.

Dates: Year round. Cost: Approx. $1,900 for 15 days, includes travel to Costa Rica, room and board. Contact: Program Coordinator, Caribbean Conservation Corporation, 4424 NW 13th St., Suite A-1, Gainesville, FL 32609; (352) 373-6441, fax (352) 375-2449; ccc@atlantic.net.

Volunteer Turtle Tagging And Monitoring. Volunteers assist scientists with several important tasks: tagging turtles, recording morphological and behavioral data, and conducting beach surveys. Tortuguero Beach is one of the most important nesting beaches for Atlantic Green turtles in the Western Hemisphere. By tagging turtles, we can identify individual animals and learn more about their behavioral patterns and survivorship.

Dates: Leatherback program Mar-May; Green Turtle program Jul-Sep. Cost: Approx. $1,500 for 8 days and $1,900 for 15 days. Includes travel to Costa Rica, room and board. Contact: Program Coordinator, Caribbean Conservation Corporation, 4424 NW 13th St., Suite A-1, Gainesville, FL 32609; (352) 373-6441, fax (352) 375-2449; ccc@atlantic.net.

Denmark

Internship Program. The World Assembly of Youth (WAY) is an international coordinating body of national youth councils and organizations. WAY recognizes the Universal Declaration of Human Rights as the basis of its actions, and works for the promotion of youth in areas such as population, development, etc. Working knowledge of English essential, knowledge of French and/or Spanish preferred. Interns are 20-30 years old.

Dates: Year round. 6-12 months minimum stay. Cost: Return trip paid by WAY. Scholarship of DKK3,000 month provided. Contact: Mr. Heikki Pakarinen, Secretary General, World Assembly of Youth, Ved Bellahøj 4, 2700 Brønshøj, Copenhagen, Denmark; (011) 45-3160-7770, fax 3160-5797; way@inform-bbs.dk.

Ecuador

Golondrinas Cloudforest Project. The Cerro Golondrinas Cloudforest Conservation Project in northern Ecuador replants deforested land in conjunction with teaching soil conservation and permaculture techniques to local community members. The beautiful subtropical valley of Mira is a great place to volunteer. Volunteers work in tree planting, nursery operations, and the setting up of an 8-acre permaculture demonstration site. Desirable experience: gardening and permaculture design, basic Spanish.

Dates: Year round. Cost: Contribution for food: $180 per month. Contact: Fundación Golondrinas, Attn. Piet T. Sabbe, c/o Calle Isabel La Católica 1559, Quito, Ecuador.

El Salvador

Melida Anaya Montes Language School. Teach small-size English classes, all levels offered. Training provided. Students are adults working in the Salvadoran opposition who need to increase their capacity for their work and/or complete their studies. CIS also seeks volunteers for their human rights work. Volunteers can receive half-price Spanish classes.

Dates: Three-month sessions beginning mid-Jan, Apr, and Aug. Mini-sessions offered Jul and Nov. Cost: No fee. Must pay living costs ($250-$400 per month). Contact: CIS MAM Language School, Urb. Padilla Cuellar, Pasaje Los Pinos #17, San Salvador, El Salvador, Centro America; Tel./fax (011) 503-225-0076; cis@nicarao.apc.org, or Language School, c/o CISPES, P.O. Box 1801, New York, NY 10159; (212) 229-1290, fax (212) 645-7280.

France

Chantiers d'Etudes Medievales. These workcamps lasting 15 days undertake to restore and maintain medieval buildings and sites. The project includes 2 fortified castles at Oltroh, near Strasbourg.

Dates: Jul 1 - Aug 31. Cost: 450FF Contact: Chantiers d'Etudes Medievales, 4 rue du Tonnelet Rouge, 67000 Strasbourg, France; (011) 33-88-37-17-20.

Doline de Roucadour (Themines, Lot). Neolithic and Bronze Age excavation of one of the most important stratigraphy in the south of France.

Dates: Jul 1997. Contact: J. Gasco, CNRS UMR150, 106 rue de la Cadoule, 34070 Montpellier, France; Tel./fax (011) 33 67 42 84 05.

REMPART. REMPART aims to preserve the French cultural heritage through the restoration of threatened buildings and monuments. It consists of a grouping of more than 140 autonomous associations organizing workcamps providing a wide variety of work projects involving the restoration of medieval towns, castles, churches, ancient walls, wind/watermills, and industrial sites. Work includes masonry, excavations, woodwork, stone cutting, interior decorating, and clearance work. Opportunities for sports, exploring the region, and taking part in local festivities. Minimum age is 14. Previous experience is not necessary. Some knowledge of French required.

Dates: Workcamps last from 2 to 3 weeks. Most of them are open during Easter holidays and from Jul to Sep. A few camps are open throgout the year. Cost: FF220 for insurance, FF45-FF55 per day for food and accommodations. Volunteers help with camp duties, pay their own fares and should bring a sleeping bag. Contact: REMPART, Foreign Secretary: Sabine Guilbert, Union des Associations pour la réhabilitation et l'Entretien des Monuments et du Patrimoine Artistique, 1 rue des Guillemites, 75004 Paris, France; (011) 33-1-42-71-9655, fax 42-71-73-00.

Vivre la Provence en Chantiers. Our association organizes annual workcamps in Provence for adults and teenagers. The aim is to restore old buildings and clean rivers. As there is a lot of demand, we recommend applying as soon as possible.

Dates: Jul-Sep. Cost: FF650 for adults, FF2,000 for teenagers. Contact: Mrs. Mireille Pons or Miss Marie Christine, Pascal Apare, Cours Jean-Jaures, 86000 Avignon, France.

Germany

International Workcamps. The international workcamps, lasting 3 to 4 weeks, are often situated near to or in homes for the elderly, Camphill village community farms for the handicapped, or different non-governmental education-centers. Volunteers (aged 18-25) are needed to help with manual work like gardening, repair work, and renovating, or social work like looking after elderly people. Special workcamp with German language courses from mid-Jul-mid-Aug.

Dates: Mar, Apr, May-Dec. Cost: DM140 (includes food, lodging, insurance). Contact:

Nothelfergemeinschaft der Freunde e.V., Postfach 101510, 52349 Düren, Germany; (011) 49 2421 76569, fax 49 2421 76468.

Rehabilitation Work. Rehabilitation for war-injured children. Peace Village International admits children from war and crisis areas for medical treatment in Germany. After completion of medical treatment the children are provided with rehabilitation measures during their stay in the institution. Volunteers prepare meals, do housework, and play with the children.

Dates: No fixed period of time. Cost: Free of charge boarding and lodging in the institution; traveling costs are the responsibility of the volunteer. Contact: Peace Village International, Mr. Andreas Simon, Lanterstr. 21, 46539 Dinslaken, Germany; (011) 49-2064 4974 0, fax 2064 4974 999.

Work with Mentally Handicapped Children. Help look after mentally handicapped young people in a residential school where "house parents," trainees, teachers, and other staff live and work together. The work includes caring for a small group of children outside of school hours, organizing recreational time, and helping with housework. Knowledge of German is necessary.

Dates: Year round. Cost: Program provides free board and accommodations, social security, and pocket money of DM350 per month. Contact: Mr. Bruno Wegmüller, Heimsonderschule Brachenreuthe, 88662 Überlingen, Germany; (011) 49-07551/8007-0, fax 8007-50.

Guatemala

Eco-Escuela de Español. The Eco-Escuela de Español offers a unique educational experience by combining intensive Spanish language instruction with volunteer opportunities in conservation and community development projects. Students are immersed in the language, culture, and ecology of the Petén, Guatemala—an area renowned for its tropical forests and ancient Maya ruins. Ecological activities integrate classroom with field-based experiences.

Dates: Every Monday year round. Cost: Classes $60 per week (based on 20 hours of individual instruction per week, Monday-Friday). Room and board with local families $50 per week. Registration fee $10. Contact: Eco-Escuela, Conservation International, 1015 18th St. NW, Suite 1000, Washington, DC 20036; (202) 973-2264, fax (202) 887-5188; m.sister@conservation.org.

Hungary and Romania

Central European Teaching Program. Work as an English Conversation teacher at the elementary or high school level. In nearly every case, students will have native Hungarian or Romanian teachers responsible primarily for teaching grammar. Conversation teachers are responsible for enhancing students' oral fluency through conversation practice, classroom drills, games, and listening comprehension, and through working with native teachers.

Dates: Sep 96-Jun 97. Cost: Program fee: $700 plus airfare. Contact: Michael Mullen, CETP Director, Beloit College, 700 College St., Beloit, WI 53511; (608) 363-2619, fax (608) 363-2449; mullenm@beloit.edu.

India

India Works Camp Programs. Joint Assistance Centre (India) is a nongovernmental voluntary group headquartered in Haryana State in the outskirts of Delhi. It coordinates conferences and training in various parts of India on disaster preparedness, working in close liaison with other groups, individuals, and small grassroots projects all over India, focusing in such areas as community welfare, health, education, youth development, and agricultural training. JAC welcomes volunteers from around the world to participate in the work of these organizations. JAC publishes information materials, books, and newsletters, and maintains a library on disasters, environment, health care, and welfare of women and children. JAC works in cooperation with various international organizations in the areas of disaster preparedness. Long term placements for periods over 3 months can be arranged.

Dates: Ongoing throughout the year. Cost: Registration $50; monthly fees $125. Long term placement fee $100. Contact: Krishna Gopalan, Friends of JAC in the Americas, P.O. Box 14481, Santa Rosa, CA 95402; (707) 573-1740, fax (707) 528-8917; jacusa@aol.com.

Project India. A unique 3-week service program open to people of all ages and backgrounds. The program is run by a highly qualified staff of educators, social workers, and cultural advisors. Positions include health care, education, social development, arts/recreation, and more. No skills or experience is required. Volunteers pay a fee which covers all expenses.

Dates: Three-week programs run year round. Cost: $1,650 covers all India based expenses. International airfare, insurance, and visa not included. Program fee is tax deductible. Contact: Steven C. Rosenthal, Cross-Cultural Solutions, 6 Aurum St., P.O. Box 625, Ophir, CO 81426; (970) 728-5551 or (800) 380-4777, fax (970) 728-4577; CCSmailbox@aol.com.

Ireland

9th Achill Archaeological Field School. Survey and excavation of a post-medieval deserted village: Slievemore, Achill, Co. Mayo. Activities include: surveying, excavation procedure, recording geology and botany of island, field trips, lectures and seminars. No previous knowledge required. Maximum 6 credits.

Dates: Weekly Jul 15-Aug 30. Cost: Weekly: IR£85 p.p. $200 course fee plus accommodations. Contact: Theresa McDonald, M.A. Director, Achill Archaeological Field School, St. O'Hara's Hill, Tullamore, Co. Offaly; (011) 353-1-505-21627, fax 506-21627.

Conservation Volunteers Ireland. A program of weekend and week-long conservation-working holidays. Volunteers will have the opportunity to mix with Irish volunteers and experience Irish culture.

Dates: Year round. Cost: Varies from IR£15-IR£19. Contact: Conservation Volunteers Ireland, P.O. Box 3836, Ballsbridge, Dublin 4, Ireland; Tel./fax (011) 353-1-6681844.

Willing Workers on Organic Farms. Voluntary work in return for food and board on farms and small holdings throughout Ireland. Learn about organic farming methods, rural Ireland and its life. Work is varied and you can volunteer from a few days to a few months.

Dates: Year round. Cost: IR £6. Contact: WWOOF, Harpoonstown, Drinagh, Co. Wexford, Ireland.

Israel

Archaeological Excavations. The Israel Antiquities Authority publishes annually a list of volunteer opportunities at archaeological excavations. Volunteers must be in good physical and mental condition, and able to do physical work for long hours in the hot sun. Accommodations, costs, dates, etc., vary by site. Some expeditions offer credit courses at additional cost. Minimum age: 18.

Dates: Year round, main season of digs from May to mid-Aug. Cost: Travel and living expenses. Contact: Harriet Menahem, Israel Antiquities Authority, 1004 Jerusalem, Israel; (011) 972-2-560-607, fax 972-2-560-628; harriet@israntique.org.il.

Interns for Peace. An independent, community-sponsored program dedicated to building trust and respect among the Jewish and Arab citizens of Israel. Develop action-oriented projects in education, sports, health, the arts, community and workplace relations, and adult interest groups. Requirements include: a commitment to furthering Jewish-Arab relations; BA, BS, or equivalent degree; proficiency in Hebrew or Arabic; a previous stay in Israel of at least 6 months; background in sports, business, teaching, health care, youth work, art, music, or community organizing (professional work experience is a plus).

Dates: Vary. Cost: Varies. Contact: Interns for Peace, 475 Riverside Dr., 16th Fl., New York, NY 10115; (212) 870-2226, fax (212) 870-2119.

Tel Dor Excavation Project. The Tel Dor Excavation Project is devoted to investigating one of the largest coastal cities in ancient Israel. Volunteers will be engaged in all facets of field archaeology, and in some of the preliminary work of artifact analysis.

Dates: $26 per day and $60 participation fee per week. Cost: Prof E. Stern or Ms. Orna Hillman, Tel Dor Excavation Project, Institute of Archaeology, Hebrew Univ., Jerusalem, Israel.

Kenya

Habitat for Humanity. IVEX conducts short-term voluntary service workcamps at the invitation of, and in partnership with, local non-profit organizations. Work projects primarily involve unskilled manual labor. In Kenya volunteers build houses with Habitat for Humanity Kenya in Western Province (south of Kitale). Volunteers will be camping, sometimes under very rustic conditions. Sightseeing expeditions through the Rift Valley and in the Western Province.

Dates: Kenya: Nov 18-29, 1996. Cost: $1,250 (tax deductible and exclusive of airfare) Contact: International Volunteer Expeditions (IVEX), P.O. Box 13309, Oakland, CA 94661-0309; (510) 339-7770, fax (510) 339-3749; oakland2@ix.netcom.com.

Kenya Voluntary Development Association. International work project involving community members in rural Kenya working alongside volunteers. The emphasis is on cross-cultural encounters as participants construct school classrooms, dispensaries, bridges, roads, and other community projects.

Dates: Apr., Jul, Aug., Dec. (every year). Cost: $200 per project; $300 for 2 projects. Contact: Gitonga Njagi, Kenya Voluntary Development Association, P.O. Box 48902, Nairobi, Kenya; (011) 254 2 225379.

Latin America

Voluntarios Solidarios. Work with grassroots peace and justice organizations in Latin America on various projects. Requires conversational fluency in Spanish or Portuguese, commitment to nonviolence, self-direction, flexibility, and minimum age of 21.

Dates: No fixed dates; serve between 3 months and 2 years. Cost: Living costs (range $75-$500/month), travel to region, insurance; $75 application fee. Contact: John Lindsay-Poland, Voluntarios Solidarios, 995 Broadway, #801, San Francisco, CA 94103; (415) 495-6334, fax (415) 495-5628; forlatam@igc.apc. org.

Volunteer in Nicaragua or Brazil. In Nicaragua you help to construct a school and a water supply and assist in a pre-school. You travel and study in the country and in Central America. In Brazil you live in a rural community, work in construction, and travel and study throughout the country. The Nicaragua program lasts 11 months, and the Brazil program lasts 6 months. Both include preparation and follow-up periods in the U.S. The programs are open to persons 18 years of age and older.

Dates: Nicaragua: Sep 15, 1996, and 1997; Brazil: Jan 4, 1997. Cost: Nicaragua: $4,600; Brazil: $3,400. Includes training, room and board, airfare, health insurance, and other direct program costs. Contact: Josefin Jonsson,

Administrative Director, IICD, Institute for International Cooperation and Development, P.O. Box 103-T, Williamstown, MA 01267; (413) 458-9828, fax (413) 458-3323; iicd@berkshire.net, www.berkshire.net/ ~iicd1.

Malta

MYHA Workcamp. Workcamp open to 16-to- 30-year-olds who want to volunteer for the MYHA and other organizations. Periods: 2 weeks to 3 months. For details send 3 IRCs or $2.

Dates: Year round. Apply 3 months in advance. Cost: A good faith deposit of $45 per night, returnable on completion. Contact: The Workcamp Organizer, Malta Youth Hostels Association, 17, Triq Tal-Borg, Pawla PLA 06, Malta; Tel./fax (011) 356-693957; myha@ keyworld.mt.

Mexico

Learn, Live, and Love Spanish in the Land of the Maya (Chiapas). Spanish lessons in private sessions or small groups (4 people max). Family stays available. School tours to Indian (Mayan) villages, jungle trips available. Extracurricular activities included: Mexican cooking, discussions, video showings. Teach English in exchange for Spanish lessons. Centro Cultural "El Puente" includes gallery weaver's cooperative, travel agency, cafe, restaurant, phone/fax service.

Dates: Year round. Cost: Highest $220 per week; lowest $75 per week. Contact: Roberto Rivas, Bastidas Centro Bilingüe de Chiapas, C. Real de Guadalupe 55, Centro Cultural "El Puente," San Cristóbal de Las Casas 29230, Chiapas, Mexico; (011) 52-967-8-41-57, fax 967-83723 or Tel./fax (800) 303-4983; cen-bili@chisnet.com.mx, www.mexonline. com/ centro1.htm.

Mar de Jade. Tropical ocean-front retreat center in a beautiful unspoiled fishing village near Puerto Vallarta offers unique volunteer opportunities in a 21-day work/study program. Work in community health program, local construction, cottage industries, and teaching. Study Spanish in small groups with native teachers. Relax and enjoy great swimming, kayaking, hiking, boating, horseback riding, and meditation. Dates: Year round. Cost: $865 for 21-day work/study. Includes room (shared occupancy), board, 12 hours per week of Spanish and 15 hours per week of community work. Longer resident program available at lower cost. Vacation/Spanish 1 week minimum: $365 room, board, 12 hours of Spanish. Vacation only: $45 per night for any length of time. Contact: Mexico: Mar de Jade/Casa Clinica, A.P. 81, Las Varas, Nayarit, 63715, Mexico; Tel./fax (011) 52-327-20184; U.S.: P.O. Box 423353, San Francisco, CA 94142; (415) 281-0164.

Third World Opportunities (Tecate). Third World Opportunities is a 2-pronged program utilizing the border with Mexico as a gigantic classroom. Learn about the realities of poverty and hunger and participate in short-term development projects including 1-week house building programs with Habitat for Humanity in Tecate, Mexico. Applicants must be at least 15 years old. Registration fee is due 6 weeks prior to event.

Dates: Call for information. Cost: $200 plus transportation (6-day events). Contact: M. Laurel Gray, Coordinator, 1363 Somermont Dr., El Cajon, CA 92021; (619) 449-9381.

Third World Opportunities (TWO). One-day or weekend experiences in Tijuana explore hunger, poverty, and border issues. A 6-day house building project in Tecate and Rosarito is conducted in the spring and summer with Habitat for Humanity. Minimum age: 15.

Dates: Call for information. Cost: $20 per person for awareness experience; $200 for 6-day house building, plus transportation. Contact: M. Laurel Gray, Third World Opportunities, 1363 Somermont Dr., El Cajon, CA 92021; (619) 449-9381.

Micronesia

Ponape Agriculture and Trade School. Volunteers with trade skills, agricultural experience, and mechanical or technical skills are needed to teach and supervise Micronesian high school students. The school is privately run and supported by the Catholic church in Micronesia.

Dates: School year: Aug 15-May 15. Only 2-year contracts are considered for volunteer acceptance. Contact: Joseph E. Billotti, S.J., Director, PATS, Box 39, Pohnpei, FM 96941, Federated States of Micronesia.

Nepal

Placement for Volunteer Service. Provides opportunities to those interested in contributing their time and skills to worthwhile community groups throughout Nepal. We arrange a limited number of volunteer placements involving either teaching or working in various organizations.

Dates: Feb, Apr, and Aug 1997. Cost: $600 program fee and visa fee depending on length of stay. Contact: Naresh M. Shrestha, Director, Insight Nepal, P.O. Box 6760, Kathmandu, Nepal; (011) 977-1-418-964, fax 223515 or 416144.

Nicaragua

North America-Nicaragua Colloquium on Health. A professional and cultural exchange between North American and Nicaraguan health workers. An academic conference is held in Managua in association with the Nicaraguan health workers union and medical university. Tour includes site visits to health and related facilities in Managua and Bluefields on the Atlantic coast. The theme will be public health and NGOs.

Dates: Aug 1997. Cost: $850 plus airfare. Contact: Lazaro Cuevas, Committee for Health Rights in the Americas, 474 Valencia

#120, San Francisco, CA 94103; (415) 431-7760, fax (415) 431-7768, chria@igc.org.

(808) 965-7828 (call for fax info); kh@ilhawaii.net, randm.com/kh.html.

Northern Ireland

Practical Conservation Work. Conservation Volunteers Northern Ireland is the largest practical conservation charity in the country, providing opportunities for volunteers over the age of 16 to take part in a variety of urban and rural projects. The organization coordinates daily task programs, conservation working holidays all over Northern Ireland and training courses in practical skills on a regular basis.

Dates: Vary. Cost: Varies according to activity, but is consistently geared towards those operating on a very limited budget. Contact: Madeleine Kelly, Conservation Volunteers Northern Ireland, 159 Ravenhill Rd., Belfast BT6 OBP, Ireland; (011) 353 1232 645169, fax 1232 644409; cvni@btcv.org.uk.

Pacific Region

Hawaii's Kalani Oceanside Eco-Resort. Kalani Educational Eco-Resort, the only coastal lodging facility within Hawaii's largest conservation area, treats you to Hawaii's aloha comfort, traditional culture, healthful cuisine, wellness programs, and extraordinary adventures: thermal springs, a naturist dolphin beach, snorkel pools, kayaking, waterfalls, crater lake, and spectacular Volcanoes National Park. Ongoing offerings in yoga, dance, hula, mythology, language, and massage. Or participate in an annual week-long event: men's/women's/couples conferences, dance/music/hula festivals, yoga/meditation/transformation retreats. Our native staff and international Volunteer Scholar participants welcome you.

Dates: Year round. Cost: Lodging $45-$85 per day. Camping $15. $550-$1,100 per week for most programs, including meals and lodging choice. Contact: Richard Koob, Director, Kalani Eco-Resort, RR2, Box 4500, Kehena Beach, HI 96778-9724; (800) 800-6886 or

Peru

California Institute for Peruvian Studies. Each year CIPS opens its field schools and archaeology program to avocationals and adventure travelers. Archaeology experiences include excavation, cultural research, survey, photography, mummy analysis, and more.

Dates: Feb-Sep 1997. Cost: $900-$2,500 depending on length of stay. Optional tours to the Amazon, Highlands, and Colca Canyon offered in conjunction with each field school. Write or call for details. Contact: California Institute for Peruvian Studies, 45 Quakie Way, Bailey, CO 80421; (303) 838-1215, fax (303) 670-3668.

Philippines

Little Children of the Philippines, Inc. LCP is a not-for-profit, interdenominational Christian agency to help develop caring communities for poor children on Negros Island in central Philippines. LCP has service programs in 7 communities covering health, housing, education, livelihood (agriculture, handicrafts), and peace formation. Research opportunities also available, especially involving handicapped and street children.

Dates: Volunteers may negotiate their own period of service during 1997. Cost: From East Coast: approx. $1,200 roundtrip airfare, $120 per month for food. Dormitory bed free. Contact: Dr. Douglas Elwood, 361 County Rd. 475, Etowah, TN 37331; Tel./fax (423) 263-2303.

Russia

Petro-Teach 1997-98. Live and work in beautiful St. Petersburg, Russia through a teacher intern program. Placement as an English language teacher in a local high school. Live with a Russian family. Group trips and excursions. Nonprofit educational program.

Dates: Aug 1997-May 1998. Cost: $2,965. Contact: John Bailyn, Adventures in Education, Inc., 81 Narcissus Rd., Rocky Point, NY 11778; (516) 821-5083.

Scotland

Volunteer Care Worker. Living and working in small Camphill commuity together with young adults with learning disabilities.

Dates: Any dates considered. Full-year stay preferred. Cost: None. £25 pocket money paid per week. Contact: Elisabeth Phethean, Beannacha Camphill Community, Banchory-Deverick, Aberdeen AB12 54G, Scotland, U.K.; (011) 44-1226-869138, fax 869250.

Sierra Leone

JMRRDO Volunteer Exchange. The camp program of the organization is to assist the rural villagers where access to services is not available. The program also helps volunteers to learn our culture and assist to improve the lifestyle of the people. The program will also establish training centers to train villagers and set-up income generating activities in each village.

Dates: Three-month, 6-month, and 1-year programs. Cost: $600, $1,200, $2,400. Contact: Mr. John Musa-Bangalie, Camp Director, JMRRDO, 42 Soldier St., Freetown, Sierra Leone, West Africa; Tel. 227822.

South America

Youth Challenge International (YCI). YCI combines community development, health work and environmental research in adventurous projects conducted by international teams of volunteers aged 18-25, and coordinated by volunteer field staff aged 26 plus. Since 1989 YCI has promoted international cooperation and understanding through dynamic living and working exchanges between the people and cultures of different nations.

Dates: Projects depart in May, Jun, and Sep, and Dec. Cost: Participants must fundraise $3,750 prior to departure. Contact: Mike Buda, Recruitment and Selection Director, YCI, 11 Soho St., Toronto, Ontario M5T 1Z6, Canada; (416) 971-9846, fax (416) 971-6863; info@yci.org.

Spain

Sunseed Desert Technology. Arid land recovery trust research center S.E. Spain aims to find and spread methods that will improve lives and environment of people in poverty in desertified areas. Full-time volunteers. Minimum 5 weeks. Working visitors 24 hours weekly.

Dates: Year round. Cost: Volunteers $70-$99, working visitors $95-$153 plus $16. Contact: Sunseed Trust, 97B Divinity Rd., Oxford OX4 1LN, England; (011) 44-1865-721-530.

Suriname

Suriname Sea Turtles. Working with local Forest Service wardens, volunteers will patrol nightly the tropical beaches of Galibi to count leatherback and green turtles, locate nesting families, and collect biological data. Participants chaperone hatchlings to the sea or move eggs to safe areas to ensure hatching.

Dates: Feb 13-21, Apr 17-25, Jun 19-27, Jul 17-25. Cost: $1,350 with international airfare from Miami. Contact: Oceanic Society Expeditions, Fort Mason Center, Bldg. E., San Francisco, CA 94123; (800) 326-7491 or (415) 441-1106, fax (415) 474-3395.

Sweden

Project Assistant. TRN is a network of NGO's, indigenous peoples and nations working for the presentation and sustainable use of the world's boreal forest. Our ongoing program consists of: coordinating consumer campaigns; serving as an information clearinghouse; organizing international meetings and conferences; researching and publishing reports, factsheets, and a bimonthly newsletter. The project assistant position is open to self motivated environmental activists interested in assisting the above activities.

Dates: Year round. Cost: Living expenses (room and board). Contact: Anne Janssen, Taiga Rescue Network (TRN), Box 116, S-96223, Jokkmokk, Sweden; (011) 46 971 17039, fax 12057; taiga@nn.apc.org.

Switzerland

Gruppo Volontari della Svizzera Italiana. Work on reconstruction projects in the Italian region of Switzerland that has suffered natural disasters. Lodging in a house in the village provided by the municipality. Participate in service projects aimed at helping the populace; e.g., help the aged, cut wood, domestic work, work in the stable and orchard. Volunteers share kitchen, cleaning, shop, and vehicle maintenance duties. Minimum age: 18.

Dates: Jun 1-Sep 30, 7-day minimum, 15-day maximum. Cost: Varies. Contact: Mari Federico, Director, Gruppo Volontari della Svizzera Italiana, CP 12, 6517 Arbedo, Switzerland; (011) 41-092-29-13-37.

Tunisia

Workcamps. Organizing voluntary workcamps during summer, school holidays, and weekends is the most important activity of ATAV. ATAV also organizes other activities such as training courses for workcamp leaders, meetings, seminars, and medical caravans.

Dates: Jul-Aug. Cost: Free. Contact: Mr. Hafidh Rahoui (S.G.), Association Tunisienne d'Action Volontaire, Maison du RCD, Lakasbah, Tunis; (011) 216 1 264899 ext 472, fax 573065.

Turkey

Workcamps and Study Tours. Gençtur organizes workcamps in small Anatolian villages with manual projects for people over 18. Lasting 2 weeks, camp language English. Enables close contact with locals. Study tour maintains close contact with students, teachers, lawyers, peasants, workers, journalists, etc.

Dates: Workcamps: Jul-Aug-Sep; Study Tours: Year round. Cost: Workcamps £45; Study Tours: depends on duration and program. Contact: Gençtur, Mr. Zafer Yilmaz, Istiklal Cad. Zambak Sok. 15/5, 80080 Istanbul-TR, Turkey; (011) 90-212-249-25-15, fax 212-249-25-54.

Uganda

Workcamps and Developmental Activities. Workcamps aim to: assist needy communities, bind communities together in all apects of life, create common understanding people to people, work for the welfare of African society and the world at large, and link an experience with comparible organizations in the world.

Dates: May, Sep, Dec. Cost: $200 per workcamp, lasts 14 days each. Contact: Mr. G. Stuart Semakula, National Chairman, Uganda Voluntary Workcamps Association, P.O. Box 3367, Kampala, Uganda; Fax (011) 256-41-234168/250668.

United Kingdom

Arbeia Roman Fort and Museum. Roman site being excavated. Volunteers will excavate, map, and survey site; catalog and photograph finds. Also flotation and pot cleaning. Tuition provided.

Dates: Jun-Sep. Cost: No fees. Must pay for own accommodations. Contact: E. Elliott, Arbeia Roman Fort, Baring St., South Shields, NE33 2BB, U.K.; (011) 44-191-4544093, fax 4276862.

Archaeological Excavation. Volunteer and

study programs in archaeological excavation techniques based on medieval settlement in mid-Wales. No previous experience necessary, but reasonable fitness required. Must be at least 16 years old.

Dates: Jul 26-Aug 16, 1997, 7-day minimum. Cost: Volunteers, food and campsite £40 weekly. Tuition, food and campsite £150. Contact: Dr. C.J. Arnold, Dept. of Continuing Education, Univ. of Wales, Newtown Powys, U.K.; (011) 44-1686-650715, fax 1686-650656.

Archaeological Excavation-Wales. Volunteer accepted on archaeological excavation of late-Roman and early medieval settlement in rural environment. Training given in varied tasks. No experience required, camp site, food and transportation provided.

Dates: Jul 26-Aug 16, 1997. Cost: £40 per week, includes campsite and food. Contact: Dr. C.J. Arnold, Gregynog, Univ. of Wales, Newtown, Powys SY16 3PW, U.K.

Archaeological Technical Training. Research excavation of post-medieval, medieval, and earlier sites in Bagshot, Surrey, England.

Dates: Aug 1997. Cost: £50 per week. Contact: Geoffrey H. Cole, MIFA, Archaeology Centre, 4-10 London Rd., Bagshot, Surrey GU19 5HN, U.K.; (011) 44-1276-451181.

Beannachar (Camphill Community). Living and working with young adults who have special needs. Minimum age 19 years. Minimum length of stay 6 months. Preferred length of stay at least 1 year.

Dates: Any. Cost: None. Volunteers receive free board and lodging and £25 per week pocket money. Contact: Elisabeth Phethean, Beannachar, Banchory-Deverrick, Aberdeen AB1 54L, Scotland; (011) 44 224 869138, fax 1224 869250.

Didcot Railway Centre. Assist restoration and operation of Great Western Railway steam locomotives, carriages and wagons, as well as signalling, buildings, etc. Activities can be tailored to the volunteer's interests.

Dates: Workweek Aug 2-8, 1997; other dates by arrangement. Cost: Varies. Contact: Great Western Society, Didcot, Oxfordshire OX11 TNJ, U.K.; (011) 44 1235 817200, fax 1235 510621.

Discover Cornwall. Week-long guided mini bus tours (Spring and Autumn). Walking. Mineral collecting, houses, gardens, archaeology, natural history, heritage. Discover unspoiled Cornwall. Cliffs and coves. Wild flowers and birds. Moorland ancient remains. Mining history and much more. Full board included. Small groups. Individuals welcome.

Dates: Mar, Apr, May, Jun, Sep, Oct. Cost: £190 includes accommodations. Some courses extra for entrance fees. Contact: Sheila Harper, Chichester Interest Holidays, 14 Bay View Terr., Newquay, Cornwall TR7 2LR, U.K.; (011) 44 1637 874216.

Holidays for Physically Disabled. Seaside holiday/respite center for adults with physical disabilities requires volunteers. No experience necessary. Simple training given. This is a very practical, hands-on working holiday. Volunteers assist staff with personal care and act as escorts on outings. Friendly, helpful staff. Excellent food.

Dates: Late Jan-mid-Dec, 1-2 week duration. Cost: Full board and lodging plus £15 per week pocket money provided; airfare not included. Contact: Mrs. Pat McCallion, Volunteer Organiser, Lulworth Court, 25 Chalkwell Esplanade, Westcliff on Sea, Essex, SS0 8JQ, England; (011) 44-702-431725, fax (011) 44-702-433165.

Independent Living Alternatives. Provides support to disabled people in London to enable them to live in their own homes.

Dates: Year round (6 months). Cost: Travel to United Kingdom. Contact: Tracey Jannaway, ILA Ashford Offices, Ashford Passage, London NW2 6TP, U.K.; (011) 41 181450 4055 or 2009.

Loch Arthur Community. A community of 70 people (families, short-term volunteers, and adults with mental handicaps) live in 6 houses on a 500-acre estate. People work on the farm, garden, workshops and in houses. Volunteers must join in all work and social and cultural activities.

Dates: Year round. Minimum of 6 months. Cost: No cost. Includes board and lodging plus pocket money. Contact: Lana Chanarin, Stable Cottage, Loch Arthur, Beeswing, Dumfries DG2 8JQ, Scotland; (011) 44-1387-760687, fax 1387-760618.

Nansen Society Ltd. U.K. (Scotland). The Nansen Society is an apolitical and non-religious charity. It was set up to help young people who have been disadvantaged in their home life, their education, or their work environment because of physical, social, or mental disability.

Dates: Year round. Cost: Room and board free/pocket money £25. Contact: Bart Lafere Nansen Society, Redcastle Station, Muir of Ord Ross Shire, IV6 7RX, U.K.; (011) 44-463-871255, fax 463-870258.

RSPB Voluntary Wardening Scheme. The Voluntary Wardening Scheme operates throughout England, Scotland, and Wales, providing an opportunity for those people interested in ornithology and conservation to gain practical experience of the day to day running of a birds reserve.

Dates: Year round. Cost: Free (does not include food and transportation). Contact: Voluntary Wardening Scheme Administrator (TA), Youth and Volunteers Department, RSPB, The Lodge, Sandy, Bedfordshire SG19 2DL, U.K.; (011) 44 1767 692365.

SHAD Haringey. Full-time volunteers required to work in the homes of people with physical disabilities, assisting them with personal care, housework and all other activities. Volunteers work a flexible rotation system. Free accommodations provided in shared flats with all bills paid plus weekly allowance.

Dates: Placements from 3 months upwards, recruiting year round. Cost: Cost of travel to project (partly subsidized by SHAD). Contact: Sue Denney, SHAD Haringey, Winkfield Resource Centre, 33 Winkfield Rd., London N22 5RP, U.K.; Tel./fax (011) 44 181 365 8528.

The Simon Community. We are a community of volunteers and homeless people working with the long-term rough sleepers of London. We have 3 residential houses and a night shelter. Voluntary workers take part in the running of the projects. Their main responsibility is to befriend those sleeping rough and provide a tolerant, accepting atmosphere.

Dates: Year round. Minimum 6-month commitment. Cost: Board and lodging provided plus pocket money (currently £25 per week). Contact: The Simon Community, P.O. Box 1187, London NW5 4HW, England; (011) 44-71-485-6639.

Welshpool and Llanfair Railway. A chance to assist in the maintenance and operation of the historic steam railway. Train services run from Easter to October. Trackwork and loco restoration take place year round. Applicants welcome at any time.

Dates: Year round, particularly Oct-Apr. Cost: Small charge to cover accommodations. Contact: David Moseley, Deputy General Manager, Welshpool and Llanfair Railway, Llanfair Caereinion, Welshpool, Powys, Wales SY21 0SF, U.K.

Winant-Clayton Volunteers, Inc. Since 1948, WCV has sponsored a summer international visitor exchange program designed for 20 U.S. and 20 U.K. citizens to work in social service settings. Winants depart in early Jun and return mid-Aug, must travel with group from New York and pay group-rate airfare. Application fee: $30, deadline Jan 31.

Dates: Jun-Aug. Cost: Free room and board; anticipate approx. $2,000 for airfare and personal expenses. Contact: Volunteer Coordinator, Winant-Clayton Volunteers, 109 E. 50th St., New York, NY 10019.

Winged Fellowship Trust Volunteer Pro-

gram. We have 5 holiday centers in England for severely physically disabled people. We need volunteers to come for 1 or 2 weeks to be the arms and legs of our disabled guests. Free food and accommodations. Travel expenses within England refunded. No experience necessary. Hard work but fun.

Dates: From Saturday to Saturday between Feb and Dec. Cost: None. Contact: Winged Fellowship Trust, Angel House, 20-32 Pentonville Rd., London N1 9XD, U.K.; (011) 44 171 833 2594, fax 171 278 0370

Worcestershire Lifestyle ILP. A local charity that aims to enable people with physical disabilities to live independently in their own home with the help of volunteer workers. For example: shopping, cooking, intimate personal care, sharing leisure pursuits, housework. Free accommodations (no bills), £51.50 per week, travel expenses, bonus.

Dates: Four to 12 months placements, ongoing. Cost: No cost. Contact: Sue Abbott, Worcestershire Lifestyles, Woodside Lodge, Lark Hill Rd., Worcester WR5 2EF, U.K.; (011) 44 1905 350635, fax 1905 350684.

United States

Camphill Special School. Volunteers for 6-12 months live in an international community based on Anthroposophy, devoted to providing a wholesome life and education to the mentally retarded child. Days are long, children demanding, 1 day off per week. Orientation course required. Challenging but rewarding. Volunteers for July summer program also only accepted. Minimum age 19; 21 and older preferred.

Dates: End of August to end of July or July only. Cost: Medical and dental exams required before arrival; no other costs. Contact: Andrea Janisch (610-469-9160) or Ursel Pietzner (610-469-9236), c/o 1784 Fairview Rd., Glenmoore, PA 19343.

The Univ. of Arizona. The Dept. of English

MA in ESL emphasizes leadership development and is designed for experienced teachers with a strong academic record and leadership experience. Specialized courses are offered in language program administration, comparative discourse, teaching language through literature, sociolinguistics, language testing, and technology. PhD in SLAT.

Dates: Applications due by Feb 1 for the following fall semester. Two years are normally required to complete the program. Cost: $1,005 registration for 7 or more units, plus approx. $244 per unit for nonresident tuition. Contact: Director, English Language/Linguistics Program, English Dept., P.O. Box 210067, The Univ. of Arizona, Tucson, AZ 85721-0067; (520) 621-7216, fax (520) 621-7397; maes1@ccit.arizona.edu.

Wales

Ffestiniog Railway Co. Help maintain a tourist railway with great historic appeal. All aspects of running a railway, meet tourists, engineering/track/building work all year. Assist in running the railway service March to November.

Dates: Year round. Cost: Bed charge £1.50 per night in Railway Hostels. Contact: Robert Shrives, Ffestiniog Railway Company, Harbour Station, Porthmadgg, Gwynedd LL49 9NF, Wales.

Worldwide

American Refugee Committee. ARC specialists provides health care and health training to persons uprooted by war or civil unrest. Program employees also promote reconciliation and self-sufficiency through education and training.

Contact: Sandee Evenson, Recruitment Director, American Refugee Committee, 2344 Nicollet Ave. S, #350, Minneapolis, MN 55404-3305; (612) 872-7060, fax (612) 872-4309; kraus024@maroon.tc.umn.edu.

Archaeology. The Archaeological Institute of America publishes the Archaeological Fieldwork Opportunities Bulletin (AFOB), a comprehensive guide to excavations, field schools, and special programs with openings for volunteers, students, and staff throughout the world. The cost is $9 for AIA members, $11 for nonmembers plus $4 shipping and handling for the first copy and 50¢ for each additional copy. All orders must be prepaid and be made in U.S. dollars or by an international money order to: Kendall/Hunt Publishing Company, Order Dept., 4050 Westmark Dr., Dubuque, IA 52002; (800) 228-0810, (319) 589-1000.

Dates: Available every January 1. Contact: Archaeological Institute of America, 656 Beacon St., Boston, MA 02215-2010; (617) 353-9361, fax (617) 353-6550; aia@bu.edu.

Catholic Network of Volunteer Service. Publishes a directory (Response) of volunteer opportunities with 184 listings of national (domestic) and international volunteer/lay missioner, full-time (long- and short-term) service programs.

Dates: Vary. Call or write for directory of programs.. Cost: Varies. Contact: Catholic Network of Volunteer Service, Phyllis Scaringe, Office Coordinator, 4121 Harewood Rd. NE, Washington, DC 20017; (800) 543-5046 or (202) 529-1100, fax (202) 526-1094.

CFCA Volunteer Program. Christian Foundation for Children and Aging founded by Catholic lay people to work with handicapped, malnourished, and abandoned children, and the elderly in 21 countries. Volunteers of varied backgrounds serve as liaisons in children's homes, neighborhoods, schools, parishes, and clinics. Must have a high school (and, for some positions, college) education. Spanish is a plus. Minimum age: 21.

Dates: Four-day orientation discernment for candidates in Kansas City are year-round. Preferred length of service 1 year. Cost: Volunteers self-funded. Room and board provided at most sites. Contact: Holly A. Neff, Director of Volunteer Services, Christian Foundation for Children and Aging, 1 Elmwood Ave., Kansas City, KS 66103; (913) 384-6500, fax (913) 384-2211.

Community Development. Two-year placements for experienced individuals in human rights, gender programming, sustainable resource use, worker and social solidarity, indigenous rights, small business and institutional development. CUSO works in Africa, the Caribbean, Latin America, Asia, and the South Pacific. Applicants should send a copy of their resume to the CUSO office nearest them. A complete list of office addresses is available from the head office.

Dates: Placements are made year round. Cost: CUSO covers all costs. Contact: Head Office, 2255 Carling Ave., Suite 400, Ottawa, ON, Canada K2B 1A6; (613) 829-7445, fax (613) 829-7996; cusocan@web.net.

Coral Cay Conservation Expeditions. CCC recruits volunteers to join coral reef and tropical forest conservation expeditions in the Caribbean and Indo-Pacific. Each month, teams of international volunteers spend from 2 weeks assisting with reef and forest survey and conservation programs. No previous expedition experience or scientific training required and all necessary training (including scuba diving) is provided.

Dates: Expeditions depart monthly throughout the year. Cost: From $1,160 (exclusive of flights). Contact: Caroline De Freze, Coral Cay Conservation, Suite 124, 230 12th St., Miami Beach, FL 33139; Tel./fax (305) 534-7638; www.demon.co.uk/coralcay/home.html.

Council Volunteer Projects. Council's International Volunteer Projects bring 10-20 volunteers from different countries together to work on an environmental or community service project for 2 to 4 weeks during the summer months. Choosing from over 600 projects worldwide, participants (aged 18 and over) join locally initiated projects to protect the environment, preserve historical sites, build low-income housing, restore community centers, or care for children, while learning and sharing the benefits of international cooperation. Dates: Jun-Sep. Cost: $250-$750, includes room and board. Contact: Council on International Educational Exchange, Information Center, 205 E. 42nd St., New York, NY 10017; (888) COUNCIL; info@ciee.org, www.ciee.org.

Cross Cultural Journeys. Our travel program encompasses journeys to remote or unusual areas of the globe to experience traditional healing practices and learn indigenous wisdom from ancient teachings. Our trips include a knowledgeable trip leader, with an average number of 15 travelers. We practice socially responsible ecotourism—leaving only positive reminders.

Dates: Year round. Cost: From $1,000-$6,000 all inclusive with attention to details and accommodations. Contact: Carole Angermeir, President, P.O. Box 1369, Sausalito, CA 94966; (800) 353-2276, fax (415) 332-0683.

Earthwatch. Unique opportunities to work with leading scientists on 1- to 3-week field research projects worldwide. Earthwatch sponsors 160 expeditions in over 30 U.S. states and in 60 countries. Project disciplines include archaeology, wildlife management, ecology, ornithology and marine mammalogy. No special skills needed—all training is done in the field.

Dates: Year round. Cost: Tax deductible contributions ranging from $695-$2,800 support the research and cover food and lodging expenses. Airfare not included. Contact: Earthwatch, 680 Mt. Auburn St., P.O. Box 9104MA, Watertown, MA 02272; (800) 776-0188, (617) 926-8200; info@earthwatch.org, www.earthwatch.org.

Fourth World Movement. The Fourth World Movement is the U.S. branch of the international organization ATD Fourth World, which is devoted to fighting extreme poverty. Two 3-month internships are held in the U.S. each year for Americans as an orientation program for those considering volunteering for at least 2 years. Minimum age is 19.

Dates: Internships held from mid-Sep-mid-Dec, and mid-Feb-May. Cost: Interns receive free housing; they pay food and spending costs. Contact: Hyacinth Egner, Fourth World Movement, 7600 Willow Hill Dr., Landover, MD 20785; (301) 336-9489, fax (301) 336-0092; 4thworld@his.com.

Global Citizens Network. Global Citizens Network provides cross-cultural volunteer expeditions to rural communities around the world. Current sites include Belize, Guatemala, Kenya, St. Vincent, the Yucatan, and New Mexico (U.S.). While immersed in the daily life of the community volunteers work on projects initiated by the local people. Projects could include setting up a library, building a health clinic, or planting trees to reforest a village. Trips last 1, 2, or 3 weeks. Specific skills are not required.

Dates: Year round. Cost: $400-$1,300 not including airfare. All trip-related expenses are tax-deductible. Limited partial scholarships available. Contact: Kim Regnier or Carol North, Global Citizens Network, 1931 Iglehart Ave., St. Paul, MN 55104; (800) 644-9292 or (612) 644-0960, fax (612) 644-0960 (by appointment).

Global Service Corps. A vacation that mixes fun with service: Live day-to-day village life in Costa Rica, Kenya, Guatemala, or Thailand. Give something back to your host community by building trails, providing health education, teaching English, or training in biointensive agriculture. You will come home excited, energized, and eager to return.

Dates: Year round. Cost: $1,495-$1,695 for 2-3 week projects, long-term project costs vary. Contact: Global Service Corps., 300 Broadway, Suite 28, San Francisco, CA 94133; (415) 788-3666 ext. 128, fax (415) 788-7324; gsc@igc.apc.org, www.earthisland.org/ei/gsc/gschome.html.

Global Volunteers. Global Volunteers provides short-term opportunities for people of all ages and backgrounds to assist mutual international understanding through ongoing development projects in 15 countries throughout Africa, Asia, the Caribbean, Europe, and North and South America. Programs are 1, 2, or 3 weeks and range from natural resources, construction and tutoring children to teaching English and assisting with health care. No special skills are required.

Dates: Over 100 teams. Year round. Cost: Tax-deductible program fees range from $350 to $1,995. Airfare not included. Contact: Global Volunteers, 375 E. Little Canada Rd., St. Paul, MN 55117; (800) 487-1074, fax (612) 482-0915.

Grail Volunteer Programme. Assist regular staff with all aspects of hospitality at small conference center. Minimum age 20.

Dates: Call for specific dates. Cost: Board and lodging and pocket money £16 per week. Contact: The Grail Centre, 125 Waxwell Ln., Pinner, Middlesex HA5 3ER, U.K.; (011) 44-181 866 2195

Habitat for Humanity. Positions are available as an International Partner (IP) with Habitat for Humanity, an international Christian housing ministry that builds houses with people in need. IPs will serve 3 years, acting as trainers, community organizers, administrators, and may participate in construction at times. Minimum age: 21 years of age, single or married (couples serve together at the same affiliate), strong history of community service, international experience preferred.

Dates: No deadline. EOE/AA. Training 7 weeks, classes held twice per year. Cost: Incremental stipend starting at $400 per month per person, re-entry escrow, housing, health insurance, transportation to and from site. Contact: Habitat for Humanity International, Attn: International Recruiter, IFPS Department, 121 Habitat St., Americus, GA 31709-3498; (800) HABITAT ext. 194, fax (912) 924-0641; IPP@habitat.org.

Health Volunteers Overseas. HVO solicits medical volunteers in Africa, Asia, the Caribbean, and South America trained in the following specialties: anesthesia, dentistry, general surgery, internal medicine, oral and maxillofacial surgery, orthopaedics, pediatrics, and physical therapy. In most cases, volunteers teach rather than just provide service.

Dates: Year round, 2-week to 1-month assignments. Cost: Includes airfare and, in some cases, room and board. Contact: Kate Skillman, Program Coordinator, Health Volunteers Overseas, c/o Washington Station, P.O. Box 65157, Washington, DC 20057; (202) 296-0928, fax (202) 296-8018; hvo@aol.com.

International Volunteer Programs. Opportunity to live, work and travel in selected countries.

Cost: $1,000 to $3,000 includes in-country room and board, transportation. Contact: Lisle Inc., 433 W. Stearns Rd., Temperance, MI 48182-9568; (313) 847-7126, (800) 477-1538, fax (419) 530-7719; www.lisle.utoledo.edu.

International Workcamps. Groups of 6-20 international volunteers come together for 2-3 weeks to provide labor for worthy nonprofits around the world. Possible projects could be working with immigrant children in London, helping an artists' collective in Posnan, Poland, taking adults with disabilities on day trips in Virginia, building a school in Tunisia.

Dates: Several hundred projects in summer, about 20 other times. Cost: $60-$250. Contact: Claire Andrews, National Coordinator, SCI-International Voluntary Service, 5474 Walnut Level Rd., Crozet, VA 22932.

Involvement Volunteering International. Involvement Volunteers Association, Inc. (IVI) aims to identify volunteer placements to suit the requirements, abilities, and experiences of individual volunteers. Placements range from environmental conservation to community-based social service. Projects may be suitable for individual volunteers with or without expertise, taking part in individual placements or as members of groups or teams of multinational volunteers. Placements may be on farms, in historic gardens or national parks; at schools teaching spoken English or special schools for disadvantaged children; at bird observatories, zoological parks or research centers. Groups and teams of up to 12 individual volunteers participate in tasks related to ecologically sustainable environmental projects and community-based projects. Volunteers can participate in any number of placements for 2 to 52 weeks. These can be planned with activities such as open water scuba diving courses on the Great Barrier Reef or native animal encounters or camping trips in the Red Centre of Australia.

Dates: Many projects are seasonal; volunteers are always needed. Cost: Approx. $350 for program, plus $40 per placement. The volunteer meets all travel costs (including insurance). Where possible the host will provide accommodations and food free, but some placements may cost up to $70 per week for food. Contact: Mr. Tim B. Cox, Involvement Volunteers Assoc., Inc., P.O. Box 218, Port Melbourne, Victoria 3207, Australia; Tel./fax (011) 61-3-9646 5504; ivimel@iaccess.com.au. and ftp2ftp.iaccess.com.au.

Jewish Volunteer Corps. The Jewish Volunteer Corps of AJWS sends skilled adult volunteers to work with grassroots organizations throughout Africa, Latin America, Asia and Russia for up to 9 months. Projects range from assisting project staff in developing community health or education programs to teaching business skills to members of cooperatives, to helping design a soil conservation plan.

Dates: Year round. Cost: Varies with placements. Stipends, and scholarships available. Contact: Manager, Jewish Volunteer Corps, American Jewish World Service, 989 Avenue of the Americas, New York, NY 10018; (800) 889-7146 or (212) 736-AJWS, fax (212) 736-3463; jvcvol@jws.org.

Learning Through Service. Learning Through Service provides 45 sites where students or recent graduates of any college may do voluntary service for a summer, semester, or longer. Eleven sites combine service with formal study for academic credit.

Dates: Two months to 2 years; beginning and ending rates vary. Cost: Some volunteer programs offer a stipend; Service-Learning programs (i.e., those that combine service with study) involve tuition fees. Contact: Program Coordinator, Association of Episcopal Colleges, 815 2nd Ave., Suite 315, New York, NY 10017-4594; (212) 986-0989, fax (212) 986-5039; anglican.colleges@ecunet.org.

Maryknoll Mission Association of the Faithful (MMAF). MMAF serves as a bridge between U.S. and overseas communities in countries like Bolivia, Brazil, Cambodia, Chile, Japan, Kenya, Mexico, Nicaragua, Peru, Salvador, Tanzania, Thailand, and Venezuela to help poor and oppressed people. Missioners serve 3 1/2 years. Prior to going overseas they take part in a 16-week orientation program from late Aug to early Dec. General age range is 24-45.

Dates: Deadline for applications is the end of Jan. Cost: Transportation to and from country of assignment is provided, plus room, board, and medical expenses. We request our associates to seek financial support for our mission work as a part of their commitment. Contact: Kathy Wright, Maryknoll Mission Association of the Faithful, Bethany Bldg., Box 307, Maryknoll, NY 10545; (914) 762-6364, fax (914) 762-7031.

Medical Ministry International. MMI International conducts over 60 annual 2-week clinics for people who have no other access to medical and surgical care. Volunteers pay fee plus airfare. MMI is a Christian organization from all traditions. Non-Christians welcome. Needed are dentists, physicians, surgeons, anesthesiologists, nurses (all areas), OR techs, health care professionals, optometrists, opticians, helpers.

Dates: Write for calendar projects. Sign up several months in advance. Cost: $450 to $700 plus, depending on destination. Participants also pay airfare. Expenses are tax deductible. Contact: In U.S.: Medical Ministry International, P.O. Box 940207, Plano, TX 75094; (214) 437-1995, fax (214) 437-1114. In Canada: Medical Group Missions Inc., 15 John

St. N, Suite 301, Hamilton, ON L8R 1H1; (905) 524-3544, fax (905) 524-5400.

Mission Service Opportunities. Opportunities are diverse with some positions requiring more experience than others. We need: educators, office workers, RN's, development and community workers, and youth and social service workers. Both national and international.

Dates: Flexible (summer, full year, 2 or more years). Cost: Varies. Depends on service project (assistance for longer-term projects possible). Contact: Mission Service Recruitment Office, Presbytarian Church U.S.A., 100 Witherspoon St., Louisville, KY 40202-1396; (800) 779-6779, fax (502) 569-5975.

Pax Tours. Pax Tours reflects our organization's commitment to peace, reconciliation, and sustainable development. Trips this year will include such destinations as the Middle East, Central and South America, and NIS countries. These international study and working tours put participants in direct contact with the people and issues behind the headlines.

Dates: Several trips throughout the year, typically 10-15 days in length. Cost: Costs vary according to region and package. Contact: Andrew Tuck, Programs Manager, Pax World Service, 1111 16th St., NW, Suite 120, Washington, DC 20036; (202) 293-7290, fax (202) 293-7023, paxwldsvc@aol.com.

Peace Brigades International. When invited, Peace Brigades International sends unarmed peace teams into areas of violent conflict or repression and provides protective accompaniment for those whose lives have been threatened. PBI fosters reconciliation and peace dialogue among conflicted parties and educates and trains in nonviolence and human rights. A 7-month commitment. Minimum age: 25.

Dates: Year round. Cost: $250 for training session. Volunteer generally pays travel costs and health insurance. Contact: PBI/USA, 2642 College Ave., Berkeley, CA 94704; Tel./fax (510) 849-1247; (peacenet) pbiusa@igc.apc.org.

Peace Corps Volunteer Opportunities. Since 1961, more than 140,000 Americans have joined the Peace Corps. Assignments are 27 months long. Volunteers must be U.S. citizens, at least 18 years old, and in good health. Peace Corps has volunteer programs in education, business, agriculture, the environment, and health.

Dates: Apply 9 to 12 months prior to availability. Cost: Volunteers receive transportation to and from assignment, a stipend, complete health care, and $5,400 after 27 months of service. Contact: Peace Corps, Room 8506, 1990 K St., NW, Washington, DC 20526; (800) 424-8580; www.peacecorps.gov.

St. Vincent Pallotti Center. The St. Vincent Pallotti Center publishes Connections 1996, a directory of organizations that provide short- and long-term volunteer opportunities with a faith-based program in the U.S. and overseas.

Dates: Year round. Contact: Andrew Thompson, National Director, St. Vincent Pallotti Center, Box 893, Cardinal Station, Washington, DC 20064; (202) 529-3330, fax (202) 529-0911.

St. Vincent Pallotti Center. We assist potential volunteers decide how they might best use their talents in one of more than 120 church-based volunteer programs. Our free annual directory Connections profiles the needs and requirements of these programs. Please contact us for a free Connections directory.

Dates: Year round. Contact: St. Vincent Pallotti Center for Apostolic Development, Inc., P.O. Box 893, Cardinal Station, Washington, DC 20064; (202) 529-3330, fax (202) 529-0911; pallotti01@aol.com, www.cua.edu/www/rel/pallotti.

Traveler's Earth Repair Network. TERN links travelers with individuals and organizations worldwide involved with sustainable forestry, organic agriculture, permaculture, restoration, and related activities. TERN provides the traveler with a detailed list of contacts (over 3,000 from over 100 countries) in the designated region of travel.

Dates: Year round. Cost: $50 (up to 5 countries). Contact: Michael Pilarski, Director, Friends of the Trees Society, P.O. Box 4469, Bellingham, WA 98227; (360) 738-4972.

Visions in Action. Visions in Action sends volunteers to Africa and to Latin America to work for nonprofit development organizations. Volunteers are placed in diverse fields such as business management, law, health care, journalism, women's issues, democratization, human rights, children's programs, and environmental concerns.

Dates: Jul: Tanzania, South Africa, Mexico. Sep: Uganda. Oct: Burkina Faso. Jan: Zimbabwe, South Africa, Mexico. Cost: $4,000-$6,000. Contact: Shaun Skelton, Visions in Action, 2710 Ontario Rd. NW, Washington, DC 20009; (202) 625-7403, fax (202) 625-2353; vision@igc.apc.org.

Voluntary Service Overseas. VSO volunteers contribute to improvements in education, health, and food production as well as technology, social development, and the growth of business. Posts are for a minimum of 2 years. Volunteers aged 20-70 must always have qualifications and must usually have relevant work experience.

Cost: VSO and local employer cover all costs. Includes airfare, accommodations, and living allowance. Contact: VSO, 317 Putney Bridge Rd., London SW15 2PN, England; (011) 44-181-780-2266, fax 181-780-1326.

Volunteers for Peace. Join volunteers from at least 3 other countries in over 800 social, environmental, conservation, restoration, archaeological, or agricultural work in over 60 countries. The length of service is 2-3 weeks; multiple placements in the same or different countries is common. Call or write VFP for a free newsletter.

Dates: Most programs are May-Sep, some Oct-Apr. Cost: $175 registration fee per workcamp covers meals and accommodations. Volunteers pay transportation costs. Contact: Peter Coldwell, Executive Director, Volunteers for Peace, Inc. (VFP), 43 Tiffany Rd., Belmont, VT 05730; (802) 259-2759, fax (802) 259-2922; vfp@vermontel.com, www.vermontel.com/~vfp/home.htm.

Willing Workers on Organic Farms. WWOOF is a network of organic farms and gardens in Western Europe, North America, and Australasia that provides room and board and learning in exchange for work. All levels of skill and experiences accepted.

Dates: Year round. Cost: £15 per year. Contact: WWOOF, Don Pynches, Coordinator, 19 Bradford Rd., Lewes BN7 1RB, U.K.; (011) 44 1273 476286.

WorldTeach. WorldTeach is a nonprofit organization based at Harvard Univ. that contributes to educational development and cultural exchange by placing volunteers to teach in developing countries (Costa Rica, Ecuador, Namibia, Poland, South Africa, Thailand, and Vietnam). Teach English, math, science, and environmental education to students of all ages. All programs last for 1 academic year; academic subjects taught vary with assignment. Teachers must have a bachelor's degree and are required to complete 25 hours of TEFL experience before departure. There is a summer program in China for undergraduates.

Dates: Year round departures vary depending on the program. Cost: Range from $3,600-$4,500. Includes health insurance, airfare, field support, and training. Contact: Anthony Meyer, Director of Recruiting and Admissions Training, WorldTeach, Harvard Institute for International Development, 1 Eliot St., Cambridge, MA 02138-5705; (617) 495-5527, fax (617) 495-1599; ameyer@hiid.harvard.edu.

WWOOFING. Learning about organic or traditional growing methods by working in exchange for keep.

Dates: Year round. Cost: $15 for list of 430 options in 40 countries. Contact: WWOOF Australia, Buchan, Victoria 3885, Australia; (011) 61-51-550-218.

CHAPTER 19

INTERNSHIP PROGRAMS

*The following listing of international internships programs was sup-
plied by the organizers. Contact the program directors to confirm costs,
dates, and other details. If you do not see the program you want in
the country of your choice, look in the "Worldwide" listings at the end
of the section for programs located in several different regions.*

Asia

Penn-in-India. Internships found on demand for interested students.

Fields: South Asian Studies, Performing Arts, Religion, Economics, Traditional Medicine. Academic credit offered. Fifteen internships per year. No prerequisites. Application materials: application, transcript, resume, letter of recommendation.

Dates: Summer: 6 weeks. Application deadline: Mar 1. Cost: $4,700 (includes room, food, international airfare, and tuition). Compensation: none. Application fee: $35. Contact: Penn Summer Abroad, Univ. of Pennsylvania, 3440 Market St., Suite 100, Philadelphia, PA 19104-3335; (215) 898-5738, fax (215) 573-2053.

Penn-in-Seoul (Korea). Internships with mul-tinational corporations, government agencies, and think tanks.

Fields: Economics, Social Sciences. Academic credit offered. Fifteen internships per year. No prerequisites. Application materials: Application, transcript, resume, letter of recommendation.

Dates: Summer: 10 weeks. Application deadline: Mar 1. Cost: $3,700 (includes room and tuition). Compensation: Varies. Application fee: $35. Contact: Penn Summer Abroad, Univ. of Pennsylvania, 3440 Market St., Suite 100, Philadelphia, PA 19104-3335; (215) 898-5738, fax (215) 573-2053.

Australia

Australian Internships. Interns are placed with research teams, Australian employers, political administrations, etc. for periods ranging from 6 weeks to a year. The positions are unpaid. Homestay (or other) accommodations are included. Placement is arranged to suit the individual provided 4 months notice is given. Most placements are in Queensland or New South Wales.

Fields: Marine and Wildlife Biology, Business, etc. No academic credit offered. Unlimited internships. Prerequisites: a) High School Graduates, b) Professional Development for Graduates and Junior/Senior college students.

Dates: Year round. Application deadline: Four months before start date. Cost: $2,040 (includes room and food) for 6-week program. Application fee: $500. Contact: Dr. Maurice A. Howe, Education Australia, P.O. Box 2233, Amherst, MA 01004; (800) 344-6741, fax (413) 549-0741; mauriehowe@aol.com.

Custom Designed Professional Development Internships. Upon application, participants are asked to describe their internship needs, after which the placement service in Australia locates suitable programs. Responsibilities vary by placement. Excellent professional development and career building opportunities. Opportunities to travel in Australia before and after the placement. Flexible duration and start dates. Interns are not usually placed as a group. On-call support service, airport transfers, academic or professional supervisor provided in Australia. Pre-trip support for air travel, visas and orientation.

Fields: Management, Marketing, Finance and Accounting, Communications (radio, television, newspaper, public relations), Law, Politics, The Arts, Social Work, Biology, Wildlife Management, Natural Resources, and Marine Science. Academic credit can be arranged through home university. One-hundred-200 internships per year. Prerequisites: Pursuing or have obtained a university/college degree. Application materials: application and transcript(s).

Dates: Six, 8, 10, 12, 16 weeks or more (52 weeks maximum) placements. Year-round start dates. Sign up at least 4 months prior to intended departure. Cost: $3,240 (6 weeks) to $4,480 (16 weeks). Includes room, 2 meals per day in homestay (or no meals in an apartment), internship placement, liaison service in Australia, airport transfers. Compensation: placements are typically unpaid due to immigration rules. Application fee: $500 deposit with application. Eighty percent refundable for cancellation after placement is found. Contact: AustraLearn, U.S. Center for Australian Universities, 110 16th St., CSU Denver Center, Denver, CO 80202; (800) 980-0033, fax (303) 446-5955; cflannery@vines.colostate.edu.

Education Australia. Study abroad for a semester or a year at Australian National Univ. (Canberra), Deakin Univ. (Victoria), Univ. of Ballarat (Victoria), Univ. of Tasmania (Tasmania), Univ. of Wollongong (New South Wales), or the Australian Catholic Univ. (several states). In New Zealand courses are offered at the Univ. of Canterbury and Lincoln Univ. (Christchurch). Liberal arts, science, business, biology, psychology, education, Australian studies, etc. Customized internships in all fields are also available. See our web page http://www.javanet.com/~edaust.

Dates: Mid-Jul-mid-Nov, mid-Feb-late Jun. Cost: Tuition approx. $4,000, accommodations approx. $2,250. Airfare. Contact: Dr. Maurice A. Howe, Executive Director, Education Australia, P.O. Box 2233, Amherst, MA 01004; (800) 344-6741, fax (413) 549-0741; mauriehowe@aol.com.

Institute for Study Abroad, Butler Univ. Internships are offered at Australian National Univ. and the Univ. of New South Wales. They take the place of 1 or 2 taught courses and are awarded 4-10 credits.

Fields: Marketing, Politics, Social Sciences, Media. Academic credit offered. Prerequisites: approval of home university, 3.0 GPA, academic preparation for internship area. Application materials: ISA general application, internship proposal form.

Dates: Semester; 15 or 16 weeks. Application deadline: Mar 15 (Fall), Nov 15 (Spring).

Cost: Varies. Compensation: None. Application fee: $40. Contact: Institute for Study Abroad, Butler Univ., 4600 Sunset Ave., Indianapolis, IN 46208; (800) 858-0229, fax (317) 283-9704.

Parliamentary Internships. The Parliamentary internship in Melbourne, Australia, is designed for students who wish to gain practical experience in a political setting while earning academic credit. Academic and practical guidance, counsel, and evaluation will be provided by a Univ. of Melbourne supervisor and by a member or officer of the Victorian parliament, who will be the student's parliamentary supervisor. Students will have full access to university housing facilities and services.

Fields: Politics. Academic credit offered. Open number of internships per year. Five applicants. Prerequisites: Junior or Senior standing; 3.0 or 4.0 GPA. Application materials: program application, college transcript, 2 evaluations. Dates: Spring. Application deadline: Nov 15. Cost: $7,745 (includes room, food, health insurance, tuition placement, and orientation). Application fee: None. Contact: Inés De Romaña, Program Coordinator, Northern Illinois Univ., Williston Hall, 4th Fl., DeKalb, IL 60115; (815) 753-0420, fax (815) 753-0825; ideromana@niu.edu.

Belgium

Environmental Information Centre. Technical management of Environmental Information Centre for Young People (library with books, magazines, reports, etc. on nature conservation). Intern also takes part in management and activities of environmental conservation youth organizations.

Fields: Environmental Education. Prerequisites: Fundamental interest in environmental education, some experience in library management.

Dates: Spring, summer, fall—mininum 4 weeks. Contact: Natuur 2000, Bervoetstraat 33, 2000 Antwerpen, Belgium; (011) 32-3-2312604, fax 3-2336499.

Belize

Internships in Belize. Interns live with host families. Following a 1-week orienation, participants work full-time in various non-governmental agencies where they are supervised and evaluated.

Academic credit offered: 15-16. Number of internships per year: Max. 20. Application fee: $20. Deadline: Sep 1 for spring, Feb 1 for fall. 2.5 cumulative GPA. Strong performance in major. Maturity and adaptability. Junior or senior status. Application materials to submit: SUNY Study Abroad Application, departmental recommendation form, application fee, internship request form, resume of experience.

Dates: Fall and spring, 17 weeks each. Cost: $4,000 includes room, food, health insurance, local transportation, international airfare, and orientation. Contact: Dr. John Ogden, Director, Office of International Programs, 228 Miller Bldg. Box 2000, SUNY Cortland, Cortland, NY 13045; (607) 753-2209, fax (607) 753-5989; studyabroad@snycorva.cortland.edu, www.cortland.edu/www/ipgms.

Colombia

Community Internships in Latin America. Emphasis on community participation for social change. Students work 3 days a week in an internship, meet together for core seminar and internship seminar, and carry out independent study project. Wide range of internship opportunities in community development and related activities. Based in Bogotá. Family homestay. Latin American faculty. Full semester's credit, U.S. transcript provided. All majors.

Dates: Early Feb-mid-May. Cost: $8,100 (1997-98). Includes tuition, room and board, field trips. Contact: Elizabeth Andress, Assistant Director, HECUA, Mail #36, Hamline Univ., 1536 Hewitt Ave., St. Paul, MN 55104-1284; (612) 646-8832 or (800) 554-9421, fax (612) 659-9421; hecua@hamline.edu, www.hamline.edu/~hecua.

Costa Rica

Teaching, Spanish Language. Nonprofit organization. The program offers English-speaking individuals an opportunity to assist an English teacher, part time, at a Costa Rican host school, while they attend Spanish language training.

Prerequisites: At least 2 years of higher education. Between the ages of 19 and 38 years old. Application fee: $60.

Dates: Mar 1-Nov 30 (1 academic year). Cost: $2,100 includes room and board, health insurance. Contact: José O. Arauz, Executive Director, World Education Forum, P.O. Box 383-4005, San Antonio de Belén, Heredia, Costa Rica; Fax (506) 239-2254.

Czech Republic

Penn-in-Prague. Internships found for interested students in the Jewish Museum in Prague and other organizations.

Fields: Language, Civilization, Political Science, Jewish Studies. Academic credit offered. Fifteen internships per year. Application materials: application, transcript, letter of recommendation, resume.

Dates: Summer: 6 weeks. Application deadline: Mar 15. Cost: $3,600 (includes room and tuition). Compensation: none. Application fee: $35. Contact: Penn Summer Abroad, Univ. of Pennsylvania, 3440 Market St., Suite 100, Philadelphia, PA 19104-3335; (215) 898-5738, fax (215) 573-2053.

Dominican Republic

Dominican Republic Program. Exposes students to career opportunities in business, human service organizations, and government agencies in conjunction with academic program featuring study of Spanish language, Dominican culture, Latin American and Caribbean Studies, and African-American Studies. Direct enrollment at Universidad Nacional PH Ureña also available for fluent Spanish speakers. Housing with host families. Field trips.

Fields: Latin American and African-American Studies. Fifteen credits per semester (fall and spring), of which 3-9 are for the internship. Nine credits for the summer (of which 3 are for the internship).

Dates: Fall (Aug-Dec): 16 weeks. Spring (Jan-May): 16 weeks. Summer (May-Jun): 6 weeks. Cost: $5,427 per semester (includes room, food, health insurance, local transport, international airfare, books, in-state tuition, and fees). Some internships may carry a stipend. Contact: Alex M. Shane, Director, Office of International Programs, LI-84, Univ. of Albany, Albany, NY 12222; (518) 442-3525, fax (518) 442-3338; oipua@albany.edu.

Ecuador

Academia Latinoamericana de Español (Quito). Ecuador's number-one private Spanish language institute in former diplomat's mansion with swimming pool, hot tub, sauna, sport facilities. Instruction by university-trained teachers, all one-on-one. Customized study programs tailored to the individual. Select host family accommodations. Excursions to haciendas, Indian markets, etc. College credit available and internships.

Dates: Year round. Cost: One-week tuition, lodging, meals $294. Contact: Suzanne Bell, Admissions Director, U.S., 640 East 3990 South, Suite E, Salt Lake City, UT 84107; (801) 268-4608, fax (801) 265-9156; latinoa1@spanish.com.ec, http://ecnct.cc/academia/learnspa.htm.

Europe

Academic Internships. Internships are prearranged prior to student arrival. Students take 2 courses in area studies, in addition to an internship 3 or 4 days per week. Academic credit is provided. Students have the option of living with a family in an independent flat, or pre-arranged flat.

Fields: Education, Social Services, Urban Planning. Academic credit offered. Open number of internships per year. 10 applicants. Prerequisites: Junior or Senior standing. Minimum 3.0 or 4.0 GPA. Spain: Minimum of 5 semesters of Spanish. Germany: Minimum 5 semesters of German. Application materials: program application, college transcript, 2 evaluations.

Dates: Fall and Spring. Application deadline: May 1 (Fall) or Nov 1 (Spring). Cost: Varies. Application fee: none. Contact: Inés De Romaña, Program Coordinator, Northern Illinois Univ., Williston Hall, 4th Fl., DeKalb, IL 60115; (815) 753-0420, fax (815) 753-0825; ideromana@niu.edu.

International Intern Program. Rural development projects in Tenerife, Cuba, Turkey, and Brazil. Project areas cover whale and dolphin conservation, organic farming, arts and crafts, Spanish language training, rural development, conservation. Projects funded on cheap working holiday basis.

Dates: May-Oct, 1-6 week stays. Cost: £65 per week covers accommodations (simple/shared) and half board. Contact: Ed Bentham, Projects Co-ordinator, International Intern Program, 55 Monmouth St., Covent Garden, London WC2 9JG, U.K.

France

Penn-in-Compiegne. Short-term (2 weeks) internships with banks, mayor's office, advertising agency, hospital, etc.

Fields: Economics, Business French. Academic credit offered. Twelve internships per year. Prerequisites: Intermediate French. Application materials: application, transcript, letter of reference.

Dates: Summer: 5 weeks of study and 2 weeks of internship. Application deadline: Mar 1. Cost: $4,100 (includes room, food, and tuition). Compensation: none. Application fee:

$35. Contact: Penn Summer Abroad, Univ. of Pennsylvania, 3440 Market St., Suite 100, Philadelphia, PA 19104-3335; (215) 898-5738, fax (215) 573-2053.

Skidmore College in Paris. A variety of internships offered for academic credit during the Fall and Spring semesters.

Fields: Business, Music, Journalism, Government. Academic credit offered. Application materials: 2 reference letters, tracking form, transcript, essay.

Dates: Sep 12-mid-Jan. 1996-97: mid-Jan-May 31. Application deadline: Mar 1 (Fall); Oct 15 (Spring). Cost: $13,686 per semester. Includes room, food, and tuition. Compensation: none. Application fee: $25. Contact: John Anzalone, Chair, Department of Foreign Language & Literature, Skidmore College, Saratoga Springs, NY 12866-1632; (518) 581-7400 ext. 2383; janzalone@skidmore.edu.

Germany

Professionals and Agriculturists. The 1-year work-study program is a cultural exchange with 3 parts: German language study in Germany to develop the facility for successful participation (about 2 months); classroom instruction at a German technical school or other institute of higher education (about 4 months); and a 5- to 6-month position with a German company or organization. The program is designed for technical, vocational, agricultural, and business fields and is meant to give participants a taste of how their professional counterparts are trained and the opportunity to experience the German workplace.

Dates: Jul-Jul following year. Cost: Funding provided: International airfare and partial domestic costs, insurance, and host family compensation during study portion of program. Own spending ($350 per month). Contact: Beate Witzler, Program Director, CDS International, 330 7th Ave., 19th Fl., New York, NY 10001; (212) 497-3500; (212) 497-3535.

Ireland

Dublin Internships. Dublin Internships provides international internships across the spectrum of majors in Dublin, Ireland. The internships are full-time and non-salaried. Credit is awarded by the student's university/college.

Dates: The Internship program schedule includes Spring and Fall semesters, Summer and Jan interim. A minimum of 3 months notice from the student is recommended. Contact: Director, Dublin Internships, 8 Orlagh Lawn, Scholarstown Rd., Dublin 16, Ireland; Tel./fax (011) 353 1-494-5277.

Internships in Dublin. Interns live with families or in apartments. Two programs available: 6-credit internship plus 9-credit classwork in Irish Studies through the Institute of Public Administration or full-time (15-16 credits) internship. IPA placements may be in Parliament, municipal government, health care administration, radio/TV, and at the Irish Times. Full-time placements available in social services, communication, film, advertising and others.

Fields: Public Administration, Parliamentary Interns, Political Science, Technology, Finance, Health and Communications. Fifteen-16 credits per semester, 10 Summer. Prerequisites: 2.5 GPA for traditional full-time internships, 3.0 for IPA internships. Adaptability and maturity. Strong performance in major. Application materials: SUNY application packet.

Dates: Early Sep-mid-Dec (Spring). Application deadline: Feb 1 (Fall); Sep 1 (Spring); Apr 1 (Summer). Cost: $4,000 (includes room, food, health insurance, and orientation). Application fee: $20. Contact: Dr. John Ogden, Director, Office of International Programs, Box 2000, SUNY Cortland, Cortland, NY 13045, (607) 753-2209, fax (607) 753 5989; www.cortland.edu/www/ipgms.

Study in Ireland and Northern Ireland. Twelve program opportunities in the Republic and the North. University study and special subject area programs including internships in the Irish parliament. Program provides a full range of services including a full-time resident director and staff in Dublin, orientation, homestay, and guaranteed housing.

Dates: Fall, spring, academic year, and summer. Semesters and terms. Cost: Varies. Call for current fees. Contact: Meghan Mazick, Beaver College Center for Education Abroad, 450 S. Easton Rd., Glenside, PA 19038-3295; (888) BEAVER-9, fax (215) 572-2174; cea@beaver.edu, www.beaver.edu/cea/.

Univ. College Cork. First opened in 1849, the Univ. College Cork (UCC) is one of 3 constituent colleges of the National Univ. of Ireland. Eight faculties comprise the educational offerings of UCC: Arts, Celtic Studies, Commerce, Law, Science, Food Science and Technology, Engineering and Medicine. Enrollment in regular UCC classes with Irish language, history, and culture, but other courses may be available. Housing arranged prior to departure from U.S. in apartments near campus. Fall, Spring, Summer, academic year.

Dates: Fall: Early Sep-mid-Dec; Spring: mid-Jan-early Jun; Summer: early Jul-end of Jul. Cost: Fall 1996 estimate: $5,995. Spring 1997: $6,366. Summer: $2,570. Academic year: $12,026. Estimates include full-day orientation before departure, application fee, apartment rental (including utilities), food allowance, health and accident insurance, airfare from NY, books and supplies. SUNY tuition not included. Contact: Dr. John Ogden, Director, Office of International Programs, Box 2000, SUNY Cortland, Cortland, NY 13045; (607) 753-2209, fax (607) 753-5989; tonerp@snycorva.cortland.edu.

Italy

American Univ. of Rome. Programs for students of international business, international relations, Italian civilization and culture, Italian studies. Credits fully transferable through affiliations with U.S. institutions. Housing in studio apartments. All courses (except language classes) in English. All programs are designed to provide students with studies of immediate relevance in a highly competitive job market.

Dates: Fall and Spring semesters plus May/Jun summer sessions. Cost: $4,475 per semester, tuition/housing $2,350. Contact: Mary B. Handley, Dean of Administration, American Univ. of Rome, Via Pietro Roselli 4, Rome 00153, Italy; (011) 39-6-58330919, fax 583 30992.

Latin America

Community Internships Lat Amer. Semester program for academic credit in Bogotá, Colombia, combines 20-hour-per-week internship with core seminar entitled "Community Participation for Social Change," taught by Latin American faculty. Internships available in wide variety of agencies. Program director assists with finding placement appropriate to individual students' interests/goals, provides orientation and on-going supervision. Also includes independent study project, family homestays, field projects, friendships with other interns from across the U.S. and with Colombians.

Fields: Social Sciences, Communications, Health Sciences, Education, Social Work, Peace Studies; open to all majors. Sixteen hours offered, equivalent to 4 semester courses or 24 quarter credits. Fifteen internships per year. Ten-20 applicants. Prerequisites: equivalent of 2 years college-level Spanish language coursework; ability to communicate verbally in Spanish. Application materials: application form, 2 essays, transcript, 2 references (forms provided).

Dates: Feb-May (15 weeks). Application deadline: Nov 1. Cost: $7,300 (1997), includes room and food. Compensation: none. Application fee: $50. Contact: Elizabeth M. Andress, Admissions Director, Higher Education Consortium for Urban Affairs (HECUA), Mail #36, Hamline Univ., 1536 Hewitt Ave., St. Paul, MN 55104-1284; (612) 646-8832 or (800) 554-1089, fax (612) 659-9421; eabejari@piper. hamline.edu.

Mexico

El Bosque del Caribe, Cancun. Take a professional Spanish course, 25 hours per week and enjoy the Caribbean beaches. Relaxed family atmosphere. No more than 6 students per class. Special conversation program. Mexican cooking classes and excursions to the Mayan sites. Housing with Mexican families. College credit available.

Dates: Year round. New classes begin every Monday. Group programs arranged at reduced fees. Cost: Enrollment fees $75, $175 per week, 1 week with a Mexican family $150. Contact: Eduardo Sotelo, Director, Calle Piña 1, S.M. 25, 77500 Cancún, Mexico; (011) 52-98-84-10-38, fax 84-58-88; bcaribe mail.interacces. com.mx.

Learn Spanish in Chiapas. Spanish lessons in private sessions or small groups (4 people max). Family stays available. School tours to Indian (Mayan) villages, jungle trips available. Extracurricular activities included: Mexican cooking, discussions, video showings. Teach English in exchange for Spanish lessons. Centro Cultural "El Puente" includes gallery weaver's cooperative, travel agency, cafe, restaurant, phone/fax service.

Dates: Year round. Cost: Highest $220 per week; lowest $75 per week. Contact: Roberto Rivas, Bastidas Centro Bilingüe de Chiapas, C. Real de Guadalupe 55, Centro Cultural "El Puente," San Cristóbal de Las Casas 29230, Chiapas, Mexico; (011) 52-967-8-41-57, fax 967-83723 or Tel./fax (800) 303-4983; cenbili@chisnet.com.mx, www.mexonline. com/centro1.htm.

Poland

Penn-in-Warsaw (Pepsi, Coopers & Lydbrand, Hewlett Packard, Citibank, etc.). Internships with American Businesses in Warsaw.

Fields: Economics, political science. Academic credit offered. Fifteen internships per year. No prerequisites. Application materials: application, transcript, resume, letter of recommendation.

Dates: Summer: 5 weeks. Application deadline: Mar 1. Cost: $3,250 (includes room and tuition). Compensation: none. Contact: Penn Summer Abroad, Univ. of Pennsylvania, 3440 Market St., Suite 100, Philadelphia, PA 19104-3335; (215) 898-5738, fax (215) 573-2053.

Spain

Simmons College in Córdoba. The Simmons in Córdoba Program, sponsored by Simmons College, offers students the opportunity to live and study—for either a semester or an academic year—in one of Spain's oldest and historically most important cities. Open to undergraduates and MA students. Fields: (Spanish) Foreign Language. Internships available for undergraduates.

Dates: Fall: Sep 3-Dec 18, 1997. Spring: Jan 12-Apr 30, 1998. Application deadline: Mar 30 (Fall); Oct 15 (Spring). Late applications are considered on a space available basis. Cost: $12,174 per semester (1996-1997). Contact: Professor Susan Keane, Foreign Study Advisor, or Racquel María Halty, Program Director, Simmons College, Foreign Languages and Literatures, Boston, MA 02115; fax (617) 521-3199; swilliams2@vmsvaxsimmons.edu.

Switzerland

Bookbinding and Book Restoration. Centro del bel libro is a professional school for artisanal bookbinding and book restoration. Courses are offered on the quarter system.

Dates: Call or write for information. Cost: Call or write for information. Contact: Christina Bordoli, Director, Centro del bel libro, Ascona, 6612 Ascona, via Collegio, Centro culturale B. Berno, Switzerland; (011) 41-91-791-72-36, fax 791-72-56.

Geneva Study Abroad. An opportunity for a part-time graded voluntary work assignment in which the student can earn academic credit. Many times our students find themselves in responsible non-routine assignments. All students are enrolled in a full course load of at least 12 semester hours.

Fields: International Relations, International Business, Economics, Human Rights, French Language Studies. One-3 credit hours offered. Prerequisites: Sophomore, Junior or Senior standing; 2.5 GPA. Application materials: application, transcript, letters of recommendation.

Dates: Fall: mid-Aug-mid-Dec. Spring: Jan-May. Application deadline: rolling. Cost: $8,700 (includes health insurance, local transportation, international airfare, tuition, and program fees). Application fee: $30. Contact: Phyllis L. Dreyer, CICP-Kent State Univ., P.O. Box 5190, Kent, OH 44242; (330) 672-7980, fax (330) 672-4025; pdreyer@kentvm.kent.edu.

United Kingdom

Academic Internships. Internships are pre-arranged prior to student arrival. Students participate in their internships 5 days per week and receive academic credit. Students can stay in apartments or live with a host family. The internships last for 9 weeks.

Fields: Most fields. Academic credit offered. Open number of internships per year. Ten applicants. Prerequisites: Junior or Senior standing. Minimum 3.0 or 4.0 GPA. Application materials: program application.

Dates: Summer. Application deadline: Apr 1. Cost: $3,940. Application fee: none. Contact: Anne Seitzinger, Program Coordinator, Northern Illinois Univ., Williston Hall, 4th Fl., DeKalb, IL 60115; (815) 752-0700, fax (815) 753-1488; ca0ams1@wpo.cso.niu.edu.

Fashion Design and Merchandising. London College of Fashion is the only college in the British Univ. sector to specialize in fashion.

Located in the center of London, students enroll in a selection of semester and summer programs with internship options. While studying in regular classes during part of the week, you can earn credits 2 days a week in professionally oriented internships in public relations, design, marketing, retailing, trend forecasting, and design companies.

Six credits offered. Twenty-four internships per year. Prerequisites: prior work experience is helpful, although it is not mandatory. Application materials: completed application form and resume.

Dates: Fall or Spring: 12 weeks. Summer: 4 weeks. Application deadline: Rolling admission. Cost: £2,195. Contact: Jan Miller, London College of Fashion, 20 John Princes St., London W1M 0BJ, U.K.; (011) 44-171-514-7411, fax 171-514-7490; lcfdali@london-fashion.ac.uk.

Hansard Scholars Programme. An opportunity for students to become involved in the workings of the British government and British politics, accompanied by a comprehensive study of British politics and British public policy. Students are mainly assigned internships with Members of Parliament, but also to political parties, think tanks, and pressure groups.

Prerequisites: 2 or more years of college. Application materials: transcript, 2 letters of recommendation, and an essay.

Dates: Spring 1997: Jan 6-Mar 28. Summer 1997: May 12-Jul 18. Fall 1997: Sep 29-Dec 19. Cost: Jan 1997: £4,500 per semester (includes housing and London travel costs). Contact: Josie Thomas, Programme Coordinator, The Hansard Society, St. Philips, Building North, Sheffield St., London WC2A 2EX, U.K.; (011) 44 171 955 7478, fax 171 955 7492; hansard@lse.ac.uk.

Institute for Study Abroad, Butler Univ. Internships are offered as part of the regular academic programs at several institutions and are taken in lieu of 1 or 2 courses. Semester-long internships occupy 2 or 3 full working days

each week for a minimum of 16 to 24 hours. Sponsoring institutions include Birkbeck College, Univ. Of Glasgow, INSTEP, Univ. of East Anglia, and Westminister Univ.

Fields: All fields. Academic credit offered. Yes. Prerequisites: approval of home university, 3.0 GPA, academic preparation for internship area. Application materials: ISA general application, Internship Proposal Form.

Dates: Sep-Dec and Jan-Jun. Application deadline: Apr 15 (year or Fall); Oct 15 (Spring). Cost: Varies. Compensation: none. Application fee: $40. Contact: Institute for Study Abroad, Butler Univ., 4600 Sunset Ave., Indianapolis, IN 46208; (800) 858-0229, fax (317) 283-9704.

Study in Great Britain. Thirty-eight program opportunities in England, Scotland, and Wales. University study and special subject area programs, including internships, for fall, spring, academic year and summer program provides a full range of services including predeparture advising, orientation, homestay, and guaranteed housing. Need-based scholarships available.

Dates: Fall, spring, acdemic year. Summer semester and terms. Cost: Varies. Call for current fees. Contact: Beaver College Center for Education Abroad, 450 S. Easton Rd., Glenside, PA 19038-3295; (888) BEAVER-9, fax (215) 572-2174; cea@beaver.edu, www.beaver.edu/cea/.

SUNY Oswego London Program. Full-time internship is 35-40 hours per week; part-time also available. Duties are prescribed by individual organizations hosting interns, of which there are over 75. Students have the option of combining study with internship.

Fields: Marketing, Political Science, Psychology, Sociology. Twelve credits offered. Prerequisites: Junior or Senior, 2.5 GPA. Application materials: SUNY Overseas Academic Program Application Packet.

Dates: Fall or Spring (14 weeks). Application deadline: Mar 15, Oct 15. Cost: $2,330 (includes tuition). Contact: Director of Office of International Education, SUNY Oswego, 102 Rich Hall, Oswego, NY 13126; (315) 341-2118, fax (315) 341-2477; intled@oswego.edu, www.oswego/intled.

The American College in London. All interns are supervised by ACL faculty who have professional experience in their fields of study. Interns may select a full-time internship or may elect to enroll in courses concurrent with the internship. Placement is with firms in central London.

Fields: International Business, Fashion Design and Marketing, Video Production, Interior Design, Graphic Design/Commercial Art. Five credit quarters per 3 semesters, 10 credit quarters per 6 semesters. Twenty-five internships per year. Prerequisites: Junior or Senior standing in field of study, 3.0 GPA, letter of recommendation from academic adviser, enrollment for a minimum of 2 terms at ACL.

Dates: Fall, Winter, Spring, and Summer terms (8-9 weeks). Application deadline: none. $250 deposit (refundable). Cost: $5,500 (includes room, tuition and fees). Application fee: none. Contact: The American College in London, Division of International Programs/Study Abroad, 3330 Peachtree Rd. NE, Atlanta, GA 30326; (800) 255-6839, fax (404) 364-6611.

Univ. of North London. Interns live in apartments in central London with other participants. Part-time interns also take classes at the Univ. of North London. Opportunities in Parliament, hospitals, promotions agencies, schools, and radio/TV. Supervision by on-site personnel. Journals and essays or projects submitted at end of program.

Fields: Health, communications, political science, publicity, marketing. Three-16 credits. Eight-12 internships per year. Application deadline: Spring: Sep 1; Fall: Feb 1. Prerequisites: 2.5 GPA. Strong performance in major. Application materials: resume, SUNY application, internship request form.

Dates: Fall and Spring, 12 weeks each. Cost: $4,700 (includes room, food, health insurance,

local transportation, international airfare, orientation). Application fee: $20. Contact: Office of International Programs, 228 Miller Bldg., Box 2000, SUNY Cortland, Cortland, NY 13045; (607) 753-2209, fax (607) 753-5989; studyabroad@snycorva.cortland.edu, www.cortland.edu/www/ipgms.

United States

Bachelor's Program in World Issues. The School for International Training's Bachelor's Program in World Issues offers a uique opportunity for undergraduates to pursue their passion to make a difference in their world. The 2-year upper-division program is divided into the first year on campus and the second year is spent on an international or domestic internship with evaluation before graduation.

Dates: Aug 28, 1996-Jun 2, 1997. Cost: $12,200 (1996-97 tuition). Contact: Ed Parker, Admissions Counselor, School for International Learning, P.O. Box 676, Kipling Rd., Brattleboro, VT 05302; (802) 257-7751, fax (802) 258-3500; admissions.sit@world learning.org, www.worldlearning.org/sit.html.

Worldwide

Agricultural Internship Program. Full-time internships in production agriculture and agribusiness. Most participants live with host families. Foreign language knowledge is helpful but not required.

Fields: Agriculture, Agribusiness, Horticulture. Prerequisites: Knowledge and experience in agriculture. Application materials: Application form.

Dates: Orientations year round; 2-12 months. Application deadline: Four months before program. Cost: $2,600-$4,900 (includes room, food, health insurance, international airfare, orientation). Compensation: None to $120 per week (includes room and food). Intern must arrange. Application fee: $15. Contact: Diane Crow, Global Outreach, Inc., P.O. Box 3291, Merrifield, VA 22116-3291; (703) 385-2995, fax (703) 385-2996; globaloutreach@compuserve.com.

Boston Univ. International Programs. Students enroll in 3 academic courses in conjunction with a professional internship experience. Students choose from internships in: Advertising, Marketing and Public Relations; Art/Architecture; Broadcasting/Film; Business and Economics; Comparative Law; Health/Human Services; Journalism; and Politics. The internship experience allows students to explore organizations from multi-national corporations to local businesses, from hospitals to community service centers, from major magazine publishers or film production studios to local radio or advertising agencies.

Academic credit offered. Prerequisites: good academic standing, 3.0 GPA, language depending on site. Application materials: 2 references, transcript, essays, academic approval. Dates: Fall, Spring, and Summer (length varies). Application deadline: Mar 15 (Summer and Fall); Oct 15 (Spring). Cost: $4,400-$8,900. Application fee: $35. Contact: Boston Univ., International Programs, 232 Bay State Rd., 5th Fl., Boston, MA 02215; (617) 353-9888, fax (617) 353-5402; abroad@bu.edu, web.bu.edu/abroad.

Brethren Colleges Abroad. Opportunities vary by location. Examples include: business at Siemens Corp. in Germany; social work at a shelter in England; political science at the Council of Europe and The Human Rights Institute in France; business in import-export companies and an international hotel chain in China and Japan; village development with The Resource Foundation in Ecuador.

Fields: Business, teaching, political science, social work. Academic credit offered. Prerequisites: participation in BCA's academic program overseas for at least 1 semester.

Dates: Before, after, or during academic semesters. Cost: Living expenses. Application fee: $150. Contact: Susan Wennemyr, Brethren Colleges Abroad, 605 College Ave., N. Manchester, IN 46962; (219) 982-5244, fax (219) 982-7755; bca@manchester.edu; http://www.studyabroad.com/bac.

Global Routes: Internship Program. Global Routes interns are assigned in pairs to remote villages where they teach in local schools and complete at least one community service project. Each intern lives separately with a local family in a simple, traditional home. Training, support, and adventure travel are an integral part of the programs. Programs offered in Costa Rica, Ecuador, Kenya, Thailand, Navajo Nation.

Dates: Year round in 3-month sessions. Cost: $3,550 summer, $3,950 during year. Includes all expenses (room, board, adventure travel) except airfare to and from country. Scholarships and fundraising information available. Contact: Global Routes, 1814 7th St., Suite A, Berkeley, CA 94710; (510) 848-4800, fax (510) 848-4801; mail@globalroutes.org, www.lanka.net.globalrts.

IAESTE-U.S. IAESTE-U.S. arranges reciprocal exchanges among 63 member countries for students of engineering, architecture, and the sciences to obtain on-the-job practical training with host employers in other countries. The IAESTE program is administered in the U.S. by the Association for International Practical Training (AIPT) in Columbia, MD.

Fields: Technical Fields. Seventy-five-100 internships per year. Three hundred-400 applicants. Prerequisites: Junior level standing, enrolled full-time at time of application. Application materials: application, reference, transcript, language certification.

Dates: Summer placements (other periods available). Application deadline: Dec 10. Cost: $150 placement. Compensation: cost of living. Application fee: $50. Contact: Jeff Lange, Program Assistant/Eric Haines, Program Director, IAESTE-U.S., 10400 Little Patuxent Pkwy., Suite 250 L, Columbia, MD 21044-

3510; (410) 997-3068, fax (410) 997-5186; iaeste@aipt.org, www.softaid.net/aipt/aipt.-hml.

International Cooperative Education Program. Paid employment and internships for college and university students for a period of 8-12 weeks in 8 European and one Asian country. Employment depends on foreign language knowledge, major, and previous work experience. Work permits and housing are provided.

Dates: From Jun-Sep. Cost: Students must pay for air transportation and have a reserve of at least $800 for initial expenses. Contact: Günter Seefeldt, PhD, Director, International Cooperative Education Program, 15 Spiros Way, Menlo Park, CA 94025; (415) 323-4944, fax (415) 323-1104.

Internships International. Quality, professional, full-time internships in all fields for college graduates. Internships are found based on the intern's needs and experiences. Internship locations are: London, Paris, Florence, Madrid, Stuttgart, Dublin, Santiago, Mexico City, Budapest, and Melbourne. Internships are non-paying but it is often possible to "moonlight" while doing an internship. This is a program for individuals who are ready to assume professional responsibility.

Fields: All fields. Prerequisites: college graduate, language ability if appropriate to location. Application materials: 2 references, photo, specific statement of purpose, resume, transcript, interview.

Dates: Flexible, depending on wishes of the intern. Application deadline: none. Cost: Intern pays all expenses (approx. $200 per week). Compensation: none. Application fee: $500 (refundable if intern not placed). Contact: Judy Tilson, Director, Internships International, 1116 Cowper Dr., Raleigh, NC 27608; Tel./fax (919) 832-1575, http://rtpnet. intercenter.net/~intintl/interns.html.

Syracuse Internships Abroad. All internships are supervised by Syracuse faculty or approved adjuncts who teach in Syracuse programs abroad. Actual work experience is assigned by an agency supervisor. Interviews and final placements take place overseas. Most internships are part of a varied semester experience including coursework, field trips, and social activities.

Fields: Business, Advertising, Political Science, Social Agencies, Drama, Human Development, Social Work, Education, Photography, Communications. Academic credit offered. Three-6 internship credits, up to 18 total credits. One hundred internships per year. Ninety applicants. Prerequisites: Sophomore status, essays, recommendations, good academic standing. Application materials: application and recommendation forms.

Dates: Fall, Spring, Summer (6 weeks or longer). Application deadline: Mar 15 (summer), Apr 1 (fall), Oct 15 (spring). Cost: $3,500-$12,000 (includes room, food, international airfare, tuition). Compensation: none. Application fee: $40. Contact: Syracuse Univ., 119 Euclid Ave., Syracuse, NY 13244-4170; (800) 235-3472, fax (315) 443-4593; dipa@suadmin.syr.edu, sumweb.syr.edu.dipa.

Whale Research Internships. Be part of a world-renowned team studying the endangered humpback whales of the South Pacific. As a Pacific Whale Foundation Research intern you'll work side by side with our researchers in the field in the Whitsonday Islands (Great Barrier Reef Marine Park) and Hervey Bay Marine Park.

Dates: Jun 19-30, Jul 1-12, Jul 14-25, July 27-Aug 7, Aug 10-21, Aug 23-Sep 3, Sep 5-16, Sep 18-21. Cost: $1,395. Contact: Judy Edwards, Pacific Whale Foundation, 101 N. Kihei Rd., Kihei, HI 96753; (808) 879-8860 or (800) 942-5311, fax (808) 879-8811; pacwhale@igc.apc.org.

CHAPTER 20

TEACHING ENGLISH: TRAINING AND PLACEMENT PROGRAMS

The following listing of teaching English training and placement programs was supplied by the organizers. Contact the program directors to confirm costs, dates, and other details.

Canada

ELC, Univ. of Victoria. English Language Centre (ELC), Univ. of Victoria provides intensive (12-week) English language programs 3 times annually for intermediate and advanced international students. Students may choose an Academic Program to improve academic and study skills for future studies or a Communicative Program to improve conversational English language skills for professional or personal development. Short-term programs are available throughout the spring and summer.

Dates: Spring and summer 1997: Mar 31-May 9 ($1,925); May 26-Jun 27 ($1,585), Jul 7-Aug 15 ($1,925), Aug 4-29 ($1,295). 1998: Apr 10-Jul 2, Sept 11-Dec 3, Jan 8-Apr 1 (tuition $2,700 per term). Contact: Maxine Macgillivray, Program Coordinator, English Language Centre, Univ. of Victoria, P.O. Box 1700 MS8452, Victoria, BC, V8W 2Y2 Canada; (604) 721-8469, fax (604) 721-6276; mmacgillivray@uvcs.uvic.ca.

TESL Certification Program. Located in Vancouver, the ESL Teacher Training Centre features TESL certificate programs. We offer full-time, part-time and correspondence courses of 1-4 months. We are a member organization of the National Association of Career Colleges and the Private Career Training Association of British Columbia.

Dates: Programs are offered year round. Cost: CAN$850. Includes course materials. Contact: ESL Teacher Training Centre, #105-2412 Laurel St., Vancouver, BC V5Z 3T2, Canada; (604) 872-1236, fax (604) 872-1275; teachabroad@ibm.net, www.arnb.com/eslttc.

Univ. of Regina Language Institute. A vari-

ety of non-credit programs are offered in 3 streams: English for Academic Purposes (EA), which prepares students for attending university; English for Business (EB) which focuses on increasing students' understanding and use of of business vocabulary and concepts; and English for Communication (EC) which focuses on increasing students' oral communication. Evening courses, conversation partners, and short-term customized courses are also available.

Dates: 1997: Jan 10-Apr 4 (12 weeks); Apr 18-Jun 13 (8 weeks); Jun 27-Aug 22 (8 weeks); Sep 12-Dec 5 (12 weeks). Cost: Winter 1997: $1,825. Spring/summer 1997: $1,625. Fall 1997: $1,945. Conversation partners: $110 per semester. Placement fee for housing: $160. Plus rent, security, and telephone deposits. Contact: Penthes Rubrecht, English as a Second Language Centre, Univ. of Regina, Rm. 211, Language Institute, Regina, SK, Canada S4S 0A2; (306) 585-4585, fax (306) 585-4971; esl@ max.cc.uregina.ca, www.uregina.ca/~esl.

Central Europe

Central European Teaching Program. English conversation teachers are needed at the elementary or high school level. Hungarian or Romanian teachers primarily responsible for teaching grammar. Conversation teachers are responsible for enhancing students' oral fluency through conversation practice, classroom drills, games, and listening comprehension, and through working with native teachers.

Dates: Sep 96-Jun 97. Cost: Program fee: $700 plus airfare. Contact: Michael Mullen, CETP Director, Beloit College, 700 College St., Beloit, WI 53511; (608) 363-2619, fax (608) 363-2449; mullenm@beloit.edu.

Czech Republic and Slovakia

FCS ESL-Fellowship Program. Teachers must be qualified, with experience, preferably TEFL/ESL. Graduate degree preferred. Teach

1-month intensive English course while living with Czech or Slovak family.

Dates: Jul and Aug only. Application deadline first week of Mar. Cost: Participants must pay for travel to and from Czech Republic and Slovakia; all receive $200 stipend. Contact: Kirsten Munro, Foundation for a Civil Society, 1270 Ave. of the Americas, Suite 609, New York, NY 10028; (212) 332-2890, fax (212) 332-2898; 73303.3024@ compuserve.com.

France

French Language Studies—Sorbonne. Intensive French language at the Univ. of Paris, Sorbonne. All levels are available, 12-15 hours of instruction weekly. All courses are taught in French. Over 100,000 students from around the world have participated in this program.

Dates: Spring semester: Feb 6-May 31; summer: Jul and Aug.; fall: Sep 11-Dec 15. Cost: Semester: $1,895 for 16 weeks. Contact: Philip Virtue, Program Director, Center for Study Abroad, 2802 E. Madison St., #160, Seattle, WA 98112; (206) 726-1498, fax (206) 285-9197; virtuecsa@aol.com.

Ireland

EFL/TEFL. DAELS: 1-year full-time postgraduate Diploma in Advanced English Language Studies: English language, linguistics, one other academic subject; Summer school: 15-23 hours per week, 1- to 10-week stay. Levels from elementary to advanced. Options in English for language teachers, business English. Cambridge CTEFLA/DTEFLA teacher training.

Dates: DTEFLA, DAELS Oct-Jun; summer school Jul-Sep. (TEFLA at intervals throughout the year.) Cost: Tuition fees DAELS: IR£1,781 per year, DTEFLA IR£1,600, CTEFLA IR£850; summer school: IR£90 to IR£165 per week. Contact: Steven Dodd/ Vivienne Lordan, Language Centre, Univ. Col-

lege Cork, Republic of Ireland; (011) 353-21-904090 or 904102.

Teaching EFL. Part-time 3-month course; full-time 1-month course both leading to the Univ. of Cambridge Certificate in Teaching English as a Foreign Language to Adults (or as renamed after 1996).

Dates: Three-month course Jan-Mar, 1997; 1-month course Jul-Aug, 1997. Cost: Tuition fees: IR£850. Contact: Steven Dodd/Vivienne Lordan, Language Centre, Univ. College Cork, Republic of Ireland; (011) 353-21-904090 or 904102, fax 904090 or 904102.

Japan

Nova Intercultural Institute. The largest conversational English school in Japan, employing over 2,100 teachers in 220 schools. Nova offers a fixed, 5-day work schedule, guaranteed monthly salary, visa, paid training, assistance with housing, flight arrangements, health insurance and an extensive support network. Maximum 3-4 students per class. Beginning to advanced levels. Forty to 45 minute classes.

Dates: Jan-Nov 1997. Cost: No application or processing fees. Contact: Trevor Phillips, Interact Nova Group, 2 Oliver St., 7th Fl., Boston, MA 02109; (617) 542-5027, fax (617) 542-3115; www.novajapan.com.

Korea

Korea Services Group (KSG). KSG provides native-speaking English conversation instructors to Korean foreign language institutes and educational institutions including public or private universities, junior colleges, high schools, middle schools, etc. Pay range is normally $19,000-$25,000 per year for foreign language institutes. Minimum requirement is usually any 4 year BA/BS, but AA/AS acceptable if major is in English or Education. Experience usually not required for language institutes. Send resume, cover letter, photocopy of passport, photocopy of transcripts, diploma, 2 passport sized photos and 2 letters of reference.

Dates: Starts monthly for foreign language institutes. Educational institutions usually start Mar 1 and Sep 1. Cost: $300 (includes most process expenses and cultural and teaching training as required). Contact: Korea Services Group U.S. Headquarters for more information; (503) 230-6932. Korea Services Group, #807-3, Mang Mi-Dong, Suyoung-Gu, Pusan 613-131, Korea.

Mexico

El Bosque del Caribe, Cancun. Take a professional Spanish course, 25 hours per week and enjoy the Caribbean beaches. Relaxed family atmosphere. No more than 6 students per class. Special conversation program. Mexican cooking classes and excursions to the Mayan sites. Housing with Mexican families. College credit available.

Dates: Year round. New classes begin every Monday. Group programs arranged at reduced fees. Cost: Enrollment fees $75, $175 per week, 1 week with a Mexican family $150. Contact: Eduardo Sotelo, Director, Calle Piña 1, S.M. 25, 77500 Cancún, Mexico; (011) 52-98-84-10-38, fax 84-58-88; bcaribe mail. interacces.com.mx.

Learn Spanish in Chiapas. Spanish lessons in private sessions or small groups (4 people max). Family stays available. School tours to Indian (Mayan) villages, jungle trips available. Extracurricular activities included: Mexican cooking, discussions, video showings. Teach English in exchange for Spanish lessons. Centro Cultural "El Puente" includes gallery weaver's cooperative, travel agency, cafe, restaurant, phone/fax service.

Dates: Year round. Cost: Highest $220 per week; lowest $75 per week. Contact: Roberto

Rivas, Bastidas Centro Bilingüe de Chiapas, C. Real de Guadalupe 55, Centro Cultural "El Puente," San Cristóbal de Las Casas 29230, Chiapas, Mexico; (011) 52-967-8-41-57, fax 967-83723 or Tel./fax (800) 303-4983; cenbili@chisnet.com.mx, www.mexonline.com/centro1.htm.

New World Teachers. Accelerated 4-week TEFL/TESL Certificate Course integrating established European Direct Method with contemporary teaching techniques. Course developed by internationally-experienced trainers and aimed at trainees with an American education; this course requires no second language. Includes extensive supervised practice teaching to foreign students, permanent access to job placement guidance, and information—including Internet resources.

Dates: Four-week intensive courses begin Jan 13, Apr 21, Jun 2, Jul 28, Dec 15, 1997. Cost: $2,750. Includes deposit, registration, books, course materials, and job placement services. Accommodations (30 days, single, private shower): $300. Contact: New World Teachers, 605 Market St., Suite 800, San Francisco, CA 94105; (800) 644-5424; teacherssf@aol.com, www.goteach.com.

Portugal

Teacher Training in Lisbon. International House Lisbon offers the following range of intensive teacher training courses. RSA/Cambridge certificate in the teaching of English to adults, RSA/Cambridge certificate in the teaching of English to young learners, RSA/Cambridge diploma in the teaching of English to adults, IHTT introductory course to TEFL.

Dates: May 6-May 31, Jul 1-26, Jul 29-Aug 23, Aug 26-Sep 20, Nov 4-29. Cost: Courses from $400 to $1,100. Contact: Paula de Nagy, International House, Rua Marqués Sá Da Bandeira 16, 1050 Lisbon, Portugal; (011) 351-3151496, fax 3530081; ihlisbon@miml.telepact.

Spain

English Schools in Spain. For those wishing to teach English in Spain the Directory of English Schools in Spain includes over 600 address, plus information on lodging, private classes, classroom activities, etc. Order from author. Checks payable to Robert Kloer.

Dates: On-going. Cost: $17.75. Contact: Robert Kloer, 3 Sunset Ave., Suncook, NH 03275.

Thailand

Teaching English at Yonok College. Suitable candidates must have a Bachelor's degree and be prepared to sign a 2-year contract. Those chosen will teach Thai university students the fundamental aspects of the English language. Teaching experience is preferred. The salary package includes a monthly stipend, housing, paid vacation time, visas, and health insurance.

Dates: May 1997-May 1999. Cost: Teachers must pay own airfare. Contact: Paul J. McKenney, Assistant to the President, Yonok College, 444 Lampany, Denchai Rd., Lamang, Thailand 52000; (011) 66-54-226-952, x 124, fax 226-957.

United Kingdom

TESOL Training and Intensive. Courses lead to Trinity College London Certificate (equivalent RSA/Cambridge). Part-time courses Sep-Jun. Intensive 4-week courses during Jul.

Dates: Contact organization for exact dates. Cost: Approx. £600. Contact: Sieglinde Ward, Course Coordinator, Surrey Youth and Adult Education Service, 25 West St., Farnham, Surrey GU9 7DR, U.K.; fax (011) 44-252-712927.

United States

AEON InterCultural U.S.A. AEON Corporation is the largest English conversation school chain in Japan with over 210 schools. Positions are salaried with subsidized housing and full benefits. We hire every month. All contracts are for 1 year. Accident and sickness insurance provided and bonus paid upon completion of contract. .

Dates: No deadline, 1-year contract beginning every month. Please send current resume and an essay entitled "Why I Want to Live and Work in Japan." Cost: No application fee. Accommodations: Fully furnished apartment. Teachers pay a maximum of ¥39,000 per month with any amount over that being subsidized. Contact: AEON Corporation, 9301 Wilshire Blvd., #202, Beverly Hills, CA 90210, or AEON Corporation, 203 N. LaSalle St., #2100, Chicago, IL 60601.

China Teaching Program. A training and placement program for those wanting to teach at institutions of higher education or at secondary schools throughout the P.R.C. Most opportunities are in TESL, some in business or law. Six-week summer training sessions held on WWU campus. Participants study Chinese language and culture, TESL methodology, etc. Minimum requirements: BA, native speaker of English. (Placement-only option may be possible.)

Dates: Application deadline for summer session 1997 is Jan 31. Cost: Approx. $1,100 (includes tuition and placement). Contact: China Teaching, Western Washington Univ., OM 530A, Bellingham, WA 98225-9047; (360) 650-3753; ctp@cc.wwu.edu.

Eastern Michigan University. The MATESOL program has a strong practical emphasis based on sound pedagogical and linguistic theory. Students take 20 hours in TESOL (theoretical foundations, pedagogical grammar and pronunciation, observation and analysis methods and materials, language testing, research seminar, practicum) and 12 more hours (at least 6 in English linguistics). There is no comprehensive exam; a thesis is optional. A typical cohort includes about 1/3 international and 2/3 U.S. students from a wide range of ages

and experiences. Limited number of assistantships.

Dates: Mar 1 deadline for fall admission; Jul 1 for winter admission. Cost: In-state, $141 per credit hour; out-of-state, $327 per credit hour. Furnished campus apartments $515 per month. Contact: Jo Ann Aebersold, TESOL Adviser, 219 Alexander, Eastern Michigan Univ., Ypsilanti, MI 48197; (313) 487-0130, fax (313) 487-0338.

EFL Teacher Training. Lado Enterprises Inc. offers an intensive Teacher Training Certificate Program in teaching English as a Foreign Language. The program is designed for inexperienced teachers, or those with no teaching experience, seeking employment overseas. This 135-hour course provides practical hands-on classroom experience using fundamental teaching principles and methodologies.

Dates: Monthly sessions held year-round. Ten-week evening program also offered. Cost: $1,950 for tuition and fees. Contact: Will Pickering, Lado Enterprises, Inc., 2233 Wisconsin Ave., NW, Washington, DC 20007; (202) 223-0023, fax (202) 337-1118.

ELS TEFL Certificate Program. Provides intensive practical training for teaching English as a foreign language to the following groups: 1) those who wish to develop skills and learn methods for teaching EFL, 2) current English (language) teachers who wish to update teaching methodologies, 3) program coordinators and administrators who are involved in curriculum design, and 4) native and non-native English speakers and international teachers who wish to teach English in their native countries or in other non-English-speaking countries.

Dates: 1997: Feb 24-Mar 21; Apr 21-May 16; Jun 16-Jul 11; Jul 14-Aug 8; Aug 11-Sep 5, Oct 6-31; Dec 29-Jan 23, 1998. Cost: $1,995 includes registration fee, course fee, books and materials, and job placement services. Contact: Victoria Cabal, Coordinator, ELS Language Centers, 5761 Buckingham Pkwy., Culver City, CA 90230; (310) 642-0982, fax (310) 649-5231; vcabal@els.com.

English For Everybody. Prague and other cities in Central/Eastern Europe. Also, Greece and Vienna. Guaranteed jobs, pre-arranged housing, airport greeting. TEFL Certificate or experience required. College degree preferred.

Cost: $450 assistance fee. Contact: English For Everybody, Spanielova 1292, 163 00 Prague 6, Czech Republic; Tel./fax (011) 42-2-301-9784. U.S. voice mail (415) 789-7641; www.vol.C2/EFE.

ESL Intensive Institute. Learn English pronunciation, listening comprehension, conversation, reading and writing. Includes an orientation to American culture and weekly field trips. By Univ. of New Hamsphire in Durham (hour north of Boston and 15 minutes from ocean). For students wanting to learn English before college or who want to improve TOEFL scores (3-10 credits, 4 hours per day).

Dates: Take 1 session or combine them for 3-, 4-, 6-, 7-, or 10-week study. Jun 2-27 (4-week session), Jul 7-25 (3-week session), Jul 28-Aug 15 (3-week session). Cost: $225 per week plus one-time fee of $130. Room and board available at a moderate additional cost. Contact: L. Conti, UNH Continuing Education, ESL Institute, 24 Rosemary Ln., Durham, NH 03824; (603) 862-2069, learn.dce@unh, www.learn.unh.edu.

ESOL/BIL MA Teacher Education Program. An integrated program of theory and practice offered by the Departments of Education, Modern Languages and Linguistics. Courses include: Methodology (including separate courses on teaching reading and teaching writing), Testing and Evaluation, Language Learning, Bilingualism, Intercultural Communication, and Instructional Systems Development. Thesis and project options. Internships available in many countries.

Dates: Fall and Spring semesters; 2- to 6-week summer sessions. Cost: 1995-96 tuition $212 per credit hour for MD residents, $353 per credit hour for non-resident. Contact: Jodi Crandall or Ron Schwartz, Univ. of Maryland Baltimore County (UMBC), Education Dept., 5401 Wilkens Ave., Baltimore, MD 21228; (410) 455-2379 or (410) 455-2313, fax (410) 455-3986; crandall@gl.umbc.edu.

Eurocentres. Immersion course of 20-25 hours per week for beginners to advanced levels. Learn in small classes with students of all ages from around the world. There is a full organizational social calendar with extended excursions available to students. Homestay living is available, options for college credit and internships.

Dates: Two- to 12-week courses offered year-round. Cost: Ranges by location and length. Contact: Eurocentres, 101 N. Union St., Alexandria, VA 22314; (703) 684-1494 or (800) 648-4809, fax (703) 684-1495; 100632.141@compuserve.com

Georgetown Univ. The RSA Cambridge Certificate in the Teaching of English as a Foreign Language to Adults (CTEFLA) course prepares those with no previous teaching experience to teach general EFL overseas. Program includes language analysis and supervised teaching experience. Passing the course leads to the internationally recognized RSA/CTEFLA and a Georgetown certificate.

Dates: Jul 8-Aug 9 (full-time). Cost: $3,300 tuition for 5-week, 150-hour course. Contact: Ms. Mary Marggraf, The Center for Language Education and Development, Georgetown Univ., 3607 "O" St., NW, Washington, DC 20007; (202) 687-4467, fax (202) 337-1559.

Hamline TEFL Certificate Course. Hamline University offers an internationally recognized TEFL Certificate Course for individuals with little or no teaching experience who wish to teach English to adults overseas. An interactive, hands-on approach enables participants to discover the principles and practices of English language teaching. Courses include lectures, workshops, and practice teaching.

Dates: Ten-week Jan-Mar Semi-Intensive; Sep-Mar Evening Extensive; 2 1-month Intensives in Jul and Aug. On-Campus room and board available for Jul Intensive. Limited

space available for Jan-Mar. Cost: Semi-Intensive and Extensive: $2,150 (15 graduate quarter credits); Summer Intensives: $1,900 (10 graduate quarter credits). Materials:approx. $60. Contact: Betsy Parrish, Associate Professor/Coordinator, TEFL Certificate Program, Graduate Continuing Studies, Hamline Univ., 1536 Hewitt Ave., St. Paul, MN 55104; (800) 888-2182, fax (612) 641-2489; blparris@ piper.hamline.edu.

Hess Language School. Recruits teachers to work with children in 60 locations around Taiwan. Must have a degree and passport of an English-speaking country. Experience working with children and living in a large city strongly preferred. Salary, assistance in finding housing, airport pickup, insurance, teaching materials, and extensive training provided. Opportunities for advancement within the company. May teach conversation, grammar, culture, etc. Typically, places 15 to 25 percent of applicants.

Dates: Hiring is done 4 times per year for 1-year contracts. Cost: No fees. Contact: Hess Language School, Main Office, Po Ai Rd., #83, 2nd Fl., Taipei, Taiwan, ROC; (011) 886-2-382-5440 x 115, fax (011) 886-2-382-0799.

MA in Education with a Major in TESOL. The 35-credit-hour program emphasizes methodological practices of the teaching of English as a second language. It prepares classroom teachers with appropriate ESL/ EFL techniques, assessment instruments, and materials. The TESL program profits from cooperation with the Center for International Education, which provides opportunities for overseas teaching experience. The university also operates an English language training program.

Dates: Multiple courses are offered each semester and every summer. Cost: $248 per credit hour. Contact: Bethyl Pearson, PhD, Company, Grand Canyon Univ., College of Education, 3300 W. Camelback Rd., Phoenix, AZ 85308; (602) 589-3300, fax (602) 589-2447; bpearso@grcanuniv.k12.az.us.

Master of Arts in Teaching Program. The School for International Training's Master of Arts in Teaching Program offers concentrations in ESOL, French, and Spanish in a 1-academic-year or 2-summer format. The program emphasizes practical teaching skills, classroom-based research, and innovative methodologies.

Dates: Aug 28, 1996-Jun 14, 1997; Jun 24-Aug 16, 1997, Jun 23-Aug 15, 1998. Cost: 1996-97 tuition for both formats is $15,800. Contact: Fiona Cook, Admissions Counselor, School for International Training, Box 676, Kipling Rd., Brattleboro, VT 05302; (802) 257-7751, fax (802) 258-3500; admissions.sit@ worldlearning.org.

Master's in TESOL. One of the most sought-after professionals in the world today is the teacher of English as a second or foreign language. Bringing together knowledge and skill from linguistics, education, humanities, and the social sciences, the Seattle Pacific Univ. Division of Humanities MA-TESOL program will prepare you for leadership and service in this growing field.

Contact: MA-TESOL Dept., Seattle Pacific Univ., 3307 3rd Ave. W, Seattle, WA 98119; (206) 281-2670, fax (206) 281-2771; daphynes@ spu.edu.

Monterey Institute of International Studies. MA program in Teaching English to Speakers of Other Languages (MATESOL) combines strong academic preparation with practical training language pedagogy, including a core of courses in applied linguistics and pedagogical theories, curriculum development, language testing, and practicum courses organized around the type of tasks encountered in the classroom. Applications must have a minimum 3.0 grade point average on a 4.0 scale, and a minimum 600 TOEFL score.

Dates: The MA program typically takes 3 semesters (fall, spring, fall; or spring, fall, spring). 37 semester units. Cost: $17,200 (fall 1997 and spring 1998). Contact: Admissions Office, Monterey Institute of International

Studies, 425 Van Buren St., Monterey, CA 93940; (408) 647-4123, fax (408) 647-6405; admit@miis.edu.

New World Teachers. Accelerated 4-week TEFL/TESL Certificate Course integrating established European Direct Method with contemporary teaching techniques. Developed by internationally-experienced trainers and aimed at trainees with an American education, this course requires no second language. Includes extensive supervised practice teaching to foreign students, permanent access to job placement guidance, and information—including Internet resources.

Dates: Four-week intensive courses begin Jan 6, Feb 3, Mar 3, Apr 7, May 5, Jun 2, Jun 30, Jul 28, Aug 25, Sep 22, Oct 20, and Nov 17, 1997. Ten-week Tuesday evening and Saturday courses begin Feb 25, Jun 3 and Sep. 2, 1997. Eight-week Tuesday, Thursday evening, and Saturday courses begin Jan 14, Apr 8, Jul 29, and Oct 14, 1997. Cost: Jan-Apr: $2,200. From May: $2,300. Includes deposit, registration, books, course materials, and job placement services. Accommodations: from $575 per month, includes all taxes in The New World Teachers Guest House near Union Sq. (walk to the school). Includes kitchen facilities, common room, television and VCR, phone and desk in room, free local calls, no long distance surcharges. Contact: New World Teachers, 605 Market St., Suite 800, San Francisco, CA 94105; (800) 644-5424; teacherssf@aol.com, www. goteach.com.

Nova Intercultural Institute. One of the largest private language schools in Japan, Nova employs 1,800 teachers at over 180 locations throughout the islands. We offer a fixed schedule, a guaranteed monthly salary, paid training, assistance with housing, and an extensive support network. Lessons are taught at a variety of levels, ranging from beginner to advanced, and are 40-45 minutes in length. Classes are limited to a size of 3 or 4 students, depending on location.

Dates: Continuous hiring year round. Cost:

No application or processing fees. Contact: Trevor Phillips, Interact Nova Group, 2 Oliver St., 7th Fl., Boston, MA 02109; (617) 542-5027, fax (617) 542-3115; www.novajapan. com.

RSA/Cambridge CETLA. Intensive 4-week TEFL training leading to the most widely recognized certification worldwide: The RSA/Cambridge CETLA. Our program offers: 35-hour pre-course assignment, unique post-course development pack, highly professional training, expert job guidance during and after training.

Dates: Every month (except December). Cost: $2,550. Includes tuition, materials and job guidance. Contact: Jeff Mohamed, English International, 655 Sutter St., Suite 200, San Francisco, CA 94102; (415) 749-5633; 103326.1743@compuserve.com.

RSA/UCLES CTEFLA. A course for those without previous TESOL experience. Input includes language awareness, phonology, methodology, classroom management, use of technology, syllabus. Trainees are observed teaching students at elementary and intermediate levels. They observe qualified teachers for 8 hours. Practical emphasis.

Dates: Jan 7-Apr 5; Apr 8-Jun 28; Jul 1-Sep 20; Sep 23-Dec 13, 1997. Cost: AUS$2,190 payable in 1 installment. Contact: Dierdre Conway, St. Mark's International College, 375 Stirling St., Highgate, Western Australia; (011) 61-9-227-9888, fax 227-9880; smic@iinet. net.au.

RSA/Univ. of Cambridge CTEFLA. The most widely recognized initial qualification for teaching English as a foreign language to adults, the CTEFLA is offered at both our Santa Monica and Portland centers year round. You need to be at least 20 years old, have a good standard of education and a recent foreign language learning experience to be qualified.

Dates: Jan-Nov year round. Cost: $2,150. Contact: John Myers, Coast Language Academy, International House, 200 SW Market St.,

Suite #111, Portland, OR 97201; (503) 224-1960, fax (503) 224-2041; lgalas@coastpdx.com.

School of Teaching ESL. Intensive 4-week courses earn 12 Seattle Univ. education credits (post-baccalaureate or graduate-status) and the Certificate in Teaching English as a Second or Foreign Language. Graduates are teaching throughout the world. Instructors have higher degrees, overseas and U.S. teaching experience, and emphasize the practical. Laboratory ESL school on site. Also available: evening program, advanced certification, Master's in TESOL through Seattle Univ.

Dates: Eleven starting dates per year for the 4-week day intensive course. Evening courses are on the Seattle Univ. quarterly system. Cost: $170 per credit ($2,040 for the 12-credit course). Includes the Seattle Univ. credit fees but not books and materials (approx. $15 per credit). Accommodations: Studio apartments on site. When those are filled, a list of alternative rentals is provided. Contact: The School of Teaching ESL, 2601 N.W. 56th St., Seattle, WA 98107; (206) 781-8607, fax (206) 781-8922; tulare@seattleu.edu.

Summer Intensive Language Program. Monterey Institute of International Studies offers elementary and intermediate language courses in a 9-week Summer Intensive Language Program for Arabic, Chinese, Japanese, and Russian, Jun 17-Aug 20, 1997. Eight-week programs in French, German, Italian, and Spanish, as well as superior-level courses in English, French, German, Japanese, Russian or Spanish for Translation and Interpretation, are offered Jun 24-Aug 20, 1997. English as a Second Language is offered year round in 8-week programs. Instruction is supplemented with tutors and cultural activities on campus for practice outside of the classroom. Customized programs are available any time during the year, call for information. Monterey is a beautiful venue for language study in a supportive small-class environment. Come join our "global village."

Cost: Nine-week program tuition $2,800,

8-week program tuition $2,600. Contact: Summer Session Office, Monterey Institute of International Studies, 425 Van Buren St., Monterey, CA 93940; (408) 647-4115, fax (408) 647-3534; jwatts@miis.edu.

Teaching English Abroad Program. This intensive program consists of 5 courses: Methods of TESOL, Language Structure and Use, Cultural Adjustment Abroad, Teaching English Internationally, and Finding an EFL Job Abroad. The program is intended for native speakers of English wishing to specialize in EFL in order to secure a teaching job overseas.

Dates: Oct-Dec and Apr-Jun. Cost: $1,210 includes all tuition (textbooks extra). Contact: Student Affairs Officer, TESL Dept., Univ. of California Irvine Extension, P.O. Box 6050, Irvine, CA 92616-6050; (714) 824-7845, fax (714) 824-3651; gfrydenb@uci.edu, www.unex.uci.edu/~unex.

TEFL in Boston. International TEFL Certificate, limit of 12 participants per course, no second language necessary, second career persons welcome, global placement guidance, humanistic orientation to cross-cultural education, teacher training at American English Language Foundation, Harvard Univ. Club or other accommodations, PDP eligible by Massachusetts Department of Education.

Dates: Full-time intensive course monthly; part-time courses offered periodically throughout the year. Cost: $1,995 includes tuition, nonrefundable $95 application fee, internship, international resume, job placement guidance, video lab, all books and materials. Contact: Thomas A. Kane, PhD, Worldwide Teachers Development Institute, 266 Beacon St., Boston, MA 02116; (800) 875-5564, fax (617) 262-0308; bostontefl@aol.com.

The Univ. of Arizona. The Dept. of English MA in ESL emphasizes leadership development and is designed for experienced teachers with a strong academic record and leadership experience. Specialized courses are of-

SMOOTH TAKEOFF TO TEACHING ENGLISH

fered in language program administration, comparative discourse, teaching language through literature, sociolinguistics, language testing, and technology. PhD in SLAT.

Dates: Applications due by Feb 1 for the following fall semester. Two years are normally required to complete the program. Cost: $1,005 registration for 7 or more units, plus approx. $244 per unit for nonresident tuition. Contact: Director, English Language/Linguistics Program, English Dept., P.O. Box 210067, The Univ. of Arizona, Tucson, AZ 85721-0067; (520) 621-7216, fax (520) 621-7397; maes1@ccit.arizona.edu.

Univ. of Cambridge CELTA. St Giles Colleges (established 1955 in London) offer 4-week intensive teacher training programs approved by the Royal Society of Arts/University of Cambridge Examination Syndicate and, in San Francisco, the California State Department of Postsecondary Education. Program focuses on practical training, teaching methodology. Information on jobs, conditions in specific countries, resume writing, interviewing included. EFL school on site for observation.

Dates: Jan 27-Feb 21, Mar 24-Apr 18, May 5-30, Jun 16-Jul 11, Sep 8-Oct 3, Oct 27-Nov 2. Cost: $2,250. Contact: Teacher Training Coordinator, St Giles Language Teaching Center, 1 Hallidie Plaza, Third Floor, San Francisco, CA 94102; (415) 788-3552; (415) 788-1923.

Venezuela

ESOL Training in Multicultural Education. Cross cultural issues in ESL offers training in multicultural educational approaches and methodology, and the opportunity for participants to learn survival Spanish. It takes place in the beautiful city of Merida nestled in the Andean mountains of Venezuela.

Dates: Contact program for dates. Cost: $1,500 for 2 weeks. Contact: Beatriz Guzman, Vice President, Venusa CPSA, 10442 Taft St., Pembroke Pines, FL 33026; (305) 433-4091, fax (305) 433-4093.

Worldwide

Diploma Program in Teaching English as a Second or Foreign Language. The Diploma Program is a noncredit, intensive, 8-week professional training program offered in summers for teachers and prospective teachers of English as a Second or Foreign Language. It covers all essential aspects of English language teaching from a practical classroom perspective. Totals 210 hours of instruction, including practicum.

Dates: Mid-Jun-mid-Aug. Cost: $2,300 tuition (plus room and board, and materials). Contact: Daniel W. Evans, PhD, Acting Director, TESL Graduate Programs, School of International Studies, Saint Michael's College, Colchester, VT 05439; (802) 654-2684, fax (802) 654-2595; sis@smcvt.edu.

English Course. This course consists of general class, conversation, TOEFL, G-MAT, SAT, and private tutoring. We recruit English teachers with BA degrees and TESL/TEFL/RSA certification, preferably those who have teaching experience in Asian countries.

Dates: Year round. Contact: Triad English Centre, JL. Purnawarman, No. 76, Bandung 40116, Indonesia; (011) 6222 431309, fax (011) 6222 431149; triad09@ibm.net.

International Schools Services. Last year International Schools Services recruited for nearly 60 ESL positions in K-12 American/international schools worldwide. Applicants must possess teaching certification and have at least 2 years of full-time K-12 teaching experience. Placement services include yearly recruitment centers and ongoing computer searches. Opportunities are as diverse as regions represented globally: salary and benefits vary congruously.

Dates: International Recruitment Centers in Feb, Mar, and Jun. Cost: Application: $100; Recruitment Center registration: $125. There are no placement fees charged to candidates who are placed through the work of ISS. Contact: Erika Pedersen, ISS, P.O. Box 5910, Princeton, NJ 08543; (609) 452-0990, fax (609) 452-2690; edustaffing@ISS@mcimail.com.

Master of Arts in Teaching English as a Second Language (MATESL). The MATESL Program is a 36-credit program (39 credits with thesis option) designed for both prospective and experienced techers. Theoretical and methodological training is integrated with practical coursework to prepare graduates for professional roles in TESL/TEFL or continued graduate study. A variety of practicum experiences are offered both domestically and abroad.

Dates: Begin in Sep, Jan, or Jun. Cost: $260 per credit. Contact: Daniel W. Evans, PhD, Acting Director, TESL Graduate Programs, School of International Studies, Saint Michael's College, Colchester, VT 05439; (802) 654-2684, fax (802) 654-2595; sis@smcvt.edu.

Mission Volunteer International. The Presbyterian Church (USA) has over 100 year's experience sending educators to work with partner institutions around the world. Engish as a Second Language teachers are needed primarily in Africa, Eastern Europe, and Asia. Training and experience preferred. Some positions require volunteer to raise cost of monthly stipend.

Dates: Year round: requires 2-year commitment. Cost: Volunteers receive stipend, housing, and insurance. Contact: Susan Heffner Rhema, Presbyterian Church (USA), 100 Witherspoon St., Louisville, KY 40202-1396; (800) 779-6779.

Peace Corps Volunteer Opportunities. Since 1961, more than 140,000 Americans have joined the Peace Corps. Assignments are 27 months long. Volunteers must be U.S. citizens, at least 18 years old, and in good health. Peace Corps has volunteer programs in education, business, agriculture, the environment, and health.

Dates: Apply 9 to 12 months prior to availability. Cost: Volunteers receive transportation to and from assignment, a stipend, complete health care, and $5,400 after 27 months of service. Contact: Peace Corps, Room 8506, 1990 K St., NW, Washington, DC 20526; (800) 424-8580; www.peacecorps.gov.

St Giles Language Teaching Center. Earn the Certificate in English Language Teaching to Adults (CELTA) approved by the Univ. of Cambridge and the California Council for Private Postsecondary and Vocational Education. The course focuses on practical training and teaching methodology. Includes access to international job postings, graduate contacts, and teaching opportunities abroad. Sessions include resume writing, and interviewing techniques. Part of a group of schools in England, Switzerland, and U.S. offering 40 years of EFL teaching and training. CELTA courses also offered in Brighton and London, England.

Dates: Four-week intensive courses begin 6 times yearly. Cost: $2,250 all inclusive. Contact: St Giles Language Teaching Center, 1 Hallidie Plaza, Suite 350-TA, San Francisco, CA 94102; (415) 788-3552, fax (415) 788-1923.

Study Abroad in Australia. Study 1 semester in a wide range of courses including humanities, arts, social sciences, economics, education, science, Australian studies.

Dates: Feb-Jun or Jul-Nov. Cost: Approx. $5,500 Contact: International Office, Univ. of New England, Armidale, NSW Australia 2351.

TESOL Certificate. The College of Sante Fe, in beautiful and historic Sante Fe, New Mexico, offers an alternative, 18-credit-hour, 2-semester TESOL certificate program. Participants must also have 6 credit hours of foreign language and possess a bachelor's degree. The TESOL certificate is for participants who wish to teach outside of the K-12 public school setting, but may qualify as an ESL endorsement for licensed teachers.

Dates: Year round. Cost: $204 per credit. Contact: Wallace K. Pond, PhD, 1600 St. Michael's Dr., Sante Fe, NM 87505; (800) 456-2673, fax (505) 473-6510; edudtp@ fogelson. csf.edu.

TESOL Minor and Certificate. An undergraduate program of courses that outlines major issues about language and trains students to teach ESL. Students may earn a public school ESL teaching endorsement or a 1-year certificate or may simply take the 3-week intensive TESOL Methods course. Field experiences may be arranged.

Dates: May 1-23 (TESOL Methods); Sep 4-Apr 26, other courses. Cost: $1,070 tuition for TESOL Methods; $5,450 tuition per semester. Contact: Carl Barnett, Goshen College, 1700 S. Main St., Goshen, IN 46526; (800) 348-7422, fax (219) 535-7609; admissions@goshen.edu; www.goshen.edu.

Training for EFL/ESL Teachers. The Australian TESOL Training Centre offers full-time intensive 4-week courses and part-time 12-week courses leading to the internationally recognized RSA/Cambridge Certificate in Teaching English as a Foreign Language to Adults (CTEFLA). We also offer 1-week introductory TEFLA courses for those wanting to learn more about this field.

Dates: RSA/Cambridge CTEFLA course start date every 5 weeks. Introductory course 1997: Apr 14, May 19, Jul 28, and Nov 10. Cost: RSA/Cambridge: Tuition AUS$2,090 plus $135 exam fee. Introductory Course: AUS$375. Contact: Gloria Smith, Australian TESOL Training Centre, P.O. Box 82, Bondi Junction, NSW 2022, Australia; (011) 61-2-9389-0133, fax 9389-6880; info@acenglish.com.au.

WorldTeach. WorldTeach is a private nonprofit organization based at Harvard Univ. which contributes to educational development and cultural exchange by placing volunteers to teach in developing countries (Costa Rica, Ecuador, Lithuania, Mexico, Namibia, Poland, South Africa, Thailand, and Vietnam). Volunteers teach English, math, science, and environmental education, to students of all ages. All programs last for 1 academic year; except for the summer program in China.

Dates: Year-round departures and deadlines vary depending on the program. Cost: $3,600-$4,700. Includes health insurance, airfare, field support, and training. Contact: Anthony Meyer, Director of Recruiting and Admissions Training, WorldTeach, Harvard Institute for International Development, 1 Eliot St., Cambridge, MA 02138-5705; (617) 495-5527, fax (617) 495-1599; ameyer@worldteachorg, www.igc.org/worldteach..

GEOGRAPHIC INDEX

TRANSITIONS ABROAD
Answering your travel questions . . . .

SPECIAL INTEREST VACATIONS (MAR/APR)

Would you like to combine a vacation abroad with a hobby or special activity you love?

• Whether it's hiking, sailing, or cooking, following your own interest is much more satisfying than fighting the crowds. Our focus this time is on low-cost special interest vacations, including a country-by-country directory.

• If you are looking for something more intellectually demanding, you can choose from our worldwide directory of credit-bearing summer as well as semester and year courses worldwide.

LANGUAGE VACATIONS (MAY/JUN)

Want to finally master Spanish, or learn enough French to travel comfortably on your own?

• In Central America, $125 a week buys full room and board plus four hours a day of private tutoring. Europe is more expensive, but a family stay is much cheaper than a hotel. Plus you make lifelong friends wherever you go. Our May/June country-by-country directory features overseas language programs.

OVERSEAS TRAVEL PLANNER (JUL/AUG)

Are your plans for your next trip abroad still not fully formed (perhaps because of money concerns)?

• If so, this most information-packed issue of the year will help you map out an affordable strategy. Our editors have located the best information sources and programs by country and region for families, seniors, persons with disabilities, and students. In short, a small encyclopedia of what you need to plan your own travel.

WORKING ABROAD (SEP/OCT)

Would you like to live abroad?

• Whether you're looking for short-term paid work, volunteer vacations, teaching jobs, or an international career this issue brings together in one place all the sources of information you need to make it happen. Also included: a directory of internship programs and our annual listing of worldwide volunteer opportunities—from Argentina to Zimbabwe.

ADVENTURE TRAVEL (NOV/DEC)

Do you prefer not to travel as a tourist?

• One of *Transitions Abroad*'s principal objectives is to promote travel that respects the culture and environment of the host country. In our November/December issue we survey tour and program operators to find those who are committed to giving something back to the communities they visit. Our special annual directory describes responsible travel programs by region and country, with the emphasis on local organizations.

• Also featured: Off-season travel bargains (remember, the less you spend, the more you see!).

Reader Response Page

Transitions Abroad relies on its editors for the best available information on alternative travel resources and programs. It relies on readers for first-hand reports. Please use the space below (or a separate sheet) to describe your own alternative travel discoveries. The most useful reports will be published in Information Exchange in *Transitions Abroad*.

Send to: Information Exchange, Transitions Abroad, P.O. Box 1300, Amherst, MA 01004-1300; fax (413) 256-0373; trabroad@aol.com. For longer submissions, ask for our Writers' Guidelines. The addresses of individual editors are listed at the end of the chapters.